Narratives, Nations, and Other World Products in the Making of Global History

Narratives, Nations, and Other World Products in the Making of Global History

Edited by Jeremy Adelman and Andreas Eckert

BLOOMSBURY ACADEMIC
LONDON · NEW YORK · OXFORD · NEW DELHI · SYDNEY

BLOOMSBURY ACADEMIC
Bloomsbury Publishing Plc
50 Bedford Square, London, WC1B 3DP, UK
1385 Broadway, New York, NY 10018, USA
29 Earlsfort Terrace, Dublin 2, Ireland

BLOOMSBURY, BLOOMSBURY ACADEMIC and the Diana logo
are trademarks of Bloomsbury Publishing Plc

First published in Great Britain 2024

Copyright © Jeremy Adelman and Andreas Eckert, 2024

Jeremy Adelman and Andreas Eckert have asserted their right under the Copyright,
Designs and Patents Act, 1988, to be identified as Editors of this work.

For legal purposes the Acknowledgements on p. xi constitute an
extension of this copyright page.

Cover image: Diego Rivera Stairwell Mural
'The History of Mexico', 1929–1935 (© Jon Arnold Images Ltd/ Alamy Stock Photo)

This work is published open access subject to a Creative Commons Attribution-
NonCommercial-NoDerivatives 4.0 International licence (CC BY-NC-ND 4.0, https://
creativecommons.org/licenses/by-nc-nd/4.0/). You may re-use, distribute, and reproduce
this work in any medium for non-commercial purposes, provided you give attribution to the
copyright holder and the publisher and provide a link to the Creative Commons licence.
Open access was funded by Princeton University, USA.

Bloomsbury Publishing Plc does not have any control over, or responsibility for,
any third-party websites referred to or in this book. All internet addresses given
in this book were correct at the time of going to press. The author and publisher
regret any inconvenience caused if addresses have changed or sites have ceased
to exist, but can accept no responsibility for any such changes.

A catalogue record for this book is available from the British Library.

A catalog record for this book is available from the Library of Congress.

ISBN: HB: 978-1-3504-4098-2
          ePDF: 978-1-3504-4099-9
          eBook: 978-1-3504-4100-2

Typeset by Integra Software Services Pvt. Ltd.

To find out more about our authors and books visit www.bloomsbury.com
and sign up for our newsletters.

Contents

List of images	vii
List of maps	viii
List of authors	ix
Acknowledgements	xi

Introduction: A world of narratives *Jeremy Adelman and Andreas Eckert*	1

Section One Stories of peoplehood

1	'This nation is a globe': Exceptionalism and universalism in the nineteenth-century United States *Matthew Karp*	19
2	Narratives of power: Political thoughts and the framework of world history in modern China *BAO Maohong*	35
3	Going beyond the 'Western impact' narrative: China as a world power, 1839–1949 *Xavier Paulès*	51
4	Fighting 'the warfare of peacetime': Japan's quest for national narratives during the late nineteenth century *SANO Mayuko*	67
5	Japan, *Tōyō* (the 'Eastern Ocean') and Asia in the World: The transition of Japanese self-consciousness from the 1850s to the 1940s *HANEDA Masashi*	87
6	Applying global history to the study of war: Transnational narratives of resilience under aerial bombardment *Sheldon Garon*	103

Section Two Empires and other great powers

7	Lighthouse of socialism for the decolonized world: Central Asia's global moment, 1956–79 *Marc Elie*	127
8	The boomerang of imperial sovereignty: Bosnia and Herzegovina in the eye of the world storm *Natasha Wheatley*	147
9	A century of convergences: Contested concepts of economic integration, 1919–2019 *Jeremy Adelman, Abigail Kret, Marlène Rosano-Grange and Bruno Settis*	165
10	Narrating progress: Developmental regimes in semi- and anti-colonial Southeast Asia *Benjamin Baumann and Vincent Houben*	183

vi   *Contents*

Section Three   Other world products

11   Narrating the common good: Stories about and around the United
     Nations *Pierre-Yves Cadalen, Connor Mills and Karoline Postel-Vinay*   203
12   Global narratives of the immigrant *Megan Armknecht, Markus Bierkoch
     and Beth Lew-Williams*   219
13   'Global integration, social disintegration: Edward Long's *History of
     Jamaica* (1774)' *Silvia Sebastiani*   239
14   World products? Narratives about workers and work in East and West
     Africa, 1904–61 *Fabian Krautwald, Kerstin Stubenvoll and Andreas Eckert* 259
15   Russia in global economic history: On modernization and its
     discontents *Alessandro Stanziani*   287
16   Mapping economic interdependence: Creating the periphery in the
     interwar period *Jeremy Adelman, Laetitia Lenel and Pablo Pryluka*   307

Coda: Narratives in an embattled world *Dominic Sachsenmaier*   329

Index   347

Images

Chapter 4

4.1	Japanese garden at Expo 1873 Vienna	74
4.2	Japanese pavilion at Expo 1893 Chicago	76

Chapter 16

16.1	Alejandro Bunge ARGENTINA, *país abanico*	311
16.2	A comparison of the United States, Europe and the Customs Union of the South	313
16.3	Sun Yat-sen, *The International Development of China*	315
16.4	Ellsworth Huntington, *The Distribution of Human Energy on the Basis of Climate*	316
16.5	Erich W. Zimmermann, *The Resource Hierarchy of Modern World Economy*	319

Map

1 *Fantan* in the six continents   59

Authors

Jeremy Adelman, Princeton University (US) and University of Cambridge (UK)

Megan Armknecht, Princeton University (US)

BAO Maohong, University of Beijing (China)

Benjamin Baumann, Heidelberg University (Germany)

Markus Bierkoch, Free University Berlin and Gottfried Wilhelm Leibniz Library in Hannover (Germany)

Pierre-Yves Cadalen, Sciences Po (France)

Andreas Eckert, Humboldt University Berlin (Germany)

Marc Elie, Centre d'études russes, caucasiennes, est-européennes et centrasiatique (CERCEC) at the École des Hautes Études en Sciences Sociales (France)

Sheldon Garon, Princeton University (US)

HANEDA Masashi, University of Tokyo (Japan)

Vincent Houben, Humboldt University Berlin (Germany)

Matthew Karp, Princeton University (US)

Fabian Krautwald, Binghamton University (US)

Abigail Kret, Princeton University (US)

Laetitia Lenel, University of Duisburg-Essen (Germany)

Beth Lew-Williams, Princeton University (US)

Connor Mills, University of Oregon (US)

Karoline Postel-Vinay, Center for International Studies, Sciences Po (France)

SANO Mayuko, Graduate School of Education, Kyoto University (Japan)

Xavier Paulès, Centre d'études sur la Chine moderne et contemporaine, École des Hautes Études en Sciences Sociales (France)

Pablo Pryluka, Princeton University (US)

Marlène Rosano-Grange, University of Oxford (UK)

Dominic Sachsenmeier, University of Göttingen (Germany)

Silvia Sebastiani, École des Hautes Études en Sciences Sociales and Centre national de la recherche scientifique (France)

Bruno Settis, University of Bologna (Italy)

Alessandro Stanziani, École des Hautes Études en Sciences Sociales and Centre national de la recherche scientifique (France)

Kerstin Stubenvoll, Humboldt University Berlin (Germany)

Natasha Wheatley, Princeton University (US)

Acknowledgements

This volume developed out of a meeting in Jeremy Adelman's dining room in Princeton in 2014. From that gathering grew a latticework of partners in Paris (École des Hautes Études en Sciences Sociales and Sciences Po), Berlin (Humboldt University and Free University), Tokyo (Tokyo University) and Princeton University. More would join that original network. We are grateful to colleagues, students, staff, and financial support from all these institutions, which are rare in an age in which universities, like many nation-states, are under pressure to raise their drawbridges to global collaborations. We especially want to underscore the support from the Council on International Teaching and Research at Princeton and to Jennifer Loessy of the History Department at Princeton.

Jeremy Adelman & Andreas Eckert

Introduction: A world of narratives

Jeremy Adelman and Andreas Eckert

Not long ago, nations were seen as relics. The end of the Cold War, a democratic wave and the triumph of the free market ushered in a global age. Widening horizons, open borders and expanding trade seemed to dissolve the nation-state into a global village. Bring on one-world thinking and transnational solidarities called the heralds of a new, post-1989, moment!

The same fate was supposed to have fallen over traditional narratives. Dispatch the familiar storytelling conventions of bounded groups; their foundational myths and heroes went the way of fairy tales, said the prophets of a new age! Swept aside by liquid identities and rootless loyalties, the heroic patriot was replaced by the unrooted cosmopolitan; the fixed subject made room for the fluid one.

The results scrambled the conventions of shared narration. There was, accordingly, a search for post-national styles of thought and imaginings. In the social sciences, methodological individualism, game theory and the triumph of interests over ideologies became the rage. In the humanities, fluidity and mixture took hold; shared narratives became 'constructions' or 'inventions' of a fading era. The transnational turn and global history played their roles in spotlighting new ways of thinking about the past that transcended old borders, familiar genres and traditional actors.

The fate of the two, nations and narration, was tethered to each other. Bounded political communities depended on stories replayed in school, rehearsed in annual bonding rituals, and memorial sites of collective heroics and tragedy. But as the figurative trumpets heralded a global age, those rituals and sites for replaying them came to be seen as anachronisms of an earlier, bordered, age. Pundits, bankers and historians declared the nation obsolete while new stories of convergence, movement and circulation were supposed to yield to a 'flat world' in the cheery, now mocked, imagery of Thomas Friedman.[1] To fit the global age, historians played their part, clearing ground for global history, a style focused on human connections, entanglements and exchanges across borders to challenge familiar national narratives and myths.

Times have changed. Nations and narratives are surging back with a vengeance. Identity politics and the urge for historical reckoning have exposed integrative institutions – especially those, like encyclopaedic museums, heroic monuments and national textbooks that purported to glue people together – to massive criticism. As the global age came under assault from the Left and Right, the rhetoric of the nation evolved into the language of resistance against fluidity and unstable boundaries; verbal weapons to counter 'invasions,' 'displacements' and 'conquests,' and the grey anonymity of the headquarters of the WTO or the European Union. The right-wing pundit-cum-politician, Éric Zemmour, has called his French variant a 'Reconquest' in open allusion to the fifteenth-century drive against Muslims in Western Europe; he likens migration to France from North Africa and the Middle East since the 1960s to a conquest that must be reversed to rescue the soul of the imperiled Gallic nation.[2]

Nowadays, we live in a moment in which all narratives are in crisis and colliding. And yet, at the same time, narratives have been more mobilized in an ever-intensifying escalation to justify claimsaking, new forms of inclusion, as well as all-too-familiar modes of exclusion.

How to make sense of this resurrection of heavily charged national narratives? One way is to treat them as the effects of global processes, to explore a global history of national ideas and the pursuit of bounding narratives as reactions to wider pressures and opportunities, including the opportunity to conquer or dominate others. Indeed, it turns out that many other social categories, and not just the nation, also emerged over the course of modern history to make sense of and to manage the ties that bind societies together. This anthology represents the work of a group of global historians committed to exchanging views across borders to help explain the ideas behind bordering and legitimating boundaries as global phenomena. While working across borders, the authors are not wistful for a return to the free-flowing days of globalization, as if a one-world narrative should be the natural successor to twentieth-century national storylines. However, the authors resist the rebounding of historical imaginations to the sanctuary of the nation, as if the nation were the natural or primordial defaults for the civic imagination and the stories that animate it; in this sense, the authors of this anthology remain true to global history's original purpose, outlined by Sebastian Conrad in his formative *What Is Global History?*: to transcend and even to explain methodological nationalism.[3] We would add, furthermore, that this applies to other methodological habits that presume the home-grown, endogenous, nature of group formations, which also presume that external forces are afterthoughts or intrusions on shared, bounded, structures.

The nation and other group concepts have been conceptual responses to external pressures and possibilities; they are world products. The authors in this book share one commitment: *to illuminate the ways in which basic social categories of modern life, starting with the creation of the nation itself, stories of empire, grandeur, race and the division of labour, have been the effects of interactions across borders.* Global interactions and integrations set off the search for narratives to explain how entangled groups might manage interdependence, its risks, hazards and temptations, by creating nations and their boundaries, and to locate their rank in hierarchies, with their legal justifications, and to create public cultures – games, museums, academic establishments, art – that make sense of, and often rush to the defence of, shared identities in a fluid world.

Global processes, this volume shows in a myriad of ways and across two centuries, informed and conditioned the methods by which societies created narratives to make sense of their place in the world, to establish a sense of belonging to – or exclusion from – wider orders and their futures. It was the pressures of world integration, migration, trade, flows of ideas that intensified with print capitalism, steam, technologies of war and finance that discharged the search to find coordinates to guide societies through the material and moral forces that laced them together. Those coordinates, for two centuries, took narrative forms.

History on the cross

This volume maps in diverse ways a global history of the nation and other world products as consequences of global interactions. Its authors have been convening long before the return of the radical patriots; they have also been aware, well before Brexit, Trump, Putin's irridentism and Modi's Hindutva-firstism, that the nation is not the only framing for extremely charged narratives. Indeed, national narratives have returned as part of a wider surge of identity-based politics and collective claims-making by minorities and majority populations alike to bolster their claims with rival stories of triumph and victimhood.

National champions are simply the noisiest, and possibly the most dangerous of the narrative resurgences given their reach into state arsenals. Indeed, national chest-thumpers have often spawned counterpoints and rival 'origin stories'. Perhaps the best example of this phenomenon in the North Atlantic realm was the *New York Times'* 1619 Project. A series of articles, profiles, videos and multi-media posts about enslavement and racial hierarchy as throughlines of American history edited by Nikole Hannah-Jones; it rocked the American political and cultural landscape for years. Celebrated and pilloried in turn, by the time Hannah-Jones gathered the pieces into a single book published by the newspaper in 2021, it was subtitled 'A New Origin Story', in not-so-veiled response to white supremacists' and Fox News' commitment to older patriotic myth-making.[4] Nor is the fight over the nation restricted to modern history. The representation of ancient Nubia (in present-day Sudan), for instance, has received a makeover. Traditionally represented by Egyptian nationalists as inferior, dark-skinned, more African than Mediterranean, the Nubian empire is now increasingly represented as the influencer of Egyptian grandeur and a force in the later making of Greco-Roman civilizations, and thus the fabled genealogy of the West itself which, in the floorplans of European and Neo-European museums, plot civilizational advances as progressive accumulations from Mesopotamia, Egypt, Athens, Rome and onwards towards a 'West' that had its 'origins' in the Upper Nile. What got fashioned in order to support Europe's civilizing mission was the original narrative itself. Those once-cherished plotlines have, in recent years, been flipped, inverted and scrambled – only to become the subjects of backlashing and drives to restore them. Everywhere, it seemed, nation-building textbooks, museums and rituals were becoming battlegrounds.[5]

The return of bordered identities and the turn to narratives have been undeniably global. From Myanmar to Hungary, Britain to Brazil, the language of nationhood has stormed back just as the place of narratives, origin stories and the symbols of group identities have become ever more celebrated, and fiercely contested. One only has to remember how the Russian President Vladimir Putin justified his invasion of neighbouring Ukraine as a restoration of Russian grandeur. He extolled a historiography of grievance and invoked Ukrainian threats to re-enact a war against fictive Nazis in Kyiv while repressing a dissident NGO at home – paradoxically – called Memoria. Ukrainians resisted, invoking memories of earlier atrocities and famines at the hands of 'Russian' despots of the 1930s. The fact that Stalin was from Georgia was a subtlety that nationalists on both sides conveniently obscured.[6]

Nor is selective remembering especially new: the late-nineteenth-century historian, Ernest Renan, reminded readers that forgetfulness was 'essential in the creation of the nation'. Indeed, over the course of the nineteenth century in Asia, Europe and the Americas, the destabilization of revolution, migration and gunboat diplomacy provoked identity crises – even in Europe where the alliance of steam technologies and citizenship ideologies conspired to motivate a search for new ideas of belonging now that kingdoms and aristocratic lineage were under assault. The rise of ethnic identities and nationalism spurred a search for older origins for nations, rooted in some mythic antiquity of, for instance, Rome, Han or Aztec greatness, or their proto-nationalist resistors. The point, as Patrick Geary has reminded us, is that national mythmaking invented medieval origins.[7] What he described for Europe transpired elsewhere – in part because the nineteenth century was suturing the world's societies together into imperial structures, commodity chains and migrant networks. Out of the increasingly interdependent world that capitalism brought us came an urgency to create and to claim national places on the world map.

The upshot was a long cycle of public, private and philanthropic energy devoted to promoting the idea of national origins for a world of nations. It was not always heroic. In the dark days of the 1930s and 1940s, for instance, nationalist narratives were seen as jingoistic, tales for intolerance and even extermination of some nations by others. George Orwell, in the middle of the Second World War, noted how the writing of history was vulnerable to spinmeisters and their mendacious ways. 'What is peculiar to our own age', he lamented in a retrospective on his days fighting in the Spanish Civil War, 'is the abandonment of the idea that history could be truthfully written'. Each side waged, in his words, combatting 'atrocity campaigns', by which he meant not just committing the atrocities but systematic lying and concealing about horrible acts in Moscow, Barcelona and Nanking. 'History stopped in 1936', he told the Hungarian émigré writer, Arthur Koestler.[8] The entanglement of memory and forgetting, truth and lies, are as recurring as the modern condition itself. But what is noteworthy is how narratives and counter-narratives have entangled nations in mixed-up, overlapping and also weaponized fates. One nation's claims necessarily entangled with others'. It is no coincidence that just as a slim majority of Britons voted to leave the European Union in 2016, the icon of imperial and national grandeur, the British Museum (itself created in 1753 as a *British* institution to reflect Albion's rise; its founder, Sir Hans Sloane, had ventured to the Caribbean to chronicle the nation made great by empire), was preparing to 're-patriate' bronze artwork pillaged from West Africa in the 1890s to a postcolonial nation, Nigeria, also seeking to reintegrate its present and future to a shared and represented past in national museums of its own. Each nation quarrelled over shared sources of its own narrative. It seems almost natural that the sorting be resolved in terms of what's right or good for the nation.[9]

Of course, selective remembering is intrinsic to all stories, picking and choosing characters, scenes and plots to fit the social purpose. Until recently, the trend was towards actors, places and storylines that favoured merging and globalizing. Nowadays, the global promise of a borderless world and liquid structures seems in retreat, and the flat-earth plotlines that took hold of imaginations that were forged in open markets, capital flows and study abroad initiatives look outdated. The nation is back. To a considerable extent, transnational forces have given way to regional bunkers, uncoupling systems and even the revival of the most fatigued of all the categories that global history once aimed to sideline: 'the West'. It was not long ago that right-wing American pundits warned about the demise – for some the 'suicide' – of the West at the hands of internationalists and multiculturalism. They needn't have been so worried. Lately, we have seen a rally for the defence of the West in the United States and across Europe, first in response to the global migrant crisis of 2015 and more recently in response to the Russian invasion of Ukraine and the Chinese government's actions in Hong Kong and Xinjiang. The West has its bravura back. But so does the Rest. The idea of a global world seems to be fracturing. Along with it so have the narratives of togetherness. In the vacuum, tales of fragility, precarity and even extinction abound.

Lest we see these trends as sequential, in one moment favouring the imperial ideal (in the nineteenth century), or national ones through much of the twentieth, and global narratives in the twenty-first, each schema has always had its critics and dissenters who favoured alternatives. In our day, this clash of narratives is not simply a reflection of the tarnished euphoria of post-Cold War globalization. It was not just a nativist reaction to events of 2015–16, a pendular swing back to the nation for a de-globalization trend. Since the founding of the World Trade Organization, its mission has been as contested as the flat-earth story it legitimated. During the fiftieth anniversary celebrations of the World Bank and IMF in Madrid, just five years after the fall of the Berlin wall, protestors gathered outside the convention shouting 'Fifty Years is Enough!' while Greenpeace activists climbed to the top of the building while King Juan Carlos was applauding the work of financiers and showered the city with fake dollar bills with the slogan 'No $'s for Ozone Layer Destruction'. Where the resistance to the happy narrative of globalization was fiercest was in the global south – burdened, long before the fall of the Berlin Wall, of having to 'adjust' to rules of the game made by others. In the wake of its nth financial meltdown in 2001, in the streets of Buenos Aires, protestors put up barricades and formed collective soup kitchens to create an alternative moral economy to the IMF-medicine doled out so the country could make its debt payments. The same malaise festered in one of the putative success stories: India. After years of protest and organizing, farmers in India joined forces in late 2020 in the shadow of the devastating Covid pandemic, to rally against bankruptcy, private investment and enclosure, causing the most severe crisis for the Modi government in New Delhi.[10]

Just as anti-globalization voices questioned the dominant celebrations of a free-flowing, liquid, world that favoured the connected haves over the less-connected have-nots, so too the current rage of the nation and the baggage of 'great replacement' theories and civilizational redemption are being challenged by refugee solidarity movements, mobilization to defund oil companies, and legal pressures to return pillaged art works and to atone for conquering pasts. In other words, the narratives have never been settled; they have always been contested.

What is more, just as globalization's discontents had always shadowed globalization, so too the importance of storytelling and narrativity never truly dissolved; narratives were not just contested and contestable; they were summoned and signified by the wider social processes we label as 'global'. Indeed, the making of the global was itself framed as a triumphal coming-to-being epic of transcending old divides; it too required a story to explain the process to its actors and to legitimate its purpose. As this anthology shows, narratives about groups, including nations, were always important to making sense of global integration and disintegration; group identities, as the authors show in a wide range of essays, functioned as responses to global processes, opportunities, pressures and threats.

These pushes and pulls to create narratives about groups and plot social categories as historical development have been global, that is, they have unfolded simultaneously across borders. But simultaneity is not the same as synchronicity. Not all narratives have mirrored each other; making and breaking them can be more fitful, even more traumatic, in some regions than others. The results were often more incomplete and unresolved. In most parts of Africa, postcolonial nationhood was a greater break with history than colonial rule had been. Much of the past was in danger of becoming irrelevant, mainly due to two developments: demographic growth and the new political logic of nation-building. To aspire to global citizenship was one thing, to exercise a national citizenship quite another. After independence, reacting to numerous internal divisions, many African states experimented with broadly inclusive nation-building strategies. New political institutions were designed to minimize centrifugal tendencies. In addition, the new regimes orchestrated cultural manifestations of nation-building, such as anthems, flags, clothes, football teams and musical items. Related efforts hardly led to overt conflicts, although tensions emerged over privileging of certain cultural forms, the sidelining of those perceived as backwards and the gendering of the national body. While nation-building comprised a vocabulary and partly also a practice, on inclusion, it also shaped assumptions about how members of the nation should live, behave and identify themselves.

Inclusion was not the only purpose. The swings also implied exclusionary tendencies, which became more pronounced in times of political and economic crisis. Since the 1990s, instead of promoting national citizenship, as implied in the idea of 'nation-building' that dominated politics in the 1970s and 1980s, African regimes in the following decades seemed to be more intent on producing 'autochthones'. Peter Geschiere also highlights the 'return of the local', as democratization and decentralization have revitalized an obsession with belonging. According to him, the idea of national citizenship, previously 'a very icon of modernity', is being called into question in debates over special rights for minorities and the cultural meaning of citizenship. In many African states where resources have come to be allocated on the basis of personal patronage, democratization and decentralization have often claimed autochthony as the most accessible way to make a priority claim on those resources. While the claims of autochthony are not replacing the state, they are grafting themselves onto the state structures.[11] While autochthony points to specific spatialized and essentialized structures of belonging to a community, a place or the soil, it does not necessarily encompass expectations against the state that are generally associated with the broader notion of xenophobia. Common to both is the production of an array of metaphors that invariably construe allochthons or strangers as threats to social order, to public health and to the purity of the social body.[12]

This urge to write scripts about belonging and claims to autochthony clears the way for blood and soil styles projects to build or defend under threat. The past has been, in current parlance, 'weaponized' in unprecedented ways worldwide. Statues of heroes are being toppled; presidents, prime ministers and potentates that once graced banknotes or university buildings are being removed; since the 1980s, when the 'reckoning' with uncomfortable truths like the Holocaust in Europe or disappeared people in Argentina picked up pace, the past has turned from being the domain of comforting truths and origin stories about our collective identities to the wellspring of our current divides. For a long time, 'history' was supposed to (although not always did) unite peoples in shared stories, incanted plotlines and revered founders.

This is no longer the case. Now the past is seen as the source of our fractious public. The contest over national symbols and stories is moving into higher gear and beyond the obvious suspects. The more familiar racist line-up of Cecil Rhodes and Woodrow Wilson, Confederate Generals and King Leopold II, was the easy target. The drive to topple, dismantle and rename is doing another round. The British Museum has announced the removal of a bust of their slave-owning founder, Sir Hans Sloane, from prominent display to a secure cabinet. 'We have pushed him off the pedestal', observes the director, Hartwig Fisher, who added, 'We must not hide anything.' A week earlier, a desecrated statue of Voltaire in Paris's elegant sixth arrondissement got whisked away for protection. Symposium after symposium discusses repeated allegations that enlightenment philosophers like Kant and Hegel were racist and helped lay the theoretical foundations of European racism. Everywhere, museum exhibitions, street names and plaza monuments that were once meant as public narrative markers are being tested for their association with – and celebration of – empire and slavery. The seamy side of greatness exposed; its emblems have been taken down.

Between the nation and the world

For two centuries the nation emerged as the organizing principle for our concept of sovereignty. However, it was tethered to and given meaning by a wider political order. Jeremy Bentham coined the term 'international' to envision an entanglement of nation-states to replace the disorder of predatory empires. Declarations of independence that spread across the Atlantic world from the latter half of the eighteenth century did double duty: they announced the entry of nations into a community of states and they announced their need for each other's recognition; declarations of independence were simultaneously declarations of interdependence, of a hope to be acknowledged and welcomed by other nations – and thereby to secure one's freedom – and to pledge one's willingness to be restrained to maintain the wider order.[13] It was so foundational to international law that it has been taken for granted, except by colonial societies who were, by definition, excluded from recognition and freedom and yearned to declare their freedom and their membership. When they worked, international laws and norms ensured that nations didn't become predators. When they failed, Nation-First zealotry took over, interdependence got weaponized; the needs of the nation authorized conquest and extermination. This is what happened in the 1930s.

The fates of nationalism and internationalism have marched together in complex ways. After the Second World War, liberal internationalism overlapped with the spread of nations under the mantle of the Third World. In her widely discussed book, Adom Getachew argued in this context that anti-colonial nationalists chose the nation-state to transform international hierarchies into a cosmopolitan order.[14] Cresting in the 1970s with efforts to redesign the international division of labour and redistribute power, Third Worldist imaginaries struggled. Then burdened by the debt crises of the 1980s, they receded just as the other internationalist vision orbiting around socialist ideas also ran aground. The emergent 'global' order brought the final round of decolonization to cover the planet with nations while tearing down barriers to the flow of capital and commodities, spreading nations while deepening interdependence between them. A wave of free trade agreements and mobile money brought new rituals – The World Economic Forum at Davos, Switzerland – and institutions – the World Trade Organization – to celebrate connectivity, liquidity and a radical sense of shared time. Unbound by place, the new barons – in the words of one 1994 Merrill Lynch recruiting brochure – sought to 'serve the needs of our clients all across geographic borders'.[15]

As the flat-earth proponents triumphed, the language of the nation became the rhetoric of resistance, especially in the global south where globalization did not come with positive connotations. For many, it meant austerity and structural adjustment, and laid the grounds for contention in the newly minted 'Global South' and spread northwards with the disenchantment with market-fuelled globalization. In Argentina, *piqueteros* railed against the pulverizing effects of austerity for citizens and payments for creditors. Taiwanese firms moved into post-Apartheid South Africa to hire dispossessed workers into their value chains, pitting trade unions and community leaders against a fledgling ANC government desperate for investment. 'We have put you in power, now you must deliver', cried one protestor in mid-1997 to a beleaguered ANC council desperate for investment.[16] Then the discontents that were largely kept to the global peripheries came home to its cores. The economic crisis of 2008 quickly disavowed the idea of a borderless world. Since 2009, the national flag has been a worldwide emblem of resistance against cosmopolitan elites and inscrutable WTO trade-dispute panels and their technocrats.

The revival of patriotic resistance against 'globalism' was not just a message for *Homo Davos*. It asserted a claim over who belonged to the nation in response to fears of invading migrants and resentment about unruly minorities. When Brexiteers like Nigel Farage mocked Brussels regulators, it was only a warm-up act for what would follow soon: frothing about the menace of migrants marching their way up the Balkans to invade where Napoleon and Hitler had failed before them because Europe had forsaken the idea of the nation and the ethnic majorities that stood at its guard. To rescue the British nation from ethnocide, it had to secede from Europe. The hysteria was not restricted to the endangered 'West'. 'I'm a Hindu nationalist, a patriot', exclaimed the then chief minister of Gujarat, Narendra Modi, before a gathering of squirming European diplomats in the German embassy in New Delhi in July 2013. Ever since the bloody riots in Gujarat that left around 2,000 people dead, mostly Muslims, Modi had been unofficially boycotted by European envoys. As he poised to become the prime minister, and as nativists Marine Le Pen and Matteo Salvini ascended in Europe, it became harder to shun Modi and Hindutva-nationalism.[17] Today, Western politicians pay court to Modi because of India's huge economic and strategic importance.

The nation was not just invoked to resist globalizers and globalists. As the examples of Farage and Modi above suggest, the nation also became the shelter to justify exclusion of those who were not part of the moral community of like-minded neighbours. Even before the pandemic of Covid-19, which took nationalism to new heights as millions of migrants were driven home and wealthy countries were unashamed in their vaccine hoarding while Russia and China used their vaccines as diplomatic weaponry, strangers were persecuted across the world as nativists sought to 'unmix' nations that globalization had mixed up. Their paroxysms were triggered by globalization's blurry borders, merging markets and mixing peoples, thereby provoking what Arjun Appadurai prophetically called the 'anxiety of incompleteness'. By this, he means an affective condition of a nation's sense that its majority is threatened. One can add the campaign and failed putsch in the United States to assert minority white rule in the name of a shrinking white majority or, in extreme, the purification efforts in the borderlands of Russia and Ukraine. The question of who is entitled to be a citizen, or to have a state in the first place, enmeshes millions into webs of tribunals, census-takers, border-police, fencing and camps that regulate and invigilate the human flow.[18]

What was – and is – the purpose of the nation and other social categories in a global world? The argument of this volume is that they have been created to manage the challenges and opportunities, comforts and discomforts, of cross-border interactions. The chapters here look at the many ways in which global integration yielded narratives about the making of places, people and processes as part of a modern, interdependent order. Like declarations of independence, these narratives performed two membership functions to elicit recognition from other parts of the order, to create bridges of mutual recognition and to bond those within the narrative circles into a common sense of peoplehood with powers and rights to manage interdependence.

In other words, trade, migration, the circulation of ideas and the ebbs of wars and peace across borders produced the need for actors to create social categories to explain legitimate, and contest these interactions. It was one of the naïvetés of the flat-earth proponents that the costs of global merging and togetherness would so far outweigh the apparently unlimited flow of cheap consumer goods, freedom to invest and access to workers that it never occurred to them that the distribution of that bounty would be unfair and yield so much havoc on daily lives. It did not take much effort to see the self-interests behind the advocacy of free trade and capital mobility. But what is often forgotten is the ways in which the costs and benefits required – indeed summoned – laws and institutions to manage and distribute them. Since the nineteenth century, nations, racial ideologies, the social catalogue of migrant, native and settler, as well as worker and 'investor' social identities emerged to classify, rank and sort the inner and outer boundaries of increasingly mixed and interdependent societies.

What is more, the needs of property and the pressures and shocks of capital and commodity booms and busts required states – increasingly legitimized as nation-states – to maximize rents and to regulate unrest. After all, it was the Chinese state that was forced to sit down with Queen Victoria's delegates in 1842 to sign the treaties that would 'open' China's ports to British goods and missionaries and give them legal shelter to operate under extra-territorial rules. In many parts of Africa, during the 1970s and 1980s economic crisis, states were obliged by international donors, to administer bitter pills, notably under the rubric of structural adjustment, that further undermined governments' capacities to provide the kind of services that would tie the citizenry as a whole to state institutions – especially in education and health – without eliminating ruling elites' control of patronage. It was the Brazilian state, after 1982, that imposed austerity on its citizens so that private bankers could recover their loans. It was the rising discontent after the financial crisis of 2008 that spurred citizens everywhere to call upon their states to shelter them from the fall-out from private bankers' short-termism. *In effect, global integration re-signified the importance of the nation-state.* A fallacy of the globalization triumphalists was to believe that global integration would ever make the nation a relic. So long as the notion of 'global citizen' was just a pipedream, real citizens would turn to their governments to cope and resist.[19]

In a competitive, over-heating, and now plague-filled, world, citizens have been left to find shelter in the bosom of the nation and summoned to its defence. Universities and schools have become battlegrounds for the national narrative. Donald Trump created a 1776 Commission to celebrate 'the patriotic educator'.[20] The Turkish government ordered the firing of almost 6,000 disloyal academics.[21] After the arrest of some 3,000 students in Hong Kong, Carrie Lam, Beijing's sergeant in the former British colony, decried how the city's campuses had failed to teach proper national values. 'What is wrong with education in Hong Kong?' she lamented. The Communist Party, meanwhile, reasserted its patriotic narrative. The city's education secretary forbade students from singing 'Glory to Hong Kong' scrapped the mandatory civics course called 'Liberal Studies', and obligated the instruction in Chinese history. Meanwhile libraries are being cleansed of anything that 'endangers national security'.[22] History textbooks must nurture 'a sense of belonging to the country, an affection for the Chinese people, a sense of national identity, as well as awareness of a sense of responsibility for safeguarding national security'.[23] In India, as part of the introduction of the 'rationalized syllabus', the Modi government attempts to remove Mughal history from high-school textbooks.

The escalation of patriotic fury could sustain some strange inversions. In Germany, in 2020, an agitated public debate emerged around the Cameroonian historian Achille Mbembe, who was accused by Felix Klein, the German government's Commissioner against anti-Semitism, and others of anti-Semitism, Holocaust trivialization and Israel hatred. Mbembe's defenders, on the other hand, saw racism and McCarthyism at work in these accusations. The controversy quickly expanded into a wide-ranging debate about memory, the Holocaust, and 'German national identity'. According to Felix Klein, Mbembe, a 'foreign' scholar in Klein's view, had 'intervened' in a debate that was, as it were, part of German identity. In doing so, Mbembe had 'formulated misleading sentences'. Klein demanded: 'He must now clarify that.' The commissioner added a statement 'that [what] is wrong from a German point of view doesn't become right just because [the call] comes from the outside in'.[24] Concealed behind these assertions is a highly problematic understanding: since Germans are responsible for the Holocaust, they now take the moral right, over and above, to dictate to others what they have to say about it.[25] Here is a classic, and ironic, confusion born of a failure to comprehend the fundamental ways in which, like nations, their narratives are entangled with each other, mirror, borrow and feud with each other. Mbembe, by raising doubts about German exceptionalism, was charged with an inability to understand or even have the moral right to echo, the German exceptionalist narrative.

Narratives and global history

Wherever the nativist Right has ascended, a caste of intellectuals has swarmed to make the case for the nation. Swapan Dasgupta of India, Jonah Goldberg of the United States and Éric Zemmour of France, the telegenic pundit and author of *Le suicide français: Ces quarantes années qui ont défait la France*, have been the prophets of despair, proclaiming a stark choice between imminent demise or national renewal.[26] The apocalyptic refrains about suicide and self-destruction are a mainstay of their alarm. They pose as the defenders of national heritage. But they do so by proclaiming themselves as storytellers. And not just any story, but the story of nations once great and now in trouble, if not doomed.[27]

Why narratives? The answer most often heard is that narratives are powerful emotional devices to connect the subject – an endangered minority, a struggling social class, a menaced nation – to the listener or reader. Even economists, less well-known for their research on passions than with their fixation with individual self-interest, have joined the fray. Some have turned to spinmeisters and narrators in the making of market life and its exuberant excesses. The most influential of them is the Nobel Prize-winning Robert J. Shiller. His book, *Narrative Economics: How Stories Go Viral and Drive Major Economic Events*, is an attempt to show that actors create characters, plotlines and morality tales to make sense of complex events and processes.[28] These stories make the interpretations easily transmissible; they simplify, make complex meanings more commensurable and thus facilitate circulation. This is where Shiller mobilizes the power of the narrative to explain how information and interpretation go, as he puts it, 'viral' because it makes them mutually intelligible. When the story makes the information go viral, it creates a reality by shaping expectations and behaviours. The dilemma, of course, is that Shiller's account of narrative is designed to explain why and how markets get unmoored from the rational calculus of *homo economicus* (hence the allusion to the out-of-control spread of disease). Narratives, in this view, matter because they provide organizing cognitive schema, impassion and mobilize actors.

Because they mobilize and demobilize, as recent world events and the toxic role of social media in political campaigns have reminded us, narratives are powerful and valuable resources. They are worldmaking devices that introduce new actors to the global stage and perform roles of legitimating and stigmatizing in-group and out-group affiliates, bond friends, create allies and make enemies.

12 *Narratives, Nations, and Other World Products*

This is why groups fight over them and why intellectuals, broadly defined, have been worldmakers in this domain of politics. Narratives bond groups through recognizable structures of character, plot and sequential order that help make meaning. Of the range of genres and types of narrative, the ones that concern the authors in this book are manifestly 'stories of peoplehood' – that is, arcs that promise and define the making of social and political allegiances out of common experiences. As the chapters in this volume attest, the narratives have taken many forms, from political speeches and museums to legal treatises and economic manifestos. They also occupy a variety of stages, from the street and casinos to the historian's desk and the podium of international conventions. And they have been produced and circulated by a plethora of actors from economists to emergency responders to labour activists.[29]

Because they are valuable, narratives are also the object of competition. Even the most triumphal or hegemonic of storylines operates in a field of alternatives. This is why the patriotic narrative has always had to vie with rivals. The plurality of voices, stages and forms means that narratives contest each other even as they mirror and emulate from each other. There has never been just one narrative upon which all stories of peoplehood have converged, but instead a repertoire. The chapters should be read as a gateway to the global history of the repertoire of stories of peoplehood. They do so in three sections. All of them illustrate how narratives jostled, competed and borrowed from each other.

Section I is concerned with bonding narratives that created attachments among co-members of entities called nations to stake claims to membership in groups. The promise here was to take advantage or shelter themselves in a world of opportunities and threats. Chapters by Matthew Karp, Bao Maohong, Mayuko Sano and Masashi Haneda outline narratives aimed at creating civic communities of nations from the United States to Indonesia because they were entangled with other civic communities called nations. In so doing, especially as forums multiplied and the technologies of circulation grew more efficient, the density of exchange and rivalry thickened. Sometimes, the imagined bonding was not even territorial, but bound by other rituals of togetherness and connection, like shared recreation across borders. Xavier Paulès's chapter on Chinese diaspora traditions of recreation and gaming is an example of bonding meanings within linguistic or ethnic groups that straddle borders. In his chapter, Sheldon Garon argues that narratives of civilian resilience in the face of aerial bombing during the Second World War were themselves the result of many years of emulating models and stories of civic preparedness that circulated the idea of 'self-defence' of the *polis* across countries and continents. Working across scales and mobilizing a range of actors, these public narratives responded to and mimicked each other to create a complex, fractious, unity of a world of narratives.

If narratives and their creators competed with each other, they also connected. Indeed, global entanglements produced other narratives of power that often transcended the nation. Some narratives appealed to and invented transnational scales of attachment that bridged communities. For most of modern history, bridging narratives have taken the form of empires and other kinds of 'great power' – from the Soviet Union and its proletarian utopia (which Marc Elie discusses at the example of Soviet Central Asian elites during the 1950s) to the association of human rights crusaders to an inescapable single world market. Indeed, peace-seeking and development were a common narrative format for transnational scales. Natasha Wheatley's chapter shows how the case of the Hapsburg empire and its intellectual heirs yielded stories of imperial order and international law to replace it. If norms and laws were scripted as bridging processes, so was trade. Commercial ties revealed, however, more discordant visions, as some saw the making of an international division of labour as stratifying, widening divides between societies even as they became more interdependent. Jeremy Adelman, Abigail Kret, Marlène Rosano-Grange and Bruno Settis outline the stages through which economists in particular imagined a bridging scale forged by a single market and a thickening web of interdependence – with plenty of feuding about whether the story of market fusion was virtuous or not. From the perspective of Southeast Asia, as Vincent Houben and Benjamin Baumann show, development discourses emerged as a way to claim the need for membership in this new scale of life to bridge the widening gap between haves and have-nots. These latter chapters show how the acknowledgement of economic interdependence yielded contentious narratives of togetherness, some uplifting, others dismayed about the power of markets as bridging forces.[30]

Latent in Sections I and II, which focus narratives' bonding and bridging functions within and between communities, is the search for something more whole. Each story of peoplehood was, by definition, a story about people *of the world*. The final section makes this more explicit. It explores the search for narratives of a wider whole motivated by need to locate one's place – as a nation, empire, member of an in-group or an out-group – in the world. Fuelling this search were claims for recognition about the legitimacy of group claims in an interdependent world. As Achille Mbembe has noted, the struggle for recognition, poignantly expressed in the struggle for decolonization, was a call for the *disenclosure* of the world.[31] To disenclose the world is to acknowledge the ways in which collective narratives imply an acknowledgement of their part in the wider frame. Indeed, one might say that all narratives of nations, empires and other great powers have also always been stories about the wholes of which each nation, empire or other collective identity was a part. Section III makes this explicit by locating people in their place in the wider world beyond the realm of political communities like nations and empires. The chapters look at 'other world products' such as work, production, migration or the idea of belonging to an 'international system'. Pierre-Yves Cadalen, Connor Mills and Karoline Postel-Vinay illuminate the ways in which the story of the United Nations yielded a post-1945 vision of peaceable integration of nations as its *racontoneurs* outlined a story of heroic actors defying odds and creating worlds. But stories of a disenclosed whole often pointed to distinctions and exclusions. Megan Armknecht, Markus Bierkoch and Beth Lew-Williams' chapter explores the ways in which the figure of 'the immigrant' played a role in national narratives, circulating in the wider whole and seeking welcome and integration within national parts. In a world of human mobility, the migrant and the in-migrant have been decisive actors in the plotlines that legitimated the range of state powers from integration to extermination. The organizing and the distinguishing powers of narratives have provided the glue for peoplehood and estrangement. Another example concerns work and the line that separated the valuable from the valueless. The struggle over the meaning – and value – of work in settings where labourers did not even enjoy citizenship rights forced them

14   *Narratives, Nations, and Other World Products*

to claim other identities and belongings, like trade union membership. By the same token, as the chapter by Andreas Eckert, Fabian Krautwald and Kerstin Stubenvoll on struggles over the meaning and narrative of work in East and West Africa shows, this contest was also a struggle over the ascribed value of African work and colonizers' work.

To imagine a whole does not imply the search for a unity. When attached to and mobilized for civic and political movements, narratives separated those with access to rights and privileges afforded to in-group members from the outliers. Dividing began early. As Silvia Sebastiani observes in her chapter, an Enlightenment effort to create taxonomies and personalities of species and races, and thus nations, evolved into biologized hierarchies that distinguished and separated beings. This urge to create narratives that explain hierarchies carried all the way to more recent efforts to map out – and contest – the unequal division of world labour, one that distinguished between the backwards and advanced, as in Alessandro Stanziani's chapter on the debate over Russia's 'retardation' in a modernizing world and a distinction between peripheral and the core regions of an integrated world, as Jeremy Adelman, Laetitia Lenel and Pablo Pryluka explore.

This volume looks at the functions of narratives as bonding, bridging and disenclosing forces that made sense of global integration – even as they explained, legitimated or contested the distinctions and divides it produced. Its goal is to illuminate the repertoire of practices of storytelling and the concepts they sired, like the nation, like empires, species, classes and places that sought meaning because they were becoming interdependent. Narratives made sense of that process. Narrators took many forms, adopted many genres. They were also increasingly interconnected, relying on shared technologies and borrowing each other's practices and norms – even if they resisted, successfully, what Chimamanda Ngozi Adichie in 2009 called 'the danger of a single story'.[32]

Notes

1   Thomas Friedman, *The World Is Flat: A Brief History of the Twenty-First Century* (New York: Farrar, Straus and Giroux, 2005).

2   https://revdem.ceu.edu/2022/01/13/three-tales-about-france-and-eric-zemmour/

3   Sebastian Conrad, *What Is Global History?* (Princeton: Princeton University Press, 2017).

4   Nikole Hannah-Jones (creator), *The 1619 Project: A New Origin Story* (New York: New York Times, 2021).

5   Holland Cotter, 'For Big Museums, It's Time to Change', *New York Times*, 22 March 2020.

6   Sergey Radchenko, 'Putin's Histories', *Contemporary European History* 32, no. 1 (2023): 57–60.

7   Patrick J. Geary, *The Myth of Nations: The Medieval Origins of Europe* (Princeton: Princeton University Press, 2002).

8   George Orwell, 'Looking Back on the Spanish Civil War' (1942), in *The Collected Essays, Journalism and Letters of George Orwell*, ed. Sonia Orwell and Ian Angus (New York: Harcourt Brace Jovanovich, 1968), V. 2, p. 256.

9   https://www.britishmuseum.org/about-us/british-museum-story/contested-objects-collection/benin-bronzes. Dan Hicks, *The Brutish Museums: The Benin Bronzes, Colonial Violence and Cultural Restitution* (London: Pluto Press, 2020).

10   The field of anti-globalization studies is now vast. Among the pioneering activists was Naomi Klein. See her *No Logo* (New York: Knopf, 1999). For an early scan, see Derek Wall, *Babylon and Beyond: The Economics of Anti-Capitalist, Anti-Globalist, and Radical Green Movements* (London: Pluto, 2005).

11   Peter Geschiere, *The Perils of Belonging: Autochthony, Citizenship, and Exclusion in Africa and Europe* (Chicago: University of Chicago Press, 2009).

12   Laurent Fourchard and Aurelia Segatti, 'Of Xenophobia and Citizenship: The Everyday Politics and Exclusion and Inclusion in Africa', *Africa* 65, no. 1 (2015): 2–12.

13   David Armitage, *The Declaration of Independence: A Global History* (Cambridge, MA: Harvard University Press, 2007).

14   Adom Getachew, *Worldmaking after Empire: The Rise and Fall of Self-Determination* (Princeton: Princeton University Press, 2019).

15   Karen Ho, *Liquidated: An Ethnography of Wall Street* (Durham, NC: Duke University Press, 2009), 242 and 302.

16   Gillian Hart, *Disabling Globalization: Places of Power in Post-Apartheid South Africa* (Berkeley and Los Angeles: University of California Press, 2002), 357.

17   https://www.hindustantimes.com/india/i-m-a-hindu-nationalist-patriotic-narendra-modi/story-AD9X3vwbidDJTtdfZKk7BO.html

18   Arjun Appadurai, *Fear of Small Numbers: An Essay on the Geography of Anger* (Durham, NC: Duke University Press, 2006), 8–9; on human flow, see Ai Weiwei, *Human Flow: Stories from the Global Refugee Crisis* (Princeton: Princeton University Press, 2020).

19   Dani Rodrik, *The Globalization Paradox: Democracy and the Future of the World Economy* (New York: W.W. Norton, 2018).

20   https://www.nytimes.com/2021/01/18/us/politics/trump-1776-commission-report.html

21   https://www.hrw.org/news/2018/05/14/turkey-government-targeting-academics

22   https://www.nytimes.com/2020/07/11/world/asia/china-hong-kong-security-schools.html

23   https://www.nytimes.com/2021/02/24/world/asia/hong-kong-national-security-law-education.html?action=click&module=Top%20Stories&pgtype=Homepage

24   Felix Klein, *Für eine Entschuldigung sehe ich keinen Anlass* [I see no reason for any excuse]. [Interview with Adam Soboczynski], *Die ZEIT*, 20 May 2020.

25   Matthias Böckmann et al. (eds.), *Jenseits von Mbembe – Geschichte, Erinnerung, Solidarität* (Berlin: Metropol, 2022).

26   Swapan Dasgupta, *The Awakening Bharat Mata: The Political Beliefs of the Indian Right* (New York: Penguin, 2019); Jonah Goldberg, *Suicide of the West: How the Rebirth of Nationalism, Populism and Identity Politics Is Destroying America* (New York: Crown, 2018); Éric Zemmour, *Le suicide français: Ces quarantes années qui ont défait la France* (Paris: Ed. Albin Michel, 2014)

27   Alain Finkielkraut, *L'identité malheureuse* (Paris: Stock, 2013).

28   Robert J. Shiller, *Narrative Economics: How Stories Go Viral and Drive Major Economic Events* (Princeton: Princeton University Press, 2019).

29   Rogers M. Smith, *Stories of Peoplehood: The Politics and Moral of Political Membership* (New York: Cambridge University Press, 2003).

30 On bridging and bonding, see Robert Putnam, *Bowling Alone: The Collapse and Revival of American Community* (New York: Simon & Schuster, 2000).

31 Achille Mbembe, *Out of the Dark Night: Essays on Decolonization* (New York: Columbia University Press, 2021), 61; Jeremy Adelman and Gyan Prakash (eds.), *Inventing the Third World. In Search of Freedom for the Postwar Global South* (London and New York: Bloomsbury, 2022).

32 https://www.youtube.com/watch?v=D9Ihs241zeg

Section One

Stories of peoplehood

1

'This nation is a globe': Exceptionalism and universalism in the nineteenth-century United States

Matthew Karp

An opposition between the national and the global is a reliable feature of historical argument all around the world. In the contemporary United States, it runs like a border through the landscape of public debate, organizing and dividing rival interpretations of American history. On one side of this well-policed frontier stand the forthright defenders of nationhood, increasingly beleaguered within the academy but stronger than ever outside it, for whom US history is still, as a number of grade-school textbooks proclaim, the story of *The American Nation*. Not every native of this land is a patriot, let alone a chauvinist, but some agreement on the irreducible significance of 'the American experiment' – its distinctive character, its autonomous existence, its particular claims to meaning – is the coin of the realm. On the other side of the border, meanwhile, are the global citizens: intellectually sceptical of the claims of the nation-state, ideologically hostile to the notion of 'American exceptionalism' and committed to a transnational, pluralistic vision of the past in which it is vital to remember that the entity we know as 'the United States' emerged *Out of Many*, and that its people have always been *Global Americans*.[1]

From a certain angle, the same essential partition has also structured two hundred and fifty years of US history itself. Today's ideological divide between nationalists and globalists, you could say, re-enacts a long-running opposition between patriots and cosmopolitans, exceptionalists and universalists. In historical terms, however, this boundary line becomes rather difficult to maintain: very often, it turns out, the foundational acts of US nation-making were also bids for global inclusion. In 1776, when American colonial leaders gathered in Philadelphia to declare themselves free from British rule, they were not marking themselves as an exception to the world, but seeking membership in it – as a newly sovereign state within an international community of sovereign states. 'The Declaration of Independence', writes David Armitage, savouring an apparent checkmate of nationalist historiography, 'was therefore a declaration of interdependence'.[2] Yet this episode may not be such a simple victory for the globalists, after all. If the Declaration effectively affirmed that America's self-rule hinged on international recognition – thus encasing the national within the global – it also announced its famously universal and self-evident truths in a document whose primary aim was the achievement of separate statehood – thus encasing the global within the national. The idea that 'all men are created equal', some exuberant nationalist might argue, was therefore created by the US nation-state.[3]

In some basic sense, of course, the national and the global are inevitably entwined across modern world history. National narratives, no matter how parochial, always imply some relationship with the rest of the world, while global visions, no matter how transcendent, have all emerged from a nineteenth- and twentieth-century planet carved into nation-states.[4] In the case of the United States, the entwinement is particularly knotty, since most American nationalists, from Thomas Jefferson to Ronald Reagan, have tended to propound an ostensibly universalistic form of exceptionalism – putting rhetorical emphasis not on blood or heritage but ideology – while American globalists, from Woodrow Wilson to Barack Obama, have tended to favour a rather exceptional form of universalism – conjuring an egalitarian world order implicitly premised on the primacy of American ideas and American power.[5]

Rather than attempt a grand but distant sketch of two hundred and fifty years of history, this chapter focuses on a particular conjuncture in the mid-nineteenth century. The era of the American Civil War may not be a representative moment – it remains both the gravest and deadliest crisis in all US history – but it is perhaps a particularly illuminating one. In the years leading up to the war, two clashing narratives about the young republic vied for supremacy in federal politics. To a greater extent than most American historians have recognized, perhaps, these national narratives pivoted from, and depended on, ideas about nineteenth-century global integration.

*

It was not so long ago that the more cosmopolitan class of American historians could be found lamenting the provincialism that seemed to isolate the US Civil War from the rest of the planet. 'Our worst navel-gazing', complained David Potter, 'has occurred in connection with the Civil War – a conflict all our own, as American as apple pie'.[6] For their part, most non-American world historians of the twentieth century shared this opinion and were not especially interested in sampling a slice. For thinkers as different as Winston Churchill and Eric Hobsbawm, America's largest war was a dramatic but ultimately second-order conflict, wherein the crashing wave of modernity – industrial capitalism and the consolidated nation-state – extinguished the last stubborn remains of an antiquated social order based on slavery. The American Civil War was a contest 'between the nineteenth century and the seventeenth', pronounced Churchill, and it was precisely in those fanciful terms that the war attracted the attention of literary romantics, while serious students of world history looked elsewhere.[7]

How much has changed in the last twenty years. No longer a peripheral or predetermined event, the Civil War has been promoted to a critical turning point in both the history of global capitalism and the international struggle for democracy.[8] Nor has this transformation been driven entirely by US historians, shrewdly seeking to convert their own specialized knowledge into the skyrocketing coin of global history. It was a notable non-Americanist, after all, who observed in 1860 that 'the most momentous thing happening in the world today' involved the 'movement among the slaves in America', and a year later called the clash between North and South 'the first grand war of contemporaneous history'.[9] Today, leading scholars of the nineteenth-century world now too depict the Civil War not merely as a bloody mopping-up operation, but a cataclysmic struggle against the vanguard of an internationally resurgent slave system, with consequences that reverberated across the hemisphere, if not the globe.[10] In some sense the deadliest war in the history of the Americas has also profited from a determined historiographical effort to liberate global history from Europe's gravitational field. As a representative event in 'the great turbulence at midcentury' that stretched from Crimea to China to Paraguay, the US Civil War did not merely follow the path already marked out by earlier European evolutions. On the contrary, its protagonists played an active part in the entangled process of nation-making and global integration that involved a large portion of the nineteenth-century world.[11] In a sense, modern scholarship has finally caught up with the Japanese scholars who compiled a multivolume history of the United States in 1872, with special attention paid to *nanbuko senso* ('The North-South War'), a political and military conflict with global implications.[12]

Even in the midst of their own crisis, nineteenth-century Americans too demonstrated a significant if partial awareness of this larger process. It is perhaps not very surprising that their attitudes displayed two of the major 'birth defects' that would mark later and more systematic efforts at modern social science. Although in 1850 the nation-state itself was still in its adolescence, Americans both North and South generally saw the world in terms of discrete national containers, the most important of which was undoubtedly the United States. And almost always, they celebrated 'progress' in a way that unconsciously replicated the particular global power hierarchies of the mid-nineteenth century, using Eurocentric categories as universal concepts, and envisioning the world as the place where Euro-Americans acted and virtually everybody else was acted upon. Nevertheless mid-century Americans, if not quite practitioners of global history in Sebastian Conrad's twenty-first-century sense, adopted a distinctly 'global perspective' on US politics. Both Northern and Southern elites sought to describe the ways in which their societies contributed to something that could legitimately be called global integration.[13]

Mid-nineteenth-century American politics was torn apart by endless arguments about slavery. At the bottom, this was a clash of social systems whose economic and ideological trajectories had diverged sharply since the American Revolution: the boisterous and expansive free-labour society of the North collided with the planter-dominated society of the South over the future of slavery in the republic.[14] After 1854, this larger conflict took the specific form of democratic political struggle, with mass parties debating the future of slavery at every election. In that respect, perhaps the most influential US narrators of global integration were not drawn from the familiar cast of intellectuals and bureaucrats we tend to associate with the construction of national mythologies and world histories alike. Instead, very often, the task fell to leading politicians themselves. When public figures like Abraham Lincoln and Jefferson Davis argued the national politics of slavery, they also crafted narratives of global progress and development. These narratives served an instrumental political purpose, but they

22   *Narratives, Nations, and Other World Products*

also represented a fascinating effort by both Northern and Southern leaders to conjure the world in a way that was persuasive to ordinary voters. The result, by 1860, was two distinct – and distinctly antagonistic – visions of the global nineteenth century.

'The world is growing wiser'

In the spring of 1850, Virginia's Robert M. T. Hunter presented his colleagues in the US Senate with a provocative global thought experiment:

> Suppose that, in 1833, African slavery had been abolished all over the world – in the colonies of France and Spain, in Brazil, in the United States, wherever, in short, it existed. I ask how such a policy would have operated upon the world at large? No cotton! No sugar! But little coffee, and less tobacco! Why, how many people would thus have been stricken rudely and at once from the census of the world?[15]

For Hunter and other antebellum Southern leaders, the defence of slavery in the United States emerged naturally from a larger argument about global commerce. The labour of African slaves, after all, was responsible not only for 'King Cotton' in the American South, but all the great staples of the Atlantic world, from São Tome to São Paulo. In the words of the essayist Louisa McCord, perhaps the most formidable of the South's pro-slavery intellectuals, 'the wonderful development of this western continent' was achieved only 'by means of slavery – her immense produce scattered all over our globe, carrying food and clothing to the hungry and the destitute; her cotton and sugar sustaining not only herself but the might of Europe's most powerful nations'.[16]

Although Britain (in 1833) and France (in 1848) had emancipated their Caribbean colonies, by mid-century Southern US leaders generally rejected the narrative that the modern world was moving away from enslaved labour. With former slaves in colonies like Jamaica and Martinique withdrawing their labour from plantations, sugar exports flagged, allowing American slaveholders to boast that Caribbean emancipation had proven a 'ruinous' failure. Enslaved Spanish Cuba, meanwhile, claimed an ever-larger share of the global market in sugar, while between 1830 and 1854 coffee production in enslaved Brazil grew by a factor of eight. The South's most prominent spokesmen, including Jefferson Davis, regularly contrasted the supposed stagnation of emancipated Spanish America with the prosperity of Brazil. R. M. T. Hunter's list of slaveholding societies included the United States, Brazil, 'the Russian, the Austrian, the Spanish dominions … governments embracing a majority of the civilized world'.[17]

The Southern narrative of global integration extended beyond a simple celebration of slavery itself: a related emphasis was the international spread of free trade. Great Britain's abolition of the Corn Laws in 1846 led to further liberalizing measures, including the repeal of the sugar duties, which had protected the emancipated West Indian colonies against direct competition with slave production. Britain's embrace of free trade triggered a decade of tariff reductions across Europe, the Americas and beyond. By 1853 the US Treasury Secretary, himself a Kentucky slaveholder, trumpeted the phenomenon in global terms: 'The free lists of England, France, Belgium, Portugal,

Brazil, Austria, Spain, Russia, Cuba, the Zoll Verein, Chili, Netherlands, Hans Towns, Norway, Mexico, and Sweden ... mark the progress of free trade among commercial nations.'[18] For pro-slavery observers, this amounted to something more than a technical adjustment within world markets. A larger transformation of political economy had occurred: the early-nineteenth-century British model of mercantile protection and slave abolition, symbolized by the sugar duties, had been supplanted by an American-led model centred on free trade in slave goods, symbolized by the exploding international market for cotton. As the world's leading producer of the world's most important slave product, the United States played an indispensable role in this great process.[19]

Alongside free trade in slave goods, American slaveholders found a second motor for global integration in the rise of Euro-American empires. Across the 1850s, from Morocco to Sumatra, powerful European states had begun to take violent possession over much of Africa and Asia. 'Never', writes Eric Hobsbawm, 'did Europeans dominate the world more completely and unquestionably than in the third quarter of the nineteenth century.'[20] This particular moment of domination produced a particularly chauvinistic global analysis, in America as well as Europe. Although Southerners sometimes criticized British hypocrisy or Russian brutality, mostly they celebrated the march of empire as the march of civilization and eagerly placed the United States alongside the great European conquerors. As one Southern essayist wrote during the US-Mexico War (1846–8), 'there is not a battle that England has fought in India, Affghanistan, or China, nor that France has fought in Africa, nor that the United States are now fighting on the rich plains of Mexico, which will not ... finally bless the people conquered'. For Louisiana Senator John Slidell, the prospective US acquisition of Cuba would fit neatly into 'the tendency of the age': the 'absorption of weaker Powers' and 'inferior races' by the stronger and the superior.[21]

A third and closely related principle, indeed, was the hardening global pyramid of race. For slaveholding leaders, key international questions could not be resolved without reference to a fixed racial order. A failure of 'respect for the natural relation of the races', charged R. M. T. Hunter, had led Great Britain to promote 'barbarism instead of civilization'. If previous generations had largely understood 'civilization' as a question of religion, culture or development, mid-century Southerners put increasing emphasis on the 'natural' laws of racial hierarchy, conveniently disclosed by the mechanism of skin colour. Southern politicians like Hunter and Davis cited the new discoveries of scientific racists – Southern, Nothern and European alike – who purported to find biological differences between humans of different phenotypes. '[T]he world is growing wiser', declared Georgia's Alexander Stephens, and its new wisdom embraced a key pillar of American slaveholding society: 'Subordination is the normal condition of the negro.'[22] In this respect, the more adventurous pro-slavery intellectuals believed, the American South could serve as a kind of laboratory for the racially ranked and coercively maintained colonial labour forces that were helping organize the planet, in places like Dutch Java, British India and Spanish Cuba.[23]

Pro-slavery Southerners did not just theorize about this emerging global order, driven by trade, empire and race: as leading officials in the US government, they worked actively to construct it. Secretary of War Jefferson Davis looked to French colonialism in Algeria for an instructive lesson in how best to subjugate the indigenous inhabitants of North American West.[24] US Commodore Matthew Perry's famous 1853–4 mission to Japan was arranged, supervised and diligently promoted by William Graham and James Dobbin, two slaveholding secretaries of the navy from North Carolina.[25] Nor was Japan the only overseas site that the Southern leadership of the US Navy sought to 'open', by persuasion or by force. The Virginia oceanographer and naval reformer Matthew Maury denounced the 'Japan-like policy' by which Brazil sought to prevent the international exploitation of the Amazon River valley. For Maury, the Amazon valley was an untapped treasure-house of wealth, whose agricultural potential as 'a slave country' should be advanced by 'the African, with the American axe in his hand'. In 1850 Secretary Graham arranged for a US Navy expedition down the Amazon, with an eye to future trade and even potential colonization.[26]

'Emancipation is a democratic revolution'

Pro-slavery leaders and their allies remained at the helm of US foreign policy across the 1840s and 1850s. Increasingly, however, they found themselves challenged by anti-slavery voices in domestic politics. After 1854, that opposition cohered in the Republican Party, which developed a comprehensive political attack on the 'Slave Power' and its malign influence over American democracy. Yet in less obvious ways, the Republican assault on the Southern master class was also a critique of the Southern theory of global integration and the elaboration of a rival narrative. To be sure, both slaveholders and their anti-slavery opponents agreed on some fundamental points. They shared a mid-Victorian faith in the idea of 'progress' as chronological, quantifiable and, in the long term, inevitable. They assumed the importance of global commercial expansion, with the United States at its forefront; and they worked from the same tinted map of world civilizations, one that highlighted the vigour of the North Atlantic nations, while throwing into relief the immaturity of Latin America, the cruelty of Russia, the 'lethargy' of Asia and the 'barbarism' of Africa.[27] In their exuberant chauvinism, and their hierarchical ideas about savagery, civilization and progress, pro-slavery and anti-slavery American leaders reflected the tradition of eighteenth-century British thought to which they were both heir.[28]

Yet within these shared parameters lived a duelling set of emphases that amounted to a violent ideological contradiction – not only about the future of slavery in the United States, but the shape of the nineteenth-century world just coming into existence. Most concretely, Republican leaders rejected the Southern vision of a world economy dependent on enslaved labour. As they saw it, a narrow focus on American, Brazilian and Cuban slave productivity could not disguise the reality that emancipation, not bondage, was leaping like wildfire across the planet. In 1854 Massachusetts Senator Charles Sumner produced a comprehensive review of slavery's global retreat: not only had Western European nations freed their bondspeople, but 'in effeminate India, slavery has been condemned'; in Constantinople, 'the Ottoman Sultan has fastened upon it the stigma of disapprobation'; the rulers of Morocco and Tunis 'have been changed into abolitionists'; and even 'despotic Russia,' with its millions of serfs, had issued a 'positive prohibition' against the expansion of bondage into Bessarabia or Poland (a restrictive proviso that, Sumner noted, mirrored the Republicans' own platform).[29]

'This nation is a globe' 25

Sumner presented the international triumph of abolition as a moral awakening. Yet leading Republicans also connected this rejection of bondage to a narrative of global economic progress that read very differently than the pro-slavery version. Where slaveholding leaders celebrated commerce on its own terms – emphasizing tariff reductions, export statistics and the widest possible dissemination of goods – Republicans typically stressed the centrality of labour in the productive process. 'It is not traffic, but labor alone, that converts the resources of the country into wealth', declared New York's William Seward. This reflected the Republicans' deep ideological commitment to the idea of free labour, an expansive category that included not only those who toiled for a living, but all who did directly productive work: farmers, mechanics, artisans and small businessmen.[30]

Yet if this free labour vision was in some respects a provincial one, involving the celebration of a particular form of small-scale capitalism in the northern United States, it had larger implications, too. It underlined the anti-slavery rejection of a global economy based on coerced labour and cheap goods: 'a world toiling and sweating for the benefit of a few capitalists ... if only it will produce raising a certain amount of cotton, sugar, and coffee, for export, one or two cents cheaper ... ' And politically it framed the Republicans, champions of 'the laboring classes' – as the German-American orator Carl Schurz put it – against a transnational cast of landlords, aristocrats and 'slaveholding capitalists', who lived 'upon the forced labor of others'. To avoid the miserable fate of 'the peasantry and poor of Great Britain', Republicans urged Northern farmers and labourers to reclaim their government from the oligarchic Slave Power. A community built around small-scale agricultural labour, argued Abraham Lincoln, 'will be alike independent of crowned-kings, money-kings, and land-kings'.[31]

Lincoln ultimately became the Republican Party's greatest figure, but across the 1850s, its leading voice on global political economy was William Henry Seward. A reform-minded senator from upstate New York, Seward championed developmentalist social and economic policy at the state and federal levels: tariff-funded internal improvements, a national bank, investment in public education. After joining the Republican Party in 1855, Seward quickly became the new organization's most significant public thinker, especially on international questions. For Seward, the true yardstick of economic progress, at home or abroad, was not the 'great accumulation of wealth', but 'diversified' development. With all the vast resources at his command, Tsar Nicholas of Russia still required 'a Massachusetts engineer' to build his railroads, 'a Baltimore mechanic' to construct his locomotives and 'a carriage-maker of Troy' (New York) to fashion his cars. Whether in Russia, Latin America or the US South, an emphasis on export goods – a priority on commerce over labour – was a deadly mistake. 'This false economy crowds the culture of a few staples with excessive industry; thus rendering labor dependent at home, while it brings the whole nation tributary to the monopolizing manufacturer abroad.'[32]

In the Republican worldview, economic progress was inextricable from the political institutions that framed it. Here, too, anti-slavery spokesmen diverged from Southern defenders of bondage. While planter-statesmen like R. M. T. Hunter occasionally adorned their speeches with vague tributes to the 'republican government', the pro-slavery theory of global development was (within a strict racial framework) resolutely materialistic: social and economic institutions produced the political order, and not the other way around. For Seward, on the other hand, political freedom was a necessary ingredient of social and economic development: 'While our constitutions and laws establish political equality', he declared, 'they operate to produce social equality also'.[33]

Above all else, the Republican narrative of global integration centred on the advance of political democracy. Since the suppressed revolutions of 1848, Seward noted, 'It has become a proverb, that Europe must soon become either republican or despotic' – and he was certain that republicanism would ultimately prevail. In the Republican mind, it was the spread of free political institutions – laws guaranteeing liberty of conscience, the sovereignty of the people and 'the absolute and inherent equality of all men' – that constituted the United States' great contribution to global progress. These American principles, incarnated by the Puritans in seventeenth-century Massachusetts, had already ensured the victory of republicanism across the Americas, from Labrador to the Straits of Magellan. Its trajectory was not merely hemispheric or transatlantic: Seward confidently projected the birth of 'future republics on the islands and continents on the Pacific Ocean, and on the heretofore neglected coasts of Africa'. The global abolition of slavery, for most Republicans, existed within this rubric. For Carl Schurz, the former German revolutionary, slavery in the South was like the kingdom of Naples, 'a social institution which is in antagonism with the principles of democratic government'. Seward was even more direct: 'Emancipation', he told the Senate, 'is a democratic revolution'.[34]

Their anti-slavery commitments notwithstanding, Republicans were not racial egalitarians, in either a national or a global context. Seward frankly asserted that black and Native Americans, due to 'their peculiar condition', constituted 'inferior masses', incapable of easy assimilation. Internationally, in a dispute with Britain over Central America's Mosquito Coast, he upheld 'the universal custom of European and American States', which decreed that 'savage tribes ... have no actual or high sovereignty', yet the terms of this Republican racial hierarchy were starkly different than the immovable pyramid envisioned by pro-slavery leaders. Condition and circumstance, not biology, explained difference: '[P]hilosophy', said Seward, 'meekly expresses her distrust of the asserted natural superiority of the white race ... ' On the Senate floor, the New Yorker's vindication of 'common humanity' brought out a crabbed rebuttal from R. M. T. Hunter, who mocked 'that extensive spirit of philanthropy' that 'loves all men equally, whether they be English, French, German, Tartar, Negro, Hottentot'. Hunter and other Southerners overstated the case, but it was true that the Republicans' formal commitment to universal humanity – the United States, said Sumner, was founded on 'the primal truth of the Equality of men' – conjured a different world order than the slaveholding vision of a globe governed exclusively by colour and blood.[35]

Pro-slavery globalists, anti-slavery nationalists

A striking contrast between these two mid-century master narratives lay in the way they imagined the relationship between American nationhood and the larger process of global integration. Again and again, pro-slavery narrators emphasized the *convergence* of the United States with the rest of the planet. Slavery, far from being a 'peculiar' institution, in fact extended over 'the majority of the civilized world'. The mid-century rise of free trade was an international rather than a particularly American story. Although the process of global integration through imperial conquest certainly involved the United States – through the war against Mexico and the settlement of the North American interior – it could hardly be said that America led the way. In the 'great race for position and empire', Britain, France and even Russia were quicker off the starter's block. Some Southerners, including Confederate Vice President Alexander Stephens, argued for a kind of pro-slavery exceptionalism: 'our new government', he boasted in 1861, 'is the first, in the history of the world' based on Black inferiority. But for the most part slaveholders understood the rise of biological racism in global rather than national terms. These international developments did not make the slave South stand out; they made the rest of the world more like the South.[36]

Anti-slavery leaders, conversely, tended to stress the distinctive features of the American experience. Sometimes this took the form of a jeremiad against the unique evil of slavery in the mid-century United States: 'Alone in the company of nations', declared Charles Sumner, 'does our country assume this hateful championship'. More frequently, for Republican politicians, American exceptionalism meant a celebration of republican equality in a world of aristocratic empires. William Seward's grand review of historical imperialisms, from Alexander the Great to Great Britain, served to distinguish the experience of the American republic, whose settler colonies quickly assumed the rights and powers of equal membership in the Union. If democracy was on the rise across the world, it was due specifically to 'the influences of the United States'.[37]

While pro-slavery leaders imagined global integration as a genuinely multipolar phenomenon – with commercial, imperial and racial solutions being worked out in parallel, from New Zealand to New Mexico – Republicans tended to describe convergence as a process by which the United States led, and the rest of the world followed. '[T]he cause of America', said Seward, 'had always been, and must ever continue to be, the cause of human nature'. Republicans trumpeted this idea, in part, to amplify the inequality and unfreedom of Southern slavery, a betrayal of American universality. 'There is a higher law than the Constitution', declared Seward in one of his most famous speeches. America's responsibility to God, and to 'the common heritage of mankind', required the restriction of slavery. From this towering perspective it became difficult to see any boundaries between the world and the United States. 'This nation is a globe', Seward continued, 'still accumulating upon accumulation ....' US national expansion represented, in effect, a form of global integration all by itself.[38]

It is not difficult to perceive how such grandiosity led, during and after the Civil War, to the creation of a US empire that soon stretched into the Caribbean and across the Pacific. As Secretary of State from 1861 to 1869, Seward himself played a large role in this process.[39] Yet in the 1850s, anti-slavery exceptionalism pointed less towards global empire than a relentlessly national political struggle. In 1856 the abolitionist Thomas Wentworth Higginson returned from Europe to find his country convulsed by debate over slavery. At a mass rally in Massachusetts, he argued that the fate of the wider world depended specifically on the outcome of this particular American struggle:

> You weigh America against Europe; and I tell you, you can hardly realize ... how little the events of Europe seem compared with those going on around us now. A single meeting of Abolitionists in some country school-house ... becomes more momentous to you, more full of prediction of the future, than all the petty manoeverings of politicians in London and Paris, Vienna and St. Petersburg ... The war in Kansas seems infinitely more than the war in Crimea; and you wonder at the glittering baubles for which men play at public life in Europe, when only here is the battle worth fighting.[40]

Higginson took a more radical line against slavery than many Republican leaders. But his transatlantic perspective on the American sectional crisis – which pitted 'a spirit of slavery such as the world has never seen' against 'a spirit of freedom such as the world has never seen' – fairly represented the worldview of the Republican Party itself. Just as the Declaration of Independence had linked inalienable truths to the sovereignty of the United States, mid-nineteenth-century Republicans wedded global principles to a national conflict. It was no coincidence that Republicans made the Declaration central to their party's identity, quoting it in their 1856 and 1860 party platforms. The global struggle for 'Universal Freedom and Equality', declared the *New-York Tribune*, the country's most influential Republican newspaper, in fact depended on the political struggle to win freedom and equality in the United States.[41]

While slaveholding elites trusted in their ultimate vindication by global markets and global scientific inquiry, Republicans sought victory in national politics. When they achieved it in 1860, with the presidential election of Abraham Lincoln, the division between pro-slavery globalists and anti-slavery nationalists only deepened. The foundation of the Confederate States of America, in large degree, was a wager on the idea that slavery would be safer in the realm of international relations than under the rule of an anti-slavery federal government. For secessionist and Confederate leaders, the national existence of the Southern republic depended not only on its internal strength, but the very process of global integration that slaveholders believed was bringing the world towards 'compulsory labour', racial hierarchy and imperial power.[42]

During the Civil War, meanwhile, anti-slavery leaders in the North only doubled down on their universalistic nationalism: the cause of global democracy required the preservation of the American Union. The war against secession, Lincoln argued, was a war on behalf of 'popular Government', intending 'to demonstrate to the world that those who can fairly carry an election can also suppress a rebellion; that ballots are the rightful and peaceful successors of bullets ....' American abolitionists likewise claimed the bloody clash between Blue and Gray as the central theatre in a global war against bondage. 'The blow we strike', declared Frederick Douglass, 'is not merely to free a country or a continent – but the whole world from Slavery – for when Slavery falls here – it will fall everywhere'.[43]

At Gettysburg in 1863, Lincoln's most famous words amounted to a wartime codicil to the Declaration of 1776, linking the global fate of its most radical idea – 'the proposition that all men are created equal' – to the intensely national struggle for the Union. The American Civil War, he said, was a test of whether 'any nation' dedicated to this idea 'can long endure'. In global terms the war was a desperate battle for liberty, equality and democracy to make sure 'that government of the people, by the people, for the people, shall not perish from the earth'.[44] But if the stakes of this battle were global, its protagonists were somewhat less so: they were American soldiers 'who here gave their lives that that nation might live'. The Gettysburg Address was an earnest appeal to universal truths as well as a grandiose burst of American exceptionalism. But above all, perhaps, it was an argument that lofty global ideals could only acquire meaning and force through particular national struggles.

*

A century and a half later, how should we make sense of this American struggle between anti-slavery nationalists and pro-slavery globalists? For all their chauvinism, both sets of narrators identified real and enduring features of global integration. By crushing the Confederacy on the battlefield, Republicans in the North advanced their vision of a planet organized by powerful, unified nation-states – led by the United States – in which chattel slavery was a relic, some forms of democratic government were the norm and the global economy was driven not by trade in agricultural staples but by diversified industrial development, protected by tariff barriers. From one perspective, this was self-evidently the world of 1920, and perhaps even 2020 too. Yet the Southern vision of global integration hardly vanished after the surrender of the Confederacy. For W. E. B. Du Bois, a generation after the Civil War, it was not Abraham Lincoln but Jefferson Davis who best anticipated his own era's imperial world order. The violent process of global conquest and modernization that scholars have termed 'the racial century', from 1850 to 1950, bore out many of the darker aspects of the Southern theory. Today, the notion of a planet effectively ranked by race, fuelled by coerced and dependent labour, and regulated by Euro-American commercial-financial capital, is too obviously still with us.[45]

The United States, of course, has played a major role in the construction of these overlapping global orders.[46] A glib if not wholly unpersuasive distillation of American history since 1865 might suggest that it followed the Southern trajectory, but with Northern rhetoric. Yet more interesting, perhaps, than a genealogical account of which narrative prevailed where and when, is the complex nature of the collision itself. In the era of the US Civil War, the most confident American globalists were also the most rigid champions of class and caste; the most egalitarian American democrats were also the most resolute political nationalists. Amid our own contemporary wars between patriots and cosmopolitans, it may be worth recalling that the lines of battle are seldom as neat as we might wish them to be.

Notes

1   Mark C. Carnes and John A. Garraty, *The American Nation: A History of the United States*, 5th edition (New York: Pearson, 2015); John Mack Faragher, et al., *Out of Many: A History of the American People*, 7th edition (New York: Pearson, 2011); Maria Montoya, et al., *Global Americans: A History of the United States*

(Boston: Wadsworth, 2017); see also Carl J. Guarneri, 'Globalizing the US History Textbook', *Journal of American History* 103, no. 4 (March 2017): 983–92; Jeremy Adelman, 'What is global history now?' *Aeon*, 2 March 2017.

2   David Armitage, *The Declaration of Independence: A Global History* (Cambridge, MA: Harvard University Press, 2007), 20–2, 29–30. See also Thomas Bender, *A Nation among Nations: America's Place in World History* (New York: Hill and Wang, 2006), 61–115; Eliga Gould, *Among the Powers of the Earth: The American Revolution and the Making of a New World Empire* (Cambridge, MA: Harvard University Press, 2012); David M. Golove and Daniel J. Hulsebosch, 'A Civilized Nation: The Early American Constitution, the Law of Nations, and the Pursuit of International Recognition', *New York University Public Law and Legal Theory Working Papers*, Paper 222 (2010).

3   For nearly all of modern history, as Hannah Arendt argued, universal, 'inalienable' human rights have required particular states to grant and protect them: Arendt, *The Origins of Totalitarianism* (New York: Harcourt, 1976 [1948]), 267–302; Samuel Moyn, *The Last Utopia: Human Rights in History* (Cambridge, MA: Harvard University Press, 2010), 12–13; Stephanie DeGooyer et al., *The Right to Have Rights* (London: Verso, 2018).

4   Christopher L. Hill, *National History and the World of Nations: Capital, State and the Rhetoric of History in Japan, France, and the United States* (Durham, NC: Duke University Press, 2008); Sebastian Conrad, *What Is Global History?* (Princeton and Oxford: Princeton University Press, 2016), 79–89; Samuel Moyn, 'Fantasies of Federalism', *Dissent* (Winter 2015): 145–51.

5   In this respect Donald Trump figures as something of an exceptional anti-exceptionalist: Stephen Wertheim, 'Trump and American Exceptionalism', *Foreign Affairs*, 3 January 2017. For a range of perspectives on the entwinement of the national and the global in US history, and how they have played out in American relations with the world, see Michael Hunt, *Ideology and US Foreign Policy* (New Haven: Yale University Press, 1987); Walter Russell Mead, *Special Providence: American Foreign Policy and How It Changed the World* (New York: Routledge, 2002); Robert Kagan, *Dangerous Nation: America's Foreign Policy from Its Earliest Days to the Dawn of the Twentieth Century* (New York: Vintage, 2006); Aziz Rana, *The Two Faces of American Freedom* (Cambridge, MA: Harvard University Press, 2010); Richard Immerman, *Empire for Liberty: A History of American Imperialism from Benjamin Franklin to Paul Wolfowitz* (Princeton: Princeton University Press, 2010); Perry Anderson, *American Foreign Policy and Its Thinkers* (London: Verso, 2014); A. G. Hopkins, *American Empire: A Global History* (Princeton: Princeton University Press, 2018).

6   David M. Potter, 'The Civil War in the History of the Modern World: A Comparative View', in *The South and the Sectional Conflict* (Baton Rouge: Louisiana State University Press, 1968), 287–99.

7   Winston Churchill, *History of the English-Speaking Peoples: The Great Democracies* (London: Dodd, Mead, 1958), 123; Eric Hobsbawm, *The Age of Capital: 1848–1875* (New York: Charles Scribner's Sons, 1975), 141–3.

8   Sven Beckert, *Empire of Cotton: A Global History* (New York: Knopf, 2014); Don Doyle, *The Cause of All Nations: An International History of the American Civil War* (New York: Basic Books, 2015). See also 'Interchange: Nationalism and Internationalism in the Era of the Civil War', *Journal of American History* 98, no. 2 (September 2011): 455–89; Richard Carwardine and Jay Sexton, *The Global Lincoln*

'*This nation is a globe*' 31

(New York: Oxford University Press, 2011); David Gleason and Simon Lewis (eds.), *The Civil War as a Global Conflict: Transnational Meanings of the American Civil War* (Columbia, SC: University of South Carolina Press, 2014); Brent E. Kinser, *The American Civil War and the Shaping of British Democracy* (Burlington, VT: Ashgate, 2011).

9   Karl Marx to Fredreich Engels, 11 January 1860, in Marx and Engels, *Collected Works* (London: Lawrence & Wishart, 1975), vol. 41, 4; Marx and Engels, *The Civil War in the United States*, ed. Andrew Zimmerman (New York: International Publishers, 2016), 53; Kevin B. Anderson, *Marx at the Margins: On Nationalism, Ethnicity, and Non-Western Societies* (Chicago: University of Chicago Press, 2010).

10 For recent work, see Robin Blackburn, *The American Crucible: Slavery, Emancipation, and Human Rights* (London: Bloomsbury, 2013); Javier Laviña and Michael Zeuske, *The Second Slavery: Mass Slaveries and Modernity in the Americas and in the Atlantic Basin* (Münster: Lit Verlag, 2014); Rafael de Bivar Marquese and Tâmis Peixoto Parron, 'Internacional escravista: A política da Segunda Escravidão', *Topoi* 12, no. 23 (July–December 2011): 97–111.

11 Michael Geyer and Charles Bright, 'Global Violence and Nationalizing Wars in Eurasia and America: The Geopolitics of War in the Mid-Nineteenth Century', *Comparative Studies in Society and History* 38 (October 1996): 619–57; C. A. Bayly, *The Birth of the Modern World* (London: Blackwell, 2004), 161–5; Jürgen Osterhammel, *The Transformation of the World* (Princeton: Princeton University Press, 2013), 543–57; Charles S. Maier, 'Leviathan 2.0: Inventing Modern Statehood', in *A World Connecting, 1870–1945*, ed. Emily Rosenberg (Cambridge, MA and London: Harvard University Press, 2012), 105–12; Bender, *A Nation Among Nations*, 116–81.

12 Michael Taylor, 'Civil War Treasures: North, South, Far East: The Civil War through Japanese Eyes', *Civil War Book Review* 17 (Summer 2015).

13 Conrad, *What Is Global History?* 3–4, 24–31.

14 On the economic, social and ideological roots of the US Civil War, see Eric Foner, *Free Soil, Free Labor, and Free Men: The Ideology of the Republican Party before the Civil War*, Revised Edition (New York: Oxford University Press, 1995 [1970]); James M. McPherson, *Battle Cry of Freedom: The Civil War Era* (New York: Oxford University Press, 1988), 3–275; Marc Egnal, *Clash of Extremes: The Economic Origins of the Civil War* (New York: Hill and Wang, 2009); John Ashworth, *Slavery, Capitalism, and Politics in the Antebellum Republic*, vol. 2, *The Coming of the Civil War, 1850–1861* (Cambridge: Cambridge University Press, 2007); and the essays of Foner, Ashworth, Steve Edwards, Neil Davidson, Robin Blackburn, Charles Post and August H. Nimtz, 'A Symposium on the American Civil War and Slavery', *Historical Materialism* 19, no. 4 (2011): 33–205.

15 Robert M. T. Hunter, speech in Senate, 25 March 1850, *Congressional Globe*, 31 Cong., 1 Sess., Appx. 381.

16 Louisa McCord, 'Slavery and Political Economy', *De Bow's Review* (October 1856): 331–49; *De Bow's Review* (November 1856): 443–67. For fuller discussion, see Matthew Karp, *This Vast Southern Empire: Slaveholders at the Helm of American Foreign Policy* (Cambridge, MA: Harvard University Press, 2016), 125–73.

17 'J. A. C.' [John A. Campbell], 'The British West Indies Islands', *Southern Quarterly Review* (January 1850): 342–77; 'The Coffee Trade – Its Production and Consumption Over The World', *New York Herald*, 20 August 1856; reprinted in the *Charleston Courier*, 16 January 1857; Jefferson Davis, Speech in Senate, 14 February

1850, *JDC*, vol. 1, 289–90; Hunter, speech in Senate, *Congressional Globe Appx.*, 31st Cong., 1st Sess., 381 (25 March 1850).

18 'Report of the Secretary of the Treasury', 6 December 1853, *Congressional Globe*, 33rd Cong., 1st Sess., App. 2; David Todd, 'John Bowring and the Global Dissemination of Free Trade', *Historical Journal* 51, no. 2 (2008): 373–97; Anthony Howe, ' Free Trade and Global Order: The Rise and Fall of a Victorian Vision', in *Victorian Visions of Global Order: Empire and International Relations in Nineteenth-Century British Political Thought*, ed. Duncan Bell (New York: Cambridge University Press, 2007), 26–46.

19 [Thomas P. Kettell], 'Stability of the Union', *Commercial Review of the South and West* (April 1850): 354–6; 'The Growth and Consumption of Cotton', *Southern Quarterly Review* (January 1848): 103–4.

20 Hobsbawm, *Age of Capital*, 135. See also John Gallagher and Ronald Robinson, 'The Imperialism of Free Trade', *Economic History Review* 6, no. 1 (1953): 1–15; Jennifer Pitts, *A Turn to Empire: The Rise of Imperial Liberalism in Britain and France* (Princeton: Princeton University Press, 2005).

21 'The Growth and Consumption of Cotton', 125–6; Report of the Secretary of War, *Congressional Globe*, 34 Cong., 3 Sess., Appx. 22 (1 December 1856); Slidell, *Congressional Globe*, 35th Cong., 2nd Sess., Appx. 90–2 (24 January 1859).

22 Hunter, speech in Senate, *Congressional Globe*, 33 Cong., 1 Sess., Appx. 221–6 (24 February 1854); Davis, speech in Senate, *Cong Globe*, 36th Cong., 1 Sess., 1682 (13 April 1860); Stephens, speech at Augusta, 7 February 1859, in *Alexander Stephens, in Public and Private ...*, ed. Henry Cleveland (Philadelphia: National Publishing Co., 1866), 647–50. On white racist thought and the rise of racist science across the nineteenth-century world, see Nell Irvin Painter, *The History of White People* (New York: Norton, 2011), 151–227; Nancy Stepan, *The Idea of Race in Science: Great Britain, 1800–1960* (London: Macmillan, 1982); John Haller, *Outcasts from Evolution: Scientific Attitudes of Racial Inferiority, 1859–1900* (Urbana: University of Illinois Press, 1971).

23 Louisa McCord, 'Diversity of the Races; Its Bearing upon Negro Slavery', *Southern Quarterly Review* (April 1851): 392–417; Daniel Lee, 'Agricultural Apprentices and Laborers', *SQR* (June 1854): 169.

24 Report of the Secretary of War, *Congressional Globe Appendix*, 34th Cong., 3rd Sess., 22 (1 December 1856); Jeffrey Ostler, *The Plains Sioux and US Colonialism from Lewis and Clark to Wounded Knee* (New York: Cambridge University Press, 2004), 1–108.

25 Pro-slavery Southerners were far from the only midcentury Americans eager to open commercial relations with Japan, but their crucial role in organizing the Perry expedition should not be neglected. Akira Iriye, *Across the Pacific: An Inner History of American-East Asian Relations* (Cambridge, MA: Harvard University Press, 1965 [1992]); John H. Schroeder, *Shaping a Maritime Empire: The Commercial and Diplomatic Role of the American Navy, 1829–1861* (Westport, CT: Greenwood Press, 1985); Jeffrey Keith, 'Civilization, Race, and the Japan Expedition's Cultural Diplomacy, 1853–1854', *Diplomatic History* 35, no. 2 (April 2011): 179–202.

26 Matthew Fontaine Maury, *The Amazon, and the Atlantic Slopes of South America* (Washington, DC: Frank Taylor, 1853); Gerald Horne, *The Deepest South: The United States, Brazil, and the African Slave Trade* (New York: New York University Press, 2007), 113–17; Karp, *This Vast Southern Empire*, 143–6.

27 William H. Seward, 'The Destiny of America', in *The Works of William H. Seward*, ed. George E. Baker (Boston: Houghton Mifflin and Company, 1884), vol. 4, 125.

Even Frederick Douglass maintained a (less severe) version of this continental pecking order: see 'The Meaning of July Fourth for the Negro', in *The Life and Writings of Frederick Douglass*, ed. Philip S. Foner (New York: International Publishers, 1950), vol. 2, 203.

28   Silvia Sebastiani, *The Scottish Enlightenment: Race, Gender, and the Limits of Progress* (New York: Palgrave Macmillan, 2013); Rana, *Two Faces of American Freedom*, 20–175.

29   Charles Sumner, *The Landmark of Freedom: Speech of the Hon. Charles Sumner ...* (Washington: Buell & Blanchard, 1854), 4. Sumner followed a long tradition of anti-slavery invocations of global emancipation, from 'Denmark' to 'Tripoli': Joshua R. Giddings, speech in Congress, 21 May 1844, in Giddings, *Speeches in Congress* (Boston: John P. Jewett and Company, 1853), 126; William H. Seward, *Speech of William H. Seward on the Admission of California* (Washington: Buell & Blanchard, 1850), 29.

30   Seward, 'The True Basis of American Independence', *Works of Seward* 4: 153–4. The classic examination of this Republican idea is Foner, *Free Soil, Free Labor, and Free Men*, esp. 11–72.

31   *Cincinnati Weekly Herald and Philanthropist*, 18 December 1844; Schurz, 'The Doom of Slavery', in *Speeches, Correspondence, and Political Papers of Carl Schurz*, ed. Frederic Bancroft (New York: G.P. Putnam's Sons, 1913), vol. 1, 137, 149–50; Seward, 'The Destiny of America', *Works of Seward* 4: 130; Abraham Lincoln, address before the Wisconsin State Agricultural Society, 30 September 1859, in *The Collected Works of Abraham Lincoln*, ed. Roy P. Basler (New Brunswick: Rutgers University Press, 1953), vol. 3, 481.

32   Seward, 'Basis of American Independence', 149–57. On Seward, see Glyndon G. Van Deusen, *William Henry Seward* (New York: Oxford University Press, 1967), 3–237; Immerman, *Empire for Liberty*, 99–126; Walter G. Sharrow, 'William Henry Seward and the Basis for American Empire, 1850–1860', *Pacific Historical Review* 36, no. 3 (August 1967): 325–42.

33   Hunter, *Congressional Globe*, 31st Cong., 1st Sess., 381 (25 March 1850); Seward, 'Basis of American Independence', 149.

34   Seward, 'The Pilgrims and Liberty', *Works*, vol. 4, 198; Seward, 'Destiny of America', 127–8; Schurz, 'Doom of Slavery', 126; Seward, *Speech ... on the Admission of California*, 42.

35   Seward, speech in Senate, *Congressional Globe Appx.*, 34th Cong., 1st Sess., 75–80 (31 January 1856); Seward, *Speech ... on the Admission of California*, 42; Seward, 'Destiny of America', 127–9; Hunter speech, *Congressional Globe Appx.*, 31st Cong, 1 Sess., 86 (31 January 1850); Sumner, *Landmark of Freedom*, 4. On early Republican racial attitudes, see Foner, *Free Soil*, 261–300; on the nineteenth-century collision between rising notions of equality and hardening ideas about race, see Siep Stuurman, *The Invention of Humanity: Equality and Cultural Difference in World History* (Cambridge, MA: Harvard University Press, 2017), 346–418.

36   Hunter, speech in Senate, *Congressional Glove Appendix*, 31st Cong., 1st Sess., 381 (25 March 1850); James D. B. DeBow et al., 'The Memphis Convention', *De Bow's Review* (March 1850): 217–32; Stephens, speech at Savannah, 21 March 1861, in *Stephens, in Public and Private*, 721. The idea of Southern convergence with the world – and Northern exceptionalism – is a notion both US and European historians have toyed with: C. Vann Woodward, 'The Irony of Southern History', in *The Burden of Southern History* (Baton Rouge: Louisiana State University Press, 1960), 187–212;

Eric Hobsbawm, *On Empire: America, War, and Global Supremacy* (New York: Pantheon, 2008), 75.

37   Sumner, *Landmark of Freedom*, 4; Seward, 'The Physical, Moral, and Intellectual Development of the American People', *Works of Seward* 4, no. 165: 168–70.

38   Seward, 'The Advent of the Republican Party', *Works of Seward*, vol. 4, 225; Seward, *Speech ... on the Admission of California*, 27–8, 45; Sharrow, 'Seward and the Basis for Empire', 326–7.

39   For a full-throated Civil War Republican defence of American 'empire ... on the very grandest of scales', see Carl Schurz, 'Peace, Liberty and Empire', speech in Philadelphia, 16 September 1864, in *Speeches of Carl Schurz* (Philadelphia: J.B. Lippincott, 1865), 269–320. On Seward and the postwar Republican pursuit of empire, see Immerman, *Empire for Liberty*, 121–7; Kagan, *Dangerous Nation*, 301–56; Jay Sexton, 'William H. Seward in the World', *Journal of the Civil War Era* 4, no. 3 (September 2014), 398–430.

40   Higginson speech at Abingdon, Massachusetts, in *National Antislavery Standard*, 5 August 1856. For similar comments from a German revolutionary and a Black abolitionist, both supporters of the Republican Party, see the speech of Gustav Struve at Newark, reported in the *New York Times*, 20 August 1856; John Mercer Langston, 'The World's Anti-Slavery Movement: Its Heroes and Triumphs', speech at Cleveland, 3 August 1858, in *Freedom and Citizenship: Selected Lectures and Addresses of John Mercer Langston* (Washington, DC: Rufus H. Darby, 1883), 41–69.

41   Charles W. Johnson (ed.), *Proceedings of the First Three Republican National Conventions of 1856, 1860 and 1864* (Minneapolis: Harrison and Smith, 1893), 43–5, 130–42; *New-York Tribune*, 4 July 1856.

42   See, for instance, John Townsend, *The South Alone, Should Govern the South* (Charleston: Evans and Cogswell, 1860); John Townsend, *The Doom of Slavery in the Union: Its Safety out of It* (Charleston: Evans and Cogswell, 1860); Stephens, speech at Savannah, *Stephens, in Public and Private*, 717–29; Karp, *This Vast Southern Empire*, 233–9; John Majewski, *Modernizing a Slave Economy: The Economic Vision of the Confederate Nation* (Chapel Hill: University of North Carolina Press, 2009), 116–19, 136–9.

43   Lincoln, Message to Congress in Special Session, 1 July 1861, *Collected Works of Lincoln*, vol. 4, 439; Douglass, 'The Mission of the War', in John Stauffer and Henry Louis, Gates Jr., *The Portable Frederick Douglass* (New York: Penguin, 2016), 330.

44   Lincoln, Address Delivered at the Dedication of the Ceremony at Gettysburg, 19 November 1863, *Collected Works of Lincoln*, vol. 7, 18–23. See also Doyle, *Cause of All Nations*, 281–98; Sean Wilentz, 'Democracy at Gettysburg, 1863', in *The Politicians and the Egalitarians: The Hidden History of American Politics* (New York: W.W. Norton, 2016), 213–32.

45   Du Bois, 'Jefferson Davis as a Representative of Civilization', in *W.E.B. Du Bois: A Reader*, ed. David Levering Lewis (New York: Henry Holt, 1995), 17–19; Karp, *This Vast Southern Empire*, 251–6; A. Dirk Moses, 'Conceptual Blockages and Definitional Dilemmas in the "Racial Century": Genocides of Indigenous Peoples and the Holocaust', *Patters of Prejudice* 36, no. 4 (2002): 31–6; Osterhammel, *Transformation of the World*, 392–415, 826–72.

46   Marilyn Lake and Henry Reynolds, *Drawing the Global Colour Line: White Men's Countries and the Challenge of Racial Equality* (New York: Cambridge University Press, 2008), 54–238; Robert Vitalis, *White World Order, Black Power Politics: The Birth of American International Relations* (Ithaca, NY: Cornell University Press, 2015).

2

Narratives of power: Political thoughts and the framework of world history in modern China

BAO Maohong

Introduction

As a perspective and process, global history has been used to develop new fields of history and rethink the written history at different levels. Certainly, the rise of global history partly resulted from the urge to respond to the challenges from continuous technological innovation and economic globalization.[1] With the economic rise of China and its integration into the world in the 1980s, global history, as a subdiscipline, appeared in China in the 1990s. However, there has been a world history framework in China since the Opium War in 1840.

From 1820 to 2010, the place of China in the world economy changed dramatically. In 1820, China's share of world GDP was one-third, its real per capita income was 90 per cent of the world average. However, the share fell to 1/20 and real per capita income fell to less than a quarter in 1950.[2] This decline resulted from the fall of the Qing empire and the depredations of colonialism and imperialism. During this period, the political leadership and intellectuals in China searched for ways to save China through national democratic revolution against feudalism and imperialism. From 1952 to 1978, China's GDP rose threefold and per capita income by 80 per cent; however, China's growth was still less than the world economy as a whole (per capita growth was 2.3 per cent a year compared with a world average of 2.6 per cent),[3] and especially in comparison to Japan and the 'Four small dragons' of Asia. The main reason for China's lagging during this boom period was that China's economy was isolated from the booming world economy and interrupted by some political movements. In other words, political leaders and intellectuals concentrated on various internal and international class struggles at the expense of the economy. From 1978 to 2010, China's share of world GDP rose from 5 per cent to 9.5 per cent and China surpassed Japan and became the world's second largest economy behind the United States. In 2001, China joined the World Trade Organization and integrated even more deeply into the world economy. During this period, political leadership and intellectuals focused on development and globalization.

In this changing historical context, China was forcefully integrated into the world capitalist system first, and then disintegrated unintentionally into two blocs during the Cold War, and finally became the current global China. In this complicated and tortuous process, China's political leaders sponsored their own worldviews as the strategic framework for the nation. Sun Yat-sen defined China as a nation-state broadly, including Pan-Asianism and global cosmopolitanism. Mao Zedong defined China in the context of the Third World and the world as a whole. Deng Xiaoping changed Mao's ideological narrative to a developmental one and contextualized China in the realm of the developing world. However, these three politicians' thoughts were usually studied from the perspectives of history of international relations, political biographies or history of the Chinese Communist Party. Their thoughts have deeply shaped the writing of world history in China.

In the traditional Chinese history framework, the dominant paradigm was the Tianxia worldview (天下观 based on the distinction of xia (夏, Han, the civilized Chinese) and Yi (夷, non-Han, the barbarians). The framework of traditional and official history was based on the relations between the middle kingdom and its surrounding tributary states. This system was replaced by nationalist history roughly after the First Opium War in 1840. Besides the input of modern history writing from Western Europe, political transformation drastically shifted history paradigms away from the traditional. As the most important figures who led the national democratic revolution and socialist revolution and construction, Sun Yat-sen, Mao Zedong and Deng Xiaoping influenced the framing of world history in China at different stages. Both frameworks for Chinese history and world history construction were usually analysed by the perspective of historiographical study.[4] In the thoughts of these three great politicians in modern China, China's national narratives were described in the framework of a three-level structure that impacted the structure of world history to some extents.

Based on these three politician's thoughts, this chapter will address the official national narratives of China in the framework of a three-level structure and their influences on world history frameworks in China. The complex interaction among these three parts (national, regional and global) in every thought will be analysed. Correspondingly, various paradigms of world history will be addressed in detail. Finally, the relationship of political narrative and world history in modern China will be observed.

Sun Yat-sen thought and contemporary world history construction

As the forerunner of national democratic revolution in China, Sun Yat-sen led the revolution that overthrew the Qing dynasty and set up the Republic of China in 1911. This revolution happened in the context of anti-colonialist and anti-imperialist wars. In Sun's thought, China, as an empire or later as a nation-state, located in Asia, was an integral part of the world that consisted of oppressors and the oppressed, colonizers and the colonized, based on the imperialist Western hegemony, that was different from the rule of moral regulation in the traditional East Asian system or tributary system. As the oppressed people, one of the main tasks of China was to change the semi-colonial and semi-feudal state through abrogating or revising unequal treaties and overthrowing Manchu rule, supported by the other oppressed people especially in Asia. In other words, liberty depended on Asia's unity and mutual aid, if the yellow people were to defeat the white people, and if the moral culture could defeat the powerful culture, then cosmopolitanism could be made true in the world finally. In his Pan-Asianism, the fall of Asia (as the origin of all cultures, including the European one) was temporary, and it would be restored after the national liberation movement. China, as the state with most population and the most influential culture, would play a critical role in cooperation with Japan that was the most advanced industrial country in East Asia. Additionally, Japan should stop invading China and voluntarily give up the unequal treaties it signed with China.[5]

Obviously, the starting point and standpoint of Sun's consideration of Asia and the world were China's national and democratic revolution. In order to win the revolution, he endorsed Pan-Asianism's vision of all Asian people uniting to fight against their white colonizers. Furthermore, the oppressed Asian people should unite the oppressed class in Western countries to overthrow the ruling class there. The aim of China's revolution was to construct a new China and new Asia and a new World based on moral principle and justice. This meant that China would be an integral and the most important part of Asia and the world. The future of China was based on worldwide racial struggle first and class struggle later.

In Sun's three-level structure, the core content was to transform China from a backward, oppressed feudal empire to an independent, democratic and advanced republic through national democratic revolution. In order to succeed in anti-colonialist and anti-imperialist struggles, China should obtain ideological, military and financial support from other Asian countries, while providing reciprocal support to them. In the Asian national liberation movement, China played a key role based on its largest population and splendid culture. However, Sun is not a Sino-centrist in his cosmopolitanism. Although the term is from Confucian classics, it encompassed utopian socialism from Europe. In other words, the cosmopolitanism was underlain by industrial production forces and mixed with the moral spirit of Chinese culture and liberty and equality of Western culture. Sun's imagination of the future world was consistent with his design of the Republic of China when he articulated his Three Principles of nationalism, democracy and people's livelihood.[6]

Sun's contextualizing of the making of the Chinese nation in Asia and the world was based on the combination of absorbing knowledge from predecessors and his own observation and practice abroad. As a student, he was trained in his hometown in China, Honolulu and Hong Kong. As a university student, he was trained as a doctor. This background made him read books in English, learn different disciplines and knowledge from the world. He inherited Hong Xiuquan's ambition (King of Taiping Heavenly Kingdom) 'to expel the Northern barbarians and to revive Zhonghua'. Here the Northern Barbarian referred to the Manchus and Zhonghua referred to the Han people. Obviously, this was the racial division based on traditional and dominant hierarchical view of Chinese and barbarians. After travelling in the United States, Japan and Western Europe and leading the national democratic revolution, he changed his Han nationalist thought to 'republic of five nationalities'.[7] Certainly, this is the concept of nation in the sense of a modern nation-state. In the 1890s when he was in Japan, he accepted the Japanese Pan-Asianism with the potential Japan-centrism. Stimulated by Japanese colonial expansion and the 1917 Russian revolution, he revised Pan-Asianism to become Sino-centric and his cosmopolitanism based on moral culture to be a new one resulting from the struggle between the colonized and the colonizers.

Partly and indirectly influenced by Sun's thought, China's world history frameworks in university instruction changed. In Chinese traditional history writing, China was at the core and other countries were recorded in the biographies of foreign savages according to their relations with China. After the Opium War, Chinese intellectuals began to understand the history of Western countries but very few of them were interested in Asian history, including Japanese history. After the Meiji restoration, especially the Sino-Japanese War of 1894–5, this situation changed. Learning from Japan after 1904, two branches of history (Chinese history and history of nation-states) were set up at Peking University. In the second branch, there were three parts, including history of the oriental or East Asian countries, history of the occidental or European countries and the United States, and world history. World history mainly dealt with the history of relations of different countries. History of the oriental was just an assemblage of Japanese history, Korean history and history of the South Seas. This meant that world history writing and teaching in China did not match the political demand completely, although it began to include Asian history and world history, mainly borrowing concepts from Japan, instead of traditional Chinese concepts and perspectives.

Concerning Asian history and world history writing and teaching, Peking University and Sun Yatsen University could be analysed as typical cases. After 1911 revolution, there were three subdisciplines in the history department of Peking University, namely general history of China, general history of the Oriental and general history of the Occidental. Besides general history of the Oriental, several selective courses on Asian history were offered, including history of exchanges in Eurasia, early modern history of Japan, history of Japan, ancient history of India, general history of India, history of Korea, history of exchanges between China and the West, history and geography of the South Seas, ethnic history of Central Asia, etc. The contemporary chairman of the history department, Prof. Zhu Xizu, hoped that his students would be trained, based on these three subdisciplines, to understand the concept of human history and research world history.[8] In the history department of Sun Yat-sen University (founded by Sun and named after him), some Asian history courses were offered, such as Asian history, history of the Oriental, national histories of Asia, national histories of the Oriental, current hundred-year history of Japan, modern history of Japan, history of India, early history of Mongols, etc.[9] In Peking University, Prof. Wang Tongling, who graduated from the Imperial University of Tokyo, taught a course titled 'history of the Oriental', in which 'the role of China in historical East Asia, the mutual relation of Chinese and races around, and relation of East Asian people and people outside East Asia were mainly analysed'.[10] In his book entitled *New History of the Oriental*, he criticized the Eurocentrism in world history and history of the Occidental from his perspective of history of the Oriental.[11] Perhaps, his historical thinking of China, Asia and world paralleled with Sun's viewpoint of China, Asia and world to some extent.

In the confusing political circumstances and tolerant intellectual context of Sun's time, his thought did not become the only and dominant guideline followed by historians. Not far from the 1911 revolution, the Republic of China entered the chaotic warlord era, Anti-Japanese war and civil war between the Kuomintang and the Communist Party. Obviously, similar to the Warring States period in ancient Chinese history, this unstable situation was helpful for various thoughts to blossom in framing world history, in which Sun's thought was just one of many choices. Fortunately, the principle of 'absorbing anything and promoting ideological freedom' has been practised at Peking University since Tsai Yuanpei became the president in 1917. Historians on the campus were free to research and teach history as they liked. However, this all changed after 1949.

Mao Zedong thought and its impact on China's framing of world history

As one of the founders of the Communist Party of China and the People's Republic of China, Mao Zedong changed his thought in the Cold War from the 'middle zone theory' to 'Three Worlds Theory'. In 1946, Mao thought that there existed a wide middle zone between the United States and the Soviet Union in the world, which could mitigate the anticipated world war and keep peace. Responding to the proposed nuclear threats from the Soviet Union after the split of Sino-Soviet relations, Mao put forward the concept of 'three worlds' when he met president of the Republic of Zambia, Mr. Kenneth David Kaunda, on 22 February 1974. On 10 April, Deng Xiaoping explained this theory further and systematically at the sixth special conference of UN Congress and made it well known all over the world.

Based on his idea of principal contradictions (the major danger in the world was struggling for hegemony and world war would result from the struggle for hegemony and against hegemony), Mao thought that there existed three worlds: the first world (the United States and the Soviet Union that were wealthy and had many nuclear weapons), the second world (European countries, Japan, Australia and Canada which were less wealthy than the first world, but more wealthy than the third world) and the third world (Asian and African and Latin American countries except Japan, all of them were poor and without nuclear arsenals).[12] In these three interactive and contradictory worlds, the third world was the main political force that has fought against the Western hegemony, and the main revolutionary driving force in historical progress. Behind this statement, there was Mao's basic appraisal of the global situation: the nuclear war was inevitable during the Cold War; China should prepare for the war earlier and more comprehensively with strong support from the third world. Furthermore, the war would result in revolution and the revolution would ultimately stop the war. It was in the world revolution that a red and new world would appear. In the thought of Mao Zedong, China was the part of the third world and the world as a whole. But as a revolutionary force, China would unite the other third world countries to defeat the hegemonists, including the US imperialist and the Soviet revisionist, and construct a new world.

In comparison with Sun's thought, Mao gave up the racial and geopolitical dimensions and completely adopted class struggle as the methodology to understand international affairs. As an independent socialist country in the context of the Cold War, China tried to defend its socialist regime and develop the cause of socialism. Earlier in 1946, Mao pointed out that the US imperialists had been preparing to attack the Soviet Union that was the defender of world peace, and further, the middle zone between the United States and Soviet Union, mostly the capitalist countries in Europe, colonies and semi-colonies in Asia and Africa, would be the buffer zone because they contradicted with the US imperialist at different levels. In other words, it was impossible for the US imperialist to attack the Soviet Union before it compelled obedience from the US ordinary people (internal oppressed class), the other capitalist countries, and colonies and semi-colonies.[13] After the signing of the Sino-Soviet Treaty of Friendship, Alliance and Mutual Assistance in 1950, China allied itself with the Soviet Union and supported national liberation movements in Asia and Africa based on its principle of class struggle and proletarian internationalism (national relations are, in the final analysis, class relations). At the Bandung Conference in April 1955, the PRC, as a third world country, shared the common historical legacy of anti-colonialism and anti-imperialism with other Asian and African countries, and affirmed its more third world identification by promoting what Mao called the 'five principles for peaceful coexistence (mutual respect for sovereignty and territorial integrity, non-aggression, non-interference in internal affairs of each other, equality and coexistence)'.[14] After China and Soviet Union parted ways in 1965, Mao had to revise his middle zone theory. Encouraged by the victory of national liberation movements in Asia and Africa, Mao regarded China and countries in Asia (except Japan), Africa and Latin America as the revolutionary force against hegemonic superpowers (the imperialist United States and the revisionist Soviet Union), the rest of the world as the second world between the first and the third, that belonged to either NATO bloc or Warsaw Treaty bloc, but contradicted with the first world. In other words, the second world was the force that the third world could unite in the anti-hegemonic revolution.

The core concept of Mao thought was proletarian revolution. Internally, it was the continued revolution under the dictatorship of the proletariat. Internationally, it was the proletarian world revolution. The final aim of these revolutions was to construct communist society all over the world. As Mao thought was regarded as a theoretical achievement of the sinicization of Marxism, the logics of his Three Worlds Theory were linear progress of five social formations and united front strategy. In Marxism, human society evolved from primitive communal society to slave society, then feudal society, capitalist society and finally socialist society (the first stage of communist society). The ultimate task of proletarian party was to overthrow the capitalist regime and its domination. However, the proletarian revolution happened mainly in the undeveloped capitalist countries (Russia) and semi-colonial and semi-feudal countries (China), not in the developed capitalist countries as predicted by Karl Marx, Mao and his party tried to take advantage of the power from the middle zone to form a united front against imperialist countries under the guidance of socialist Soviet Union first and then unified the third world to fight against the imperialist United States and the revisionist Soviet Union.

The Three Worlds Theory based on revolution and war as the major themes of the times originated from both the Communist International and his own theorization. At the sixth national congress of the Communist International in 1928, war was considered to be the central issue and the proletarian parties were requested to launch proletarian revolution to fight against imperialists.[15] During the first half of the Cold War, this judgement was still valid, especially for Chairman Mao. Mao formed his own theory about China's revolutionary path and socialist construction, based on comprehensive mixing of Marxism and observation of Western European politics and his social investigation and research. From Mao's history of reading, it is evident that his understanding and analysis of world history and international relation were based on class struggle. It is from the perspective of class analysis that he constructed his own 'Three Worlds Theory' and international strategy.

Inspired by the thought of Mao Zedong (as the guiding or dominant ideology of the People's Republic of China), the world history framework in China was revolutionized completely after 1949. All the members in Yan'an were required to read and study Mao's texts on the interpretation of Marxism and revolution of China in the Party Rectification Campaign launched in 1941. After that, Mao's thought was modelled as a uniform ideology that guided the cause of the party, including its academic research and cultural construction. After the PRC was established in October 1949, people's democratic dictatorship was also implemented. For the people, democracy has been enjoyed; for the non-people, dictatorship has been imposed. As a part of non-people, the intellectuals could join in the socialist construction after they educated themselves in accordance with Marxism and Mao thought or were re-educated by the communist party and the people. The incident of anti-Hu-Feng Counter Revolutionary Clique caused intellectuals to give up the bourgeois character and believe in Mao's revolutionary truth. With turning the 'blossoming and contending of one hundred flowers' campaign to the anti-rightist campaign, the intellectuals who spoke out their critical opinion were labelled as rightists or counter-revolutionaries for crackdown. In 1965, an ideological study campaign was carried out, beginning with the criticism of Wu Han's 1961 play *Hai Rui's Dismissal of Office*. Wu was a historian who specialized in Ming dynasty. His play was regarded as a defence of Marshall Peng Dehuai, one of Mao's critics. The politicization of history writing shocked and frightened all historians. Subsequently, the drastic 'The Great Proletariat Cultural Revolution' further frightened the historians to be 'the political correct'. In other words, in order to protect themselves, some historians had to pursue the pragmatic principle of 'better left than right' in their historical research and writing.

Learning from the Soviet Union, history writing was divided into two separate parts: Chinese history and world history. Both of them were reconstructed in the framework of evolution of five production modes with the class struggle as the main dynamics of it. In July 1956, Ministry of Higher Education organized historians to examine and approve the syllabus of world history. In April 1957, the authorized syllabus was published and implemented in all universities. In April 1961, the Propaganda Department of the CPC Central Committee held a meeting on textbooks of liberal arts and authorized Prof. Zhou Yiliang to edit the world history textbook.[16] At these two meetings, it was ordered that all history teaching and research should be guided by Marxism, Leninism and Mao thought.

Prof. Zhou Yiliang tried to collect and revise the manuscripts edited by masses (a group combining workers, peasants and soldiers in which professional historians just played a role as advisors) in various universities but failed. Then, he and Prof. Wu Yujin coedited the four-volume *General History of the World* that was published first in 1962 and second in 1972. These four-volume books covered world history from *Homo sapiens* to the Russian October Socialist Revolution that was divided into three stages, including Ancient Volume (Primitive communal society and slave society), Medieval volume (Feudal society) and Modern volume (A & B: Capitalist society). The proposed contemporary volume (Socialist society) was not completed. Although this set of books learned from the *General History of the World* edited by the Soviet Union Academy of Science in its framework based on Marxism, Leninism and Stalinism, it increased the pages of history of the third world to balance Eurocentrism and to strengthen the viewpoint of worldwide class struggle. Although these books lacked chapters of Chinese history, they included the economic and cultural relations of China and the other countries in the Ancient volume and Medieval volume, four subchapters on Chinese history in four chapters titled the invasion of Western colonialists and struggles against feudalism and colonialism in Asian Countries, and Peasant revolt and bourgeois reform and revolution in Asian countries in Modern volume (A & B).[17]

From the interesting introduction to reprint in the 1972 version, editors rethought the deficiency or defects in the 1962 version from the contemporary political ideology (Proletarian Cultural Revolution). Firstly, Marxism, Leninism and Mao Thought were not put into effect, and bourgeois idealism was not criticized comprehensively in the writing, because it was affected by the revisionist education line at that time. Secondly, the great struggle of the masses in different historical times was not discussed completely; on the contrary, the activities of the exploiting class became the historical focus. Thirdly, as the driving force of historical development, class struggle was not emphasized. The role played by the ruling and exploiting class in socio-economic and cultural prosperity was exaggerated and appraised further. Fourth, writing world history did not serve contemporary proletarian politics with its emphasis on bourgeois objectivism and was not helpful for the broad masses of workers, peasants and soldiers and their cadres to understand contemporary international situation correctly.[18] In one word, all these defects in world history writing resulted from not understanding Marxism, Leninism and Mao thought very well.

Why Chinese world historians wrote more on the history of the third world in their multivolume books of *General History of the World*, as mentioned above, was that Mao wanted them to pay more attention on the rise of the third world and its history. After the reorganization of universities and departments in the autumn of 1952, Peking University authorized Prof. Zhou Yiliang to set up the teaching and research section of the history of Asian countries, and to offer courses on ancient, modern and contemporary history of Asian countries. After the Bandung Conference in 1955, for every country in the Third World, Chairman Mao even requested to publish at least one book translated from foreign language and one book compiled by Chinese masses, in order to meet the needs of Chinese diplomats and cadres at different levels.

Prof. Zhou Yiliang suggested his department offer various courses on African history to train specialist of African studies. Prof. Yang Renbian, a historian specialized in the history of French Revolution, changed his field to African history in the autumn of 1958 and organized a group with three junior scholars and three graduate students for MA degree to learn and research African history. Responding to the intellectual need on Latin America, junior scholar, Luo Rongqu, changed his field from the history of Sino-Soviet friendship relation to Latin American history. After Prof. Yang and Luo joined in, the teaching and research section of the history of Asian countries became one section encompassing Asian, African and Latin American history.

With the unfolding of the Proletarian Cultural Revolution, it was necessary to construct a more revolutionary version of world history. In 1974, the three-volume *Concise World History* edited by world historians in the History Department of PKU was published by People's Press. Similar to the *General History of the World* coedited by Prof. Zhou and Prof. Wu, world history was divided into three stages, including ancient history (three social stages from *Homo sapiens* to British bourgeois revolution in 1640: primitive communal society, slave society and feudal society), modern history (capitalist society from 1640 to 1918 was divided into two stages: the first was from 1640 to the Paris Commune Revolution in 1871, in which feudal autocracy was destroyed and capitalism was established by the rising and progressive bourgeois; the second was from 1871 to 1918, in which bourgeois became reactionary and capitalist system went into decline) and Contemporary history (from 1918 to 1945, imperialism and colonialism went into decline and finally became extinct while socialism headed to victory). In the editor's note, four guiding principles were pointed out. Firstly, historians tried their best to implement Marxism, Leninism and Mao thought and to make world history as a discipline to serve proletarian politics. Secondly, historians tried their best to deconstruct class reconciliation theory and to reconstruct the long history of civilizations as the history of class struggle. Thirdly, historians tried their best to break the determinism of emperors, generals and ministers and prove that the people were the true masters of history. Fourthly, historians tried their best to deconstuct 'Eurocentrism' and to reconstruct world history as the history of people all over the world, especially the third world.[19] Obviously, this set of books were more ideologized and politicized than Zhou and Wu's set.

China's framing of world history from 1949 to 1978, as a completely ideologized and politicized one, matched Mao thought very well. The most extreme was that all schools and universities at different levels aimed at training students as the successors of the proletarian revolution. Almost all university students, officials and cadres at all levels were indoctrinated in class struggles and the belief in the final success of socialism against capitalism. Furthermore, they worshipped Mao unreasonably. However, the paradox in Mao thought could be observed in the different versions of *General History of the World*. The evolution of five production modes was the law summarized from the unique European history by Karl Marx; however, this law was overgeneralized as the universal law of human history. Needless to say, this was the typical Eurocentrism. Mao argued that the third world, as a rising revolutionary force, would push forward the revolution against capitalism and further build socialist society all over the world. Although historians added more pages on the history of the anti-colonial and national

Deng Xiaoping thought and its impact on China's world history construction

With the passing of Mao Zedong in 1976, Maoism weakened as a dominant ideology. After almost a two-year transition period, Deng Xiaoping took office as the head of the second generation leadership. As one of the leading members of Mao's leadership group, Deng insisted on raising the flag of Mao thought, on the one hand, while practising his own socialism theory with Chinese characteristics (concretely manifested in his reform and open door policy), on the other hand. The making and practice of Deng's thought depended upon his observation and judgement of the changing world situation.

Although Deng disseminated the Three Worlds Theory in public, he changed Mao thought in accordance with the deep change of the world in 1980s, when the tension between two blocs began to ease. On 4 March 1985, Deng Xiaoping said that world war had abated, although the risk of world war still existed. The real strategic issues in the world were how to keep peace and promote development in which the latter was at the core.[20] As the biggest developing country in the world, the main task of China was to push forward economic development and unremittingly enhance the overall national strength as soon as possible, instead of revolution. Developing economy needed international peace and keeping peace depended upon economic development. In order to reach this aim, China had to open to the whole world (including developed countries and developing countries), but mainly to the industrial countries, while China always stood on the side of developing countries, but did not want to be the leader of developing countries. In other words, in order to catch up to the developed countries, China tried to acquire advanced scientific technique and management experience and attract large investments from developed countries. From the perspective of the developing countries, he asserted that the world should be harmonized with the five principles for peaceful coexistence, instead of drawing lines according to ideology and social systems.

In comparison with Sun thought and Mao thought, Deng went beyond the political ideology of revolution and war. Sun aimed at setting up an independent and democratic republic of China, Mao aimed at guarding and constructing his socialist people's republic of China and Deng aimed at industrializing and modernizing China. However, contrary to Mao's revolutionary idealism, Deng was a pragmatist whose symbolic slogan was that 'it does not matter whether the cat is white or black, as long as it catches mice'. The experience of working as a probationer in Renault S. A. and visiting various industrial countries made him become a complete materialist. Additionally, after he took power in 1978, he tried to legitimize Chinese Communist Party and its socialist system as the ruling party and the permanent system with its ability to make Chinese people wealthy in the background of collapsing national economy, which resulted from Mao's Proletarian Cultural Revolution. 'Poverty is not socialism', 'the advantage of socialism should be embodied in its labor productivity higher than that of a capitalist country', Deng repeated on different occasions. So, China, as a member state of the developing countries, should concentrate on economic development to catch up the developed countries rapidly. It was economic development that could minimize the gap between the developed and the developing countries, and further changed the unequal international economic order. Interestingly, he did not mention that socialism would be victorious all over the world. He pointed out that the world would be multipolar and any country had its own right to choose its developmental model and state regime.

The core concept of Deng thought is development that should be understood from the perspective of the whole world and human as a whole. The most important in the development is production force. Deng said repeatedly, the fundamental task of socialism is to develop social production force. Furthermore, the advanced production force represents the superiority of socialism. The way to improve production force is to practise the reform and open door policy with the help of market forces. Concerning the world market, he said, developed countries should clearly realize that economy in developed countries could not be developed further if economy in developing countries did not develop.[21] As the biggest developing country in the world, China should learn all the advanced civilizational achievements, whether or not from capitalist countries. In Deng thought, development was the same with modernization, including four aspects (industry, agriculture, national defence, and science and technology). Guided by four kinds of modernization, China would become a medium-developed country by the middle of the twenty-first century. As a member state of developing countries, China supported the development of other developing countries via mechanisms for South-South cooperation and the Group of 77. However, China did not ally with any country.

The change of Deng's thought originated from his reading and thinking in Jiangxi Province. He became a Marxist when he worked in France and learned in Soviet Union from 1920 to 1927. At the Sun Yat-sen Univerity in Moscow, he not only studied the theory of Marxism and Leninism, but also observed the practice of New Economic Policy instead of wartime Communism. This experience inspired him that it is possible and reasonable to allow the development of private ownership in Socialist country, because it allows for the development of production forces and the whole national economy. Before the Great Proletarian Cultural Revolution, he followed and supported Mao thought. But from 1969 to 1972, he lived in Jiangxi after he was defeated politically. Based on his reading of the classical works of Marxism, and historical books of China and the world, he rethought some basic themes, such as 'what is socialism?', 'how to construct socialist country?' Perhaps, he remembered what he saw in the Soviet Union. The thinking of Deng in Jiangxi is similar to Mao's thinking in Yan'an. The commonality of them was to design the future of China (the focus of Mao was to set up the People's Republic of China; the focus of Deng was to make China wealthy via reform and open door). The contrast was in how Mao published some articles and works; however, Deng left nothing, no articles, no marks in books he read. This resulted in difficulty to understand the origins of his thought.

Deng has emphasized the role of science and technology in economic development. In France, he realized that poor efficiency in salary earning and economic growth in China was due to the lack of advanced technology. In Jiangxi's factory, he saw the backwardness in technology and management. When he visited Singapore, Japan and the United States, one of the main tasks was to import advanced industrial technology and management systems by signing the treaties of economic and technological cooperation. He was very active in sending Chinese students and scholars to study abroad. Prof. Luo Rongqu is one of those who did research in the United States. Additionally, even during the Greater Proletarian Cultural Revolution, he suggested his daughter and son enter university to learn medicine and technology. Perhaps, to some extent, this was influenced by his wife who graduated from the physics department of Peking University. Undoubtedly, this helped him to deepen his understanding of development and put forward his assertion of 'Science and technology was the first production force'.

In comparison with Mao's revolutionary romanticism of international affairs, Deng observed the international affairs from the perspective of objective realism. While in Jiangxi, he listened to the short-wave radio to keep up with international affairs. From January 1978 to March 1979, he visited eight countries, especially Japan and the United States, where he found that China lagged behind the industrial countries in the economic booming period and tried his best to create peaceful international circumstances for China's development. In other words, the experience of living abroad and many national visits made him change his judgement of the international situation from following Mao's thought to his own thought.

In the context of practising reform and open door policy, China's world history framework changed dramatically. Modernization theory and world process of modernization replaced class struggle and revolution and became the dominant paradigms in world history writing and teaching. Interestingly, this was sponsored by Peking University historians. Modernization studies was led by Prof. Luo Rongqu. On 12 May 1981, Luo visited Prof. C. E. Black, who was the well-known historian specializing in dynamics of modernization and comparative studies of modernization of Japan and Russia. Inspired by his historical perspective of modernization and interdisciplinary or multidisciplinary approach, Prof. Luo began to think about modern world history from the perspective of modernization.[22] In 1982, his programme of comparative studies of various modernizations was approved to be supported financially as 'the 7th five-year plan' key programme by the National Social Science Foundation that was managed by the Propaganda Department of the CPC Central Committee. In 1986, he set up the center for process of world modernization. He said that he borrowed the perspective of modernization to revisit the modern history of the World and China in order to meet the theoretical need of socialist modernization construction in China.[23] From his new perspective of historical development (one axis vertically: production force, instead of production relations, was regarded as the main dynamics of social development; plural developmental models horizontally: various social-economic structures, various political structures and cultural models in different regions and countries), Luo thought that world modernization process consisted of three waves: the first was the early industrialization originated from British industrial revolution in the late eighteenth century and diffused to Western Europe till the mid-nineteenth century; the second was that Europe and North America were industrialized and the non-Western world responded to the challenge from industrial Western world from the late nineteenth century to early twentieth century; and the third was industrialization improved in the industrial world and the developing world has been involved in industrialization since the mid-twentieth century.[24] In the modernization of developing countries, the state played a more important role than free market in the developed countries.

Although Luo's modernization theory was based on Marxism, it had a different thinking on many themes in modern world history with Zhou's world history. Luo emphasized production force as the dynamics of historical development, instead of class struggle, agricultural society and industrial society as the main forms of society, instead of feudalism and capitalism.[25] Luo paid more attention to reform than revolution in world history. In exploring the models of development, Luo emphasized the role of interaction of state, market and culture as the shaping force. He also revived the positive or constructive role of colonialism and imperialism in modern world history, to balance emphasizing negative or destructive role of them in traditional Marxist and nationalist history writing. His programme entitled 'History of Colonialism' was approved and supported financially as 'The 8th Five-Year Plan' key programme by the National Social Science Foundation.

Although Luo was inspired by modernization theory in the United States, he reconstructed it based on Marxism. He learned Marxism in the ideological reform movement and later believed in it, although he was never a member of the CPC. Stimulated by Deng's economic developmental initiative, Luo tried to provide a theoretical support for China's socialist modernization by reconstructing the modern history of China and the World.[26] This historical explanation corresponded to the catch-up strategy pursued by developing countries and China. In 1989, his paper 'On Historical Development View of One Axis and Multiple Lines' was awarded the excellent paper prize in commemorating the tenth anniversary of the Third Plenary Session of the 11th Central Committee by the Propaganda Department of the CPC Central Committee. Regretfully, he passed away in 1996 and did not push forward his theoretical research and concrete world history writing (including history of colonialism). However, his theory influenced many junior scholars in history and other disciplines. Inspired by his theory, university students and cadres at all levels came to rethink the left ideology in China and understand development and globalization. In other words, his world history framework helped to train supporters of socialism modernization in China.

To some extent, Luo's world history framework responded to Deng's socialist theory with Chinese characteristic. Although Deng's theory was practical and plain, it guided China to successfully transform from a backward country to the second largest economy and GDP in the world. The most outstanding was that Deng's theory was depoliticized and development was defined as the main task of the developing countries and China. Luo's modernization theory did not try to deconstruct Euro-Americentrism, but further rationalized the worldwide spread of modernization, which originated in Western Europe. Developing countries could not copy the Western modernization model, but should graft or implant modernity on their culture or reconstruct imported modernity. Both of these contradictory orientations were emphasized in his books.

Brief conclusions

The world and regional integration narratives of China were based on China's national interest. Of course, the definitions of China's national interest changed in different times (Sun's anti-imperialism and national democratic revolution, Mao's anti-world war and proletarian revolution, Deng's peace and development) and were contextualized in the particular judgement and appraisal of world situation. China's sovereignty stood out on a larger scale at different times. The stratification of the world in three politicians' thoughts helped to identify the place of China in the world. China's footholds changed from Sun's Pan-Asianism to Mao's Third World to Deng's Developing Countries. These resulted in the de-politization and de-ideologization of China's main tasks: from revolution to modernization; from ideological struggle to economic development.

As the dominant paradigms of views of China and the world, thoughts of Sun, Mao and Deng partly influenced the world history framing in China. Being a national democrat, Sun's thought triggered a few of contemporary historians to explore history of the oriental and world history to some extent. Being a proletariat revolutionist, Mao's thought guided and regulated the world history framing from 1949 to 1978. Being the chief architect of reform and open door policy, the impact of Deng's thought on world history framing was not dogmatic. The reference of world history frameworks in China came mainly from Japan, the Soviet Union and the United States. The framework of scalar division of history in Japan influenced the world history framing in Sun's Republic of China. Maoist historians studied world history according to the *General History of the World* in Soviet Union. Modernization theorists borrowed some concepts and analysis from their counterparts in the United States. However, the latter two shared the same foundations of Marxism. Both of these inner and outer elements made the world history framing share not only the common historical logic with foreign model paradigms but also gave them Chinese characteristics.

Inspired by the shift of dominant paradigms of guiding thoughts, world historians in China constructed their own view of world history. Certainly, these different versions of world history were the products of various times. As B. Croce said, 'all history is contemporary history'. These three world history narratives paralleled with three periods in modern China. This reflected that history writing was used to serve the Chinese people to learn more successful experiences from world history. Applicability of historical narratives was emphasized, instead of its ideological characteristics. Meanwhile, as professional historians, they tried to comply with academic principles and norms. In other words, dominant paradigms of guiding thoughts and world history construction served each other in China.

Notes

1   Sebastian Conrad, *What Is Global History?* (Princeton: Princeton University Press, 2016); Akira Iriye, *Global and Transnational History: The Past, Present, and Future* (Basingstoke and New York: Palgrave Macmillan, 2013).

2   Angus Maddison, *Chinese Economic Performance in the Long Run, Second Edition, Revised and Updated: 960–2030 AD* (Development Center of OECD, 2007), 17.

3   Angus Maddison, *Chinese Economic Performance in the Long Run, Second Edition, Revised and Updated: 960–2030 AD* (Development Center of OECD, 2007), 18.

4   Huaiyin Li, *Reinventing Modern China: Imagination and Authenticity in Chinese Historical Writing* (Honolulu: University of Hawaii Press, 2013); Luo Xu, 'Reconstructing World History in the People's Republic of China since 1980s', *Journal of World History* 18, no. 3 (Sep., 2007): 325–50; Luo Xu, 'The Rise of World History Studies in Twentieth-Century China', *History Compass* 8, no. 8 (2010): 780–9; Edward Wang, ed., *Chinese Studies in History* (World History vs. Global History? The Changing Worldview in Contemporary China), 42, no. 3 (Spring 2009).

5   Sun Yat-sen, 'Speech to Kobe Chambers of Commerce', in *Complete Works of Sun Yat-sen* (vol. 11) (Zhonghua Book Company, 1986), 401–9.

6   Qi Qizhang, 'On Sun Yat-sen's Cosmopolitanism', *History in Anhui*, no. 1 (1999): 58–60.

7   Including the Manchus, the Hans, the Mongolian, the Huis and the Tibetan.

8   Zhu Xizu, 'Introduction to New History', in James Harvey Robinson, *New History* (translated by He Bingsong) (Beiping: Commercial Press, 1929), 1–2.

9   Shang Xiaoming, 'Asian History Education in Universities during the Republic of China', in *Clio at Beida*, vol. 17 (Beijing: Peking University Press, 2012), 139.

10   Xiaoming, 'Asian History Education in Universities during the Republic of China', 154.

11   Wang Tongling, 'Preface', in *New History of the Oriental(A)* (Shanghai: Commercial Press, 1922), 3.

12   Mao Zedong, 'Talk with Kenneth David Kaunda', in *Selected Works on Diplomacy of Mao Zedong* (Beijing: Central Document Press, World Affairs Press, 1994), 601.

13   Mao Zedong, 'Talk with Anna Louise Strong', in *Selected Works of Mao Tse-Tung*, vol. 4 (People's Press, 1991), 1193.

14   Rebecca E. Karl, *Mao Zedong and China in the Twentieth-Century World* (Durham, NC: Duke University Press, 2010), pp.89–90.

15   Dai Longbin (ed.), *Historical Documents of the International Communist Movement*, vol. 45 (Beijing: The Central Compilation and Translation Press, 2013), 49.

16   Zhou Yiliang, *After All, It Is a Scholar* (Beijing: Beijing October Literary and Art Press, 1998), 51.

17   Zhou Yiliang, and Wu Yujin (eds.), *The General History of the World* (Ancient Volume) (Beijing: People Press, 1972), Chapter 31, pp. 415–19; Medieval volume, Chapter 39, pp. 523–39; Modern volume (A), subchapter 5 of Chapter 3, pp.102–12, subchapter 1 of Chapter 18, pp.429–33, Modern Volume (B), subchapter 1 of Chapter 23, pp. 116–22, subchapter 3 of Chapter 27, pp. 256–62.

18   Introduction to reprint, in Yiliang, Yujin eds., *The General History of the World*, 1–2.

19   The writing group of *Concise World History* in History Department of Peking University, *Concise World History* (People Press, 1974), 1.

20   Deng Xiaoping, *Selected Works of Deng Xiaoping*, vol. 3 (Beijing: People Press, 1993), 105.

21   Xiaoping, *Selected Works of Deng Xiaoping*, 96.

22   Lin Beidian, Zhou Yingru (eds.), *The Footprint of an Explorer: The Academic Life of Luo Rongqu* (Beijing: Commercial Press, 2006), 466.

23   Lin Beidian, Zhou Yingru, *The Footprint of an Explorer*, p.352; Luo rongqu, *Exploring History* (Commercial Press, 2009), 3.

24 Luo Rongqu, *A New View on Modernization* (Beijing: Commercial Press, 2006), 5–6.
25 Chapter 7: From Revolution to Modernization: The Paradigmatic Transition in Reform Era Historiography, in Li, *Reinventing modern China*.
26 Rongqu, *Exploring History*, 95–117.

3

Going beyond the 'Western impact' narrative: China as a world power, 1839–1949

Xavier Paulès

Introduction

In China, the period between 1839 (beginning of the First Opium War) and 1949 (creation of the People's Republic of China) is ritually referred to as 'the century of humiliation' (*bainian guochi* 百年國恥). Highly emotional indictments against these decades of 'humiliation', 'slavery', when China was a victim of imperialism, are more than ever *de rigueur* in the political discourse, medias and high-school textbooks. Such an interpretation serves, of course, a political aim. This pre-communist century is depicted as an age of weakness and humiliation because China ought to be waiting to be 'liberated', as according to the official history terminology, the Chinese Communist Party seizure of power in 1949 is referred to as the 'Liberation (*jiefang* 解放)' and supposed to have resulted in China regaining its freedom and its rank among the nations.[1]

The reader may get the feeling that by referring in my title to China during the period 1839–1949 in making use of the term 'world power', I intend to deliberately contradict that vulgate. This is indeed the case. Yet against the very dark depiction of the century 1839–1949 just mentioned, my aim is not to substitute too rosy a picture and argue that China was not relatively weak compared to the then dominant powers: Great Britain, France, Germany, Japan, the United States, etc. Instead, elaborating on a precious insight by Joseph Nye: 'soft power does not depend on hard power';[2] it is my intention to suggest that China's military, diplomatic and political weakness do not necessary imply that China was unable to exert a strong and wide influence on the rest of the world.

Among Chinese scholarly circles, the interactions of China with the rest of the world during the 1839–1949 period have been seen through the lenses of two main historical narratives. The 'Western impact' narrative describes how China received the modernizing influence of the West. The 'nationalist narrative' depicts China as a victim of imperialist influences. Even if they at first glance may look antithetical, however, both narratives share the same precept that during the 1839–1949 period, as far as its relations with the rest of the world were concerned, China was first and foremost under massive Western influence.

52   *Narratives, Nations, and Other World Products*

The last main narrative connecting China with the rest of the world takes the shape of Overseas Chinese studies (*Huaqiao huaren yanjiu* 華僑華人研究, in this chapter I shall use two terms indiscriminately: 'Overseas Chinese studies' and '*Huaqiao* studies'). The exponential growth of its diaspora is no doubt a crucial element of the relations between China and the rest of the world as the number of Overseas Chinese witnessed a tenfold increase between the middle of the nineteenth century and 1949 (from about 1 million to 10 million). Moreover, it became a worldwide phenomenon, as Chinese migrants settled in such faraway places as Australia, the United States or Peru, which had previously remained out of their reach. The only continent where Chinese population numbers remained insignificant was Europe.

One of the main features of *Huaqiao* studies is their overall framing into a paradigm of *inclusion*: they put dramatic emphasis on the connections between the diaspora and the motherland.[3] They pay some attention to the life of Chinese overseas communities, but in that matter, it is remarkable that they are far more interested in their inner organization, their economic and political achievements rather than in their relations and impact over the local populations.

This chapter will elaborate on how and why the Western impact/nationalist narratives as well as *Huaqiao* studies have all overlooked the fact that concomitantly to a political decline, Chinese influence not only remained strong, but greatly expended, as a side effect of the development of its diaspora. The idea of a 'Chinese influence' is especially relevant in the sphere of cultural exchanges as long as one takes 'culture' in its most comprehensive sense.

The two dominant narratives

The 'Western impact narrative' and the 'nationalist narrative'

The Western impact narrative was initiated in the West (mostly the United States) during the post-Second World War period by John Fairbank[4] and his many followers (historians like Albert Feuerwerker, Joseph Levenson, Rhoads Murphey or Mary Wright). These historians staged a relatively unchanging China facing the challenge of the modern West, both a threat and a model. The sequence of events and transformations was shaped, from start to finish, by problems posed for China by the West.[5] For one part, the predominance of such an 'impact-response' approach derived also from the fact that before the opening of Chinese archives in the 1980s and even more so the 1990s, Western scholars were making use almost exclusively of Western and Japanese sources. Therefore, as a whole, they were inclined to pay a disproportionate attention to Western-related facets of the history of China.

However, as can be expected, the 'Western impact' narrative did not remain completely identical through six decades. In particular, the importance of 'alternative channels' (Douglas Reynolds) of Western influences has been pointed out.[6] By far the most important was Japan. Its role as an intermediary between China and the West has been thoroughly investigated by many scholars among whom the most prominent is Joshua Fogel.[7] For example, it is no exaggeration to state that the modern Chinese

Going beyond the 'Western impact' Narrative   53

language was largely shaped under the influence of Japanese. In the last decade of the nineteenth century and the beginning of the twentieth, a great number of neologisms entered the Chinese language via Japanese like 衛生 *weisheng* (hygiene, jap. *eisei*), *shehui* 社會 (society, jap. *shakai*) or *jingji* 經濟 (economy, jap. *keizai*).

Moreover, the 'West' (a notion that for no few scholars ended up to be a mere substitute for the 'United States') as a paradigm has been challenged. Scholars made more finely grained researches underlining the respective roles of countries like Italy (Margherita Zanasi) or Germany (William Kirby),[8] providing a more comprehensive picture. Very recently, researches have demonstrated the crucial role of Russians in the passing of Western classical music to China.[9] Another significant shift, the relations between China and non-Western countries are no more a mere footnote in the overall picture of China's cultural exchanges.[10]

The 'Western impact' narrative is nowadays clearly losing momentum in the West (especially since Paul Cohen criticized it in his milestone 1984 book *Discovering History in China: American Historical Writing on the Recent Chinese Past*, advocating instead a China-centred approach).[11] But it is worthy to underline that it is nowadays still very influential in China.

One of the reasons why it remains influential is that Chinese historians are no more writing exclusively about the 1839–1949 period as a teleology of revolution as was the case during the 1949–78 Maoist era.[12] The 1950s, 1960s and 1970s were the heydays, in China, of the 'nationalist narrative'. It characterized the relations between China and the rest of the world as centred on the forced 'opening' of China consecutive to the Opium Wars (1839–42 and 1856–60). The concept of imperialism as the main heuristic concept and driving force became overly prominent after 1949. Only recently has its influence as a historical paradigm tended to fade away.

Since the 1980s, even if 1839–1949 is still seen as a period of dramatic weakness, the trend among Chinese historians has been to shift away from narratives of revolution and imperialism to narratives centred on China's quest for modernization. In that perspective, for them, the paradigm of the 'Western impact' still has a strong appeal, hence the numerous studies on the long quest for China to 'catch up' with the Western powers, and also on how Chinese ways of life and thought got altered during the period.

Outbound cultural exchanges?

In the overall context of the dominance of these two narratives of the interactions of China with the rest of the world during the 1839–1949 period, how are, more specifically, cultural exchanges depicted? The two bulky collective volumes edited in 2008 by the late He Fangchuan 何芳川, *History of China's Cultural Exchanges* (*Zhongwai wenhua jiaoliu shi* 中外文化交流史),[13] are still representative of the state of the field of Chinese historical research on cultural exchanges. What is the most striking in He's volumes is how the perimeter of 'cultural exchanges' is restricted. There is a heavy emphasis on the circulation of scientific and technical knowledge as well as highbrow forms of culture (literature, philosophy). China's cultural exchanges are described in a way that overlooks more vulgar forms of culture or everyday ways of life (food, clothes, entertainment, music). Allusions to more popular forms of culture are scarce if not non-existent in most chapters of He's book.[14] The pioneering study on the circulation of everyday objects by Frank Dikötter[15] has had a very little impact in China. Second, even if He's book harbours the ambition of drawing a comprehensive map of China's cultural exchanges, there is a marked emphasis on China's relations with the West. It is remarkable, for example, that despite the fact that Buddhism made its way to China from there, the chapter dealing with China/India relations has thirty-eight pages (in a 1,026-page-long book) and is shorter, for example, than the chapter about the relations between China and Spain.

He Fangchuan's volumes are not centred on a particular period of time. When one looks more specifically at the period under our consideration, the same features are present and even exaggerated in the case of the relations with the West. It certainly does not come as a surprise as, even if they were to a certain extent in competition, the Western impact and the nationalist narratives do share the common assumption that during the 1839–1949 period China was first and foremost under the massive Western cultural influence. One side effect of this posture is a tendency to jump (implicitly) to the conclusion that, unlike during older periods, the cultural influence of China over the rest of the world amounts to nil.[16]

Overseas Chinese (*Huaqiao*)[17] studies development

How global history enjoyed an enthusiastic reception by Chinese historians

Since two decades, global history has been developing at a steady pace in China. Beijing Normal University created a global history research centre in 2004, and many other universities have followed suit.[18] At the same time, a steady flow of translations has taken place, making classical works of global history by Western scholars like Leften Stavros Stavrianos (*A Global History: From Prehistory to the 21st Century*), as well as more recent scholarship by Sebastien Conrad (*What Is Global History?*) or Sven Beckert (*A Global History of Cotton*) available in the Chinese language. Several academic reviews like *Global History Review* (*Quanqiushi pinglun* 全球史評論) founded in 2005 are devoted to global history. Global history is now fully a part of teaching and research within most history departments all over China. The very concept of globalization (全球化 *quanqiuhua*) has even gained currency beyond historical academic publications and has a strong impact on the general public sphere.

Nonetheless, a survey of publications related to global history in China reveals that, with a few exceptions,[19] the history of Chinese migrations has remained the preserve of an older and already well-established field of research: Overseas Chinese studies.

Basic facts about Chinese emigration during the 1839–1949 period

It is necessary to underscore that for China the century under our consideration witnessed inner and outer migrations of unprecedented magnitude. For example, great eastbound movements of populations took place to fill the terrible losses of lives in the region of the Low Yangzi, in the decades following its devastation by the great Taiping

Rebellion (1850–64). Also, between 1891 and 1942, 9 million migrants from Shandong and Zhili/Hebei moved to Manchuria.[20] The development of the Chinese diaspora was part of this general trend. Chinese emigration was certainly not a new thing. Chinese communities had already been present since at least the Song dynasty in Southeast Asia.[21] Chinese merchants built powerful trade networks to the extent that some scholars refer to the 1740–1840 period as the 'Chinese century' in this region.[22]

The development of the diaspora during the 1839–1949 period was not devoid of continuities with the preceding centuries. Despite controversies existing among scholars concerning the number of people who migrated, all agree that, as before, the great majority of the migrants continued to head to Southeast Asia. Contrary to a common cliché, it seems that (as before) most Chinese migrants were not indentured (according to Adam McKeown, between 1840 and 1930, only about 4 per cent were indentured).[23] A third crucial element of continuity was that almost all migrants originated from two provinces: Guangdong and Fujian.[24] Nonetheless, the migration waves departed from previous ones in two ways: first, the scope of the outflow of migrants leaving China was without precedent (no less than 20 million according to the most recent estimates)[25]; second, Chinese migrants now reached places far beyond the traditional sphere of Chinese migration, places where they had until then been altogether absent, like America or Australia.

Huaqiao studies in China since the 1980s

Huaqiao studies have established themselves as a very substantial field of research which can be traced back to pioneering works by scholars like Liu Shimu and Chen Da[26] during the 1930s. *Huaqiao* studies existed during the 1949–78 Maoist era, but their development on a massive scale dates back to the early 1980s. In the new political context of the late 1970s, Deng Xiaoping 鄧小平 launched reformist policies which involved in particular moving towards a market economy as well as a great deal of opening to the hitherto vilified capitalist countries. China desperately needed investments and the *Huaqiao* were targeted as potential investors. Very significantly, the first Special Economic zones *jingji tequ* 經濟特區 (Shenzhen, Shantou, Zhuhai and Xiamen) were all located in areas that had experienced massive emigration since the mid-nineteenth century. It is quite remarkable that making use of *Huaqiao* to foster the development of China amounted more or less to a return to the policy the Qing had enforced at the end of the nineteenth century: the Chinese migrants were considered a precious asset who could help the mother country with two trump cards: their wealth, which could help overcome the dramatic lack of capital in China (by the means of investments or remittances), and the various kinds of knowledge they had accumulated overseas.[27] So one of the academic consequences of the political turn initiated by Deng Xiaoping is that Overseas Chinese *should* be exalted: a strong impetus was given in the 1980s to scholarly research on *Huaqiao* with, for example, the creation of journals like *The Journal of Overseas Chinese History Studies* (*Huaqiao huaren lishi yanjiu* 华侨华人历史研究) in 1986, still one of the leading reviews on the field, and the edition of volumes of primary sources like the ten volumes of the *Collection of Historical Sources on Overseas Chinese Labor* edited by the veteran Chen Hansheng

陈翰笙.[28] The University of Jinan 暨南 in Guangzhou successfully established itself as a hub for *Huaqiao*-oriented studies, where scholars like Zhu Jieqin 朱杰勤 tirelessly devoted their efforts to extoll past and present Overseas Chinese national loyalty and commitment to the motherland.[29]

The reason why (as already mentioned) *Huaqiao* studies have a strong focus towards the economic achievements of Overseas Chinese is quite evident.[30] In full tune with the new 1980s political rhetoric, it was deemed legitimate and even profitable that a portion of the people get rich first (*xian fuqilai* 先富起来); it is understandable that a significant share of the *Huaqiao* research consists of extoling self-made men who made a fortune overseas and depicting them as zealous patriots only eager to contribute to the development of the motherland.[31] The most famous of them is probably Chen Jiageng 陳嘉庚 (aka Tan Kah Kee), who founded the University of Xiamen in 1921, but there are dozens of biographies describing other successful overseas businessmen. More generally, when *Huaqiao* studies investigate the life of Overseas Chinese, they adopt a resolutely top-down approach, extolling the achievements of the community leaders. A great deal of attention is paid to what is sometimes called the 'three treasures' (*sanbao* 三寶) of the overseas communities, namely their associations, their Chinese-language journals and their educational institutions.[32]

A loophole and its causes

As already alluded to, the development of *Huaqiao* studies from the 1980s onwards was, so to speak, an academic response to a political problem. It is rather telling that nowadays searching for any book dealing with the history of *Huaqiao* in the 'history and geography' (歷史, 地理) section of a library in China is a disappointing endeavour. According to the current classification system of Chinese libraries, such books are only to be found under the section 'Law and politics' (政治, 法律).[33] This observation, far from being anecdotal, means that the history of the *Huaqiao* is therefore seen in China as a *political* issue more than a historical one.

This fact hints, more generally, at a dissociation of *Huaqiao* studies from history as a discipline. It makes it understandable why *Huaqiao* specialists have not assimilated the influence of global history as Chinese historians so enthusiastically did. It may be one of the reasons why the particular concern for circulations (of goods, habits and knowledge), which is one of the main perspectives of global history, has not really percolated to *Huaqiao* studies.

On the very contrary, and it is the key point, this scholarly literature depicts Overseas Chinese first and foremost in the light of their relations with the motherland[34] (it is worth underlining that the very term 'Huaqiao' 華僑, far from being neutral, conveys a nuance of nostalgia for home)[35] and certainly not as potential agents of the propagation of Chinese influence. Instead, a disproportionate attention is paid to issues such as the remittances Overseas Chinese sent to their families at home, their investments in China and the help they provided to support China resistance during the 1937–45 Sino-Japanese War.

As a consequence, *Huaqiao* studies have paid little attention to the relations of reciprocal influence between Overseas Chinese communities and their country of settlement. Despite its promising title, even the recent book by Zhang Yudong 張禹東 and Chen Jingxi 陳景熙, *Overseas Chinese Organizations and the Dissemination of Chinese Culture* (*Huaren shetuan yu Zhongguo wenhua chuanbo* 華人社團與中華文化傳播) has very few insights into the introduction of elements of Chinese culture into the societies of the places where Chinese migrants settled.[36] The organizations under scrutiny in the book are only catering to the Overseas Chinese themselves.

The *Huaqiao* studies also insist on considering the migrants first and foremost as 'Chinese'. This is the consequence of a postulate, the cultural unity of China. Questioning it is still a highly controversial issue in China.[37] It is for this reason, for example, that in China the regional languages are called 'dialects' (*fangyan* 方言), when they are, from a linguistic point of view, genuinely distinct languages (much more distinct, for example, than French and Italian).[38]

Admittedly, *Huaqiao* studies frequently distinguish between different components of the diaspora. But these components are defined either by the country or region of destination (Malaysia, Cuba, North America, etc.) or by the province of departure (namely, Fujian or Guangdong). However, the province level has only one interest, that of not threatening the unassailable predicament of the unity of the diaspora. But it is of no value in accounting for the highly fragmented nature of the diaspora. This fragmentation was following cultural lines. The diaspora was comprised of five main distinct constituents: 'Cantonese' (migrants originating from the Pearl River delta region), 'Hokkien' (coastal part of southern Fujian), 'Hakka' (hilly districts from Guangdong and south Fujian), 'Teochow' (Chaozhou and Shantou region) and 'Hainan' (isle of Hainan), each with their linguistic and cultural idiosyncrasy. None of these people were speaking mandarin as their mother tongue.

It comes as no surprise that *Huaqiao* studies also tend to downplay the fact that animosity and fierce competition between the constituents of the Chinese diaspora was the rule rather than the exception. Little to no attention is paid to the feuds and fights, in some instance deadly, that took place between them, like the massive Singapore Hokkien-Teochew riots of May 1854 which took a death toll of no less than five hundred lives. Such conflicts persisted even after the second half of the nineteenth century.[39] For example, consecutive to diverging reactions to the 1911–12 Revolution in China, the Kuala Lumpur 1912 riots resulted in ten deaths.[40]

The postulate of the indissoluble unity of the diaspora is one of the causes for the disinterest for the circulation of popular culture and everyday life practices in *Huaqiao* studies: yet arguably the greatest part of the popular culture the migrants took away with them overseas was more genuinely Cantonese and Hokkien, for example, than 'Chinese'.

A very revealing case study: The circulation of Chinese gambling games

Gambling games are an excellent example of those social practices, strongly embedded in the regional cultures of the migrants, which have not been deemed worthy of attention. If they are mentioned (most often in a very cursory fashion) in *Huaqiao*

58 *Narratives, Nations, and Other World Products*

studies, it is to underline their allegedly destructive role, their connections with secret societies or the fact that they were constituent of a prejudiced and clichéd vision against the Overseas Chinese.[41] Given their general orientations, the lack of interest by *Huaqiao* studies in gambling games is not surprising.

But what about the considerable flow of scholarly literature devoted to the history of games and gambling games in China? Did they pay any attention to the outbound circulation of Chinese games? Again, in tune with the 'Western impact' and nationalist narratives mentioned previously, it turns out that when dealing with the circulations of games, specialists like Ge Chunyuan eagerly mention the fact that many Western games (poker, roulette, horse and dog races) found their way into China due to the impulse of 'imperialist' forces.[42] But, on the other hand, they completely disregard the possibility that Chinese gambling games have taken the opposite direction and made their way to other countries. To be fair, such an attitude only partly results from the influence of the Western impact and nationalist narratives. It is also the consequence of the sources Chinese specialists of the history of gambling are resorting to. They read only Chinese sources, without tapping into the diplomatic and colonial archives, or local Western newspapers, where a wealth of evidence and details about the circulation of Chinese gambling games can be found.

Against such a backdrop, the fact that some Chinese gambling games were passed from the Overseas Chinese communities on to the local people in the country where they lived comes to our knowledge only as cursory mentions, made in passing by Western scholars in studies which are much more general in scope. For example, the great historian Denys Lombard mentions that cricket fighting became very popular among the population of Java (where it was known as *adu jangkrik*).[43] Roger Caillois, in his classical study, mentions that the lottery *zihua* 字花 (also known as *huahui* 花會) had become widely popular in Cuba under the name *Rifa Chiffà* (literal meaning: *Chiffa* lottery, *Chiffa* being the Cantonese pronunciation of *zihua*).[44] Only in the very last years did the dissemination of Chinese games become the research focus of a handful of scholars, all of them from outside of China. They have described, in particular, how Chinese migrants actively promoted lotteries of different sorts in Korea and how mahjong became widely popular at the beginning of the twentieth century in the United States outside the Chinese communities, to the point that it is possible to mention it a nationwide 'mahjong fad'.[45]

Yet no in-depth study on the worldwide circulation of a given Chinese gambling game exists. In a recent article,[46] I started investigating the worldwide circulation of a Cantonese gambling game, *fantan* 番攤. It is difficult to imagine today how very popular this game was, which is nowadays only played in a few casinos (and on a very small scale) in Macau and Cambodia. During the 1850–1949 period, *fantan* was striving in the Pearl River Delta (which was the heart, in both geographical and economic terms, of Guangdong province). There the casinos specifically dedicated to it, the *tanguan* 攤館, were flourishing businesses.[47] The worldwide ubiquity of *fantan* at the turn of the twentieth century (see Map 1) was a by-product of the diversity of the destinations of Cantonese emigration: it was present in the six continents. Outside Asia, it was played in North America (the United States, Canada), South America (Peru, Cuba), Europe (in London), Africa (South Africa) and Oceania (Australia, New Zealand). It was indeed a worldwide phenomenon.

Going beyond the 'Western impact' Narrative 59

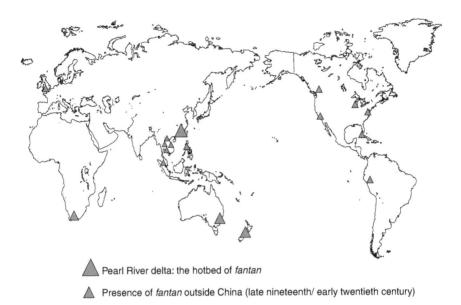

▲ Pearl River delta: the hotbed of *fantan*
▲ Presence of *fantan* outside China (late nineteenth/ early twentieth century)

Map 1 *Fantan* in the six continents.

Of course, such a map can be misleading. Some spots on the map (like London) are only based on a handful of evidence of the presence of *fantan* and correspond to a very limited presence of the game, whereas others (like Vietnam) correspond to hundreds of gambling dens and thousands of players. And in the case of very large countries, like the United States or Canada, for example, the fact that only a few major cities are figured certainly does not imply that *fantan* was not played elsewhere in the country.

As a whole it appears that the most relevant distinction must be made between two kinds of place, based on the fact that *fantan* did or did not cross the boundaries of the Chinese communities to take root in the local population. In places like the United States, Australia and New Zealand, *fantan* remained a Cantonese migrant's thing. But in certain Southeast Asian countries, the game widely spread among local people. In Vietnam, for example, *fantan* spread not only in the biggest cities, like Saigon and Hanoi, but as well as in towns of secondary importance, such as Fai-Foo (nowadays called Hoi An). It made its way down to the countryside, where Chinese itinerant merchants proposed *fantan* to Vietnamese farmers. A hint at its acculturation, the game of *fantan* was known under a name in the local language as *baquan* (sometimes written as *bacouen* or *bacouan*). In Siam, the situation was similar; *fantan* became very popular under the Thai name of *thua*. Its popularity among Thai people even led to the common expression in the Thai popular vocabulary with the phrase *chaeng si bia*, meaning 'to explain in full detail', whose literal meaning was 'to explain to the extent of four cowries' (this was a reference to the drawing process of *fantan*).[48]

The case of *fantan* is eminently relevant when we consider another dimension of the problem. As we have mentioned, *Huaqiao* studies consider the migrants as 'Chinese' rather than 'Cantonese' or 'Hokkien'. *Fantan* was a genuinely *Cantonese* game, the

60 *Narratives, Nations, and Other World Products*

product of a gambling culture whose hotbed was the Pearl River delta. It was unknown in north and central China.

The conclusion drawn from the example of *fantan* is that many cultural transfers by the diaspora have been downplayed because the items that have been transferred were the products of one of the distinctively regional cultures which were flourishing at the time in south China.

The dissemination of Chinese popular cultures between 1839 and 1949

The dissemination of *fantan* and other Chinese gambling games is only one manifestation of a larger fact: during the century 1839–1949, Chinese cultural influence greatly extended overseas as a side effect of the massive development of the diaspora.

Southeast Asia

As we have already mentioned, the vast majority of Chinese migrants went to Southeast Asia. The overall influence of these Chinese communities was enhanced by the fact that they were beefed up by this influx of new migrants. In some countries, they ended up amounting to a significant percentage of the population in the mid-twentieth century (12 per cent of the population of Thailand was then of Chinese descent).[49] One of the consequences of this new demographic weight was that these communities exerted a very significant cultural influence over the local populations.

It would be misleading to assume that Chinese cultural influence in Southeast Asia is completely overlooked by Chinese scholars. But scholarship has tended to focus almost exclusively on the late-nineteenth-century nationalist writers, the May Fourth Movement intellectuals and pro-communists writers. Some attention has been paid to the influence of Kang Youwei (康有为), Liang Qichao (梁启超) or Lu Xun (鲁迅). The dissemination of masterpieces of Chinese literature like *Sanguo yanyi* (三國演義) (which was heavily influential in Thailand and got translated no less than six times into Vietnamese between 1909 and 1937) was also deemed worthy of attention.[50]

By contrast, it is necessary to underscore the fact that the Chinese influence extended through more trivial channels which are equally worthy of attention. Other genres representative of Chinese popular culture massively percolated into Southeast Asian countries. *Wuxia* (武俠 knight's errant) novels were a case in point: in the 1930s in Java there were half a dozen periodicals in the local language which were dedicated to this alien genre. In Thailand, the tremendous success of the daily newspaper *Siam Rat* was due to its serialized *wuxia* stories translated into the Thai language.[51] Another popular genre, the mandarin ducks and butterfly literature (*yuanyang hudie pai* 鴛鴦蝴蝶派), was also successfully exported to Southeast Asian countries. It was enthusiastically received, for example, by the Vietnamese public.[52]

In many places of Southeast Asia, the influence of Chinese languages was strongly felt. Mandarin played no role; of course, it was all about local languages. A case in point is Khmer: as demonstrated in an article by Pou Savero and Philipp Jenner, about three hundred loan words were taken from Chinese languages (Hokkien, Teochew, Cantonese), sometimes through Thai or Vietnamese.[53] The situation was rather similar in Siam with Thai language.[54]

Another sphere of influence is the one of popular religion. The flourishing of redemptive societies in China in the first half of the twentieth century has been the topic of a great deal of research in the last two decades.[55] They had also a very deep impact outside China, in Southeast Asia, most notably in Vietnam Malaysia and Singapore. The Cao Dai sect (a syncretic Vietnamese religious movement that appeared in the early 1920s in Cochinchina) is the most important (but certainly not the only one) scion of the Chinese redemptive societies.[56]

Besides gambling already mentioned, other social practices are worthy of attention. The dissemination of opium smoking in Southeast Asia was closely associated with the Chinese diaspora. With a few exceptions, such as in Cambodia and the Philippines, local populations in turn adopted this practice. Admittedly, the proportion of smokers remained much higher everywhere among the Overseas Chinese. Nevertheless, the fact remains that, for example, in Annam and Tonkin, the Chinese accounted for only about 10 per cent of smokers in the 1900s. There were about 250,000 smokers in French Indochina as a whole, out of a population of about 16 million.[57]

Other parts of the world

During the second half of the nineteenth century a minority of the Chinese migrants (which still amounted to the sizeable number of about 1 million) reached faraway places such as North and South America where Chinese people had never been seen before. There, as a whole, the cultural impact of the diaspora over the local population was relatively weaker. But this should not lead us to believe in the total absence of cultural transfers: certainly less buoyant than in the case of Southeast Asia they nonetheless took place. The local populations were pickier in their borrowing from the Chinese migrants. Food was a case in point: Chinese gastronomy aroused the interest of many Westerners in North America during the 1920s. Many cookbooks featuring Chinese recipes were published and widely circulated. And such an interest in Chinese food was no flash in the pan: on the very contrary, it reached wider stratums of the population: during the following decade, US Chinatown restaurants were patronized by many non-Chinese customers.[58] Though not on the same scale as Khmer, the influence of Chinese language on American English was not negligible either.[59] The dissemination of Chinese medicine is another case in point, yet remarkably understudied. In France, acupuncture was very fashionable during the interwar period.[60]

Conclusion

During the century following the Opium Wars, the decline of China in Asia, in terms of politics and diplomacy, was no doubt glaring. Even if the scope and depth of the 'Western impact' is still a matter of debate among scholars, there is no doubt that

China was a country under massive Western cultural influence. Yet, given the fact that massive Chinese emigration took place during the 1839–1949 period, it would seem only natural to inquire whether the Chinese did have or not an impact on the countries where they settled. Clearly Chinese did have an impact, especially on the region where the diaspora had been present for a long time: Southeast Asia. By stating this, I do not intend to hint at the continuation of the old fascination of the traditional local elites for Chinese culture and language (such a fascination was nonetheless a reality, and a reality that, for example, was still lamented by French colonial authorities as late as the 1910s).[61] The 'Chinese impact' went well beyond narrow intellectual spheres: there was a deep penetration at grassroots level within the local populations of social practices that went also beyond the scope of highbrow cultural realms. I have elaborated at some length on the example of gambling games. But many more ways of life, of speech and forms of popular culture were at stake.

In what sense was China, as stated in the title, 'a world power'? To put it squarely: because China did have a much deeper influence on the world during the period between 1839 and 1949 than in the pre-1839 period. In this chapter, I have investigated the various reasons why such an important historical reality was left virtually untouched by Chinese scholars. These reasons have mainly to do with the fact that it contradicts, or at least is not easy to frame, the dominant historical narratives concerning the 'century of humiliation' and the still dominant paradigms of imperialism and 'Western impact' on China. Another reason has to do with the idiosyncrasies of the field of *Huaqiao* studies, with their heavy political implications and the subsequent emphasis on the relations of Overseas Chinese with their motherland. Last but not least is the fact that the concerned ways of life may often be considered trivial, and, moreover, instead of being a part of an essentialized and celebrated 'Chinese' culture, they were actually pertaining to distinctively southern Chinese local cultures (Cantonese, Hokkien, Hakka, Teochow, Hainan).

A common assertion of both the Western impact and nationalist narratives is that the main event concerning the relations between China and the rest of the world during the modern era is that China was forced to open after the Opium Wars.[62] I think this is irrelevant for two reasons. First, it is worthy to underline that China was not closed before that period; the commerce with Europe, in particular, was striving. Second, and more importantly, it is the outcome of an outrageously Eurocentric vision. The main factor that dramatically altered the relations between China and the rest of the world during the period was *not* the so-called 'opening' of China by Western powers but the massive emigration that took place during this period of time. Less conspicuous, less dramatic maybe, it is nonetheless this emigration that had the deepest and most lasting effects in the long run.

Notes

1   Xavier Paulès, *The Republic of China, 1912 to 1949* (Cambridge: Polity Press, 2023), 275.

2   Joseph Nye, *Soft Power. The Means to Success in World Politics* (New York: Publicaffairs, 2004), 9.

3 The term 'diaspora', of Greek origin, is no doubt a controversial one and some scholars have objected to its extension beyond the dispersion of Jews around the world. I nonetheless follow the more and more general trend deeming it acceptable to refer to migrants settled in distant lands who maintain ties of different types with their homeland, in particular the feeling of a shared history. For a discussion on the term, with specific reference to African diaspora, see Patrick Manning, *The African Diaspora, a History through Culture* (New York: Columbia University Press, 2009), 2–4.

4 See for example the very influential book: John Fairbank and Teng Ssu-yü, *China's Response to the West. A Documentary Survey, 1839–1923* (Cambridge: Harvard University Press, 1954).

5 Paul Cohen, 'Nineteenth-Century China: The Evolution of American Historical Approaches', in *A Companion to Chinese History*, ed. Michael Szonyi (Hoboken: Wiley Blackwell, 2017), 154–68.

6 Douglas Reynolds, *China, 1898–1912: The Xinzheng Revolution and Japan* (Cambridge: Harvard University Press, 1993).

7 See for example Joshua Fogel, *The Cultural Dimension of Sino-Japanese Relations. Essays on the Nineteenth and Twentieth Centuries* (Armonk/London: M.E. Sharpe, 1995), and the collective volume Joshua Fogel (ed.), *The Role of Japan in Liang Qichao's Introduction of Modern Western Civilization to China* (Berkeley: Center for Chinese Studies, *c.* 2002).

8 William Kirby, *Germany and Republican China* (Stanford: Stanford University Press, 1984); Margherita Zanasi, *Saving the Nation: Economic Modernity in Republican China* (Chicago: University of Chicago Press, 2006).

9 See the special issue of *Twentieth Century China*, 37, no.1 (January 2012).

10 Claudine Salmon (ed.), *Literary Migrations, Traditional Chinese Fiction in Asia (17–20th centuries)* (Beijing: International Culture Publishing Corporation, 1987).

11 Paul Cohen, *Discovering History in China: American Historical Writing on the Recent Chinese Past* (Cambridge: Cambridge University Press, 1984).

12 Li Huaiyin, *Reinventing Modern China: Imagination and Authenticity in Chinese Historical Writing* (Honolulu: University of Hawai'i Press, 2013), especially chapter 7, pp. 204–35.

13 He Fangchuan 何芳川 (ed.), *Zhongwai wenhua jiaoliu shi* 中外文化交流史 (*History of Cultural Exchanges between China and Foreign Countries*) (Beijing: Guoji wenhua chuban, 2008, 2 vols.).

14 The remarkable chapter by Fu Zengyou 傅增有 about the relations with Thailand nonetheless stands as an exception: He, *Zhongwai wenhua jiaoliu shi*, vol. 1, pp. 308–72.

15 Frank Dikötter, *Exotic Commodities. Modern Objects and Everyday Life in China* (New York: Columbia University Press, 2006).

16 This is for example the case in the recent book by Zhang Zhaojun 張昭軍 and Sun Yanjing: 孫燕京, *Zhongguo jindai wenhua shi* 中國近代文化史 (*A History of Culture in Modern China*) (Beijing: Zhonghua shuju, 2018).

17 The term *Huaqiao* 華僑 which can be roughly translated as 'Overseas Chinese' has its origins in the 1890s but came into general use only after the 1911 Revolution.

18 Gu Yunshen, 'Global History in China: Inheritance and Innovation, a Case Study of the Development of World History in the History Department of Fudan University', in *The 'Global' and the 'Local' in Early Modern and Modern East Asia*, ed. Benjamin Elman and Jenny Liu Chao-Hu (Leiden/Boston: Brill, 2017), 95–101.

19 For example, 丁汀 Ding Ting and 張侃 Zhang Kan, '閩南華僑的跨境流動與追求幸福的家庭策略 – 以20世紀20-80年代石獅永寧蔡氏家書為中心的討論

(Cross-border Movement of Overseas Chinese in Minnan and the Pursuit of Happy Family Strategy – A Case Study of Yongning's Cai's Family Letters from 1920s to 1980s)', 全球史評論 *Quanqiushi pinglun* 15 (2018): 100–24.

20 James Reardon-Anderson, *Reluctant Pioneers. China's Expansion Northward, 1644–1937* (Stanford: Stanford University Press, 2005), 114–15 and 128–9.

21 Anthony Reid, *A History of Southeast Asia. Critical Crossroads* (Chichester: Wiley, 2015), 65–8.

22 Richard Von Glahn, *The Economic History of China: From Antiquity to the Nineteenth Century* (Cambridge: Cambridge University Press, 2016), 391.

23 Adam McKeown, 'The Social Life of Chinese Labor', in *Chinese Circulations. Capital, Commodities, and Networks in Southeast Asia*, ed. Eric Tagliacozzo and Chang Wen-Chin (Durham: Duke University Press, 2011), 66.

24 Exceptions to this general rule are very rare: see the example of a Hubei district in Zhang Jiayan, *Coping with Calamity: Environmental Change and Peasant Response in Rural China, 1736–1949* (Copenhagen: NIAS Press, 2015), 37.

25 McKeown, 'The Social Life of Chinese Labor', 66.

26 Chen Da 陳達, *Nanyang Huaqiao yu Min Yue shehui* 南洋華僑與閩粵社會 (*South Seas Huaqiao and Society in Guangdong and Fujian*) (Shanghai: Shangwu yinshu guan, 1938).

27 Eric Guerassimoff, 'Des coolies aux Chinois d'Outre-mer. La question des migrations dans les relations sino-américaines (années 1850–1890)', *Annales. Histoire, Sciences Sociales* 1 (2006): 94–6.

28 Chen Hansheng 陈翰笙 (ed.), 華工出國史料匯編 *Huagong chuguo shiliao huibian* (*Collection of Historical Sources on Overseas Chinese Labor*) (Beijing: Zhonghua shuju), 10 vols., 1981–5.

29 Zhu Jieqin 朱杰勤, *Dongnanya Huaqiao shi* 東南亞華僑史 (*History of Overseas Chinese in Southeast Asia*) (Beijing: Zhonghua shuju, 2008) (first edition 1989).

30 Xu Yuming 許玉明, *Zhongguo qiaowu tonglun* 中國僑務通論 (Guangzhou: Jinan daxue chubanshe, 2012).

31 Bureau of the Overseas affairs of the People's government of Guangzhou municipality 廣州市人民政府僑務辦公室 (ed.), *Guangzhou qiaowu yu qiaojie renwu* 廣州僑務與僑界人物 (*Figures of the Overseas Chinese Affairs and Community from Guangzhou*) (Guangzhou: Guangzhou chubanshe, 2000).

32 Zhang Yudong 張禹東 and Chen Jingxi 陳景熙, *Huaren shetuan yu Zhongguo wenhua chuanbo* 華人社團與中華文化傳播 (*Overseas Chinese Organizations and the Dissemination of Chinese Culture*) (Beijing: Shehui kexue wenxian chubanshe, 2018), p. 89.

33 Whereas since 1929 Chinese libraries had been using a system based on the Dewey classification, in 1971 the Beijing Library (now the National Library of China) initiated, along with thirty-five other libraries, the creation of a new classification. The new system was more in tune with the political and ideological context of China during the Cultural Revolution. This system (*Zhongguo tushuguan fenleifa* 中國圖書館分類法, often abbreviated in *zhongtufa* 中圖法) was revised several times and is still in use in Chinese libraries.

34 This is true of research works dealing with the Chinese diaspora at a general level like (the titles speak for themselves): Zhuang Guotu 庄國土, *Huaqiao huaren yu Zhongguo de guanxi* 華僑華人與中國的關係 (*The Overseas Chinese and Their Connections with China*) (Guangzhou: Guangdong gaodeng jiaoyu chubanshe, 2001), and Zheng Wanli 鄭萬里 et al., *Menghui dongfang: Huaqiao huaren bainian xinling*

shi 夢迴東方: 華僑華人百年心靈史 (Guangzhou: 商訊文化 Shangxun wenhua, 2011) (Dream back to the East: the history of one hundred years of Overseas Chineses thoughts and feelings). But studies more narrowly focused on a given area share the same perspective: see for example Lin Yuanhui 林遠輝 and Zhang Yinglong 張應龍, *Xinjiapo Malaixiya Huaqiao shi* 新加坡馬來西亞華僑史 (*A History of Overseas Chinese in Singapore and Malaysia*) (Guangzhou: Guangdong gaodeng jiaoyu chubanshe, 2016), 431–8.

35 It implies 'the sense of enforced migration, duty to return and nostalgia for home': Wang Gungwu, 'A Note on the Origins of Hua-ch'iao', in *Community and Nation: Essays on Southeast Asia and the Chinese*, ed. Wang Gungwu (Sydney: Georg Allen & Unwin, 1981), 119.

36 Zhang Yudong 張禹東 and Chen Jingxi 陳景熙, *Huaren shetuan yu Zhongguo wenhua chuanbo* 華人社團與中華文化傳播 (*Overseas Chinese Organizations and the Dissemination of Chinese Culture*) (Beijing: Shehui kexue wenxian chubanshe, 2018).

37 Shelly Chan, *Diaspora's Homeland. Modern China in the Age of Global Integration* (Durham/London: Duke University Press, 2018), 7.

38 Viviane Alleton, *L'écriture chinoise, le défi de la modernité* (Paris: Albin Michel, 2008), 166.

39 Carl Trocki, *Opium and Empire: Chinese Society in Colonial Singapore, 1800–1910* (Ithaca: Cornell University Press, 1990), 35–49, 82, 110–11.

40 Public Record Office (Kew), CO 273/387: Report of the commission appointed to inquire into the disturbances in Kuala Lumpur and district at the Chinese New Year, 1912.

41 Chao Longqi 潮龍起, 危險的愉悅 : 早期美國華僑賭博問題研究 (1850–1943 年) (Dangerous Pleasures: Research on the Problem of Gambling among Overseas Chinese in the USA, 1850–1943)', *Huaqiao huaren lishi yanjiu* 华侨华人历史研究, 2010/2: 41–53.

42 Ge Chunyuan 戈春源, *Zhongguo jindai dubo shi* 中國近代賭博史 (*History of Gambling in Modern China*) (Fuzhou: Fujian renmin chubanshe, 2005), 225–34 (especially 229).

43 Denys Lombard, *Le Carrefour javanais, essai d'histoire globale* (Paris: éditions de l'EHESS, 1990), 276.

44 Roger Caillois, *Les jeux et les hommes* (Paris: Gallimard, 1967), 286–91.

45 Kang, Jin-A, 'Chinese Lottery Business and Korea, 1898–1909: The Cantonese Company *Tongshuntai*, and East Asian Trade Networks', *Translocal Chinese: East Asian Perspectives* 11, no. 1 (2017): 150–81; Annelise Heinz, *Mahjong: A Chinese Game and the Making of Modern American Culture* (New York: Oxford University Press, 2021).

46 Xavier Paulès, 'An Illustration of China's "paradoxical soft power": The Dissemination of the Gambling Game *fantan* 番攤 by the Cantonese Diaspora, 1850–1950', *Translocal Chinese: East Asian perspectives* 11, no. 2 (Fall 2017): 187–207.

47 For a general presentation about *fantan*, see Xavier Paulès, 'Gambling in China Reconsidered: *fantan* in South China during the Early Twentieth Century', *International Journal of Asian Studies* 7, no. 2 (2010): 179–200.

48 James Warren, *Gambling, the State and Society in Thailand, c. 1800–1945* (London/New York: Routledge, 2013), 29.

49 William Skinner, *Chinese Society in Thailand: An Analytical History* (Ithaca: Cornell University Press, 1957), 183.

50 He, *Zhongwai wenhua jiaoliu shi*, vol. 1, pp. 275, 338–40, 419.

51 Brigitte De Beer-Luong, 'Les tribulations d'un journaliste chinois dans les mers du Sud', *Archipel*, no. 23 (1982): 110, https://revue-archipel.fr/revue_en.html.

52 Yan Bao, 'The Influence of Chinese Fiction on Vietnamese Literature', in *Literary Migrations. Traditional Chinese Fiction in Asia (17th–20th centuries)*, ed. Claudine Salmon (Beijing: International Culture Publishing Corporation, 1987), 278–84; Claudine Salmon, 'Malay Translations of Chinese Fiction in Indonesia', in Ibid., pp. 423–6.

53 Saveros Pou and Philipp Jenner, 'Some Chinese loanwords in Khmer', *Journal of Oriental Studies* 11, no. 1 (1973): 1–90.

54 He, *Zhongwai wenhua jiaoliu shi*, 340–2.

55 David Palmer and Vincent Goossaert, *The Religious Question in Modern China* (Chicago: University of Chicago Press, 2010), 93. The term 'redemptive societies' was coined by Prasenjit Duara in 2001 to draw attention to their common project of saving both individual and the world as a whole.

56 See Jérémy Jammes, *Les oracles du Cao Dài étude d'un mouvement religieux vietnamien et ses réseaux* (Paris: Les Indes savantes, 2013), 57–68.

57 Xavier Paulès, 'Opium', in *L'Histoire du monde au XIXe siècle*, ed. Pierre Singaravélou and Sylvain Venayre (Paris: Fayard, 2017), 501–5.

58 John Roberts, *China to Chinatown: Chinese Food in the West* (London: Reaktion, 2002), 144–51, 187–8.

59 Cannon Garland, 'Chinese Borrowings in English', *American Speech* 63, no. 1 (1988): 25.

60 Lucia Candelise, 'Georges Soulié de Morant. Le premier expert français en acupuncture', *Revue de synthèse* 131, no. 3 (2010): 373–97.

61 Pierre Brocheux and Daniel Hémery, *Indochine, la colonisation ambigüe, 1958–1954* (Paris: La Découverte, 2001), 221.

62 This event is considered a watershed to the point that according to Chinese historiography, the first Opium war marks nothing less than the beginning of China modern times (*jindai* 近代).

4

Fighting 'the warfare of peacetime': Japan's quest for national narratives during the late nineteenth century

SANO Mayuko

Introduction

In June 1873, a group of high-level Japanese politicians and bureaucrats visited the Expo Vienna 1873 that had opened in the city the previous month. The group, known as the Iwakura Embassy, was headed by Iwakura Tomomi,[1] then the *Udaijin* or Minister of the Right, the highest member of the government. The embassy's journey around the globe, which began in late 1871 and continued until the summer of 1873, is one of the best-known historical stages of Japanese modernization. The embassy visited the United States, Great Britain, France, Belgium, the Netherlands, Germany, Russia, Denmark, Sweden, Italy, Austria and Switzerland; their visit to Vienna occurred towards the end of their tour.

For the information of readers who may be unfamiliar with the Japanese historical context, a new government was formed in Japan in 1868 after the Tokugawa shogunate was overthrown. The feudal regime had been stable since 1603 and had kept the country under a policy of seclusion from the 1630s until the 1850s, while maintaining inter-state relationships with the kingdoms of Chosen and Ryukyu and conducting limited commercial activities with Chinese and Dutch merchants. In the nineteenth century, the shogunate fairly quickly familiarized itself with the changing international environment and prepared to reopen the country to the rest of the world.[2] The new government, which positioned the emperor and his court at the top of its hierarchical structure, mainly comprised former feudal powers that had harshly objected to the shogunate's policy of reopening the country in the early stages, due to their views on Westerners as barbarians. Consequently, they had experienced some local but direct military confrontations with Great Britain and other Western powers. However, such collisions had impressed them with the advancements in Western technology and this had encouraged them to change their ideas. When the revolution occurred in 1868 (the so-called Meiji Restoration), they came to believe that a thorough and rapid opening of the country was necessary for Japan's survival in the international community.[3]

In the context of survival as an independent nation, which will prove to be the core story of this chapter, the new government's main priority was expressed with the well-known slogan *fukoku kyohei,* which roughly translates as 'enrich the nation and strengthen the military'. The Iwakura Embassy was despatched as one part of such efforts and had three objectives: first, to conduct formal visits on behalf of the emperor to announce the establishment of the new regime to countries with which Japan had already concluded bilateral treaties under the Tokugawa shogunate; second, during the visits, the embassy's members were to explore the possibility of revising those treaties containing certain elements that were disadvantageous for Japan[4]; and third, they were to observe various aspects of Western civilization first hand. For a large portion of the highest government members to remain away from home for nearly two years in the early stage of nation-building was a grave and bold act, but the government nonetheless endured their absence. Undoubtedly, the above-mentioned third objective eventually bore abundant fruits.

Now returning to Vienna, the official report of the embassy *Beiou Kairan Jikki* states that the members of the embassy found the expo most convenient as it enabled them to learn about many countries by visiting a single place. This added to, expanded on, and also summarized what they had observed during their visits to various countries and enabled a close comparison between them.[5] The report's author, Kume Kunitake, who was secretary to Minister Iwakura, added his own genuine impression, asserting that the expo was like a miniature garden of the world, which seems fairly poetic but was an accurate description of the expo. Based on this observation, they reached the following understanding of the expo as an enterprise:

[This] competition is the warfare of peacetime and, in an enlightened world, is the most important concern of all. This issue must be given attention.[6]

An expo is a large-scale international event collecting and displaying world products, the history of which commenced with the Great Exhibition of the Works of Industry of All Nations in London in 1851. New York (1853–4) and Paris (1855) soon followed, with the second round taking place in London (1862) and Paris (1867), and the sixth such occasion was in Vienna (1873).[7] Countries that could invest their resources to host such an event were of course limited and, for many other countries worldwide, to be invited to participate and occupy a good position there turned out to be a core and immediate concern. Japan was one such country and would prove to be the country that most firmly bound its fate with the successive expos.[8]

When the 1851 Great Exhibition was held, Japan was not part of it, even if it was called the exhibition of 'All Nations'. This was naturally the case since Japan had not been opened for diplomatic relations with any Western nations, including Great Britain, the host country of the event. It was at the second Expo London in 1862, where Japan (under the Tokugawa shogunate) was invited and actually participated for the first time. Japan was welcomed, but obviously a latecomer to the world.[9] The shogunate took part in Expo 1867 Paris, and the Expo 1873 Vienna became the first occasion for the newly established government.[10]

After observing the Expo Vienna, Japanese policymakers devoted significant attention to the 'warfare of peacetime', which would assign fair importance to the development of industry and other non-military aspects of the country, and ultimately entail a well-balanced pursuit of *fukoku kyohei*. This attention necessitated the launch of explicit efforts to explain aspects of their own country to the external world to achieve optimal results from their participation in such peaceful wars. While the means for such an explanation had to be devised, the contents to be explained had to be produced and compiled. This chapter spotlights these processes and aims to examine them as an important path through which national narratives were created in the context of nineteenth-century Japan. I hope this work will illuminate a meaningful case for integration into the overall analysis of the world of narratives.

The arguments in this chapter are genuinely empirical and are divided into two historical stages. The next section will address the temporal scope around the Iwakura Embassy, when the generation of a national narrative evolved as an embedded, inseparable component of the state's operations, while the third section will mainly cover the 1880s and 1890s, during which the search for a national narrative became more pronounced. In these contexts, the overall processes were part of government strategies, and the major actors we will encounter in the following pages were policymakers in the national government. In each section, several representative figures will be introduced. The concluding section will review the entire process and will close by touching on later developments.

This chapter does not only regard 'narratives' as expressions in words. While ideas may be conveyed by text in some cases, they may also be represented by objects, including artistic and industrial works, and more impressively through their intentional combination, that is, an exhibition. What the Iwakura Embassy gleaned from the Expo Vienna verifies this fact, and therefore policymakers attempted to mobilize all exhibitable items, sometimes combined with certain texts, to construct their national narratives. The successive expos, the rare occasions of world-scale interchange in the nineteenth century, undoubtedly served as a major medium for Japan (and also other countries at the time) to disseminate its narratives internationally. Naturally, mention of expos will often occur as a major component of this chapter's analysis; however, the chapter encapsulates a wider scope of cultural policymaking in the country, including matters such as the development of museum collections, the preservation of cultural properties and art education.

The birth of a 'two-faced' strategy

Daigaku-kengen (proposal to preserve ancient artefacts and create a museum) of 1871 as the starting point

In 1871, the invitation to attend the Expo Vienna reached the Japanese government. This eventually prompted an irreversible turn in the nature of Japan's national narrative making, but to fully understand this shift, it is important to view the wider picture of the cultural policy movement that took place in Japan during that same year, when the Expo Vienna became a prominent endeavour.

Let us begin with an expression used by the contemporaries, by which we can reference the general social trends following the Meiji Restoration (1868); *enkyu*

70 *Narratives, Nations, and Other World Products*

shoshin, which literally means 'detesting the old and respecting the new'. As a natural feeling among people after a revolution, the trends were apparently strengthened by the government policy which focused on earnestly and rapidly introducing Western ideas and technologies into Japanese society to achieve the aforementioned objective of *fukoku kyouhei*. Further accelerated by another policy that intended to unify the emperor's authority and Shintoism, and to separate Shintoism and Buddhism, which had historically been intermingled in the lives of ordinary people, the mood of *enkyu shoshin* seems to have gone too far. One peculiar result was the nationwide phenomenon whereby the old property of Buddhist temples was destroyed by the general population (primarily from 1868 to 1871). In addition to this phenomenon, the civil war associated with the revolution was a preceding and important cause of the widespread destruction of all types of historical properties (the *Boshin* War, which was fought between the parties supporting the Tokugawa shogunate's rule and the revolutionary power for 1868–9).

Confronted by this situation, the *Daigaku* (predecessor of the Ministry of Education) took action from within the government. They drafted a proposal (*Daigaku-kengen*) urging the government to manage the crisis and submitted it to the *Dajokan* (the head political entity before the cabinet system was introduced) in 1871. How did the bureaucrats who oversaw the education and intellectual system of Japan at this time understand the crisis and what did they suggest? The whole text as cited below is worth examining because it clearly marks the first stage in Japan's modern history, where the public concern for the nation's culture arose.

> We will not utter too many words on the important issue of erecting a museum, as it has already been proposed by the Ministry of Foreign Affairs. However, we have been informed that since the *Boshin* War, many of the country's treasures have been lost, which we find extremely lamentable. In recent years, those who are not fully aware of the real state of European society seem to erroneously understand that people there are inclined to the idea of rapid civilisation and only respect newly invented, rare objects in an aimless manner. Eventually, an evil mode in which the old is to be simply detested and the new is welcomed is prevailing here, and the destruction of historical antiquities is not even noted. We hear that some have been destroyed to the extent that they may no longer be restored. It is regrettable indeed that we are losing objects and artefacts on a daily basis that may serve as evidence in a study of the past. Museums exist in Western countries not only to trace society's history from the past to the present, but also to investigate old objects and institutions. Such a function is necessary for *Daigaku* as well, and we sincerely hope that the above-mentioned antiquities and other items will not be lost. However, as the government is currently so occupied with both domestic and external affairs, the establishment of a museum may not be carried out immediately. If this is the case, it is desirable for the government to issue an edict directing all local governments to make the best possible effort to protect the historical treasures that have been handed over from one generation to the next as well as any other miscellaneous articles that should be preserved as evidence in a study of the past, and also to, respectively, appoint staff to sketch

Fighting 'the warfare of peacetime' 71

those articles and collect and edit the accompanying information. If the current situation continues for another year without further attention, we may witness the destruction of most of this country's antiquities and treasures or see their transformation into completely different forms; therefore, we are submitting this proposal for the government's urgent attention. Concluded. (25th day, 4th month, 4th year of Meiji [12 June 1871]).[11]

Among many important elements, it is particularly noteworthy that this proposal is based on the understanding that the preservation of antiquities is useful in securing the evidence necessary for tracing the past. First, we must note that a certain desire to trace one's own history (vis-à-vis the West) was already existent at this stage. It is not necessarily clear whose history is being discussed in the text, but if the proposal was issued by a government organization for government action, it is natural to interpret that the focus was on the history of the people they governed, that is, the nation.

That same year, the Edict for the Preservation of Antiquities and Old Items (*Koki kyubutsu hozon-kata*) was introduced.[12] The preamble of the edict repeats the above-mentioned idea regarding the preservation of antiquities, and the contents correspond to the proposal's request to instruct the local governments to take direct action to protect as many articles as possible. The local governments were also ordered to submit a detailed list of protected articles and their owners. Today, this is considered the beginning of Japan's policy actions to protect its cultural property, for which Japan is now internationally renowned in the field of cultural policy.

The proposal included another important element, which was the idea of creating a national museum. Although I used the term 'museum' in the English translation above as a technical term that is more understandable today, the original Japanese word is *shuko-kan*, which literally means the 'house for collecting old things', and clearly explains the writers' understanding of the suggested institution's nature. In relation to the matter of the museum, we find an interesting paradox in the text: while the major purpose of such a house was to secure Japan's historical evidence vis-à-vis an increase in Westernization, its necessity was apparently justified as European countries possessed equivalent institutions, and the establishment of a museum was understood as one aspect entailed in the importation of Western social systems. It can be said that this contradiction, an example of which symbolically appeared in this document, comprised a base for Japan's process of modernization.

Within *Daigaku*, the leading figure behind this proposal was Machida Hisanari (1838–97), one of the very few Japanese who had experienced living abroad before the Meiji Restoration – in London, to be precise. He was a former retainer of a feudal domain (*han*) called Satsuma, which was ultimately a major force in overthrowing the Tokugawa shogunate. He was secretly sent to London with young colleagues from that domain to learn about Western civilization at a time when such overseas journeys were still strictly banned by the shogunate, except for circumstances in which a representative was sent on designated shogunal missions. After the Meiji Restoration, he first served in the foreign service, but soon moved into the educational and cultural sector; he eventually devoted his entire career to starting Japan's first national museum and became its first director.[13]

72 Narratives, Nations, and Other World Products

His early overseas experiences had a significant influence on his later thoughts, and two different museums in London, the South Kensington Museum (today's Victoria & Albert Museum) and the British Museum, apparently served as models for the institution Machida wanted to introduce in Japan. A paper he later prepared in 1873 shows his correct understanding that the latter more genuinely entailed collecting and preserving a broad range of historical articles, including books and documents, while the former was dedicated to more practical purposes.[14] Although he clarified his intention to reference both ideas in developing a Japanese museum, the institution originally proposed in the above-cited proposal in 1871 shared more similarities with the British Museum.

Invitation to the Expo 1873 Vienna

The invitation to the Expo 1873 Vienna was conveyed to the Japanese government through the Austrian legation in February 1871. The government clearly perceived this expo as an occasion of supreme importance through which Japan could situate itself in a respectful position within international society. Although the government was particularly busy preparing for the departure of the Iwakura Embassy through 1871, the final decision to participate in the expo was made before the embassy left at the end of the year. The issuance of *Daigaku-kengen* and the following edict occurred between this decision and the invitation, while the two separate discussions, one focused on the museum and antiquities and the other on the expo, were independent matters and not necessarily connected.

The preparations for the Japanese exhibition in Vienna were entrusted to the government members who remained in Japan during the absence of the Iwakura Embassy members. Besides the political head of the team (Okuma Shigenobu), it was Sano Tsunetami (1822–1902, a bureaucrat associated with the Ministry of Public Works), who was appointed to supervise the preparations first hand.[15] Another important figure was Gottfried Wagener, a German expert in chemistry who was in Japan at the time to help modernize the ceramics industry[16]; he was appointed official advisor to the Japanese government for the Vienna preparations. In January 1872, the temporary bureau for Vienna preparations was officially established under *Seiin*, the then-supreme organ of government, which issued a proclamation to Japanese nationals regarding the country's participation in the expo in which all interested parties were invited to provide articles for exhibition. Throughout the year, the task of collecting objects for the expo from around the country continued.

In fact, this work was somewhat similar and even complementary to the ongoing efforts of the other group aimed at protecting antiquities and obtaining them for the planned national museum. Records show that the staff from the bureau of preparation for Vienna soon visited the museum department of the Ministry of Education (which succeeded the *Daigaku* in 1871) to obtain information about the objects they 'already possessed'. Further, Machida and his subordinate colleague Tanaka Yoshio, the representative members of the museum department, were also formally appointed to engage in the Vienna project. Eventually, the museum department and the bureau of preparation for Vienna conducted collaborative research on various related matters,

Fighting 'the warfare of peacetime' 73

including the treasures held by Shinto shrines and Buddhist temples in the old capitals (Kyoto and Nara).[17]

In this way, these two separate endeavours became merged organizationally and, metaphorically speaking, comprised a set of wheels on one cart – the 'cultural policy cart' that characterized the first step in Japan's modernization. As a result, the preparations for Vienna, which were a special national project, allowed a good budget and human resources that could also assist in carrying out the museum project; moreover, the philosophy and expertise of the museum department, and the access to items they had already collected, proved to be of enormous help for the Vienna project. When the Ministry of Education (the museum department) finally materialized its first temporary exhibition in Tokyo in 1872, and displayed its collection, the exhibition was held at the same time as a memorial event in which the objects that would be sent to Vienna for the 1873 Expo were showcased. This exhibition is officially noted as the founding moment of today's Tokyo National Museum.[18]

It is natural to suspect that this happy collaboration would have concluded with more than mere organizational sharing. Indeed, on the one hand, given that the museum and antiquity projects were in progress simultaneously, Japan's exhibition at the Expo Vienna had an affirmed characteristic of representing the nation's culture using specimens of the past rather than from contemporary society. This focus was reinforced by Wagener's famous advice that Japan should not bring contemporary industrial products to Vienna, as doing so would inevitably reveal the country's underdeveloped state to the international community; instead, it should concentrate on showing original, exquisite artefacts to attract the European audience.[19] On the other hand, combined with the Vienna project, Japan's first national museum, which was expected to provide evidence of Japanese history, inevitably absorbed the viewpoint of introducing Japan to the external world in the compilation of its collection in its earliest stage.

Japan achieved great success in Vienna. Another citation from the report of the Iwakura Embassy, who directly observed the Japanese exhibition at the expo site, is evidence of this fact:

> The exhibits of our own Japan at the exhibition won particular acclaim from visitors. One reason was that the Japanese exhibits were <u>different</u> from European ones in design and taste, so that to European eyes they had the charm of exoticism ....[20]

The 'different' (underlined by Sano) in the original Japanese is actually closer in meaning to 'rare' or 'strange'. The rareness or strangeness resulted in diffusing 'the charm of exoticism' and promoted Japan in the international arena as a country with a unique charm of that kind, which successfully attracted the curiosity of a Western audience. At that time, this rareness was partly a natural result of true lifestyle differences, but more substantially, it was an intended achievement of the preparations that were made; thus, it was a told story.

Of most importance here was that the embassy members observed this effect in direct connection with their understanding of the opportunity that they called 'the

Figure 4.1 Japanese garden at Expo 1873 Vienna. Source: 'Expositions where the modern technology of the times was exhibited' (National Diet Library Digital Exhibitions) Available online: https://www.ndl.go.jp/exposition/

warfare of peacetime'. Japan learned from its success, and during the following decade and a half, it made every effort in the successive expos in Europe and the United States to emphasize the uniqueness and exoticism of Japanese culture to acquire positive attention, although this chapter will not further delve into this period.

Emphasizing the *fukoku kyohei* policy domestically, this method of conveying exotic stories to the external world was useful in securing a certain honourable position in the international community, when Japan's modern technology and industry were still underdeveloped, and it bought time for Japan to catch up with more developed Western states. It even generated revenue for Japan, as the government prepared design sketches of ceramics and other artistic objects based on the collected antiquities and had artisans to reference them to create more attractive productions for the Western market.[21]

This may be deemed a 'two-faced strategy'. It was rather innocently introduced to distinguish the external storytelling from the domestic requirements for modernization, which was necessary to cope with the dramatically rapid increase in international exposure, but was soon perceived as critically useful and was consciously applied. In this context, the two wheels of the 'cultural policy cart' that we examined in this chapter – the preservation of antiquities (tantamount to securing evidence of the

Fighting 'the warfare of peacetime' 75

nation's history) and the promotion of an exotic Japan at various expos – both served as interdependent components comprising the external side of the 'two-faced strategy', and were simultaneously nurtured by the motivation to generate effective narratives for the outside world.

Remaking narratives

Questioning exoticism: A turn from the Expo 1889 Paris to the Expo 1893 Chicago

In the course of continued implementation of the 'two-faced strategy', however, a major change was observed in the views of Japanese leaders, beginning at the end of the 1880s. The first such change is referenced in the government report on Japan's participation in Expo 1889 Paris, in a statement titled 'An opinion on participation in overseas expos'. The report was prepared by Yanagiya Kentaro, the acting head of Japan's bureau of preparation for that expo. Here, he encouraged 'serious reflection' on the already-established style of Japan's participation in past expos. The statement is roughly divided into two parts: the first pertains to the architectural characteristics of the buildings prepared for the country's exhibitions, and the second discusses the exhibits in such buildings. Both parts criticize erroneous imitations or the introduction of 'Western styles' at past expos and present a new policy for adoption for future expos, which emphasizes a focus on authentic representations that are 'purely Japanese', based on unique cultural traditions handed down for hundreds of years, rather than displaying items that have been adjusted to appeal to European tastes.[22]

On the surface, this is seemingly a contradiction of the observations made in the previous section; further explanation is perhaps needed. Yanagiya's criticism addressed the situation that duly resulted from the 'two-faced strategy'. Having eagerly pursued the external side of the strategy, with the intention of securing the best-possible standing for Japan in the international community, by the late 1870s, such efforts had resulted in the creation of 'Japanese' products that had never actually been seen or used in the daily lives of Japanese people. The emergence of a category called *yushutsu-kogei* (crafts specifically prepared for export) during that period testifies to the existence of this situation.[23] As shown by the well-known 'Japonisme' boom, such efforts achieved a certain amount of commercial success, but some European art specialists were already beginning to write about the regrettable change in Japanese products.[24]

Yanagiya's opinion was the first serious reaction to the situation from among the Japanese directly concerned with expo operations. This certainly opened a new chapter for Japanese exhibitions – narrative making – at expos. An obvious change soon occurred on the occasion of the next expo, which was held in Chicago in 1893.[25] In the government's overall policy towards participation in that expo, which was eventually published in the report after its conclusion, it can be observed that Yanagiya's alert was squarely adopted.

Regarding the Japanese pavilion, a major decision was made asserting that its construction must be modelled after that of an existing ancient temple, to 'reflect the supreme sophistication of traditional architecture', and to ultimately 'represent what is to be a great empire of the East to verify the nation's long history'.[26] This constituted a pronounced shift in Japanese policymakers' priority from one in which a story was offered to earn superficial popularity with foreigners, to that which focused on the authenticity of Japanese cultural contents that could be conveyed to the world. The selected model was *Houou-do* in *Byodo-in*, a representative Buddhist temple constructed in 1053 in the ancient capital of Kyoto. This was later considered the first example of a series of Japanese expo pavilions modelled after a specific example of representative traditional Japanese architecture, which continued until the Expo 1915 San Francisco.[27]

Another important effort was made to secure a renewed position for Japanese fine arts. As a background, it is important to note that, besides the popularity of Japanese antiquities, Japan's original water paintings, for example, had never been accepted as elements of fine art at past expos because they were different from Western works of art and had been considered applied art objects or categorized as Oriental art. The Japanese organizers decided that this treatment was 'detrimental to the pride of the Japanese arts', and was moreover 'opposing to a path to encourage artists and thus contribute to the development of the field'. The bureau of preparation for the Expo

Figure 4.2 Japanese pavilion at Expo 1893 Chicago. Source: 'Expositions where the modern technology of the times was exhibited' (National Diet Library Digital Exhibitions) Available online: https://www.ndl.go.jp/exposition/

Chicago designated an officer to travel to the United States in 1891 to conduct advance negotiations with the organizers of the expo to advocate adjusting this treatment of Japanese art. This was apparently the first time that the Japanese government had taken such an action for the particular purpose of securing a more honourable position in an expo. The action was successful, and Japanese art objects, not only paintings but also unique ceramics and lacquerware, eventually appeared alongside Western artworks in the same physical space at the expo.[28]

The individual sent to the United States to negotiate this change was Tejima Seiich (1850–1918), the director of the Tokyo School of Engineering; he was entrusted with handling all negotiations with the Chicago organizers. As a former retainer of the Suruga-Numazu *han* (feudal domain), Tejima had learned English as one of the earliest students sent to the United States after the Meiji Restoration. Subsequently, he had mainly served in the Ministry of Education, and by the time of the Expo Chicago, he had been directly involved in Japan's participation in overseas expos, starting from the Expo 1876 Philadelphia. He was later engaged in the same type of negotiation with the organizers of successive expos, as the Japanese government made it a significant focus; these negotiations continued again until the Expo 1915 San Francisco.[29]

Finally, another important figure was Kuki Ryuichi (1852–1931), who supervised Tejima as the vice-president of the bureau of preparation, or as the de facto head under successive presidents who were high-profile politicians. He had been appointed to his primary role as director of the National Museum in 1889. Focusing on Kuki as a key player in this context will allow us to become better acquainted with the nature of Japan's efforts leading up to the Expo 1893 Chicago, the framework of which was associated with the question of preserving the country's cultural elements, as had been the case at the time of the Expo 1873 Vienna.

Craving for history

Kuki Ryuichi, a former retainer of the Ayabe domain, was educated after the Meiji Restoration at *Keio Gijuku* (today's Keio University), a private educational institute established by Fukuzawa Yukichi (1835–1901), one of the most influential intellectuals of the time, known as a leading importer of Western knowledge. Kuki then joined the Ministry of Education in 1872, the year after the aforementioned Edict for the Preservation of Antiquities and Old Items was introduced. As a young elite official, he was involved in many of the initial research activities on cultural properties conducted by the Ministry at this time, and he also experienced the Expo 1878 Paris. He was deeply interested in and inclined towards preserving Japan's traditional culture, even when this entailed engaging in harsh confrontation with Fukuzawa, his former professor and muse.[30] As such, Kuki became involved in the Meiji government's cultural policymaking.

Having been rapidly promoted to the position of under-secretary at the Ministry at the age of twenty-eight (1880), he was appointed to serve as the Japanese minister to the United States in 1884. When he returned to Japan in 1887, he joined the Ministry of Imperial Household. Here, it is important to bear in mind that the already-established national museum had been transferred to the Ministry of Imperial Household in 1886, following various organizational changes that had occurred since its inauguration. The transfer of the museum was not necessarily carried out for conceptual purposes; instead, it was the result of administrative reforms connected to the establishment of the cabinet system in 1885 and was also part of the government's strategies to increase the imperial estate.[31] However, this transfer unavoidably influenced the nature of the museum and its collection, which was now defined as representing culture on the highest level of Japanese society.

It is unclear whether Kuki's latest appointment was related to this transfer of the museum, but the combination of his presence and the museum's new position determined the course of Japan's cultural management. The museum was renamed the Imperial Museum in 1889 (and further renamed the Imperial Household Museum in 1900) under Kuki's supervision.[32] After becoming the director, Kuki prepared a huge set of official documents explaining the organization, budget and duties of the museum. Here, quoting some paragraphs from a document contained within the set may be useful as they display his thoughts at the time. With the aforementioned Yanagiya's reflective opinion at the forefront of a certain process, this provided a more substantive foundation for Japan's new narrative making, the path for which would be supervised by Kuki himself:

Summary of Administrative Mandates of the Imperial Museum
1. The work of the history department aims to represent the improvement of this country's culture and to articulate the actual state of society for each era and also demonstrate the evolution of the people's way of life. The culture of this country has been influenced by Paekche, Goryeo, Silla, Sui, Tang, Yüan, Ming, etc., and the objects from those countries should be displayed in order as original elements associated with this country's history; this must be gradually extended to all countries concerned. Thus, all historical documents should be arranged in order and be accessible to the public.

...
3. The departments of fine arts and of arts and crafts ... should first articulate the artworks of this country as well as those of China and Chosun, which are related to the art of this country. Once preparations are complete, they should also plan to demonstrate Oriental art in general, and also gradually address Western artworks.
4. Many Western artworks currently held by the museum are of particularly poor quality; it is desirable to identify and discard these accordingly. The artworks from Japan that are of an average quality should be treated in the same manner.
5. The collection should be pursued according to the course of history; the works that should serve as representatives of each of the great artists of each era must be collected comprehensively to attain perfect order. ...[33]

We may reorganize these notifications and highlight three major characteristic ideas: (1) the clear intention for the museum collection to chronologically represent Japanese culture and thus outline Japan's history; (2) the intention to do so by depicting products of the highest quality from the past (vis-à-vis collecting all artefacts, as was

Fighting 'the warfare of peacetime'

done in the 1870s); and (3) the understanding of Japan's culture as the product of wider cultural interaction since ancient times across the East Asian region. If (1) shows the accumulation thus far of the experiences and related tasks entailed in creating a national historical collection since the 1870s, (2) reflects an important shift undergone by Japan's cultural policy management at the time. While (2) may be understood as corresponding with the aforementioned direction around the Expo 1893 Chicago, which placed the utmost importance on the authenticity of Japan culture to be narrated, (3) now suggests another perspective. This perspective, which is to view Japanese culture as a result of interaction with its Asian neighbours, seemingly disrupts the authenticity of the nation's culture; however, this was deeply desired to strengthen Japan's historical authenticity, and was thus introduced in cultural policy discourses at this time.

As an extension of this thought and policy exercise, Kuki and his museum colleagues aspired to produce the first book on Japanese art history for the principal purpose of disseminating it at the Expo 1900 Paris.[34] Kuki's preface for this book thoroughly explains that the above perspective (3) has become further embedded in and intermingled with clearer policy intentions, and that it now sustains the dignity of the Japanese nation; Asian connections emphasize Japan's long history and cultural uniqueness. Situating Japan within the wider context of Asian civilization was to grant equal value to the nation's art to that of the West, which had originated in Ancient Greece.

Further, we must discern another element, the most fundamental to have emerged in this context: that is, the burning desire for history. Japanese policymakers had engaged in the 'warfare of peacetime' since the early 1870s, and their conclusion thus far appeared to be that amidst various efforts to create national narratives, it was historical narratives that they would have to most earnestly establish, as history could affirm the nation's dignified standing – their vital goal; history would verify the nation's unshakeable presence since before the recent involvement in the wider international community.

The completion of the above-mentioned art history book was a remarkable achievement in this regard. In addition to this famous work, other history books on different aspects of Japanese society were published on occasions of participation in expos; for example, one book focused on manufacturing industries (for Expo 1876 Philadelphia), another addressed traditional music (for Expo 1878 Paris) and another concerned agriculture (for Expo 1900 Paris). Further, a more definitive introductory book on Japanese society and history, *Le Japon à l'exposition Universelle de 1878*, was published under the direction of the Imperial Commission of Japan for the Expo Paris 1878.[35] Although the art history book of 1900 has independently served as an optimal subject among Japanese art historians because it provided a basic structure for the 'history of Japanese art', on which today's education is still based, it is also important to see it as an outstanding result of the broader efforts towards generating the country's history, which was conceived as crucially important among Japanese policymakers by the 1880s to attain a better international standing. Further, these history books provide concrete evidence of the interaction between external motives and domestic reactions regarding national narrative making.

Conclusion

For late-nineteenth-century Japan, as has been observed in previous sections, making national narratives – that is, telling stories about the nation – was a central means of surviving and securing a more honourable place in the international community; thus, it constituted a major weapon in fighting the 'warfare of peacetime'. The motivation for national narrative making stemmed from the entanglement of ideas that occurred in the country, largely due to the society's sudden exposure to the external world; as the exposure increased, the motivation became concretized and more explicit. Meanwhile, the narratives, required for the nation's survival, evolved from those that emphasized cultural uniqueness vis-à-vis European cultures to those that conveyed the dignity believed to have been rooted in Japan's long history, and further, to those that would authenticate the nation's pride by situating Japanese culture in the context of broad cultural interactions with its Asian neighbours. Towards the end of the nineteenth century, the narrative-making efforts were more focused on history writing.

Such narratives were essentially produced by policymakers and functioned as precursors, or political engines, for nation-building. In that sense, if the contents of narratives changed over time, the structure of narratives remained nurtured by the 'two-faced' strategy, which always involved a certain distance between the artificial face, that is, the created narrative for disseminating towards the outside, and the domestic reality. At the Expo 1873 Vienna, this two-faced structure was generated by Japan's sense of behindness with respect to the leading Western nations, and the consequent urgency to join the march of modernization and achieve membership in the international community, while hiding its real face. However, when the Iwakura Embassy perceived that Japan lagged behind other countries by only forty years, based on their direct observation of major European countries and the United States,[36] which was an unexpectedly short period of time for them, the motivation to catch up with the West became relevant and deeply embedded in their mindset.

The Japanese actions towards national narrative making were required, above all else, to catch up with other nations,[37] and the overall theme for the conduct of policymakers could be summarized as 'restoring pride'. This historical reality is not to be overlooked, though I consent with Carol Gluck's 'modernity in common' as an inspiration for twenty-first-century discussions to convert the stereotyped scholarly attitudes by asserting that no early or late modernization exists.[38] As the basis for the historical analysis as pursued here, the empirical understanding of people's feelings at the time is indispensable.

Who, then, received the stories that the Japanese policymakers of the era so earnestly produced? Of course, the recipients partially comprised the audience of the expos and also the Japanese visitors to the national museum. However, it is unrealistic to believe that the entire population of Japan was immediately influenced by these narratives. For the overseas audience, it is already known that their firm expectations for an 'exotic' Japan did not easily change and rather encouraged them to misinterpret the story of 'authenticity' that Japan gradually became more interested in conveying; the first amiable impression of Japan lasted for a much longer period than Japan had desired.[39]

Fighting 'the warfare of peacetime' 81

The narrative-making efforts of policymakers, originally directed towards the external world, were, instead, echoed by their own steps in nation-building; in the first place, the told narratives served as their own goal for the relatively close future. Further, I can say that the most important recipients of the narratives comprised the future generations in Japan who were (and still are) given education based on a framework of national history, the foundation of which was largely prepared by Meiji policymakers.

Before concluding this chapter, it may be useful to lightly touch on situations that occurred later as an extension of what we have observed. First, alongside the preparations for the aforementioned art history book (published in French in 1900), Kuki Ryuichi directed nationwide research on cultural properties, particularly those held in temples and shrines. This research laid the foundation for the Ancient Temples and Shrines Preservation Law, which was eventually enacted by the Diet in 1897,[40] and replaced the Edict for the Preservation of Antiquities and Old Items of 1871. The important difference between the new law and the former edict was the new law's clear intention to select, for national preservation, superior specimens to represent Japanese history and serve as excellent models of the arts, while the former aimed to collect and preserve any objects.

This difference implied an irreversible change. While the original edict suggested that any object from the past that still existed could be proof of the nation's history, the new law departed from that stance and introduced the idea that some artefacts were appropriate and effective in epitomizing the nation's history while others were not. This reflected a shift emerging in the background that history writing was becoming more proactive and politically motivated.

The selective nature of the 1897 law was maintained until when it was revised into the National Treasures Preservation Law in 1929, the scope of which encapsulated more than shrines and temples. Since that time, the same perspective has been handed over and adopted in the existing Law for the Protection of Cultural Properties (1950).

Another consequence of the events examined in this chapter was the specialization of the cultural diplomacy field in the early twentieth century. The two-faced strategy was particularly useful when Japan decided to fight in the Russo-Japanese war (1904–5) and at the same time to participate in the Expo 1904 St. Louis.[41] Following this experience, the 'culture' sector gradually gained more recognition as a field of expertise in the context of diplomacy. Eventually, *Kokusai Bunka Shinko Kai* (known as KBS, the predecessor of today's Japan Foundation as the specialized organization for promoting Japanese culture abroad and enhancing cultural exchange under the auspice of the Ministry of Foreign Affairs) was established in 1934. It may be seen as Japan's first organization dedicated to the 'warfare of peacetime', as a marked result of the accumulated efforts of policymakers for producing national narratives that had originated in the nineteenth-century expo participations.

Achieving recognition or visualization of a specialized policy field, however, often signifies its gradual marginalization. In the Japanese case of cultural diplomacy, this seemingly occurred, with the establishment of KBS and even further in later twentieth century. In contrast, as we have seen in the former pages, the cultural representation of a nation had apparently been pursued as a central political issue when it had rather vaguely been incorporated into Japan's general diplomacy and politics. Therefore, the

82   *Narratives, Nations, and Other World Products*

period of focus in this chapter undoubtedly represented a heyday in policymakers' production of national narratives in the context of Japanese history, and after all, those narratives and the narrative-making processes were never national but essentially a world product.

Notes

1   Hereinafter, I write the names of Japanese figures with their surnames first and given names after, following the original style in the Japanese language. However, the authors' names mentioned in the footnotes including my name are in the reverse order for consistency, regardless of their cultural backgrounds.
2   For Tokugawa officials' rather quick and effective reactions, in contrast with the prevailing, opposite understanding, see Hiroshi Mitani, *Perii raiko* (The arrival of Commodore Perry) (Tokyo: Yoshikawakobunkan, 2003); Mayuko Sano, *Bakumatsu gaikogirei no kenkyu: Obei gaikokan tachi no shogun haietsu* (Diplomatic ceremonial of the last decade of the Tokugawa shogunate: The Western diplomats' audiences with the shogun) (Kyoto: Shibunkaku Shuppan, 2016).
3   For a detailed account of general revolution processes in Japan in the English language, it is recommended to reference the first couple of chapters in the following book, although international factors are not sufficiently discussed therein: Junji Banno, trans. J. A. A. Stockwin, *Japan's modern history 1857–1937: A new political narrative* (London and New York: Routledge, 2014). For another notable work that spotlights movements of local domains in Japan in the path towards the revolution, see Robert I. Hellyer, *Defining engagement: Japan and global contexts, 1640–1868* (Cambridge, MA; London: Harvard University Asia Center, 2009). It should also be mentioned that for the past decade, there has been an increasing international research trend analysing the course of Japan's Meiji Restoration in a global context, rather than understanding it as a single country's political history.
4   This chapter refrains from explaining the famous story of the normalization of unequal treaties that required enormous effort from the Meiji Government until the early twentieth century. For a reliable scholarly argument on this matter, see Kaoru Iokibe, *Meiji joyaku kaiseishi: Hoken kaifuku e no tenbo to nashonarizumu* (Meiji treaty revision: The prospects for unified jurisdiction and nationalism) (Tokyo: Yuhikaku, 2010).
5   The English translation of the entire report is available due to the significant efforts of a group of prominent English-speaking Japan specialists. The visit to the Expo Vienna is included in the last volume: *The Iwakura Embassy 1871–1873, A true account of the Ambassador Extraordinary & Plenipotentiary's journey of observation through the United States of America and Europe* (vol. V), ed. Kunitake Kume, trans. Graham Healey and Chūshichi Tsuzuki (Chiba: Japan Documents, 2002), 9–41.
6   *The Iwakura Embassy*, 11. (Translation partly amended by author.)
7   The history continues up to today. The one in 2025 is planned to take place in Osaka, Japan. Since expos involve extremely diverse aspects of human activities, through not only their exhibited items but also their organizing processes, they have provided an unlimited range of scholarly topics. However, studies broadly dealing with the history of expos are rather limited, with a representative example: Paul Greenhalgh, *A history of world's fairs and expositions, from London to Shanghai 1851–2010*

Fighting 'the warfare of peacetime' 83

(London: Papadakis, 2011). I should also mention a valuable anthology focusing on the involvements of smaller nations in the history of expos: Mart Filipová, ed., *Cultures of international exhibition 1840–1940: Great exhibitions in the margins* (Surrey (UK) and Burlington (US): Ashgate, 2015). Based in Japan, I have been organizing, since 2010, an interdisciplinary team research of a global perspective on the history of expos (developed to be the Society for Expo-logy), and published: Mayuko Sano, ed., *Bankokuhakurankai to ningen no rekishi* (Expos and human history) (Kyoto: Shibunkaku Shuppan, 2015); Mayuko Sano (ed.), *Banpakugaku: Bankokuhakurankai to iu sekai o haaku suru houhou* (Expo-logy: Expos as a method of grasping the world) (Kyoto: Shibunkaku Shuppan, 2020).

8   See Mayuko Sano, 'Nothing but nation building: Promoting Japan's national image at early expos', *BIE Bulletin 2019*, 90–111.

9   For details of the processes of this participation, see Mayuko Sano, 'Banpaku no hito, Razafodo Orukokku (A man of expos, Sir Rutherford Alcock): 1851, 1862, 1878, 1886', in Sano, ed. *Expos and human history*, 29–35.

10 Besides the official designation of each expo (such as 'the Great Exhibition of the Works of Industry of All Nations'), there are historically various ways to call these events, typically 'international exhibition' in the UK, 'exposition universelle' in France, and 'world's fair' in the United States. Currently, the BIE (Bureau International des Expositions), the international organization established based on the Convention Relating to International Exhibitions (1928) to administer the expos, has adopted 'expo' as a neutral term to apply to all these events. In this chapter, I will follow this new custom to simplify the argument except for occasions when necessary to particularly employ another term.

11 *Tokyo Kokuritstu Hakubutsukan hyakunen-shi* (The 100-year history of the Tokyo National Museum, Vol. I) (Tokyo: Tokyo National Museum, 1973), 37–8. (Translation by author.)

12 Ibid., 39–40.

13 Hideo Seki, *Hakubutsukan no tanjo* (The birth of a museum) (Tokyo: Iwanami Shoten, 2005).

14 *The 100-year history*, 108.

15 Sano had had experiences relating to the Expo 1867 Paris, when Saga domain, the local authority to which he had belonged under the shogunate system, had acted to be part of it in its own name besides the shogunate.

16 He was one of many *o-yatoi gaikoku-jin* (foreign employees) who were commissioned by the central or local governments (and sometimes private bodies) to help improve various sectors of Japanese society, mainly during the 1870s.

17 *The 100-year history*, 47–72.

18 'History of the TNM', available on the website of the Tokyo National Museum: https://www.tnm.jp/modules/r_free_page/index.php?id=143&lang=en (accessed 28 December 2019). The Museum gradually assumed the form of a permanent public institution, and in 1882, it was opened in a fully formal style on the same site as that of today's Tokyo National Museum.

19 Mitsukuni Yoshida, *Kaiteiban Bankokuhakurankai: Gijutsu bunmei-shi teki ni* (Expos: from a perspective of the history of technology and civilisation, Revised version) (Tokyo: Nihon Hoso Kyokai, 1985), 68–9.

20 *The Iwakura Embassy*, 31.

21 This aspect of the government's efforts has been ferreted out mainly by historians specializing in Japanese arts and crafts. For a representative work, see Hiroko

Yokomizo, 'Meiji seifu ni yoru kougei zuan no shido ni tsuite: *Onchi Zuroku* ni miru seihingazu-kakari no katsudo to sono shuhen (The Meiji government's instructions about art design: Functions of product design section with a focus on the design collection *Onchi Zuroku*)', *Proceedings of the Tokyo National Museum* 34 (1999): 5–172.

22 *Kaigai hakurankai honpo sando shiryo* (Collection of documents regarding Japan's participation in overseas expositions), vol. 3 (Tokyo: Hakurankai Kurabu, 1928), 132–40. (The citations from this source are translated by author.)

23 See Toyoro Hida, 'Meiji kogei-ron: Kokumin kokka ni okeru shokuninteki "gigei" no yakuwari (A study on arts and crafts in Meiji: Roles of *gigei,* the artisanal work, for a nation state)', in *Dento kogei saiko, Kyo no uchi-soto: Kako hakkutsu, genjo bunseki, shodai tenbo* (Rethinking the traditional crafts, in and outside of Kyoto: Looking into the past, analysing the present state, and prospecting the future), ed. Shigemi Inaga (Kyoto: Shibunkaku Shuppan, 2007), 128–49.

24 See Sano, 'Nothing but nation building', 100–2.

25 Chicago was the first expo in which Japan took part based on an official decision by the Imperial Diet, introduced in 1890 as the legislative organ under the Imperial Constitution, which was promulgated in the preceding year.

26 *Rinji Hakurankai Jimukyoku houkoku* (Report of the Temporary Bureau for the Participation in Chicago World's Fair) (Tokyo: Rinji Hakurankai Jimukyoku, 1895), 493–4.

27 Mayuko Sano, 'Bunka no jitsuzō to kyozō: Bankoku hakurankai ni miru Nihon shōkai no rekishi (True and false images of culture: A history of promoting Japan at expos)', *Kokusai kankeiron kenkyū* (Studies on international relations) 9 (1995): 88–91, 104.

28 Ibid., 393.

29 *Tejima Seiichi sensei den* (Biography of Prof. Tejima Seiichi) (Tokyo: Tejima Kogyo Kyoiku Shikin-dan, 1929).

30 See Shinji Takahashi, *Kuki Ryuichi no kenkyu* (Studies on Kuki Ryuichi) (Tokyo: Mirai-sha, 2005).

31 *The 100-year history*, 243–5.

32 In 1952, the museum was detached from the imperial court and renamed the 'Tokyo National Museum' (as it is called today) as a result of Japan's overall democratization reform following the end of the Second World War.

33 *The 100-year history*, 250. (Translation by author.) It is said that during this period, Kuki was closely supported by his young colleague Okakura Kakuzo (1863–1913), or the later famous philosopher Okakura Tenshin, who was an initiator of the Tokyo School of Fine Arts established in 1887 (Today's Faculty of Fine Arts, Tokyo University of the Arts), although they separated rather soon thereafter. Okakura's symbolic phrase 'Asia is one' is the opening sentence of his *The Ideals of the East with special reference to the art of Japan* (London: J. Murray, 1906).

34 Therefore, it was first published in French as *L'Histoire du l'art du Japon* (Commission impériale du Japon à l'Exposition universelle de Paris, Paris: Maurice de Brunoff, 1900) and was not published in Japanese until that following year.

35 Additional examples should be identified and researched, although such books were spontaneously planned and published, and unfortunately not systematically preserved or archived.

36   This understanding of a delay by 'forty years' can be found in many parts of the accounts of the Iwakura Embassy, but most impressively in a chapter dedicated to their observation of the city of London: *The Iwakura Embassy,* vol. II, 57.

37   In this light, Takehiko Kariya's argument applying the same notion of 'catching-up' to the post-Second World War Japan is convincing, though stemming from a limited perspective of the history of education and dealing with a different era. See Kariya, *Who killed Japan's modernity? What comes after 'catch-up'?* (Tokyo: Iwanami Shoten, 2019).

38   Carol Gluck, 'Modernity in common: Japan and world history', in *Internationalizing Japan studies: Dialogues, interactions, dynamics* (*TUFS International Symposium 29–31 January 2016*) (Tokyo: Institute of Japan Studies, Tokyo University of Foreign Studies, 2017), 26–38.

39   Sano, 'True and false images of culture', 89–92.

40   *The 100-year history*, 248.

41   See Sano, 'True and false images of culture', 91.

5

Japan, *Tōyō* (the 'Eastern Ocean') and Asia in the World: The transition of Japanese self-consciousness from the 1850s to the 1940s

HANEDA Masashi

Introduction

The self-consciousness of a group of people can vary over time, depending on its location in the world and surrounding situation. Thus, the purpose of this study is fivefold. First, it demonstrates that the self-consciousness of the Japanese people changed considerably between the Meiji Revolution[1] and the end of the Second World War, in response to Japan's political, economic and military strength in the global context. During that time, both officials and intellectuals attempted to find a suitable and meaningful position for Japan in the world.

Second, the concept of 'Asia' was previously known as a geographical term in the Tokugawa era (1603–1867), while the concept of *Tōyō* (the 'Eastern Ocean') was introduced to the Japanese language in the mid-nineteenth century. Hence, this study examines these concepts in order to better understand the manner in which the self-consciousness of Japanese officials and intellectuals evolved in parallel with their understanding of Japan's global position.

Third, after focusing on the influential worldview of the Tokugawa era, this study discusses the ways in which the concept of *Tōyō* was interpreted in the travel accounts by Kume Kunitake, the official diarist of the Iwakura Mission to the United States and Europe in the 1870s. For example, he repeatedly expressed his opinions regarding the global standing of the Japanese people. He also reported that Japan (a country of *Tōyō*) should strive to be equal with the nations of *Seiyō* (the 'Western Ocean'), which were far ahead in terms of their economic and military development. In this case, the concepts of *Tōyō* and *Seiyō* resemble the ideas of the Orient and the Occident found in the traditional European orientation. However, the significations of these two conceptual pairs are distinct from one another, at least initially.

Fourth, this study examines the narratives of Japanese self-consciousness in history teaching by focusing on *Tōyōshi* ('the history of *Tōyō*') and how a different meaning of *Tōyō* was introduced in high-school curriculums during the 1890s. It is important to note that the *Tōyōshi* textbooks written in the late nineteenth century did not

88   *Narratives, Nations, and Other World Products*

encompass the history of Japan. Apparently, the Japanese intellectuals did not envision a *Tōyōshi* that included Japan's past.

On a side note, the word 'Asia' bears a striking similarity to *Tōyō*. However, Asia and *Tōyō* did not designate the same geographical sphere. In fact, Asia's range was much wider and larger than that of *Tōyō*, and this discrepancy remained when *Tōyōshi* was introduced. Meanwhile, although Tōyō was more important for Japanese statesmen and intellectuals in the nineteenth century, the situation gradually changed in the first half of the twentieth century, when Asia became a critical keyword for the self-consciousness of Japanese elites. This change was based on two episodes: (1) the promotion of the idea of a 'Muslim world' in the 1930s and (2) the government's attempt to write an Asian history in the middle of the Second World War. Of course, both the aforementioned episodes were based on the Japanese military's expansion and a review of Japanese self-consciousness.

In sum, the present study alludes to the confluence of the Japanese and Western worldviews in postwar Japan. It also refers to the legacy of the prewar worldview and how its interpretation of history merged with the confrontational 'West versus the rest of the world' perspective in postwar Japan. Moreover, three concepts are used as reference points in this study: *Tōyō*, Asia and the Orient. It is hoped that the discourses on these concepts will not only illustrate the ambivalent nature of the Japanese self-consciousness, but they will also demonstrate the extent to which Japan's position in the world (as embedded in the minds of Japanese intellectuals) has often been closely entangled with global circumstances. In this case, the national narrative of the Japanese identity must be discussed through its evolution in the international context.

The discovery of *Tōyō* and *Seiyō*

The importance of China and Chinese elements in pre-modern Japan

The identification of oneself in one's geographical space is one of the most common means of human self-awareness. In this regard, the principal islands of the Japanese archipelago are situated close to one another, off the eastern shore of the Eurasian landmass. Given their location, size, proximity and their clear separation from the Korean peninsula and mainland China, it would have been relatively easy for people living on these islands to imagine themselves belonging together.[2]

One of the most influential positions taken by the Japanese people until the early nineteenth century was that the world consisted of three countries: Japan (*honchō*), China (*kara*) and India (*tenjiku*). This long-held historical perspective was also widely acknowledged by the twelfth century.[3] However, this orientation did not imply that the Japanese actually believed that the world was made up of only three countries. In fact, it was well known that there were many other countries, with neighbouring Korea being the closest.

In the sixteenth and early seventeenth centuries, the Japanese archipelago was frequently visited by missionaries, merchants and sailors from the Iberian Peninsula and northwestern Europe. In the Japanese categorization, both the Portuguese and the

Spanish were placed in the same category of *nanbanjin* ('southern barbarians'), while the Dutch and English were named *koumoujin* ('red-haired people'). At that time, Japanese intellectuals commanded geographical awareness and specific knowledge of many countries between Europe and Japan. For example, in the seventeenth century, folding Japanese screens, called *biombo* by the Europeans, depicted paintings of people en route Japan from Europe.[4] *Kunyu Wanguo Quantu*, a map created by Matteo Ricci in Beijing at the beginning of the seventeenth century, also reflected the newfound European geographical knowledge of the world that was subsequently imported to Japan. Meanwhile, Dutch ships continually brought an assortment of informative world maps illustrated in Europe. Thus, Japanese intellectuals at the time realized that, according to these maps, the world was comprised of five regions: Asia, Europe, Africa, the Americas and Oceania.

However, the pejorative nomenclature for the European presence and its influences indicate that these inputs were curbed in the Tokugawa era. In fact, until the early nineteenth century, every aspect of Japan and Japanese society was inspired by Chinese elements or by Indian religious traditions interpreted from a Chinese perspective. Moreover, Chinese goods and cultural artefacts were objects of admiration and were regarded as being imbued with values that were far more substantial than the European cultural items brought to Japan by the Dutch. At that time, the Western half of the Eurasian landmass and the Americas were still out of the sight of most Japanese people,[5] until the arrival of the American fleet under Commodore Matthew Perry in 1853.

The arrival of the *kurofune* ('black ships') was a tremendous shock for both the officials of the Tokugawa government and Japanese intellectuals, whose perspectives dramatically shifted. More specifically, they discarded their conventional interpretation of the world comprised of three countries and began regarding Europe and the United States as the most important components of human existence on Earth.

Full-fledged encounter with European modernity

A reading of one particular text, recorded and compiled in the 1870s (less than ten years after the establishment of the new Meiji government), can elucidate how Japanese intellectuals dramatically changed their worldview. In this regard, in 1871, a large diplomatic mission of Japanese statesmen and scholars, headed by a top official named Iwakura Tomomi, was sent to the United States and Europe by the Meiji government.[6] The log of this journey was recorded by Kume Kunitake, the official diarist of the mission, and published in 1878.[7] This text eloquently exhibits the fundamental and perspectival pivot that occurred among Japanese intellectuals at that time.

What is interesting, in connection with the Japanese self-consciousness, is Kume's usage of the terms *Seiyō* and *Tōyō*. For instance, he described (in detail) the political, economic and social evolution of the United States and Europe, and categorized them as *Seiyō*.[8] From his standpoint, it was clear that the United States and Europe jointly constituted a singular world unit, since their respective parties visited the Japanese archipelago with similar aims of concluding trade agreements. Moreover, they were distinguished from other countries, such as China and Japan, due to their superior technological and military strength.

90 — *Narratives, Nations, and Other World Products*

The term *Seiyō* emanates from the Chinese word *xīyang*, which has been in use since ancient China. In addition, the two words employ the same Chinese character. The signage for *xīyang* appears in two places in *Kunyu Wanguo Quantu*: (1) *xiao* ('small'), designating the western Indian Ocean, and (2) *dā* ('large'), indicating the Atlantic Ocean. In this regard, the countries of *xīyang* signified those along the maritime route to the south and to the west from Guangzhou. Southeast and South Asian countries were therefore included in the original concept of *xīyang*. As for Japan, Japanese intellectuals in the Tokugawa era introduced the term and pronounced it in the Japanese way as *Seiyō*. However, the meaning was basically the same as the original Chinese term, that is, it signified the countries situated along the route between Europe and Southeast Asia, including African and South Asian countries.[9] Interestingly, its meaning changed after the arrival of Commodore Perry in 1853, which indicates the influential power of the United States and Europe. Fukuzawa Yukichi, a well-known intellectual in the Meiji period, also used the term *Seiyō* to signify European countries and the United States in his 1866 book titled *Seiyō Jijō* ('Information of the West').

It is possible that the concept of *Seiyō* originated from that of the West or Occident in European languages. However, this term was actually invented without any direct influence from these concepts. Moreover, it is generally assumed that the current concept of the West emerged in the 1890s, as an idea of British imperial rhetoric,[10] while the history of 'Western civilization', which explicitly connects European history with that of the Americas after the European arrival, was first taught in American universities after the First World War.[11] Yet, the term *Seiyō* was already in use in the mid-nineteenth century.

Kume also compared the various aspects of *Seiyō* with the features of *Tōyō* (its counterpart) and, in some instances, with Japan itself.[12] For him, Japan's characteristics often represented those exemplified by *Tōyō*, as shown in the following excerpt:

> From the earliest days of intercourse between the *Tōyō* and the *Seiyō*, the two have not really understood each other since they have totally different outlooks, with customs and characters the opposite of the other's in every respect, down to the smallest detail. Since our Embassy embarked on the American ship in Yokohama, we have been journeying through a realm of foreign customs. And just as our behavior is surprising to Americans, their customs seem baffling to us with so many fundamental differences in every area, even though I was quite a practiced observer. I found it difficult to fulfill my responsibilities as official recorder and capture all the nuances of these differences. (... ...) In conjugal and family relations in Japan, a wife is dutiful to her mother-in-law and father-in-law, and children display filial respect for their parents. [In America] however, it is the custom for the husband to serve his wife.[13]

The concept of *Tōyō* also comes from the Chinese word *dongyang*, meaning 'the ocean that faces the eastern coast of the Chinese mainland'. Thus, the countries of *Tōyō* included Japan, Ryukyu, the Philippines, etc. Japanese intellectuals also modified the original meaning of this term and began to use the word to signify the countries located on the eastern end of the Eurasian landmass such as China, Korea and Japan. It is important to note that, according to the original Chinese meaning, China is neither *xīyang* nor *dongyang* because it is located in the centre of the Eurasian landmass. However, once the two terms were transferred into Japanese and acquired a new meaning, China was categorized as a part of *Tōyō*, along with Japan.[14]

Over time, China and Chinese culture, which were objects of admiration and sources of inspiration for Japanese intellectuals, lost their supremacy in the Japanese mindset. China was eventually degraded and included in the same group of *Tōyō*, as Japan's equal.[15] Moreover, less than twenty years after Commodore Perry's visit, Japanese officials and intellectuals no longer maintained their conventional supercilious attitude vis-à-vis the European people.

Although Kume often underlined the contrast between *Tōyō* and *Seiyō* in his text, he believed that the disparity between the technological and industrial advancements of *Seiyō* and *Tōyō* was not critical. He also argued that *Seiyō*'s prosperity only began in the beginning of the nineteenth century, and that it was mainly realized by the rapid development of science and technology.[16] Meanwhile, if *Tōyō* successively introduced the same progressive spirit, then it would have easily become equal to *Seiyō*, as stated in the following excerpt:

> To speak of the error of being over-hasty to put knowledge to work is enough to suggest that *Tōyō* is far behind *Seiyō* on the path of development, but the fact is that even Britain and France, the most advanced countries, have taken a mere fifty years to reach their present prosperity. The development of *Tōyō* and *Seiyō* has not been wholly unlike. Surely the bettering of the condition of the people has been a common principle. (…) Civilizations of *Tōyō* and *Seiyō* are not completely heterogeneous and irreconcilable. There is no difference, between the two spheres, of smart employment of various resources and technologies and creating a rich and happy life.[17]

In sum, it is true that Kume often used the terms *Seiyō* and *Tōyō* in opposition. However, it must be noted that he did not reduce the world to only two contrasting zones. Instead, he sometimes utilized the concept of *Nanyō* ('the Southern Ocean') to indicate the countries in South and Southeast Asia,[18] while using *Seiyō* to emphasize the power it wielded over the rest of the world.

Tōyō and *Seiyō*, compared to the Orient and the Occident

In general, the concepts of *Tōyō* and *Seiyō* did not exactly correspond with the European or Western notions of the Orient and the Occident. As explained earlier, both *Tōyō* and *Seiyō* were of Chinese origin and their significations were closely related to real geographical locations. For example, the *Tōyō*-designated countries in the eastern part of the Eurasian landmass included China, Korea and Japan, while the *Seiyō*-designated countries, located to the west of Japan, included the European powers[19] and the United States. In addition, *Nanyō* was used in a similar vein to indicate the nations in South and Southeast Asia.

It is noteworthy that at that point *Tōyō* did not signify either Asia or the Orient in the European sense of the words. Originally, in Europe, the term 'Orient' basically represented the regions in which the ancient civilizations were born, that is, Mesopotamia, the eastern coastal regions of the Mediterranean Sea, and Egypt. Afterwards, as the European nations expanded their forays towards the east in the nineteenth century, the term 'Orient' began to encompass the entire geographical area of Asia. China, Korea and Japan were also gradually integrated into the broad scope of this term.

In fact, the dichotomous view of the Occident[20] versus the Orient formulated in Europe around the nineteenth century. Moreover, Europe's former admiration and yearning for the Orient in the eighteenth century transformed into curiosity, exoticism and even contempt in the nineteenth century. In parallel, the Orient became the object of a scientific research domain called 'Oriental Studies',[21] after which *Société Asiatique* (the first academic society on Asia) was established in France in 1822 and the Royal Asiatic Society of Great Britain was founded in 1823. It is important to note that these societies incorporated the term 'Asia' in their names, even though the academic discipline was called *Orientalisme* or 'Oriental Studies', and their mainstream research (until the latter half of the nineteenth century) mainly consisted of philological studies on the ancient Near East and India.[22] In this respect, the terms 'Orient' and 'Asia' covered (at least theoretically) almost the same geographical sphere in the European languages.

Despite being considered one of the countries of Asia, European knowledge of Japan was extremely limited before Commodore Perry's visit in 1853.[23] However, once the country opened up, information on Japan began to pour into European countries and the United States, after which it captivated the interests of many people. Interestingly, the Asiatic Society of Japan (the first European-style academic society in Japan) was established in Yokohama in 1872, at the exact time of the Iwakura Mission to the United States and Europe.

In sum, as the Europeans were producing their dichotomous worldview of Europe or the Occident versus the Orient, Japanese intellectuals attempted to apprehend the world and Japan's position in it by using the concepts of *Tōyō* and *Seiyō*. At first glance, these two sets of ideas appear to be similar, but upon closer examination, they are very different in their meanings.

The perspective shift in historical understanding

The initial framework of teaching history

After repeatedly witnessing the invincible military power and advanced technology of *Seiyō* in the 1850s and 1860s, the Meiji government shifted its viewpoint and attempted to systematically (and forcefully) introduce the political and social institutions of *Seiyō* to Japan. The restructuring of the educational system was one such endeavour. In 1872, (just four years after the establishment of the new government), a new rule for the school system mandated that elementary schools include history as a subject.

The following two points are noteworthy in this initial stage of history education. First, Japanese history, referred to at the time as the 'History of the Empire', was separated from the histories of other countries and taught independently, even though both domestic and international aspects were included in the framework of the subject. In those days, it was quite normal for Japanese officials and intellectuals to believe that Japan had its own unique history. Chinese-style history writings had been imported since the eighth century, and the chronological narratives of dynasties under the reigns of various emperors enjoyed a long tradition in Japan.[24] Thus, Japanese officials and intellectuals were used to such historical writings. In 1869, once it became stable, the government had taken the initiative of writing a comprehensive history of Japan.[25] In this case, recording the history of the former dynasty/government became one of the missions of the following dynasty/government.

Second, apart from Japanese history as an independent subject, the histories of other countries were also taught in elementary schools. In fact, the advanced technology and strong military power demonstrated by the respective navies of *Seiyō* countries in several incidents/conflicts along the Japanese coast were repeatedly emphasized. Such experiences also convinced the political elites in Japan that it was important to learn the histories of other nations, especially those that belonged to *Seiyō*.

However, at that time, no textbooks on the histories of *Seiyō* countries existed. Hence, in 1876, the Ministry of Education created and published a two-volume Japanese translation of *Parley's Universal History on the Basis of Geography*,[26] which was a popular history textbook in the United States. As the title elucidates, this book outlined the histories of numerous countries and peoples of the world under five geographical sections: Asia, Africa, Europe, the Americas and Oceania. Although the segment of European history occupied more than half of the entire book (i.e. 111 out of 193 chapters), it did not adopt the influential German style that diachronically narrated human history from the beginning of the Orient to modern 'civilized' Europe.

Each country was also classified within a geographical framework and its history was distinguished from that of other countries. For example, instead of placing the history of the Hebrew people and early Christianity in the first part of the book (i.e. in German style), this narrative was included in the section on Asia due to its geographical location. Meanwhile, since there was no mention of the Orient, the textbook did not appropriately correspond to the oppositional perspective of *Tōyō* and *Seiyō* that Kume and the others in the Iwakura Mission had adopted. In other words, at that time, the subject of history was divided into two parts, that is, Japanese history and the history of the rest of the world,[27] with neither *Tōyō* nor *Seiyō* commanding its own history.

The birth of *Tōyōshi* (the 'history of Tōyō')

Within twenty years of the Iwakura Mission, Japan transformed from 'the United States of feudal lords' into one of the world's 'civilized' countries by adopting Western political and economic methods as well as social systems and institutions. For example, the ban on Christianism was lifted, a conscription system was adopted and the privileged class of samurai warriors lost their military function. In addition, Hokkaido, Ryukyu and Ogasawara islands were integrated under Japanese sovereignty, and Japan's national border (as a sovereign state) became fixed. In 1889, the constitution was issued, after which a bicameral parliament, called the 'Imperial Diet', was inaugurated the following

94 *Narratives, Nations, and Other World Products*

year. Subsequently, quarrels began with Qing China over various rights and interests in Korea and Taiwan.[28]

In 1894, a reform of the education system was initiated by the Ministry of Education, just after the First Sino-Japanese War broke out. This was also when the committee of the Tokyo Normal High School discussed the history syllabus. One of its members, Naka Michiyo (a leading historian of Chinese history), argued that the history of foreign countries should be divided into two segments: the history of *Seiyō* and the account of *Tōyō*.

The history of *Tōyō* outlines the vicissitude of eastern countries, at the centre of which is China. Paired with the history of *Seiyō*, these two aspects can be included in the history of the world. However, when teaching the history of *Tōyō*, it is important to focus on the interactions between Japan and these countries as well as the relations between the *Tōyō* and *Seiyō* countries themselves.

All of the attendees at the aforementioned meeting agreed with Naka's argument, and for the first time, the words *Tōyōshi* (the 'History of *Tōyō*') and *Seiyōshi* (the 'History of *Seiyō*') were mentioned in a regulation passed by the Tokyo Normal High School. Shortly thereafter, they appeared in the corresponding edict by the Ministry of Education.[29] For the first time, *Tōyō* and *Seiyō* were accorded their own histories.[30]

Since *Tōyōshi* was a new subject, a new textbook was mandated. Of the several textbooks written after the edict was instituted,[31] the most trustworthy, popular and influential was Kuwabara Jitsuzo's *Tōyōshi for High School Students,* published in 1898. In the preface of the textbook, Kuwabara defined the concept of *Tōyōshi* as follows:

> *Tōyōshi* clarifies the vicissitude of nations and the rise and fall of countries mainly in Eastern Asia. The history of the world consists of *Tōyōshi* and *Seiyōshi*.
>
> Geographically speaking, we can divide Asia into five parts: 1. Eastern Asia, which is the area, surrounded by the Himalayas in the south, the Pamirs in the west and the Altai mountains in the north, 2. Southern Asia, 3. Central Asia, which is the sphere surrounded by the Hindukush in the south, the Pamir in the east, and the Syr Darya in the north, 4. Western Asia, and 5. Northern Asia.
>
> In the framework of *Tōyōshi*, the history of Eastern Asia is mainly described, but, at the same time, the history of Southern and Central Asia needs to be outlined, as they have had direct and indirect relations with the history of Eastern Asia. Since the weather is too cold and severe, and there are few populations in Northern Asia, no important affairs affecting the history of Eastern Asia have taken place there. Western Asia has had close relations with European affairs and cannot be separated from Europe and its history. Therefore, the history of Northern and Western Asia is out of the range of *Tōyōshi*.[32]

The following points may be noted from the aforementioned excerpt. First, Japanese history is clearly separated from *Tōyōshi*. Of course, Japanese history had been independently taught in elementary schools since the 1870s, as a distinct subject from the history of the rest of the world. However, as a sovereign nation-state, Japan required its own history, which could be taught to its children so they could eventually become Japanese nationals and deserving subjects of the Emperor.

Japan, Tōyō (the 'Eastern Ocean') and Asia in the World   95

It is also important to remember that Japan was regarded as a country belonging to *Tōyō* at the time of the Iwakura Mission in the 1870s. In addition, the concept of *Tōyō* itself was created just before that time by Japanese intellectuals who faced the supremacy of European and American powers, and aimed to classify Japan and China in the same group. Then, why did Kuwabara not include Japanese history in the history of *Tōyō*?

Second, it must be remembered that the textbook was written just after the Japanese military victory over Qing China in 1895. Unlike the 1870s, when the Iwakura Mission visited various nations around the world, the status of Japan in the world was no longer (at least in the eyes of the Japanese intellectuals) the same as that of Qing China. In fact, Japan was poised to leave *Tōyō* and become one of the world's major powers, along with Europe and the United States.[33] Moreover, since Taiwan had become a Japanese colony, Japan was able to dispatch its army to Beijing at the time of the Boxer Rebellion in 1900, after which it would sign the Anglo-Japanese Alliance in 1902. At that point, *Tōyō* had to be externalized.

At the same time, according to the Japanese worldview and understanding, the countries of *Tōyō* did have their unique histories. Meanwhile, many Europeans believed that only Europe had a history. From their viewpoint, other countries outside of Europe had remained stagnant and, as a result, they lacked their own histories.

Finally, it must be highlighted that *Tōyōshi* was not identical to Asian history. Kuwabara clearly contended that Western Asia should not be included in *Tōyōshi*. Instead, this region should be incorporated within the framework of European history. However, this viewpoint greatly differed from that of Europe, where the Orientalists and other intellectuals firmly believed that Western Asia was basically equivalent to the Near East, a part of Asia or the Orient, and culturally separated from Europe.

Discovery of the Muslim world and the history of Asia

Japan won both the Sino-Japanese War in 1894–5 and the Russo-Japanese War in 1904–5, after which it participated in the First World War, conforming to the Anglo-Japanese Alliance. Moreover, in the 1930s, it had become one of the world's colonial powers, by annexing Taiwan and Korea, and establishing a puppet state in Manchuria. Thus, when Japanese leaders established mainland China and Southeast Asia as their next targets, it was natural that the religion of Islam and the Muslims living in these regions came into their view. Until that time, due to the geographical distance, Japan had no close relations with the Muslim people.[34]

It was also at that time when the term *kaikyōken* (equivalent to the 'Muslim world') was created through the interactions between Tatar Muslim refugees and Japanese intellectuals interested in Islam, and used during the latter half of the 1930s.[35] In fact, some Japanese intellectuals who found the concept of *kaikyōken* meaningful believed that it was not just an idea, but also a real and concrete geographical space between Europe and China. They also regarded the people living in this sphere as victims of the colonialist countries of *Seiyō*. According to them, Japan, as the leader of the non-*Seiyō* countries, should confront the *Seiyō* powers, in collaboration with the people of *kaikyōken*.[36]

96 *Narratives, Nations, and Other World Products*

Meanwhile, in the latter half of the 1930s, many institutes and societies related with *kaikyōken* were also established, after which many research journals and books on *kaikyōken* were published,[37] and related public events were held.[38] As a result, the concept of *kaikyōken* rapidly spread and permeated among the Japanese public. From the viewpoint of the government and the military, *kaikyōken* was highly important, since they planned to advance into regions where many Muslims lived in order to govern them. Thus, the research on this sphere was strongly encouraged and financially supported.

Based on the importance of *kaikyōken* at that time, it is not surprising that the Japanese intellectuals focused on the concept of 'Asia', which not only covered the sphere of *Tōyō*, but also that of *kaikyōken*. Meanwhile, the government promoted the concept of *Dai-tōa Kyōeiken* (The Greater East Asia Co-prosperity Sphere[39]), in which Japan (as the leader of Greater East Asia) should support other Asian peoples, including Muslims, and defeat the Western powers, in collaboration with them. However, the concept of *Tōyō* was not large enough to contain the ideals of the Japanese government and military. Thus, they used 'Asia', instead of '*Tōyō*', to justify their intention of expanding the sphere under their control.

In line with this shift of political importance from *Tōyō* to Asia, the Ministry of Education changed the framework of history teaching. In fact, they attempted to replace *Tōyōshi* with a new concept, called *Dai-tōashi* ('History of Greater East Asia'), and requested professors of *Tōyōshi* at the Tokyo and Kyoto Imperial University to describe a history in which Japan's excellent culture spreads throughout all of Asia. In this case, the Ministry of Education's plan was to translate the new history into various languages and distribute it to the Greater East Asia Co-prosperity Sphere.[40]

However, Miyazaki Ichisada, a well-known historian of Chinese history at Kyoto University who took part in this rewriting project, found it impossible to forge such an unimaginable history. Thus, he suggested that they write a history from the following perspective: human culture born in West Asia and developed to the highest level in Japan (the eastern end of Asia), after which it spreads throughout all of Asia. Government officials subsequently accepted his idea and asked professors to describe such a history. Although the historians began to work on this project, the Second World War had ended before the entire text was ready to be published.[41]

What is important about this story is that the historians actually planned to write an 'Asian history' that integrated the history of West Asia. In parallel with the Japanese overseas expansion, the history of West Asia, which had been regarded as a part of *Seiyōshi*, found its place in the framework of Asian history for the first time in Japan. In other words, the framework of understanding the past shifted from *Tōyō* to Asia, based on a strategy by the Japanese government and military.

Conclusion

After the Japanese defeat in the Second World War, the framework of *Tōyōshi* in history teaching, especially in secondary schools, fundamentally changed. The tentative guideline, issued by the Ministry of Education in 1947, clearly acknowledges this fact. For example, in the preface, the meaning of learning *Tōyōshi* is explained as follows:

Tōyōshi's assignment is to demonstrate how *Tōyō*'s original culture was born and developed, how it has changed after interacting with other cultures, especially how the influence of modern *Seiyō*'s culture changed it and made students understand the current situation in the right way. In a sense, however, most of the contemporary culture comes from *Seiyō*'s one, and it seems that *Tōyō*'s old culture was interrupted on the way and is not connected with today, ... but that is not true. ... We cannot say that the weakened *Tōyō* was ruined and *Seiyō* replaced it. It is natural that *Tōyō*'s old-fashioned culture was overwhelmed by the modern *Seiyō*'s superior culture. *Tōyō* needs to keep learning and digesting *Seiyō*'s excellent culture. However, *Tōyō*'s five-thousand-year tradition never dies. After absorbing and assimilating *Seiyō*'s original modern culture, the renewed *Tōyō*'s inherent character will appear. This is the only way that *Tōyō* can contribute to the world culture.[42]

Interestingly, this excerpt is filled with an inferiority complex, with a touch of self-encouragement. It also represents the mood of Japanese society just after its defeat in the Second World War. Although Japanese history is separated and not included in *Tōyōshi* (as the guideline suggests), Japan was certainly a part of *Tōyō* at that time.

Upon examining the details of the guideline, the history of the Muslim world is, in fact, included in *Tōyōshi*. It not only covers the history of China and its neighbours, but also that of all other regions in Asia. This was the worldview just before and during the Second World War. Since then, *Tōyōshi* has become almost equivalent to *Ajiashi*, the history of Asia today.

Meanwhile, the meaning of *Tōyō* has become almost the same as that of the Orient in European languages and the understanding of the world in the Western manner. Since *Tōyō* (Orient) is inferior to *Seiyō* (Occident), there is no other path for *Tōyō* to follow than the one taken by *Seiyō*. There is neither the optimism of Kume in the 1870s, who stressed that there is no fundamental disparity between *Tōyō* and *Seiyō*, nor the self-confidence of Naka and Kuwabara in the 1890s, who believed that Japan had left *Tōyō* to become a world power. In this regard, we could say that Japanese intellectuals then admitted the correctness of the Western view of the world and accepted it for the first time.

Japan would need several more decades in order to recover its self-confidence and create its own perspective of the world and its history, based on a new level of self-consciousness.

Notes

1   I follow Mitani Hiroshi's opinion that the political turmoil in Japan during the 1860s should be understood as a 'revolution', rather than a 'restoration'. For more details, see Mitani Hiroshi, *Aikoku, Kakumei, Minshu* (Patriotism, Revolution, and Democracy) (Tokyo: Chikuma Shobo, 2013).

2   It is a question of relativity, compared, for example, with Middle Eastern or Central European countries. As Andrew Gordon pointed out in the beginning of his book on Japanese modern history, there were limited cases in which the general public felt that they shared a common 'Japanese culture' in the pre-modern era. Instead, many

people had a stronger sense of belonging to the town/village in which they lived and the feudal territory (*han/kuni*) where their town/village was situated. Being 'Japanese' was the sentiment that they might have had when only meeting people with different customs and physical features. The idea of 'one Japan as a sphere' and 'one Japanese as a nation' was, for the most part, created in modern times. For more details, see Andrew Gordon, *A Modern History of Japan. From Tokugawa Time to the Present* (New York: Oxford University Press, 2014 [First edition published in 2002]), 4.

3   See *Konjaku-monogatari*, a collection of more than one thousand tales (probably written in the twelfth century) consisting of three parts: tales of India, China and Japan, respectively.

4   See 'Twenty-eight Cities in the World', created in the early seventeenth century and conserved in the Imperial Household Agency; and Sannomaru Shozokan's 'Western Kings on Horseback', created in the early seventeenth century and possessed by the Suntory Museum of Art (Tokyo). Also see *Biombo. Japan Heritage as Legend of Gold* (Tokyo: Catalog for an exhibition held at the Suntory Museum of Art from September 1 to 21 October 2007).

5   Since the latter half of the sixteenth century, Portuguese, Dutch and other countries' merchants and sailors made frequent visits to Japan. However, most of the goods that they brought came from other Asian countries such as silk from China, cotton textiles from India, and various dyestuffs and sugar from Southeast Asia. It should be noted that, unlike the later period, the status of Dutchmen and other Europeans among overseas people was not high. For example, see the choice of the high-ranked harlots in Nagasaki: Koga Jujirou, *Maruyama Yujo-to Tō Kōmō-jin* (Prostitutes of Maruyama and the Chinese and the Red-Haired People) (Nagasaki: Nagasaki Bunken-sha, 1968).

6   On 23 December 1871, the Iwakura Mission, consisting of twenty-three members, thirty-nine attendants and twenty-six students, sailed from Yokohama to San Francisco, and returned to Yokohama on 13 September 1873, after visiting the United States, the United Kingdom, France, Belgium, the Netherlands, Germany, Russia, Denmark, Sweden, Italy, Austria and Switzerland.

7   See Kume Kunitake, *Tokumei Zenken Taishi Bei-Ō Kairan Jikki* (*A True Account of the Ambassador's Extraordinary and Plenipotentiary's Journey of Observation through the United States of America and Europe*), 5 vols. (Tokyo: Hakubunsha, 1878). For the English translation see *The Iwakura Embassy 1871–73: A True Account of the Ambassador Extraordinary and Plenipotentiary's Journey of Observation through the United States of America and Europe*, 5 vols., ed. Graham Healey and Chushichi Tsuzuki (Matsudo: Japan Documents, 2002). However, the translators did not focus on the terms *Tōyō* and *Seiyō*, but they simply translated *Tōyō* into the East, Orient and Asia, and *Seiyō* into the West. Thus, when citing the English translations, I will use the original terms *Tōyō* and *Seiyō* in place of their English translations.

8   It should be noted that North European countries, such as Denmark and Sweden, and Russia are included in this group.

9   Arai Hakuseki, an important political figure in the middle of the Tokugawa regime, also used this term in his book titled, *Seiyō Kibun* (*Accounts on Seiyō*), written around 1715.

10 See Georgios Varouxakis, 'The Godfather of "Occidentality": Auguste Comte and the idea of the "West"', *Modern Intellectual History* 16, no. 2 (2019): 413. In this chapter, Varouxakis stressed that Auguste Comte (1798–1857) had already employed the term, the meaning of which was not always the same as that used later. Comte also

placed France, England and the United States into a group and called it 'l'Occident'. In any case, it is clear that the concept itself did not take final shape until the end of the nineteenth century.

11 See Gilbert Allardyse, 'The Rise and Fall of the Western Civilization Course', *The American Historical Review* 87, no. 3 (1982): 703.

12 For example, the production of cotton textiles (Kume, vol. 1, 384, English translation, vol. 1, 383), a trial (Kume, vol. 3, 145–6, English translation, vol. 3, 134–5), and pieces in a museum (Kume, vol. 3, 264–5, English translation, vol. 3, 234).

13 See Kume, vol. 1, 250, English translation, 253–4.

14 For example, when Kume wrote about the history of coins in the world, he presented Chinese and Japanese coins in the same framework of *Tōyō* (Kume, vol. 1, 339–40, English translation, vol. 1, 343). He also stated that Shanghai was one of the largest port cities in *Tōyō* (Kume, vol. 5, 386, English translation, vol. 5, 351).

15 Kume not only severely criticized the slump in Qing's academia and artefacts, but he also deplored the Japanese intellectuals' belief that all Chinese products were excellent (Kume, vol. 5, 388, English translation, vol. 5, 351).

16 Kume, vol. 2, 53–4, English translation, vol. 2, 57.

17 Kume, vol. 2, 278–9, English translation, vol. 2, 274–6. Kume did not suppose that there was an insurmountable disparity between *Tōyō* and *Seiyō*, unlike the case between the Orient and Europe.

18 For example, see Kume, vol. 2, 277, English translation, vol. 2, 272.

19 Geographical Europe and the United States are not the same as *Seiyō*. Kume also distinguished Great Britain, France and Germany from Spain and Portugal, stating that the latter had yet to be sufficiently 'civilized' (Kume, vol. 5, 355, English translation, vol. 5, 323).

20 The term 'Occident' and the concept of Europe were interchangeable in French in the nineteenth century, while this term and the concept of the West were rarely used in English before the 1890s. For more details, see Varouxakis, 'The Godfather of "Occidentality,"' 412–13. This also indicates that the United States was basically excluded from the notion of the Occident in the nineteenth century.

21 See Edward Said, *Orientalism* (New York: Pantheon Books, 1978).

22 According to the centenary publication by the *Société Asiatique* in 1922, the field of Oriental Studies (*Orientalisme*) included thirteen disciplines, with seven concerning the ancient Middle East (1. *L'Egyptologie*, 2. *L'Assyryologie*, 3. *La philology hébraïque, l'exégèse biblique, l'archéologie sémitique*, 4. *Les études araméennes*, 5. *Islamisme*, 6. *Les études arméniennes* and 7. *Les études iraniennes anciennes*). Although Chinese Studies (*La sinologie*) and Japanese Studies (*Les études japonaises*) were also included in the list, it is evident that the main focus of this society was on the philological studies of the ancient Middle East. Subsequently, the centenary publication by the Royal Asiatic Society in 1923 indicated that half of the articles published over the previous century focused on India, thus emphasizing the importance of the country to the United Kingdom in those days.

23 It was through Engelbert Kaempfer, who resided in Nagasaki in 1690–2, Carl Peter Thunberg in 1775–6 and Philipp Franz Balthasar von Siebold in 1823–9 that the Europeans obtained information on Japan. Meanwhile, the Tokugawa government strictly prohibited the export of any materials or information related to Japanese land and politics.

24 *Nihonshoki*, the first work of this style, was edited and published in 720. Since then, many books in the same genre were published. For instance, *Dai Nihonshi* (*The Great*

100   *Narratives, Nations, and Other World Products*

History of Japan) was compiled in the seventeenth century under the initiative of a lord in the Mito branch of the Tokugawa family.

25   This edict also aimed to establish an institute of history writing in 1869.

26   The author of this book is Samuel G. Goodrich (1793–1860). The book was first published in 1837 and reprinted many times thereafter. Under the same author, there is a book with another title in which the contents are basically the same: *Peter Parley's Common School History*. Although there is no mention of the history of Japan in either of these textbooks published before Goodrich's death in 1860, the subsequent translation contains a short chapter on Japan, which mentions the first Japanese diplomatic mission to the United States in 1860. This indicates that the first translation was published after the death of the author by someone with such information. Regarding Goodrich and his series of textbooks, see Sato Takami, 'S. G. Goodrich and Parley's Universal History' (in Japanese), *Eigakushi Kenkyu (Journal of the History of English Studies)*, no. 2 (1970): 1–24.

27   It seems that the framework of the subject had yet to be fixed, since they published a different textbook called *Shiryaku* ('Abstract of History'), which consisted of three parts: the Empire (Japan), China and *Seiyō*. Many textbooks similar to *Parley's Universal History on the Basis of Geography* were published during that time, including *Bankokushi (History of Ten Thousand Countries of the World)* in Japanese.

28   There are many references on the transformation of Japan during the Meiji era. For example, Andrew Gordon's *A Modern History of Japan* represents the interpretations of researchers outside of Japan, while Makihara Norio's *Bunmeikoku-o Mezashite (Towards a Civilized Country)* (Nihon-no Rekishi (History of Japan)) (Tokyo; Shogakkan, vol. 13, 2008) represents the perspective of one of the leading Japanese historians.

29   See Yamamuro Shinichi, *Shisōkadai-toshiteno Ajia. Kijiku, Rensa, Touki (Asia as a Thought Task: Axis, Sequence, and Project)* (Tokyo: Iwanami Shoten, 2001), 434–5 and Nakami Tatsuo, 'Nihon-teki Tōyōgaku'-no keisei-to kōzu (Formation and Structure of Oriental Studies in Japanese Style)', in *Tōyōgaku: Teikoku' Nihon-no gakuchi* (Oriental Studies, Academic Knowledge of Japanese Empire), ed. Kishimoto Mio (Tokyo: Iwanami Shoten, 2006), 13–54.

30   Based on the fact that *Seiyō*, in addition to *Tōyō*, had its own history called *Seiyōshi*, it is worth noting. The history of European countries had been taught at the Imperial University since 1887 by Ludwig Riess, a disciple of Leopold von Ranke, a renowned German historian invited by the Japanese government. However, the title of his lectures was simply 'History'. Meanwhile, *Bankokushi* had been taught in high schools for more than twenty years, and its core was the history of European countries. By that point, the name *Seiyōshi* had not yet been used.

31   As for the education of the history of the world in the Meiji era, see Okazaki Katsuyo, *Nihon-niokeru sekaishi kyōiku-no rekishi (I-1): Fuhenshi-gata bankokushi-no jidai (History of World History as a Subject of School Education (I-1): On an Age when World History was Taught and Modeled after a Pattern of Universal History)*, Saitama Daigaku Kiyō (Kyōyō Gakubu) 51, no. 2 (2016), *Nihon-niokeru sekaishi kyōiku-no rekishi (I-2): Bunmeishi-gata bankokushi-no jidai 1 (History of World History as a Subject of School Education (I-2): On an Age when World History was Taught and Modeled after a Pattern of Enlightenment 1)*, Saitama Daigaku Kiyō (Kyōyō Gakubu) 52, no. 1 (2016), *Nihon-niokeru sekaishi kyōiku-no rekishi*

(I-3): *Bunmeishi-gata bankokushi-no jidai 2* (*History of World History as a Subject of School Education (I-3): On an Age when World History was Taught and Modeled after a Pattern of Enlightenment 2*), *Saitama Daigaku Kiyō (Kyōyō Gakubu)* 52, no. 2 (2017).

32 See *Kuwabara Jitsuzo Zenshū* (*Complete Works of Kuwabara Jitsuzo*), vol. 4 (Tokyo: Iwanami Shoten, 1968), 17–18. Regarding Kuwabara's *Tōyōshi*, see Yoshizawa Seiichiro, 'Tōyōshigaku-no keisei-to chūgoku: Kuwabara Jitsuzo-no baai (Formation of Tōyōshigaku and China: Kuwabara Jitsuzo's Case)' in *Tōyōgaku, Teikoku Nihon-no gakuchi*, ed. Kishimoto Mio, 55–98.

33 The phrase *Datsu-a Nyū-ō* (Leave Asia, Enter Europe) represents one way of thinking by some Japanese intellectuals in those days. However, the author of this phrase is not Fukuzawa Yukichi (as is often stated), but Suzuki Kentaro (Editorial, *Sanyō Shinpō*, 14 April 1887).

34 'Abdül Reşit Ibrahim (1857–1944), an influential Tatar pan-Islamist, visited Japan for the first time in 1909. At that time, he met some Japanese political leaders, such as Itō Hirobumi and Ōkuma Shigenobu, and asserted that the Japanese people should convert to Islam, since it fit well with Japanese customs and thinking. He also believed that it would make the Muslim world stronger when confronting Western powers. For details regarding his travels to Japan and other countries, see *Âlem-i İslâm ve Japonya'da İntişâr-i İslâmiyet* (*The Islamic World and Dissemination of Islam in Japan*), Istanbul 1910 (the book was translated into Japanese by Komatsu Hisao and Komatsu Kaori, and published under the title *Japonya* in 2013 by Iwanami Shoten). It appears that Ibrahim was the first Muslim to visit Japan under his own will. Subsequently, many Tatar Muslims, missionaries and refugees came to live in Japan, especially after the Russian Revolution.

35 Haneda Masashi, « La découverte du 'monde musulman' dans le Japon des années, 1930» in *Miscellanea Asiatica. Mélanges en l'honneur de Françoise Aubin*, eds. Denise Aigle, Isabelle Charleux, Vincent Goossaert and Roberte Hamayon (Sankt Augustin: Institut Monumenta Serica, 2010), 317–43.

36 Regarding Okubo Koji's address to Muslims in China in 1939, see Haneda Masashi, *Isuramu-sekai-no sōzō* (*Creating the Notion of the Islamic World*) (Tokyo: Tokyo-Daigaku Shuppankai (The University of Tokyo Press), 2005), 238–40.

37 *Kaikyōken Kenkyūsho* (the Research Institute on Kaikyōken) was established in 1938, after which it began publishing a monthly journal titled, *Kaikyōken*. *Kaikyō jijō* (*Islamic Affairs*). In 1939, *Kaikyō sekai* (The Islamic World) was distributed. In the same year, *Dai-nippon Kaikyō kyōkai* (Islamic Society of the Great Japan) was established. Konoe Ayamaro, the then prime minister, attended the opening ceremony of this society. The aim of this society was to promote friendship and mutual understanding between Japan, the Japanese people and the Islamic world.

38 One of these events was a series of expositions about *Kaikyōken*, held at department stores in Tokyo and Osaka in 1939.

39 Regarding the genealogy from Pan-Asianism to this concept made public in 1940, see Yamamuro Shinichi, *Shisōkadai-toshiteno Ajia*, Matsuura Masataka, ed., *Ajia-shugi-wa nani-wo katarunoka: Kioku, Kenryoku, Kachi* (*What Tells Pan-Asianism? Memory, Power, and Value*) (Kyoto: Mineruva Shobo, 2013).

40 Kishi Toshihiko, 'Higashi Ajia ("East Asia")', in *Chiikishi-to Sekaishi* (*Regional History and World History*), ed. Haneda Masashi (Kyoto: Mineruva Shobo, 2016), 44.

41 Miyazaki Ichisada, *Miyazaki Ichisada Zenshū* (*Complete Works of Miyazaki Ichisada*), *Vol. 18: Asian History* (Tokyo: Iwanami Shoten, 1993), 428–30. Based on his manuscript written before the end of the Second World War, Miyazaki published his interpretation of Asian history in the 1947 work *Ajiashi Gaisetsu* (*Outline of Asian History*) (Tokyo; Kōbundō).

42 https://www.nier.go.jp/guideline/s22ejs3/index.htm

6

Applying global history to the study of war: Transnational narratives of resilience under aerial bombardment

Sheldon Garon*

The Second World War was the most global conflict in history. Yet narratives of its home fronts remain the preserve of national history and national mythologies. Walk into a museum in London, and you'll learn about the nation's 'Finest Hour', when Britons stood up to relentless German bombing in the Blitz. Remembering 'The War of Resistance against Japan' (1937–45), Chinese museums celebrate civilian resilience in the face of Japan's four-year bombing campaign against the rearguard capital Chongqing. For the USSR, it is the story of the Soviet people's superhuman sacrifice and defiance in the Great Patriotic War. In the 900-day siege of Leningrad by German forces, 1 million inhabitants died of starvation or bombardment, yet the city held firm. Among the defeated Axis countries, memories are less heroic, but equally national. While no public museum in Germany today would commemorate the people's spirited defence against Allied air raids, local exhibitions recall the backbreaking efforts of townspeople to rebuild their pulverized cities *after* the war. Iconic are the 'rubble women' (*Trümmerfrauen*), who cleared broken bricks and stones from their neighbourhoods. And at Japanese exhibitions, we experience the extraordinary ability of women and children to endure dire food shortages and survive the aerial destruction of sixty-six cities. The National Showa Memorial Museum (Shōwakan) dedicates itself to communicating to 'future generations ... the everyday hardships of the [Japanese] people in wartime and postwar (c. 1935–1955)'.[1]

Historians typically study such narratives as the products of postwar memory in individual nations. This chapter argues instead that narratives of resilience under bombardment had been developing long before 1945 – from the time of the First World War and interwar years, as well as during the Second World War. Nor did these stories emerge primarily within national histories, but rather as part of a transnational

---

* Note: This work was supported by the European Commission (Marie-Sklodowska-Curie Actions – COFUND Programme) as part of the French Institute for Advanced Study Fellowship Programme; the Humboldt Foundation under the Humboldt Research Award; and the Harry Frank Guggenheim Foundation grant.

process in which states and societies monitored and adopted discourses of resilience in other countries. Nation-states came to believe that wars could be won – or at least, not lost – by persuading civilians to stand up to the enemy's attacks. Although postwar memories appear so 'national', the earlier narratives of resilience were often remarkably similar as they crossed borders, shaping each other as they went.

War and global history

This transnational understanding of narratives of the home front is part of my larger effort to apply the methods of global history to studying wars.[2] A case in point is aerial bombardment. By the end of the Second World War, cities across Europe and East Asia lay in ruins. The history of bombing is usually told episodically. German and Italian pilots indiscriminately bombed civilians in the Spanish Civil War; Japanese planes raided Chinese cities; Britain survived the Blitz thanks to Spitfires and valiant air-raid wardens; the Anglo-Americans firebombed Dresden; and atomic bombs obliterated Hiroshima and Nagasaki.

A transnational analysis demonstrates, however, that none of these episodes unfolded in isolation.[3] The practices involved in bombing cities originated neither in one country nor from one ideology. During the 1930s, international peace groups denounced aerial attacks by Germans, Italians and Japanese as 'fascist'.[4] Yet in the Second World War, the greatest destroyers of cities turned out to be two of the greatest democracies – Britain and America. Nor does imperialism or racism explain very much. Historians often assert that Europeans and Americans bombed colonial subjects – and then the Japanese people – with a savagery they would not have unleashed on Caucasians.[5] In fact, white people evinced few qualms about bombing other white people. In both world wars, air forces targeted densely populated urban areas in Europe. And there was nothing all that unique about the US firebombing of Japanese cities in 1945. The strategic decisions were in large part based on what the Allies had learned from their 'area bombing' of German cities.

Accordingly, I argue that the destruction of cities in the Second World War resulted from a long process of transnational learning dating back to the First World War and accelerating through the interwar decades and wartime. Much of this was related to the new concepts of total war, home fronts and civilian morale. Nation-states vigorously investigated each other's strategies to win wars not simply by defeating the enemy's armed forces but also by bombarding urban 'nerve centres' and crushing popular morale. Just as urgently, nations emulated each other's efforts to defend their own home fronts by mobilizing the entire populace in civil-defence efforts. The circulation of such knowledge was global and multi-directional. The Japanese, for example, were both takers and makers of these ideas and practices. By the late 1930s, Japan's naval air force emerged as the leading practitioner of the long-distance bombing of cities. As Japanese aircraft repeatedly struck Chinese urban areas, the world watched in horror but also with curiosity. The RAF and British civil-defence officials, for their part, were keen to draw 'air lessons' from East Asia that could be operationalized in the anticipated war in Europe.

Applying Global History to the Study of War   105

Although transnational or global history is currently one of the most dynamic fields in history, few have applied its methods to study war on a global scale. The best comparative and transnational work on war and society focuses on the European belligerents during the First World War.[6] By contrast, transnational histories of the Second World War barely exist. Some military historians have linked the naval and ground campaigns in the European and Asia Pacific theatres.[7] Rarely do they compare or connect home fronts. Richard Overy, who is exceptional in comparing the war on civilians globally, observes that the Asia Pacific War (1941–5) has been commonly understood as a mere 'appendix' to the defeat of the European Axis states.[8] None of the global histories of the Second World War utilize Japanese- or Chinese-language sources. Linguistic limitations aside, historians have generally been averse to situating Nazi Germany or Imperial Japan within a transnational framework despite ample evidence that these authoritarian states actively learned from others. For instance, Germany's largest mass organization, the Reich Air Defence League, was not so exceptionally National Socialist; it was modelled on existing nationwide civil-defence leagues in Poland, the Soviet Union and elsewhere. Nor did Japanese militarists force children to die defending the cities; instead, officials carried out the massive evacuation of younger children as they had observed in Britain during the Blitz.[9] I have no wish to draw moral equivalences between the Axis and the Western Allies. But when it comes to wartime mobilization and strategies, should historians continue to divide the world neatly into thuggish Nazis, fanatical Japanese, totalitarian Soviets and liberal democratic Anglo-Americans?

There is yet another reason why global historians have shied away from examining the world wars. As Jeremy Adelman recently observed, many scholars assume that global history is the study of 'globalization'. By this, they mean cosmopolitanism, migration, freer trade, international cooperation and 'integration'.[10] Not surprisingly, global historians tend to regard war as the ultimate disjuncture. Borders close. People, commodities and capital no longer move freely. Adelman calls on us to reckon with 'disintegration as well as integration'. I propose that we also think more expansively about the unexpected *interconnectedness* that arises among nations at war.

Indeed, while the two world wars severely constricted flows of integration, the belligerents devoted enormous resources to creating new connections. Never before had states expended so much money and manpower on gathering information from abroad. Warring nations frenetically investigated and emulated the military strategies of allies and enemies, while just as seriously surveying how others were defending their home fronts.[11] Although many shipping routes shut down, oceanic super-highways took their place as the United States, Canada, New Zealand and Australia supplied Great Britain and Allied forces with food and materiel.[12] Ordinary people crossed borders and seas in extraordinary numbers as soldiers, nurses, labourers and merchant seamen. Some 140,000 Chinese workers, for example, were sent halfway around the world to the Western Front in 1917–18.[13]

Globalizing the study of war challenges another critique of the transnational method. Global history, asserts Adelman, privileges those who move between nations over those who got 'left behind'. However, one need not venture from home to be affected by global forces. Consider the spread of self-consciously 'middle-class' values of thrift and domesticity around the world, even to remote Japanese villages by the 1930s.[14] But nothing transformed everyday life globally as much as the Second World War. By 1942, one would have observed strikingly similar features of wartime life in Nazi Germany, Imperial Japan, the Soviet Union and democratic Britain. These included ration coupons, blackouts, evacuations and neighbourhood-based civil defence units. Women everywhere were being mobilized to fight incendiary bombs and to direct communal efforts at food distribution and war saving. Such commonalities were no coincidence. The practices and the very concept of the 'home front' had been transnationally constructed between the First and Second World Wars.[15]

How then shall we truly globalize the history of the Second World War? The inclusion of Japan and China is a vital first step. Yet we must go beyond mere inclusion to reveal the critical connections between the European and Asia-Pacific theatres of war. This is a formidable task, but not impossible. It calls for leveraging one's language skills, plus a willingness to venture outside the comfort of one's national history. I myself am a historian of Japan who has also done extensive archival research in Germany, Britain, France and the United States. Multi-archival work is essential, considering that secondary sources rarely discuss the vibrant linkages among nations. If we are mindful of what good global history requires, the transnational method permits us to challenge the core assumptions behind the national mythologies.

Totale Panik

How one's population would react to air raids emerged as a key storyline in commentaries and fiction around the world by the early twentieth century. Within a few years of the Wright brothers' famous flight in 1903, nations from France to Japan were building fleets of airplanes. In the First World War, these squadrons were deployed not only at the front, but also to attack the enemy's cities and factories. We are accustomed today to thinking of human beings as resilient. Certainly, that is the message of many foundations and NGOs that seek to build on this resilience to help people recover from natural disasters and conflicts.[16]

One hundred years ago, few visionaries would have agreed. Far from expecting cities to stand up to aerial attacks, writers and strategists predicted panic and social collapse. In 1907, H. G. Wells set the tone in his darkly prophetic novel, *The War in the Air*. German Zeppelins attack New York City, sparking a worldwide air war and the 'collapse of the civilisation that had trusted to machinery'. 'Everywhere went the airships dropping bombs, ... and everywhere below were economic catastrophe, starving workless people, rioting, and social disorder.' Wells could think of nothing comparable in the history of warfare, except cases of a 'nineteenth century warship attacking some large savage or barbaric settlement' or the more modern urban experience of the 'Communist insurrection of Paris' during the Franco-Prussian War.[17]

Wells was hardly alone among science fiction writers. During the 1920s and 1930s, people around the world read story after story about urban dwellers reverting to savagery following air raids.[18] In a widely translated novel in 1931, the German author Hanns Gobsch graphically depicted 3 million Parisians fleeing an impending poison-gas attack from the air:

The authority of the State failed at every point .... The forces of law and order were utterly powerless against the desperate rush of this human herd, fighting for its life .... By to-morrow France will be a ruin and a wilderness. Starving and murdering, the human beasts will fly at one another.[19]

In far-off Japan, too, the popular science fiction writer Jūza Unno – himself a big fan of H. G. Wells – published a novel in 1932 about a US firebombing and gas raid on Tokyo. No one fights the fires; the people panic; hundreds are trampled to death and many more die from poison gas.[20]

Sober military men were no more sanguine about human beings' capacity to stand up to aerial bombardment. On the eve of the First World War, a British defence expert predicted that an air attack on London would be 'more effective against the national life than in any other capital of the world'. It quite possibly would cause 'such panic and riot' as to 'force the Home Government to accept an unfavourable peace'.[21] A decade later, Italy's Guilio Douhet, the era's most influential theorist of strategic bombing, envisioned poison-gas and incendiary attacks that would 'envelop a great city like London or Paris' and 'destroy completely great centers of population'.[22]

The First World War put this pessimistic narrative to the test. Although air forces had not yet reached the scale to devastate urban infrastructure, German Zeppelins and airplanes repeatedly bombed London and Paris. Air raids killed some 1,239 Britons and 267 Parisians.[23] Londoners did not descend into barbarism, yet representations of their experiences became hotly contested. Guided by government directives, the media commonly celebrated the heroism, stoicism and calmness of the civilian population, particularly women. Psychologists joined in. The nation, asserted an article in *Lancet*, was endowed with 'the traditional British phlegm' and 'our public, as a whole is calm, and its conduct exemplary'.[24] As would happen in many countries over the next three decades, Britons contrasted their own resilience with the enemy's timorousness. The Germans, recalled a prominent air-defence official, expected their Zeppelins to create panic among Londoners just as air raids would have done in Berlin. But the enemy failed to appreciate the 'unyielding nature of that stubborn courage which gathers strength from adversity and has ever been the proudest attribute of our national character'.[25]

While British authorities publicly lauded the cheerfulness of their people under fire, officials and experts questioned whether civilian populations would be capable of enduring aerial attacks in the future. Reports of London in 1917–18 described 'mad rushes for shelter', as 'many civilians lived in constant fear of bombardment'. On nights when air raids were expected, 100,000–300,000 would crowd into Underground stations. Stampedes, resulting in a large number of deaths and injuries, broke out in London and Paris stations.[26] Writing to the War Cabinet in 1917, E. R. Henry, chief commissioner of the Metropolitan Police, concluded that 'most classes of the community, especially the poorer classes, feel in fact somewhat terrorised by these repeated air-raids'. Henry contrasted the stoic behaviour of the English with the panicked responses of the large Eastern European immigrant communities in the East End. Referring no doubt to the Jews, he reported that these 'aliens' impulsively fled to the shelters because many 'belong to nationalities that have always been oppressed, and ... they become more easily intimidated than our own people'.[27]

The question of British resilience in the First World War soon became central to an inter-service debate over whether aerial bombardment crushed civilian morale or strengthened it. The interwar RAF was emphatic that urban populations could not stand up to the destructiveness of the world's expanding air forces. Recalling the raids of 1915–18, an influential staff officer judged it 'ridiculous' to suggest that 'the nightly exodus of the population from Hull in the face of threatened air raids or alarms was evidence of a "stiffened morale" or that the disordered rush into London tubes was a sign of a growing will to win and a strengthened determination to resist'.[28] During the 1920s, Hugh Trenchard, air marshal and chief of the Air Staff, took a dim view of the ability of civilians to defend their cities. The 'best means of defence', he insisted, 'lay in the prosecution of a vigorous offensive'.[29] The objective of air forces, argued Trenchard, was to 'destroy the morale' of the enemy. In this 'contest of morale between the respective civilian populations', the people of the nation that 'suffered most from air attacks, or which lacked in moral tenacity' would pressure their government to capitulate.[30] To be sure, some British officials were more concerned than Trenchard about protecting the civilian population. In 1924, the government's subcommittee on air raid precautions began secretly meeting to prepare for attacks on London in the next war. Members discussed plans for the orderly evacuation of non-essential residents and other 'useless mouths', but they too appeared uninterested in mobilizing civilians for the active defence of their neighbourhoods. No one captured the lack of faith in popular resilience as famously as Prime Minister Stanley Baldwin in 1932. 'The bomber will always get through', he declared. There was nothing that could be done to protect the man in the street: 'The only defence is offence, which means that you have to kill more women and children more quickly than the enemy if you want to save yourselves.'[31]

Baldwin's chilling words reflected a growing conviction among air forces and military writers that future wars might be won by destroying whole cities. Visions of frightened, undisciplined civilians circulated around the globe. Witness the role of Japan in the making of these transnational narratives. Allied with the Entente in the First World War, the Japanese government had dispatched a large number of rising officers and elite bureaucrats to survey home-front policies in Europe. Some observed mass panics resulting from German air raids on London and Paris. In an influential report of 1919, the army's Provisional Military Investigative Commission warned of even worse consequences for Japan if enemy aircraft were to firebomb its cities made of wood. Such raids would likely 'eviscerate civilian morale'.[32]

And then it happened. In the aftermath of the Great Kantō Earthquake of 1923, fires killed nearly one hundred thousand people in Tokyo and Yokohama. Social order collapsed as roving bands of Japanese vigilantes massacred several thousand Korean migrants and hundreds of Chinese. For those charged with national defence, this was ominous. General Kazushige Ugaki, vice-minister of the army, wrote in his diary: 'Chills run down my spine when I think that the next time Tokyo suffers a catastrophic fire and tragedy on this scale, it could come at the hands of an enemy air attack'.[33]

Few scholars have grasped the importance of the Kantō Earthquake in the global history of bombing. To Basil Liddell Hart, perhaps the era's most influential military writer, the destruction of one of the world's largest metropolitan areas illustrated how an aerial attack might similarly demoralize the life of an entire nation. Imagine, he asked, 'London, Manchester, Birmingham, and half a dozen other great centres simultaneously attacked, the business localities and Fleet Street wrecked, Whitehall a heap of ruins, the slum districts maddened into the impulse to break loose and maraud, the railways cut, factories destroyed. Would not the general will to resist vanish ... ?'[34] While the example of the Tokyo-Yokohama earthquake encouraged the proponents of strategic bombing, the spectre of social chaos simultaneously spurred states into making greater efforts at air defence. To demonstrate the perils of being unprepared in 'Total War', Nazi Germany's civil-defence magazine later profiled the Kantō Earthquake, along with the San Francisco Earthquake of 1906. Left to their own devices, humans would invariably succumb to 'Totale Panik'.[35]

Manufacturing, mobilizing and marketing resilience

As countries contemplated a second world war, many nations began questioning the pessimistic narratives of social collapse. By the early 1930s, a new spirit animated efforts to prepare populations to stand up to aerial assaults. These measures were commonly called 'passive' air defence to distinguish them from 'active' defence, such as anti-aircraft batteries and fighter planes. Yet there was little that was passive in the new vision. 'Civilian defence' meant not simply the protection of civilians by means of shelters and evacuations, but also the active participation of civilians in their own defence. From Europe to East Asia, millions would serve as air-raid wardens, first-aid workers, auxiliary firefighters and fire watchers in neighbourhoods and workplaces. No longer would the bombed accept aerial attacks with resignation. In nation after nation, the women, youth and older men who took part in civil defence became known as 'soldiers on the home front'. They were to defend their country no less fiercely than their countrymen at the front.[36]

Japan and Germany were among the pioneers in civil defence. Shocked by the mass panic in the Kantō Earthquake, Japanese authorities resolved to drill urban residents in how to bear up to air raids and natural disasters alike. In 1928, Osaka held the world's first mass air-raid exercise, involving 2 million people as members of state-organized youth, women's and veterans' associations. Residents took part in a city-wide blackout, first-aid activities and anti-gas manoeuvres. On the eleventh anniversary of the Kantō Earthquake on 1 September 1934, the state carried out air-defence drills in Tokyo, Yokohama and Kawasaki. Some 5 million residents were mobilized. These exercises were widely reported in Europe. Germany's civil-defence magazine called them the costliest air-raid drills to date.[37] Beginning in 1937, the Japanese state constructed a nationwide system of civil defence reaching down to the neighbourhoods. Officials feared bomber attacks from the Soviet Union, as well as raids from China with whom Japan was fighting an all-out war that broke out in July.

German leaders likewise translated feelings of national vulnerability into the organization of civil defence. In 1927, conservative nationalists prevailed upon the Weimar government to establish a robust programme of 'passive air defence' as Germany's only option against massive air raids by its many neighbours. An active defence was deemed impossible because the Treaty of Versailles prevented Germany from maintaining fighter planes and bombers while severely limiting anti-aircraft guns. In 1933, the new Nazi regime rapidly expanded the Weimar-era system of civil defence into the Reich Air Defence League (Reichsluftschutzbund, or RLB). Extending down to individual apartment houses, the RLB counted 13 million members by 1939. In the context of the 1930s, the RLB was not exceptional. Nationwide air-defence leagues were simultaneously emerging in the Soviet Union, Poland, Finland, Denmark, Sweden, Italy, Czechoslovakia and elsewhere.[38]

During the 1930s, nations created a new language of civilian discipline and resilience that went well beyond propaganda appeals, for it was rooted in the reorganization of daily life. In Germany, both Weimar and Nazi authorities defined the core principle of civil defence as 'self-protection' (*Selbstschutz*). Japanese officials translated the concept as 'household air defence' (*katei bōkū*). In those two nations and many others, the responsibility for defending the nation fell to ordinary men and women where they lived. As experts increasingly recognized, the greatest threat from the air might not be poison gas or high-explosive bombs, but rather small incendiary bombs weighing one or two kilograms. Falling by the thousands through rooftops, these 'stick bombs' were expected to overwhelm professional firefighters. The firebombs would have to be fought, one by one, by thousands of residents at home before the fires spread to whole districts. As early as 1932, Weimar Germany's Ministry of Interior proposed organizing each apartment block into a 'house fire brigade', including some 'brave' women and supervised by a house air-raid warden. The imperative for neighbourly cooperation was recognized in the incorporation of house units into a street-level *Luftschutzgemeinschaft* (air-defence community).[39] In Japan, the base unit was the single-family house. By 1940, every ten to fifteen households were compelled to form a 'neighbourhood association' (*tonarigumi*). The principle of 'self-protection' governed most civil-defence schemes – whether German, Japanese or British. States required residents to stock sand, ash, buckets, water pumps and gas masks, but rarely paid for them.[40]

More than anything else, national leaders feared that people would panic before or during air raids. Residents would abandon their homes and leave no one behind to stop small fires from becoming conflagrations. Accordingly, states imposed military-like discipline on civilians. The Nazis demanded that Germans view civil defence as a 'duty to the National Socialist state', making participation compulsory in the Air Defence Law of 1935.[41] Modelled on the Nazi legislation, Japan's own Air Defence Law (1937) likewise stipulated fines and imprisonment for those who shirked their duties. The revised Japanese law of 1941 required residents to engage in 'stop-gap firefighting' during the air raids, and prefectural governors could prohibit anyone from leaving a bombed neighbourhood. Even the British turned to conscription in 1941–2 to compel men and women to serve as Fire Guards in neighbourhoods and workplaces when voluntary methods were insufficient.[42] To ensure that civilians fulfil their duty, officials around the world insisted on 'training, training, and more training', as German authorities put it.[43] The RLB established schools for local civil-defence leaders and ran ongoing exercises for all residents in blackouts, anti-gas defence and firefighting. Japan did not experience significant air raids until the end of 1944, but everyday life in wartime was filled with incessant air-raid drills. The key word globally was 'preparation'. From Weimar Germany to Japan, civil-defence pamphlets presented strikingly similar illustrations that contrasted the orderly image of the 'prepared city' – protected by calm men and women – with that of 'unprepared city' of panicked residents and corpses.[44]

It was no coincidence that so many nations exhorted their people to stand up to aerial attacks in similar ways. Civil defence developed during the interwar years in a remarkably transnational fashion, as states investigated and emulated each other's practices.[45] Working through their embassies and military attachés, German officials systematically gathered information on air-defence programmes in Britain, France, Italy, the Soviet Union, Poland and Japan. Following the Nazi takeover, the new Air Ministry and Ministry of Interior cooperated with the Foreign Office to compile periodic reports on the latest civil-defence developments in some twenty countries. These included Japan and China, the latter of which was under heavy air attack by the former. From the mid-1930s, Nazi Germany itself came to be seen as the most advanced nation in air defence. Numerous foreign delegations from Europe and overseas visited Berlin to survey its shelters, the Reich Air Defence School and the nationwide RLB network. In 1934, for example, the Republic of China requested the Air Ministry's advice on establishing a school and overall civil defence on 'the German model'. In addition to seeking information on early warning systems and first-aid, the Chinese specifically desired German materials on training the populace by means of films, pamphlets and teaching pictures.[46] Japanese delegations of officers, civil bureaucrats and urban planners made several visits to Germany between 1934 and 1941.

Transnational learning promoted narratives of resilience in two ways. As they investigated other nations' practices, state officials and experts shaped the civil-defence institutions and propaganda that would discipline their own populations. At the same time, officials directly conveyed images of other peoples' preparations to their countrymen, aiming to motivate them in contests of resilience. In general, images travelled more easily across borders than text, as witnessed in the circulation of similar recruiting and savings-campaign posters in the world wars.[47] We see this in the richly illustrated civil-defence magazines of Nazi Germany and Japan, *Die Sirene* (The Siren) and *Kokumin bōkū* (Civil defence). Both were targeted at local civil-defence leaders. While depicting advances in several countries, *Sirene* singled out Japan as a key model in the nationwide organization of the populace.[48] Following the outbreak of the second Sino-Japanese War in 1937, the German magazine presented a series of vignettes of Japanese civilians donning gas masks and drilling to decontaminate streets. The headlines screamed 'Japan is Ready!', just as they would soon proclaim 'every German house ready for air defence'.[49] In both *Sirene* and *Kokumin bōkū*, colourful covers also highlighted the vital role of girls and women in civil defence.[50] Whether in Germany or Japan, images abounded of women and men engaged in competitive drills to pass as many buckets as possible to extinguish fires.[51] The two magazines similarly depicted women courageously fighting incendiary bombs with sand or water pumps.[52]

Once the Second World War broke out, the belligerents passionately communicated their people's superior resilience while ridiculing that of the enemy. In 1940, the RLB president informed *Sirene* readers that British 'morale is more than dismal'.

Air-raid alarms sent millions to the shelters where the English allegedly sat with 'dumb resignation'. British bombing supposedly had the opposite effect on Germans. 'What doesn't kill us, makes us strong', he boasted invoking Nietzsche.[53] American propagandists denigrated Japanese civil defence in the crudest of terms. The Looney Tunes film *Tokio Jokio* depicted a buck-toothed Japanese 'losing face' after waiting the mandated five seconds and then roasting a hot dog over an incendiary bomb.[54] Japanese authorities were perhaps exceptional in these contests. Even at the height of the Pacific War against the Western Allies, *Kokumin bōkū* not only offered heroic images of their German and Italian allies, but also featured positive stories and photos of London firefighters, British female civil-defence workers and Soviet girls engaged in first-aid activities.[55]

It is difficult to measure the impact of transnational images on ordinary people, but one could argue that they helped normalize narratives of popular resilience around the world. Global historians generally assume that those 'left behind' do not directly experience transnational knowledge, unlike cosmopolitan elites and state actors. I beg to differ. The bombing war threatened nearly every urban centre in the European, Asia-Pacific and Eurasian theatres of the Second World War. Propaganda and media made one's nationals aware that others were also being bombed and that resilience had become a competitive matter. Far from being 'left behind' in experiencing global connections, many civilians surely wished they'd been left alone.

By the late 1930s, the prevailing transnational consensus had changed radically from earlier decades, when many had predicted the breakdown of civilization in the wake of air raids. In the smaller wars preceding the Second World War, the parties under attack pointedly *marketed* their resilience to gain international support. In March 1938, the people of Republican-held Barcelona won high marks for withstanding repeated bombing runs by Italian and German aircraft in the Spanish Civil War. British officials were keenly interested in the 'lessons from Barcelona' for their own civil defence. Consulting closely with Barcelona municipal authorities, one civil-defence officer from London reported back that the 'morale of the whole of the population of a city cannot be broken' if 'passive defence measures have been properly organised', as they were in Barcelona. Accordingly, there had been 'no stampede' by a 'nerve-racked population. No wild and unreasoned panic. No terrible and uncontrolled hysteria and certainly no thought of beseeching the Government to seek an immediate and unconditional peace'.[56] His superiors similarly echoed local informants. Bombing civilians in Spain, insisted the British Air Raids Precautions Department, had not broken their morale. On the contrary, it had 'stimulate[d] the hatred and endurance of the people'.[57]

In the Second Sino-Japanese War, the Chinese Nationalist government lost most battles against the invading Japanese, but like Republican Spain, it won the contest of international public opinion. Propagandists encouraged stories in the Western press about the Chinese people's resilience against the relentless Japanese bombardment of Chongqing. Addressing the nation in May 1939, the Nationalist leader Chiang Kaishek noted that Japanese had failed to terrorize the residents of bombed Chinese cities. Far from it. The people of Chongqing 'have gone about their work as usual and have shown the same calm and steady courage'. By 1941, Chinese propaganda was comparing Chongqing's defiant spirit to that of Londoners under the Blitz.[58]

Applying Global History to the Study of War   113

Meanwhile, back in London, Winston Churchill was exhorting his own people. Everyone knows his 'Finest Hour' broadcast on 18 June 1940. But who remembers his words about the anticipated German bomber onslaught? He earnestly hoped 'our countrymen will show themselves capable of standing up to it, *like the brave men of Barcelona*, and will … carry on in spite of it, at least as well as any other people in the world'.[59] There was indeed a global circularity in the narratives of resilience.

Resilience challenged

Looking back on recent developments in Spain, Finland and Poland, British intelligence officials in October 1940 affirmed that the outcome of the Second World War would depend 'largely on the staying power of the civilian population'.[60] However, as bombing grew in intensity, states discovered it was far more challenging to maintain narratives of endurance than to manufacture them. Germans and Britons became locked in a contest of resilience, as their air forces simultaneously bombed each other's urban areas. Both sides continually improved their civil-defence structures, often based on surveillance of the enemy's advances.[61] To prevent morale from 'cracking', the Germans and British developed similar relief programmes for air-raid victims. They established feeding and rest centres, organized temporary housing and repaired damaged homes. The two peoples were, moreover, listening to each other's narratives. As Dietmar Süss notes, the Nazis boasted about their inclusive *Volksgemeinschaft* (national community), while the British responded with the catchphrase 'People's War' which likewise aimed to rally the entire populace.[62]

It is noteworthy that the British propaganda began telling the story of popular resilience *before* the cities suffered heavy German raids in the Blitz (September 1940–May 1941). The 'Myth of the Blitz', argues Angus Calder, was not simply a postwar memory, but was actively constructed by the British government and media at the time. From the perspective of global history, however, there was nothing new about this myth even in 1940. It rested on long-standing transnational narratives of avoiding panic, remaining 'cheerful' and mobilizing every man, woman and adolescent as 'soldiers on the home front'. The Myth of the Blitz also built upon the previous marketing of resilience by the Spanish Republicans and Chinese Nationalists. The British government was desperate to secure US support against Hitler. Officials worked closely with American journalists to script heroic stories of ordinary Britons standing up to German bombing. On the night of 24 August 1940, Edward R. Murrow made one of his famous live broadcasts to America during a light air raid. Despite sirens and a searchlight bursting into action, he intoned, the people around Trafalgar Square were 'walking along quite quietly' as they entered the shelter. He even crouched down to record the sound of Londoners' calm, unhurried footsteps.[63]

Their 'unconquerable spirit' was soon immortalized in 'London Can Take It'. Produced by the Ministry of Information and narrated by American correspondent Quentin Reynolds, the film was seen by millions in the United States and Britain. Each night, Londoners of all walks of life were shown putting on their civil-defence uniforms to form 'the greatest civilian army ever assembled'. Buildings were destroyed;

114   *Narratives, Nations, and Other World Products*

people were killed. Yet each morning, like a 'great fighter in the ring', the townspeople got up 'from the floor after being knocked down'. They opened their stores; they went to work. The Nazi propagandist Joseph Goebbels had gotten the Britons wrong, the narrator tells us. The bombing had raised their morale 'higher than ever before'. The transnational mantra was unmistakable. Reynolds witnessed 'no panic, no fear, no despair in London Town'.[64]

The narrative of resilience became so entrenched by the start of the Blitz that it shaped the daily reports on British morale by the Ministry of Information – split as it was by the twin tasks of information-gathering and propaganda. Investigators seemed determined to find silver linings in the looming dark clouds. Indeed, the morale surveys often read like weather reports. Londoners had come through a weekend of extensive raids with 'courage and calmness' in late August, but on 19 September, 'people are not so cheerful today'. By August 1941, the monitors observed war weariness and growing apathy, yet they happily noted there had been more 'cheerfulness' last week.[65] Strange as it may seem, 'cheerfulness' had become the standard of measure. Why anyone would be cheerful after seeing neighbours killed or homes flattened was a question few surveyors asked themselves.

The British narrative of courage and calmness frayed amid worsening bombing in late 1940 and the first half of 1941. Ridiculed by other agencies of government for their pollyannish assessments, the Ministry of Information's reporters increasingly recognized that heavy raids were demoralizing civilians. The German attack on Coventry in November produced a greater 'shock effect' than any other raid, agreed officials. More than five hundred people were killed, and the city centre was badly damaged. In the immediate aftermath, 'great depression' and 'hysteria' reportedly set in. The central authorities were particularly concerned about the practice of trekking – that is, the 'nightly exodus' in the repeatedly bombed coastal cities of Plymouth, Portsmouth, Southampton and Hull. Fearing subsequent raids, thousands of Britons walked or took transport into the countryside each night. They often slept in unsanitary conditions and then trekked back into town for the coming workday. After one deadly raid on Portsmouth in spring 1941, some 90,000 trekked. An estimated 30,000 continued to trek nightly, even during a period free of air raids. Roughly half were men. Officials complained that the nightly trek was 'causing confusion' and straining local services – especially transportation, feeding and accommodation. Worse, the trekkers were reportedly shirking their responsibilities to safeguard their homes and neighbourhoods from incendiary bombs.[66]

The nightly exodus continued the longest in Hull, lasting from 1941 through 1943. National leaders did not hide their displeasure. The Ministry of Home Security instructed local newspapers to avoid reporting on trekking and instead to praise people who 'stick it' in bombed towns. Speaking in Hull in summer 1941, Minister of Health Ernest Brown was blunter still. If the government encouraged trekking, 'we should lose the war'.[67] The townspeople of Hull countered by questioning the efficacy of the resilience narrative itself. They blamed Churchill for having dared the Nazis to 'do your worst' just four days before one raid on the port.[68]

In the end, as the Air Ministry concluded, British morale was never 'broken' in any town, despite the shock of Coventry. Although there had been instances of 'havoc', civil-defence mechanisms had been effective enough to prevent social collapse.[69] Nonetheless, we must recognize that the British were truly fortunate. They escaped the scale of bombardment visited upon their enemies. Unlike the RAF and US Army Air Force, the Luftwaffe had not invested in long-range heavy bombers that could deliver concentrated attacks on urban areas. Moreover, the worst phase of German bombing lasted no more than a year in 1940–1. This was thanks to Hitler's capricious decision to move most of the bombers to fight his new war against the Soviet Union in summer 1941. The Luftwaffe made sporadic attacks on British towns over the next three years, and the Germans killed several thousand Londoners with V-1 flying bombs and V-2 rockets in the last year of the war. Neither campaign posed an existential threat.[70] Had German bombing truly intensified throughout the war, we would not be looking back on England's 'Finest Hour'. The myth of British endurance survived and thrived precisely because the Blitz itself did not endure.

German narratives of resilience, by contrast, confronted steadily worsening levels of bombardment. The story of standing up to air raids had been persuasive enough during the first two and half years of the bombing war. Well-trained men and women in the residential 'self-protection' units coped with small fires and bomb damage, deferring to the police and Luftwaffe's mobile firefighting service in heavier attacks. Led by Minister of Propaganda Goebbels, the Nazi Party offered civil-defence teams a social contract of sorts: protect your neighbourhoods and the regime will protect your families. In autumn 1940, Hitler personally committed the Reich to constructing massive air-raid shelters for the people. Following British raids, Nazi Party organizations – notably women in the Welfare Organization (NSV) – intervened to offer the homeless hot meals, real coffee (a prized commodity) and temporary housing or evacuation.[71]

The Nazis' social contract came unstuck during the last two years of the war. Tales of resilience had prevailed in 1940–2. British bombers were notoriously inaccurate, and they faced formidable German air defences. But Bomber Command's offensives became deadlier from spring 1943 with large-scale attacks on the Ruhr industrial area. Firebombing raids on Hamburg in late July and early August 1943 killed some 37,000 people and drove nearly 1 million to flee the city. The Allied offensive against Germany vastly increased in scale when the US Army Air Force joined with Bomber Command. By spring 1944, the Luftwaffe had lost many of its best-trained pilots. Allied aircraft were able to bomb cities all over Germany at will. From September 1944 to May 1945, Allied air forces dropped three-quarters of the entire war's tonnage of bombs targeted at Germany.[72]

Nazi leaders kept talking about civilian 'self-reliance' in the war's last phase, but the message resonated poorly. Goebbels grew alarmed by the devastating attacks of 1943. The populace of Wuppertal had 'lost its nerve', he wrote in his diary of the first town to be consumed by a firestorm. In the wake of Operation Gomorrah against Hamburg, Goebbels observed a 'panic' that threatened to paralyse the popular will to resist. The SD intelligence service reported sensational rumours about the devastation in Hamburg, warning of rebellion in the bombed districts akin to the November 1918 protests at the end of the First World War.[73] Allied air forces expanded their range to attack towns in southern and eastern Germany that had rarely experienced bombing. Their less prepared inhabitants proved less resilient. Attacked in February 1945, Augsburg lacked any air-raid bunkers. Public air-raid shelters accommodated only 5,500 people out of population of 185,000.[74] Germans were no longer receiving the protections they had been promised. The Luftwaffe could not defend them; the Party lacked the resources to help victims; Hitler had stopped building large public shelters, and increasingly cities and homes could not be rebuilt. The overwhelming scale of destruction also revealed the dirty little secret behind German resilience. The tremendous capacity to clear rubble and corpses and rebuild cities had not been based on brave German men and women, but rather on the deployment of millions of European forced labourers, Soviet POWs, and concentration camp inmates. In the final months, even those labourers became insufficient to the task.[75] Although the German people began the war with an international reputation of determination and endurance, survivors exited with few heroic myths of having stood up to Allied bombing.

For wartime Japanese, myths of civilian resilience under fire remained largely aspirational. The Japanese experience was, in a sense, the mirror image of Britain's. Japan suffered no heavy bombardment until the last five months of the war. America's sixteen-bomber Doolittle Raid in April 1942 had done little damage. The Japanese state proudly showcased the constant drilling of residents in civil defence from the late 1930s. The nation's long history of regimented village and neighbourhood associations, boasted officials, made Japan uniquely prepared against air raids, surpassing even the Germans.[76] Nonetheless, Japan, like Nazi Germany, faced a crisis of confidence by late 1943. The spark was in fact the same. In yet another instance of transnational connection, Japan's military and civil-defence authorities were jolted by their diplomats' first-hand reports of the Allied bombing of Hamburg in July 1943 and the large-scale raids on Berlin that autumn.[77] Anticipating similarly heavy bombing of Japanese cities, officials for the first time confronted the woeful inadequacy of neighbourhood civil defence.

From early 1944, the Japanese government changed its air-defence policies in highly visible ways that diminished the people's confidence in their ability to withstand aerial assaults. Whereas the state had previously called upon families – including mothers and children – to stay in the cities to fight firebombs, it began evacuating some 800,000 schoolchildren from the big cities to the countryside. The authorities also ordered the demolition of hundreds of thousands of wooden homes to create firebreaks against incendiary bombing. Some 1,844,000 people became homeless and were forced to evacuate, even before the bombs fell. Germans might cling to the myth of popular resilience because forced labourers performed the back-breaking and dangerous tasks of civil defence. By contrast, Japan's smaller body of foreign labourers (mainly Korean) could not be spared for air-defence work. With younger males fully mobilized for war, the state commanded older Japanese men, women and 'mobilized students' (aged fourteen and older) to demolish structures and clear the rubble.[78]

Whatever resilience remained in Japan's exhausted, malnourished populace was crushed by the devastating US raids on the largest cities in March 1945. On the night of 9–10 March, 279 B-29s bombed Tokyo's most densely populated working-class area. An estimated 100,000 people died in the ensuing firestorm. In this and other raids, neighbourhood associations – armed with buckets and hand pumps – sometimes extinguished flames at the edges of the fire zones, but they were powerless to stop the

Applying Global History to the Study of War   117

conflagrations at the core. After repeatedly attacking six of the largest cities, the B-29s firebombed fifty-eight small and medium-sized cities during summer 1945. Japanese civilians responded to these infernos not by fanatically defending their cities, but by fleeing. An astounding 8.5 million people left the big cities for the countryside, most of them in the weeks after the March raids.[79]

Excepting some die-hard army officers, the regime too acknowledged the end of popular endurance. In its report of July, the Home Ministry's 'thought police', the Special Higher Police, offered the government an extraordinary bleak assessment of civilian morale under bombardment. In the immediate aftermath of air raids on the big cities, the people had reportedly reacted with defiance and a 'willingness to carry on'. But as the days passed, popular sentiment shifted to 'feelings of terror' that spread to the entire nation. The millions who fled the cities did so in an 'unplanned, self-willed manner'. Even in smaller cities not yet bombed, townspeople were seized by 'extreme panic', leaving their homes every night to sleep in the villages – much like the trekkers of Hull. The police warned not only of widespread defeatism, but of looming class warfare from the legions of dispossessed.[80] Japanese greeted the end of the war much as the Germans. They were determined to survive but held few memories of having 'taken it'.

Nationalizing while universalizing the narrative

After 1945, what had once been a transnational narrative of resilience fractured into a number of national stories. Britain's Myth of Blitz was perhaps the most persistent. Crafted in 1940, it survived the bombings and resonated with postwar efforts to break down the barriers of a class society. Postwar commemoration of the Chinese people's endurance under Japanese bombardment followed a more meandering course. For decades the Communist leadership paid little attention to the defence of Chongqing, for that was the capital of their archrivals, the Nationalists. Only recently has Beijing embraced Chongqing as a symbol of China's tenacity and for its contribution to the Allied victory.[81]

For postwar West Germans, understandings of resilience shifted from standing up to bombardment to the heroic popular efforts to rebuild shattered cities after the war. This is not to say that Germans plunged into reconstruction oblivious to the bombings, as W. G. Sebald famously suggested. On the contrary, Süss argues, Hamburg openly memorialized the victims of Operation Gomorrah during the 1950s. Political leaders frequently related the city's rapid reconstruction and modernization – and those of many other towns – to the discipline, unity and perseverance that citizens had displayed under aerial attack in wartime.[82]

In their own postwar narratives of rebirth, Japanese leaders likewise extolled the people's remarkable contributions to reconstruction. But they did so with little reference to the aerial destruction of sixty-six cities. The notable exception was atomic-bombed Hiroshima, which deliberately marketed its renaissance as a world-city of peace to secure national and international funds for rebuilding. Unlike Hamburg, Tokyo and the other firebombed cities rarely commemorated the air raids until the 1970s.[83] Japanese authorities drew instead upon the wartime spirit of material sacrifice. To exhort the Japanese people to keep on saving and working hard for national recovery, the officials repeatedly invoked 'the healthy discipline' imposed by war savings campaigns. Witness the spectacle of Vice Minister of Finance Hayato Ikeda speaking in Hiroshima in 1947. After praising citizens for their extraordinary efforts to rebuild the devastated city, he encouraged them to save all their unspent money so as to finance the manufacture of Japanese goods for export. Only by living 'austere lives' will 'our country exist in the future'.[84] Despite some differences, the narratives of postwar resilience converged in West Germany and Japan. By the early 1960s, the term 'Economic Miracle' was widely applied to Japan as well as Germany.

While these narratives of resilience remained largely national after 1945, they occasionally came together to form an oft-cited 'universal truth'. Over the past six decades, many have touted the resilience of human beings under fire. They hold that bombing in the Second World War did not break civilian morale; if anything, it strengthened the will to resist.[85] The evidence for this is exceedingly thin. The relatively light bombing of Britain may have occasionally stiffened morale, but in other instances it provoked terror and nightly trekking. To be sure, bombing was not decisive in defeating Germany, yet the Nazi regime may have been an extraordinary case. Nazi leaders relied on millions of forced labourers to construct air defences and rebuild cities, and they were willing to sacrifice the entire nation in a fight to the finish. Those who believe that bombing stiffens morale tend to overlook the experiences of the other belligerents. In Japan and Italy, saturation bombing often terrorized civilians, sparked mass exoduses and helped persuade leaders to surrender.[86] Let us also consider the narrative itself. The axiom that bombing boosts morale has its own history, dating back to the wartime claims of the Spanish Republicans, Chinese Nationalists and the British as they appealed for international support. Shorn of its historical context, the transnational myth of resilience under bombardment remains alive and well today.

Applying the tools of global history to the study of war permits us to ask new questions about historical memory, whose analysis has long been limited in time and space. Surely, we can no longer discuss 'national narratives' as if they can be traced back to origins in 'traditional British phlegm', 'German ideology' or Japanese Bushido. In the modern world of interconnections and globalized warfare, narratives of civilians under fire crossed borders as rapidly as military strategies and tactics. At the same time, as this chapter demonstrates, transnational narratives did not necessarily produce one storyline. They were shaped and reshaped as they confronted new realities, such as the intensity of the bombardment or the effectiveness of a nation's civil defence.

This chapter also reminds us that war memory is not a process that suddenly begins *after* a war. In my own field of Japanese history, so many studies of war memory scarcely 'mention the war' itself. Can we truly understand memories like resilience on a global scale if we have not investigated the nature of the warfare in each location, people's varying wartime experiences and their interactions with the evolving transnational narratives? War memory might best be thought of as connected narratives that developed in prewar and wartime, as well as in postwar. Global history may not be the only way to study memory and war, but we miss much of the richness of the human experience in its absence.

Notes

1 Shōwakan, https://www.showakan.go.jp/about/, accessed 31 July 2023; also, Angus Calder, *Myth of the Blitz* (London: Jonathan Cape, 1991); Rana Mitter, *China's Good War: How World War II Is Shaping a New Nationalism* (Cambridge, MA: Belknap Press, Harvard University Press, 2020), 179–81; Leonie Treber, *Mythos Trümmerfrauen* [Myth of the rubble women] (Essen: Klartext Verlag, 2015).

2 Sheldon Garon, 'Transnational History and Japan's "Comparative Advantage"', *Journal of Japanese Studies* 43, no. 1 (Winter 2017): 80–92.

3 Sheldon Garon, 'On the Transnational Destruction of Cities: What Japan and the United States Learned from the Bombing of Britain and Germany in the Second World War', *Past & Present* 247, no. 1 (May 2020): 235–71.

4 Tom Buchanan, *East Wind: China and the British Left, 1925–1976* (Oxford: Oxford University Press, 2012), 63–4.

5 Sven Lindqvist, *A History of Bombing*, trans. Linda Haverty Rugg (New York: New Press, 2001), 105–6; John W. Dower, *War without Mercy: Race and Power in the Pacific War* (New York: Pantheon Books, 1986), 11, 40–1.

6 John Horne (ed.), *State, Society and Mobilization in Europe during the First World War* (Cambridge: Cambridge University Press, 1997); Jay Winter and Jean-Louis Robert (eds.), *Capital Cities at War: Paris, London, Berlin 1914–1919* (Cambridge: Cambridge University Press, 1997); for global coverage, see Ute Daniel et al. (eds.), *1914–1918 Online: International Encyclopedia of the First World War*, https://encyclopedia.1914-1918-online.net/themes/

7 Craig L. Symonds, *World War II at Sea: A Global History* (New York: Oxford University Press, 2018); Gerhard L. Weinberg, *A World at Arms: A Global History of World War II*, 2nd edition (Cambridge: Cambridge University Press, 2005).

8 Richard Overy, *Blood and Ruins: The Great Imperial War, 1931–1945* (London: Allen Lane, 2021), xii.

9 Garon, 'Transnational Destruction of Cities', 256, 262.

10 Jeremy Adelman, 'What Is Global History Now?' *Aeon*, 2 March 2017, https://aeon.co/essays/is-global-history-still-possible-or-has-it-had-its-moment

11 Garon, 'Transnational Destruction of Cities'.

12 Lizzie Collingham, *The Taste of War: World War Two and the Battle for Food* (London: Allen Lane, 2011), 96–115.

13 Xu Guoqi, *Strangers on the Western Front: Chinese Workers in the Great War* (Cambridge, MA: Harvard University Press, 2011).

14 Sheldon Garon, *Beyond Our Means: Why America Spends While the World Saves* (Princeton: Princeton University Press, 2012), 48–57, 91, 231–5, 246–51; see also Christof Dejung, David Motadel and Jürgen Osterhammel (eds.), *The Global Bourgeoisie: The Rise of the Middle Classes in the Age of Empire* (Princeton: Princeton University Press, 2019).

15 Sheldon Garon, 'Japon: la guerre des autres?' in *Une histoire de la guerre – Du XIXe siècle à nos jours*, ed. Bruno Cabanes (Paris: Seuil, 2018), 538–51.

16 For example, International Organization for Migration, 'Building Resilience Helps People Carry on during Wartime', 29 June 2022, Ukraine, https://ukraine.iom.int/stories/building-resilience-helps-people-carry-during-wartime, accessed 1 August 2023.

17 H. G. Wells, *The War in the Air* (New York: Macmillan, 1908), 251, 254.

18 Lindqvist, *History of Bombing*, 46, 54, 63, 67.

19 Hanns Gobsch, *Wahn-Europa 1934, eine Vision* (1931); in English, *Death Rattle*, trans. Ian F. D. Morrow (Boston: Little, Brown, 1932), 302–4, 308.

20 Unno Jūza, *Kūchū sōsō kyoku* [Air Raid Requiem], 1932; see Cary Lee Karacas, 'Tokyo from the Fire: War, Occupation, and the Remaking of a Metropolis' (PhD diss., University of California, Berkeley, 2006), 41–4.

21 Louis Jackson, 'The Defence of Localities against Aerial Attack', *Journal of the Royal United Services Institution* 58, no. 436 (June 1914): 711, 712–13.

22 Giulio Douhet, 'The Probable Aspects of the War of the Future', April 1928, in *The Command of the Air*, trans. Dino Ferrari (New York: Coward-McCann, 1942), 182.

23 Richard Overy, *The Bombing War: Europe, 1939–1945* (London: Allen Lane, 2013), 20–1.

24 'Air Raid Psychology', *Lancet* 190 (14 July 1917): 55.

25 Alfred Rawlinson, *The Defence of London, 1915–1918* (London: Andrew Melrose, 1923), 4; also Susan R. Grayzel, *At Home and under Fire: Air Raids and Culture in Britain from the Great War to the Blitz* (Cambridge: Cambridge University Press, 2012), chap. 3.

26 Harford Montgomery Hyde and George R. Falkiner, *Air Defence and the Civil Population* (London: Cresset Press, 1937), 52–3.

27 E. R. Henry (Metropolitan Police Office), 'Moral Effect of Air-Raids in the Metropolis, and Measures Taken to Provide Shelter', Memorandum by the Chief Commissioner of Police, E. R. Henry, 1 October 1917, CAB 24/27, The National Archives of the UK [hereafter TNA], Kew.

28 Norman Bottomley, 'Some Comments on C.O.S. 156: Notes by Squadron Leader Bottomley', 26 May 1928, in 'War Aim of an Air Force', Air Ministry, 'Air Policy', 1918–1938, AIR 9/8, TNA.

29 Sub-Committee on Air Raid Precautions, minutes of meeting, 5 June 1924, appendix to 3rd meeting, CAB 46/1, TNA.

30 'War Office Staff Exercise, Buxton, 9–13 April 1923, 2nd Conference: Address by Chief of the Air Staff', 2–3, AIR 9/8, TNA.

31 Hansard, HC Deb, 10 November 1932, vol. 270, 630–41.

32 Rinji Gunji Chōsa Iin, *Sansen shokoku no rikugun ni tsuite* [The Belligerents' armies] (Tokyo: Rinji Gunji Chōsa Iin, 1919), 74–7.

33 Entry of 6 September 1923, *Ugaki Kazushige nikki* [Diary of Kazushige Ugaki] (Tokyo: Misuzu Shobō, 1971), 3:445–6; J. Charles Schencking, *The Great Kantō Earthquake and the Chimera of National Reconstruction in Japan* (New York: Columbia University Press, 2013), 76–7.

34 B. H. Liddell Hart, *Paris, or the Future of War* (London: Keagan Paul, Trench, Trubner, 1925), 47–8.

35 'Totale Panik: Wenn die Natur Krieg führt' [Total panic: when Nature goes to war], *Die Sirene*, no. 7 (April 1937): 170–2.

36 'Soldaten der Heimat', *Sirene*, no. 2 (January 1943): 20.

37 *Sirene*, no. 3 (February 1935): 68; Garon, 'Transnational Destruction', 259.

38 Garon, 'Transnational Destruction', 256.

39 Reichsminister des Innern, 'Abschnitt VII: Brandschutz', 19 October 1932, Politisches Archiv des Auswärtigen Amts [hereafter PA], Berlin.

40 Sheldon Garon, 'Defending Civilians against Aerial Bombardment: A Comparative/ Transnational History of Japanese, German, and British Home Fronts, 1918–1945', *Asia-Pacific Journal: Japan Focus* 14, no. 23 (1 December 2016), https://apjjf. org/2016/23/Garon.html

41 *Sirene*, no. 10 (March 1934): 3.

42 Garon, 'Defending Civilians'.

43 *Sirene*, no. 1 (January 1937): 3.

44 C. Ohlenhof and H. von Mutius, *Selbstschutz im Luftschutz* [Self-protection in air defence] (Berlin: Volkschutz-Verlag, n.d. [ca. 1932]), 40–1; Chūbu Bōei Shireibu, *Kokumin bōkū* [Civil defence] (Kobe: Kokubō shisō fukyūkai, 1938), 28–9.

45 Garon, 'Transnational Destruction', 257, 259.

46 Auswärtiges Amt to Reichsluftfahrtministerium, 'Auf das Schreiben vom 19.d.M'. 26 July 1934, IIF Luft, R32819, PA.

47 Garon, *Beyond Our Means*, 170–1.

48 'Ziviler Luftschutz in aller Welt: Die deutschen, italienschen und japanischen Massnahmen vorbildlich' [Civil defence around the world: examples of German, Italian, and Japanese measures], *Sirene*, no. 21 (October 1938): 583–4.

49 *Sirene*, no. 19 (September 1937): 511–13, no. 1 (January 1939): 2.

50 *Sirene*, no. 11 (June 1935), no. 23 (November 1940); *Kokumin bōkū* [hereafter *KB*] 2, no. 6 (June 1940).

51 'Die Feuerprobe bestanden! 300 Eimer wandern von Hand zu Hand' [Passing the test by fire: 300 buckets passed from hand to hand], *Sirene*, no. 18 (August 1940): 394–6; *KB* 5, no. 10 (October 1943): inside cover, 20–4.

52 'Selbstschutz gegen Terror: Wir bekämpfen britische Brandbomben' [Self-protection against terror: we fight British incendiary bombs], *Sirene*, no. 8 (April 1943): 89–93; Kokubō shisō fukyūkai, *Katei bōkū* [Household air defence] (Osaka: Ōsaka kokubō kyōkai, 1937); Garon, 'Defending Civilians'.

53 Ludwig von Schöder, '"Die Stimmung mehr als trübe"' [Their morale is more than dismal], *Sirene*, no. 16 (August 1940): 346.

54 *Tokio Jokio*, dir. Norman McCabe, 1943.

55 *KB* 1, no. 6 (December 1939): inside cover; 4, no. 3 (March 1942): 38–41; 4, no. 5 (August 1942): inside cover; 5, no. 5 (May 1943): 8–11.

56 N. de P. MacRoberts, *A.R.P. Lessons from Barcelona: Some Hints for Local Authorities and for the Private Citizen* (London: Eyre and Spottiswoode, 1938), 3–5; also, Letter from Sir Philip Gamble (Commissioner of the Metropolitan Police) to Major N. de P. MacRoberts, 18 April 1938, MEPO 2/3632, TNA.

57 'Effects of Air Raids in Spain and China', *Confidential Admiralty Monthly Intelligence Report*, no. 231 (15 August 1938): 48, ADM 223/826, TNA.

58 Chiang Kai-shek, 'Bombing of Civilians and Open Towns', 16 May 1939, quoted in Edna Tow, 'The Great Bombing of Chongqing and the Anti-Japanese War, 1937–1945', in *The Battle for China*, ed. Mark Peattie, Edward J. Drea and Hans van de Ven (Stanford: Stanford University Press, 2011), 273; Alan Baumler, 'Keep Calm and Carry On: Airmindedness and Mass Mobilization during the War of Resistance', *Journal of Chinese Military History* 5 (2016): 26–9.

59 Italics mine. Quoted in Calder, *Myth*, 30.

60 Memo, Intelligence Branch (Ministry of Home Security), 25 October 1940, HO 199/16, TNA.

61 See 'ESPIONAGE AND INTELLIGENCE, Blackout and Civil Defence Measures in Germany: Intelligence Reports', 1942–45, Ministry of Home Security, HO 186/2046, TNA.

62 Dietmar Süss, *Death from the Skies: How the British and Germans Survived Bombing in World War II*, trans. Lesley Sharpe and Jeremy Noakes (Oxford: Oxford University Press, 2014), 16.

63 Calder, *Myth*, 1–2, 212–17.

64 'London Can Take It', dir. Humphrey Jennings and Harry Watt, 1940.

65 *Daily Report on Morale*, 26 August, 19 September 1940, INF 1/264; *Home Intelligence Weekly Report*, no. 45 (6–13 August 1941): 1–2, INF 1/292, TNA.

66 *Summary of Special Report on Coventry*, 19 November 1940; *Home Intelligence Weekly Report*, no. 19 (5–12 February 1941): 2–3; no. 30 (23–30 April 1941): 3; no. 35 (28 May–4 June 1941): 7; *Home Intelligence Special Report on Conditions in Portsmouth*, 19–24 May 1941, INF 1/292, TNA.

67 Holdsworth to Editor (Yorkshire Post), secret, *c.* October 1941; Robert G. Tarran [Sheriff, Kingston on Hull], 'Report on My Interest and Activities in the Trekking Problem since the Two Heavy Raids on the 6/7th and 7/8th Mau [May]1941', 26 July 1941, HO 186/1861, TNA.

68 'Effects of Enemy Attack upon Hull on 18 July 1941', report by Hull and East Riding Information Committee, 28 July 1941, secret, 3, INF 1/292, TNA.

69 Air Intelligence (Liaison), 'The Blitz'. 14 August 1941, Appendix A, 1, 3, 7, AIR 40/288, TNA.

70 Overy, *Bombing War*, 59–60, 75–6, 88–90, 108–9, 118–25, 191–6.

71 'Civil Defence in Germany', Ministry of Home Security, Intelligence Branch, 15 August 1941; 'Notes on German Civil Defence: General Organisation', Inspector-General's Department, Home Office, March 1946, both in HO 186/2949; 'Civil Defence in Germany', 1 January 1943, HO 186/2046, TNA.

72 Overy, *Bombing War*, 321–3, 333–5, 377–8.

73 Joseph Goebbels, *Die Tagebücher*, 26 May 1943 and 4 September 1943, quoted in Süss, *Death from the Skies*, 76–7.

74 Jörg Friederich, *The Fire: The Bombing of Germany, 1940–1945*, trans. Allison Brown (New York: Columbia University Press, 2006), 279, 283–4.

75 Süss, *Death from the Skies*, 77–8, 102, 105, 108, 202, 219–22, 423.

76 Yamamoto Shigeru, 'Tonarigumi no katsuyaku wa Doitsu ijō' [Japanese Neighbourhood associations' efforts surpass even Germany's], *KB* 3, no. 11 (December 1941): 53.

77 Garon, 'Transnational Destruction', 259.

78 Garon, 'Defending Civilians'; United States Strategic Bombing Survey, Civilian Defense Division, *Final Report Covering Air-Raid Protection and Allied Subjects in Japan* (Washington, DC: USSBS, 1947), 169.

79 USSBS, *Air-Raid Protection*, 29–32, 57; Garon, 'Transnational Destruction', 267.

80 Naimushō Keihokyoku Hōanka, 'Kūshū gekka ni tomonau minshin no dōkō' [Trends in morale as air raids worsen], in *Nihon no kūshū*, ed. Matsuura Sōzō (Tokyo: Sanseidō, 1981), 10: 62–5.

81 Mitter, *China's Good War*.

82 Dietmar Süss, 'Memories of the Air War', *Journal of Contemporary History* 43, no. 2 (April 2008): 339–40; cf. W. G. Sebald, *On the Natural History of Destruction*, trans. Anthea Bell (New York: Random House, 2003), 4–7.

83 Ran Zwigenberg, *Hiroshima: The Origins of Global Memory Culture* (Cambridge: Cambridge University Press, 2014), 23–4, 28–37; Cary Karacas, 'Place, Public Memory, and the Tokyo Air Raids', *The Geographical Review* 100, no. 4 (October 2010): 524–5.

84 'Jikan chochiku kōen shiryō' [Vice minister's address], 5 April 1947, Aichi bunsho, Chochiku: Chochiku zōkyōsaku, vol. 2, doc. 1, Shōwa zaiseishi shiryō, Ministry of Finance, Japan; Garon, *Beyond Our Means*, 256–8.

85 For example, Hans Rumpf, *The Bombing of Germany*, trans. Edward Fitzgerald (New York: Holt, Rinehart and Winston, 1962), 233–34; for a refutation of this myth, see Phillip S. Meilinger, *Airpower: Myths and Facts* (Maxwell Air Force Base, Alabama: Air University Press, 2003), 47–51.

86 Garon, 'Transnational Destruction', 265–70.

Section Two

Empires and other great powers

7

Lighthouse of socialism for the decolonized world: Central Asia's global moment, 1956–79

Marc Elie

At the turn of the 1970s, the capital of Soviet Kazakhstan, Almaty, dreamed of hosting the Winter Olympics.[1] At the foot of the high mountains of the Tian Shan range, Almaty offers stunning alpine landscapes. Since the early 1960s, the Kazakh leadership had been developing ski and skating resorts above Alma-Ata. Kazakhstan, although on the periphery of the Soviet Union, could envision a future as a full-grown nation shining internationally, the Olympic flag flying high above its capital. It seemed that Turkestan, once a poor, colonially exploited southern border region of the Russian Empire, was now a thriving centre of socialist development and prosperity; that socialism had propelled the Central Asian nations – Uzbekistan, Turkmenistan, Kyrgyzstan, Tajikistan and Kazakhstan – to new economic and political significance both inside and outside the Soviet Union.

For some twenty years, between the death of Joseph Stalin in 1953 and the second half of the 1970s, Central Asia lived through a global moment and a Soviet socialist golden age. The synchronicity of decolonization, the Cold War and destalinization created unique opportunities for Central Asia. For Moscow, the former Turkestan became a development front from which to extract wheat, cotton and gas. Major scientific-military projects were located in the Kazakh steppes, like the Semipalatinsk nuclear test site and the Baikonur cosmodrome.

But Moscow needed these areas not only as providers of raw materials and remote spaces for military exercises: they wanted to showcase 'development' in Central Asia in its economic, social, cultural and political aspects. Moscow promoted the Central Asian republics as ambassadors of Socialist socio-economic accomplishments in the recently decolonized countries of the 'East', especially Muslim nations. The message that Soviet Central Asia was to send out was that socialism was a global model enabling liberation from colonial oppression, the building of effective states, national emancipation and economic prosperity.[2]

In their turn, the Central Asian elites embraced Moscow's openness policy towards a more constant engagement with the decolonized nations of the 'Third World'. They were agile in using their newly acquired role as emissaries of socialism as a bargaining lever to get more investments for their republics and more political prerogatives to administer them. Using the language of decolonization, they renegotiated Soviet federalism to put it on a less exploitative foundation than it had had under Stalin. In the 1960s, the five republics reached a high degree of national autonomy in the Soviet framework of limited sovereignty. Their populations reached a modest but stable level of prosperity which compared favourably to neighbouring countries.[3]

This chapter shows that the post-Stalin Soviet federal and economic integrative framework made it possible to propel the Central Asians into the globalization initiatives of the Soviet Union: the network of international socialist solidarity, the offer of Soviet development aid and cultural exchange with decolonized nations. In these fields the Central Asian cultural and political elites enjoyed a new role as representatives of the Soviet integration project and of their nation and culture. In this global moment they saw themselves as participants in global processes of socialist influence abroad that were an alternative to the capitalist offering.

Since the 2000s, interest in the encounter of the 'Second World' with the 'Third World' has grown in Russian studies.[4] Moving beyond the Cold War confrontation of the two world powers, the field has discovered how new nations born during the fall of the European colonial empires and a new Soviet leadership after the death of Stalin entered into intense political, military, economic and cultural exchanges.[5] In 1957, the Soviet public welcomed youth from colonial and postcolonial nations to the Moscow Youth Festival, a key event that unlocked and loosened up Soviet culture. How did decolonization challenge and change the Soviet Union, which claimed to have resolved the 'nationality question' once and for all?[6]

Pursuing the implications of this enthusiasm for the Third World in the Second World, researchers have been challenging the notion of globalization in the twentieth century as a uniquely Western process. They have proposed the concept of 'red' or 'alternative globalizations'.[7] Although the pluralization of global interconnectedness is an important contribution to historiography, I refrain in this article from using the terms 'alternative' or 'socialist globalizations' for fear of conjuring up a debate about 'alternative modernization'.[8] My emphasis is less on processes than on a particular moment, a window of opportunity that Central Asia seized with some success: in these two decades, existing Soviet ideas about how to navigate global entanglements (national liberation, economic dependency and Cold War antagonisms) were operationalized and adapted by Central Asian elites in practical situations like encounters with Third World leaders and negotiations with Moscow for funds and prerogatives.

I will stress two key changes for Central Asian actors who had to make sense of decolonization, destalinization and the Cold War, which brought opportunities to enhance their agency within their republics, in their relationship with Moscow and the Soviet Union's foreign relations. The first is the change of scale. With their embrace of decolonized countries, the world opened up for Soviet people. The change was especially dramatic in Central Asia, which was no longer languishing on the southern periphery of a great empire closed to the outside world, but shining at the centre of the Asian continent, at a time when the USSR was striving to become an Asian power. Reviving the ideas of the 1910s and 1920s, socialism presented itself as a global ideology addressed to all oppressed peoples. There were certainly various flavours of socialism, but the USSR could believe that its brand brought stability and power, and Central Asia had the potential to be a proud example of that.

A second change pertains to how Central Asian elites perceived and influenced the place of the region in Soviet federalism. They compared their nations to the newly decolonized nations and discovered that they shared many challenges and values with them, most importantly a rural economy, a strong dependence on metropolizes and the belief that industrialization was the highway to development and prosperity.[9] In the Soviet Union, the republics were declared equal but actually economically ranked. In this stratification Stalinism had left Central Asia at the bottom of the territorial pyramid. A central question for Central Asian political and cultural leaders was how to attain equality with the Western peoples of the Soviet Union. During destalinization there was room for manoeuvre for national leaders to shift the place of their republics in this construct, and they avidly exploited it, although with mixed and limited results.

I begin by sketching out how, after the initial promise of emancipation under Bolshevik rule and its partial implementation, Central Asia was violently downgraded to a semi-colonial condition under Stalin. The central sections of the article are devoted to how Central Asian elites under Nikita Khrushchev and Leonid Brezhnev pushed for changes in Soviet federalism, played a greater role as national leaders, embraced economic development in their republics and became emissaries of Soviet socialism to developing countries. The closing section shows why this global moment came to an end in Central Asia, followed, ten years later, by the opening of new connections to global transformations during the region's accession to independence.

From imperfect decolonization to colonial exchange

The Bolshevik leaders under Lenin and Stalin at the end of the Civil War engineered an original solution to the challenge of administering the ethnic diversity of the former Tsarist Empire, a problem known in Russian as the 'nationality question'. Elsewhere in Europe at the end of the First World War, the crumbling empires had given rise to nation-states. The peace settlement promoted the reign of states based on one nation on the ruins of the German, Austro-Hungarian and Ottoman empires, as well as a great deal of French and British colonialism in the Mediterranean and Africa. The Soviet Union took a different route, undermining the European triumph of the nation-state and the colonial empire. They proposed decolonizing Russian peripheries not by creating independent states, but by binding quasi-states with broad cultural and economic rights in a federal framework under strong revolutionary leadership from Moscow. This policy could certainly be read – and was actually read by many – as the re-establishment of Moscow's control over the former Russian dynastic domain.[10] But the order created was initially deliberately different from its Tsarist predecessor in that the indigenous populations were called upon to rule themselves.

In the course of the Civil War (1918–21), the Bolsheviks recaptured the peripheries of the former Russian Empire. In Central Asia as elsewhere, they promised wide-ranging rights to the national minorities to gain their support against the whites. To consolidate Moscow's hold on the former empire, the agreement of 1922 founding the Soviet Union secured extensive prerogatives for the 'Soviet republics' and lesser ones for the 'autonomous republics' within them. The 1922 arrangements were mainly the work of Lenin and Stalin.[11]

Accompanying this original federal construction, a vigorous policy of promoting locals to functions of responsibility within the state and party apparatus in their Soviet or autonomous republics created an indigenous political and managerial elite that controlled the national republics. The support given by Moscow to national languages and cultures helped develop and strengthen a sense of national belonging among minorities. Terry Martin has aptly labelled the early Soviet Union an 'affirmative action empire' to underline that the new state went to considerable lengths to roll back Russification, develop national languages and emancipate minorities within their own cultures. Significantly, these rights were territorial: with a few exceptions, each recognized people enjoyed its own territory in which it could develop its institutions, language and culture.[12]

'Titular nationalities', that is, the ethnic groups that gave the republics their names (the Uzbeks in Uzbekistan, the Turkmens in Turkmenistan, etc.), were the main targets of these policies, but not their only beneficiaries, as even peoples without their territorial representations within the USSR received far-ranging cultural and linguistic rights, such as the Jews and the Poles. Nationalities were seen in a Marxist framework as evolving social bodies who would move from backwardness to enlightenment when developing under socialist policies. Initially, the republic statuses were seen as evolving towards more sovereignty, following the cultural and economic development of each nationality. Thus, Kazakhstan, first an autonomous republic within the Russian Soviet republic, was promoted in 1936 to become the 11th Soviet republic.

In Central Asia, national communists embraced this way of managing ethnic and religious diversity. Contrary to the classical view, the five republics of Soviet Central Asia were not artificially created by Moscow in a policy of 'divide and rule'. First, national movements were no Bolshevik creation: they had been developing in Turkestan from the beginning of the Russian colonization in the mid-nineteenth century.[13] National communists seized the compromise proposed by the Bolshevik: the national elites gained the right to govern their traditional territories in their own language in exchange for their support of the revolutionary socialist 'civilizing mission'.[14] Thus, the young postcolonial elites removed Europeans from their power positions throughout Turkestan, both in cities and in the countryside, where the end of the Tsarist government had only reinforced land grabbing by European settlers.[15] To these elites, the revolution was a path of national liberation.[16]

The Central Asian nations were no creations of Moscow in a second sense: it was Central Asian elites that managed the process of creating borders and political entities in Central Asia. Until the Revolution, Russian-dominated Central Asia was divided into two large entities or 'Governor-Generalships' covering the Kazakh steppes to the North and Turkestan to the South, with the Khanate of Khiva and the Emirate of Bukhara retaining formal independent status as protectorates. Ten years of difficult negotiations between representatives of the different Central Asian nationalities resulted in the creation of six national-territorial entities, in place of the three initially envisioned by the Bolsheviks. Apart from the Uzbeks, Turkmens and Kazakhs, the institutional rights of the Kyrgyz, Tajiks and Karakalpaks were recognized. All of them were eventually recognized as full-blown Soviet Republics, but for Karakalpakstan, which remained an autonomous region within Uzbekistan.[17]

With the goal in mind of spreading revolution to the whole world, the Bolsheviks appeared as a strong anti-colonial force on the international scene. They linked the nationalist struggle in the various colonies together in a general interpretative framework and in an international militant network to support them. They renounced the secret privileges that the Tsarist regime had extorted from ailing empires – the Chinese, the Persian and the Ottoman.[18] Lenin endowed the 'East' (*vostok*) with special importance in the anti-colonial struggle: he called for 'awakening the peoples of the East'. The European colonial powers – including Russia – were the oppressors and the 'East', the oppressed. In 1935, Stalin added a dichotomy between the Soviet East, already liberated from oppression by virtue of Bolshevik power, and the outside East, still languishing under the colonial yoke. The Soviet East included the North and South Caucasus, Central Asia and the Tatars of the Volga region. The outside East included East Asia, the Middle East, Africa and sometimes even Latin America.[19]

The failure of revolution in Central Europe forced the Bolshevik leaders to turn to spreading revolution in the colonies of the European capitalists. As Trotsky famously put it in 1919, 'the road to [revolution in] Paris and London [lay] via the towns of Afghanistan, the Punjab and Bengal'.[20] Central Asia had a central role to play as a door to China and British India. The Communist International, or Comintern, created several institutions in Tashkent to coordinate the revolutionary efforts towards the East. Its Eastern Section convened a Congress of the Peoples of the East in Baku (Azerbaijan) in 1920. A Central Bureau of Communist Organizations of the Peoples of the East and a Communist University of the Toilers of the East established in Moscow in 1921 completed the network of institutions addressing both the inner and the outer 'Easterners', reinforcing a sense of shared challenges and solutions for colonial regions: alumni of the University include Deng Xiaoping, Ho Chi Minh and Manabrenda Nath Roy.[21]

Decolonization proceeded within the Soviet framework. Teaching in the national languages became the main vehicle of literacy in populations that were largely illiterate (less than 5 per cent of Uzbeks and less than 10 per cent of Kazakhs could read in 1926). The administrative and economic elite co-opted more and more local cadres in a process known as 'indigenization' (*korenizatsiia*).[22]

However, these initial efforts at national emancipation came to a bitter end under Stalin's rule. First, in a process that began in 1930 and was completed during the Great Terror of 1937–8, the national elites were physically destroyed (shot, sent to camps). Second, the policy of rapid industrialization put most power in the hands of ministries in Moscow, and not in those of the republics' leaders. Forced collectivization and sedentarization led to the destruction of one-fourth of the Kazakh people.[23] Third, rule via the party and the secret police curtailed the national rights or rendered them ineffective, even if *korenizatsiia* itself was not abandoned. First Secretaries of the republics and leading Chekists were more often than not Europeans. Kazakhstan was led by non-Kazakhs from 1920 until 1960 with only two exceptions.

Stalinists rewrote the national histories of each ethnic group so as to reinforce the continuities with Russian tsarism. The Central Asians were presented as in need of Russian guidance. Historical narratives that underlined the revolutionary break with Russian colonialism were silenced, and their promoters accused of 'nationalism'.[24] Now it appeared that Kazakh and Kyrgyz nomads, Uzbek and Tajik farmers had voluntarily joined the Tsarist Empire.[25] Stalin declared that Russians were the most advanced people and as such had the duty to enlighten more backward nations and lead them on the path towards socialism.[26]

With the first Five-Year Plan, cotton self-sufficiency became the driving mantra of the Stalinist leadership in dealing with the three cotton-growing Central Asian republics of Uzbekistan, Tajikistan and Turkmenistan. Cotton had precedence over subsistence farming: the agricultural authorities discouraged the growing of rice, Turkestan's staple crop. Cotton was exported raw to foreign countries or processed in the Soviet Union, but both export and processing occurred outside of Central Asia. After the war, cotton was declared a central resource for rebuilding the country and production targets for growers were raised substantially. As far as cotton, the main Central Asian resource, was concerned, the economic relationships between producers and consumers were on a colonial footing.[27]

Destalinization as a second decolonization

The death of Stalin opened up the possibility for a reconfiguration of the relationships between Moscow and its semi-colonial southern periphery. Destalinization brought about major shifts in both domestic and foreign policy. Whereas Stalin had a pessimistic view of the world stage, where the Soviet Union had to make territorial gains to protect itself from growing capitalist encirclement and aggression, Khrushchev believed that the wind of history was blowing in Soviet sails. With many others he detected a socialist moment in the 1950s: the wave of decolonization submerged and crushed the capitalist empires of France, Britain, the Netherlands and Portugal.[28] A huge opportunity was emerging for revolution abroad: the dream of World Revolution was revived.

In Asia, three revolutionary communist regimes had defeated capitalist and colonial forces: in China, Mao Ze Dong took power in 1949. Contrary to Stalin, who was wary of the Chinese communists, his heirs enthusiastically supported Mao with a huge programme of technology transfer and development. In Vietnam, Ho Chi Minh inflicted a serious military defeat on a French expeditionary corps and, with Chinese and Soviet help, forced the French government to the negotiation table. French Indochina was history. The Korean War may have been disastrous for all sides, but it led to the creation of a North Korean communist state under the leadership of Kim Il-sung in 1948. In India, the anti-colonial forces took power, the British had to leave in 1947 and a progressive government under Jawaharlal Nehru leaned to the left and had a friendly attitude towards the Soviet Union. Khrushchev even contemplated the possibility that the bourgeois government of India could be toppled by a socialist revolution, like the Provisional Government of Alexander Kerensky by the Bolsheviks.[29]

Khrushchev and his colleagues interpreted these regime changes as the beginning of a triumphant communist crusade across the colonial world. In Africa and the Middle East in the mid-1950s, it was clear that the French and the British would soon have to give up their colonial possessions and protectorates. An immense field for Soviet influence was opening up: agrarian reform, education and industrialization Soviet-style were on the horizon.

New developments in the decolonized nations in the mid-1950s acted as a wake-up call for the Soviet leadership. Especially the movement for Afro-Asian solidarity challenged the USSR's new posture as the main support for the new nations: at the Bandung Conference in 1955 they refused to invite a Soviet delegation led by Nuritdin Mukhitdinov, first secretary of the Uzbek Communist Party, because they placed the USSR among the imperialist nations of the West and did not consider the Soviet republics to be independent countries. Ten years later, the Soviet delegation was not invited to the second Bandung Conference for the same reason. This failure to be part of Afro-Asian solidarity and be taken seriously as an Asian power and decolonizing force led the Soviet leadership to reconfigure its relationship with the republics so as to have them move away from underdevelopment.[30] In response to this change there was growing agency for the leadership of the five Central Asian republics both within their republics and in formulating the goals of Soviet policy.

The embrace of decolonization as a revolutionary force stood in stark contrast to the attitude that had prevailed throughout the first half of the 1950s, when the Soviet leadership was wary of the 'bourgeois nationalist' liberation movements. It was made possible by an ideological revision officialized at the 20th Party Congress in 1956. Now a social revolution was no longer a prerequisite for an anti-imperialist alignment. The bourgeois elites of oppressed colonies were promoted to true anti-imperialist forces and allies of the Soviet Union in the struggle for socialism.[31] Most former colonies were rural countries. Soviet Central Asia itself was not industrialized prior to its sovietization and remained predominantly rural for the whole Soviet period and until the present day. But the five republics showed that nations could jump from colonial agriculture to socialism bypassing the step of bourgeois capitalism.[32]

In his report to the congress, Khrushchev further hailed a new era of history, 'when the peoples of the East ... have become a new and mighty factor in international relations'.[33] The 20th Congress marked the birth of a 'new Eastern policy' which reinforced the agency of Central Asian elites in formulating the policy of the Soviet state towards decolonized nations.[34]

The post-Stalin leadership declared that war with the United States was not inevitable. Thus, they removed enormous pressure from international relationships. The two 'camps', communist and capitalist, could live peacefully side by side ('peaceful coexistence'). For Khrushchev the confrontation with the West would be decided by economic development at home and expansion of socialism abroad and not by war between the superpowers, which, in the nuclear age, could leave no winner. In the decolonized world, the United States and the USSR fought over minds and bellies, financing development projects in India, Afghanistan and many other countries.[35]

The 20th Congress is well known for Khrushchev's speech denouncing some of Stalin's crimes. Stalin was condemned for the destruction of communist cadres in the 1930s and 1940s, which included the republics' elites. Many of the economic, political and cultural personalities that had been killed under Stalin were now rehabilitated. Thus a lot of the fear that had paralysed republic leadership disappeared. Central Asian intellectuals challenged the Stalinist interpretation of their republics' national histories without risking their life or freedom for alleged 'nationalism'.

The vision of a revolution on the march and the rehabilitation of several national leaders changed the position of Soviet Central Asia and facilitated a reordering of the five republics' relationships with Moscow. Nikita Khrushchev loosened the network of control bearing on the republics' elites. He implemented a sweeping policy of devolution, which shifted many prerogatives to the republics, especially in science and engineering, education and culture, construction and economic development.[36] Even justice and police were somehow decentralized, allowing for a greater differentiation of criminal policy. A second wave of indigenization began: the 'titular nationalities' took over the main levers of power in places which were ethnically moderately to extremely diverse.

National leaders of their republics

As a result, the First Secretaries and government chairmen of all five republics were in the hands of the titular nationality. To win the power struggle in Moscow against his rivals in the Politburo, Khrushchev leaned on the regional and republican secretaries, whom he could appoint in his function as First Secretary of the Party. The promotion of new personnel to replace Stalinist cadres helped create a support base for his policies in Moscow. In Central Asia Khrushchev made forty-year-old Mukhitdinov first secretary of Uzbekistan on the way back from his voyage to Afghanistan, India and Burma in 1955.[37] In Tajikistan he chose Tursunbai Uldzhabaev a year later. But the main reshuffle occurred at the beginning of the 1960s. Khrushchev installed a new generation of First Secretaries most of whom remained in place into the 1980s: Turdakun Usubaliev in Kyrgyzstan, Sharof Rashidov in Uzbekistan, Dzhabar Rasulov in Tajikistan, Dinmukhamed Kunaev in Kazakhstan and Balysh Ovezov in Turkmenistan. But some important controls remained in the hands of Europeans from Central Asia: the republic KGB bureaus, the military and many posts of Second Secretary and Deputy, which had the function of supervising the dealings of their Central Asian bosses.[38]

The Party First Secretaries of the republics were able to considerably strengthen their leadership.[39] To be legitimate in the eyes of the Central Asian elites, the Soviet state had to resume the decolonization of Central Asia, which Stalin had interrupted. Destalinization meant putting more political prerogatives and economic powers into their hands. The consequences of this 'republicanization' were the creeping autonomization and nationalization of Soviet republics, which progressed under Khrushchev's successor Brezhnev.[40] The client-patron relationship of republic elites with Moscow was evolving: Moscow grew gentler with its territories. Paternalism (Brezhnev) replaced terror (Stalin) and mobilization (Khrushchev). Far more discussion was possible: Brezhnev called the First Secretaries – the territorial leaders – on the phone almost every day to stay tuned to the situation in the republics.[41]

In the eyes of the post-Stalin leadership in Moscow, Soviet Central Asia, with a predominantly Muslim population and borders to Iran, China and Afghanistan, could be a model of decolonization and socialist development for the emerging nations of the 'East' (*vostok*). But this argument worked both ways: not only could Moscow display to the world the republics of Soviet Central Asia as an example of successful modernization of former (Tsarist) colonies, but these republics' leaders could also lobby for more rights and funds in Moscow, arguing that if the republics were really to serve as models of decolonization, they should be developed along socialist lines.[42] The socialist path of development implied industrialization. Under Stalin, Soviet Central Asia, with the exception of part of Kazakhstan, had been largely spared by industrial development. Some industry was evacuated to Central Asia during the war.

One example will show how Central Asian leaders seized the new opportunity offered by destalinization and decolonization to reinforce their power base. In construction, engineering and the applied sciences, the republics became their own bosses. The project for a controversial giant dam (115 metres) above Alma-Ata in the 1960s illustrates the growing autonomy of republic elites in designing and implementing massive building schemes. Opinions were divided on how best to protect Kazakhstan's capital from devastating mudflows. In 1921, a mudflow had killed several hundred inhabitants of the young city. Every few years, a mudflow would cut through roads and residential zones, destroying vital infrastructure and often killing people. In the 1950s, two protection schemes were in contention. The one favoured by specialists from Moscow and Leningrad, as well as by nature conservation activists in Alma-Ata, was to disperse the raging stream through a network of reinforced canals, using zoning to keep the areas along the most dangerous rivers free from buildings. Traditional anti-erosion measures, like tree planting, would limit the material that the mudflow could collect on its way down.

Kazakhstan Party and Government elites, on the contrary, favoured the construction of a single giant dam on the most dangerous stream, that of the Malaya Almaatinka River, at a narrow spot called the Medeu (Russian *Medeo*) Gorge. The main promoter of the project was Kunaev. Trained as a mining engineer, he embodied the second wave of indigenization. He had been the president of the Kazakh Academy of Sciences (1952–6). He shared the transforming ethos of many Soviet engineers, who believed in the virtue of massive technical schemes to solve issues with the natural environment. Against the protest of many mudflow specialists, ecologists and writers, Kunaev imposed the dam scheme which was to be built using two giant explosions.[43]

Kunaev exploited to the fullest the autonomy conceded by Moscow in scientific and technical matters to push forward the dam idea. He needed financial support from Moscow to fulfil his idea, as well as technical assistance from scientists specializing in explosions in Akademgorodok, the newly created Siberian city of science near Novosibirsk. Kunaev nonetheless used the project to develop a strong national expertise in mudflow hydrology at the republic's meteorological agency and the Academy of Sciences: whereas in the 1950s hydrologists from Moscow and Leningrad led the research on mudflows by way of expeditions to Kazakhstan, in the 1960s all hydrological research was done domestically. Other slope hazards like snow avalanches also benefitted from Kunaev's attention and received financing, and these places grew to become leading scientific hubs in the Soviet Union. Eventually, in 1973, Kunaev combined these forces in a new scientific and engineering body, *Kazglavselezashchita*, separate from the meteorological service and the Academy of Sciences. It researched, designed and built all mudflow-protection schemes across Kazakhstan. It was an operational body, active in both mudflow prevention and rescue operations across the republic. Its staff answered to Kunaev alone.

136   *Narratives, Nations, and Other World Products*

As much a protective scheme as a prestigious project, the Medeu Dam became a visiting card for Almaty. Countless delegations came from all over the world to observe this unique solution to the mudflow hazard. What is more, the dam was central to developing the mountains: it became the doorway to the 'white gold' of snow and ice tourism. At the foot of the dam, the Kazakh leadership built an open-air skating rink that offered perfect ice all year long. A grand hotel was added to the site. Up in the Almaatinka valley they built a ski resort at Shimbulak, which became the training base for the Soviet alpine ski team.[44] In other republics of Central Asia, nature-taming schemes also served the nationalization of construction capacities and technical expertise: the building of a giant dam in Nurek, Tajikistan and the 'greening of the desert' in Turkmenistan.[45]

Experts of the East

Khrushchev reinforced the stature of the Soviet Union as an Asian power. For that he put forward the Central Asian republics. The Soviet Union had its own 'vostok' (East) in these republics and Far Eastern territories. This inner East could speak better to Asia, he believed.

Khrushchev lamented the lack of Soviet expertise about the East. He believed that Central Asians had a better understanding of the 'East' and should be instrumental in reshaping Soviet Eastern policy: 'Our problem is that here, in Moscow, we have no representatives of the East – of such people who would know the problems of Asia and Africa and follow their events.'[46] This changed over the following years: leaders from Muslim republics were co-opted to the highest executive body, the Politburo (or Presidium, as it was known under Khrushchev): Mukhitdinov (1957–61) and Rashidov (as a candidate member, from 1966) from Uzbekistan and Kunaev from Kazakhstan (1971–87), and in the 1980s, Heydar Aliev from Azerbaijan. All of them were called upon to play an important role in the definition of foreign policy towards the Third World, especially Muslim countries.[47]

Khrushchev repressed religion at home during a strict atheist campaign at the turn of the 1950s.[48] Islam as well as other denominations suffered from this hostile attitude: the number of mosques was reduced by two-thirds in 1960.[49] But Khrushchev used Islam to further his diplomatic agenda: after the Bandung Conference in 1955 and the Suez crisis in 1956, the Soviet leadership began employing secular Muslims to talk to independent Middle East countries like Syria, Lebanon, Egypt and Iraq. Sharaf Rashidov, Uzbek first secretary, led the Soviet delegation to the Afro-Asian Peoples' Solidarity Conference in Cairo in 1957–8, and Mukhtar Auezov, a prominent Kazakh writer, became vice-chairman of the Solidarity Council of the Afro-Asian Countries based in Cairo in 1958. The Tajik writer Mirzo Tursun Zade chaired the Soviet Afro-Asian Solidarity Committee (SKSSAA) in 1956 and led the Soviet delegation to the Conference of Peace Partisans in Baghdad in 1959.[50]

Khrushchev entrusted Mukhitdinov from Uzbekistan with renewing Soviet Eastern expertise and co-opted him to the Central Committee and then, in 1957, the Politburo as the first Central Asian Communist to reach the highest level of power.[51] After the

Lighthouse of Socialism for the Decolonized World 137

20th Congress, Anastas Mikoyan reordered the system of knowledge about former colonial countries. New academic journals were created. Bobozhan Gafurov, a Tajik Orientalist and first secretary of the Tajik Communist Party, became director of the Institute of Oriental Studies of the Academy of Sciences in Moscow, a key position from which he expanded and reformed expertise on non-Western regions of the world. He renamed the institute 'Institute of the Peoples of Asia' to try and remove the Orientalist bias associated with the tradition of the institute. Orientalist Institutes were enlarged in Central Asia and the Caucasus to further Arab, Turkic and Iran studies.[52]

Brezhnev put an end to the anti-religious campaigning, allowing Islam to develop in Central Asia to the point that many Muslims felt no contradiction between their religion and being Soviet, belonging to an atheist country, and even being members of the Communist Party.[53] Now not only secular Muslims, but religious leaders were used in soft power efforts, allowing the Soviet Union to reach out to anti-Soviet states like Saudi Arabia and Iran.[54]

'Ex Oriente lux': Emissaries of socialist development

In his conversation with an Iraqi delegation to Moscow in February 1959, Khrushchev invited his guests to take inspiration from the southern Soviet nations which had a Muslim population. Six months before the encounter, the Iraqi army led by General Abd al-Karim Kassem had overthrown King Faisal and proclaimed a republic. Diplomatic relationships with the Soviet Union (broken in 1955) were restored.

> We want the Republic of Iraq to promptly shine out like a diamond among the Arab countries. The Republic of Iraq possesses all conditions for that. Travel to Tashkent, to Baku and look at what the Soviet Union has done in these Muslim countries! These countries are located next to Iran. Compare the achievements of Uzbekistan, Turkmenia, Azerbaijan with Iran! And you'll see that the Soviet republics of Central Asia and the South Caucasus are far more advanced than Iran, Turkey and so on.[55]

Khrushchev used the economic comparison between Soviet republics and their Muslim neighbours to insist that embrace of socialism was the best way to achieve socio-economic success. Khrushchev offered economic aid to the Iraqi delegation in the form of credits, agriculture consultants and trade in chemicals to ease Iraq's dependence upon British industry. As in the cases discussed by Sanchez-Sibony (India, Indonesia, Ghana), the USSR did not initiate the aid, but responded to Iraqi requests.[56] Like most decolonized peoples, the Iraqis, however, even under the Ba'ath Party, did not embrace Soviet-style socialism, but tried to use the Cold War confrontation between the USSR and the United States to their advantage during the 1960s (this changed, however, in the 1970s when Iraq and the Soviet Union signed a major treaty).

Official Soviet documents show restrained enthusiasm concerning the prospect of the Soviet Union playing a leading role in decolonized countries. Take the 22nd Party Congress in October 1961, seven months after the failed US-led Bay of Pigs invasion

138   *Narratives, Nations, and Other World Products*

of Cuba and two after the East German comrades had built a wall to separate their country from the capitalist Federal Republic of Germany. It was a truly magnificent event in that scores of delegates from newly decolonized countries participated in the congress. In his report to the congress, Khrushchev explained to the delegates the main change in the relationships between the 'socialist world', the 'capitalist world' and the newly created countries.

> The imperialist countries have lost their past monopoly on the supply of means of production to the non-socialist world market, and in the realm of credit, loan and technical services. The peoples of Asia and Africa, who liberated themselves from the colonial foreign yoke, look with increasing frequency at the socialist countries, adopt their experience in organizing selected branches of economic and social life. They look at the world socialist system for intercession and support in their struggle against the infringements of colonizers upon their freedom and independence.[57]

Central Asian elites were proud of the level of prosperity attained in their republics. They compared favourably with their neighbours in terms of both national rights and economic development: Kazakhs and Uighurs were oppressed in Chinese Xinjiang, while the populations of Pakistan, Afghanistan and Iran lived through political upheavals, wars and underdevelopment.[58] This was not only Central Asian self-perception, but a view shared by Western economists.[59]

Mukhitdinov held a major conference on Orientalism in July 1957 in Tashkent. Delegates came from Soviet republics as well as from China, North Korea, Vietnam and the Warsaw Pact countries.[60] In his opening speech, Mukhitdinov insisted that the USSR should shift its focus from Europe to Asia if it was to make full use of decolonization. He linked Soviet international policy towards the 'foreign East' to Soviet nationality policy towards the 'inner East'. His roles as a negotiator and leader of the Uzbek republic were two sides of the same coin. He was convinced that with decolonization Soviet nationality policy would move from being an inner-Soviet question to a global one. He welcomed Nehru to Tashkent, negotiated with Nasser, met with Ho Chi Minh in Hanoi. At the same time, at the turn of the 1960s, he fought against the recentralizing and russifying tendencies of some in the Soviet leadership, especially Chief Ideologist Mikhail Suslov, who spoke of a 'fusion' of Soviet nationalities, a notion intolerable for many republic leaders eager to protect their national cultures. The backlash from Suslov and others led to the fall of Mukhitdinov in 1961 from his position as Presidium member and Uzbek first secretary. In 1968, Brezhnev made him ambassador to Syria, the most important partner of the USSR in the Middle East. Thus Mukhitdinov remained an important asset in Soviet policy towards the Muslim world.[61]

A Conference of Writers from Africa and Asia, held by SKSSAA in Tashkent in 1958, was a central event of the 'decolonization of the mind'. This 'literary Bandung', opened by a speech from Khrushchev, marked a spectacular rapprochement of the Soviet Union with the cultural elites of recently and yet to be decolonized countries.[62] The Tashkent Conference jump-started the acquaintance of the Soviet public with literature that was almost entirely unknown to them. Soviet delegates encountered suspicion and had trouble understanding the call of African delegates for *négritude* and pan-Africanism.[63]

Supporting the Orientalist institutes in the republics, Gafurov wrote: 'Yes, we have [our own] national questions that await solutions, but a more pressing problem that cannot be put off is the development of the countries and peoples of Asia and Africa.'[64] In 1958, Friendship Societies were created in almost all the republics to address specific countries. The soft power efforts of the Friendship Societies of the republics of Central Asia were to focus on China, India, Mongolia and Arab countries.[65]

Latin American visitors to Central Asia were impressed by what they saw. In 1969, at a conference in Frunze, the capital or Kyrghyzstan, representatives from Bolivia, Chile, Panama and Venezuela reflected on how similar the settings were in their own countries to the post-revolutionary Kazakhstan.[66] Argentinian Communist leader Rodolfo Ghioldi, Dominican singer Efrain Morel and Peruvian poet Gustavo Valcarcel underlined in their books on their Soviet experience how they saw the Soviet modernization of Kazakhstan as a model for Latin America.[67]

Closing global opportunities

The special moment when the Central Asian elites were agents of global socialist interconnections came to a close towards the end of the 1970s: military conflicts, especially the Soviet intervention in Afghanistan, the persistence of economic inequalities against the background of growing economic difficulties and cultural alienation of national minorities weakened both the capacity of the Soviet Union to carry out a decolonizing policy, and the agency of Central Asian intermediaries within Soviet federalism and the international influence of the USSR.

The conflict with China had ambivalent consequences for Soviet Central Asia's global forays. Behind the personal and ideological feud of Khrushchev and Mao – the immediate cause of the Sino-Soviet split – lay a profound strategic opposition between the two communist empires for hegemony in the socialist movement and over regions which straddled their border.[68] Central Asia lay 'at the epicenter' of the conflict, split as it is between the five Soviet republics and Xinjiang to the East, which is under China's control.[69] Mao kept complaining that Stalin had annexed Xinjiang to the Soviet 'sphere of influence' and handled it as a 'semi-colony'.[70] Soviet Kazakhstan and Chinese Xinjiang shared some 1,800 kilometres of border. The Soviet assistance programme in China saw many experts from Central Asia working in Xinjiang. In 1961, the Soviet leadership cancelled its assistance programme and withdrew its experts. During the disastrous 'Great Leap Forward' many Kazakhs and Uighurs left Xinjiang to look for shelter in Soviet Kazakhstan. In 1962, the USSR closed its border to China.

The military significance of Central Asia rose dramatically. The Chinese detonated their first atomic bomb in 1964. Atomic tests were held on each side of the Sino-Soviet Central Asian border: on the western side lay the main Soviet nuclear test range near the city of Semipalatinsk of Eastern Kazakhstan, while the Chinese tested their bombs at Lop Nor in eastern Xinjiang.[71] Chinese and Soviet forces clashed on the Amur River in the Far East in March 1969, and once again at the Kazakh border on 13 August 1969.[72] If anything, however, the conflict impelled the Soviet leadership to demonstrate that China could not pretend to the role that Mao wanted for his country, that of sole leader of the international socialist movement. The Chinese leadership attacked the Soviet Union for its 'revisionism' and 'conciliatory stance' towards the capitalists. They claimed that only China could lead socialist international solidarity. In response, Soviet engagement with the Third World increased in the 1970s. In particular, the Brezhnev government built a 'coherent and powerful Islamic strategy' in which Muslims from Central Asia played a leading part.[73]

This policy came to an end when the Soviet government decided to intervene in Afghanistan to support the government, their ally. The republics of Central Asia were at the forefront of the war. Afghanistan shares a border with Turkmenistan, Uzbekistan and Tajikistan. Soviet troops included many Central Asian recruits. Ethnically and linguistically there is much in common between the three republics and Afghanistan, which explained why, even before the Soviet intervention, Central Asian experts acted as translators and advisors to the socialist government of Afghanistan.[74] However, the intervention severely damaged the USSR's policy towards the Muslim world, when several regional powers and Cold War foes – Iran, Pakistan, Saudi Arabia, the United States and China – supported the anti-government mujahedin rebellion in Afghanistan. The recourse to military intervention in Afghanistan was tantamount to a recognition that the revolutionary wave envisioned by Khrushchev had been broken.[75]

In parallel to the hardening of the USSR's international stance, the economic situation in the Soviet bloc began degrading in the second half of the 1970s. Consequently, the Soviet government sought more pragmatic economic relationships with Third World countries. Most of the enthusiasm of the 1960s for development aid and international socialist friendship had gone by the next decade.[76] Central Asia ceased to play the positive role of lighthouse of socialist development and concord towards the East.

In the fields of economics, culture and federalism, the promises of destalinization did not come to full fruition. The traditional conflict between, on the one hand, the division of labour and specialization at the scale of an immense and diverse Soviet territory, and, on the other, economic diversification in each republic continued to be resolved at the expense of the republics. Specialization even increased with efforts to organize in one economic interdependent system not only the Soviet Union, but also its Western neighbours, as well, in the Comecon. Seen from Moscow it made sense for the good of the Soviet economy to process cotton in Central Russia and Ukraine that had a long history of textile industry, and not in Central Asia, but it was detrimental to the industrial development of the cotton-growing republics. Against this tendency, Central Asian economists argued for the industrialization of their republics, like leading Tajik economist Ibadullo Narzikullov. They saw the growing population of Central Asian republics as a resource for building and operating new plants, whereas Moscow planners imagined using the large Central Asian labour force for industrial development in Siberia.[77]

The promise of industrialization did not materialize, for reasons that pertain both to the economic policies of Moscow and to the life choices of Central Asia's inhabitants who preferred to remain in the countryside. Russian ethnographers analysed this reluctance to join the industrial workforce as a sign of enduring backwardness and a cultural difference that could not be bridged.[78] Central Asia appeared to many economists and sociologists to be non-transformable, non-assimilable in the Soviet mould: in Central Asia, the rural population did not move easily to the cities and industrial centres, slowing social transformation and depriving industry of the necessary workforce. Cities remained to a great extent Russian: 41 per cent of the population of Tashkent, the fourth most populated city in the USSR, was Uzbek, and 45 per cent was European.[79] Although Central Asia's population expanded considerably, it remained predominantly rural.

For many Central Asians, the specialization of their republics in raw materials from the agricultural sectors – wheat and cotton – proved that the central powers did not take the point of view of the inhabitants seriously. The trade resembled an unequal exchange worthy of the postcolonial world: the cotton-growers had to raise production from year to year on Moscow's orders, but they got less and less in exchange, and the gap in standard of living with the western regions of the USSR kept widening. The 'cotton affair' brought the unequal exchange to light: the leadership of the cotton-growing republics had falsified cotton production data submitted to the centre. The result was that Moscow repressed the corrupt leadership in the republics and sent in many Russians, curtailing indigenization, and validating the disastrous notion that corruption was 'Eastern' and could only be contained by Europeans.[80]

In Central Asia, contrary to the western republics, the vernacular languages lost ground to Russian. Russian was seen by the Central Asian elites as their language of communication. All social promotion implied moving from one's native language to Russian. The promise of language emancipation made at the beginning of the Soviet Union was not kept. Languages other than Russian retained only local significance.[81] The policy of Khrushchev and Brezhnev reinforced the trend towards Russification. Khrushchev's school reform allowed non-Russian families to send their children to Russian schools. And under Brezhnev the weight of Russian in teaching the curriculum was considerably reinforced.[82] Higher education was carried out in Russian in Central Asia. In contrast, in Lithuania, indigenization was almost complete under Brezhnev: more than 85 per cent of scientific personnel were Lithuanian and 90 per cent of the curriculum at Vilnius University was delivered in Lithuanian.[83] Thus, in both economic and cultural terms, Central Asia looked neglected and retarded in comparison with the European republics.

The history of Central Asian nations was not entirely decolonized. It remained based on a neo-imperial assumption that the Russian Empire was a benevolent and peaceful force of progress that benefitted all nations that came under its rule. Tajiks, Turkmens and the other peoples of Central Asia were required to accept that their nations had voluntarily entered the Russian Empire.[84]

Conclusion

Forty years after imagining hosting the Winter Olympics, independent Kazakhstan revived the Olympic dream. Almaty, still the major city of independent Kazakhstan, but not its capital anymore, applied for the 2022 Winter Olympics. In 2015, the city made it to the last round, but lost to Beijing. The dream came closer to realization than ever before.

The five republics of Soviet Central Asia became independent in 1991, although a majority of their inhabitants would have preferred to retain a federal structure uniting them to Russia.[85] One of the reasons for this attachment is that the Soviet Union was their vehicle for navigating the world. During the course of twenty years, the nations of Central Asia had thought of themselves as models for the decolonizing world. Emancipated by the Soviet nationality policy reinvigorated after Stalin, the nations of former Turkestan entered a mutually profitable relationship with Moscow, in which their elites were cultural, economic and religious ambassadors for the interests of the Soviet Union abroad, and national leaders of their republics with growing powers.

The change of scale in opportunities – from the fearful execution of Moscow's orders under Stalin to negotiations with leaders of the Third World – led Central Asian elites to believe that they could change the economic arrangement within the union. Industry would bring prosperity and equality with the better-off regions of the union. In their understanding, the industrialization and nationalization of their republics within the Soviet Union were linked to decolonization abroad and the role that they believed Soviet socialism could play in Third World nations' access to modernity. This global moment in which decolonizations inside and outside the Soviet Union were connected ended when the Soviet government renounced the transformative appeal of socialism in the Third World and socio-economic stratification among the Soviet republics solidified instead of diminishing.

A decade later, a new global moment carried off the union: a third decolonization wave tore apart Moscow and the Western and Caucasian republics in 1989–91, at the same time as the fall of multi-ethnic states like Yugoslavia and Czechoslovakia. This time round, it was not the languages of socialism and development that could frame the process. The global horizon was integration into the European Union, NATO and neo-liberalism. Central Asia remained at the periphery of this global trend and under the political, economic, military and cultural influence of Moscow.

Since Russia's full-scale invasion of Ukraine in February 2022, a new era has begun for the five countries, an uncertain and dangerous one: there is the opportunity to further emancipate from Moscow, but at the cost of key economic relations. It is unclear what global frameworks these countries could strive to integrate beyond the Chinese 'Belt and Road Initiative' of transport infrastructure development.

Notes

1   Marc Elie, 'Governing by Hazard: Controlling Mudslides and Promoting Tourism in the Mountains above Alma-Ata (Kazakhstan), 1966–1977', in *Governing Disasters: Beyond Risk Culture*, ed. Sandrine Revet and Julien Langumier (New York: Palgrave Macmillan, 2015), 23–58.
2   On development as ideology and practice in Central Asia the standard work is Artemy M. Kalinovsky, *Laboratory of Socialist Development: Cold War Politics and Decolonization in Soviet Tajikistan* (Ithaca: Cornell University Press, 2018).

3 Kalinovsky, *Laboratory of Socialist Development*.
4 Among the pioneering works: Constantin Katsakioris, 'L'union soviétique et les intellectuels africains', *Cahiers du monde russe* 47, no. 47/1–2 (2006): 15–32; Moritz Deutschmann, *Die zentralasiatischen Sowjetrepubliken und die sowjetische Außenpolitik in der Dritten Welt während der Entstalinisierung: Vom 'eigenen' zum 'ausländischen' Orient* (GRIN Verlag, 2010); Masha Kirasirova, '"Sons of Muslims" in Moscow: Soviet Central Asian Mediators to the Foreign East, 1955–1962', *Ab Imperio*, no. 4 (2011): 106–32.
5 Kalinovsky, 'Not Some British Colony in Africa: The Politics of Decolonization and Modernization in Soviet Central Asia, 1955–1964', *Ab Imperio* 2013, no. 2 (2013): 191–222; Constantin Katsakioris, 'The Soviet-South Encounter: Tensions in the Friendship with Afro-Asian Partners, 1945–1965', in *Cold War Crossings: International Travel and Exchange across the Soviet Bloc, 1940s–1960s*, ed. Babiracki, Patryk and Zimmer, Kenyon (College Station: Texas A&M University Press, 2014), 134–65; Moritz Florin, *Kirgistan und die sowjetische Moderne: 1941–1991* (Göttingen: Vandenhoeck & Ruprecht Verlag, 2015); Steffi Marung, 'A "Leninian Moment"? Soviet Africanists and the Interpretation of the October Revolution, 1950s–1970s', *Journal Für Entwicklungspolitik* 33, no. 3 (2017): 21–48; Tobias Rupprecht, *Soviet Internationalism after Stalin: Interaction and Exchange between the USSR and Latin America during the Cold War* (Cambridge: Cambridge University Press, 2017); Kalinovsky, *Laboratory of Socialist Development*; James Mark, Kalinovsky and Steffi Marung, eds., *Alternative Globalizations: Eastern Europe and the Postcolonial World* (Bloomington: Indiana University Press, 2020); James Mark and Paul Betts, eds., *Socialism Goes Global: The Soviet Union and Eastern Europe in the Age of Decolonisation* (New York: Oxford University Press, 2022).
6 Deutschmann, *Die zentralasiatischen Sowjetrepubliken*; Kirasirova, '"Sons of Muslims" in Moscow'; Kalinovsky, *Laboratory of Socialist Development*.
7 Oscar Sanchez-Sibony, *Red Globalization: The Political Economy of the Soviet Cold War from Stalin to Khrushchev* (New York: Cambridge University Press, 2014); Mark, Kalinovsky and Marung, eds., 'Introduction', in *Alternative Globalizations*, 1–31.
8 Michael David-Fox, 'Multiple Modernities vs. Neo-Traditionalism: On Recent Debates in Russian and Soviet History', *Jahrbücher für Geschichte Osteuropas* 54, no. 4 (2006): 535–55.
9 Kalinovsky, *Laboratory of Socialist Development*.
10 Richard Pipes, *The Formation of the Soviet Union: Communism and Nationalism, 1917–1923*, 2nd Revised edition (Cambridge: Harvard University Press, 1997).
11 Francine Hirsch, *Empire of Nations: Ethnographic Knowledge and the Making of the Soviet Union* (Ithaca: Cornell University Press, 2005).
12 Terry Martin, *The Affirmative Action Empire: Nations and Nationalism in the Soviet Union, 1923–1939* (Ithaca: Cornell University Press, 2001).
13 Adeeb Khalid, *The Politics of Muslim Cultural Reform: Jadidism in Central Asia* (Berkeley: University of California Press, 1998).
14 Isabelle Ohayon, 'Chapitre 2. Gouverner La Diversité. La Question Nationale', in Alain Blum, Françoise Daucé, Mare Elie and Ohayon, *L'âge Soviétique. Une Traversée de l'Empire Russe Au Monde Post-Soviétique* (Paris: Armand Colin, 2021), 72.
15 Khalid, *Central Asia: A New History From the Imperial Conquests to the Present* (Princeton: Princeton University Press, 2021), 178; Niccolò Pianciola, 'Décoloniser l'Asie centrale ? Bolcheviks et colons au Semireč'e (1920–1922)', *Cahiers du monde russe* 49, no. 1 (2008): 101–44.

16 Khalid, *Central Asia*, 149.

17 Hirsch, *Empire of Nations*, 160–5.

18 Khalid, *Central Asia*, 172.

19 Masha Kirasirova, 'The "East" as a Category of Bolshevik Ideology and Comintern Administration: The Arab Section of the Communist University of the Toilers of the East', *Kritika: Explorations in Russian and Eurasian History* 18, no. 1 (2017): 7–34. Lenin is quoted by Kirasirova.

20 Quoted by Khalid, *Central Asia*, 172.

21 Kirasirova, 'The "East"'.

22 Ohayon, 'Chapitre 2', 72–3.

23 Ohayon, *La sédentarisation des Kazakhs dans l'URSS de Staline: collectivisation et changement social (1928-1945)* (Paris: Maisonneuve et Larose, 2006).

24 Khalid, *Central Asia*, 308.

25 Florin, *Kirgistan*, 74–81.

26 Martin, *Affirmative Action Empire*, 451–60.

27 Christian Teichmann, *Macht der Unordnung: Stalins Herrschaft in Zentralasien 1920-1950* (Hamburg: Hamburger Edition, 2016).

28 Chris Miller, *We Shall Be Masters: Russian Pivots to East Asia from Peter the Great to Putin* (Cambridge: Harvard University Press, 2021), 217–18.

29 Miller, *We Shall Be Masters*, 219.

30 Kirasirova, '"Sons of Muslims" in Moscow', 112–13.

31 Katsakioris, 'L'union soviétique et les intellectuels africains', 18.

32 Khalid, *Central Asia*, 381.

33 Quoted by Kirasirova, ' "Sons of Muslims" in Moscow', 116.

34 Kirasirova, '"Sons of Muslims" in Moscow'.

35 Odd Arne Westad, *The Global Cold War: Third World Interventions and the Making of Our Times* (Cambridge; New York: Cambridge University Press, 2007), 4–5.

36 Elie, 'Governing by Hazard'.

37 Deutschmann, *Die zentralasiatischen Sowjetrepubliken*, 72.

38 Khalid, *Central Asia*, 317.

39 Elie, 'Coping With the "Black Dragon". Mudflow Hazard and the Controversy over the Medeo Dam in Kazakhstan, 1958-1966', *Kritika: Explorations in Russian and Eurasian History* 14, no. 2 (2013): 313–42.

40 Tetsuro Chida, '"Nationalizing" the Soviet Republics: Centrifugal Tendency of the Republican Politics in Soviet Central Asia during the Brezhnev Era', in *The Caucasus and Central Asia, Twenty Years after Independences: Questioning the Notion of 'South Countries.'* Conference Proceedings (Almaty, 2011), 26–30.

41 Susanne Schattenberg, *Brezhnev: The Making of a Statesman* (London; New York: I.B. Tauris, Bloomsbury Publishing, 2021).

42 Kalinovsky, 'The Cold War in South and Central Asia', in *The Routledge Handbook of the Cold War*, ed. Kalinovsky and Craig Daigle (Abingdon, Oxon; New York: Routledge, 2014), 180.

43 Elie, 'Coping With the "Black Dragon"'.

44 Elie, 'Governing by Hazard', 48–9.

45 Kalinovsky, 'A Most Beautiful City for the World's Tallest Dam: Internationalism, Social Welfare, and Urban Utopia in Nurek', *Cahiers Du Monde Russe* 57, no. 4 (2016): 819–46; Julia Obertreis, *Imperial Desert Dreams: Cotton Growing and Irrigation in Central Asia, 1860-1991* (Göttingen: V&R unipress, 2017).

46 Kirasirova, '"Sons of Muslims" in Moscow', 114.

Lighthouse of Socialism for the Decolonized World   145

47   Deutschmann, *Die zentralasiatischen Sowjetrepubliken*, 68.
48   Alexandre Bennigsen, *Soviet Strategy and Islam* (New York: St. Martin's Press, 1989), 30.
49   Bennigsen, *Soviet Strategy and Islam*, 30.
50   Bennigsen, *Soviet Strategy and Islam*, 31; Philipp Casula, 'The Soviet Afro-Asian Solidarity Committee and Soviet Perceptions of the Middle East during Late Socialism', *Cahiers Du Monde Russe* 59, no. 4 (2018): 499–520.
51   Kirasirova, '"Sons of Muslims" in Moscow', 115.
52   Ibid., 119.
53   Khalid, *Central Asia*, 344.
54   Bennigsen, *Soviet Strategy and Islam*, 55.
55   Andrey Fursenko, ed., *Prezidium TsK KPSS. 1954–1964. Chernovye Protokol'nye Zapiski Zasedaniy. Stenogrammy. Postanovleniya*, vol. 3. Postanovleniya. 1959–1964 (Moskva: ROSSPEN, 2008), 840; partly quoted by Kirasirova, ' "Sons of Muslims" in Moscow', 128–9.
56   Sanchez-Sibony, *Red Globalization*, 11.
57   *22nd Congress of the Communist Party of the Soviet Union. 17–31 October 1961. Verbatim report*, Gosizdat, 1962, vol. 1, p. 22.
58   Florin, *Kirgistan*; Khalid, *Central Asia*, 304.
59   Kalinovsky, *Laboratory of Socialist Development*, fn. 25.
60   Kirasirova, '"Sons of Muslims" in Moscow', 118.
61   Deutschmann, *Die zentralasiatischen Sowjetrepubliken*, 73.
62   Katsakioris, 'L'union soviétique et les intellectuels africains', 20–1.
63   Ibid.
64   Kirasirova, '"Sons of Muslims" in Moscow', 120.
65   Ibid., 122.
66   Rupprecht, *Soviet Internationalism*, 65.
67   Ibid., 65.
68   Jeremy Friedman, *Shadow Cold War. The Sino-Soviet Competition for the Third World* (Chapel Hill: The University of North Carolina Press, 2015).
69   Khalid, *Central Asia*, 378.
70   Miller, *We Shall Be Masters*, 226–7.
71   Khalid, *Central Asia*, 379.
72   Radchenko, Sergey, 'The Sino-Soviet Split', in *The Cambridge History of the Cold War. 2 Crises and Détente*, ed. Melvyn P. Leffler and Odd Arne Westad (Cambridge: Cambridge University Press, 2010), 367.
73   Bennigsen, *Soviet Strategy and Islam*, 55.
74   Khalid, *Central Asia*, 391.
75   Miller, *We Shall Be Masters*, 235.
76   Mark, Kalinovsky and Marung, 'Introduction'.
77   Kalinovsky, *Laboratory of Socialist Development*, 69–73.
78   Ibid., 5–6; Khalid, *Central Asia*, 402.
79   Khalid, *Central Asia*, 345.
80   Riccardo Mario Cucciolla, 'Legitimation through Self-Victimization. The Uzbek Cotton Affair and Its Repression Narrative (1989–1991)', *Cahiers Du Monde Russe* 58, no. 58/4 (2017): 639–68.
81   Florin, *Kirgistan*, 182–3.
82   Malte Rolf, 'Die Nationalisierung der Sowjetunion. Indigenisierungspolitik, nationale Kader und die Entstehung von Dissens in der Litauischen Sowjetrepublik der Ära

Brežnev', in *Goldenes Zeitalter der Stagnation ? Perspektiven auf die sowjetische Ordnung der Brežnev-Zeit*, ed. Boris Belge and Martin Deuerlein (Tübingen: Mohr Siebeck, 2014), 212.

83 Rolf, 'Die Nationalisierung der Sowjetunion'.

84 Florin, *Kirgistan*, 83.

85 Henry E. Hale, 'Cause without a Rebel: Kazakhstan's Unionist Nationalism in the USSR and CIS', *Nationalities Papers* 37, no. 1 (2009): 1–32.

8

The boomerang of imperial sovereignty: Bosnia and Herzegovina in the eye of the world storm

Natasha Wheatley

The portent of marginality

In one of the set pieces of popular modern history, Gravilo Princip assassinates a Habsburg Archduke, Franz Ferdinand, in Sarajevo in June 1914 and unwittingly sparks the First World War. The easternmost peripheries of the Habsburg Empire here come soaked in a kind of aestheticized obscurity, heightening the historical drama: there on the streets of the Bosnian city, in the abstruse borderlands of an already abstruse empire, lay some half-invisible loose thread that, when tugged, could pull right through the cloth of the world of states, bringing it all apart. Bosnia and Herzegovina thereby surfaces in the book of world history as a sore pressure point along what Hessel Duncan Hall memorably called the 'international frontier'.[1]

In his idiosyncratic 1948 monograph, the former member of the League secretariat described this frontier as 'the main line of structural weakness in the earth's political crust'. It was the zone where the great powers' interests and spheres of influence rubbed up against each another and overlapped. The main 'crises and eruptions of world politics' occurred not in metropolitan centres where hegemony was clear: they broke out in the volatile borderlands between regional hegemonies, just as 'a volcano is a local vent for widespread pressures in the molten depths of the earth's crust'. This frontier produced tension and conflict but also the need to compromise: the powers were 'constantly at work on the frontier trying to patch up the peace by international agreements of various kinds', which led to a range of different 'international territorial regimes'. This optic allowed Hall to group together a wild variety of seemingly disparate quasi-sovereignties from all over the globe – including protectorates, condominiums, demilitarized zones, minorities treaties, mandates and extraterritorial concessions – as 'phenomena of the international frontier'.[2]

Though the story might not appear in the same schoolbooks, Bosnia and Herzegovina's zoning along the fiery ridge of that frontier in fact emerged well before 1914. It reaches back to the twilight hour of Ottoman rule in Europe, when, in 1875, rebellious Christian Herzegovinian peasants revolted against their Muslim landlords and drew Ottoman troops into a messy guerrilla war that quickly spread throughout

148   *Narratives, Nations, and Other World Products*

Bosnia. As refugees spooled out over the region and Serbia and Montenegro announced their support for the uprising, the precarious balance of Russian and Habsburg interests in the area – long steadied, however artificially, by the sovereign integrity of the Ottoman empire – threatened to turn the great 'Eastern Question' into a great eastern war. After Russia went to war with Turkey and the resulting peace treaty of San Stefano (with its swollen Slav states) horrified everyone else, the great powers assembled in Berlin under Bismarck's watchful eye in the summer of 1878 to thrash out a new territorial settlement for the Balkans. Austria-Hungary walked away from the Congress of Berlin with a curious prize: an international mandate, enshrined in the Treaty of Berlin itself, to 'occupy and administer' Bosnia and Herzegovina. Formally, the provinces would remain under Ottoman sovereignty; though the 70,000 Austro-Hungarian troops who marched into the territory two weeks later did not, of course, tread any lighter for this nominal qualification.

According to many, the Habsburg empire thereby acquired its first 'colony'. Nineteenth-century commentators, like historians today, saw this moment as Austria-Hungary's entry into the world of late nineteenth-century *Kolonialpolitik* – into the vast, accelerating, hemispheric game of empire. We can understand the occupation of Bosnia and Herzegovina as part of that global story along a number of different axes. An older historiography presented it as quintessential diplomatic history: though not hamstrung by the vice of a narrow national frame (indeed, Bosnia and Herzegovina and the 'south Slav question', which spanned Slavic populations inside the empire and beyond it, illustrated why Habsburg domestic policy could not be separated from foreign policy), this literature concentrated on the machinations of a small cohort of aristocratic men directing the foreign offices of the Great (European) Powers. Predictably enough, historians have since grown sensitive to the cultural and discursive register of the Habsburg turn eastwards: its ambitions in Italy and Germany thwarted; the Habsburg state embraced a new self-understanding as civilizer of a backward east.[3] Officials spoke of civilizing missions and remedies for underdevelopment, of making order and keeping peace, clearly echoing the languages of legitimacy pedalled by European imperialists the world over.[4] Indeed, Austro-Hungary's emphasis on the inability of the Turkish state to preserve order and security, especially for its Christian inhabitants, also ties the occupation to the empire-soaked history of humanitarianism,[5] and further to the logic of today's neo-colonial 'Responsibility to Protect' doctrine, which prioritizes the factual capacity of the state over formal legitimacy and sovereignty.[6]

This archive of civilizational rhetoric has proved too tempting for some: today it offers the raw material for scholars seeking the methodological de-provincialization, even decolonization, of Habsburg history through the application of postcolonial theory. They focus on literary texts and other cultural objects that depict uncouth Slav 'others' awaiting enlightenment, wastelands awaiting development, pre-modern chaos awaiting rational order.[7] While historians like Pieter Judson remain understandably sceptical that the Habsburg Monarchy can be meaningfully interpreted as an empire in the same sense as the British or French versions,[8] even proponents of this new 'postcolonial' approach concede that it must rely heavily on the example of Bosnia and Herzegovina. It was the 'only territory within the Austro-Hungarian Monarchy', writes scholar Clemens Ruthner, 'that could be approached through the paradigm of

The Boomerang of Imperial Sovereignty 149

colonialism not only in a figurative sense'.[9] This is a large interpretive burden for two little lands. This volatile spot on the earth's crust thus marks out a volatile spot in our historiographical frontiers, too – a small piece of high imperialism beached on the European mainland, and a small European outpost for postcolonialism.

It is precisely this liminal status – as a colony 'at home', a domestic or 'internal' colony – that, I suggest, contains a different sort of global history. Rather than situate Bosnia and Herzegovina in the imperial world via postcolonial readings of culture, this chapter takes up their place in a world of empires instead through the stories of sovereignty they provoked.[10] These stories were multidirectional and capture the articulation of sovereign selfhood as an inter- and intra-imperial conversation.[11] The territories proved an inflection point for larger questions of state and sovereignty because they placed so much pressure on the borderline between the 'inside' and 'outside' of the state, revealing the production of both selves and categories as an international process.

The occupation was in fact symptomatic (and in some senses prophetic) of a set of imperial legal techniques that spread like wildfire around the world in the 1870s, 1880s and 1890s. As Europeans scrambled for Africa – and not only Africa – they exported European sovereignty in pieces: they played out a set of instrumental experiments in dividing and rearranging its component parts, thereby spawning new strains of semi-sovereignty. Different names and designations for half-standing proliferated in this global process of naming the units of world order. 'Protectorates' abounded. By ostensibly cleaving off 'external' sovereignty from internal autonomy, these forms of incomplete, flexible legal title generally allowed European powers to extract the desired advantages without shouldering the full cost of administration that would accompany formal annexation.[12] In this transcontinental 'marketplace of sovereignty', 'private' actors and 'public' prerogatives bed-swapped promiscuously; 'rogue empires' were hard to tell apart from their more official cousins.[13] At the same time, and alongside the simultaneous (and co-implicated) professionalization of international law,[14] the protagonists grew increasingly attentive to questions of international legitimacy. Dubious acquisitions like King Leopold's Congo territories were famously laundered 'legitimate' at the Berlin Conference of 1884–5, when Bismarck again played host, this time to sanction a cabinet of African quasi-sovereignties rather than those (like Bosnia and Herzegovina, Cyprus, and Egypt) already dotted along the fraying edges of the Ottoman state.[15]

These intertwined processes – imperial expansion through parcelled sovereignty; a newly professionalized, theoretical attention to sovereignty (including obsessive attempts to catalogue its myriad possible mutations); and practices of international legitimacy – tie Bosnia and Herzegovina into a global legal story that stretches from the Balkans to Borneo. The legal issues sparked by Austria-Hungary's occupation of Bosnia and Herzegovina were legion. Did the territories lie inside the state, as a component part of its constitutional order, or were they located legally somewhere 'else'? Neither option enabled a legally coherent account of the sovereign standing of the territories. Scant clarity was won when the empire formally annexed the provinces in 1908; in what reads like a scene from Robert Musil's *The Man without Qualities*, a parliamentary committee was still earnestly at work on the conundrums associated with the legal status of the provinces when the First World War broke out.[16]

150   *Narratives, Nations, and Other World Products*

But this process was not simply outward facing, comprising the European conjuring of its inferior others. The case of Bosnia and Herzegovina shows with picturesque clarity how these stories of sovereignty were 'double-faced', or really, double-edged. The ambiguous status of the Balkan territories in fact ricocheted back to Vienna, with dramatic results. These modest territorial acquisitions at the external periphery of the empire washed back unexpectedly as 'domestic' constitutional crises, rocking the foundations of the Habsburg state. Processes of making sovereignty abroad thus bled into processes of making it at home: legal narratives that made sense of transformations in the far-flung imperial world tangled reflexively into legal stories of self.[17] In exploring that loop, I frame law as a genre of narrative. When law assigned categories like 'quasi-sovereignty' or 'colony' or 'constitutional', it demarcated the line between Us and Outside-of-Us, folded individual instances into a broader patterns and sequences, provided context, suggested implications and generated meaning. In naming and arranging things, it made them legible.[18] Through the language of the law we can see Bosnia and Herzegovina as a pivot point where narratives of state-making and worldmaking collide.

In tracing what we might call the boomerang of imperial sovereignty, I thus float Bosnia and Herzegovina as a kind of exchange house or percolation device for historical scales. It functions not only as a valve that allows us to move up and down the scalar ladder between borderland, colony, state, empire, region and globe, but as heuristic device for exploring the reciprocal transformation of those scales, something akin to what Cyrus Schayegh has recently termed 'transpatialization'.[19] When the legal status of the borderland-colony Bosnia and Herzegovina emerged as a thorny conundrum, it had the effect of throwing up and 'back' a set of foundational questions about the nature of the state that 'possessed' it – and indeed about the nature of statehood *tout court* – forcing the reconceptualization of a series of relations inside the empire. In exploring how these spaces worked upon each other, I take global history's interest in the co-implication of scales[20] not only as a rubric for (our own) historical analysis, but also as a question in and for the history of legal knowledge: namely, a history of law's own naming of scales, of the permeability and mobility of its own scalar and scaling categories. Law has an indigenous, often formalized set of scales – they are inherent in the logic of jurisdiction itself: chains of norms or prerogatives that (in theory) cascade sequentially, in strings of derived authority. The story of Bosnia and Herzegovina's occupation allows us to watch law's names – things like 'colonial', 'sovereign', 'constitutional', 'international' and the 'state' – move vertically (through scales) and horizontally (across space) in an unsettled application to the world. That is, we can open up a history of law's conceptual navigation of scale – its own disciplinary practices of world ordering.

Jurisdictional scaling: Where does one state end, and another begin? Where does one state end, and 'the international' begin?

After the Berlin Treaty gave Austria-Hungary an international mandate to 'occupy and administer' Bosnia and Herzegovina, it quickly incorporated the provinces into its customs domain and introduced military service, alongside other classical markers of state power over territory and population. At the same time, the Treaty had explicitly preserved the Sultan's sovereignty. What, then, was the relationship between the Habsburg state and the Balkan territories? Did the relationship exist in international or in imperial constitutional law? That is, in which of law's jurisdictional scales should the territory be shelved? Any determination required answers to further fraught questions, including: how 'real' was this reserved Turkish sovereignty? (The realer Turkish sovereignty, of course, the less likely the territories could be swallowed into the Habsburg constitutional order.) To answer *this* question, jurists had to decide whether to prioritize the letter of the law or the cold 'reality' of Austro-Hungarian control, and *this* in turn seemingly forced them into a legal-philosophical position on the relationship between 'fact' and 'law' in general. Such questions about the relationship between factual rule and formal legal title became global features of legal debate in the age of high imperialism, where European powers often preferred to deny they possessed sovereignty *de jure* while wielding de facto control. Martti Koskenniemi's standard history of international law depicts it as a late, counterintuitive heyday for fictional sovereignty.[21]

Whether occupied Bosnia and Herzegovina was legally 'inside' (i.e. regulated by constitutional law) or 'outside', the Austro-Hungarian Empire coupled with the question of whether it was inside or outside the Ottoman one. Was it possible for the territories to be inside two states at once? Or *outside* them both at once? – suspended in a kind of stateless vortex? If Turkish sovereignty over the provinces seemed fictional to many, it was the prospect that the new Young Turk regime of 1908 might render it 'real' by summoning Bosnian delegates for the re-opened Ottoman parliament that spooked Austria-Hungary into formal annexation. Here the legal orders of the two neighbouring continental empires tangled together, in ways that speak to new scholarly interest not only in cross-imperial legal pluralism but in the shared space and shared history of the Habsburg and Ottoman domains.[22]

The Austrian jurist Joseph Ulbrich thus faced some delicate decisions when he sat to write the first textbook of Austrian constitutional law in the early 1880s. The constitutionalization of the empire between 1848 and 1867 had encouraged the inauguration of 'Austrian constitutional law' as a university subject: the legal and academic articulations evolved in tandem.[23] Tellingly, though, the nascent scholarly field lacked standard works or synthetic accounts. In this first attempt to render Habsburg imperial law into a systematic, logical whole, Ulbrich effectively portrayed Bosnia and Herzegovina as tied into all these jurisdictions at once – a jumble of jurisdictional scales, or the world in a province. He argued that the constitutional relationship between Bosnia and Herzegovina and the Ottoman empire had not been severed by Austria-Hungary's occupation and administration. True, 'this right of occupation and administration is not connected to any temporal limit; but it does not only satisfy the interests of the monarchy, but rather also those of the other contracting parties in the establishment of an ordered state of affairs in these lands to prevent threats to world peace'.[24] With the multilateral Berlin Treaty as the wellspring of right, the jurisdictional sweat of the other great powers was mixed into the compound. For that reason, it could not be a narrowly defined constitutional relationship to Austria-Hungary: 'The territories have more been taken over merely administratively [...] as a legal subject of international law'. In analyses like Ulbrich's, it was not simply that imperial constitutional law opened up porously to international law – as in many other imperial formations in this moment[25] – but that the curious arrangement in Bosnia and Herzegovina portended a novel sort of internationalized sovereignty. The Austrian legal scholar Georg Jellinek, who would become perhaps the most influential public law jurist of the German-speaking world by the turn of the century, emphasized this dimension, too. In Jellinek's argument, the 'intervention' possessed a comprehensive multilateral legitimacy in large part because 'anarchy' there threatened not only regional peace but world peace.[26] Some would later refer to it as a precedent for the (ostensibly) internationalized sovereignty of the mandate system administered by the League of Nations between the world wars.[27]

As against the occupied territories, Ulbrich continued, 'the two lands of Austria-Hungary are in and of themselves *abroad [Ausland]*'.[28] Yet the line demarcating legal foreignness was fuzzy: Ulbrich conceded that 'because Austro-Hungarian agencies are operative in the occupied lands, that removes the need for the particular protection of Austrian or Hungarian citizens, for example through consulates'.[29] At once foreign and de facto at home, imperial citizens in the occupied lands were like bits of the state's insides seeping over beyond its borders, or Bosnia and Herzegovina smuggled the great 'legal outside' under the umbrella of the state's domestic agencies – the empire's internal *Ausland*. This was a different but similarly suggestive version of the uncoupling of sovereignty, territory and citizen/subject increasingly found in the extraterritorial European consular jurisdictions in places like in China and Japan, where unequal treaties allowed Europeans to carry their home jurisdictions with them like luggage.[30]

Jurisdiction is law's way of registering and producing space: these various constructions capture Bosnia and Herzegovina as jurisdictional sorting house, absorbed into multiple legal-spatial scales at once: zoned partly inside the space-scale of the empire-state, partly in a cross-imperial legal space-scale where Habsburg and Ottoman jurisdictions co-mingled, and partly folded under the increasingly global jurisdiction of international law and the pooled authority of the Great Powers, experimenting with new forms of collective legal sanction: a tragi-comic portrait of making state territoriality in the age of high imperialism.

An adolescent science and the typological gaze: Bosnia and Herzegovina in the global legal picture

Sovereignty was the foundational concept of the young discipline of international law. As a cohort of jurists began describing themselves as international lawyers, founding professional associations and publishing textbooks, they needed to constitute not only a new discipline but also the world that it ostensibly governed. They set about coding the world map through the prism of their key concepts. Their efforts to classify the spectrum of existing political formations according to gradations of sovereignty produced global legal typologies that often grouped widely dispersed regions in unfamiliar ways. These typologies were legal narratives of a sort: they arranged the world according to a particular legal grammar and logic, offering ways to understand

The Boomerang of Imperial Sovereignty   153

new phenomena and establishing connections across time and place. They also threaded Bosnia and Herzegovina into global tableaux of quasi-sovereignties.

Bosnia and Herzegovina provoked a colourful search for legal names. It could be termed 'an occupation under the title of protectorate' – a '*pseudoprotektorat*'[31]; or a 'contractual occupation' – an occupation by contract[32]; or perhaps 'a unified particular administrative area' (*ein einheitliches besonderes Verwaltungsgebiet*) or an 'autonomous province'.[33] The chosen name established patterns and affinities between different world regions, producing geographies visible only through the slanted kaleidoscope of international law. The American scholar Charles Fenwick labelled Bosnia and Herzegovina an 'administered province', which meant it shared a category with Cyprus and Cuba.[34] The prominent French-German jurist Robert Redslob favoured 'dependent land', which bundled Bosnia-Herzegovina with Alsace-Lorraine, Finland and the British dominions of South Africa, Australia and Canada.[35] (Interestingly, these global legal maps of incomplete sovereignty did not conform to the strict separation of the European and non-European worlds ostensibly foundational to the historical development of international legal concepts.)[36] Franz von Liszt's fine-boned typology of territorial acquisition created an especially eclectic map. 'A disguised form of derivative acquisition', he wrote in his international law textbook, 'is the takeover of an area "for occupation and administration" under nominal continuation of the hitherto existing state authority (also, but very unhappily, described as "Condominium inégal")'.[37] In this bracket he grouped the Austro-Hungarian occupation of Bosnia and Herzegovina, the position of the United States in the territory of the Panama Canals, and various extraterritorialities like the treaty between England and the Congo state from 12 May 1894 and the Chinese treaty with Germany from 1898 about the cession of Kiautschou Bay.[38]

The wild profusion of mooted legal names illustrates the ungivenness of the world as a legal object. International law groped haphazardly towards ways of understanding and organizing an increasingly integrated global order. Practitioners of the new science sensed its youth. Georg Jellinek argued stridently that theory needed to respond to empirical realities: the foundational concepts of public law must be permanently re-evaluated as the world of states rolled onwards in endless transformation. Danger awaited if one attempted to grasp 'the life of the present with the categories of the past'.[39] A major weakness of current juridical thought, he wrote in 1896, lay in its insufficient conceptualization of an 'inbetween level' (*Zwischenstufe*) between the 'state', on the one hand, and the 'province', on the other. There are political formations, he argued, that are subordinated under a state government, but that have not entirely 'merged' with that state – 'that are in fact not states themselves, but present the rudiments of a state'. They had some of the irreducible properties or features of states while falling short of the category proper. He called them 'state fragments' (*Staatsfragmente*).[40] In his telling, Bosnia and Herzegovina fit his new category perfectly. It possessed two key features of statehood: its own territory (which was only its own) and own citizens (which belonged only to it) – markedly different to the situation in a federal state, say, where these things were shared. 'Both Turkish provinces are neither Austrian nor Hungarian state territory, their citizens have neither Austrian nor Hungarian citizenship'. And yet, they were not states.

154   *Narratives, Nations, and Other World Products*

In an 1892 analysis of the legal standing of Bosnia and Herzegovina, Hans Schneller grappled still more explicitly with the conceptual inadequacy of international legal knowledge. The occupation of Bosnia and Herzegovina – like that of Cyprus, Egypt and Tunis – was a subject of great political as well as academic controversy, he sighed. 'Scholarship stumbles over not insignificant difficulties in the attempt to register and to classify these newly-created, idiosyncratic relationships in an adequate way.'[41] In the diagnosis of the brilliant Austrian legal scholar Friedrich Tezner, intellectual problems surfaced with particular sharpness when form and content diverged. 'To this day, constitutional legal science has managed no satisfactory construction of the phenomenon of the severing of the essence of legal power from its appropriate form': 'One thinks of the contrast between the legal standing of the English parliament and the formal rights of the king, of the modern forms of *occupation* of Turkish territories under the preservation of the *sovereignty* of the sultan … One can only be humbly resigned in the face of creating a *terminology* for these relationships.'[42]

Law lacked the words. Cases like Bosnia and Herzegovina exposed its epistemological limitations. Modern legal methodology prided itself on a scientific, positivist approach founded upon source analysis rather than speculative natural or organic theories, wrote the Prague legal scholar Emil Lingg. But the official source materials for Bosnia and Herzegovina were so meagre, and so coy. Because the agreements spoke just of the takeover of administration, carefully avoided any definitive definitions, and were largely of a mere international law nature, scholarship had come to deny the existence of a constitutional relationship between Bosnia and Herzegovina and the Austro-Hungarian monarchy, and either explained the administration of these two provinces as 'provisional' – 'a singularity formed by a mere transitional step and incapable of scientific conceptual determination' – or alternatively looked to establish a new category of international-legal state-union [*Staaten-Verbindungen*] for this relationship.[43] But neither of these options was tenable, Lingg argued. A provisionality that lasts twelve years and which will seemingly continue for a long while yet, is no passing phenomenon whose singularity one can set aside. 'If the existing state theory does not fit this relationship, then it is only a telling proof that it is not exhaustive.'[44] Global legal typologies may have been forging new maps of the world, but they were also pushing up against the limitations of legal science itself. Conundrums like Bosnia and Herzegovina forced practitioners to confront the inadequacy of existing names, which in turn drove them back to first principles, and to reflect on how legal reasoning related to a world of facts in the first place. Categorical challenges of this sort document a young legal science struggling to comb the globe into coherent conceptual narratives.

A reversible legal geography: The boomerang of split sovereignty

The legal opacity of Bosnia and Herzegovina was a condition that affected more than the empire's fingers and toes: it attacked the very heart, threatening relationships between the imperial state's vital organs. 'When Austria-Hungary concluded the Treaty of Berlin with the other signatory powers', wrote the jurist Theodor Dantscher von Kollesberg in 1880, 'it so happened that this Treaty unleashed phenomena inside the empire that have not surfaced in any of the contracting powers.'[45] Bosnia and Herzegovina ricocheted back from those global canvasses to force a new narration of the sovereign self as well.

Ten years before the occupation, in the *Ausgleich* of 1867, imperial elites had attempted to settle continual constitutional strife by way of a bold experiment: the Habsburg monarchy was re-modelled into a dual polity composed of two equal and equally sovereign states: the Kingdom of Hungary, on the one hand, and a conglomerate of the 'Austrian' lands, on the other. (The latter, formally titled 'The Kingdoms and Lands Represented in the Imperial Parliament', was known only more colloquially as 'Austria' or Cisleithania.) A new constitutional architecture carefully preserved the dual (duelling?) sovereignties. Only three common ministries were established: one for foreign affairs, another for defence and a third for the finances for defence and foreign affairs. These shared or joint ministries were not responsible to any comprehensive imperial forum but rather to 'delegations' dispatched regularly from the 'Austrian' and the Hungarian parliaments, respectively, which met alternately in Vienna and Budapest.

So the Habsburg Empire became the Austro-Hungarian one, with the hyphen hiding manifold juridical uncertainties.[46] How could a state be two and somehow still always one? Hungarian jurists and politicians argued that there was no third, over-arching state entity subsuming both states; and even Austrian ones had to concede, often with great frustration, that no 'third' state could in fact be 'found' in the 1867 *Ausgleich* laws. While the problem of this legally vanishing, or legally invisible empire was already galvanizing academic debate, the occupation of Bosnia and Herzegovina turned it into an administrative, logistical and political crisis and not only a theoretical-philosophical one. Who or what possessed the new colony? Who was the 'self' that could own or interpellate the other? The 'Austrian' state would not permit it to be a 'Hungarian' protectorate or colony, and vice versa.[47] This moment of bold colonial expansion shone an unflattering mirror back onto a disappearing metropole: it sent jurists scrambling to ascertain and sure up the internal legal architecture of the state.

'Bosnia and Herzegovina is attached with the same band to the one monarchy and to the other', reasoned Redslob. 'It is thus a systematic necessity to ask above all about the nature of state-theoretical organization which encompasses both monarchies. Only when we have won clarity about the relationship between Austria and Hungary can we investigate the political and legal standing of Bosnia-Herzegovina.'[48] Tezner was less optimistic: 'a final, organic solution scarcely seems possible on the foundation of dualism'.[49] Bosnia and Herzegovina exposed the embarrassing logical incoherence of the empire: if the Habsburg Monarchy had traditionally been a so-called empire without colonies, now there was a colony without an empire – at least in legal terms. Could the colony perhaps be possessed twice over – by both Hungary and Austria separately but simultaneously, a doubled subordination? Without any clear answers, the territories were administered out of the common finance ministry as a kind of permanently provisional stop-gap arrangement.

The juridical headaches proved impossible to contain. If the Treaty of Berlin – the origin of the right to occupy – needed to be ratified by the empire's representative organs to become operative law (and opinion was divided here), then which representative organ could perform such a function? The empire didn't have a parliament of its own: how could *either* the Austrian *or* the Hungarian one ratify it in the name of the whole Dual Monarchy? Like countless other jurists, Kollesberg explained to his readers, almost apologetically, that occupation of Bosnia and Herzegovina forced one to backtrack and answer the most basic, foundational questions about the nature of the Austro-Hungarian Empire. 'First it must be clear or made clear which state form – or perhaps *state forms* – Austria-Hungary represents.'[50] One soon stumbled on a 'particularly strange phenomenon'. While everyone recognized the 'international legal existence' of 'Austria-Hungary' – this was, after all, the entity that had signed the Treaty of Berlin – the 'constitutional [*staatsrechtliche*] existence' of such a state was doubted from many sides. 'Austria-Hungary, *one* state outwardly, is supposed to be *two* states inwardly.'[51] 'What confusion, what uncertainty in the theory about this Austria-Hungary!', he exclaimed. 'What state-conceptual [*staatsbegrifflichen*], logical impossibilities are brought forth, what positive-constitutional falsities are claimed!'[52]:

> The common ministry, as soon as foreign states and their diplomats observe it and engage officially with it – the common ministry seen from the front and the outside – is one ministry; when one's own citizens and state organs, for example the delegations, observe this ministry and enter into official, organic contact with it – the ministry seen from behind and from inside and oriented to the inside – there are supposedly two ministries![53]

A schism had yawned open between the state as viewed from the front and outside, on the one hand, and the state viewed from behind and inside, on the other. The state and its sovereignty appeared as two radically different phenomena from these alternate vantage points.

Of course, the bifurcation of 'internal' and 'external' sovereignty was precisely the characteristic legal feature of colonial protectorates, that legal edifice then spreading round the world like a rash. As the mid-century jurist Charles Alexandrowicz phrased it, 'the Protectorate means a split sovereignty and its purpose is to vest in the Protector rights of external sovereignty while leaving rights of internal sovereignty in the protected entity'.[54] But European powers were not supposed to be vulnerable to the Janus face of split sovereignty, the schizophrenia of one self facing outwards and another inwards; that legal pathology was symptomatic of those parts of the world zoned outside the magic circle of civilization. No, European states were supposed to possess that wholesome legal unity of self, an 'I' unburdened by qualifications and clauses; and it was the damaged or incomplete sovereignty of those non-European entities that reflected back the crystalline completeness of their own.[55] Like a weapon that turns, unexpectedly, to injure its maker, the occupation of Bosnia and Herzegovina *reimported the schizophrenia of split sovereignty into the heart of the imperial state*. The question of how to hold a colony had exposed a disconnect between its inside self and its outside self, bringing the spectre of disaggregated legal selves boomeranging back into the metropole. It was the state's colonial periphery, its frayed legal edges – a kind of sovereign marginalia – that flipped the world over on its pivot.

Remaking selves – from the outside in

Where some wrung hands and gnashed teeth, others saw an opportunity. The internal dilemma posed by the possession of Bosnia and Herzegovina might just prove the basis for a new work of state integration and centralization, or so some hoped. The task of administering Bosnia and Herzegovina had exposed the radical inadequacy of the common, empire-wide ministries and competencies. That colonial prerogative thus invited the expansion of those common prerogatives and institutions, argued the law professor Karl Lamp. The shared responsibility and common mission of colonial rule could galvanize new cooperation and investment, could spur a new, integrative story of self for the dual monarchy – a little like the couple who hopes a child will breathe new life and purpose into their relationship. Lamp speculated that a strengthening of the power position of the monarch, an extension of the jurisdiction of the common ministry, the creation of a new representative imperial organ and the organization of a bureaucratic body under the common government independent from the Austrian and the Hungarian government would all be legal effects of the 1908 annexation of Bosnia and Herzegovina and the 1910 promulgation of constitution for the territories. The latter formed 'a powerful new counterweight to the tendencies towards separation that dwell to a greater or lesser extent in all state unions', and would 'direct the monarchy in its further development on the path to federal organisation'.[56] It wasn't only that the line between the inside and the outside of the state was porous, or that the state's outsides imported awkward sovereign truths into the imperial core: these relations did not leave the entities in question unchanged, but worked upon one another as practical projects of reform as much as conceptual reorganizations.

But perhaps that re-constitution of an integrated legal self required not so much the creation of new institutions as change in perspective. Scholar-turned-politician Josef Redlich certainly saw it that way: he identified a different way of transforming all the legal chaos unleashed by the question of Bosnia and Herzegovina into a new account of the wholeness of the Habsburg state. Redlich's two-volume, 900-page epic, *Das österreichiche Staats- und Reichsproblem* (*The Austrian State- and Imperial Problem*) still marks him as the empire's most significant legal chronicler.[57] But well before those volumes had appeared, he also headed the Austrian parliamentary commission charged with trying to 'legalize' the annexation of Bosnia and Herzegovina and determine its relationship to the empire's constitutional order, especially the law of succession, known as the Pragmatic Sanction. Redlich's parliamentary report discussed the Hungarian argument that the act of annexation was not the act of a common monarch. This reflected the dominant Hungarian perspective that fully denied the existence of a single, unified monarchy. This whole view of the imperial order, repeated *ad nauseam* by Hungarian ministers, journalists and politicians, naturally affected the relationship between Hungary and the once-occupied-now-annexed lands. Such views, he asserted, rode roughshod over the fact that all Austrian and all Hungarian constitutional arrangements in relation to Bosnia had their exclusive foundation in the Treaty of Berlin that, in accordance with the principles of international law, granted the mandate for occupation and administration to *the monarchy* and only to it. 'Through this act neither Austria nor Hungary acquired an independent right, rather, exclusively the from-the-outside-in unified monarchy [*die nach außen hin einheitliche Monarchie*], just as the bearer of this mandate since the Berlin contract has been exclusively the common monarch.'[58]

Both the occupation and annexation had 'occurred' in international law, and so they should be rightly analysed, from a jurisdictional perspective, in that frame, too. And in international law, Austria-Hungary was clearly a *single* actor. If he agreed with Kollesberg that Habsburg sovereignty appeared radically different viewed from the 'inside' and the 'outside', he did not seem to find this a mark of shame, or at least let pragmatic objectives drown out any embarrassment. For that disjuncture was useful. That view from international law offered a way to bypass Hungarian arguments about their undiluted sovereignty: it offered a jurisdictional meta-perspective, a legal bird's eye view, that smoothed out the divisions that looked so intractable from ground level. If all else failed, the Treaty of Berlin could be relied upon to fashion the empire into a unified legal subject. From Redlich's perspective, the empire's legal identity was a truth that may be knowable only from the outside the self.

Ironically, then, those classic late-nineteenth-century rituals of international legitimacy – the congresses and contracts and treaties – here had a more unexpected vocation: they made the Austro-Hungarian Empire whole even if its own constitutional law was incapable of proving this point itself. Ironically, the Congress of Berlin here 'created' – or at least made plausible, legal, legible – one of the Great Powers, and not only shaky new states like Serbia or the Congo Free State. One needed to conceptualize the state from the outside in: it needed to talk about itself in a kind of conceptual third person. International law became the language for imperial-legal stories of selfhood – a syntax and grammar that allowed the two states to be one where constitutional law let the state unravel, a language of disaggregation and dissolution. The question of legal scale, of jurisdiction, was also one of perspective: international law offered a different place to start the story, and made a different protagonist visible as a result.

Notes

1   H. Duncan Hall, *Mandates, Dependencies and Trusteeship* (Washington: Carnegie Endowment for International Peace, 1948), 4, 8.

2   Hall, *Mandates, Dependencies and Trusteeship*, 4, 8. In arguing that the international frontier had exerted a formative influence on the development of international life and politics, Hall drew an analogy to Turner's frontier thesis: 'It has long been recognized that the expanding national frontier in the case of certain states such as the United States has exercised a major influence on the national life – political, economic, and cultural. The international frontier has exercised a no less profound influence in modern history on the relations of the states and peoples of the world. It has been a major factor in the development and shaping of international arrangements and institutions' (4). In this cross-pollination of analytical scales, interpretive frameworks themselves emerge as one of our 'other world products'.

3   See Pieter Judson, *The Habsburg Empire: A New History* (Cambridge, MA: Harvard University Press, 2016), 319–32; Robin Okey, *Taming Balkan Nationalism: The Habsburg 'Civilizing Mission' in Bosnia 1878–1914* (Oxford: Oxford University

Press, 2007). For Bosnian intellectuals' own view of the modernization efforts of both empires and their creation of a European Islamic intellectual tradition, see importantly Leyla Amzi-Erdogdular, 'Alternative Muslim Modernities: Bosnian Intellectuals in the Ottoman and Habsburg Empires', *Comparative Studies in Society and History* 59, no. 4 (2017): 912–43.

4 To give one example: 'Österreich-Ungarn hat die Erwartung Europas nicht getäuscht. Es hat in den beiden Ländern wirklich Ruhe und Ordnung geschaffen und eine eifrige und opervolle Verwaltung hat sie aus halbbarbarischen Zuständen zu west-europäischer Zivilisation emporgehoben'. August Fournier, *Wie wir zu Bosnien kamen: Eine historische Studie* (Vienna: Reisser, 1909), 82.

5 In which the Ottoman Empire obviously plays a central role. See Davide Rodogno, *Against Massacre: Humanitarian Interventions in the Ottoman Empire, 1815–1914* (Princeton: Princeton University Press, 2012); Gary Bass, *Freedom's Battle: The Origins of Humanitarian Intervention* (New York: Knopf, 2008); Samuel Moyn, 'Spectacular Wrongs', *The Nation*, 24 September 2008.

6 On the 'Responsibility to Protect', see Anne Orford, *International Authority and the Responsibility to Protect* (Cambridge: Cambridge University Press, 2011); Mark Mazower, *Governing the World: The History of an Idea, 1815 to the Present* (New York: Penguin, 2012), 378–405.

7 See especially Clemens Ruthner and Tamara Scheer (eds.), *Bosnien-Herzegowina und Österreich-Ungarn, 1878–1918: Annäherungen an eine Kolonie* (Tübingen: Francke, 2018). On the occupation and annexation of Bosnia-Herzegovina as an opening for the application of postcolonial theory to the Habsburg lands, see further Johannes Feichtinger, Ursula Prutsch and Moritz Csaky (eds.), *Habsburg Postcolonial: Machtstrukturen und Kollektives* Gedächtnis (Innsbruck: StudienVerlag, 2003); Clemens Ruthner, 'Central Europe Goes Post-Colonial: New Approaches to the Habsburg Empire Around 1900', *Cultural Studies* 16, no. 6 (2002): 877–83; Clemens Ruthner, Diana Reynolds Cordileone, Ursula Reber and Raymond Detrez (eds.), *WechselWirkungen: Austria-Hungary, Bosnia-Herzegovina, and the Western Balkans, 1878–1918* (New York: Peter Lang, 2015).

8 For scepticism about the usefulness of a toolbox of racialized 'othering' and hegemony in a state which otherwise had citizenship, legal equality and very fluid national identification – a scepticism that Edward Said himself shared – see Pieter Judson, 'L'Autriche-Hongrie était-elle un empire?', *Annales: Histoire, Sciences Sociales* 63, no. 3 (2008): 563–96; Tara Zahra, 'Looking East: East Central European "Borderlands" in German History and Historiography', *History Compass* 3 (2005): 1–23; Edward W. Said, *Culture and Imperialism* (New York: Vintage Books, 1993), xxii, see also xxiii. Indeed, the central thrust of Judson's newest work is that Habsburg state-building was not qualitatively different from Western European versions: Judson, *The Habsburg Empire*.

9 Clemens Ruthner, 'Introduction: Bosnia-Herzegovina: Post/colonial?' in *WechselWirkungen: Austria-Hungary, Bosnia-Herzegovina, and the Western Balkans, 1878–1918*, ed. Clemens Ruthner, Diana Reynolds Cordileone, Ursula Reber and Raymond Detrez (New York: Peter Lang, 2015), 1.

10 On Habsburg Central Europe as a central crucible for the production of modern sovereignty and ideas about it, see Natasha Wheatley, *The Life and Death of States: Central Europe and the Transformation of Modern Sovereignty* (Princeton: Princeton University Press, 2023).

160   *Narratives, Nations, and Other World Products*

11   See generally Jane Burbank and Fred Cooper, *Empires in World History: Power and the Politics of Difference* (Princeton, NJ: Princeton University Press, 2010); Antony Anghie, *Imperialism, Sovereignty and the Making of International Law* (Cambridge: Cambridge University Press, 2005); Jennifer Pitts, *Boundaries of the International: Law and Empire* (Cambridge, MA: Harvard University Press, 2018); Gerrit Gong, *The Standard of 'Civilization' in International Society* (New York: Oxford University Press, 1984); Karen Barkey, *Empire of Difference: The Ottomans in Comparative Perspective* (New York: Cambridge University Press, 2008). For other new research on Austria-Hungary in a world of empires, see Alison Frank, 'The Children of the Desert and the Laws of the Sea: Austria, Great Britain, the Ottoman Empire, and the Mediterranean Slave Trade in the Nineteenth Century', *American Historical Review* 117, no. 2 (2012): 410–44.

12   See Anghie, *Imperialism, Sovereignty,* 87–90.

13   Steven Press, *Rogue Empires: Contracts and Conmen in Europe's Scramble for Africa* (Cambridge, MA: Harvard University Press, 2017). The 'world was a marketplace for sovereignty', Press writes on 235, open to monarchs, entrepreneurs and missionaries alike.

14   See Martti Koskenniemi, *The Gentle Civilizer of Nations: The Rise and Fall of International Law, 1870–1960* (Cambridge: Cambridge University Press, 2001).

15   See, for example, Andrew Fitzmaurice, 'The Justification of King Leopold II's Congo Enterprise by Sir Travers Twiss', in *Law and Politics in British Colonial Thought: Transpositions of Empire*, ed. Shaunnagh Dorsett and Ian Hunter (New York: Palgrave Macmillan, 2010), 109–26; Press, *Rogue Empires*.

16   As the Austrian politician and some time minister Joseph Maria Baernreither would tease in proposing some unconventional administrative reforms for Bosnia before the Austrian parliament in 1910: 'aber bedenken Sie doch, wie exzeptionell Bosnien in staatsrechtlicher Beziehung zu uns steht. Ja, die Professoren werden uns alle aus dieser Verlegenheit nicht heraushelfen, wenn sie definieren sollen, in was für eine Kategorie staatsrechtlicher Bildungen Bosnien gehört. (*Heiterkeit*)'. [Joseph Maria Baernreither], *Rede des Dr. Baernreither, gehalten in der Delegation des Reichsrates am. 14. November 1910 über die bosnischen Angelegenheiten* (Vienna: k. k. Hof- und Staatsdruckerei, 1910), 7.

17   For the concept of 'stories of peoplehood' from a political science perspective, see Rogers Smith, *Stories of Peoplehood: The Politics and Morals of Political Membership* (Cambridge: Cambridge University Press, 2003).

18   For an exploration of law as a language and framing power that constrains political imagination 'within the conventions of authoritative speech and writing', see Martti Koskenniemi, *To the Uttermost Parts of the Earth: Legal Imagination and International Power* (Cambridge: Cambridge University Press, 2021), 6.

19   Cyrus Schayegh, *The Middle East and the Making of the Modern World* (Cambridge, MA: Harvard University Press, 2017), 2 and generally.

20   See Sebastian Conrad, *What Is Global History?* (Princeton: Princeton University Press, 2016), esp. 135–40.

21   Koskenniemi, *The Gentle Civilizer of Nations,* 155.

22   On the entangled (legal) history of the Habsburg and Ottoman Empires, see Emily Greble, *Muslims and the Making of Modern Europe* (Oxford: Oxford University Press, 2021); Jared Manasek, 'Refugee Return and State Legitimation: Habsburgs, Ottomans, and the Case of Bosnia and Herzegovina, 1875–1878', *Journal of Modern European History* 19, no. 1 (2020): 63–79; Ruthner and Scheer, *Bosnien-Herzegowina*

The Boomerang of Imperial Sovereignty 161

und Österreich-Ungarn; Adam Mestyan, 'A Muslim Dualism? Inter-imperial History and Austria-Hungary in Ottoman Thought, 1867–1921', *Contemporary European History* 30, no. 4 (2021): 478–96.

23 See Wheatley, *The Life and Death of States*, chapter 2.

24 'Dieses Okkupations- und Verwaltungsrecht ist an keine zeitliche Grenze gebunden; es befriedigt aber nicht allein das Intresse der Monarchie, sondern auch das der übrigen Vertragsmächte an der Herstellung geordneter Zustände in diesen Ländern zur Abwendung von Gefahren für den Weltfrieden'. Joseph Ulbrich, *Lehrbuch des Oesterreichischen Staatsrechts: Für den akademischen Gebrauch und die Bedürfnisse der Praxis* (Berlin: Verlag von Theodor Hofmann, 1883), 792–3.

25 On analogous debates in the British context, see Lauren Benton, 'From International Law to Imperial Constitutions: The Problem of Quasi-Sovereignty, 1870–1900', *Law and History Review* 26, no. 3 (2008): 595–619.

26 The legal title granted to Austria-Hungary at the Congress of Berlin originated in 'der dort unaufhörlich herrschenden Anarchie, welche nicht nur die benachbarten Provinzen Oesterreich-Ungarns, sondern bei der Lage der Dinge sogar den Weltfrieden bedrohte, also in dem Vorhandsein eines jener wenigen Fälle, in welchen die Intervention in die inneren Angelegenheiten eines Staates fast allseitig als gerechtfertigt erklärt wird'. Georg Jellinek, *Die Lehre von den Staatenverbindungen* (Berlin: Verlag von O. Haring, 1882), 115.

27 As Quincy Wright explained to his readers in 1930, international law 'is familiar with the dissociation of sovereignty from its partial or entire exercise temporarily or permanently'. 'The same is true of rights of control and administration as exercised by Austria-Hungary under the treaty of Berlin from 1878–1908 in Bosnia and Herzegovina and by Great Britain in Egypt'. Quincy Wright, *Mandates Under the League of Nations* (Chicago: University of Chicago Press, 1930), 395.

28 'Die okkupirten Länder sind zu Oesterreich-Ungarn in kein staatsrechtliches Verhältnis getreten'. 'Dieselben sind vielmehr von Gesammtstaat als völkerrechtlichen Rechtssubjekte bloss in Verwaltung übernommen'. 'An und für sich sind die beiden Länder Oesterreich-Ungarn gegenüber *Ausland*'. Ulbrich, *Lehrbuch des Oesterreichischen Staatsrechts*, 793. Emphasis in original.

29 'Da oesterreichisch-ungarische Behörden in den okkupirten Ländern wirksam sind, so entfällt daselbst das Bedürfniss eines besonderen Schutzes der österreichischen oder ungarischen Staatsbürger, z. B. durch Konsulate'. Ulbrich, *Lehrbuch des Oesterreichischen Staatsrechts*, 794.

30 See for example Turan Kayaoglu, *Legal Imperialism: Sovereignty and Extraterritoriality in Japan, the Ottoman Empire, and China* (Cambridge: Cambridge University Press, 2009); Pär Cassel, *Grounds of Judgment: Extraterritoriality and Imperial Power in Nineteenth-Century China and Japan* (Oxford: Oxford University Press, 2012). See also Lale Can, 'The Protection Question: Central Asians and Extraterritoriality in the Late Ottoman Empire', *International Journal of Middle East Studies* 48 (2016): 679–99.

31 Boghitchevitch, *Halbsouveränität*, 174.

32 Jellinek, *Staatenverbindungen*, 116.

33 For the last two, see the survey in Josef L. Kunz, *Die Staatenverbindungen*, Handbuch des Völkerrechts, vol. 2, part 4 (Stuttgart: Verlag von W. Kohlhammer, 1929), 224–7. In our own day, the historian John Deak terms it an 'internal colony'. John Deak, *Forging a Multinational State: State Making in Imperial Austria from the Enlightenment to the First World War* (Stanford: Stanford University Press, 2015), 261.

162   *Narratives, Nations, and Other World Products*

34   Charles G. Fenwick, *Wardship in International Law* (Washington: Government Printing Office, 1919).

35   Robert Redslob, *Abhängige Länder: Eine Analyse des Begriffs von der ursprünglichen Herrschergewalt: Zugleich eine staatsrechtliche und politische Studie über Elsaß-Lothringen, die österreichischen Königreiche und Länder, Kroatien-Slavonien, Bosnien-Herzegowina, Finnland, Island, die Territorien der nordamerikanischen Union, Kanada, Australien, Südafrika* (Leipzig: Verlag von Veit & Comp., 1914).

36   Antony Anghie has contributed the most famous account of that foundational distinction, which he terms the 'dynamic of difference'. Anghie, *Imperialism, Sovereignty*.

37   Franz von Liszt, *Das Völkerrecht: Systematisch dargestellt*, 10th edition (Berlin: Julius Springer, 1915), 102.

38   Liszt, *Das Völkerrecht*, 103.

39   Georg Jellinek, *Ueber Staatsfragmente* (Heidelberg: Verlag von Gustav Koester, 1896), 8.

40   'die zwar nicht selbst Staaten sind, aber die Rudimente eines Staates darbieten'. Jellinek, *Ueber Staatsfragmente*, 11.

41   Hans Schneller, *Die staatsrechtliche Stellung von Bosnien und der Herzogowina* (Leipzig: Kommissionsverlag von H. G. Wallmann, 1892), 11.

42   Friedrich Tezner, 'Das staatsrechtliche und politische Problem der österreichisch-ungarischen Monarchie (Schluß)', *Archiv des öffentlichen Rechts* 31 (1913): 170. Emphasis in original.

43   ' … eine provisorische, einer wissenschaftlichen Begriffsbestimmung unfähige, eine blosse Uebergangsstufe bildende Singularität'. Emil Lingg, 'Die staatsrechtliche Stellung Bosniens und der Herzegowina: Ein Beitrag zur Kritik der Lehre von den Staatenverbindungen', *Archiv des öffentlichen Rechts* 5, no. 4 (1890): 482.

44   Emil Lingg, 'Die staatsrechtliche Stellung Bosniens und der Herzegowina: Ein Beitrag zur Kritik der Lehre von den Staatenverbindungen', *Archiv des öffentlichen Rechts* 5, no. 4 (1890): 482.

45   Theodor Dantscher von Kollesberg, *Der Monarchische Bundesstaat Oesterreich-Ungarn und der Berliner Vertrag nebst der Bosnischen Vorlage* (Vienna: Alfred Hölder, 1880), 1.

46   Or even, in Hermann Bidermann's phrase, 'juridical monstrosities' (*juristische Ungeheuerlichkeit*): see his *Die Rechtliche Natur der österreichisch-ungarischen Monarchie* (Vienna: k. k. Hofbuchdruckerei Carl Fromme, 1877), 44. See further Wheatley, *The Life and Death of States*.

47   At the same time, neither 'state' wanted it especially, for it would entail a dramatic increase in the number of 'Slavs' and potentially upset the already-tense ethno-national situation.

48   Redslob, *Abhängige Länder*, 202.

49   Tezner, 'Das staatsrechtliche und politische Problem der österreichisch-ungarischen Monarchie (Schluß)', 183.

50   Kollesberg, *Der Monarchische Bundesstaat*, 2. Emphasis in original.

51   Kollesberg, *Der Monarchische Bundesstaat*, 4.

52   Ibid., 5.

53   'Das gemeinsame Ministerium, sobald die fremden Staaten und deren Diplomaten dasselbe betrachten und mit ihm amtlich verkehren – das gemeinsame Ministerium von vorne und aussen gesehen – ist Ein Ministerium; wenn die eigenen Staatsangehörigen und Staatsorgane, z. B. die delegationen, dieses Ministerium

betrachten und mit ihm in amtliche, organische Berührung treten – das Ministerium von rückwärts und innen gesehen und nach Innen gewendet – soll zwei Ministerien sein.' Kollesberg, *Der Monarchische Bundesstaat*, 7.

54 Charles Alexandrowicz, *The European-African Confrontation: A Study in Treaty Making*, 62. See also Koskenniemi, *The Gentle Civilizer*, 124–5.

55 Which is, most famously, Anghie's argument in *Imperialism, Sovereignty*.

56 'das alles sind rechtliche Wirkungen der neuen Verfassung, welche den Trennungstendenzen, die mehr oder weniger jeder Staatenunion innewohnen, ein neues mächtiges Gegengewicht bieten' – and 'die Monarchie in ihrer weiteren Entwicklung auf den Weg *bundesstaatlicher* Organisation verweisen'. Karl Lamp, 'Die Verfassung von Bosnien und der Herzegowina vom 17. Februar 1910', *Jahrbuch des öffentlichen Rechts der Gegenwart* 5 (1911): 229.

57 Josef Redlich, *Das österreichische Staats- und Reichsproblem: Geschichtliche Darstellung der inneren Politik der habsburgischen Monarchie von 1848 bis zum Untergang des Reiches*, 2 vols (Leipzig: Der Neue Geist Verlag, 1920 and 1926).

58 'Bericht des Referenten im Ausschusse für bosnische Angelegenheiten, Reichsratsabgeordneten Professor Dr. Josef Redlich: betreffend 1. die Regierungsvorlage über das Protokoll vom 26. Februar 1909, betreffend die Reglung der zwischen der österreichisch-ungarischen Monarchie und dem Osmanischen Reiche bestehende Fragen; 2. den Gesetzesentwurf, betreffend die Art der Bestreitung der an das Osmanische Reich für die in Bosnien und der Herzcegovina gelegenen Staatsgüter zu leistenden Entschädigung; 3. den Gesetzesentwurf, betreffend die Erstreckung der Souveränitätsrechte Seiner k. u. k. Apostolischen Majestät sowie der Bestimmungen der Pragmatischen Sanktion auf Bosnien und die Hercegovina', 1912, Österreichische Nationalbibliothek, Sammlung für Alte Handschriften und Drucke, Nachlass Josef Redlich, Cod. Ser. n. 53589 Han.

9

A century of convergences: Contested concepts of economic integration, 1919–2019

Jeremy Adelman, Abigail Kret, Marlène Rosano-Grange and Bruno Settis

Introduction

This chapter is about the struggle over rival visions of global interdependence, visions that rested on competing stories about integration. During the nineteenth century, the debate for many societies was whether to integrate, in large part because the machines for integration were formal and informal empires; by the 1890s, the last spasms of resistance were being snuffed out, squashed or relegated to distant margins. Once settler colonialism and finance capital had, for all intents and purposes, enclosed the world into one economic unit, the debate turned to how to manage this unequal human creation. For the past century, the debate was not whether societies should integrate economically with each other, but how. We trace three rival models of unequal integration which vied for influence and legitimacy in different historic moments.

Our story draws attention to a running tension between international economic integration and national political politics: integration across borders created opportunities and hazards, rewards and risks that had to be distributed within borders. This has been an important subject of research in the field of international political economy, where the stress has been on national policy responses to international shocks and shifts.[1] It fell to states to manage the political economy of capitalist distribution. If scholars of international political economy draw attention to inter-scalar effects of integration, our concern is with the ways in which cross-border flows and pressures created the idea of the markets that needed regulating – or, alternately, deregulating – in order to understand and handle interdependence. This forced the observers we study to reckon with the role of nation-states in international markets.

This chapter is thus about the search for models that framed the policies and regimes, models that took narrative form, with an eye to contributing to the intellectual history of political economy. It is less about policy responses or regime types than about the concepts that informed them, framed options and guided choices. It aims to bring the history of the world economy into views of global intellectual history which has, for the most part, been dominated by political and legal thought. It is tempting to conclude that this is the result of the ways in which international relations between states have informed a century of thinking about global order, and the grip that political

166   *Narratives, Nations, and Other World Products*

science has had over conceptualizing it. It may well also reflect the demoted status of the history of economic ideas in the conceptualizing of economic power, though recently some intellectual historians have plumbed the history of neoliberalism.[2] Either way, this chapter seeks to illuminate how economic concerns were central to thinking about global order as well as how economic policymakers struggled to develop models, narratives and concepts for managing global interdependence that criss-crossed national sovereignties.

Transwar period

The world market presented itself as a problem that transcended nations and empires at the close of the First World War; it was the crisis of the postwar that set in motion the first systematic and global round of reflection and debate over the elements of the international economy and the role of the state in managing it. Until then, the orthodoxy had been that adherence to the gold standard would discipline societies to the rule of price stability while the theory of free trade, even if honoured only in the breach, would ensure that nations would prosper by doubling down on their comparative advantage. The disequilibrium of the war changed forever the landscape of thinking about markets as the natural engines of integration that would invariably fold all societies liberal structures. There were, to be sure, early signs that all was not well, resistance in colonies and a growing array of voices denouncing the hypocrisy of the civilizing mission. For the most part, they did not affect core thinking. The war changed all that. The weakness of empires, and the rise of an alternative ideological appeal to internationalism in the form of Bolshevism, fundamentally changed the horizon of global interdependence. No longer could the discipline of the market and the long-run faith in comparative advantage command the same consensus. Internationalists were shocked to watch rivalries between states escalate so quickly; the long convergence of the nineteenth century now seemed so fragile; after 1919, burdened by debts, inflation and mass unemployment, the idea of relying on the self-correcting impulses of the market was anathema.

The First World War induced the first attempts to explain world integration as a specific historical condition, a condition whose time had passed or was in need of some institutional and political scaffolding to keep the free-trade order from collapsing into competition and *sauve qui peut policies*. It also saw the emergence of contending narratives and radical critique which tapped into earlier discontents with the world system. But there was one thing upon which the rival narratives tended to agree: if nineteenth-century theories of convergence thought in terms of ever-more order, fusion and interdependent equilibrium, the war shattered all that. New ideas of economic integration were premised on disequilibrium and tendency to crisis and possibly – hopefully, for some – revolution. This meant the need to manage what the free market and nation-states so evidently could not.[3]

The result was the birth of two basic narratives of economic integration from within the core of the European world economy. These were not the only narratives on offer as the periphery was also a source and subject of analysis in this conjuncture,

A Century of Convergences 167

as explored in another chapter in this anthology by Adelman, Lenel and Pryluka. The first challenger came from the pen of a Marxist, Vladimir Lenin. Lenin's theory and revolutionary praxis tore away the confidence in the evolutionary destiny of single capitalist societies. In *Imperialism, the Highest Stage of Capitalism*, published in 1916 in Russian, Lenin proposed his vision of capitalism as worldwide social formation in its most consistent form. In the 1917 French and German editions of the pamphlet, he labelled it a 'world system', defined by 'colonial oppression and of the financial strangulation of the overwhelming majority of the population of the world by a handful of "advanced" countries'.[4] What followed was an analysis of the Russian economy as the embodiment of its contradictions – a backward country, but one that should be considered fully capitalist inasmuch as it was embedded in the capitalist world system and dependent from foreign finance capital. Russia's position in the hierarchy of the Great Powers was that of the country 'economically most backward, in which modern capitalist imperialism is enmeshed, so to speak, in a thick web of pre-capitalist relations', but a similar position as a 'commercial colony' was held by Argentina, or Portugal, sovereign countries dependent on British finance. War provided the political detonator for revolutionary possibilities that were rooted in the structure of 'uneven development' within an interdependent capitalist world.

In Lenin's view, the disorder was not the result of the archaic power of nationalism. This had been the view of hopeful liberals; their hopes were pinned on a narrative of economic convergence that would sweep away old cultural and political habits and tame the nationalist furies. For Lenin, disorder was the result of how global capitalism actually functioned; it was the *effect* of integration. In capitalist countries, the dialectics of competition and monopoly, free markets and cartels (as a specific development of the second industrial revolution), made production ever more social while the rewards ever more privatized to a small clique. And they became the drivers of expansion, betraying their own rhetoric of liberal integration and free markets: 'capitalism has been transformed into imperialism', Lenin famously noted, because it was forced to export its swelling pools of surplus capital to the rest of the world. The ensuing scramble intensified integration, while heightening rivalries and feuds. Lenin created a narrative of capitalism characterized not by its lock-step stages of country-by-country development, but by uneven development between them, competition between monopolies and alliances, unsteady hierarchies in world markets and power politics; he was building a narrative in which unification and disruptive effects paradoxically were one and the same. Once the world became an economic unit, the 'struggle for the division of the world' began.[5] Lenin was not alone in thinking systemically and seeing that integration rested on, and needed, inequality of its parts.

If the crisis of war produced critical reflections on a world economy made of uneven and unstable parts, liberals also had to revisit their faith in the means to tether them together – the market. A counterpoint to the critical narrative of congenital disequilibrium came from John Maynard Keynes, who charted an alternative narrative. He outlined what might be called the first liberal narrative of global economic integration that broke from the older, nineteenth-century mechanical and evolutionary stories of convergence, one that identified fundamental structural properties and flaws of integration. To rescue markets as integrative machinery, they had to be embedded in new institutional formations. Like Lenin he conceded that there was something basically wrong with the world economy; unlike them, he thought it could be made right.

Keynes finished *The Economic Consequences of the Peace* in the dying days of 1919; the armistice was a year old when he sent it to the printer. He accused the victors of sowing the seeds of an eventual destruction by imposing what he called a 'Carthaginian Peace' on the losers, especially Germany. The reason had to do with an underlying interdependence which they blithely ignored. 'The invite their own destruction', he prophesized, 'being so deeply and inextricably intertwined with their victims by hidden psychic and economic bonds'.[6] The failure of the men of 1919 was not being able to recognize that the world of the nineteenth century was gone for good, and that they had to devise a new one. What closed the cycle of open market convergence were historical conditions that the war wiped out. The tragedy of Versailles and the League was having been designed by men who wanted to restore a world economy on conditions that no longer existed.

To make this case, Keynes looked back to outline an arc for the history of European capitalism. The basic historic condition was the windfall that came from integrating the resources and land of the New World after 1492 into the hunger of the Old. An era of four centuries of merging the peoples, land and resources was now over. The Old World, Keynes noted, 'staked out a claim in the natural wealth and virgin potentialities of the New'. But by 1914, those once-open frontiers were closing; the land was filling up. Besides, New Worlders themselves were starting to consume the surpluses that once flowed east since 1492; scarcity of wheat, the staple of the Malthusian imaginary, was resuming its pride of place as the constraining factor in human betterment. 'The date was evidently near when these (grains) would be an exportable surplus only in years of exceptionally favorable harvest'. Gone was the illusion of inevitability about ever-expanding frontiers. The result was a scramble for more: more resources, more markets, more possessions – and inevitable clash of the great powers. The problem now was that, instead of seeing that pre-1914 integration begat the war, the victors of that war wanted to turn back the clock. This represented 'the policy of an old man', who 'sees the issue in terms of France and Germany, not of humanity and of European civilisation struggling forwards to a new order'.[7]

Instead of thinking globally, in a new way, the victors thought nationally in an old way. The irony, Keynes underscored, was that this made Europe even more dependent on the largesse – and, as it turns out, the fickleness – of American resources and goodwill to pay for the disequilibrium they built. He was prescient about the need for Wall St to bail out Germany to keep up payments to Britain and France.

Keynes made two important contributions to the narrative thinking about the global political economy. First, he accented to historically contingent nature of integration – in contrast to the universalizing and one-way narratives of the nineteenth-century views which hoped that interdependence might put an end to war for good. To Keynes, the combination of the open frontiers of the New World and the myth of industrial accumulation without mass participation (which, as we will see later in this chapter, flipped with the discovery of the concept of Fordism) was provisional – and thus contingent factors in a worldmaking epic. His second move: to emphasize the changes in leadership and organization, that is, dramatis personae and the victory of their enlightened self-interest for the story. If the nineteenth century patched the world together with empires, the gold standard and a London at the centre of world finance, what would replace it now that the war sundered the empires, kicked the legs out from under gold and turned Britain from creditor to debtor? In the end, Keynes had no answer to the question – except to emphasize that going backwards was disastrous, and that a new generation had to make history. 'The forces of the nineteenth century have run their course and are exhausted', he concluded famously. 'Never in the lifetime of men now living has the universal element in the soul of man burnt so dimly.'[8]

The war thus produced rival narratives of global economic integration and the very idea of a world market produced by converging and competing parts whose alignments were now shaky. After 1921, much of the heat and feuding over how to reassemble a shattered world market passed, briefly. The Soviet Union turned inwards. The flames of insurrection in India and China died down. The world economy, for a moment, appeared to recover, thanks to the help of American loans to rickety Central European banks. Trade and migration recovered some – though only some – of their Victorian dynamism. Without a pressing social crisis or disequilibrium, the contestation after 1918 subsided. Rulers even defaulted back to the rigidity of the gold standard as a stabilizer; indeed, their return to orthodoxy would prove calamitous a few years later after the crash in the New York stock market brought the entire financial system to its knees.

Depression and new models

So it was that it was the crisis at the core of the capitalist system spurred a search for new narratives of what was going wrong and how to make things right. If the postwar analysts spotlighted how economic tensions yielded a political calamity, retrospectives after 1929 pointed to economic forces that spurred a political failure. Now, it was not the menace from Bolsheviks that motivated the search for new means to manage market life, but the rising tide of nationalism, from the United States in the form of the Smoot-Hawley tariffs, the formation of imperial blocs like the Ottawa Agreements, Japanese Co-Prosperity in the Pacific or the Reichsmark bloc, and then the more explicit predatory policies as fascist countries bulked up for war. Italy's break with the fragile postwar consensus was driven by Benito Mussolini's dreams of empire in Africa; likewise, militarists and magnates in Japan were behind the invasion of Manchuria in 1931 and the attack on China of 1937. Last but not least, part of the Nazi project was to build its neo-imperial *Lebensraum* and to apply to Eastern Europe the methods of colonial rule.

As the Wall Street crash reverberated through the world economy and brought on protectionist and predatory responses, there was once again a round of soul searching and narrative quests to explain what happened, why the failure? In the depths of the Depression, some turned to the international and economic origins of contemporary nationalism and the authoritarian turn in national politics. By the late 1930s, two exiled thinkers were hard at work creating narratives of the world economy and its fragilities. Karl Polanyi and Albert O. Hirschman were the offspring of the crisis of Mitteleuropa, both witnesses to economic implosion, and both – in contrasting ways – were anxious to find a new way to manage interdependence. Polanyi echoed Keynes and pointed to the need to restore national sovereignty within interdependence to manage global markets by embedding them in regulatory nation-states; Hirschman, by contrast, yearned for a new model of sovereignty altogether, one which would transcend shopworn nineteenth-century internationalism for good with a model that would bury *national* self-determination in favour of a new international order.

Polanyi's *The Great Transformation* (1944) turned to a deeper historical narrative. Originally called *Origins of the Cataclysm*, it then became *Anatomy of the 19th Century*. These would have been more vivid, and more accurate, titles. They were bleak and did not convey his ambition to create an epic about capitalism that would convince readers that the world would be better off by turning its back once and for all on nineteenth-century liberalism's commitment to open markets and global interdependence. In this sense, he was writing in the same Jeremiad mode as Keynes had done: in crisis times, rulers aimed to restore the past, with disastrous consequences. What Polanyi sought was a narrative about the past of what Lenin had called the 'world system' in order to envision an entirely new one. For Keynes, this had been the mistake of 1919; instead of reforming a liberal civilization with a fresh narrative, the architects of the post-First World War had built its tomb. They tried 'recasting the regimes that had succumbed on the battlefields'.[9]

In a fashion, Polanyi's story picked up where Keynes left off. The rise of the world economy in the nineteenth century rested on four 'institutions': a balance of power between states, the international gold standard, the liberal state and the self-regulating market, which he credited with producing 'unheard-of material welfare'. This great transformation was responsible also for 'the hundred years' peace'. It was also a 'stark utopia'. It was stark because of its brutal physical and moral consequences; it was utopian because it depended on great acts of will and denial of reality. The commodification of land, labour and capital was the result of an organized, wrenching, dislocation from collective moorings in 'the traditional unity of a Christian society'; societies with markets ceded to market societies, bent to live and die in exchange.[10]

What started as an uprooting from communities of reciprocity and redistribution and the victory of individual gain came full circle with welfare systems, both democratic and authoritarian, in the 1930s. The market restoration of the 1920s had failed; gold collapsed, the old balance of imperial powers fizzled, the self-regulating market produced mass unemployment and the liberal state got swept away. Now, Polanyi argued, the marketplace was being restored to its rightful place at the service of society. 'In retrospect', he noted, 'our age will be credited with having seen the end of the self-regulating market'.[11] Managed currencies, protectionism and make-work declared the arrival of moral economy and the prospects for rebuilding a world economy that was not based on the illusion of free markets as the compass for interdependence. He anticipated the ways in which a new compromise around welfarism might give some ballast to a new form of interdependence, one that relied on more communitarian resorts than the liberal-individualist framework of the first hundred years of global economic interdependence. But it is noteworthy that, while he lambasted the nineteenth-century liberal internationalists for their faith in the free flow of commodities across borders, Polanyi had no model for reintegration above the national scale: he could not envision interdependence without some shared community. His narrative imagined disembedded global markets eclipsed by embedded national ones. He could not see the ways in which Atlantic Charterists (the Charter issued by President Roosevelt and Prime Minister Churchill in 1941) had forged a narrative of their own about managed interdependence and its institutional correlate in the form of the Bretton Woods system.

One who did seek a model of global economic interdependence that tackled squarely the problem of national sovereignty was Hirschman. If Polanyi could not relinquish his belief that the nation was, ultimately, the bastion of the moral economy because it was within the patriotic community that markets could get re-embedded, for Hirschman, national sovereignty had been the source of the problem in an inter-dependent economic system. He envisioned a narrative that projected a new – albeit thin – notion of solidarity and mutuality that transcended borders. Why? Because the coincidence of a world market for commodities with uneven state power would lead big countries inevitably to bully weaker ones, inter-dependence was, so long as the scales of national units were unequal, vulnerable. The only solution would be to curb the cherished principle of national sovereignty in order to place international welfare on a more secure plane.

So, Hirschman flipped the underpinnings of the model of economic integration. If Polanyi had wanted to emphasize the ways in which states, and the liberal elites that ruled them, *created* an asymmetrical order, Hirschman began with the premise that states and rulers seized the opportunities afforded to them because they inhabited an *already* imbalanced interdependent world. Indeed, it was this asymmetry that induced predatory state behaviour and the temptation to build muscular, expanding, imperial, states because the global trading order fused big and small powers together. This was the kernel of his narrative in *National Power and the Structure of Foreign Trade* (1945).[12]

In *National Power*, Hirschman wanted to show how strong states manipulated foreign trade to bolster state power at the expense of weak states; the breakdown of the world system and the clash between big blocs were hardly an irrational, nationalist, pathology. It was an understandable response to a basic contradiction, a contradiction that grew with time so long as the world economy stitched societies together but left the management of market risks to nation-states. In this sense, Hirschman saw economic relationships as intrinsically unharmonious and inclined to disequilibria. There was nothing discontinuous about the long arc of imperial integration of the nineteenth century through the turmoil of the interwar years. But he distanced himself from his Marxist roots by seeing patterns of exploitation beyond class terms; empire was not – as he noted from his readings of Lenin – the result of cyclical capitalist crises; empire was ingrained in the nature of commercial interdependence. In this sense, he wanted to challenge liberal *and* Marxist tendencies to see aggrandizement as the expression of desperate reactionary elites that the moralists were all too happy to denounce while ignoring the underlying source of the problem. Hirschman aimed to bring some 'realism' to the understanding of political economy and economic analysis to the study of realpolitik. Hirschman urged readers to see German aggression not simply as a response to the punitive terms of the Versailles peace; it reflected a larger challenge. Economic aggression had to be seen in more systemic ways, as woven into the very fabric of national sovereignty. A real peaceable order had to confront the source of the problem – a contradiction from which liberal, democratic regimes were not immune. If there was a 'natural temptation' to use trade as 'an instrument of national power', Hirschman felt it was therefore obligatory to sacrifice the means of national power-holders' access to commercial weaponry. The core of his injunction came down to this: 'nothing short of a severe restriction of economic sovereignty' would preserve a world that wanted peace with the gains from trade. The only way out, to achieve peace with welfare, was a narrative that revealed the necessity of a wholesale break from the formula that governed global trade since Machiavelli: 'This can be done only by a frontal attack upon the institution which is at the root of the possible use of international economic relations for national power aims – the institution of national economic sovereignty.'[13]

For its time, this was an audacious argument. It anticipated the language of interdependence that we now associate with globalization, though it was far more committed to the necessity of fairness and equity as conditions of interdependence that later neoliberals ignored. As Polanyi and Hirschman sent their books to press in the waning years of the Second World War, there was in fact an effort to rebuild the world market based neither on the re-creation of the national moral economy nor according to a post-national vision. At Bretton Woods, New Hampshire, bankers, economists and diplomats convened to design the elements of a new economic order that would reflect the ideas behind the Atlantic Charter signed by the British and American leaders in 1941 as a model of postwar peace.

Trente Glorieuses

Atlantic Charterism was a kind of compromise, a middle ground between Polanyi's story about the need for restored nation-state vigilance of global markets and Hirschman's global markets which could tame and discipline the national power seekers. The delegates at Bretton Woods, in drafting the terms for the International Bank for Reconstruction and Development (World Bank) and the International Monetary Fund, would strike a balance between the need for states to be able to regulate national economies while strapping them to a multilateral market order, to embed the national markets into a wider order while accepting the role of states to manage their stability to curb the social forces that led to the mayhem of the 1930s. This section considers how this comprise rested on framing narratives of capitalism and interdependence that gave this new arrangement some legitimacy and resilience for three decades, after which it was besieged by the forces that would give way to our globalization.

We point to two key concepts that stemmed from narratives of capitalist interdependence. Both sought to redress a double challenge: how to ensure that consumption kept pace with production within national markets *and* ensure that the resources of colonized peoples that had been seized by old empires continue to meet the industrial needs of empires as they retreated. The first was what became called 'Fordism', which provided a narrative solution to inequities of the old industrial model.

A Century of Convergences

It relied on an institutional bulwark in the form of the Bretton Woods system and domestic welfare to embed new markets, fuse them together and sustain a framework for a post-Euro-centric system which aligned (non-imperial) state power to norms and rules of markets. The second was an international drive towards 'development' to rebuild the fraying ties between postcolonial societies and their former masters, recast as a story of hope, a hope that interdependence could exist without empire. Both were key to the building of a postwar consensus, a consensus that was coming unravelled by the end of the 1960s and which would yield a new search for coordinates in the 1970s, which will concern us in the final section.

The rise and fall of the Fordist narrative mapped on to postwar reconstruction and was based upon the cornerstones of industrial development, international cooperation and American hegemony. It was not just a coincidence that Antonio Gramsci focused on this term, Fordism, as he reflected on the American industrialist's (Henry Ford, founder of the Ford Motor Company) recognition of the ineluctable relationship between mass production, the assembly line and mass consumption. Gramsci could not yet foresee the rise of the shopping mall, though there was already some conceptualizing of mass consumption at the time he was writing – from Thorstein Veblen to Walter Benjamin. However, Gramsci's insight was mainly set in a national framework, albeit in its relation with international processes. His conceptual goal had been to explain how the alienation that came from the routinized assembly lines, standardized production and the disciplining of tasks did not yield to a revolutionary consciousness as mainstream Marxism had predicted. Rather, Gramsci – while never abandoning his hope for a socialist utopia – recognized the shrewdness of employers like Ford who, instead of whipping his workers into obedience, paid them enough of a salary that they could afford the car they helped produce. The brilliance was twofold. First, Fordism buoyed a growing domestic market to soak up domestic production, in a way resolving the problem that concerned Keynes' *General Theory*, how to prevent business cycles from spinning into crises of under-consumption. Second, by re-identifying the worker as a consumer, Fordism blunted the proletariat's self-conception as oppressed wage-labourer and reframed it to wage-consumer; along the way, the capitalist was able to conduct a discreet campaign to cleanse the rebellious worker's body, right down to taming sexual urges and private passions (Gramsci was fascinated by American prohibition movements, for instance). Aligning mass consumption and mass production channelled what Gramsci called 'animality' for possessing things into the rationalization of industrial production of those things, thereby moralizing capitalism and mechanized production. Herein lay the terms of a new capitalist compromise, one in which the capitalist would be willing to pay a living wage in order to see the market expand.[14]

To Gramsci, Fordism was almost interchangeable with Americanism. He ended his ruminations in what would eventually become called his *Prison Notebooks* with a question: is American civilization invading Europe? Was this 'Fordist' system being imported into the Old World? The answer was no. America was condemned to 're-masticate' what Europe created. However, when it came to the ability to moralize the market and give new significance to the wage-labour relationship, Fordism did hasten what would have been inevitable in Europe with the rise of welfare and mass consumption. 'In Paris', he noted, possibly with a dig at the emergent hair-dye firm Oréal (later l'Oréal), 'Americanism can appear like a form of make-up, a superficial foreign fashion'.[15]

Fordism – even as it went by other coinages – was an important guiding principle for the compromises and balances of the post-1945 decades, and gave meaning to the double expansion of mass consumption and mechanization under the roof of integrated corporate structures and sheltered by welfare and Keynesian macroeconomic management. It was a keyword for reimagining the virtuous harmony of the national market and the nation-state.

But what about the world system that had been the condition for Europe's civilization? The struggle against European colonialism forced a search for a different narrative of economic integration – one that made catching up with industrial societies a cornerstone of a more equitable world system. The topic of how postwar integration fuelled a postcolonial narrative is covered in other chapters in this anthology (see Chapter 10). Still, it is important to underscore here that the remaking of the world system had to consign the old imperial convergence narrative which required that peripheries join and submit to the uplifting powers of foreign markets, capital and control, in favour of a successor. For instance, Jawaharlal Nehru railed against British exploitation, and his vision represented an important step in how narratives of global economic interdependence forked in the 1920s and 1930s, as one vision saw membership in global empire as a key to modernization, while others argued that only a break with empire would put colonies on the path to development. 'The only way to right [injustice and exploitation] is to do away with the domination of any one class over another.' 'The exploitation of India and other countries', he exclaimed in *Whither India?*, 'brought so much wealth to England that some of it trickled down to the working class and their standard of living rose'.[16] Since colonies actually lost by staying within the prevailing system, the solution was to drive the British out of India, to break with the old imperial-uplift story of progress and replace it with a new one – a narrative that argued that convergence would only come with an end to empire.

The long dismantling of empire after 1945 cleared the way for that new narrative of uplift. Nehru championed the idea of national planning – coordinated big pushes to get India out of its colonial trap by integrating a domestic economic space. This was a kind of peripheral New Dealism. Parts of the Indian elite glanced at the American projects for reactivating the economy as a model for activating their own industrial capacities and a premium on the integration of a domestic, eventually 'national', market. Taking a page out of the Tennessee Valley Authority, they aimed to build multipurpose dams on the Mahanadi River in the Damodar Valley, which would become the signature of India's economic independence. While some British and American observers fretted about the country's global alignment as Nehru drew from the Soviet planning model to accelerate history and the passage from a rural society to an industrial economy, the effort was more of a hybrid. The point, as far as the eventual head planner, the physicist Prasanta Mahalanobis, was concerned, was to reverse the haemorrhaging of resources from the colony to the metropole by becoming a new manufacturing power bristling with its own heavy-metal plants. By coupling statistics with steel, Indian social scientists could effect a fundamental change in the global economic geography: they could halt centuries of one-sided accumulation under the aegis of colonialism and reconnect decolonized peripheries, increasingly self-identified as a 'Third World' after the 1955 Asian-African Conference in Bandung, Indonesia, as economically and political sovereign co-members of a new, more equitable and inclusive, world order.[17]

National welfare for industrial societies under the Fordist compromise and national development for postcolonial ones were two sides of world market reintegration after empire, with a new bevy of international financial agencies and trade agreements to keep states from resorting to commercial competition policies, provided the framework of interdependence and an equipoise between national and international scales – of resolving the abrasive relationship between nation-states and world markets, national sovereignty and global interdependence.

As a framing for the *Trente Glorieuses*, the three decades following 1945, Fordism and development would be liberating for many and served as the language of liberal internationalism. But they also yielded detractors with other conceptions of interdependence. One was the idea of European integration, of curbing national sovereignty of European states in order to create more regional autonomy and to defuse any threats of future conflict by making nations into tighter trading partners. An important figure in this movement was Jean Monnet, who made his wartime service in Washington as advisor to President Roosevelt, and who saw first hand the rising power of the United States in the global economy. He recognized for France in particular, the advantages to be integrated in a global system. But he also advocated transitional measures to be strong enough to confront global competition, including from the United States.[18] Monnet advocated a New Deal for European integration, that is, a technocratic supranational organization in charge of the modernization of Western European through decartelization and liberalization within the region, creating 'a Union that has the power to lower customs barriers, create a large European market, and prevent the reconstitution of nationalisms'.[19] He did not, however, advocate a single regional state to match the making of a single unified market. Monnet promoted a project of integration in order to prepare European economies for wider global integration.[20]

Even as the embedded narrative of managed interdependence was reaching its peak in the 1960s, it was coming under the lens of critics. By the 1960s, Third World thinkers, inspired by events in Vietnam and Cuba, began to call for a different model of socialist solidarity to rid the world of neocolonialism. The Cuban government convoked left-wing delegates from Africa, Asia and the Middle East to gather in the capital to flesh out a model and plan for outlining a socialist pathway to economic development, one that could rival the orthodoxy coming from Washington. The brainchild of the Moroccan politician, Mehdi Ben Barka, before he was assassinated in 1965, early meetings in Cairo, Accra and elsewhere gathered momentum for something called the Organization of Solidarity with the People of Asia, Africa and Latin America. It was in Havana, at the Tricontinental Conference, that the movement took official shape.

By fusing socialism, development and the anti-imperial struggle, the Tricontinental mapped out an alternative imaginary of solidarity and integration across borders. The signature document for socialist developmentalism was an address by the Argentine-born icon of armed struggle, Che Guevara. Since the early 1960s, Che had been campaigning against the notion of 'peaceful coexistence' of the capitalist imperial world and the postcolonial proto-socialist one struggling for liberation. For the global guerrilla, there could be no true development so long as 'imperialists' structured international dependence on their own terms; only a decisive, violent, break with the Washington order would put the Third World on the path to development. Much to the discomfort of the Soviets, who were having a hard time with Third World firebrands, Che called for the proliferation of insurgencies and a militarization of the narrative of contestation.[21]

By the late 1960s, the postwar consensus was coming apart from within with competition from a more integrated Europe and a rebuilt Japan and challenged from without by critics of global trade and finance. The condition of its buoyancy, the leadership of the United States, unravelled, as trade deficits, pressure on the dollar, and war crippled it. The Bretton Woods System 'ended' on 15 August 1971 when Richard Nixon took the United States off of the Gold Standard. But the end of the narratives that accompanied this order – the Keynesian consensus, cooperation through trade and international organizations, the linkage between growth and development – would come undone over the course of the next decade and yield to a new narrative of convergence.

The struggle for alternatives in the 1970s

During the decade of malaise and uncertainty of the 1970s, the fundaments of the Fordist compromises and developmentalism, overseen by national states' autonomy to manage market integration, came apart and cleared the stage for new narrative of integration, one that turned away from inter-state action to loosened, private, cross-border convergence. It was the flow of capital and commodities above all that would redefine the interdependent makeup, one that would dis-embed the market from structures of state sovereignty.

The term that's often employed to describe this emergent regime is neoliberalism. It is not to be conflated with nineteenth-century style '*laissez-faire*' economics. What buoyed neoliberals was not a romantic narrative that wanted to turn the clock back. If anything, neoliberals had a narrative that wanted to accelerate time in order to liquify social relations into a global social fusion. Indeed, there was, from the start, a strong push to sustain market-based convergence that severed the management of exchanges from the politics of empire/nation-states and placed the tasks in the hands of technocratic, cross-border, classes. In this sense, Monnet and the European integration narrative were prophetic. This narrative was expressed early in the European integration debate by German officials connected to a network of ordoliberal thinkers. For example, Hans-Joachim Mestmäcker was an influential advisor of Hans von der Groeben, the president of the common market committee during the negotiations of 1955 and the future competition commissioner. Together, they developed a holistic conception of competition, a *Wirtschaftsverfassung* for Europe,[22] different from the US tradition of anti-trust law that US officials were trying to implement in Europe. For Mestmäcker and von der Groeben, competition was the way to merge European markets into a unique market. Nor were market fundamentalists on the same page. This German ordoliberal narrative of competition

A Century of Convergences

was firmly criticized by economists and jurists from the University of Chicago. On the basis of the thinking of scholars such as Robert Bork or Richard Posner, the British professor of competition law Valentine Korah and the American lawyer Barry Hawk denounced the outsized legal power of the Commission as meddling since markets tend towards a natural equilibrium.[23] They had sway over the European Court of Justice. Mestmäcker led the counter-offensive in academic circles and European Economic Commission institutions and eventually won the debate for European competition policy.[24]

These ideas of market-based integration swayed and accelerated the pace of European fusion. When Bretton Woods collapsed in 1971, the first oil shock of 1973 sparked a quest for a return to stability without US leadership but based on market flows – which channelled into a narrative about prices and eventually monetary union, this time led not by Washington but by Bonn and West German financiers. The German chancellor Helmut Schmidt as well as German officials were influenced by the ordoliberal analysis of the crisis. For Schmidt, 'the root of all current evils was the failure to get a grip on inflation; in these circumstances, tradition Keynesian policies were irrelevant'. Austerity and wage control had to be implemented to fight inflation. At the same time, states with surpluses were summoned to coordinate their spending. The second oil shock of 1979 pushed the West German government to a firm embrace of the ordoliberal model at a trans-European scale. Coordinated currencies and eventually the making of the Euro would stimulate the competitiveness of European firms though an interventionist industrial policy and challenge the hegemony of the US dollar.[25]

While the project of European integration along ordoliberal lines was taking shape in the 1970s, the decade also saw international efforts to redress the inequality among nations – increasingly conceived along North-South lines – that accompanied global economic integration. The developmental state did not deliver economic power to accompany the political independence of the postcolonial states; it only led further into the periphery rather than to prosperity. Disenchantments with development along the lines of Nehru and others of the 1950s Third Worldist bent turned more radical interpretations to argue for overcoming dependency through revolution. A more fundamental break with the past would put underdeveloped societies on a new trajectory. While there were Neo-Marxist critics like Andre Gunder Frank and Samir Amin who argued that integration into the capitalist world system was itself the cause of underdevelopment, the option to (or desire for) exit was fading. But in a world of asymmetrical power, was there a way to reconcile economic integration *and* national development?[26]

The Third World regrouped into a new, more contestatarian bloc in the 1970s, under the banner of the Group of 77 members of the United Nations calling for a new world order. Leaders of the G77 thought they could achieve this by changing the rules of international trade to level the playing field for the developing nations and stop the drainage of wealth from the Third World. In 1972 Luis Echeverría Álvarez, the president of Mexico, travelled to Chile to meet with counterparts to draft a Charter of Economic Rights and Duties of States and outlined a New International Economic Order (NIEO) in which developing countries would assert their control over their resources and fight back against multinational firms, retain the rents from their exports and proclaim the right of the Third World to sit at the table where global decisions were being made. Here was a new vision of convergence that re-asserted the power of national states to govern the rules of interdependence and thereby make the world system more equitable.[27]

By the end of the decade, attempts to reconfigure the relationship between the global North and South had stalled, but the energy crisis, food shortages and the persistence of poverty kept the management of the world economy at the top of the international agenda. As the head of the International Commission on Development Issues, former West German Chancellor Willy Brandt recast the problems of interdependence in the language of morality and mutual interests and proposed a model of economic integration premised on the internationalization welfare and globalization of Keynesianism. In the introduction to the Commission's report, he wrote that 'in the world as in nations, economic forces left entirely to themselves tend to promote growing inequality. Within nations, public policy has to protect the weaker partners. The time has come to apply this precept to relations between nations within the world community'.[28] The report recommended reforms familiar from the NIEO: commodity price stabilization, regulation of transnational corporation and better access to markets in the North, along with massive transfers of capital from the North to the South which would finance development in the South while also priming the pump to lift the world economy out of stagflation.

By the time the Brandt Commission's report was released in 1980, the world had recently seen a second oil crisis, revolution in Iran, the renewal of East West tensions and a revived enthusiasm for the market, which was now bolstered by conservative electoral victories in Europe. In this environment, Brandt's vision for Keynesianism at an international scale seemed less like a bold way forward and more like an attempt to turn back the clock to an earlier juncture, a tendency that Keynes himself had warned against after the First World War. There was no going back to the growth and stability of the *Trente Glorieuses*. And despite Brandt's attempts to conjure up a sense of international solidarity, the problem Polanyi saw in trying to reconcile welfare and interdependence without a shared community seemed more glaring than ever.

Breaking the impasse

If the crisis of the 1970s saw the competition between rival models of convergence heat up, the shocks of the end of that decade tilted the balance in favour of a market-based conception of togetherness. But it did not necessarily remove institutions from the picture. Far from it, states remained important for disciplining societies that could not remain within the lane-markers of price stability and open markets. After the breakdown of efforts to reform the global economic system in the 1970s, the question of how developing countries could better position themselves in the global economy shifted from the international to the domestic scale. Now problems of relative backwardness were attributed to bad domestic policies, rather than the dynamics of dependence or neocolonialism. The developing countries needed to get their house in order before casting blame on the system at large, and the proper functioning of the global economy required them to do so. For countries of the Third World, this meant using the levers of state policy to dismantle the structures of development – from privatization and deregulation to removing protection for native industries and promoting exports; the state was important for reconfiguring developing societies for a new international division of labour, with the hope that foreign capital and foreign markets would lift them from their plights. The model became a dogma, and the phrase 'Washington Consensus' was its shorthand.

The term 'Washington Consensus' was first used by the economist John Williamson in a 1989 paper outlining the consensus he observed in *both* Latin America and the United States around ten policies: fiscal discipline, reordering public expenditure priorities, tax reform, liberalizing interest rates, competitive exchange rates, trade liberalization, lower barriers to foreign direct investment, privatization, deregulation and property rights. Earlier that year when Williamson testified on Capitol Hill in favour of the Brady Plan for debt relief, his assertion that Latin American governments were reforming their economic policies was met with complete disbelief.[29] Williamson's subsequent articulation of the Washington Consensus was meant to capture a broad shift that was not on the radar of those lawmakers, namely the move away from the orthodoxies of development economics (planning, state ownership, import substitution, industrialization) towards a new set of priorities: macroeconomic stabilization, a larger role for the market and export-led growth models that occurred over the past decade.

In the 1990s, the term took on a life of its own and came to represent a powerful and pervasive conception of global economic integration. For critics, 'Washington' was a monolith from which economic orthodoxy originated and was imposed, and the 'consensus' stood for any number of malign ideologies including neoliberalism, Reaganism, monetarism and *laissez-faire* economics. The policies outlined in Williamson's ten points were interpreted as prescriptive rather than descriptive, representing a universally applicable set of principles that represented common sense. This was no longer the time of the three worlds of the Cold War, each operating according to its own set of economic laws. There was now a single global economy emerging that operated according to a single logic. In order to develop, countries needed to put policies in place that would attract investment and technology, lest they be left out of the global flows of capital and goods. Liberalization, privatization and deregulation weren't just the proper policies to follow at the national level, they were policies that would lead to the best outcomes for the global economy.

Conclusion

For a brief, albeit worldmaking, moment, this 'consensus' about the new balance of markets and states in the making of interdependence appeared to reign supreme. It found its way into the popular discourse on what would be called 'globalization' through the writings of Thomas Friedman. Friedman's syndicated *New York Times* column and bestselling books presented an easily digestible conception of globalization as an inexorable process beginning after the Cold War, which brought prosperity, democracy and stability to those who understood and played by its rules, and disorder and deprivation to those who do not mould themselves to the preferences of the market. It was, in a sense, an ironic return to the mechanical and evolutionary stories of convergence from the nineteenth century that Keynes had broken with. In Friedman's telling, integration was driven by the mutually reinforcing dynamics of capital mobility and technological innovation. Fibre optic cables and microprocessors allowed capital to ricochet between Wall Street, The City of London, Hong Kong and financial hubs in the developing world (now dubbed 'emerging markets' to make them more enticing to investors) and the internet was flattening differences across borders. Friedman had a penchant for strings of comparative adjectives – faster, closer, deeper, farther, cheaper – that repeat like mantras, reinforcing the sense of acceleration and inevitability that underlie his conception of global affairs.

In a 1997 *New York Times* column, Friedman imagined an exchange between Malaysian Prime Minister Mahathir Mohamad and US Treasury Secretary Robert Rubin. Mohamad often appeared in Friedman's writings as a symbol of misplaced Third World fury and a stubborn refusal to come to terms with the realities of the new world order. Friedman's imaginary Rubin scolded an imaginary Mohamad for putting the blame for Malaysia's economic troubles on currency speculators: 'You keep looking for someone to complain to, someone to take the heat off your markets. Well guess what, Mohamad, there's no one on the other end of the phone! The global market today is an electronic herd of anonymous stock, bond and currency traders, sitting behind computer screens.' Malaysia *used* to play by the rules and was rewarded with investment, and when it stopped, the herd took off to greener pastures. For Friedman, no one was in charge. There was no choice.[30]

Not everyone bought into the optimistic sweep of Friedmanian conceptions of globalization with no one at the helm or available to answer for its consequences. For dissenters, globalization was not an abstract force at work in the world, but was the result of decisions made by global elites and the interests of multinational corporations. The protests at the 1999 WTO Ministerial Conference in Seattle – dubbed 'the Battle for Seattle' – were bookended by equally large (and even more violent) clashes between activists and police at the G8 meetings in Cologne in June of 1999 and Genoa in July 2000. McDonald's, Microsoft and Nike – the darlings of Friedman's narrative – became the target of highly visible protests around the world. French farmer Jose Bove and his *Confederation Paysanne* attacked a McDonald's in southern France in protest of WTO policies on beef exports; pictures of children sewing shoes in Nike sweatshops in South Asia sparked boycotts of the brand; and *Adbusters*' 'Corporate America Flag' replaced the stars and stripes with corporate logos, creating a snarky icon for the loose movement. Canadian writer Naomi Klein's 1999 exploration of how brands shape our society and politics, *No Logo*, became a bestseller and the 'manifesto of the anti-globalisation movement'.[31]

For almost two decades following 1989, however, the voices of dissent appeared to be howling in the prevailing winds. It was another crash, in 2008–9, that finally sundered the certainties and hegemonic narratives of globalization, not unlike the effects of 1929.

Ever since, there has been a standoff over the meanings of convergence.

A Century of Convergences

In our day, nativism, fences, walls and herding refugees into barbed-wire camps on a scale unseen since 1945, indeed the very concept of interdependence as a global good which lay at the root of the post-1945 world order is being questioned. Even the prospect of a shared commitment to bend back the carbon emission curve is on the ropes.

Nowhere is this absence of guiding models and narratives for global meaning-making more pronounced than in the domain of the economy. There was once a common-sense view that cross-border trade and investment were good; by lacing the world together into a pool of common interests, an interdependent economy restrained conflict, it brought prosperity, and, under some contentious conditions to be sure, it might even bring development for the world's have-nots. That package makes less sense than ever. Why depend on strangers? Who wants the burden of strangers depending on us? This crisis of global narratives and norms is at once a crisis in economic historiography, an impasse in the guidance systems that have steered the players in the world economy to a sense of historic purpose, one that passed through them from a past to a future.

Notes

1   For classical accounts, see Peter Katzenstein, *Small States in World Markets: Industrial Policy in Europe* (Ithaca: Cornell University Press, 1985); Peter Gourevitch, *Politics in Hard Times: Comparative Responses to International Economic Crises* (Ithaca: Cornell University Press, 1986); Peter A. Hall, *Governing the Economy: The Politics of State Intervention in Britain and France* (New York: Oxford University Press, 1986).

2   Angus Burgin, *The Great Persuasion: Reinventing Free Markets since the Great Depression* (Cambridge, MA: Harvard University Press, 2012); Quinn Slobodian, *Globalists: The End of Empire and the Birth of Neoliberalism* (Cambridge, MA: Harvard University Press, 2018).

3   Daniel Laqua, 'Transnational Intellectual Cooperation, the League of Nations, and the Problem of Order', *Journal of Global History* 6, no. 2 (July, 2011): 223–47.

4   https://www.marxists.org/archive/lenin/works/1916/imp-hsc/pref02.htm

5   https://www.marxists.org/archive/lenin/works/1916/imp-hsc/ch06.htm

6   Keynes, *The Economic Consequences of the Peace* (London: Macmillan, 1919), 5.

7   Ibid., 22–4 and 36.

8   Ibid., 297.

9   Karl Polanyi, *The Great Transformation: The Origins of Our Time* (New York: Farrar and Rinehart, 1944), 23.

10   Ibid., 3 and 102.

11   Ibid., 142.

12   Albert O. Hirschman, *National Power and the Structure of Foreign Trade* (Berkeley and Los Angeles: University of California Press, 1945).

13   Ibid., 79.

14   Quentin Hoare and Geoffrey Nowell Smith, *Selections for Prison Notebooks of Antonio Gramsci* (New York: International Publishers, 1971), 298.

15   Ibid., 318.

16 Jawaharlal Nehru, 'Whither India?' (1933), in *India's Freedom* (London: Unwin Books, 1962), 21.

17 Stephen Clarkson, *The Soviet Theory of Development: India and the Third World in Marxist-Leninist Scholarship* (Toronto: University of Toronto Press, 1978); Adom Getachew, *Worldmaking after Empire: The Rise and Fall of Self Determination* (Princeton: Princeton University Press, 2019).

18 Jean Monnet, *Mémoires* (Paris: Fayard, 1976), 813–15.

19 Ibid., 482–3.

20 Ibid., 610.

21 Jon Lee Anderson, *Che Guevara: A Revolutionary Life* (New York: Grove Press, 1997), 682–84.

22 That is, an 'economic order based on competition'. Hans von der Groeben, 'Wettbewerbspolitik in der europäischen Gemeinschaft', *Bulletin der EWG*, no. 7/8 (1961): 10.

23 Valentine Korah, *Competition Law of Britain and the Common Market* (The Hague: Martinus Nijhoff Publishers, 1982), 284–85; Barry Hawk, 'EEC and US Competition Policies. Contrast and Convergence', in *Enterprise Law of the 80s. European and American Perspective on Competition and Industrial Organization*, ed. F. Rowe, F. Jacobs and M. Joelson (Chicago: American Bar Association, 1980), 49.

24 See the special issue coordinated by Mestmäcker who gathered several specialists of German and US competition laws in order to attack the Second Chicago School: Ernst-Joachim Mestmäcker, 'Introductory Remarks' and 'Competition Policy: German and American Experience', *Zeitschrift für die Gesamte Staatwsissenschaft* 136, no. 3 (1980): 385–407.

25 Helmut Schmidt, *Men and Powers: A Political Retrospective* (New York: Random House, 1989), 173–7. For more, see Schmidt speech to the Bundesbank, 30th of November of 1978, http://www.margaretthatcher.org/document/111554

26 Andre Gunder Frank, *The Development of Underdevelopment* (New York: Monthly Review Press, 1966); Samir Amin, *L'accumulation à l'échelle mondiale* (Paris: Editions Anthropos, 1970).

27 Christy Thornton, *Revolution in Development: Mexico and the Governance of the Global Economy* (Berkeley and Los Angeles: University of California Press, 2021), 168–71.

28 *North-South, A Program for Survival: The Report of the Independent Commission on International Development Issues* (London: Pan Books, 1980), 3.

29 John Williamson (ed.), *Latin American Readjustment: How Much Has Happened* (Washington, DC: Peterson Institute for International Economics, 1989).

30 https://www.nytimes.com/1997/09/29/opinion/foreign-affairs-excuse-me-mohamad.html

31 Naomi Klein, *No Logo: Taking Aim and at the Brand Bullies* (New York: Random House, 1999).

10

Narrating progress: Developmental regimes in semi- and anti-colonial Southeast Asia

Benjamin Baumann and Vincent Houben*

As a concept, development denotes, at the very least, change over time along some kind of progression. Things move upwards and onwards, forwards and not back. As a historical process, the concept could be used as merely a descriptor of the changes in a particular society or relationship, to signify precisely that shift along some kind of agreed-upon metric. However, as with several such concepts, the notion of forward progression through set stages is itself a product of particular historical processes, and for this reason requires some disaggregation. For the purpose of this chapter, we will use 'development' to refer to an historical object: the idea and associated practices held by historical actors in the nineteenth and twentieth centuries, in their efforts to describe or compel the movement of societies through stages of progression. We will focus on how the concept emerged in colonial and postcolonial governance and was adopted idiosyncratically in two key sites. We are also concerned with how the idea that one could, through human endeavour, compel a society to grow, prosper and match the level of 'more developed' groups affected the politics and lived experience of those who lived in these places.

Through two related yet contrasting cases, that of the Siamese monarchy and Siam/Thailand and the Dutch East Indies and independent Indonesia, we will show how the sites of 'development' as a concept and aim demonstrate continuities between semi-colonial/monarchical and postcolonial/democratic governance. Furthermore, rather than the practices of development moving unidirectionally from 'the West' outwards, we will show how the circulation of these practices mirrored the emergence of nationalism, internal colonization and twentieth-century geopolitics in a region that came to be known as Southeast Asia – partly because of these practices and their implementation. The objective of this chapter is not to reify 'development' as an unproblematic historical reality, nor to reduce it to mere discourse – rather, we explore how sets of actors in Southeast Asia narrativized their own pasts, presents and futures,

---

* A first draft of this chapter was co-written with Disha Jani. Disha was part of our team during the workshop series in Princeton and Berlin and we thank her for her insightful input and critical comments on first drafts of this chapter.

184 *Narratives, Nations, and Other World Products*

with the aim towards something understood as 'development' and 'progress'. What kinds of narratives were produced out of these attempts? And what is the relationship between such narrativization and the practices of governmentality?

From a global perspective, it is difficult to ignore the immense impact of European colonialism on the concept and practices of development as they emerged in the late nineteenth and early twentieth centuries. In particular, the period is marked by the emergence of Britain and France at the helm of global empires, with Germany, the Netherlands, Tsarist Russia, the United States, the Ottoman Empire and Japan carving out their own spheres of direct rule and economic control. Colonial governance and the technologies of rule that accompanied it varied across the globe, though the overwhelming expansion of British economic and political influence in the nineteenth century and the synchronization of regional markets into something like a global economy meant that the circulation of commodities and labour became irreversibly transnational. Our focus is on Southeast Asia, a region that is itself the product of the geopolitical regionalizations that characterize Cold War development politics. The socio-cultural collectives[1] that constitute the region[2] have a millennia long history of interaction and exchange between multiple types of polities, while in the nineteenth and twentieth centuries, being home to interlocking types of political organization and centralization. Siam, never directly colonized by a European power, enacted its own process of 'internal' colonization – consolidating centralized monarchical rule over a 'peripheral hinterland' and transitioning to a 'civilized modernity' in the form of the nation-state now known as Thailand. Indonesia was an example of what is considered the classical example of colonial relations in the period of high imperialism – a European power, in this case the Dutch, governed the territories by acquiring sovereignty through violent military and coercive economic means. Both sets of actors participated in political practices and intellectual exchange that sought to govern the people they considered represented by their political projects, in attempts to guide their conduct and secure a particular kind of sovereignty propped up by particular practices of governance. We have found useful the Foucauldian concept of governmentality in explicating these processes; historians of colonialism have more recently worked over the concept into the more specific 'colonial governmentality' (Scott 2005).

The literature on colonial governmentality is rich and grew out of critiques of and responses to Michel Foucault's elaboration of that concept and its relationship to the geography of power in the West. It describes the way in which colonial governments disciplined, ordered and knew the people they ruled, in conjunction with practices of power enacted by European states on 'their own' populations (that is to say, on other Europeans). Scholars of colonialism and postcolonial critics have questioned the usefulness of this Eurocentric model for understanding the notion of power and how it functioned in colonial spaces, and so colonial governmentality is both a modification of Foucault's notion and a fundamental re-working. For colonial governmentality to work, it could not be the 'tropicalization of its Western form' despite the fact that it shared with European governmentality its origins in responses to epidemics, defecation, death and famine, and was meant to treat people as populations capable of manipulation (Prakash 1999). The idiom of anti-imperial political writing, then, as it emerged in the proceedings of the League of Nations, made claims about the kind of sorting, knowing and controlling of people that was required, not to govern them inside of a political form, but to orient them towards that form's realization.

Knowledge was the foundation of colonial governmentality's management of conduct. The threat of revolt loomed behind the colonial state's collection of information, as did the impulse (even in the absence of a centralized state) to learn more so as to better access the local economy and extract wealth. This shift created not only new scholarly disciplines, like anthropology and later area studies, but also a new kind of subject, who was marked by difference from the European subject; indeed, colonial governmentality is specifically 'the knowledge and discipline of the other ... positioned as a body of practices to be applied onto an alien territory and its population' (Prakash 1999: 10). The colonial state's project existed in an uneasy synthesis of the innovations of the civilizing mission and the holdovers of the local. For instance, Karuna Mantena has shown how imperial thinking after the turbulent 1850s – the 1857 Rebellion in India, the Morant Bay Rebellion in Jamaica, the Fenian uprising in Ireland and the Māori Wars in New Zealand – meant that a universalist stance in imperial ideology (liberal imperialism) gave way to a culturalist stance that emphasized difference (Mantena 2010). This meant that 'native' social formations and political systems would be incorporated into the political forms of imperial power, rather than eradicated entirely, if they were deemed useful to the colonial project.

At the same time, the differentiated subject of colonial governmentality could not be ruled like the liberal subject of Europe envisioned by utilitarian theorists such as Jeremy Bentham and James and John Stuart Mill. Colonial governmentality dislocated this process to the colonial sphere and showed how difference and the hybridity of local and colonial governance acted upon the lives of colonized people (Bhabha 1994). New hierarchies, legal orders and forms of knowledge created new kinds of subjects in the colonies; subjects, who could be atomized into individuals, could be aggregated via calculation and census taking, who were seen as a population when taken together, and ordered by the law. In this way, the practices of colonial government created subjects as it acted on them.

The idea of development has a great deal to do with the relationship between political sovereignty, territorial autonomy and the economy (Goswami 2004; Thongchai 1994; Wheatley 2017). For an entity to exist as one that could be studied in its development or compelled to 'develop', it needed to exist as a unit in space and time with clearly demarked boundaries. All the sets of actors addressed in this chapter toggled between political practices and conceptual framings at the local, national, regional and global scale, which shows the extraordinary elasticity of this object called 'development' in this region, and during this period. In the nineteenth century, the nation-state grew in a Romantic European imagination and became enshrined both in the political programmes of that region's nation-building and in the annals of its history-writing (Anderson 2006; Case 2018; White 1973). Between the world wars, a well-documented process of state-making and mandatory rule was carried out by the victorious powers via the postwar treaties and the League of Nations, carving independent nations out of the disintegrating German, Austro-Hungarian and Ottoman lands, and the colonial possessions of the losing powers in Asia, Africa and the Middle East (Martin 2016; Pedersen 2015; Roshwald 2002; Weitz 2008). The 1917 revolution in Russia and subsequent export of Leninist internationalism criss-crossed the globe alongside its liberal internationalist variant, Wilsonian self-determination (Dogliani 2017; Manela 2007). Though not an inevitable telos for this process of political ferment and social upheaval, by the 1940s, the prerequisite for freedom and prosperity became recognition as a singular entity in the international community of sovereign states, characterized by, among other things, membership in the United Nations (Banivanua-Mar 2016; Mazower 2009; Walker 2019).

Anti-colonial nationalism's task in this period was to make an argument for the relationship between a territory, a group of people and place in the global economy that would elevate the standard of living of that group of people. For others, political equality enshrined in a constitution combined with a planned economy would allow for the 'development' of their nation forward into the prosperity that colonialism had robbed, but that the colonial powers achieved. Continuities persisted, because 'colonial states ... were designed to be development states: their telos, from the start, was focused on resources, revenue, and production rather than political participation' (Tilley 2011: 17).

As anti-colonial nationalists took the reins of postcolonial nation-states at the height of decolonization, the project of knowing and controlling their populations moved from the colonial state to the new one without changing the epistemic premises of developmentalist knowledge (Benton 1999; Cooper 2014; Prakash 1999). This project included managing their place in the global economy through the law, trade and international organizations. Theories of development, most notably modernization theory and variants of Marxist political economy, both guided and justified large-scale industrial projects, land reform, public works and population control. By the middle of the twentieth century, experts in economics, sociology, medicine, population, as well as the policy bureaus of the American and Soviet superpowers dominated the global proliferation and implementation of developmental discourses (Bashford 2014; Connelly 2008; Timothy 2002). European states began to account for the problems of the 'end of empire' with welfare programmes, new regimes of migration, policing and ideals of citizenship for the post-imperial nation-state. International agencies codified the world in terms of more and less economically developed countries, terms which grew to eclipse the Cold War political designations of First, Second and Third Worlds.

This contribution focuses on development as a history of ideas of what essentially was a floating signifier across spatio-temporal scales, beginning in the 1850s and ending roughly around 1960. Development became a globally shared language and set of practices but its meaning differed markedly depending on specific historical contexts across multiple spatial scales (Macekura and Manela 2018: 3–9). Instead of taking the West as a point of departure, the rise of developmental thought is linked to non-Western spatial modes – that of internal colonialism, the rise of nation within empire and the late imperial global order. These spatial modes are rendered through consecutive case studies on Siam from the second half of the nineteenth century until the present, and Indonesia from 1900 until 1940. Our core argument is that development as a form of narrative-making was highly contextual, therefore not merely based on a single genealogy while sharing the essentially modern trajectory of progress.

Siam's internally colonizing narrative of development

Thailand is the only Southeast Asian nation that was formally never colonized. Thailand was chosen as a name over Siam in the renaming of the country in 1939 to make explicit that Thailand is the land of 'the Thais'.[3] The renaming was part of a nationalist project initiated by Siamese monarchs in the late nineteenth century and continued by non-aristocratic political elites after the Siamese revolution of 1932 that ended absolute monarchy. Reynolds argues that in this time of transition fraught with internal crises, the renaming was an attempt to monopolize 'the nation semantically for Thai speakers' (Reynolds 2002: 4). As the term *thai* also means 'free', the elites hoped that the name change would emphasize the uniqueness of Thailand's encounter with the colonial powers in the region. In the era of high colonialism, Thailand's quasi-independence and the implied epithet 'free' of the new ethnonym would instil pride and equality with the West in the country's citizenry. As such, the renaming was believed to be capable of creating a sense of national identity in an ethno-linguistically highly diverse population, when it, in fact, privileged the population of Thailand's central plains and especially the urbanized residents of Bangkok, as their local dialect became the national standard (Keyes 1997: 209; Reynolds 2002: 1–4).

The ethnoynm 'Thai' had little practical relevance as a socio-cultural category in everyday contexts before the kingdom's official name change. The homophone category 'Tai', on the other hand, was very meaningful and placed at the imaginary apex of the kingdom's social hierarchy. The practical meaningfulness of this social category derived from the non-modern social ontology of the *mueang*[4] that imagined qualitatively different social collectives than the modern social ontologies that spread to the region during its colonization and introduced race, society, nation-state, ethnic group, tribe, etc. (Baumann 2020; Baumann and Rehbein 2020; Houben 2020). The Siamese empires that emerged from the social ontology of the *mueang* are usually classified as 'cosmic' or 'galactic' polities (Tambiah 1977). This scholarly classification emphasizes the parallelism of macrocosm and microcosm characterizing conception of state and kingship (Baumann 2020: 42). In the Siamese *mueang*, the socially dominant people were classified as Tai, rather than that some 'ethnic Tai' were everywhere socially dominant (Turton 2000: 6). O'Connor emphasizes, therefore, that in order to answer who 'the Tai' were, we need an approach 'that does not already assume modernity's answer [...] Tai, it turns out, is an achieved status' (O'Connor 2000: 35, 38). The country's conspicuous name-change from Siam to Thailand, thus, fostered an 'ethnic chauvinism' that became an essential aspect of the official imagination of national belonging in Thailand (Reynolds 2002: 1). The thus emerging ideas of Thainess and ethnicity are inextricably linked to an idiosyncratic narrative of development under the Thai topos *siwilai*.

Siwilai was one of the first words that was transliterated from English to Thai in the middle of the nineteenth century as a translation for civility and one of the few words that survived in its transliterated form until today (Thongchai 2000: 529). The topos became crucial for the imagination of what it means to be 'Thai' in Siam's newly emergent public sphere (Thanapol 2009). *Siwilai* gradually replaced the Hindu-Buddhist idea of civility that characterized the non-modern Siamese empires

(O'Connor 2003: 295–7). This religiously derived idea is usually portrayed as being premised on a centripetal socio-spatial logic in which the degree of civilization increases the closer one gets to the *mueang's* centre, which was the king's court. This imagination of civility was closely tied to Hindu-Buddhist conceptualizations of purity and monarchy-backed Buddhism imagined itself as the centre of purity-cum-civility. Buddhist temples, therefore, constituted the centre of every settlement modelled upon this non-modern socio-spatial logic and morally righteous rulership – in the form of the Thammaracha – was in Siam indispensably tied to Buddhism. While the Siamese monarchs staged themselves as upholders and protectors of the Buddhist faith, they adopted, nevertheless, a secularized rhetoric of civilization during their encounters with the colonial powers. This rhetoric was premised on the secular twin concepts of progress and development, which increasingly superseded the religious value of purity (Baumann 2020: 54–6).

Although nationalist Thai historiography is based on the premise that Thailand was never a colony, critical Thai studies conceive the Siamese and later Thai elites' modernizing reforms as a conscious 'project', rather than a teleological process of enlightened modernization and rational development based on the growing differentiation of the social body in Elias' sense (Elias 2000; Vandergeest 1993). By appropriating the topos *siwilai* in the sense of refined courtly manners and etiquette in the late nineteenth and early twentieth centuries, an idiosyncratic reformulation of civility became central for the royal elites' deliberate attempts to become members of the 'Victorian ecumene' (Peleggi 2002: 15). Later, non-aristocratic political elites added new layers of meaning and the meaning of *siwilai* became increasingly shaped by nationalism than by royalism. Dress and decorum remained, nevertheless, essential to signify the state of being *siwilai*, and various Cultural Mandates issued in the 1940s declared traditional clothing styles and customs, like the chewing of betel, as to be damaging the prestige of the country (Jory 2022; Reynolds 2002: 6). Despite the gradual replacement of the religious value of purity with secular notions of development and progress to imagine the civility of the urban Thai subject, being *siwilai* remained closely associated with Thai Buddhism.

The rationalization of Thai Buddhism's official image was, therefore, an essential aspect of the elites' project modernity. The Sangha reforms in the late nineteenth century did not only centralize the Sangha administration to enhance its controllability, but also turned Buddhist temples into agents of the nationalist state (O'Connor 1993: 335). The royally sponsored Thammayut Order of monks was founded by King Mongkut (Rama IV) in the 1830s as a Protestant version of the popular Mahanikai Order. In an attempt to counter Christian critiques of the 'superstitious' character of Thai religion, the Thammayut order increasingly incorporated Western symbols of rationality by emphasizing reason, order and self-control (Gray 1986: 253). This rationalized and royally sponsored interpretation of Thai Buddhism became wedded to the official imagination of national identity as it is still epitomized in the common Thai dictum 'to be Thai is to be Buddhist' (Larsson 2022: 5). The primitive country bumpkin adhering to superstitious animist practices and popular Buddhism was thus created as a central foil to imagine the modernity of the civilized Thai Buddhist in the country's urban centre. The practical meaning of *siwilai* gradually shifted in this process from refined courtly manners towards rationalized notions of development (*charoen*) and progress (*patthana*), social values epitomized by the colonial powers and the newly invented Thai Buddhist orthodoxy (Thongchai 2000: 530). The elites' 'project modernity' was thus a direct response to the presence of the colonial powers in the region while revolving around idiosyncratic notions of religiously backed development and progress.

Herzfeld calls the thus emerging socio-cultural configuration crypto-colonial, which he defines as the outcome of a

> curious alchemy whereby certain countries, buffer zones between the colonized lands and those yet untamed, were compelled to acquire their political independence at the expense of massive economic dependence, this relationship being articulated in the iconic guise of aggressively national culture fashioned to suit foreign models. Such countries were and are living paradoxes: they are nominally independent, but that independence comes at the price of a sometimes humiliating form of effective dependence.
>
> (Herzfeld 2002: 900–1)

Semi-colonial is another term used by Peter A. Jackson to describe the characteristic configuration of Thailand's public sphere that emerged from the selective adaptation of Western cultural elements and their organic hybridization with local elements (Jackson 2004a, b; Pattana 2005).

The major difference between Thailand and its externally colonized regional neighbours is that the Siamese and later Thai elites actively mediated Western culture's impact on their subjects as internal colonizers (Baumann 2020: 56). In his discussion of the Southeast Asian variety of internal colonialism, Scott emphasizes the

> massive reduction of vernaculars of all kinds: of vernacular language, minority peoples, vernacular cultivation techniques, vernacular land tenure systems, vernacular hunting, gathering, and forestry techniques, vernacular religion, and so on. The attempt to bring the periphery into line is read by representatives of the sponsoring state as providing civilization and progress – where progress is, in turn, read as the intrusive propagation of the linguistic, agricultural, and religious practice of the dominant ethnic group.
>
> (Scott 2009: 13)

As the Siamese quest for *siwilai* constitutes a form of cultural imperialism, Loos is correct when she identifies King Chulalongkorn (Rama V) as a colonial competitor with Britain on the Malay peninsula (Loos 2006: 17). The most distinguishing feature of the quest for *siwilai* was the institutionalization of a bifurcated disciplinary gaze that monitored the civilizing process of the recently invented Thai subject. Jackson calls this bifurcated disciplinary gaze the 'Thai regime of images' (Jackson 2004b).

Whereas the urban elites tightly monitored the circulation of images in the emerging nation-state's public sphere, they showed remarkable disinterest in monitoring practices in other contexts of social life. Siam's semi-colonial governmentality was in this respect significantly different from European governmentality and the colonial

190 *Narratives, Nations, and Other World Products*

governmentalities that where modelled upon it, which fostered the subject's self-regulation in public and everyday contexts alike. This is usually called self-surveillance. The constant monitoring of one's behaviour as a result of having embodied the state's panoptic gaze is the central characteristic of modern governmentality (Foucault 1991).

However, the self-surveillance of the newly created Thai subject unfolded significantly different. Under the bifurcated logic of the Thai regime of images the subjects of the internally colonizing Thai state learned to monitor their behaviour according to the rules of the elites' quest for *siwilai* in contexts that were classified as public, whereas they were allowed to deviate from these performative rules in contexts beyond the judgemental gaze of Western observers.

One particularly interesting context to map this bifurcation and understand how Thailand's semi-colonial governmentality was tied to idiosyncratic understandings of development and progress is the introduction of Western-style toilets.

The introduction of modern toilets shielded by physical walls and their incorporation into the Thai house from which toiletry spaces were originally absent (Tambiah 1969, Turton 1978) turned human defaecation into a paradigmatically domestic affair. This domestication was an essential aspect of King Chulalongkorn's sanitary reforms that started in Bangkok in the late nineteenth century. The sight of human faeces was probably omnipresent in Bangkok during his reign (1865–1910). Without a sewage system, Bangkok's inhabitants used to defaecate along the banks of the many canals that formed the primary transportation system in central Thailand until the middle of the twentieth century. Given the common portrayals of King Chulalongkorn as a benevolent monarch who saved Siam from direct colonization, one may be tempted to invoke public health concerns to explain these policies. The Thai architect M. L. Chittawadi Chitrabongs (2011) reminds us, however, that his sanitary reforms were aesthetic makeovers driven by monarchic ideas of civility more than policies designed to improve his subject's living conditions through development. As the Western-educated monarch was very sensitive about how European residents and visitors perceived Bangkok, he issued several decrees that hid human defaecation from their judgemental gaze.

Chittawadi describes the goal of the king's sanitary reforms as the creation of a public image that depicted Bangkok as a modern metropolis inhabited by civilized urbanites. In the king's understanding this image would be pleasing to the gaze of Western residents and visitors, while simultaneously depriving the colonial powers of the legitimacy to intervene in Siam's internal affairs as civilizing forces. The symbolic character of King Chulalongkorn's reforms becomes evident when one realizes that water closets in the royal palace and public lavatories on the streets of Bangkok lacked flushing mechanisms or a sewage system (Chittawadi 2011: 173). The king's reforms, therefore, failed to address the hygienic problem of sewage disposal, even as they successfully rendered defaecation publicly invisible.

The purely visual nature of King Chulalongkorn's sanitary reforms conforms to Jackson's arguments about the bifurcated logic of Thailand's semi-colonial governmentality. According to Jackson, in the crucible of Thailand's semi-colonial encounter, Siamese elites acted as internal colonizers and brokers of Western epistemologies, fashioning public and private realms that were structured by contrasting sets of cultural premises and performative logics. Many actions of the Thai elites that may look like developmental policies to Western observers were thus not so much attempts to develop the country in the sense of techno-scientific progress, but rather aesthetic makeovers under the politico-semiologic aegis of the quest for *siwilai*.

Although the primary goal of King Chulalongkorn's sanitary reforms was to create an image of Bangkok that depicted it as an international metropolis inhabited by civilized subjects of a modern state, the introduction of faecal discipline established and institutionalized a modern understanding of the divide between public and private realms as an aspect of urban Thai habitus.[5] King Chulalongkorn's sanitary reforms illustrate how the quest for *siwilai* initiated a selective adaptation process that disciplined Siamese subjects through modern techniques of the body that reinforced the hegemony of an idiosyncratic narrative of development under the topos *siwilai*. The lifestyle of the civilized urban citizen became thus opposed to the 'primitive' lifestyle of the rural masses, using regional vernaculars in everyday life, defaecating along canals and in the field while practising a syncretic form of popular Buddhism. The teleological notion of progress that is enshrined under the idiosyncratic topoi *charoen* and *patthana* at the heart of Siam's quest for *siwilai* is thus essentially normative. Its meaningfulness derives from the identification and devaluation of various 'primitive' Others and their role in imagining the civilized Thai Self in the urban centres of the newly created nation-state. Thus, the Thai elites adopted not only the teleology of progress and development during their semi-colonial encounter, but also the dualist logic of modern identity politics where the Thai Self needed various primitive Others to imagine its civility. The spread of mass-communication technologies, public schools and water closets to the countryside during the twentieth century finally completed the discursive integration of the rural masses under the internally colonizing narrative of *siwilai*.

Genealogies of development in colonial Indonesia

As was the case in Siam, during the second half of the nineteenth and early decades of the twentieth century the state in Indonesia took a leading role in promoting development. This process was narrativized as well as practised within the parameters of colonial governmentality, which was in turn framed as a shared vocabulary circulating among the Western imperial powers. French ideas on a mission civilisatrice or the British notion of the white men's burden resonated within Dutch ideas on modernization through development, which constituted the core epistemological frame of the European colonial project. The structural entanglement between modernity and development led to its further pursuit during the postcolonial period (Mignolo 2007).

The Dutch colonial project was a classic case of high imperialism. Its first priority was the carving out of a single bounded space within which colonial governmentality could effectively be imagined and realized. Within insular Southeast Asia, a territorial scramble between British and Dutch was basically resolved through the 1824 Sumatra Treaty, which relegated the Malay Peninsula and Singapore to the British and other islands in this region to the Dutch. The so-called Dutch East Indies as a territorial unit, prefiguring the geobody of postcolonial Indonesia, emerged from this act of colonial boundary drawing. Different from Siam, where several Western powers continued to vie for influence which gave the Siamese monarchy room to manoeuvre and ultimately save its relative autonomy, the indigenous power holders within the Archipelago were now facing one single imperial power. As a result, in the course of the nineteenth century, the Dutch colonial state gradually expanded its sway both horizontally across the map, annexing one indigenous polity after the other, and in a vertical sense by deepening its interference in indigenous society. As a result an exemplary colonial formation emerged, in which economic as well as social development was pursued to serve the benefit of the colonizer. The Dutch official label for Indonesia was that of a 'wingewest', that is, an area for profit.

However, the Dutch imperial formation in the Indies was also specific in several ways. First, the Dutch had been present in the Indies Archipelago since the early seventeenth century, engaging in trade but also creating a territorialized mercantile network which involved the occupation of Asian trading ports and creating an extensive base on the island of Java. After the Sumatra Treaty of 1824 Dutch territorial expansion was considered to be 'internal', that is, within an area of influence that was already internationally recognized. Therefore, there existed more continuity within the colonial project than was the case in other Afro-Asian areas. Second, after a major rebellion was subdued on Java, already by the middle of the nineteenth century the colonial state started to systematically exploit the rural resource base of the island. The Cultivation System (1830 and 1870) established a state-led scheme in which the Javanese peasants were forced to cultivate huge quantities of cash crops (sugarcane, indigo, coffee) on their own lands and hand them over as their tax contribution. Whereas elsewhere the predominant format of capitalist exploitation was linked to the plantation, in Java colonial export production mobilized the village, forcing peasants and landless to reserve local rice fields for market production but without benefitting in the spoils (Elson 1994). Third, although Dutch territorial expansion after 1880 felt the ramifications of modern imperialism elsewhere, it was rather late until effective rule had been established throughout the Archipelago. Since 1871 the Dutch had been tied down by a major military confrontation with Aceh (Nord-Sumatra), which delayed the conquest of the rest of the so-called Outer Islands (Borneo, Celebes, Papua) to the early twentieth century. In a temporal sense, the Dutch were therefore part of a second wave of imperialism exemplified by the Japanese in China and the Americans in the Philippines (Locher 2012).

The rhetoric of development as cornerstone of the colonial modernizing project started to emerge after 1900, when the so-called Ethical policy was officially adopted in the metropole. The rise of the Christian parties in Dutch parliament strengthened voices which argued that one could not only exploit the population of Java but also had to give something in return. This consciousness was seen as resulting from a 'debt of honor'. Queen Wilhelmina spoke in the crown address of 1901 to Dutch parliament of 'a moral vocation'. Instead of unilaterally ruling over the people of the Indies, the Dutch now framed the colonial system in terms of 'association' between East and West towards a common goal – that of modernizing the colony. Lurking behind this was the idea of civilization both in the cultural and moral sense that resembled the Siamese understanding of *siwilai*, which informed discursive strategies of Western rule and progress (Bloembergen and Raben 2009). Similar to American initiatives on the

Philippines, social policies were started with the aim of offering more education to colonial subjects, enlarging areas for rice cultivation by means of irrigation projects and other efforts. The introduction of new technologies (railways, steamships, newspapers) dramatically raised the general public awareness of modernity and development.

Dutch official narratives were highly self-congratulatory on the achievements of their Ethical policy. In the introduction to a two-volume survey on the Dutch East Indies published in 1911, the colonial politician Hendrik Colijn wrote that the possession of 'our' East-Indies colony was driven by a sense of duty, moral mission and natural self-interest with the goal of bringing these rich lands to fluorescence and development. The Ethical policy was seen by the Dutch people as an epochal project for their small country, which entailed the development of the land and its people in a Western direction (Houben 2015: 211–12). Internal dissent did occur, as the paternalism implicated in 'ethical' development was discursively attacked by critical European voices within the colony. In a series of letters to the daily *Bataviaasch Handelsblad*, the Dutch Resident of Rembang ridiculed the manner in which the Ethical policy was executed in practice. He mocked the arrogance of young colonial officials telling experienced local people how to develop, arguing that much of the established colonial knowledge was off the mark when compared to realities on the ground (Gonggrijp 1944).

The epistemic hegemony of narratives of development in the context of colonial modernity was quickly appropriated by Indonesian, Western-educated actors. Through them the topos of development was reversed as well as re-scripted in order to fit the powerful emancipatory potential of anti-colonial nationalism. A first turning point in the switch from a colonial towards an Indonesian understanding of development was laid out in 1913 in the pamphlet 'If I were a Dutchman' by Suwardi Suryaningrat, written on the occasion of the Dutch celebration of hundred years independence from Napoleonic rule. He protested against the request by colonial authorities that the indigenous population should take part in these festivities since it was precisely colonial rule that denied them their own independence (Anderson 2006: 107–8). In the same booklet Tjipto Mangoenkoesoemo attempted to unmask the double speak of the Ethical policy, since it pretended to prepare the Indies people to stand on their own feet but precluded this at the same time by suggesting that they were like children in need of continuous guidance. The lack of capacity that was entrusted to 'our people' (*bangsa kita*) needed therefore to be rejected. In response both were then exiled from the colony, together with the radical Eurasian leader Eduard Douwes Dekker, the first one who publicly envisaged Indies political independence.

Since 1913 Indonesian and largely Western-educated elites appropriated the narrative of development but modified it in order to serve nationalist aspirations. The Dutch colonial idea had been encapsulated in the idea of '*opheffing*', that is, 'lifting up' from a situation of backwardness in the direction of Western modernity but without relinquishing benevolent colonial rule, being framed in terms of a timeless 'association' between East and West. In contrast, Indonesian nationalism saw development not in hierarchical terms but as the lateral as well as upward movement of a people (*bangsa*) towards independence. The key notions within this strand of thinking were development in the sense of bringing emancipation to fruition (*perkembangan*) and attaining progress (*kemajuan*). In contrast to the colonial thinking that also characterized the appropriation of the twin concepts of development and progress in Siam, both these terms were inclusivist, at least at the outset when *bangsa* was understood to include all ethnicities living within the territory of the East Indies. Ultimately this inclusive and secularized format of nationalism gained the upper hand over other ethno-religious as well as regional nationalisms in the Archipelago or global ideologies like socialism or communism.

The Ethical policy was gradually abandoned in the 1920s because its financial costs were considered too high. Conservative Dutch people both at home and in the Indies were convinced that it had been this policy that had provoked Indonesian nationalism to emerge in the first place. In the meanwhile, the narrative of Indonesian nationalist development evolved further. Instrumental in the increasing politicization of the concept of development was the Indonesian student association Perhimpunan Indonesia in the Netherlands and its magazine *Indonesia Free* (*Indonesia Merdeka*). Its leader and future vice-president of Indonesia, Mohammad Hatta, played a key role in this student association. In the magazine *Indonesia Free* Hatta published a series of editorials, in which he narrated the basic premises of nationalist development. The three goals of the student association were to make students coming from the colony aware that they were above all Indonesians, make ugly colonial realities known to the Dutch public and to develop an own coherent nationalist ideology. The ideas that emerged in Holland were transferred back to Indonesia when Indonesian students returned to the Indies after finishing their studies, carrying smuggled copies of the *Indonesia Free* magazine back home. In addition, ideas of national development were circulating within Asia, whereby Indonesian intellectuals closely watched developments in Japan, India and the Philippines. Inspired by Mahatma Gandhi, Hatta argued that an independent Indonesia could only be achieved on the basis of mass action through self-help and non-cooperation. According to him a fundamental divide existed between 'our group' (*kaum sini*) in the sense of 'the Indonesians' and 'the others' (*kaum sana*). This meant that independence could only be attained on the basis of own strength and self-reliance. So, instead of accepting the colonial narrative of association of East and West, Indonesian nationalists and those in other Southeast Asian colonies expressed their expectation of rupture and eventual confrontation between both spheres of the world.

The politicization of development under a nationalist agenda was watched with increasing suspicion by the Dutch authorities. When anti-colonial revolts broke out in West Java and West Sumatra in 1927 and 1928, they intervened by arresting the former Indonesian student leaders. Hatta wrote his own defence speech, in which he reiterated the principles of nationalist development. The Indonesian people should free themselves from the feeling that only a foreign ruler was capable of improving their economic and social situation. The principle of non-cooperation should therefore be extended in a positive direction. The Indonesian people should become active in promoting their own well-being, thereby making use of the results of modern science and technology (Houben 1996: 93–6). In those years, similar ideas of a self-managed, autonomous development were shared across the colonized world.

During the late colonial era the Dutch colonizers introduced an idea of development that was framed in hierarchical terms, denying those who were supposed to develop their own agency. Also, the ultimate goal of development, the autonomy and independence of those colonized after having reached an advanced stage of development, was denied to the Indonesians. In a second stage, starting in 1913, educated Indonesians were able to expose these unspoken assumptions on the Dutch side and revert them into an emancipatory direction. During the 1920s narratives of Indonesian-led development were yet again transformed as they became much more politicized and geared towards concrete political action through self-help.

The legacies of development as different forms of narrative making reached well beyond the colonial period. After the Indonesian-Dutch war of decolonization had come to an end in December 1949, the economic and political turmoil of the 1950s triggered a further deepening of horizontalist developmentalist narratives in the name of national unity. President Sukarno adopted an increasingly populist governmental style, stressing that 'unlimited' democracy only hurt the commoner and the revolution should be pushed further until a socially just society (*masyarakat keadilan sosial*) was finally attained. He promoted the ideology of Marhaenism, named after a poor farmer whom he supposedly met, in order to define the Indonesian 'little people' as national citizens instead of a proletariat enmeshed in the universal logic of class struggle (Legge 1972: 72–4).

During the authoritarian New Order Suharto regime (1966–98), a deliberate return to the technocratic Dutch format of development occurred, privileging economic growth and increased social inequality over horizontal nation-building. *Pembangunan* ('development' in the sense of engineering or building something) instead of *perkembangan* ('development' as a natural process of change) became the key ideological tool to uphold state authority, in which Suharto was paternalistically represented as the father (*bapak*) of development. Pembangunan carried the image of something new and modern, engineered by specialists and technocrats rather than the common people and something exemplified by concrete physical stuff like infrastructure and industry (Heryanto 1988: 1–24). This type of development reduplicated the policies of Dutch colonial times, which the Indonesians since the 1960s often referred to as 'normal times' (*zaman normal*).

Conclusion

The related yet contrasting historical sites dealt with in this chapter – semi-colonial Siam and colonial Indonesia – show how notions of development and progress as narratives and practices of governmentality were shared by actors located on different scales governed by both colonial and anti-colonial orientations. The late nineteenth and early twentieth centuries thereby constituted a particular period in which the circulation of the idea of development moved between colonization and nationalism. Despite development narratives constituting a globally shared language, it has been shown how the meanings attributed to it differed according to context.

In Siam the monarchical state sought to encounter the colonial powers in Southeast Asia by crafting a national identity based on a newly formulated idea of Thainess, built on the pre-existing non-modern notion of the *mueang* and royal as well as Buddhist notions of *siwilai* or civility. A selective appropriation of colonial governmentality was turned inwards in order to generate an own format, which was more focused on the image of development than its material substance. In Indonesia, likewise colonial governmentality was mostly geared towards using development as the epistemological frame of a project of Western modernization rather than sincere attempt to give colonial subjects more leverage to develop. Thus, as was the case in Siam, development narratives and colonial control were closely intertwined. Yet, contrary to Siam, where development long remained the prerogative of the royal family, top-level bureaucrats and urban merchants, a young generation of Western-educated actors emerged in colonial Indonesia, who were able to use nationalism as leverage to turn development into an anti-colonial venture. Instead of pursuing teleological and idiosyncratic notions of development by mirroring practices and discourses employed by the colonial power to legitimize their own colonial conquest, as was the case in Siam, Indonesian nationalist ideas of progress were more open-ended and socially inclusive. Articulated by a decolonial movement they set the stage for the predicaments and struggles that were to emerge during the period of postcolonial state-building, which nevertheless remained premised on colonial narratives of development.

Notes

1   We prefer the category 'collectives' here as the commonly encountered alternatives 'societies' and 'communities' are partly products of the developmentalist thinking that characterized the colonial powers' imperial projects (Baumann 2020: 51).

2   For alternatives to this still dominant form of geo-political regionalization see Paul Mus' 'Monsoon Asia' or James Scott's 'Zomia' (Mus 2011, Scott 2009). While both of these regions encompass collectives that are usually classified as 'Southeast Asian', the authors' varying emphases of ritual, lowland and upland differences as well as political strategies to evade the state produce totally different units of analyses.

3   The Thai-speakers of contemporary Thailand are just one branch of the larger Tai-Kadai language family. Speakers of this language family can be found from Assam in the West and Annam in the East to Southern China in the North and the Malay Peninsula in the South (Terwiel 2023). The ethnonym Thai refers to the Thai-speaking majority population of contemporary Thailand.

4   The word *mueang* is usually translated as meaning town, country and or realm (Haas 1964: 410). Holt classifies the word, however, as 'nearly untranslatable' as it is rooted in a non-modern language game that produces non-modern forms of life (Holt 2009: 29). The term non-modern here does not imply the notion of progress in the sense of pre-modern, but is used to identify forms of social collectivity that seem to contradict modern common sense. If modern common sense rests on a naturalist ontology and imagines the individual human person as the smallest unit of all social collectives, Siam's non-modern common sense was animistic and imagined the human person as a dividual. As such, it was itself a social collective of human and nonhuman components. This non-modern social ontology was premised on participation and affective, whereas modern social ontology is premised on classification and mentalist (Baumann 2020: 43).

5   We are following the French historian Dominique Laporte here, who argues that it was the domestication of human defecation that created the modern divide between public and private realms (Laporte 1993) and not Foucault, who regards the divide as inviolable truth (Foucault 1986: 23).

Bibliography

Anderson, Benedict R. 2006. *Imagined Communities. Reflections on the Origin and Spread of Nationalism*. London and New York: Verso. Original edition, 1983.

Banivanua-Mar, Tracey. 2016. *Decolonisation and the Pacific: Indigenous Globalisation and the Ends of Empire*. Cambridge: Cambridge University Press.

Bashford, Alison. 2014. *Global Population: History, Geopolitics, and Life on Earth*. New York: Columbia University Press.

Baumann, Benjamin. 2020. 'Reconceptualizing the Cosmic Polity: The Tai Mueang as a Social Ontology'. In *Social Ontology, Socioculture and Inequality in the Global South*, edited by Benjamin Baumann and Daniel Bultmann, 42–66. New York: Routledge.

Baumann, Benjamin, and Boike Rehbein. 2020. 'Rethinking the Social: Social Ontology, Sociocultures and Social Inequality'. In *Social Ontology, Sociocultures and Inequality in the Global South*, edited by Benjamin Baumann and Daniel Bultmann, 6–22. New York: Routledge.

Benton, Lauren. 1999. 'Colonial Law and Cultural Difference: Jurisdictional Politics and the Formation of the Colonial State'. *Comparative Studies in Society and History* 41, no. 3: 563–88.

Bhabha, Homi K. 1994. *The Location of Culture*. London and New York: Routledge.

Bloembergen, Marieke, and Remco Raben. 2009. *Het koloniale beschavingsoffensief: wegen naar het nieuw Indië, 1890–1950*. Leiden: KITLV uitgeverij.

Case, Holly. 2018. *The Age of Questions: Or, a First Attempt at an Aggregate History of Eastern, Social, Women, American, Jewish, Polish, Bullion, Tuberculosis, and Many Other Questions over the Nineteenth Century, and beyond*. Princeton: Princeton University Press.

Chittawadi, Chitrabongs. 2011. 'The Politics of Defecation in Bangkok of the Fifth Reign'. *Journal of the Siam Society* 99: 172–96.

Connelly, Matthew. 2008. *Fatal Misconception: The Struggle to Control World Population*. Cambridge, MA: Harvard University Press.

Cooper, Frederick. 2014. *Citizenship between Empire and Nation: Remaking France and French Africa, 1945–1960*. Princeton: Princeton University Press.

Dogliani, Patrizia. 2017. 'The Fate of Socialist Internationalism'. In *Internationalisms: A Twentieth Century History*, edited by Glenda Sluga and Patrica Clavin, 38–60. New York: Cambridge University Press.

Elias, Norbert. 2000. *The Civilizing Process. Sociogenetic and Psychogenetic Investigations*. Oxford: Blackwell Publishing.

Elson, Robert. 1994. *Village Java under the Cultivation System, 1830–1870*. Sydney: Allen and Unwin.

Foucault, Michel. 1986. 'Of Other Spaces'. *Diacritics* 16, no. 1: 22–7.

Foucault, Michel. 1991. *Discipline and Punish: The Birth of the Prison*. London: Penguin Books.

Gonggrijp, G. 1944. *Brieven van Opheffer aan de redactie van het Bataviaasch Handelsblad*. Maastricht: Leiter-Nypels.

Goswami, Manu. 2004. *Producing India: From Colonial Economy to National Space*. Chicago: University of Chicago Press.

Gray, Christine. 1986. 'Thailand: The Soteriological State in the 1970s'. PhD, University of Chicago.

Haas, Mary. 1964. *Thai-English Student's Dictionary*. Stanford: Stanford University Press.

Heryanto, Ariel. 1988. 'The Development of "Development"'. *Indonesia and the Malay World* 46: 1–24.

Herzfeld, Michael. 2002. 'The Absent Presence: Discourse of Crypto-Colonialism'. *The South Atlantic Quarterly* 101, no. 4: 899–926.

Holt, John Clifford. 2009. *Spirits of the Place: Buddhism and Lao Religious Culture*. Honolulu: University of Hawai'i Press.

Houben, Vincent. 1996. *Van kolonie tot eenheidsstaat. Indonesië in de negentiende en twintigste eeuw. Semaian 16*. Leiden: Vakroep Talen en Culturen van Zuidoost Azië en Oceanië.

Houben, Vincent. 2015. 'Koloniale Moderne in Nederlandsch-Indië. Grenzen und Gegenströme'. In *Andere Modernen. Beiträge zu einer Historisierung des Moderne-Begriffs*, edited by Wolfgang Kruse, 209–18. Bielefeld: Transcript.

Houben, Vincent. 2020. 'Colonial Social Ontology and the Persistence of Colonial Sociocultures in Contemporary Indonesia'. In *Social Ontology, Sociocultures and Inequality in the Global South*, edited by Benjamin Baumann and Daniel Bultmann, 19–37. London and New York: Routledge.

Jackson, Peter A. 2004a. 'The Performative State: Semi-Coloniality and the Tyranny of Images in Modern Thailand'. *SOJOURN* 19, no. 2: 219–53.

Jackson, Peter A. 2004b. 'The Thai Regime of Images'. *SOJOURN* 19, no. 2: 181–218.

Jory, Patrick. 2022. *A History of Manners and Civility in Thailand*. Cambridge: Cambridge University Press.

Keyes, Charles F. 1997. 'Cultural Diversity and National Identity in Thailand'. In *Government Policies and Ethnic Relations in Asia and the Pacific*, edited by Michael Brown and Sumit Ganguly, 197–231. Cambridge, MA: MIT Press.

Laporte, Dominique. 1993. *History of Shit*. Cambridge, MA and London: MIT Press.

Larsson, Tomas. 2022. 'Royal Succession and the Politics of Religious Purification in Contemporary Thailand'. *Journal of Contemporary Asia* 52, no. 1: 2–22.

Legge, John. 1972. *Sukarno: A Political Biography*. Sydney: Allen & Unwin.

Locher-Scholten, Elsbeth. 2012. 'Imperialism after the Great Wave: The Dutch Case in the Netherlands East Indies, 1860–1914'. In *Liberal Imperialism in Europe*, edited by Matthew Fitzpatrick, 25–46. New York: Palgrave MacMillan.

Loos, Tamara. 2006. *Subject Siam: Family, Law, and Colonial Modernity in Thailand*. Ithaca and London: Cornell University Press.

Macekura, Stephen, and Erez Manela. 2018. 'Introduction'. In *The Development Century: A Global History*, edited by Stephen Macekura and Erez Manela, 1–20. Cambridge: Cambridge University Press.

Manela, Erez. 2007. *The Wilsonian Moment: Self-Determination and the International Origins of Anticolonial Nationalism*. New York: Oxford University Press.

Mantena, Karuna. 2010. *Alibis of Empire*. Princeton: Princeton University Press.

Martin, Terry. 2016. *The Affirmative Action Empire: Nations and Nationalism in the Soviet Union, 1923–1939*. Ithaca: Cornell University Press.

Mazower, Mark. 2009. *No Enchanted Palace: The End of Empire and the Ideological Origins of the United Nations*. Princeton: Princeton University Press.

Mignolo, Walter. 2007. 'DELINKING. The Rhetoric of Modernity, the Logic of Coloniality and the Grammae of De-coloniality'. *Cultural Studies* 21, no. 2/3: 449–514.

Mus, Paul. 2011. 'India Seen from the East: Indian and Indigenous Cults in Champa'. In *Monash Papers on Southeast Asia*, edited by Ian Mabbett and David Chandler, 15–91. Clayton: Centre of Southeast Asian Studies, Monash University.

O'Connor, Richard. 1993. 'Interpreting Thai Religious Change: Temples, Sangha Reform and Social Change'. *Journal of Southeast Asian Studies* 24, no. 2: 330–9.

O'Connor, Richard. 2000. 'Who Are the Tai? A Discourse of Place, Activity and Person'. In *Dynamics of Ethnic Cultures across National Boundaries in Southwestern China and*

Mainland Southeast Asia: Relations, Societies and Languages, edited by Yukio Hayashi and Guangyuan Yang, 35–50. Chiang Mai: Ming Muang Printing House.

O'Connor, Richard. 2003. 'Founders' Cults in Regional and Historical Perspective'. In *Founders' Cults in Southeast Asia: Ancestors, Polity, and Identity*, edited by Nicola Tannenbaum and Cornelia Ann Kammerer, 269–312. New Haven: Yale University Press.

Pattana, Kitiarsa. 2005. 'Beyond Syncretism: Hybridization of Popular Religion in Contemporary Thailand'. *Journal of Southeast Asian Studies* 36, no. 3: 461–87.

Pedersen, Susan. 2015. *The Guardians: The League of Nations and the Crisis of Empire*. New York: Oxford University Press.

Peleggi, Maurizio. 2002. *Lords of Things: The Fashioning of the Siamese Monarchy's Modern Image*. Honolulu: University of Hawaii Press.

Prakash, Gyan. 1999. *Another reason: Science and the imagination of modern India*. Princeton: Princeton University Press.

Reynolds, Craig. 2002. 'Introduction: National Identity and Its Defenders'. In *National Identity and Its Defenders: Thailand Today*, edited by Craig Reynolds, 1–32. Chiang Mai: Silkworm Books.

Roshwald, Aviel. 2002. *Ethnic Nationalism and the Fall of Empires: Central Europe, Russia, and the Middle East*. London: Routledge.

Scott, David. 2005. 'Colonial Governmentality'. In *Anthropologies of Modernity: Foucault, Governmentality, and Life Politics*, edited by Jonathan Xavier Inda, 23–49. Oxford: Blackwell.

Scott, James C. 2009. *The Art of Not Being Governed: An Anarchist History of Upland Southeast Asia*. New Haven and London: Yale University Press.

Tambiah, Stanley. 1969. 'Animals Are Good to Think and Good to Prohibit'. *Ethnology* 8, no. 4: 423–59.

Tambiah, Stanley. 1977. 'The Galactic Polity: The Structure of Traditional Kingdoms in Southeast Asia'. *Annals of the New York Academy of Sciences* 239: 69–97.

Terwiel, Barend Jan. 2023. *The ,Soul' of the Tai Re-Examined: The Khwan Concept and the Tham Khwan Ceremony of the Tai-Speaking Peoples*. Edited by Benjamin Baumann. Glienicke: Galda Verlag.

Thanapol, Limapichart. 2009. 'The Emergence of the Siamese Public Sphere: Colonial Modernity, Print Culture and the Practice of Criticism (1860s–1910s)'. *Southeast Asia Research* 17, no. 3: 361–99.

Thongchai, Winichakul. 1994. *Siam Mapped. A History of the Geo-Body of a Nation*. Honolulu and Chiangmai: University of Hawai'i Press.

Thongchai, Winichakul. 2000. 'The Quest for "Siwilai": A Geographical Discourse of Civilizational Thinking in the Late Nineteenth- and Early Twentieth-Century Siam'. *Journal of Asian Studies* 59, no. 3: 528–49.

Tilley, Helen. 2011. *Africa as a Living Laboratory: Empire, Development, and the Problem of Scientific Knowledge, 1870–1950*. Chicago: University of Chicago Press.

Timothy, Mitchell. 2002. *Rule of Experts: Egypt, Techno-Politics, Modernity*. Los Angeles: University of California Press.

Turton, Andrew. 1978. 'Architectural and Political Space in Thailand'. In *Natural Symbols in South-East Asia*, edited by G. Milner, 113–32. London: University of London.

Turton, Andrew. 2000. 'Introduction to Civility and Savagery'. In *Civility and Savagery: Social Identity in Tai States*, edited by Andrew Turton, 3–33. Richmond: Curzon Press.

Vandergeest, Peter. 1993. 'Constructing Thailand: Regulation, Everyday Resistance, and Citizenship'. *Comparative Studies in Society and History* 35, no. 1: 133–58.

Walker, Lydia. 2019. 'Decolonization in the 1960s: On Legitimate and Illegitimate Nationalist Claims-Making'. *Past & Present* 242, no. 1: 227–64.

Weitz, Eric. 2008. 'From the Vienna to the Paris System: International Politics and the Entangled Histories of Human Rights, Forced Deportations, and Civilizing Missions'. *AHR* 113, no. 5: 1313–43.

Wheatley, Natasha 2017. 'Spectral Legal Personality in Interwar International Law: On New Ways of Not Being a State'. *Law and History Review* 35, no. 3: 753–87.

White, Hayden. 1973. *Metahistory: The Historical Imagination in Nineteenth-Century Europe*. Baltimore: Johns Hopkins University Press.

Wittgenstein, Ludwig. 1984. *Culture and Value*. Translated by Peter Winch. Chicago: University of Chicago Press.

Section Three

Other world products

11

Narrating the common good: Stories about and around the United Nations

Pierre-Yves Cadalen, Connor Mills and Karoline Postel-Vinay

Dag Hammarskjöld, the United Nations Organization's second secretary-general, was weary of great power politics. He welcomed decolonization and believed that the UN's General Assembly with its growing number of newly independent states should have a bigger say in international governance.[1] The Swedish diplomat was markedly at odds with Charles de Gaulle who firmly believed in the right of a few powerful nations to decide on war and peace – the five Second World War victors who were, and still are, sitting on the Security Council. Yet the French president did share with Hammarskjöld the idea that the world needed a place like the UN where 'all nations could meet on an equal footing and discuss together the matters of the universe'.[2] But whereas the former thought that ultimately the world's nations were indeed 'united' by a common narrative embedded in the UN's Charter, the latter envisioned the global organization as a site of anti-hegemonic contestation and formulation of counter-narratives. History proved Hammarskjöld right. With an ever-expanding mandate covering increasingly complex issues, coupled with the multiplication of players in international affairs, the UN has become a formidable production site of countless competing stories. The UN's Charter itself, rather than an unanimously agreed-on, clear-cut roadmap, has turned out to be a loose script that beckons for multiple dreams, visions and plots, sustaining a polymorphous definition of common good.[3]

Yet, as the two cases discussed in this chapter underscore, it was unlikely that the UN could ever be as consensual as Charles de Gaulle believed it should be. From the start, the organization was built on a fundamental tension between an ambition to foster a singular narrative of global common good and the pledge to invite as many storytellers as there were sovereign states on the planet. If the peaceful coexistence of all nations and peoples was the ultimate goal, what that goal entailed has been deeply contested, reflecting a variety of needs, interests and beliefs, fed by different experiences of global connectedness. As Jeremy Adelman and Andreas Eckert point out in the introduction of this volume, the reality of global interconnectedness, the need to adjust or the drive to react to one's entanglement within a growing web of global interactions have fed peoples' narrative search and the construction of social categories, or 'world products', such as nation, empire or race. The UN, both as an outcome of, and a reflection on global integration, is arguably a world product par excellence. Established on 24 October 1945, it materialized at long last, after the failure of the League of Nations, the old ambition of world governing for the sake of universal peace. It is a unique institution not just because it is the only international organization that aims at planetary representativeness, but also because of its retention power that echoes the very nature of global integration. Once in, never out.

Getting out of the UN is nearly impossible because the organization is much more than an association of states bound by treaties; it is an entity where realities of global integration are deeply intertwined, and whose existence provokes both hope and exasperation. Its grand aims locate it in the repertoire of the moral meta-narratives of international politics. This assemblage of aims is what we call here 'common good'. It is, more specifically, a layered assemblage that reflects the successive missions the UN has envisioned, with the help of commissions chaired by experienced policymakers, and as many endeavours to define the commonality of purpose of the world's nations. Willy Brandt's proposal, known as the Brandt Report, published in 1980, was about bridging the North-South divide and surviving together. It was followed in 1982 by Olof Palme's proposition, around disarmament and common security. Then in 1987 came Gro Harlem Brundtland's publication that introduced the notion of sustainable development as a new horizon for the UN's global call for action.

So the scenario for the implementation of world peace evolved. In the late 1940s and 1950s, the main storyline was the protection of the rights of nations and the global search for state sovereignty. Later on, the harsh socio-economic conditions of the newly independent nations came to the forefront, illuminating the relation between global development and global stability. The 1980s also witnessed the rising threat of nuclear weapons, pushing the focus of the UN's grand narrative back from North-South to East-West. By the end of the Cold War, the possibility of total annihilation inspired by military analysis such as Mutual Assured Destruction (MAD) concurrently highlighted our earthly condition and vulnerabilities. It transformed the common human-centric understandings of security. Nature became part and parcel of the world represented by the UN, and environmental protection was increasingly deemed as a core feature of global security.

But facts and events do not, as such, make narratives. Stories need storytellers. By the end of the Cold War, the number of raconteurs on the international scene had notably increased: national actors that did not have a voice before decolonization, transnational actors who found ways to talk across borders despite the rigidities of the bipolar order setting. That trend sharply increased after the fall of the Berlin Wall. The centrality of sovereign states in cooperation and regulation, which defined the UN's architecture, was challenged by the growing involvement of non-state actors since the early 1980s in a continuously expanding number of issues pertaining to global governance. In the beginning of the millennium, the rise of non-Western powers – exemplified by the creation of the BRIC (Brazil, Russia, India, China) forum in 2009 – accompanied the diversification of both narrators and narratives of common good. Or rather it considerably improved the audibility of the latter. It also sheds a cruder light on the quaintness of institutional arrangements that were shaped by the post-1945 international balance of power, such as the composition of the UN's core body from which both Africa and Latin America are conspicuously absent.

The research cases presented here are located at the two temporal extremes of the trajectory of the UN as we know it today. Together they involve a remarkable diversity of actors and sites – from the military base towns of Japan in the 1950s to the forests of the Andes in the 2000s – and hence give an idea of the complexity of factors and processes implicated in the making of the UN's narrative space. The first one takes place during the very early days of the organization: less than a decade after its establishment, and only two years after the launching of its first Security Council-authorized military action, on the Korean peninsula. It follows events that occurred in the city of Kobe when Japan had just recovered its sovereignty after more than six years of Allied occupation. The UN was then an abstract presence – the weird abstraction to which Dag Hammarskjöld referred to – but its dominant narrative of common good, which was the quest for national dignity, and therefore the enforcement of state sovereignty, had a very concrete resonance on the ground. The second research case takes us to the beginning of our new millennium and to Evo Morales's Bolivia. It looks at the reinvention of environmental politics at a time when, more generally, new national actors in Latin America – such as Morales and other indigenous leaders – were redefining domestic and international political practices. Now the UN was a familiar figure, with its blue apparel of doves, helmets and flags. It was, and is, an institution that had been acknowledged, called upon, hailed, loved and hated, and might have even turned into the 'drawing made by the people themselves' that Hammarskjöld hoped for, albeit not necessarily a coherent one. The ownership of the UN's narrative of common good has considerably widened since the years of the Korean War, and that narrative has become thicker, made of a complex fabric of ideas and ambitions. But, as we will see, what has not changed is the strength of the national narrative framework. As yet the UN is fundamentally a gathering of nations and not a union of peoples, and national interests have a decisive shaping power on the formulation of narratives of common good.

National sovereignty as a narrative of the common good

The Kobe incident and national sovereignty in Korean War–Era East Asia

The Korean War was the result of a particular interaction across a particular border, in this case the invasion of the North Korean military across the thirty-eighth parallel. The UN war effort subsequently required many more cross-border interactions, including the stationing of hundreds of thousands of US and British Commonwealth personnel on bases in Japan. These various interactions produced narratives from the moment the conflict began. At the broadest level, a narrative put forward by the UN itself placed territorial justice squarely at the centre of a conception of the common good in international relations. Indeed, Security Council Resolution 82, which laid the groundwork for the eventual decision to commit military forces to the Korean Peninsula, began by framing the invasion as a violation of Korean sovereignty. The resolution noted that 'the Government of the Republic of Korea is a lawfully established government having effective control and jurisdiction over' the territory of Korea below the thirty-eighth parallel, an authority that was 'based on elections which were a valid expression of the free will of the electorate of that part of Korea'. It was the violation of this lawful sovereignty by armed attack that led the council to determine that the North Korean invasion was a 'breach of the peace'.[4]

Such a narrative of the common good may initially appear internally consistent when articulated at the abstract level of a Security Council resolution. A number of inconsistencies begin to crop up, however, when one examines the international politics behind the conflict, much less the practical realities of prosecuting a war that required the coordination of more than two dozen ally nations and the deployment of millions of military personnel. At the level of international politics, a number of historians have pointed out how the impetus behind the UN intervention in Korea had far more to do with the national interests of the United States than any universalist conception of the common good.[5] A voluminous body of scholarship underlines the fact that the Korean War was a contradictory moment in a number of interlinked histories, from that of the nascent United Nations to that of the burgeoning Cold War.[6] While keeping these high-level debates in mind, this section sets its sights lower to the ground. It argues that the abstract gears of the aforementioned narrative of the common good were often seized up by the concrete sand of a thousand particularities and details.

Specifically, this section will examine one of these grains of sand: the 'Kobe incident', a 1952 diplomatic crisis between Great Britain and Japan that was a direct result of the stationing of soldiers in Japan for the UN war effort. On 29 June 1952, the HMS *Belfast*, taking a break from active duty around the Korean peninsula, steamed into Kobe on a 'goodwill mission'. Two sailors aboard the *Belfast*, Able Seamen Derek Smith and Peter Stinner, took the opportunity to go ashore for a night of bar hopping. Unfortunately, as a newspaper later put it, 'one beer led to another, and then came the incident'.[7] The pair were apprehended late that night by the local Japanese police, arrested for stealing a taxicab after they had assaulted its driver and robbed him of around 1,700 yen. At the time, it was common practice for local Japanese authorities to turn detained military personnel over to British authorities for punishment. In this case, however, the Japanese officials refused. Instead, the two sailors remained in Japanese custody until they were tried, convicted and sentenced to thirty months in prison on August 5. The sentencing in turn prompted a formal request for the release of the men by British Foreign Secretary Anthony Eden on August 6, launching the diplomatic crisis proper.[8]

Much like the war in Korea, this was a fight over a question of jurisdiction. With the promulgation of the San Francisco Peace Treaty in April 1952, Japan had regained its full sovereignty after more than six years of occupation by Allied troops. The transition from occupation to independence raised new questions about the legal position of the hundreds of thousands of soldiers who lived in or passed through Japan during the Korean War. The United States largely resolved these issues by effectively negotiating a Status-of-Forces Agreement (SOFA) with Japan in 1951, as part of the broader negotiations surrounding the San Francisco Peace Treaty. Great Britain, meanwhile, was left scrambling to nail down a new legal position for its military personnel in Japan. Ongoing negotiations centred on two alternatives: Japan wished to implement a NATO-style SOFA, in which off-duty troops who committed crimes would be prosecuted by their host country rather than their home country; Great Britain, on the other hand, insisted that they should have full jurisdiction over their own personnel, as the United

States did under the terms of the agreement it had signed in 1951. Here we can already see the beginnings of new narratives that challenged the universalist story of the UN. If the UN claimed that Korea's 'jurisdiction' was inviolate in Security Council Resolution 82, Great Britain saw Japan's jurisdiction as a subject for negotiation.

When the crisis came, the universal narrative of the common good quickly collided with national narratives articulated by officials in Great Britain and Japan. The UN narrative held that Great Britain and Japan were equals, united in an effort to uphold global peace. British officials, meanwhile, had their own story. In February 1952, a few months before the crisis in Kobe, British Ambassador to Japan Esler Dening had written of Japan:

> [T]he Sleeping Princess who, after six years in her glass case, was restored to life by the kiss of peace of forty-eight nations at San Francisco, differs very largely from the lady of the fairy tale. She has a number of aches and pains, her limbs are stiff and uncertain from lack of use and she is certainly a little bedraggled and bewildered.

Great Britain, on the other hand, was 'Prince Charming ... rich, handsome and strong'. Dening admitted that the road ahead did not look entirely smooth; Japan remained somewhat sceptical that the prince was 'as charming as his name'. Still, there was good reason to hope that Japan would see reason; all that remained was to negotiate a new 'marriage settlement'.[9] If the UN narrative emphasized unity and equality, this British fairy tale insisted that Japan was in a distinctly subordinate position at the beginning of 1952. A few months later, the Kobe incident confronted British officials with a choice between international cooperation and national pride, a choice between the narratives of the United Nations and those of the UK. When put to the test, they seemed to have little difficulty choosing which storyline to follow.

Competing narratives of the Kobe incident

The Kobe incident quickly generated new and competing narratives in Japan and Great Britain. National interest in Japan was particularly intense; the *Mainichi shinbun*, *Yomiuri shinbun* and *Asahi shinbun* all published editorials on the sailors, and the incident was front-page news for at least one – and often all three – of the major national papers every day for the rest of August.[10] Japanese media members and politicians produced narratives about the crisis that drew directly on the history of imperialism in East Asia, as well as the regime of extraterritoriality that had existed in Japan under the so-called 'unequal treaties' of the late nineteenth century. One opposition Diet member warned that, without prompt action, Japan might 'become like Korea or Manchuria', a target of encroachment by external powers.[11] A representative for the Yoshida administration later admitted that memories of extraterritoriality were 'still fresh' in Japan and that granting extraterritorial rights to a foreign army was 'totally unacceptable' in the minds of many Japanese.[12] An editorial in the *Yomiuri shinbun* argued that a sense of national consciousness, which had 'withered [*ishuku*]' during the Occupation, was reawakened by the signing of the San Francisco Peace Treaty. The paper warned that international insults like the Kobe incident could have very easily caused a more extreme form of nationalism to 'flare up [*moeagaru*]' in postwar Japan.[13]

This was precisely what British narrators of the Kobe incident argued had already happened. Although the case received far less attention in British media, a number of articles claimed that the Japanese actions were motivated by bigotry and anti-British feeling. The *Times* wrote that the 'savage sentence ... betokens a degree of anti-foreign feeling which westerners had hoped had been eradicated from Japanese nationalist sentiment'.[14] The *Daily Express* informed its readers that the Japanese press had 'started a hate campaign against British troops in Japan', and the *Manchester Guardian* ran a column under a headline that claimed that Japan was 'Feeding the Flames of Xenophobia'.[15] Ambassador Esler Dening and his colleagues at the embassy were equally outraged by what they saw as the mistreatment of their countrymen. After the sailors were sentenced, Dening wrote that the sentence was 'savage, wholly unjustified and animated by anti-foreign sentiment'.[16] Even as Japan placed the Kobe incident in a longer narrative of imperialism and foreign encroachment, Great Britain located the crisis in a narrative about the lasting legacies of Japanese criminality and xenophobia during the Second World War.

These narratives competed directly with the story of formal equality and international cooperation simultaneously being put forward by the UN. Perhaps nothing better symbolizes this fact than one of the stratagems that Dening suggested to secure the release of Smith and Stinner. In early August, during what was perhaps the most intense phase of the crisis, Dening argued that Great Britain should threaten to block Japan's bid to join the UN. If Great Britain hinted that it might veto Japan's request for membership, Dening proposed, Japanese officials might be convinced to release the two sailors. To test the waters, he suggested, the threat could first be put to the Japanese ambassador to Britain; on 9 August, Dening asked (somewhat strangely), 'Might it not be possible discreetly to make his flesh creep?'[17] Perhaps unsurprisingly, the British Foreign Office's reaction to this suggestion was decidedly negative. One of Dening's colleagues wrote that the plan was 'ill-advised', and a British official stationed in Washington wrote that his 'blood rather curdled' at the very suggestion.[18] Nonetheless, the proposal is suggestive of just how little weight Dening assigned to Britain's status in Japan specifically as it pertained to the UN war effort. To prevent any damage to Great Britain's national status in Japan, Dening was willing to undermine an ally's attempt to join the very international body that was ostensibly responsible for keeping the peace in Korea.

After months of backchannel negotiations, the Kobe incident was finally resolved on 5 November, when a Japanese appeals court upheld the conviction of the sailors but suspended their sentence for three years. The court maintained that Japan did in fact have proper jurisdiction, but Smith and Stinner were allowed to board a British vessel to return home. Dening was pleased that the crisis was over but did not feel that Japan had done Great Britain any great favour, writing that he saw 'no reason to encourage the Japanese in the belief that they have behaved with any particular generosity'.[19] No one seemed entirely pleased, as British officials continued to grouse privately and the Diet's opposition parties continued to criticize the Yoshida administration for several more months. Meanwhile, the wider SOFA negotiations ground on. It was not until more than a year later, in February 1954, that Japanese and British negotiators once and for all cemented the formal legal status for UN personnel in Japan. In the end, Japanese officials got their way, as the new SOFA was based almost entirely on the NATO model.

National sovereignty for whom?

Though now little more than a historical footnote in the larger history of the Korean War, the Kobe incident offers an interesting perspective on the various narratives produced when UN soldiers crossed territorial borders for that conflict in the early 1950s. For one, the incident shows how shallow the roots of international cooperation could sometimes be in the early postwar years. Even as the UN was attempting to put forward a narrative based on equality among nations, the old colonial, racial and international hierarchies appeared to linger. Once the crisis began, British officials quickly accused their Japanese counterparts of anti-foreign bias and demanded that the sailors be released. The cooperative rhetoric embodied in Security Council Resolution 82 was nowhere to be found in Ambassador Denning's suggestion that Great Britain block Japan from UN membership even as Japan was lending active support to the UN's war effort in Korea. Media members in both countries articulated the crisis in terms that appealed to nationalist sentiments. Thus, the fledgling UN narrative found itself struggling to compete with national narratives that drew on already-existing histories of imperial projects and international relations in East Asia. As the following section will show, this conflict between the universal and the particular was not a problem solely for the narrative around territorial justice. When it came to environmental justice, too, actors on the ground sometimes took the UN's narratives into their own hands.

Environmental justice and the Bolivian forest as an empowerment narrative

Reframing the global narrative of environmental justice

We will indeed see that national narratives are still, several decades after the Kobe incident, decisive in the process that leads to the definition of the global common good. The global common good, as an idea, is constantly reinterpreted before eventually being projected internationally. In other words, global common good narratives are always going bidirectionally, from the local to the global and from the global to the local. In contemporary Bolivia, presided by Evo Morales from 2006 to 2019,[20] the ever-growing international importance of environmental issues, and the resulting powerful idea of environmental justice, gave the government in La Paz an opportunity to produce a new national narrative – a counter-narrative to previous ones – designed to have a global reach. But what the Bolivian President Evo Morales' narrative strategy has revealed, either at the United Nations General Assembly or in other multilateral fora, is precisely a difference in directionality. Whereas the Kobe incident offered a clear direction from the local to the global, where national narratives confronted an international one, the Bolivian example exposed another, almost reversed, trajectory. Here, the narration of the common good goes from the global to the local, and more specifically, the national. It borrows from and reshapes a global narrative of common good – the narrative of environmental justice – to produce a national narrative, aiming at international projection.

Common good is fundamentally attached to peace at the UN level, and the actual links between peace and the ecological issue[21] are the very basis for the Bolivian national counter-narrative to achieve a global dimension. One apparently universal notion served this diplomatic purpose: the Forest, as a part of 'Nature', or 'Mother Earth', the Andean '*Pachamama*'.[22] This universal notion is a useful tool to build a 'political fiction', which is, as stated by Patrick Boucheron in his Collège de France's lectures, 'not necessarily feigned: it does not always create a possible world, but it produces a thought experiment'. And the historian adds: 'This dual definition – fiction imitates the world, but it is its own world – allows for the pragmatic description of a variety of practices and conducts'.[23]

We will try to explain now the reason why forests are an effective world and subject to build an international counter-narrative precisely articulated to the common good. Why can forests be useful to imagine an alternative narrative received within the general frame of the UN's common good?

The Bolivian forest: A globalized national counter-narrative

First and foremost, the particularity of forests is to be found in their materiality. Even if 'the Forest' can lend to the production of many narratives, one cannot ignore that each forest forms a local ecosystem of its own while belonging to a much larger ecosystem. The UN has always been a site of contested narratives where, since the 1970s, 'nature' has progressively become a crucial battlefield for international politics.[24] Nature, therefore, turned both into a global common and an increasingly decisive political stake in world affairs, leading to an evermore intense competition of narratives. Bolivia experienced, with Evo Morales' election, an important political shift regarding the rights of 'Mother Nature' – 'la Pachamama'. This notion then became an international asset in order to produce an ecological counter-narrative that provided Bolivia with international recognition. Although what looked like a new emplotment created by one of the poorest countries in Latin America has always been and continues to be a way for the Bolivian government to gain global legitimacy as both a state actor and the producer/promoter of a transnational vision.

Three dimensions are particularly salient in the Bolivian attempt at reconfiguring environmental narratives within the UN, along the lines of common good principle. Firstly, a forest is a territory, and cannot consequently escape from the principle of sovereignty. Secondly, the forest as a narrative is an empowerment tool, through which the Bolivian state has taken ownership of academic and civil society ideological movements. From there, and thirdly, the Bolivian projection of its forest narrative means building an imaginary that can be used for what could be called a new government of the empowered.

The sovereign defence of the forest

The Amazonian forest is the bearer of a fundamental tension. On the one hand, the Amazonian forest has been constructed as a single entity, ecologically relevant and crucial for the survival of indigenous ways of life. On the other hand, the unique legitimacy of sovereignty was reinserting Amazonia in the normal and current process of state territorial appropriation[25]; it was a way to guarantee the development policies. The *proceso de cambio*[26] or 'process of change' in Bolivia gave a central position to the indigenous culture and politics, modifying substantially the Bolivian international position regarding the classical territorial narrative. Indeed in 2009 Bolivia self-proclaimed itself an indigenous multinational state, making the indigenous rhetoric a central feature of the international projection of its new regime.

The interaction between a singular Bolivian configuration and the global counter-narrative articulated by the Bolivian diplomacy gave birth to the International Day of Mother Earth adopted by the General Assembly (resolution 63/278) in 2009: this negotiation was led by Pablo Solón, a quite well-known environmentalist in Bolivia, and he considered this international step as an important diplomatic victory for Bolivia.[27] This is a typical example of 'political reconfiguration' through narrative invention, following a process described by Paul Ricoeur.[28]

This narrative based on the *Andean* worldview meets the issue of forests in the context of UN negotiations. What could appear as a paradox here is the relative absence of Amazonian communities within this narrative. The unifying factor between different communities is then to be found in another narrative, which could be described as a powerful metanarrative: the common good. At the intersection of Christianity, environmentalism, socialism and indigenism, this notion constitutes a useful punctuation for this new narrative. Any traditions can be reconfigured through the ambiguous notion of community. At this point, forest became for the Bolivian diplomacy a narrative that could conveniently evolve upon the basis of the common good metanarrative, convenient for Bolivian diplomacy and relevant to the UN sphere.

Common good and the Pachamama as narrative partners

Then, the narrative construction of Bolivia within the UN aims at building a counter-narrative that would nevertheless respect the metanarrative structure of the UN: even more, it would offer a new interpretation of what the common objectives of World Nations could be.

From the Bolivian perspective, the counter-narrative on climate change constituted a window of opportunity. The political agenda of the Bolivian diplomacy was limpid, and implied that the ecological issue was both giving this peripheral country a global echo, and allowed the singularization of their position.[29]

It is also essential to analyse the specificity of the ecological issue. The paradox of the articulation between the Bolivian counter-narrative, the UN metanarrative and their very definition is lying in the current and permanent possibility of their annihilation. In other words, if no one cooperates in order to maintain the forest – and other environmental commons – as an ecosystem which mitigates climate change, the political and material basis of the political narrative coming from the new Bolivian government would vanish. The main feature of both the Bolivian counter-narrative and the metanarrative of the UN is without any doubt a strong instability.

However, this instability does not prevent both the Bolivian counter-narrative and the metanarrative to meet at the UN and then to be a source of legitimization each one for the other: the UN needs national counter-narratives to justify its metanarrative, based on the free expression of equal Nations. The vastness of the notion of Common Good, even if it is culturally rooted and partly Eurocentric, allows the metanarrative to work quite efficiently as a potential gathering of different worldviews.

Forest as an empowerment narrative

One striking example of such a process is the integration of the indigenous perspective within the Forest narrative. Indeed, the narrative of the Forest is not the same whether one integrates or not the indigenous communities within the story. For the most conservative environmentalists, there is no positive human impact on the forests,[30] which have then to be emptied.[31]

For instance, the Tipnis, a Bolivian national park and indigenous territory, was a place of many struggles against the liberal governments during the 1990s. Those struggles were mainly led by the *cocaleros*, the coca growers. At the head of their union was Evo Morales. The international support of the UN and the EU was crucial in their political formation and capacity for later political events.[32] Their relations to the Amazonian communities living inside the very park were quite weak though. Their link to the territory was relying on their work as peasants. It was and still is an economical one. The ground is considered by the *cocaleros* as a potential source of wealth.

In order to understand the difference between the Amazonian communities and the indigenous peasants, it is possible to analyse the conflictual situation linked to the construction of roads within the park: the Amazonian communities considered it as an assault on their living space. In their view the *cocaleros* were 'men of roads' whereas they were 'men of rivers'.[33]

The main narrative evoked in the first part, defining now the interaction between the Bolivian government and the UN, has almost erased the narrative of those *hombres de los ríos* (men of rivers), which explained the *a priori* paradox of their absence from the Bolivian counter-narrative about the Forest.

Even if a nuanced and synthetic version of the Amazonian communities' narratives has been integrated to the governmental narrative, some material processes are going on, which erode their middle-run capacity to live in the forest.

According to Diego Pacheco, one of the Bolivian negotiators for COP, other parties in the negotiations of the COP17 at Durban were surprised to hear the critics from Bolivia against the material conceptualization of a forest: what is a forest to you all, indeed, was their interrogation.[34] Is this a part of our consciousness and lives as human beings integrated to a greater natural entity or an element of nature subjugated to our possibilities of action? In this very opposition lies the political importance of narratives.

The government of the empowered: A global and political counter-narrative

History as a discipline is at the core of any narrative formation. For there is no narrative without references to the past, an effective narrative contains the ambiguities of this very past. Despite its novelty, the reconfiguration cannot be based on any *tabula rasa*. It is thus interesting to observe the continuity between the national development narrative from the 1970s and the forest narrative from the last decade. The former was mainly based on the dependency theory[35] that linked the economic situation in Latin America to the wealth of Northern capitalist countries.[36] As for the latter, the notion of ecological debt is essential and largely based on the same theoretical ground[37]: the contribution to climate change is almost neutral for a country such as Bolivia, implying that the main contributors to its mitigation have to be the Northern nations. Forest is at the core of such an argument: the vice-president of Bolivia, Álvaro García Linera, argued that there were 5,400 trees per habitant in Bolivia, whereas there were 140 trees per habitant in Germany[38]: efforts are already made by Bolivia, and the international community have to take this fact into account, given their economic predominance.

This global narrative of the forests is thus to be considered as a unifying one, addressed to the UN and the international community in order to globalize the stakes and draw a straight global line between the empowered and the powerful: in other words, the political use of this narrative is to displace the conflict from a national or local perspective to a global one, involving all the social forces and determining actors in the analysis. In a nutshell, this new emplotment is meant to search unity where conflict is the dominant and persistent reality. It evolves on the edge, between the indigenous *cosmovisión* or worldview and a more euro-centric perspective, that would consider, with Élisée Reclus, that 'mankind is nature becoming conscious of itself'.[39]

The paradoxes of a counter-hegemonic sovereignty

The counter-narrative that Bolivia defended is based on a paradox that can enlighten more generally the analysis of counter-narratives held at the General Assembly of the UN. As it is built on the international status of Bolivia, that of a peripheral country, this counter-narrative works to be closer to the transnational and social movements at a global scale. However, even if Bolivia is a peripheral state, it is still a state. And the international claim for an anti-capitalist protection of the environment is also a claim for sovereignty and international recognition. Here lies the paradox between the forest as a core element of the Bolivian counter-narrative and the forest as a global space that is structured by a transnational dimension and a global militancy.

Sovereignty is both a condition for the projection of a counter-narrative and an inner limitation of the counter-narrative. In the eventuality of a direct conflict upon a forest, the counter-narrative's integrity would suffer from the priority given to sovereignty over the global protection of the Amazonia. The identity of the narrators is then particularly interesting, because they have various stories to tell. At the UN, the Pachamama's protection is a powerful counter-narrative, but Evo Morales, his vice-president and the entire government have another imperative: they have to tell simultaneously another story, that of a state strengthening itself nationally and internationally. This paradoxical position leads to inevitable tensions that, in turn, reveal a deeper reality: national interests, strictly defined, are inescapable as is the framework of the UN's metanarrative.

Conclusion

A global organization such as the United Nations relies on a fundamental hypothesis: the possibility of a narrative that can be shared on a planetary scale. Which brings about a fundamental question: whose narrative is it? Who owns it? At the moment of its creation, the UN belonged to the history of institutions described by Craig Murphy,[40] that is, an institution imagined and conceived by a small Western governmental elite, and eventually established by a few big national powers. The Charter, that delineated its original narrative, was very much the product of a handful of persons even if it was discussed within the larger circle of the Allied representatives at Dumbarton Oaks. Yet the Charter, and the institution it sustained, was a call for a much wider conversation and became a de facto invitation to define and redefine the 'common good' that the fundamental text was supposed to enshrine. The UN offered a framework, and soon became an actual site for the production of multiple narratives. It also became a major node for the formation and dissemination of ideas, and for the global projection of norms.[41] In that sense the organization is as much an assembly as it is a laboratory-cum-workshop.

As the two research cases presented in this chapter illustrate, the narrative production triggered by the establishment of the UN has been far from homogeneous, both temporally and spatially. The numerous narrations occurred within a variety of scales and units, at different moments in the history of international politics. The Kobe incident, a multi-scalar event in itself, led to the expression of a counter-narrative of territorial justice to the Charter-sponsored narrative about the rights of nations and world peace. It revealed, however, not just a disjunction of narratives – the national versus the global – but also a circulation: how the initial world peace narrative could be re-interpreted, destabilized, re-adjusted by the voices from the ground. Half a century later, this circulation was fully at play in the domestic politics and foreign policy of Bolivia. But the international scene had changed in the meantime: it was considerably more democratic, following decolonization and, later on, the rise of non-state actors. The indigenous president Evo Morales is, among many others, one metaphoric figure of that change. It gives a measure of a transformation that was hardly thinkable a few decades before, when frail states, whether Japan or others, were struggling to be heard, whereas from the perspective of some dominant actors and their representatives – like the British diplomats encountered in the Kobe story – the former were not really supposed to be heard at all.

The promise of empowerment made by the UN at its inception has in some measure materialized. Taking ownership of the 'sovereignty as common good' narrative was, in the 1950s, a difficult fight, if not a bloody one, as many decolonization processes have shown. At the beginning of the twenty-first century, the tropes of narratives of common good have multiplied, and the possibility for owning and using them for oneself has expanded. All international actors – states and non-state actors – can claim access to the 'environment as common good' narrative; this global access is almost a given. Hence was the opportunity for the Bolivian government of using the global narrative of environmental justice to create a novel national plot, for both international and domestic purposes. Such opportunity is, furthermore, not limited to ecology. It is more generally the global narrative of the 'common good' and its many tropes (territorial justice, human security, sustainable development, etc.) that can be mobilized by local, national or transnational narrators for their own benefit. In that sense, we could tentatively conclude that the very notion of a global narrative has become a common good.

So, coming back to Hammarskjöld's prophecy, one could indeed argue that the people, 'just the people', have finally made the UN's narrative their own. This larger and more diverse ownership might obscure but does not, however, erase the paramount characteristic of the institutional functioning of the UN. It has never ceased to be an organization where, ultimately, decisions are taken by nations with sovereign rights. And this makes the UN an increasingly paradoxical narrative stage. It still belongs to the realm of *Realpolitik*, allowing for the expression of diversely narrow national visions, and it is at the same time an expanding central public space, something of a mammoth Greek *agora*, where a multifarious mix of communities and individuals deploys their worldviews. It has grown, almost organically, out of the stories of Japanese military base towns and of those of the Andean forests, and of thousands of other ones. It is narratively a powerful place, and its narrative power generates high expectations as well as deep frustrations. Once the UN appears, like the naked king, without its discursive glory, it suddenly looks like an organization with limited capacity and in dire need of reform, a reality that even its most fervent supporters acknowledge.[42] The Syrian poet Racha Lotfi, contemplating the deadly chaos of Aleppo in 2016, wished that the UN would talk less and act more. The management of the Covid-19 pandemic by the international organization was, again, a source of disappointment. The gap between the tediousness of decision-making processes and the sense of urgency triggered by global problems such as large-scale food insecurity leads to frustration and distrust. But however shaky the future of multilateralism might look, and however feeble the institution actually is, the global stage it created over several decades will probably not be dismantled anytime soon.

Notes

1   Henning Melber, *Dag Hammarskjöld, the United Nations and the Decolonisation of Africa* (London: Hurst, 2019).

2   Charles de Gaulle, press conference given at Elysée Palace, 4 February 1965.

3   The historiography of the UN reflects this polymorphousness, from the classic accounts of Evan David Luard's *History of the United Nations* (London: Macmillan, 1982 and 1989) to the more critical one of Sunil Amrith and Glenda Suga, 'New Histories of the United Nations', *Journal of World History* 19, no. 3 (September 2008).

216   *Narratives, Nations, and Other World Products*

4   United Nations Security Council, 'Resolution 82: Complaint of Aggression upon the Republic of Korea', *UNSCR: Search Engine for the United Nations Security Council Resolutions*, 25 June 1950, http://unscr.com/en/resolutions/82

5   See, for example, William Stueck's discussion of how the United States initially 'used the United Nations largely as an instrument of its own policies in Korea' but was eventually constrained by other nations who used the UN as a forum to influence US policy during the war: William Stueck, 'The United Nations, the Security Council, and the Korean War', in *The United Nations Security Council and War*, ed. Vaughan Lowe, et al. (Oxford: Oxford University Press, 2008), 265–79.

6   See, for example: Rosemary Foot, *The Wrong War: American Policy and the Dimensions of the Korean Conflict, 1950–1953* (New York: Cornell University Press, 1985); Aaron Forsberg, *America and the Japanese Miracle: The Cold War Context of Japan's Postwar Economic Revival, 1950–1960* (Chapel Hill, NC: University of North Carolina Press, 2000), 83–112; Masuda Hajimu, *Cold War Crucible: The Korean Conflict and the Postwar World* (Cambridge, MA: Harvard University Press, 2015); William Stueck, *Rethinking the Korean War: A New Diplomatic and Strategic History* (Princeton: Princeton University Press, 2002); Stueck, 'The United Nations'.

7   'Why We Are in Kobe Jail', *News Chronicle*, 12 August 1952, in Great Britain Foreign Office, *Foreign Office Files for Japan and the Far East, Series Two: British Foreign Office Files for Post-War Japan*, Part 1. (Adam Matthew Publications, Marlborough, England, 2005) [hereafter, FOFJ], Reel 13, FJ1192/620 (FO371/99462).

8   This narrative is based on Foreign Office documents and Japanese- and English-language media sources from the time. The Kobe incident itself has received remarkably little attention from historians in either Japan or Great Britain. For one exception, see Uchiyama Masakuma, 'Dai ni Kōbe suihei jiken', *Keiō gijuku sōritsu nijūgo-nen kinen ronbunshū: hōgakubu seijigaku kankei* 10 (1983): 395–421. The term 'Kobe incident' comes from British documents. The term '*suihei jiken*' [sailors incident] or '*Eisuihei jiken*' [English sailors incident] was more common in Japanese newspapers at the time.

9   Esler Dening to Anthony Eden, Memorandum on 'Japan: Annual Review for 1951', 4 February 1952, in FOFJ, Reel 2, FJ1011/1 (FO371/99388).

10   See, for example: 'Reisei ni hōteki kaiketsu o nozomu', *Asahi shinbun*, 9 August 1952, 1; and 'Eisuihei saiban to warera no shuchō', *Mainichi shinbun*, 8 August 1952, 1.

11   'Foreign Affairs Committee, Meeting 36, Session 13', *National Diet Proceedings Retrieval System*, National Diet of Japan, 18 June 1952.

12   'Judicial Affairs Committee, Meeting 3, Session 15', *National Diet Proceedings Retrieval System*, National Diet of Japan, 13 November 1952.

13   'Minzoku ishiki to suihei jiken', *Yomiuri shinbun*, 12 August 1952, 1.

14   'British Sailors' Sentence: Reticence in Tokyo', *The Times*, 7 August 1952, 4.

15   'Sailors: New Flare-Up', *Daily Express*, 9 August 1952, 1; Tiltman, Hessell. 'Japan's Orgy of Emotion: The Kobe Case: Feeding the Flames of Xenophobia', *Manchester Guardian*, 20 August 1952.

16   Esler Dening to Robert Scott, Telegram No. 1319 on 'Detained Seamen', 5 August 1952, in FOFJ, Reel 12, FJ1192/415 (FO371/99456).

17   Esler Dening to Robert Scott, Telegram No. 1353 on 'Detained Seamen', 9 August 1952, in FOFJ, Reel 13, FJ1192/512 (FO371/99459).

18   John Pilcher to Esler Dening, Memorandum on 'Detained Seamen', 12 August 1952, in FOFJ, Reel 13, FJ1192/512 (FO371/99459); J. E. Coulson to Michael

Williams, Personal Correspondence, 12 August 1952, in FOFJ, Reel 13, FJ1192/513 (FO371/99459).

19 Esler Dening to Foreign Office, 'Detained Seamen', 5 November 1952, in FOFJ, Reel 14 FJ1192/711 (FO371/99466).

20 On Bolivian politics and the Amazon forest during this period see *inter alia*: John Crabtree, 'From the MNR to the MAS: Populism, Parties, the State and Social Movements in Bolivia since 1952', in *Latin American Populism in the Twenty-First Century*, ed. Carlos de. La Torre and Cynthia Arnson (Baltimore: Johns Hopkins University Press, 2013), 269–94; David Recondo, 'Participatory Decentralization in Bolivia: The Genealogy of an Institutional Transplant', in *Democracy at Large. NGOs, Political Foundations, Think Tanks and International Organizations*, ed. Boris Petric (Basingstoke: Palgrave MacMillan, 2012), 125–45; Susanna Hecht and Alexander Cockburn, *The Fate of the Forest. Developers, Destroyers and Defenders of the Amazon* (Chicago: The University of Chicago Press, 2010); Pierre-Yves Cadalen, 'When Populists Govern: Bolivia, Ecuador and Populism', in *Discursive Approaches to Populism Across Disciplines. The Return of Populists and the People*, ed. Michael Kranert (London: Palgrave MacMillan, 2020, 313–37); Forrest Hylton and Sinclair Thomson, *Revolutionary Horizons: Past and Present in Bolivian Politics* (New York: Verso, 2007).

21 Harald Welzer, *Les guerres du climat. Pourquoi on tue au XXIe siècle* (Paris: Gallimard, 2009).

22 Franck Poupeau, 'La Bolivie entre Pachamama et modèle extractiviste', *Ecologie & politique*, no. 46 (2013): 109–19.

23 Patrick Boucheron, 'Fictions politiques. Chaque époque rêve la suivante', lecture given at the Collège de France, January 2017.

24 Razmig Keucheyan, *La nature est un champ de bataille. Essai d'écologie politique* (Paris: La Découverte, 2014).

25 Bertrand Badie, *La fin des territoires. Essai sur le désordre international et l'utilité sociale du respect* (Paris: Fayard, 1995).

26 The *proceso de cambio*, literally 'process of change', is the name given by the government to the political phase following Evo Morales' election in 2006.

27 Interview with Pablo Solón, head of Fundación Solón, La Paz, 15 July 2016.

28 Paul Ricœur, *Le temps raconté* (Paris: Seuil, 1991), 12.

29 Personal interview with Diego Pacheco, Vice-Minister for development planning, La Paz, 14 July 2016.

30 Keucheyan, *La nature est un champ de bataille*.

31 Guillaume Blanc, *L'invention du colonialisme vert* (Paris: Flammarion, 2020).

32 Personal interview with Magdalena Medrano, ex-Secretary of the Mother Earth department in Cochabamba, Cochabamba, 3 August 2016.

33 Personal interview with Sarela Paz, anthropologist, Cochabamba, 9 August 2016.

34 Personal interview with Diego Pacheco, vice-minister for development planning, La Paz, 14 July 2016.

35 Elaborated by Raúl Prebisch and further developed by Samir Amin and André Gunder-Franck, the dependency theory was mainly based on the idea of an international division of labour between the South that produced low-value goods and the North that produced most of the high-value goods.

36 Andre Gunder-Frank, *Le développement du sous-développement en Amérique latine* (Paris: Maspero, 1970).

37 Esperanza Martínez, *Yasuní. El tortuoso camino de Kioto a Quito* (Quito: Abya Yala, 2009); Grupo de Trabajo sobre Deuda Externa y Desarrollo, *Deuda externa, desarrollo y ecología* (Quito: Ecuador, FONDAD, 1992).

38 Interview with Alvaro García Linera, vice-president of the Plurinational State of Bolivia, La Paz, 21 August 2016.

39 Élisée Reclus, *L'homme et la terre* (Paris: Librairie universelle, 1905), 1. Despite the fact that both statements could appear different, the political implications of both can be the same. This possibility is also what gave existence to the Bolivian narrative which articulated the indigenous traditions with a Marxist perspective.

40 Craig Murphy, *International Organization and Industrial Change: Global Governance since 1850* (Cambridge: Polity Press, 1994).

41 See *inter alia*, Roger Normand and Sarah Zaidi, *Human Rights at the UN: The Political History of Universal Justice* (Bloomington: Indiana University Press, 2008) and Kirsten Haack, *The United Nations Democracy Agenda: A Conceptual History* (Manchester: Manchester University Press, 2011).

42 Sumihiro Kuyama and Michael Fowler (eds.), *Envisioning Reform. Enhancing UN Accountability in the Twenty-First Century* (Tokyo: United Nations University Press, 2009).

12

Global narratives of the immigrant

Megan Armknecht, Markus Bierkoch and Beth Lew-Williams

The word 'immigrant' is relatively young. In a snide footnote to his *Travels Through the Northern Parts of the United States in 1807 and 1808*, Edward Augustus Kendall mentioned its invention: '*Immigrant* is perhaps the only new word, of which the circumstances of the United States has [sic] in any degree demanded the addition to the English language.' By the time the travelling Englishman encountered it, the word had been in occasional use for three decades in the newly formed United States. In 1806, it had appeared in a dictionary for the first time. Noah Webster's *A Compendious Dictionary of the English Language* defined the term as 'one who removes into a country'. His more voluminous sequel *An American Dictionary of the English Language*, first published in 1828, clarified that an immigrant is 'a person that removes into a country for the purpose of permanent residence.'[1]

From there the term spread to other languages, in a journey across the globe that seems only fitting. The effect can still be heard today. In French, 'immigrant' is 'immigrant', as it is in Afrikaans, Russian, Bulgarian and Cebuano. In Italian, it is 'immigrato', 'inmigrante' in Spanish, 'imin' in Japanese and Korean, 'yímín' in Mandarin, and 'imigran' in Sudanese. Derivatives can also be found in Albanian, Danish, Estonian, Irish, Maltese, Polish, Portuguese, Romanian, Serbian, Ukrainian, Uzbek, Yoruba, Indonesian, Javanese and Haitian Creole. As mass migrations took hold worldwide in the nineteenth and early twentieth century, so too did this new term.[2]

Immigrant wasn't just a new term, however; it was a novel concept. People have always moved, at times across vast distances, but it was not until the nineteenth century that many of these long-distance travellers were imagined to be immigrants.[3] The immigrant is a modern invention that evolved alongside the world's early nation-states, starting with the United States but not ending there. Beginning in the nineteenth century, the process of global integration prompted both mass migration and the emergence of nation-states. To grapple with these concurrent transformations, the framers and policymakers of these new nations told immigration stories to themselves and their constituents, re-conceiving human mobility in specific normative terms that upheld modern concepts of sovereignty, territory and nationalism. Circulating through a rapidly integrating world, these narratives became standardized and simplified.

By the turn of the twentieth century, a global image of the ideal immigrant had begun to take shape: he was a free agent (and a free worker) intending to make a permanent move across a political boundary with the hopes of becoming a member of a new polity (and contributing to the national economy). Although the ideal immigrant was often described in economic and political terms, gender and racial beliefs also saturated this normative category. At the time, Western nations often questioned whether non-white people and women could be 'free agents', or whether they were inherently servile, dependent and incapable of self-government. The emphasis on membership – and with it, assimilation, naturalization and loyalty – also contained racial and gender assumptions. The normative immigrant was imagined to be a citizen-in-waiting, and many Western leaders believed race and sex determined one's ability to earn and exercise full citizenship. Narratives about the ideal immigrant and laws meant to select for him also produced narratives about non-normative forms of mobility and created new forms of stratification. By giving legal preference designed to include certain types of migrants, lawmakers excluded other migrants, rendering them stateless, undocumented and/or temporary. In other words, narratives about the ideal immigrant had meaningful, sometimes violent, consequences on his unwanted counterpart.

While scholars have long described the immigrant as a central *problem* for modern nation-states, it is more accurate to describe the immigrant as a *product* of modernity.[4] The state impulse to simplify, categorize and control left an indelible mark on the meaning of the immigrant and the people imagined to embody the term. Lawmakers were not the only ones to imagine that mobile people could be neatly slotted into categories, however; scholars have made similar assumptions. Too often historians rely on state-produced definitions of the immigrant, treating him as a transhistorical figure and naturalizing immigration as the default category of human mobility.[5]

The following is a brief history of the immigrant from the early modern period – before the term emerged – through the twentieth century – when it gained global prominence. We begin with early European theorists of international law who considered the ethics of sovereignty and mobility. Although their writings would eventually form the basis for modern immigration law, these intellectuals had no notion of the modern immigrant. Second, we look at patterns of human mobility in the early modern period. Lived experience of migrants did not conform to theories of international law, but neither did they approximate modern concepts of immigration. Third, we discuss the birth of the concept of the immigrant and its proliferation through an increasing interdependent world. Even as the immigrant became accepted as the normative form of human movement, however, migrants continued to defy simple categorization. In the final section, we turn to the narratives nineteenth- and twentieth-century migrants told about themselves. At times, migrants' own narratives reified the normative immigrant, as they contorted their experiences to embody the privileged category. At other times, migrants' narratives offer alternate ways to think about human mobility. Throughout the chapter, we remain attentive to the construction, circulation and naturalization of narratives – whether produced by the state, by migrants or by scholars, including ourselves.

Global Narratives of the Immigrant

Early modern theories of migration

Early theorists of international law offer a glimpse of the terms, categories and notions that presaged a consolidated concept of the immigrant. From the sixteenth through the eighteenth century, prominent European intellectuals, including Francisco de Vitoria (1480–1546), Hugo Grotius (1583–1645), Samuel van Pufendorf (1632–94), Christian von Wolff (1679–1754) and Emer de Vattel (1714–67), saw human mobility as a vital concern in debates about the often conflicting demands of human rights and national sovereignty. Although they took different positions on a nation's obligation to the migrant, these men held similar assumptions about the nature of migration itself. As they imagined people in motion, however, none assumed these subjects would take a form resembling the modern immigrant. Rather, they tended to narrate the lives of 'strangers' or 'foreigners' in different terms: as stories of exiles, travellers, conquerors and emigrants. Nevertheless, nineteenth-century policymakers and jurists would later depend on their theories to craft early immigration laws.

Early modern debates surrounding international law focused particular attention on the figures of the refugee and the traveller. When Grotius argued, for example, that 'a fixed abode ought not to be refused to strangers', he pictured those 'strangers' to be 'expelled [from] their own country, seek[ing] a retreat elsewhere'. Pufendorf took a different view, placing an emphasis on state sovereignty and the state's discretion for refusing admission, but he continued to call attention to the 'stranger' who was 'driven on the coasts by necessity, or by any cause that deserves pity and compassion'. Wolff insisted on the right of the state to deny entrance: 'just as the owner of a private estate can prohibit any other person from entering upon the same'. He softened his statement in regard to refugees 'who have been expelled from their homes' and harmless travellers who sought the 'right of passage' for 'recovering health', 'study' or 'commerce'. Like his predecessors, Wolff was particularly concerned about the treatment of exiles, arguing that 'permanent residence ... cannot be denied to exiles by a nation, unless special reasons stand in the way'. Vattel agreed, 'The sovereign may forbid the entrance of his territory either to foreigners in general, or in particular cases, or to certain persons, or for certain particular purposes'. But with a mind towards refugees, he did allow for some notable exceptions. 'When a real necessity obliges you to enter into the territory of others' he allowed, 'you may force a passage when it is unjustly refused'. Although they took different positions on the rights of foreigners, these intellectuals presupposed that most strangers would be exiles seeking refuge or travellers seeking only a right of passage.[6]

At times, these leaders in international law acknowledge that some of the people traveling the world were European conquerors and colonists. According to Vitoria, Spaniards arrived in Mexico and South America as 'strangers and travelers' who had no natural right to conquer the territory of 'barbarians'. And yet he found it possible to justify their actions based on the right of humanitarian and missionary intervention as well as the barbarians' duty to hospitality and their supposed mental incapacity. Grotius took a similar tact. He cautioned that foreigners must not engage in 'thievery and rapine' of 'occupied' territory, but he did not believe that much of the New World was occupied, since it was not under agricultural cultivation. 'If within the territory of a people there is any deserted and unproductive soil', he reasoned, 'this also ought to be granted to foreigners if they ask for it'. Vattel agreed, distinguishing between the occupied lands of 'the civilized Empires of Peru and Mexico' and 'uncertain occupancy' of North America. To conquer the former was 'a notorious usurpation', but to settle the latter was 'entirely lawful'.[7]

In addition to their attention to the colonist, traveller and exile, these theorists also spent considerable time pondering the rights of the 'emigrant', that is, he who wished to leave his country of origin. Grotius argued that nations had the right to regulate emigration in order to prevent mass exit. While individual emigrants should be allowed free passage, he believed that 'the nationals of a state cannot depart in large bodies … for if such migration were permissible the civil society could not exist'. Wolff was also outspoken about the state's ability to limit departure, arguing that there was no natural right to emigration. For Pufendorf and Vattel, an emigrant's departure was a natural rightVattel wrote, 'every man has a right to quit his country, in order to settle in any other, when by that step he does not endanger the welfare of his country'.[8]

In the seventeenth and eighteenth centuries, these founders of international law were more concerned with colonists, emigrants, refugees and travellers, than with the people who would come to be known as immigrants. This is hardly surprising, given that few people fell neatly under Webster's (not-yet-drafted) definition at the time.

Early modern migration

Mobile peoples in the early modern period did not resemble the modern immigrant, but neither did they fall easily into the normative categories used in early modern debates over international law. Theorists' notions of colonists, emigrants, refugees and travellers belied an even more complicated terrain of actual human movement.

Take, for example, the travelling merchant. Theorists debated the rights of the foreign merchant, but none described in any detail the complicated ways in which merchants moved. Merchants rarely predetermined the extent of their movement or the length of their stay, choosing instead to move in response to shifting trade connections and power networks. For example, as early as the twelfth century the merchant Wang Yuanmao, who was born and raised in the town of Quanzhou in South China, went to Champa, a collection of independent polities in what is today known as central and southern Vietnam. After ten years of doing business in Champa and forging good connections with local authorities he returned to Quanzhou with a fortune. Like many Chinese merchants, Yuanmao left his village without a plan for how long he would be away, spent a considerable portion of his life abroad, but ultimately returned to the place of his birth.[9] Yuanmao's experiences defy easy categorization. What might he have called himself? An emigrant? A sojourner? A travelling merchant? The uncertainty that accompanies human mobility blurs the distinction between these terms.

Early modern merchants do not slot neatly into the modern-day concept of the immigrant, and neither did colonial settlers. Hoping to strengthen their political power and bolster their imperial projects, many empires came to welcome colonial settlement

Global Narratives of the Immigrant 223

over the seventeenth century, drawing in migrants keen to move due to poverty or systematic prosecution. In what would become South Africa, for instance, the Dutch Empire learned to use colonial settlement as a way to stabilize colonial rule and reap additional profit. Dutch East India Company began by allowing company servants to engage in farming by granting them the status of 'free burghars' in Cape Town. This became a first step in turning the station into a permanent settlement. These early colonial settlers were joined, in the 1670s, by French Huguenots who embraced the company's offer for refuge and criminals and slaves who were expelled and brought in from Southeast Asia to support the local economy. These settlers expanded into land originally held by the indigenous population of the Khoikhoi, while strengthening the Dutch local presence in opposition to other colonial powers such as the British.[10]

A similar process can be seen in eighteenth-century Central Europe when the Austrian Habsburg monarchy directed migrants towards territories it had recently conquered in Transylvania, Galicia and Bukovina. German migrants from the Palatine who moved into these newly acquired Austrian Eastern-European territories understood themselves as co-contractors and reclaimers of land for agriculture. Based on the agreement for settling in these provinces the settlers demanded the provision of houses, adequate amount of farmland and horses. In return, they promised to become 'strenuous and useful citizens of the state and of your royal majesty', as settlers in Cservenka in today's Serbia expressed it in a letter to the Emperor Joseph II in 1786.[11] These colonial settlers understood the obligations they were expected to fulfil as newcomers in the Austrian Empire, namely, to extend the power of the crown.

In other words, colonial settlers who set off from imperial metropoles bound for peripheral colonies did not come as immigrants, they came to conquer and colonize. These settler colonists were not 'removing into a country' like modern-day immigrants, they were, in effect, moving the boundaries of their empire. As Lorenzo Veracini has observed, 'while settlers systematically disavow or deny the indigenous sovereignties they encounter, either by signing treaties they do not intend to honour, or by asserting different versions of the *terra nullius* doctrine, migrants need to recognise the sovereignties they come across (if only to elude them, if they can).' The English in North America, for instance, brought with them the British Empire and the assumption they would remain British subjects. They had not left their homeland behind, they had extended its reach, with the consent and acknowledgement of the crown. Living in the American colonies did not make them 'foreigners'; indeed to allow such a term would undermine the sovereignty of the empire.[12]

However, 'foreigners' did exist within every settler colony of the seventeenth and eighteenth centuries. There were Germans in the English Colonies, Chinese in the Spanish Empire, Dutch in New France and many others. Empires recognized the presence of these foreigners at the time and often sought to regulate them by preventing their entry, baring their naturalization or limiting their rights. Or they worked to make them into loyal subjects, as the Austrian Monarchy did. Although scholars have often called these people immigrants and these laws immigration control, this terminology is problematic. These foreigners were also colonial settlers, intent on permanently occupying these lands by asserting sovereignty over indigenous populations, and it was their status as competing colonists that often made them targets of regulation and exclusion. Observing Spanish, Portuguese, French and British colonial laws regulating foreigners, David Scott FitzGerald and David Cook-Martin observe that the statutes were primarily intended to 'keep[] out subjects of major colonial rivals'. By regulating the presence of 'foreigners', each empire hoped 'to achieve military security from other competitor colonies'.[13] These laws, in other words, regulated rival settler colonists rather than immigrants.

Although the forefathers of international law rarely mentioned the slave trade when considering the rights of foreigners, enslaved people made up a significant proportion of mobile people in the early modern world. Between the sixteenth and nineteenth century, slave traders trafficked approximately 12 million Africans, forcibly moving them from the inland to the coast and then across the Atlantic. And while white settler colonists regularly imagined the indigenous of Africa, Asia and the Americas to be static and immobile, in fact they moved as well, some over the course of seasons and others over generations. Neither of these groups approximate the immigrants of later centuries who 'remove[d] into a country for the purpose of permanent residence'. The movement of enslaved people was involuntary and, therefore, their settlement (whether permanent or not) lacked intent.

In sum, the early modern period saw a wide swath of human movement, but little that assumed the modes of modern immigration. Rather, movement in the early modern period embodied the categories imagined by theorists (travellers, exiles, colonists and emigrants) and then some. While it was rare for people to voluntarily cross a political boundary with the intent to settle permanently and become a full member of new polity, people often moved in many less intentional, unidirectional and permanent ways.

Signs of gradual change began to emerge in the latter half of the eighteenth century, as states increasingly worked to shape migratory patterns and imagine foreigners as long-term settlers. In the aftermath of imperial expansion, for example, Russia invited foreign colonists like Germans, Scots, Serbs and Swiss in order to consolidate parts of the country. While these migrants were certainly not considered 'immigrants' in the modern sense, their migration was organized and showed rudimentary elements of the state regulation that would later shape international migration in the nineteenth century. The Russian empire had made resettlement a 'growing as a sphere of government activity' and began to 'all but require[] every resident of the empire to be recorded in a particular locale [...]'. Here we can see an early example of a state extending its power over the individual migrant, controlling his or her movement and settlement, and determining who should be entitled to either action in its territory.[14]

Nation-states and modern theories of the immigrant

The proliferation of nation-states, especially in the 'New World' of North and South America, began the consolidation of a modern concept of the immigrant. Immigration and naturalization laws offer a view (albeit a partial one) into how states reconceived of mobile people as immigrants starting in the nineteenth century. Although the modern immigrant emerged from a host of legal, cultural, scientific and bureaucratic sources,

Global Narratives of the Immigrant 225

laws and the framers behind them had an outsized impact on reimagining human mobility in the nineteenth century and circulating these immigration narratives around the globe.

Rarely did immigration laws explicitly define the ideal immigrant, but nonetheless they slowly built a consensus around who occupied this normative category. They did so in two distinct ways: by preferring those people deemed desirable and by excluding those seen as undesirable. In the process, they drew justification from early modern international law without recognizing that early theorists were more concerned with travellers and refugees than people approximating the modern immigrant. Moreover, policymakers applied these new immigration laws to migrants without acknowledging that the complexity of human movement defied simple state categorization. Two early nation-states, the United States and Argentina, provide examples of how states developed and circulated new narratives in which the modern immigrant played a starring role.

In the United States, the birth of the republic came with a demand for free migration. In the Declaration of Independence, American revolutionaries complained that King George III had slowed the arrival of foreigners: 'He has endeavored to prevent the population of these States; for that purpose obstructing the Laws for Naturalization of Foreigners: refusing to pass others to encourage their migration hither, and raising the conditions of Appropriations of Lands.' Wishing to maintain British dominance in the colonies, the monarch attempted to discourage the migration of continental Europeans and hamper their naturalization. In their Declaration, revolutionaries signalled that the new nation would view 'foreigners' in a different light.

America's founders believed that European settler-colonists had brought civilization with them to North America. In the Federal Convention of 1787, for example, James Madison argued, 'America was indebted to emigration for her settlement and prosperity. That part of America which had encouraged [emigrants] most, had advanced most rapidly in population, agriculture, and the arts.' America's forefathers disagreed on how many migrants were ideal for the young nation and how quickly they should be able to naturalize, but they agreed that 'emigrants' had provided the basis for the republic.[15] And they took steps to ensure that new arrivals would continue the tradition of European colonial settlement in North America. In 1790, Congress passed an act to limit the privilege of naturalization to 'free white persons'.

With the exception of the short-lived, ineffectual and controversial Alien Acts of 1798, Congress passed no federal immigration laws until the mid-nineteenth century. The major obstacle was the resistance of slave states. Fearing that federal immigration laws could threaten the slave trade, southern statesmen decried federal interference in the movement of people. However, some states, including New York and Massachusetts, began to draft alien passenger laws. Imagining passengers as potential permanent residents, state legislators sought to weed out undesirable ones. These laws themselves did not include any mention of immigrants or 'immigration', but the Supreme Court, which overturned these laws in the *Passenger Cases* (1849), described many of these alien passengers using the new term. In the controversial *Passenger Cases,* eight justices authored separate opinions. They deeply disagreed on the constitutional basis of immigration laws, but what they shared was an implicit assumption of who

226 *Narratives, Nations, and Other World Products*

constituted an immigrant. Together, they drew distinctions between the immigrant and the merchant, trader or visitor, due to his divergent purpose and degree of permanency. In addition, they described the normative immigrant as male. Justice J. Grier, for example, referred to the 'immigrant and his family' who intended to 'come and settle themselves within our limits'. Justice McKinley distinguished the immigrant by his voluntary movement as well. 'The slaves are not immigrants', he explained, 'and had no exercise of volition in their transportation from Africa to the United States'.[16] The *Passenger Cases* reflect a growing consensus in the United States around the normative category of the immigrant.

Starting in the 1860s, the US Congress began to pass laws intended to encourage some migrants while discouraging others. The Civil War drove the federalization of US immigration policy. Not only did slave states no longer stand in the way, but also Reconstruction ushered in a new era of citizenship in the United States. The 1866 Civil Rights Act and then the Fourteenth Amendment gave rise to modern American citizenship, granted certain privileges and immunities, and promised federal protection of these civil rights. This brought new urgency to the state project of selecting who would be granted the privileged status of citizenship. Early immigration laws named those migrants considered undesirable (including criminals, paupers, lunatics, contract labourers, Oriental prostitutes and Chinese labourers) and left unspoken the assumption that able-bodied, free, moral, monied white migrants were ideal.[17]

The actions of the United States did not go unobserved. Argentinian intellectual Juan Batista Alberdi, for example, took careful note of immigration to the United States and the laws passed to facilitate it. In his landmark work, *Bases y puntos de partida para la organización política de la República Argentina* (1852), he devoted a section to the topic of '*inmigración*'. He observed, 'The United States is such an advanced people because it has been made up incessantly of European elements' and credited 'abundant immigration from Europe' for this development. State policy had played a vital role. Pointing to the new state of California and the 'generous liberties' granted to migrants there, Alberdi credited these policies for 'mak[ing] the immigrant forget he is a foreigner, persuading him to settle in this homeland'.[18] Not only did Alberdi admire America's population of migrants, he shared Americans' new definition of the immigrant.

When legislators turned to crafting an Argentine constitution a year later, they drew directly from Alberdi's writings and, therefore, the example of the United States. At a time when the term 'immigration' was still rare in English, and 'inmigración' rarer still in Spanish, the Argentine constitution borrowed the American term. Article 25 of the 1853 constitution declared: 'The Federal Government shall encourage European immigration, and it may not restrict, limit or burden with any tax whatsoever the entry into Argentine Territory of foreigners whose purpose is tilling the soil, improving industries, and introducing and teaching the sciences and the arts.'[19] The Argentine framers did not, however, directly draw from the letter of US law. The US Constitution made no bid to encourage immigration and American lawmakers in the early nineteenth century had avoided explicit preferences for European migrants.

And when the United States started to bar certain undesirable migrants in the late nineteenth century, Argentina did not follow suit. When debating the Law of

Immigration and Colonization (1876), Argentine lawmakers showed recognition of US immigration policy, but also a determination to follow local tradition. The law continued to prefer European migrants under the presumption that they were more civilized and amenable to state control, but refrained from excluding other races or nationalities. At the level of enforcement, however, the Argentine government showed racial preferences. In the 1880s, Director of Immigration Samuel Navarro actively discouraged the recruitment of Chinese migrant labour and cited the example of Chinese exclusion in the United States.[20]

In fact, laws barring Chinese migrants provide a key example of narratives of the normative immigrant circulated and converged. Among the twenty-two independent nations in the Americas, at least nineteen passed laws to explicitly exclude Chinese migrants and others, like Argentina, used more subtle means towards the same ends. Other British settler nations, including Australia, New Zealand and South Africa, targeted Chinese as well. These nations did not all share similar economic or political conditions – for example, some saw significant Chinese immigration while others experienced little – but several factors drove the explosion of Chinese restriction laws. While Argentines drew vague inspiration from the United States, other nations, like Canada, passed laws in direct response to the United States. Following America's restriction of Chinese labour in 1882, Canada passed a head tax on Chinese migrants to prevent the migration stream from diverting north. Other nations bowed to geopolitical pressure. Concerned that Chinese migrants were using Mexico as a backdoor to the United States, American diplomats convinced their southern neighbour to restrict Chinese starting in the early twentieth century. Imperialism also spread Chinese exclusion policies. When the American troops occupied the Philippines, Puerto Rico, Cuba and Guam in 1898, they brought Chinese exclusion with them.[21]

With the transnational circulation of immigration policy, including Chinese restrictions laws, came the convergence of narratives surrounding the nature of human mobility and how to regulate it. Through these laws, nation-states defined which peoples and which forms of movement constituted normative immigrants. Increasingly, states began to view undesirable migrants, including the Chinese, as not really immigrants at all. Describing the Chinese as involuntary, unfree and temporary, policymakers made a case for ideal immigrants to be voluntary, free and permanent. By targeting a group known to be heathen and racially inferior, western policymakers implied that the ideal immigrant was both Judeo-Christian and white.

Like immigration laws, naturalization laws simultaneously excluded some and included others, thereby promoting each nation-state's conception of the ideal immigrant. As Daniel Tichenor has explained, naturalization laws provided legal means for the state to define itself 'through the official selection and control of foreigners seeking permanent residence on their soil'.[22] Naturalization laws permitted some immigrants to claim citizenship rights while others could not, allowing the state to privilege 'certain visions of nationhood, social order, international engagement' over others.[23] By providing a clearer path to citizenship for those whom the state deemed as 'ideal', these laws contain explicit and implicit definitions of the normative immigrant.

Although nationality laws were in place in pre-modern times, many of these laws dealt with subjecthood, rather than foreign aliens seeking residence in a nation. For

228   *Narratives, Nations, and Other World Products*

example, Great Britain's nationality acts date from the sixteenth century, but these acts focused on natural-born subjects. Great Britain did not have a nationality act providing for the naturalization of aliens until 1844. Prior to the Act of 1844, 'nationality could be obtained only by special acts of Parliament or by letters of denization'.[24] Denization did not have the same rights as naturalization did, as it 'restricted inheritance rights business activity'.[25] The shift to naturalization laws in the nineteenth century arose from Great Britain's concern with making and keeping wealth within the empire. As Margit Beerbuehl argues, 'in 1844 the fear that foreigners might make their fortunes in England and then take them to their countries of origin, draining the kingdom of revenue, was a major reason behind the reform of nationality regulation. Naturalization thus became a tool in England's mercantilist economic policy'. For Great Britain in the nineteenth century, the ideal immigrant was someone who produced wealth, and contributed to the rise of a global economy powered by Britain's mercantile and industrialization systems. Naturalization policies, therefore, favoured foreign merchants.[26]

Although empires, like Great Britain, began adopting nationality policies in the nineteenth century (and were some of the first entities to do so) there is a correlation between the emergence of naturalization laws with the emergence of independent nation-states.[27] Indeed, the invention of modern national citizenship – often credited to the French Revolution – served as a model for new nation-states of the early – to mid-nineteenth century.[28] This not only included France and other European nations, but Latin American republics. These Latin American republics provide examples of how nation-states used naturalization laws to encourage specific types of people to immigrate. For example, Paraguay's Constitution of 1870 required foreigners seeking naturalization to have 'resided two consecutive years in the country and have during this period either owned real estate, had some capital invested in business, practiced some profession, or been engaged in some industrial occupation, science, or art'.[29]

Other Latin American republics also required naturalization-seeking immigrants to prove their dependability in employment, their intention to stay in the country and their potential to contribute to the nation's wealth and infrastructure. Each of these requirements created state narratives about the kinds of immigrants the state wanted to attract: able, hard workers who would contribute to societal and national success. For example, Costa Rica's Naturalization Law of 1889 allowed aliens to naturalize if they 'had a profession, employ or income, with which to live', while Argentina's Law Number 346 in 1869 allowed foreigners to naturalize if they proved their service to Argentina through, among other things, serving in Argentina's army or navy, establishing a new industry, introducing a new invention, or constructing railroads in any of its provinces.[30] For these states in Latin America, the ideal immigrant was explicitly shown in the naturalization laws: men who could contribute to the economic or structural growth of the nation-state, and become productive citizens.

Indeed, all of these naturalization laws and the image of an ideal immigrant applied to men. Naturalization laws mentioned women, but only insofar as they related to men. Foreign women were naturalized only if they married a state national. For example, in 1892, the Netherlands declared that in questions of naturalization, a 'wife follows the nationality of her husband', that 'naturalization granted to the husband is of legal effect also for his wife', and that 'a request to become naturalized cannot be made by

Global Narratives of the Immigrant   229

a married woman.[31] Similarly, Dutch women who married foreigners forfeited their nationality.[32] The gendering of naturalization laws was common practice well into the twentieth century, showing that the state imagined and defined the ideal immigrant as an able-bodied, working male. Even if a woman might prove herself to be productive, economically solvent and an asset to the growth of the nation-state she immigrated to, she could not change her nationality on her own merits. Therefore, for a woman, naturalization depended on her marital status, and her husband's ability to claim citizenship.

Like immigration laws, naturalization laws proliferated in the late nineteenth century as nation-states influenced one another, as they sought for regulation and order against the scale of mass migration. As Mira L. Siegelberg argues, mass migration drove national and international jurists to 'develop legal principles to regulate the movement of people across oceans and into new polities', as jurists, theorists and politicians attempted to categorize statelessness, immigration and naturalization.[33]

In addition to mass migration, a new emphasis on self-determination also increased the amount of naturalization laws around the world. Although the reality of self-determination has been seen as more of a rhetorical ideal, the breaking and shaking up of empires during and after the First World War culminated in a slew of revised naturalization laws and new countries. This changing world order allowed for new countries to determine who could immigrate to their nations and define what it meant to be Latvian, or Bulgarian, or Afghan.

Although most naturalization laws defined the ideal immigrant on the basis of sex, ability and class, after the First World War, some naturalization laws focused on loyalty as well. These loyalty laws bear resemblance to the language of assimilation favoured in the United States.[34] Through nationality and naturalization laws, new nation-states could determine what constituted loyalty and who counted as an ideal citizen. In this way, migration both connected and separated the world through globalization and nationalization. These ideas spread along with naturalization laws through the twentieth century.

By 1919, Henry Pratt Fairchild, an American sociologist surveying the global movement of people, declared the normative definition of immigration to be clear. He defined immigration as 'a movement of people, individually or in families, acting on their own personal initiative and responsibility, without official support or compulsion, passing from one well-developed country (usually old and thickly settled) to another well-developed country (usually new and sparsely populated) with the intention of residing there'. Fairchild sought to distinguish immigration from other forms of migration. Within his typology, movement to a less-developed nation constituted 'conquest', arrival of a less-developed people meant 'invasion', and relocation to 'empty lands' was 'colonization'.

Rather than speak in the language of race, Fairchild deployed a rhetoric of civilization and barbarism. According to Fairchild, immigration was only possible between two nations that shared a similar 'stage of civilization', 'culture', 'climate' and 'circumstances of life'. Therefore, he observed, 'There has never been any immigration between the temperate zones and the tropics.' Since he assumed there were no 'civilized' nations in tropical climates, all such movement constituted conquest, invasion or colonization. Immigrants required 'a high degree of civilization' because they acted as free agents. 'They must be trained to act on individual initiative, and must have sufficient personal enterprise to undertake a weighty venture without an official or state backing.'[35] For Fairchild, 'immigration' – presumed to be the permanent movement of free, enterprising individuals from one 'civilized' nation to another – was 'a distinctly modern' form of movement.

Modern migrants

Although nation-states converged around the normative category of the modern immigrant in the late nineteenth and early twentieth centuries, mobile people continued to defy simple categorization. By exploring how migrants defined themselves, rather than how they were defined by the state, we can begin to see the artifice of the state-produced narrative of the modern immigrant.

The fact that simple categorization was not applicable to the complex and shifting nature of human movement was soon understood by twentieth-century scholars. In this context, they tried to find a terminology that would capture the realities more accurately. In his classic book *Soziologie* Georg Simmel tried to address this in his chapter on 'The Stranger'. 'The potential wanderer: although he has not moved on, he has not quite overcome the freedom of coming and going', he observed.[36] Simmel's theoretical discussion stressed the contingency of movement: one who moved from a social group to another might choose to stay in the new group or may not. The study of mobility must allow for this degree of uncertainty and possibility. Migration as something open-ended and in-between was likewise in the focus of Robert Ezra Parks's concept of the 'Marginal Man' which he described as a potential outcome of migration: 'One of the consequences of migration is to create a situation in which the same individual (...) finds himself striving to live in two diverse cultural groups.'[37] Both Simmel and Park described a phenomenon that ever since has been acknowledged as embodying key characteristics of migration. The integration of migrants into society is an ongoing process, which depends on legal and economic opportunities, both in the society from where migrants come and to where they go, and is affected by cultural proclivities.[38]

This perspective argues against the prevalent assumption that the final stay of so-called 'immigrants' in a society is self-evident, pre-determined at the moment of departure. Likewise, these findings push against the rhetoric of the state, which often tries to label arrivals as 'immigrants', presupposing their permanent settlement. In truth, the final stay of so-called 'immigrants' in a society is not a self-evident fact. The difference between a sojourner and a settler, for example, may depend on 'success in the new home; failure; homesickness; a call to return to take over the family farm or other property; rejection of life overseas'.[39] Migrants' lives do not enfold linearly, rather are continually affected and shaped by doubt, contingency and uncertainty.

Nation-states, of course, prefer more simple stories about immigrants and the narratives that they tell hold disproportionate power – both in the world and in scholarship. It is hardly surprising that immigration policy depends upon state-defined categories, but it is concerning that the field of migration studies does as well.

One way to break free of this narrative loop is to listen closely to how migrants themselves understood and narrated their motion. Sometimes, as it will be shown, migrants were not quite ready to accept an end to their migration process; other times migrants wanted to end their journey much faster than governments or societies would allow.

Some migrants always imagined their journey as roundtrip, including Chinese sojourners in the late-nineteenth and twentieth centuries.[40] 'I had always planned on returning to China,' explained one elite Chinese migrant in Hawai`i in the twentieth century.[41] Although many migrants originally view themselves as sojourners, they also experience changes of heart and circumstance. A study on Israeli migrants in Chicago in the second half of the twentieth century termed a similar group of migrants 'permanent sojourners'. This seeming oxymoron describes 'immigrants [who] maintain their general intentions of returning to Israel. However, they do not have any concrete plans of returning and cannot point to a specific finite duration of their stay in the host country.'[42] The term 'permanent sojourner' exemplifies the difficulty of finding fitting terms to describe the complexity of migratory processes.

This difficulty is also apparent in the personal statements of migrants. A statement of an Israeli woman who had worked as a speech therapist in the United States for twenty-one years highlights the emotional effect of a migrant's uncertain future: '(…) I purposely do not get involved in American life, and do not try to feel that I belong here, because I want to return to Israel.' Another Israeli migrant named Yaakov, an owner of a car repair garage, expressed similar doubts concerning his stay in the United States: 'Five years ago I wanted to return to Israel. In order to open a similar business to the one that I have here, I had to get a license (…). To cut a long story short, I did not get the required license.' Had he received his licence he would have returned to Israel, making him a sojourner of the mind but an immigrant due to economic realities. Yaakov's experience captures the potential conflict between a person's legal status and his subjective experience.[43]

These examples are not exceptions but, rather, can be found regularly in accounts by migrants. A study on Turkish immigrants in the United States asserted that the state of 'ambivalent desire' came up most frequently. In this state, immigrants had not decided to return but 'long to go back at some point'.[44] Impulses for this emotional state can come from familial concerns, economic insecurity and legal status. For example, Burcu, a woman in her early thirties who had just married and was pursuing a graduate degree in the United States, expressed worries concerning the advanced age of her parents. These concerns pertained especially to her father getting sick: 'And that time will come […], he might need us […]. […] Am I going to be able to bring him here? And … maybe he can stay here? How? When? […] That distance question is always in my head.'[45] As various migration studies highlight, an uncertain and torn emotional status, to a certain degree, is a common aspect of migrants' lives.[46] If situations accrue that lead to an unbearable situation of torment or discontent, migrants might actually return. However, in many cases, this level of frustration is often not reached, but, rather, the involved emotions can linger on for years.

Migrants' ability to imagine permanent settlement is often tied to their legal status. The uncertainty a legal status can produce was influentially described by

232   *Narratives, Nations, and Other World Products*

anthropologist Victor Turner. Turner subsumed such a situation under the title liminality, a liminal condition between farewell to a former social group and before the full belonging to a new group.[47] For example, since the agreement between Germany and Turkey in 1961, Turkish migrants were termed 'guestworkers' by the German government in order to stress that their stay was designated to be temporary and instrumental. Due to the lack of opportunities in Turkey and the higher living standard in Germany, however, many Turkish migrants extended their stays in Germany despite their inconsistent legal status. For example, Dilek, who was forty-four years old in 2012 and who came as a child to Germany as part of a family of 'guestworkers', describes the typical uncertainty that shaped the stay of Turkish migrants in Germany: 'Everything was prepared for the return next summer. The money was saved, saved and saved. "Next year we will go back forever." That had a negative effect on me, because you can't set yourself proper goals. Also, in terms of education, career plans or friendships [...] I never really felt at home.'[48] Such circumstances produced, according to the sociologist Rogers Burbarker, 'delicate problems of membership' for migrants because 'partial membership for immigrants, then, too often becomes a final station rather than a way station on the road to full citizenship.'[49] These examples emphasize the multiplicity of migrant experiences and the difficulty of classifying human mobility with any accuracy. Moreover, they reveal the artifice of state-based definitions of human mobility and point to the problems scholars encounter when they borrow legal concepts.

Clearly, migrants themselves sometimes identify as 'immigrants' and, in the process, help to reify the category. It is often advantageous for migrants, in their bid for legal rights, to adapt to state-made categories. In her work on Chinese exclusion in the United States, Kitty Calavita highlights the 'misfit between preconceived [state] categories (...) and the complex, fragmented, and overlapping social reality'. In order to enforce the law, border inspectors had to decide whether individuals either belonged to an exempt group of merchants and elites who could enter the country, or an 'undesirable' group of 'coolie labourers' who could not. The reality was that the 'myriad occupations of aspiring entrants could not be so easily dichotomized'. Once the state designated binary categories of 'exempt' and 'excluded', however, Chinese arrivals attempted to style themselves as the former. Calavita found, 'the very devices used by enforcement officials to identify the Chinese (...) were sometimes appropriated by aspiring Chinese immigrants as tools of resistance and evasion.' Chinese migrants, for example, dressed up in their identification photographs, appearing in borrowed silken robes mostly associated with Chinese from the upper classes.[50] By conforming to state-made categories, even as they sought to work around them, Chinese migrants inadvertently reinforced the idea that human motion could be neatly classified by immigration law.

Migrant activists sometimes played a more explicit role in shaping immigration policy and, thereby, the category of the 'immigrant'. Chinese, Japanese and South Asian activists successfully lobbied the US Congress to dismantle Asian exclusion laws in the 1940s and 1950s, paving the way for legal immigrants from Asia and a pathway to citizenship.[51] Similarly, Salvadoran migrants who fled to the United States during the

Salvadoran Civil War in the 1980s fought to designate themselves refugees. Activists from this well-organized group worked hard for Salvadorans' status as refugees which granted them political asylum, a possibility which US immigration law contained but which was only applied to Salvadorans because of the activists' engagement. Notably, these migrant activists have not challenged the notion that the 'immigrant' should be the preferred category of human mobility; rather they have advocated to be included within the immigrant ranks.[52]

When narrating their individual lives, migrants often describe their movement and settlement in non-linear, contingent and uncertain ways. Their diverse experiences remind us that, for many, the notion of the immigrant is more of a socio-legal construct than a lived reality. In response to immigration laws, however, migrants tend to identify themselves within legal categories that are legible and desirable from the perspective of the state. In a bid for privileges and rights, most migrants wish to be viewed as 'immigrants' (and, therefore, citizens-in-waiting), whether or not the term captures their social position and identity.

*

Starting in the mid-nineteenth century, early nation-states began to produce and circulate admiring narratives about the ideal immigrant. They celebrated the 'free', 'civilized' agent, guided only by his own personal enterprise, who chose to remove into a new country and become a member of its polity. This simple story of the immigrant was seductive and powerful, particularly for receiving nations. It fed beliefs about a nation's desirability – how it's civilization, progress, prosperity could draw immigrants in – and built up notions of the nation's sovereignty – how its leaders, laws and bureaucracy could determine who should be kept out. In other words, immigrants were constitutive of early nation-states, not only as workers or citizens, but also as characters in modern narratives of the globe. The image of the immigrant offered solace during a period marked by the upheaval of rapid industrialization, expanding capitalism, increased mobility, new state formations and reorganized social life. Nation-states sought to build a sense of order by imagining migration to be unidirectional, desirable immigrants to be citizens-in-waiting, and state bureaucracies to be powerful enough to cull new arrivals.

The naturalization of the nineteenth-century European immigrant as the ideal form of human mobility has had unsettling consequences for today's policymakers, scholars and migrants. When policymakers assume that immigration is the dominant and preferred form of mobility, they are more likely to write laws that treat other forms of motion as abnormal and suspect. When historians use the category of the immigrant without regard to period or context, they can reinforce these state assumptions. And when migrants' lives do not fit within normative notions of immigration, they can find themselves marginalized, denigrated and deprived of legal status. In the twenty-first century, amidst a global rise of nationalism and nativism, it is particularly vital to recognize the immigrant as a construct, one weighed down by the stories modern nation-states told about themselves.

Notes

1 Edward Augustus Kendall, *Travels Through the Northern Parts of the United States in 1807 and 1808* (New York: L. Riley, 1809) 2: 150; Neil Larry Shumsky, 'Noah Webster and the Invention of Immigration', *The New England Quarterly* 81, no. 1 (March 2008): 126–35; Noah Webster, *A Compendious Dictionary of the English Language* (Hartford, CT: Hudson & Goodwin, 1806); Noah Webster, *An American Dictionary of the English Language* (New Haven, CT: H. Howe, 1828).

2 Amanda Erickson, 'The 1829 Dictionary Entry that Reshaped How Americans Think about Immigrants,' *Washington Post*, 18 January 2018, https://www.washingtonpost.com/news/worldviews/wp/2018/01/18/people-used-to-move-heres-how-that-changed-and-why-they-became-immigrants-instead/; 'How to Say Immigrant in Different Languages', In Different Languages, https://www.indifferentlanguages.com/words/immigrant (accessed September 2019). In this chapter, we use the term 'immigrant' to refer to a historically constructed category and we reserve the term 'migrant' to describe a person in motion. For ease of reading, we have not placed quotation marks around every instance of 'immigrant'.

3 Recent research highlights that migration took place throughout human history on a global scale, cf. Jan Lucassen and Leo Lucassen, 'The Mobility Transition Revisited, 1500–1900: What the Case of Europe Can Offer to Global History', *Journal of Global History* 4, no. 3 (2009): 347–77; Patrick Manning, *Migration in World History*, 2nd edition (London & New York: Routledge, 2012); Immanuel Ness, ed., *The Encyclopedia of Global Human Migration* (Chichester: Wiley, 2013); Jan Lucassen and Leo Lucassen, eds., *Globalising Migration History. The Eurasian Experience* (Leiden: Brill, 2014).

4 See, for example Agnes Czajka, 'Migration in the Age of the Nation-state: Migrants, Refugees, and the National Order of Things', *Alternatives: Global, Local, Political* 39, no. 3 (August 2014): 151–63; Christian Joppke, *Immigration and the Nation-State: The United States, Germany, and Great Britain* (Oxford: Oxford University Press, 1999); Eithne Luibéid, 'Immigration', in *Keywords for American Cultural Studies*, 2nd edition, ed. Bruce Burgett and Glen Hendler (New York: NYU Press, 2014), 125–9; Reed Ueda, 'Historical Patterns of Immigration Status and Incorporation in the United States', in *E Pluribus Unum?: Contemporary and Historical Perspectives on Immigrant Political Incorporation*, ed. Gary Gerstle and John Mollenkopf (New York: Russell Sage Foundation, 2001), 292–327; Theresa Alfaro-Velcamp and Robert H. McLaughlin, 'Immigration and Techniques of Governance in Mexico and the United States: Recalibrating National Narratives through Comparative Immigration Histories', *Law and History Review* 29, no. 2 (2011): 573–606; Eytan Meyers, 'The Causes of Convergence in Western Immigration Control', *Review of International Studies* 28, no. 1 (January 2002): 123–44.

5 As Reinhard Koselleck reminds us, terms used to describe historical circumstances are usually abstractions that do not represent real historical events. As we try to understand a distant time and place, the best we can do is to try to reconstruct 'the language used by its members to conceptualize their arrangements'. Cf. Melvin Richter, 'A Note on the Text of Reinhart Koselleck: »Offene Fragen an die >Geschichtlichen Grundbegriffe<«', *Archiv für Begriffsgeschichte* 54 (2012): 250.

6 Vincent Chetail, 'Sovereignty and Migration in the Doctrine of the Law of Nations: An Intellectual History of Hospitality from Vitoria to Vattel', *The European Journal of International Law* 27, no. 4 (2017): 901–22.

7   Antony Anghie, 'Vattel and Colonialism: Some Preliminary Observations', in *Vattel's International Law from a XXI St Century Perspective*, ed. Vincent Chetail and Peter Haggenmacher (Leiden: Brill, 2011), 237–53; Georg Cavallar, 'Vitoria, Grotius, Pufendorf, Wolff and Vattel: Accomplices of European Colonialism and Exploitation or True Cosmopolitans?', *Journal of the History of International Law* 10, no. 2 (2008): 181–209.

8   Adam McKeown, *Melancholy Order: Asian Migration and the Globalization of Borders* (New York: Columbia University Press, 2008), 27; Chetail, 'Sovereignty and Migration in the Doctrine of the Law of Nations', 901–22.

9   Chin Kong James, 'Merchants and Other Sojourners. The Hokkiens Overseas, 1570–1760', (Ph.D. diss, Department of History, University of Hong Kong, 1998), 10–15.

10 Cf. Kerry Ward, *Networks of Empire: Forced Migration in the Dutch East India Company* (Cambridge: Cambridge University Press, 2009), 39, 157, 271.

11 '[..] und wir werden auch alle unsere Kräfte anwenden, tüchtige und nützliche Bürger des Statts, und Euer k. K. Majestät zu werden [...]', quoted from Màrta Fata, *Migration im kameralistischen Staat Josephs II. Theorie und Praxis der Ansiedlungspolitik in Ungarn, Siebenbürgen, Galizien und der Bukowina von 1768–1790* (Münster: Aschendorff, 2014), 313.

12 Lorenzo Veracini, *The Settler Colonial Present* (London: Palgrave, 2015), 35–47, esp. 41; Klaus Bade, *Migration in European History*, trans. Allison Brown (Malden, MA: Wiley-Blackwell, 2003); Stephen Castles, Hein de Haas, and Mark J. Miller, *The Age of Migration: International Population Movements in the Modern World* (Basingstoke: Macmillan International Higher Education, 2013).

13 David Scott FitzGerald and David Cook-Martin, *Culling the Masses: The Democratic Origins of Racist Immigration Policy in the Americas* (Cambridge, MA: Harvard University Press, 2014), 38; Kunal M. Parker, *Making Foreigners: Immigration and Citizenship Law in America, 1600–2000* (New York: Cambridge University Press, 2015); Sarah Cleveland, 'Powers Inherent in Sovereignty: Indians, Aliens, Territories and the Nineteenth Century Origins of Plenary Power over Foreign Affairs', *Texas Law Review* 81, no. 1 (2002): 81. King George III's desire to limit non-British Europeans, in particular Germans, because of their lack of allegiance would receive condemnation in the US Declaration of Independence (1776).

14 Willard Sunderland, 'Catherine's Dilemma: Resettlement and Power in Russia, 1500s–1914', in *Globalising Migration History. The Eurasian Experience (16th–21st Centuries)*, ed. Jan Lucassen and Leo Lucassen (Leiden, The Netherlands: Brill, 2014), 55–70, here 66f.

15 In his *Notes on the State of Virginia* (1781), Thomas Jefferson observed, 'The present desire of America is to produce rapid population by as great importations of foreigners as possible.' But he cautioned that too large an influx of migrants could threaten the young nation, since newcomers might lack republican principles. Thomas Jefferson, *Notes on the State of Virginia*, 2nd edition (Philadelphia: Printed for Mathew Carey, 1794), 92–3.

16 *Passenger Cases*, 48 U.S. 283 (1849).

17 The first, in 1862, prohibited American traders from participating in the 'cooly' trade in Cuba, likening Chinese indenture migration to the slave trade. In 1864, Congress passed 'An Act to Encourage Immigration', setting aside 25,000 dollars to facilitate migration into New York, and in 1870, it outlawed discriminatory state taxes on persons 'immigrating' from 'any other foreign country'. 'An Act to Encourage Immigration', 4 July 1864 (repealed 1868), 38–246, H.R. 411, 13 Stat. 385. In 1875,

the Page Act outlawed the immigration of Oriental prostitutes and, from all nations, criminals and contract labourers. In 1882, Congress passed the Chinese Restriction, which barred new Chinese labourers for ten years, and a General Immigration Act, which instituted a head tax and prohibit 'lunatics', 'idiots' and 'any person unable to take care of him or herself without becoming a public charge'. Beth Lew-Williams, *The Chinese Must Go: Violence, Exclusion, and the Making of the Alien in America* (Cambridge, MA: Harvard University Press, 2018), 235–44.

18 As translated in Natalio R. Botana and Ezequiel Gallo (eds.), *Liberal thought in Argentina, 1837–1940*, translated from the Spanish by Ian Barnett (Carmel, IN: Liberty Fund Incorporated, 2013), 140.

19 'Artículo 25. – El Gobierno federal fomentará la inmigración europea; y no podrá restringir, limitar ni gravar con impuesto alguno la entrada en el territorio argentino de los extranjeros que traigan por objeto labrar la tierra, mejorar las industrias, e introducir y enseñar las ciencias y las artes'. Argentina's Constitution of 1853, accessed September 2018, https://www.constituteproject.org/.

20 FitzGerald and Cook-Martin, *Culling the Masses*, 309.

21 Mae Ngai, 'Trouble on the Rand: The Chinese Question in South Africa and the Apogee of White Settlerism', *International Labor and Working Class History* 91, no. 91 (Spring 2017): 59–78; Lew-Williams, *The Chinese Must Go*, 194–234; McKeown, *Melancholy Order*; FitzGerald and Cook-Martin, *Culling the Masses*.

22 Daniel J. Tichenor, *Dividing Lines: The Politics of Immigration Control in America* (Princeton: Princeton University Press, 2001), 2.

23 Tichenor, *Dividing Lines*, 2.

24 *A Collection of Nationality Laws*, ed. Richard W. Flournoy and Manley O. Hudson (New York: Oxford University Press, 1929), 59.

25 Margit Schulte Beerbuehl, trans. Cynthia Klohr, *The Forgotten Majority: German Merchants in London, Naturalization, and Global Trade, 1660–1815* (New York: Berghahn Books, 2015), 15.

26 Beerbuehl, *The Forgotten Majority*, 14, 27.

27 Will Hanley, 'What Ottoman Nationality Was and Was Not', *Journal of the Ottoman and Turkish Studies Association* 3, no. 2 (November 2016): 277–98, 277.

28 Rogers Brubaker, *Citizenship and Nationhood in France and Germany* (Cambridge, MA: Harvard University Press, 1992), 35.

29 Flournoy and Hudson, *Nationality Laws*, 471.

30 Ibid., 187, 11.

31 Ibid., 442.

32 Ibid., 443.

33 Mira L. Siegelberg, *Statelessness: A Modern History* (Cambridge, MA: Harvard University Press, 2020), 35–6.

34 For example, see scholarship on the Ottoman Empire, Will Hanley, 'What Ottoman Nationality Was and Was Not', 278, 292, 297; Siegelberg, *Statelessness: A Modern History*, 29; Flournoy and Hudson, *Nationality Laws*, 569.

35 Henry Platt Fairchild, *Immigration: A World Movement and Its American Significance* (New York: Macmillan, 1919), 1–26; McKeown, *Melancholy Order*, 344.

36 Georg Simmel, 'The Sociological Significance of the "Stranger,"' in *Introduction to the Science of Sociology*, ed. Robert E. Park and Ernest W. Burgess (Chicago: The University of Chicago Press, 1921), 322.

37 Robert Ezra Park, 'Human Migration and the Marginal Man', *American Journal of Sociology* 33, no. 6 (1928): 881.

38   Richard Alba and Victor Nee, *Remaking the American Mainstream. Assimilation and Contemporary Immigration* (Cambridge, MA: Harvard University Press, 2005), 36–42.
39   Mark Wyman, 'Emigrants Returning. The Evolution of a Tradition', in *Emigrant Homecomings. The Return Movement of Emigrants 1600–2000*, ed. Marjory Harper (Manchester & New York: Manchester University Press, 2005), 21.
40   For a critique of an inflationary use of labelling Chinese migrants as sojourners see Karen Leigh Harris, 'A History of the Chinese in South Africa' (Ph.D. diss., Department of History, Univeristy of South Africa, 1998), 13.
41   Clarence E. Glick, *Sojourners and Settlers. Chinese Migrants in Hawaii* (Honolulu: University Press of Hawaii, 1980), 92.
42   Natan Uriely, 'Rhetorical Ethnicity of Permanent Sojourners. The Case of Israeli Immigrants in the Chicago Area', *International Sociology* 9, no. 4 (1994): 439.
43   Natan Uriely, 'Rhetorical Ethnicity of Permanent Sojourners,' 439–41.
44   Aysem R. Şenyürekli and Cecilia Menjívar, 'Turkish Immigrants' Hopes and Fears around Return Migration', *International Migration* 50, no. 1 (2012): 4.
45   Ibid., 10.
46   Cf. Peter Kivisto and Vanja La Vecchia-Mikkola, 'Immigrant Ambivalence toward the Homeland: The Case of Iraqis in Helsinki and Rome', *Journal of Immigrant & Refugee Studies* 11, no. 2 (2013): 198–216; Buster C. Ogbuagu, '"Diasporic Transnationalism": Towards a Framework for Conceptualizing and Understanding the Ambivalence of the Social Construction of "Home" and the Myth of Diasporic Nigerian Homeland Return', *Journal of Educational and Social Research* 3, no. 2 (2013): 189–212; For a general assessment cf. a special issue of *Emotions, Space and Society* and its introduction. Paolo Boccagni and Loretta Baldassar, 'Emotions on the Move: Mapping the Emergent Field of Emotion and Migration', *Emotion, Space and Society* 16 (2015): 73–80.
47   Cecilia Menjívar, 'Liminal Legality: Salvadoran and Guatemalan Immigrants' Lives in the United States', *American Journal of Sociology* 111, no. 4 (2006): 999–1037.
48   Eveline Reisenauer and Jürgen Gerdes, 'From Return-Oriented to Integration-Related Transnationalisation. Turkish Migrants in Germany', *Revue européenne des migrations internationales* 28, no. 1 (2012): 115. See also, Andrea Klimt, 'European Spaces: Portuguese Migrants' Notions of Home and Belonging', *Diaspora* 9, no. 2 (2000): 259–85; Ahmet Icduygu, 'Unintended Turkish Immigrant Settlement in Australia', *International Migration* 32, no. 1 (1994): 71–93.
49   William Rogers Brubaker, 'Introduction', in *Immigration and the Politics of Citizenship in Europe and North America*, ed. William Rogers Brubaker (Lanham: University Press of America, 1989), 5, 17.
50   Kitty Calavita, 'Collisions at the Intersection of Gender, Race, and Class: Enforcing the Chinese Exclusion Laws', *Law & Society Review* 40, no. 2 (2006): 249–81.
51   Jane Hong, 'The Repeal of Asian Exclusion', *Oxford Research Encyclopedia of American History*, 2019, https://oxfordre.com/americanhistory/view/10.1093/acrefore/9780199329175.001.0001/acrefore-9780199329175-e-16 (accessed 6 May 2019).
52   Susan Bibler Coutin, 'From Refugees to Immigrants: The Legalization Strategies of Salvadoran Immigrants and Activists', *The International Migration Review* 32, no. 4 (1998): 901–25.

13

'Global integration, social disintegration: Edward Long's *History of Jamaica* (1774)'

Silvia Sebastiani

A world-island: An introduction

This chapter explores how global interactions shape historical narratives by focusing on a single work, the *History of Jamaica*, published anonymously in three volumes in 1774.[1] Its author, the English planter Edward Long (1734–1813), distinguished himself for being one of the most fervent defenders of the slave trade and the institution of slavery in the second half of the eighteenth century. Long claimed that 'Negroes' were an originally distinct branch of humankind, naturally inferior to 'white men'. He even argued, more than anybody else in his times, the close proximity between Africans and orang-utans, insisting on their sexual intercourse and consanguinity. Labelled as 'the father of English racism', the name of Edward Long is today inserted in any history of race as the anti-hero of the age of abolitionism.[2]

However, historians of racism have mostly focused on one single chapter – that on 'Negroes' which opens the third book of the second volume of the *History of Jamaica* – whereas the rest of Long's extensive as well as contradictory enquiry about the Caribbean island and its population has remained under-explored. My book on *The Scottish Enlightenment* has not been an exception: it looked at Long's work as the translation of the British philosophical discourse on race into the practical idiom of the colonial empire, concentrating on the horrific image of the enslaved Africans it conveyed.[3] By contrast, historians of the British Caribbean have tended to regard Long's *History of Jamaica* more as a source of information than as an object of study in its own right.

My attempt here is different. I'll examine Long's *History* as simultaneously a national, an imperial and a worldmaking narrative. I'll investigate the taxonomy it yielded and the social categories it created for legitimating the global system in which Jamaica was a vital part. I'll try to show that Long both acclaimed and contested such a system of economic and human interdependency by giving voice to the interests and aspirations as well as to the worries and fears of English planters. Global commerce and a mixed population, composed for the most part of enslaved Africans, made of Jamaica a 'world-island', that is, an island that encompassed the world. World here represents not the literal totality of global connections, but the seat of the particular anxieties that were activated, for Long, by world (rather than purely national or English) scales. Plantation and slavery were at the heart of his narrative, which presented Jamaica as a hub of global integration through trade, but also as the possible theatre of social disintegration through the 'contamination' of the 'white blood'. His declared purpose was to defend English national identity, the interests of the British Empire, as well the 'white civilization' *tout court*. I thus take the *History of Jamaica* as a case study for reflecting on the shaping of an ambivalent discourse about globalization and its consequences on race, at the very beginning of the age of revolutions.

Long's *History* was characterized by the relationship – and dichotomy – between natural history and political economy, between the static and determinist structures of nature, including human nature, and what drives change and development in the island. How do these opposing narratives relate and interact? What I suggest is that Long combined two conflicting objectives. On the one hand, he gave shape to a fixed *natural history*, with human history folded into it; on the other, he wrote the history of the *making* of a colony and stressed the increasing of Jamaican production under the British. In doing so, Long made transformation a key element of his narrative, which challenged the static scheme he derived from natural history. Long's understanding of race resulted from the entanglement of these two divergent purposes.

By referring to polygenesis and the great chain of being, Long presented human races as fundamentally timeless, unchanging and fixed. Yet, he assumed that they could be altered through degeneration, adaptation and interbreeding. Africans were placed outside of history, yet they could enter history indirectly, by 'contaminating' the 'white race' and causing its decline. At the same time, Long conceived black Creoles, that is, Africans descendants born in Jamaica, as an improved 'species', far superior to the 'original Negroes' born in Africa. Creoles and 'mulattos' were the manpower allowing the proliferation of sugar plantations – although only under the vigilant supervision of the white English, according to Long.

My argument proceeds as follows: first, I'll focus on Long's historical narrative, paying attention to the process of globalization and the shaping of the British empire in its relationship with national history. Second, I'll look at the other side of the coin, and deal with the making of race and the dangers emerging from an integrated global world. Jamaica appeared, then, as a site of different but entangled stories and languages, which were in tensions with each other. While describing the process of global integration, Long pointed to the risks of social disintegration.

Long's 'useful knowledge' of Jamaica: Historical narrative, political economy and global commerce

How to write a history of a colony? Long's *History* did not begin with the geography of Jamaica and its natural history, as one might have expected in the wake of a long historiographical tradition harking back to Acosta. This structure had generally been adopted by Enlightenment histories, such as William Robertson's monumental *History of America*, published three years later (3 vols., 1777), or Hans Sloane's earlier natural

'Global integration, social disintegration'   245

key of welfare. Such an effervescence of productivity also raised the 'value of land', so supporting both 'the landed and trading interests of this country'.[24] Long's idyllic statement of the virtue of slavery for global capitalist production is worth to be quoted extensively:

> If, upon the whole, we revolve in our minds, what an amazing variety of trades receive their daily support, as many of them did originally their being, from the calls of the African and Weft India markets; if we reflect on the numerous families of those mechanics and artisans which are thus maintained, and contemplate that ease and plenty, which is the constant as well as just reward of their incessant labours; if we combine with these the several tribes of active and busy people, who are continually employed in the building, repairing, rigging, victualling, and equipping, the multitudes of seamen who earn their wages by navigating, and the prodigious crowds who likewise obtain their bread by loading, unloading, and other necessary attendances upon ships; if we remember, that the subsistence [sic] of all these ranks and degrees of men, thus usefully employed, constitutes a new fund of support to the landed and trading interests of this country; that their various consumptions contribute to raise the value of land, to cause a regular and constant demand for immense quantities of our native commodities, as well as to procure a vent for our numberless manufactures; and that all this is equally regular, permanent, and certain; we may from thence form a competent idea of the prodigious value of our sugar colonies, and a just conception of their immense importance to the grandeur and prosperity of their mother country.[25]

In short, Long made the entire economy depend on the slave trade and slavery. It was 'the prodigious value of our sugar colonies' that made Britain 'greater'.[26] Even Africans had much to gain in being enslaved 'in the colony': whereas they were 'slaves, abject slaves in Africa, [...] subject to all the severities of the most brutal and licentious tyranny', they became protected by law in Jamaica, where 'a tacit agreement' was stipulated with their masters, who held not 'an unlimited power' over them, but assured them a dignified standard of life.[27]

But such an apparently peaceful and industrious picture paved the way to another scenario, one pervaded by fear. It is no coincidence that Long recurred extensively to a term which was not so common in the language of his time: 'anxiety'. He spoke of 'present urgent anxiety', 'unceasing anxiety of mind' in relation to the precarious conditions of the planters, who were tormented by creditors and had to face continuous losses, of crops as well as – he lamented – of enslaved workers dying of diseases. Samuel Johnson's *Dictionary of the English Language* (1755) defined 'anxiety' as 'trouble of mind about some future event; suspense with uneasiness; perplexity; solicitude'. Long also employed the second medical meaning recorded by Johnson, that is, 'lowness of sprits, with uneasiness of the stomach', for describing the diseases of the passions and sensibility which attacked 'the natives of this island', 'men of lively imaginations and great vivacity', which could lead them even to death.[28] During the 1760s, slave revolts were frequent.[29] Two years after his arrival in Jamaica, Long experienced one of the largest and most violent, known as Tacky's war – after the name of its 'generalissimo in

246   *Narratives, Nations, and Other World Products*

the woods', as he put it.[30] The revolt broke out in 1760, in the middle of the Seven Years' War (1756–63), which historiography has identified as the first commercial conflict on a world scale, while stressing its significance in 'the making of the British empire'.[31] In his *History*, Long devoted several dark pages to Tacky's insurrection, which remained etched in his memory as a source of constant terror.[32]

Once back in England, Long's distress did not vanish but was directed to a correlated issue: the opposition to slave trade which was growing in the public opinion of the metropole. In 1772, the Somerset case set legal limits to slave-owners by establishing that masters could not force enslaved Africans to leave England against their will and by extending the *habeas corpus* to them too.[33] Lord Mansfield's judgement became a *casus belli* for Long. Long accused the new legislation of endangering the 'right' of property of those who had 'deemed their negroes to be fit objects of purchase and sale, transferrable like any other goods and chattels'.[34] Furthermore, by integrating *de iure* Africans into a common humanity, it encouraged mutiny and debauchery, together with interbreeding and *métissage*.

The new political, economic and juridical atmosphere created new anxieties. Long warned British citizens of the immense peril which was 'now' spreading in England too: that of the 'contamination' of the 'white race'. The acclamation of the benefits of global commerce and capitalist interdependency went hand in hand with the denunciation of the risks of social disintegration, due to the pollution of blood. The optimistic language of political economy gave way to the apprehensive language of disorder and disease. Long's *History of Jamaica* was pervaded as much by the confidence as it was by the fear of globalization.

Slavery, complexion, corruption

It is difficult to exaggerate the impact that the new abolitionist climate and Somerset trial had on the *History of Jamaica*. Soon after his return to the metropole, Long published two texts of very different genres, a satirical play and a political pamphlet. Both shared the same harsh criticism of the law for adopting anti-slavery stances. *The Trial of Farmer Carter's Dog Porter, for Murder* (1771) was, as the title reveals, the story of the prosecution of a dog, named Porter, accused of having murdered a hare, belonging to a local landowner (who ate it for dinner). The trial, which culminates in the hanging of the dog, was displayed as a farce. First of all, the accused was an animal who could not talk (but 'the law can, not only make dogs to speak, but explain their meaning too'). Furthermore, it was innocent. Magistrates, lawyers, councillors and all witnesses were presented as ridiculous, senseless and arbitrary. The only one arousing author's sympathy is the owner of the 'poor' dog, farmer Carter, who fiercely denounced judges' corruption ('You pretend to be Judges ... ').[35] Through his voice, Long accused the whole system of justice for having turned into a masquerade, a '*just-ass*'. When read in the context of the beginning of an abolitionist legislation, Long's satire acquires its full meaning.

After Somerset's sentence in 1772, Long's tone and rhetoric became 'serious' – as he put it.[36] The *Candid Reflections upon the Judgement Lately Awarded by the Court of King's Bench, in What Is Commonly Called The Negroe Cause* was a direct, ferocious and meticulous response to Lord Mansfield's judgement, published in the same year of the ruling it opposed. It was signed 'by a planter', so to make clear the position of its author, who spoke not in his personal capacity but on the behalf of a large proportion of 'active' British citizens. Long contested Mansfield's 'Delphic *ambiguity*'[37] by reasserting the fundamental dictates of common law and colonial codes as well as the right of property which legitimated slavery. Slavery was, according to him, integral to the English constitution, and in perfect agreement with the principles of British trade. In contrast with the wisdom of the previous legislation, the new one was 'a direct invitation to *three hundred thousand blacks*, now scattered over our different colonies' to come to Britain, the new 'land of *Canaan*'.[38] The consequences of such a reckless act were massive. Long depicted an apocalyptic scenario, one marked by blood, revolt, debauchery, miscegenation and 'every evil', both in England and in the colonies. He appealed to the Parliament (his last hope) to set limits to 'the ferment of this law poison, by a suitable and seasonable antidote'.[39]

In Long's account, American slavery was nothing other than the continuation of ancient *villenage*, which in England has grown 'into desuetude by the gradual extension of our national commerce', and the changing requirements of the global market: 'On the decline of villenage within the realm, a species of it sprang up in the remoter parts of the English dominion, the *American plantations*; clearly introduced by the very same enlarged commerce which had extinguished it in the mother state'.[40] Therefore, the same global commerce that made slavery obsolete in Britain made it necessary in America. No sugar plantations could subsist without 'Negroe labourers' and 'Negroe slaves' – terms that Long employed as synonymous.

If in *The Trial of Farmer Carter's Dog* Long ridiculed magistrates for their pretention to understand dog's language, in the pamphlet he accused Lord Mansfield of inventing 'the art of washing *the black-a-moor white*'. Long transformed the biblical passage of Jeremiah 13.23 ('Can the Ethiopian change his skin, or the leopard his spots? Then may ye also do good that are accustomed to do evil?') into a tool for racializing humanity. He wrote: 'the thing that *Solomon* thought impossible when he said, "Can the *Æthiop* change his skin?" What the wise *Aesop* esteemed a prodigy in nature; has, in the present wonder-working age, ceased any longer to be *miraculous*'.[41]

The expression *to wash an Ethiop [or a Blackamoor] white* has a very long history harking back to Aesopic *Fables*, which Jean Michel Massing has meticulously reconstituted.[42] In 1741, Ephraim Chambers used this axiom to explain the meaning of the word 'trope' in his *Cyclopaedia*: 'TROPE, TROPUS, in rhetoric, a word or expression used in a different sense from what it properly signifies. Or, a word changes from its proper and natural signification to another, with some advantage. [...] As, when we say an *ass*, for a *stupid person*; *thunderbolt of war* for a *great captain*; to *wash the black-moor white*, for a *fruitless undertaking*'.[43] Srinivas Aravamudan has stressed the very significant role that the trope played in eighteenth-century colonial discourse.[44] He argues that by changing the original sense of a word or of an expression into a 'more significant' discourse (in Chamber's words), tropes performed specific functions which attain different meanings in different periods. The 'supplementary signification' that the expression *to wash the black-moor white* acquired as a metaphor for *fruitless undertaking* was that of a 'negative outcome': a 'failure'. Within the colonial context in which Long wrote, this became the 'sign of *failed whitening* or *unachievable whiteness*'.[45] As Aravamudan puts it, '*blackness* begins to signify *unchangeability*, just as much this *unchangeability* suggests, in turn, *uselessness*: hence, fruitless undertaking. By associative reduction, the blackamoor thereby lapses into the stereotype of *unchangeable uselessness*.[46]

Long played with all these meanings at once. By accusing Lord Mansfield of attempting the impossible, Long condemned 'Negroes' to immobility, and through this to perpetual slavery. In a vicious and circular reasoning, Blacks' unchangeable complexion made of them a *merchandise*. In his own copy of *Candid Reflections,* the anti-slavery campaigner Granville Sharp, who had played a key role in supporting James Somerset, glossed and opposed point by point Long's assertions, in extensive manuscript notes written at the margins of Long's text. Sharp also unveiled the 'glaring misapplication of the proverb' by which Long had equated 'Negroes' to natural 'slaves'. 'The Author's rhetorical Trope about their [Negroes'] being washed white, is so impertinent to the present point, that it disgusts' – Sharp wrote. 'For no lawyer was ever yet so ignorant as to suppose that a Man's Freedom depended upon his Complexion; or that Negroes are Slaves because they are black.'[47]

In the *History of Jamaica* Long effected a change of scale, accompanied by a further naturalization of the differences between Blacks and whites. His response to abolitionists now based 'African slavery on biology'.[48] With a meaningful shift from a legal and politico-economic argument to a 'physical motive', Africans were now described as 'naturally' inferior to whites, both in body and in mind.[49] Long employed the old scheme of the great chain of being for conceptualizing the descending gradation from white to black, and from the human to the animal. In addition, he used the language of naturalists for contending that Africans belonged to a different 'species' of men. In line with natural world, Long argued, men belonged to one 'genus' divided into 'species', clearly separated from each other.[50] He also maintained that the differences in complexion did not depend on climate, but 'must be referred to some other cause', as English would not 'by living in Guiney, [...] exchange hair for wool, or a white cuticle for a black'.[51] The chain of being and a polygenetic credo shaped the general system of Long's world, universalizing the principle of hierarchy.[52]

Within this framework, slavery emerged as a relative term, which changed meaning depending on whom it was applied to. Long invited sensitive British citizens, imbued with freedom from birth, to refrain from judging the feelings of Africans, who had always lived in the midst of barbarism and slavery. 'If we are impartial', Long argued pretending once again to have a disinterested voice,

> we ought to examine the subject; not using slavery as an indefinite term, but considering how far just our particular idea or definition of it is, when applied to this or that set of men, who live in a different part of the world; since what is deemed slavery in one place, is far from being reputed so in another: a Briton therefore, who has always lived in fruition of a rational freedom, must not judge of every other man's feelings by his own ...[53]

Not only were Africans incapable of understanding and appreciating English freedom that they didn't know, but they were also 'scarcely' different 'from the wild beasts of the wood in the ferocity of their manners' as well as in their 'savage [...] disposition'.

'*Global integration, social disintegration*'   249

Such men must be managed at first as if they were beasts; they must be tamed, before they can be treated like men.[54]

The parallel between 'Negroes' and 'orang-utans'[55] that Long developed at length in the following pages, while echoing the contemporary scientific debate, was instrumental in showing the proximity and 'consanguinity' between the two. Actually, he even claimed that apes were more educated and sensitive than Africans. Without entering into this wide-ranging debate, which deeply permeated Enlightenment reflection on the 'science of man' and on which I have been working for years,[56] I would like to stress one point which is crucial for the economy of this chapter: the major divide for Long was not between animal and human, but between Black and white.

By recurring to the orang-utan, Long meant to demonstrate that the orang-utan had 'much nearer resemblance to the Negroe race, than the latter bear to White men'.[57] He knew perfectly well that Africans were humans, but was keen to provide evidence that they could, and did, interbreed with orang-utans.[58] Insisting on the fecundity of their relationships was particularly significant within the context of the European debate, as Buffon had made the capacity to reproduce the main criterion for belonging to the same species.[59] Long's strategy was twofold. On the one hand, he asserted that he did 'not think that an Oran-Outang husband would be any disgrace to an Hottentot female' (with an inversion of role between the husband-ape and the female-African).[60] On the other hand, he pretended that the union between Blacks and whites produced an infertile offspring. 'Mulattos' would be real 'mules', unable to procreate when 'intermarried [...] with those of their own complexion' (they could instead breed with individuals of the complexion of their parents, either white or black).[61] Long even invoked his local knowledge to suggest that the exceptions depended on illicit intercourses, whereas all the chaste relationships he could observe in Jamaica had the same result: infertility. The controversial reference to Buffon should not escape notice. Buffon had made it clear that:

> If the negro and the white could not reproduce together, if even their offspring remained infertile, if the mulatto were truly a mule, there would be then two well distinct species; the Negro would be to man what the donkey is to a horse: or rather, if the white was a man, the Negro would no longer be a man; he would be a distinct animal, like the ape, and we would be entitled to think that the white and the Negro would not have a common origin. But even this supposition is given lie to by fact; and since all men can communicate and reproduce together, all men come from the same stock and are of the same family.[62]

Long supported the opposite view, while endorsing Buffon's definition of species. He attempted to demonstrate that human nature was not the same, but was fragmented in different species and degrees. This is why he insisted on the very doubtful 'fact' that 'mulattos' were of 'the mule-kind' and their 'matches have generally been defective and barren'.[63]

Indeed, Long expressed his deepest anxieties about globalization when dealing with the 'dark inheritance' and the corruption of the 'white blood', caused by the sexual 'commerce' between Blacks and whites.[64] His apprehensions vis-à-vis the *métissage*

250   *Narratives, Nations, and Other World Products*

gave rise to a negative narrative of integration. 'Corruption', 'contamination', 'pollution', 'taint' were key words in Long's world view, marked by an obsession with the sexual relations of white men of 'every rank, quality, and degree' with 'Negresses and Mulattas, free or slaves'.[65] Not only did the mixing of Black and white produce 'a vast addition of spurious offsprings of different complexions', but it also went against nature since they were 'two tinctures which nature has dissociated, like oil and vinegar'.[66]

This wake-up call to the dangers of degeneration through contamination was sounded against the backdrop of Jamaican laws, which recognized the children of third-generation Africans as white. As Long deplored, these descendants 'are called English, and consider themselves as free from all taint of the Negroe race'.[67] The example of Spanish America provided a historical reference of the degenerative results of racial hybridization. Long remarked:

> Let any man turn his eyes to the Spanish American dominions, and behold what a vicious, brutal, and degenerate breed of mongrels has been there produced, between Spaniards, Blacks, Indians, and their mixed progeny.[68]

To avoid a similar fate, Long encouraged the 'white men of that colony' to free themselves from the 'goatish embraces' of 'black women' (here reduced to reproductive cattle) and 'perform the duty incumbent on every good citizen, by raising in honourable wedlock a race of unadulterated beings'.[69] Long's insistence on chastity, as well as the invitation to his fellow-citizens in Jamaica to 'abate of their infatuated attachments to black women', suggests however a scenario a quite different from the one that he exhibited: not rejection but attraction, or perhaps libido, fantasy and repulsion at once. As Robert Young notices, 'theories of race were also covert theories of desire'.[70]

In *Candid Reflections*, Long had already addressed the issue of the tainting of blood as a major problem not only in the colonial world but also in the domestic space of the metropole. England itself was already infected, or at least its lower classes were. In addition to differences between races, he pointed out differences between social classes, mixed with a dose of sexism:

> The Lower class of women in England are remarkably fond of the blacks, for reasons too brutal to mention: they would connect themselves with horses and asses, if the laws permitted them. By these ladies they generally have a numerous brood.[71]

The staining of the 'race' was the doing of white women of lower classes who engaged in intercourse with Black men, the latter being assimilated with horses or donkeys. Alongside Africans and apes, Long delineated a continuum between humans and animals, whose positions were determined along race, class and gender lines. From the lower classes, the 'pollution' could spread and pervade the middle rank and the higher orders too. Without containing such danger, 'the whole nation' would have been transformed into swarthy '*Portuguese* and *Moriscos*', degraded in body as well as in mind.

The nation already begins to be bronzed with the African tint ... In the course of a few generations more, the English blood will become so contaminated with this mixture, and ... this alloy may spread so extensively, as even to reach the middle, and then the higher orders of the people, till the whole nation resembles the Portuguese and Moriscos, in complexion of skin and baseness of mind. This is a venomous and dangerous ulcer, that threatens to disperse its malignancy far and wide, until every family catches infection from it.[72]

Ulcer, malignancy, infection: the language of sickness and (sexually transmitted) diseases was once again associated with the integration of Blacks in Britain.

However, in the *History of Jamaica* the description of the populations residing in the colony is not only in black and white. Long opened the chapter on 'the inhabitants of this island' by distinguishing various 'classes' of people: 'Creoles, or natives; Whites, Blacks, Indians, and their varieties; European and other Whites; and imported or African Blacks'.[73] He sketched a chart of racial intermixture between whites, Blacks and Indians, generating 'several different casts', in its 'Direct lineal Ascent from the Negroe Venter' as well as its 'Retrograde' line, which recorded Spaniards' sophisticated nomenclature. Long claimed that the Spaniards in the New World had 'invented' 'a kind of science among them', even if not as sophisticated as that proposed by the Dutch.[74] 'These distinctions, however', Long explained, 'do not prevail in Jamaica; for here the Terceron is confounded with the Quateron; and the laws permit all, that are above three degrees removed in lineal descent from the Negro ancestor, to vote at elections, and enjoy all the privileges and immunities of his majesty's white subjects of the island'.[75] If Long was ironic vis-à-vis Dutch and Spanish meticulousness, English exceeded in the opposite extreme, by confounding 'all the Blacks in one class', and supposing them 'equally prompt for rebellion': 'an opinion' that he considered 'grossly erroneous'.[76]

Long made a clear descending hierarchy between 'Mulattos', Black Creoles and Africans (born) in Africa. The latter only were condemned to the unchangeable realm of inferiority, while all other inhabitants of the British colonies were deemed capable of education as well as improvement.[77] 'Mulattos', freed Blacks, enslaved Black Creole, all could progress and contribute to the improvement and security of Jamaica. Indeed, Long paid much attention in separating enslaved Black Creoles, born in Jamaica, from enslaved Africans. In contrast with 'imported Africans', whose 'intractable and ferocious tempers naturally provoked their masters to rule them with a rod of iron', black Creoles could, 'with a very moderate instruction in Christian rules, be kept in good order without the whip'.[78] The differences between them did not concern 'only manners', but also the 'beauty of shape, feature, and complexion'.[79] Long even accorded some space to the impact of climate which he had previously excluded as the cause of Black complexion. But he mostly insisted in the positive effects of commerce, education and Christianity. His plan was to transform 'mulattos' and Black Creoles into allies of the planters' cause by inserting them 'into colonial circuits of defence and trade', so to make Jamaica both wealthier and more secure (for whites).[80] Accordingly, Long proposed two different legal codes, instead of a single *Code Noir*.

252   *Narratives, Nations, and Other World Products*

The logic of political economy and the defence of Jamaica marked the limits of Long's polygenism. His *History* brought conflicting views of human differences together. It mixed, in Roxann Wheeler's words, 'his contention of a permanent gulf between Africans and Europeans with a belief in the reformist possibilities of consumerism and Christian education'.[81] In this sense, Suman Seth is right to stress that 'race-science during the Enlightenment in the West Indies looks very different to metropolitan race-science in the same period, for reasons very specific to the location of its production'.[82] The 'fundamental ambivalence' of Long's arguments about racial fixity depended on his colonial location.[83] Histories of blood, race, nation and sex intersected with the commercial dynamism of colonial society. Long's *History* was pervaded by ambivalences and anxieties, which were directly connected with the processes of globalization.

Conclusions

What is global about *The History of Jamaica*? My suggestion is that Long's history was at once national, imperial *and* global. It was a history of race and political economy which aspired to generalize from a close analysis of Jamaica. From his specific position of planter and local knowledge-broker, Long contributed to the contemporary debates on the shaping of racial categories, on the one hand, and on political economy and consumption, on the other, while displaying their intimate connections. His work invites to reflect on the positive as well as negative narratives of globalization in the age of Enlightenment. As this chapter has shown, Long's relationship with globalization was characterized above all by anxiety and fear. For him, fear was not only a product of colonization, but of its global scale. It was the global scale of war which raised the terror of slave revolt; it was the global scope of slavery and worldwide mobility which prompted anxieties of inter-racial reproduction.

I would like to conclude by evoking a last point, which allows us to fully grasp the global significance of *The History of Jamaica*. Moving from Jamaica and England to Europe and the German world, Long's history became a source of the most influential attempt of racial taxonomy in the eighteenth century: *De Generi humani varietate nativa*, published by the Göttingen anatomist Johannn Frederich Blumenbach in 1775. *The History of Jamaica* was still mentioned in the third revised and expanded edition of 1790, which famously classified humankind into five races (Caucasian, Mongolian, Malayan, Ethiopian and American), based not on skin colour but on craniometry. Blumenbach dedicated this third edition to the President of the Royal Society Joseph Banks, to whom, a few years later, he asked the identity of the author of the *History of Jamaica*, thus showing a persistent interest in Long's work.[84] What seems significant to me is that the father of modern physical anthropology recurred to *The History of Jamaica* for the description and classification of 'mulattos'.[85] A convinced monogenist, who deeply believed in the effects of climate on human complexion and morphology, Blumenbach referred to Long's account for displaying how individuals could adapt and transform themselves in different environments, how they mixed together and changed. It was in the sections on 'hybrids' and 'changes' that the *History of Jamaica* was mostly quoted, while no mention was made of Long's polygenetic statement. Blumenbach's selective reading of the *History of Jamaica* shows that Long's anxiety-ridden notion of the global as a dimension of adulteration and mixing was one of his most ominous legacies. The elaboration of racial theories, to which Blumenbach made a crucial contribution, was built on a multiplicity of sources and references to authorities such as Long, whose own work was an expression of his colonial interests and of his sentiments towards family, nation and empire. By inserting the *History of Jamaica* in his treatise, Blumenbach thus made Long's anxieties, as well as his interests and sentiments, important sources for what would become modern anthropology. In doing so, he took *The History of Jamaica* far beyond the Atlantic world.

Notes

1   [Edward Long], *The History of Jamaica, or, General Survey of the Antient and Modern State of That Island: With Reflections on Its Situation, Settlements, Inhabitants, Climate, Products, Commerce, Laws, and Government* (3 vols., London: printed for T. Lowndes, 1774) – hereafter cited as HJ. I presented this chapter twice at Princeton, first in 2018, when I was a member of the Institute for Advanced Study, and then in January 2020, right at the beginning of the Covid-19 pandemic crisis that had detrimental consequences for collaborative work such as ours. In both cases, I benefited enormously from the feedback from the editors and other authors of this volume, to whom my thanks go. I am also grateful to Bruce Buchan and Cécile Vidal for their helpful comments on an earlier version of this chapter. Many of my reflections took shape within the 'Edward Long reading group' and in the rich discussions with Markman Ellis, Miles Ogborn and Catherine Hall, to whom I am particularly indebted. When I wrote this chapter, Catherine Hall was in the middle of writing her much needed book on *Lucky Valley. Edward Long and the History of Racial Capitalism* (Cambridge: Cambridge University Press, forthcoming 2024), which readers now have at their disposal.

2   Peter Fryer, *Staying Power: The History of Black People in Britain* (London and New York: Pluto Press, 2010), 70.

3   Silvia Sebastiani, *The Scottish Enlightenment. Race, Gender and the Limits of Progress* (New York: Palgrave/McMillan, 2013), chap. 4.

4   Hans Sloane, *A Voyage to the Islands Madera, Barbadoes, Nieves, St Christophers, and Jamaica; with the Natural History of the Herbs and Trees, Four-Footed Beasts, Fishes, Birds, Insects, Reptiles, & c. Of the Last of Those Islands* (2 vols., London: Printed by B.M. for the author, 1707 and 1725). See Miles Ogborn, 'Discriminating Evidence: Closeness and Distance in Natural and Civil Histories of the Caribbean' and Silvia Sebastiani, 'What Constituted Historical Evidence of the New World? Closeness and Distance in Robertson and Clavijero', *Modern Intellectual History* 11, no. 3 (2014): 631–53 and 675–93.

5   Trevor Burnard, *Mastery, Tyranny, and Desire: Thomas Thistlewood and His Slaves in the Anglo Jamaican World* (Chapel Hill: University of North Carolina Press, 2004), 13–22; Jack P. Greene, *Settler Jamaica in the 1750s: A Social Portrait* (Charlottesville: University of Virginia Press, 2016). For the precise context in which Long operated, see now Hall, *Lucky Valley*.

6   Elizabeth Bohls, 'The Gentleman Planter and the Metropole: Long's *History of Jamaica* (1774)', in *The Country and the City Revisited: England and the Politics of Culture 1550–1850*, ed. Gerald Maclean, Donna Landry and Joseph P. Ward (Cambridge: Cambridge University Press, 1999), 180–96. See also Elizabeth Bohls, *Slavery and the Politics of Place: Representing the Colonial Caribbean, 1770–1833* (Cambridge: Cambridge University Press, 2014).

7   Richard Grassby, *Kinship and Capitalism. Marriage, Family and Business in the English Speaking World, 1580–1740* (Cambridge: Cambridge University Press, 2001); Sarah Pearsall, *Atlantic Families: Lives and Letters in the Later Eighteenth Century* (Oxford: Oxford University Press, 2008); Catherine Hall, *Macaulay and Son: Architects of Imperial Britain* (New Haven: Yale University Press, 2012).

8   Emma Rothschild, *The Inner Life of Empires. An Eighteenth-Century History* (Princeton: Princeton University Press, 2011), 172.

9   Catherine Hall, 'Whose Memories? Edward Long and the Work of Re-Remembering', in *Britain's History and Memory of Transatlantic Slavery*, ed. Katie Donington, Ryan Hanley and Jessica Moody (Oxford: Oxford University Press, 2016), 136. See also Catherine Hall, *Civilising Subjects: Metropole and Colony in the English Imagination, 1830–1867* (Cambridge: Polity Press, 2002). I borrow the last quotation to Stuart Hall speaking about the work of his wife Catherine, in *Familiar Stranger: A Life between Two Islands* (Durham and London: Duke University Press, 2017), 81.

10   Mary Ballard was the widow of John Palmer, and the second daughter and heir of Thomas Beckford. On Edward Long's family, see Hall, *Lucky Valley.*

11   Sir Henry Moore was the husband of Edward Long's sister Catherine Maria. He embodied the role of 'colonial governor', also becoming governor of the Province of New York between 1765 and 1769. See Joseph S. Tiedemann, 'Moore, Sir Henry, first baronet (1713–1769)', *Oxford Dictionary of National Biography* (Oxford: Oxford University Press, 2004).

12   Long described in depth the functions of the Vice Admiralty Court and of the Assembly in *HJ*, vol. I, 53ff.

13   *HJ*, vol. II, 228.

14   Arnaldo Momigliano, *Sui fondamenti della storia antica* (Turin: Einaudi, 1984), 3–45, 294–327.

15   Mark S. Phillips, 'Reconsideration on History and Antiquarianism: Arnaldo Momigliano and the Historiography of Eighteenth-century Britain', *Journal of the History of Ideas* 57 (1996): 297–316; Mark S. Phillips, *Society and Sentiment. Genres of Historical Writing in Britain, 1740–1820* (Princeton: Princeton University Press, 2000).

16   *HJ*, vol. I, 2, emphasis added.

17   Review of *The History of Jamaica*, *Monthly Review*, LI (1774): 129–36, 431–41, quotations p. 134 and 441.

18   *HJ*, vol. I, 6.

19   [Edward Long], *Candid Reflections upon the Judgement Lately Awarded by the Court of King's Bench in Westminster Hall on What Is Commonly Called The Negroe Cause, by a Planter* (London: T. Lowndes and Co., 1772), 30.

20   Jean-Marc Besse and Guillaume Monsaingeon (eds.), *Le temps de l'île* (Marseille: Mucem/Parentheses, 2019).

21   Stuart Hall, 'New Cultures for Old', in *A Place in the World? Places, Cultures and Globalization*, ed. Doreen Massey and Pat Jess (Oxford: Oxford University Press, 1995), 175–211.

22 His literary ambitions are confirmed by the fact that Long published two works before leaving to Jamaica: *The Prater*, a periodical printed in thirty-five instalments in 1756, in the wake of the *Spectator*; and *The Anti-Gallican; or, the History and Adventures of Harry Cobham, Esquire. Inscribed to Louis the XVth, by the Author* (London: printed for T. Lownds, 1757), a novel which, at the beginning of the Seven Years' War, sharply criticized French style. In addition, Long had a musical education, and played a Cremona violin.

23 Elizabeth Bohls, 'The Gentleman Planter and the Metropole,' 180–1. Markman Ellis stresses similar tensions in '"Incessant Labour": Georgic Poetry and the Problem of Slavery', in *Discourses of Slavery and Abolition. Writing in Britain and Its Colonies 1660–1832*, ed. Brycchan Carey, Markman Ellis and Sarah Salih (London: Palgrave, 2004), 45–62.

24 *HJ*, vol. I, 494.

25 *HJ*, vol. I, 494. On this passage, see the sharp analysis offered by Catherine Hall, 'Gendering Property, Racing Capital', in *History After Hobsbawm: Writing the Past for the Twenty-First Century*, ed. John H. Arnold, Matthew Hilton and Jan Rüger (Oxford: Oxford University Press, 2018), 20–1.

26 Duncan Bell, *The Idea of Greater Britain: Empire and the Future of World Order, 1860–1900* (Princeton: Princeton University Press, 2007). Bell refers to a later period, but some of the issues he discusses are already at work in the 1770s.

27 *HJ*, vol. I, 401.

28 *HJ*, vol. I, 557; vol. II, 437, 542–3.

29 *HJ*, vol. II, 451. See Andrew Jackson O'Shaughnessy, *An Empire Divided: The American Revolution and the British Caribbean* (Philadelphia: University of Pennsylvania Press, 2000), 38.

30 Vincent Brown, *Tacky's Revolt: The Story of an Atlantic Slave War* (Cambridge, MA; London: Harvard University Press, 2020).

31 Christopher A. Bayly, *Indian Society and the Making of the British Empire* (Cambridge: Cambridge University Press, 1988).

32 *HJ*, vol. II, 447–62.

33 From among an extensive literature, see Christopher Leslie Brown, *Moral Capital: Foundations of British Abolitionism* (Chapel Hill: University of North Carolina Press, 2006).

34 Long, *Candid Reflections*, 41.

35 Edward Long, *The Trial of Farmer Carter's Dog Porter, for Murder. Taken Down Verbatim et Literatim in Short-hand, and Now Published by Authority, from the Corrected Manuscript of Counsellor Clear-Point, Barrister at Law. N. B. This is the Only True and Authentic Copy; and All Others are Spurious* (London: T. Lowndes, 1771), 11 and 36. For a useful contextualization of this process within other animal trials in early-modern Britain, see Piers Beirne, 'A Note on the Facticity of Animal Trials in Early Modern Britain; Or, the Curious Prosecution of Farmer Carter's Dog for Murder', *Crime, Law and Social Change* 55 (2011): 359–74; Yoriko Otomo, 'Law', in *The Edinburgh Companion to Animal Studies*, ed. Lynn Turner, Undine Sellbach and Ron Broglio (Edinburgh: Edinburgh University Press, 2018), 307–20, esp. 308–11. Instead, I'm not convinced by the arguments both advance for questioning Long's authorship of *The Trial*. When one takes into account Long's whole literary production, it is far from unlikely that he did write this text. See Hall, *Lucky Valley*.

36 Long, *Candid Reflections*, iv. Yet even in this case, Long cannot help but use irony.

37 Long, *Candid Reflections*, 57.

38 Long, *Candid Reflections*, 64.

39 Long, *Candid Reflections*, 62.

40 Long, *Candid Reflections*, 3.

41 Long, *Candid Reflections*, iii.

42 Jean Michel Massing, 'From Greek Proverb to Soap Advert: Washing the Ethiopian', *Journal of the Warburg and Courtauld Institutes* 58 (1995): 180–201.

43 Ephraim Chambers, *Cyclopaedia: Or an Universal Dictionary of Arts and Sciences* (4th edition, 2 vols., London: printed for D. Midwinter et al., 1741), vol. 2, no page number, emphasis in the original.

44 Srinivas Aravamudan, *Tropicopolitains: Colonialism and Agency, 1688–1804* (Durham: Duke University Press, 1999).

45 Aravamudan, *Tropicopolitains*, 4. I employ here Aravamudan's terminology and analysis, which I consider highly pertinent, but I emphasize the discontinuities represented by Long's use of the trope. Long's work is not part of the texts examined by Aravamudan, who especially focuses on literature. See also Srinivas Aravamudan, *Enlightenment Orientalism. Resisting the Rise of the Novel* (Chicago and London: The University of Chicago Press, 2012).

46 Aravamudan, *Tropicopolitains*, 4.

47 Granville Sharp's manuscript annotations in Long, *Candid Reflections*, IV. Sharp's copy, with his copious manuscript notes, is held at the Yale University Library, Beinecke Rare Book and Manuscript Library, Ntg45 G5 772L.

48 Seymour Drescher, *The Mighty Experiment: Free Labor versus Slavery in British Emancipation* (Oxford: Oxford University Press, 2002), 75.

49 I follow here Miles Ogborn, *The Freedom of Speech. Talk and Slavery in the Anglo-Caribbean World* (Chicago and London: University of Chicago Press, 2019), 6–16. Ogborn convincingly argues that, in his shift towards nature, Long has been inspired by the second and expanded edition of the *Considerations on the Negroe Cause, Commonly So called, Addressed to the Right Honourable Lord Mansfield*, by the assistant agent for Barbados Samuel Estwick, published in 1773 (first ed. 1772). By contrast, Suman Seth questions the direct connection between Long's polygenism and his anti-abolitionism, in *Difference and Disease. Medicine, Race, and the Eighteenth-Century British Empire* (Cambridge: Cambridge University Press, 2018), chap. 6.

50 *HJ*, vol. II, 356.

51 *HJ*, vol. II, 262. On polygenesis in Britain's Enlightenment, see Sebastiani, *The Scottish Enlightenment*.

52 Winthrop D. Jordan, *White over Black. American Attitudes toward the Negro, 1550–1812* (Chapel Hill: University of North Carolina Press, 1968), 228 and 482–97.

53 *HJ*, vol. II, 401.

54 *HJ*, vol. II, 401.

55 'Orang-utan' (spelled in many different ways) is a term of Malayan origin literally meaning 'man of the wood'. All along the eighteenth century it was used as the generic noun for describing all the great apes (both Asiatic and African) then known.

56 See Silvia Sebastiani, 'Challenging Boundaries. Apes and Savages in Enlightenment', in *Simianization. Apes, Gender, Class, and Race*, ed. Wulf D. Hund, Charles W. Mills and Silvia Sebastiani (Berlin: Lit Verlag, 2015), 105–37; Silvia Sebastiani, 'A "Monster with Human Visage": The Orangutan, Savagery and the Borders of Humanity in the Global Enlightenment', *History of the Human Sciences* 32, no. 4 (2018): 80–99; Silvia

Sebastiani, 'Enlightenment Humanization and Dehumanization, and the Orangutan', in *The Routledge Handbook of Dehumanization*, ed. Maria Kronfeldner (London and New York: Routledge, 2021), 64–82. I'm now completing a book on the boundaries of humanity in the Enlightenment, focusing on how the great ape contributed to the shaping of human and social sciences.

57 *HJ*, vol. II, 371.

58 *HJ*, vol. II, 364.

59 Georges-Louis Leclerc, compte de Buffon, *Histoire naturelle générale et particulière* (36 vols., Paris: Imprimerie Royale, 1749–89), vol. IV (1753), 385–6 (my translation).

60 *HJ*, vol. II, 364. Long's terminology shifted between 'African', 'Hottentot' and 'Negro', with no clear distinction. See Nicholas Hudson, '"Hottentot" and the Evolution of European Racism', *Journal of European Studies* 34, no. 4 (2016): 308–32; François-Xavier Fauvelle-Aymar, *L'Invention du Hottentot. Histoire du regard occidental sur les Khoisan (XVIᵉ – XIXᵉ siècle)* (Paris: Publications de la Sorbonne, 2002).

61 *HJ*, vol. II, 335–6. Long accepted that in very few cases 'mulatto' men and women produced, but he assured that the offspring did not survive to maturity.

62 Buffon, *Histoire naturelle*, vol. IV (1753), 388–9.

63 *HJ*, vol. II, 335.

64 Brooke N. Newman, *Dark Inheritance. Blood, Race, and Sex in Colonial Jamaica* (New Haven: Yale University Press, 2018).

65 *HJ*, vol. II, 328. For a survey on the pervasive ideas of moral corruption and degeneration in the eighteenth century, see Bruce Buchan and Lisa Hill, *An Intellectual History of Political Corruption* (New York: Palgrave Macmillan, 2014).

66 *HJ*, vol. II, 331. On the question of mixing textures, see Mechthild Fend, *Fleshing out Surfaces. Skin in French Art and Medicine, 1650–1860* (Manchester: Manchester University Press), chap. 5.

67 *HJ*, vol. II, 332.

68 *HJ*, vol. II, 327.

69 *HJ*, vol. II, 328.

70 Robert J. C. Young, *Colonial Desire: Hybridity in Theory, Culture and Race* (New York: Routledge, 1995), 8.

71 Long, *Candid Reflections*, 47.

72 Long, *Candid Reflections*, 48.

73 *HJ*, vol. II, 260.

74 *HJ*, vol. II, 260–1.

75 *HJ*, vol. II, 261.

76 *HJ*, vol. II, 444.

77 Roxann Wheeler, *The Complexion of Race. Categories of Difference in Eighteenth-Century British Culture* (Philadelphia: University of Pennsylvania Press, 2000), chap. 4.

78 *HJ*, vol. II, 411 and 497.

79 *HJ*, vol. II, 410.

80 Wheeler, *The Complexion of Race*, 209–33.

81 Wheeler, *The Complexion of Race*, 210.

82 Seth, *Difference and Disease*, 20.

83 Suman Seth, 'Materialism, Slavery and *The History of Jamaica*', *Isis* 105, no. 4 (2014): 770.

84 Blumenbach to Banks, Göttingen, 28 December 1794, BM Add MS 8098, fol. 221.

85 Johannn F. Blumenbach, *De Generi humani varietate nativa* (Göttingen: Typis Frid. Andr. Rosenbuschii, 1775) and *De Generis Humani Varietate Nativa. Editio tertia* (Gottingae: Apud Vandenhoek et Ruprecht, 1795). For an English translation: *The Anthropological Treatises of Blumenbach and the Inaugural Dissertation of John Hunter on the Varieties of Man*, trans. and ed. Thomas Bendyshe (London: Longman for the Anthropological Society, 1865), 112ff. (for the first edition) and 214ff. (for the third edition). Blumenbach also quoted Long in the section on the orang-utan, among other 'famous men, who [...] ill-instructed in natural history and anatomy, [...] are not ashamed to say that this ape is very nearly allied, and indeed of the same species with themselves' (p. 95).

14

World products? Narratives about workers and work in East and West Africa, 1904–61

Fabian Krautwald, Kerstin Stubenvoll and Andreas Eckert

Introduction

Historians of Africa have had an uneasy relationship with the global. In the 1960s and 1970s, Marxist scholars detailed how the continent's integration into worldwide networks of the slave trade led to its economic underdevelopment.[1] At the same time, studies on the emergence of wage labour employed proletarianization as a supposedly universal model of analysis. Since the 1980s, studies of African workers' rhetoric, activism and cultural life have instead shown that the continent does not easily fit teleological narratives such as proletarianization or globalization.[2] This has led to an impasse: 'If proletarianization and globalization both seem like concepts that are either too Eurocentric or too general to be applied to labor in Africa, how then can we connect the history of labor in Africa with the history of labor elsewhere in the world?'[3] As a solution, Gareth Austin has called for the 'reciprocal comparison' of African regions with other areas of the globe.[4] We explore an alternative, endogenous path by comparing how workers in East and West Africa shaped narratives of labour and their global circulation. Such narratives have influenced Africans' interaction with the world for a long time. The integration of Africa, the Americas and Europe into a triangular trade rested on the idea of African slaves as fungible commodities, as products for and of labour. In the nineteenth century, European colonialists and missionaries imported an industrial time-regime to the continent, which often conflicted with but was not necessarily anathema to vernacular work ethics.[5]

We argue that during the first half of the twentieth century, questions of work became central to emerging, globally inflected perceptions of politics and society in colonial Cameroon and Tanzania.[6] African workers, nationalist politicians and colonial officials struggled over what made a worker and work in different arenas, including newspaper columns and petitions to the League of Nations and the United Nations. In doing so, they created audiences that reached from the local farm and shop floor to the halls of global diplomacy. While many spoke out against the injustices of colonialism, others defended what they considered its merits. In vernacular newspapers, authors argued over the figure of the migrant worker and the effects of labour migration. In petitions, union activists and workers further developed a language of politics that they had begun to fashion in contests with the colonial state. The resulting entanglement of older traditions of work, colonial notions of wage labour and global ideologies of socialism and racial uplift reflected Africans' past and present global interactions.

In recent years, historians of African labour have increasingly turned to paradigms of global history.[7] Authors now stress non-economic dimensions of wage labour such as the importance of familial and affective ties as push and pull factors of migration.[8] We hope to incorporate these findings into a conceptual history of work that goes beyond categories of analysis developed in the West.[9]

Cameroon and Tanzania lend themselves to a comparison from a global perspective. In some areas, both experienced the growth of long-distance precolonial trade networks, followed by the simultaneity of slavery, other forms of unfree labour and commodified labour relations under colonialism.[10] Since about the eighth century CE, Islam united the East African coast with what is today northern Cameroon in the global intellectual community of the *umma*. Islamic law and custom influenced what was subsumed under work, ranging from slavery, trade and credit to the rhythm of the workday itself.[11] Finally, they exhibit a similar trajectory of colonial rule. After a period under German rule between 1884 and 1918, the two colonies were re-allocated as mandated territories to Britain and France after the First World War.

Mandate status under the League of Nations and, after the Second World War, trusteeship status under the United Nations offered the possibility of third-party scrutiny over colonial policy. Susan Pederson and others have argued that the League became an important forum through which subalterns and imperial reformers could mobilize moral capital against colonial powers.[12] Oversight by the Permanent Mandates Commission and petitions pushed colonial administrations to justify the persistence of forced labour and other grievances.[13] The League, in particular, engendered new styles of reading, writing and argumentation that provided petitioners with means to criticize colonialism.[14] It is less clear, however, whether trusteeship status changed the material conditions of work. Trust territories were primarily characterized by 'colonial powers' adeptness at out-manoeuvring or ignoring UN resolutions.[15] But petitions' lack of impact made the dangers associated with petitioning no less real for African workers. On the one hand, petitions highlight their hope in international organizations as global arbiters – even if it was an ultimately displaced one. On the other hand, petitions illustrate social change *within* the respective territories, ranging from the expansion of education to gender relations. Our comparison examines the interplay of these processes by analysing how local actors engaged with colonial and global discourses of labour. To this end, we draw on the growing literature on African print publics. Scholars such as Karin Barber have highlighted how colonial newspapers engendered public spheres in which new forms of selfhood and group identity developed, often despite censorship. Examining such arenas of negotiation as well as 'African modes of self-writing' allows us to understand how actors approached global discourses of work through their own idioms, how one influenced the other and vice versa.[16]

First, we sketch the emergence of narratives about work and the migrant worker on both sides of the continent based on debates in vernacular colonial newspapers. Albeit propaganda instruments, such publications became an early forum in which African and European authors and readers could exchange their views on labour migration. We then turn from these print negotiations about the meaning of work towards how Africans used the medium of petitions to voice grievances about working conditions to a global audience. Finally, we examine how the very same petitions reflected a spectrum of competing visions about work, society and the role of European rule in Africa.

Producing Migrant Workers

Both West and East Africans participated in long-distance trade networks before colonial rule. Since the 1770s, global demand for slaves and ivory spurred the caravan trade from the Indian Ocean to the Congo basin. By the middle of the nineteenth century, tens of thousands of porters annually carried tusks and escorted slaves to be sold on the coastal markets of Pangani and Bagamoyo. While slaves were put to work on plantations in Zanzibar and the coast, tusks were exported and worked into medical instruments and pianos.[17] In exchange, porters carried valued commodities such as American textiles, guns and beads inland.[18] The men who bore loads hailed from different societies, and through their work brought back not only commodities and savings, but also an awareness of the world beyond home. Indeed, precolonial porterage produced its own culture, work ethos and identities.[19] The figure of the porter became a symbol for economic and cultural exchange, but also for the dangers of the road and exploitative working conditions.[20] Although the diverse societies in what is today Cameroon did not experience a similar growth of commodified labour relations before 1884, porterage based on slave and non-slave labour was still widespread. Trading caravans crisscrossed the northern savannah. While leaders of coastal and grassland societies such as the Duala engaged in considerable trade in people and goods such as ivory, palm oil and rubber, the heterogeneous societies of the rainforest conducted more small-scale barter trade.[21]

German colonial rule built on these diverse networks, expanding (or disrupting) them through direct and indirect force. Military and scientific expeditions would have been impossible without porters. Missions were not only spiritual but economic enterprises in need of workers.[22] The quest for exportable raw materials increased demand for labour at plantations, in towns and, to a lesser extent, at mines. In German Cameroon, 'caravan culture' became closely linked to a rubber boom and relied on migrant labour, especially from Liberia. Transport work in this sector was characterized by a mix of wage, slave and forced labour. While young men bore the brunt of this work, women also formed a considerable part of the labour force.[23] In East Africa, the number of annual long-distance migrants to the coast increased from about 40,000 in the mid-1890s to 100,000 in 1907.[24] While the construction of roads and railways required labour, finished infrastructure increased workers' mobility further. Both Cameroon and Tanzania saw the construction of railway lines to aid the export of primary goods. Both also developed extensive plantation sectors.[25] By 1903, German planters between Pangani and Usambara employed about 10,000 workers on sisal and other plantations.[26] Between 1904 and 1914, the number of workers on the plantations

262   *Narratives, Nations, and Other World Products*

around Mount Cameroon increased from about 9,000 to 20,000.[27] By the First World War, migrant labour thus became a defining feature of the colonial economies of both territories.

What kind of narratives African societies developed about migrant labour could – but did not necessarily have to – differ from colonial narratives. One forum in which these views intersected were colonial newspapers. Around the turn of the twentieth century, German East Africa experienced the fastest growth of vernacular print media in the region.[28] Founded in 1904, the government newspaper *Kiongozi* (The Guide or Leader) was nominally non-denominational and aimed to include the colony's growing Muslim population.[29] Meanwhile, the Catholic *Rafiki yangu* and Protestant *Pwani na Bara*, both of which were founded in 1910, addressed mission adherents.[30] While German government teachers and missionaries edited these publications, African government teachers, officials and catechists wrote most of their content. All three were subject to censorship. German editors rejected large numbers of submissions. When accepted, they weeded out Islamic loanwords in coastal dialects because of their alleged role in spreading Islam. The newspapers thus served as propaganda instruments that allowed German colonialists to translate their civilizing mission into the vernacular. After the creation of Germany's African empire in 1884, the 'labour question' formed the single most important factor in this mission because colonial economies required large numbers of workers.[31] Since the demand for labour could often not be satisfied, 'educating the negro to work' became the avowed goal of officials, settlers and missionaries.[32] These efforts drew on a parallel discourse in the metropole that aimed to transform potentially dangerous proletarians into civic-minded workers.[33]

In the pages of colonial newspapers, officials and missionaries similarly promoted a gospel of diligence. If workers wanted to receive wages and live 'a good life', they had to work every day.[34] Time was essential. Workers had to understand the European way of telling time to pay taxes promptly and send children to school at the right age.[35] African agents of the colonial state such as the *maakida* (sg. *akida*), who oversaw tax collection in a given district, also spread this gospel. Akida Raphael Mpelembe, for instance, claimed that wage labour for Europeans had solved the problem of recurring famines by allowing farmers to earn additional income through wages, which allowed them to buy foodstuffs.[36] Author Mshirazi claimed that while 'insubordination will bring us damage and great sorrows', obedience would allow readers to reap 'beautiful and sweet fruit' in the form of 'a good life and profit'. Because the Germans offered 'good advice', *Kiongozi*'s readers had to behave like the oysternut plant (*mkewe*), which followed the shape of its host tree while meandering up the stem.[37] Similarly, the poet and government teacher Mwabondo Mwinyi Matano from Tanga emphasized that asking for higher wages was dependent on working diligently.[38]

Despite their propagandistic nature, the newspapers reveal African workers' ambivalent relationship to the colonial work ethos, which ranged from criticism and rejection to participation. According to Mshirazi Chui, who was probably a German teacher, '[m]any people often say that "[i]n working for ourselves we only benefit the Europeans."' Dismissing such 'words of stupidity', he called on workers to save part of their wages and invest them in farms. In this way, they could either achieve self-reliance in staple foods such as cassava or acquire additional income by planting coconuts, which did not require a lot of labour input.[39] By criticizing 'European work' (*kazi ulaya*), African workers not only pointed to the exploitative nature of colonial labour relations, but also to the problem of reconciling wage and forced labour with additional agricultural work to meet subsistence needs.[40] However, *kazi ulaya* also carried prestige for workers from inland societies because it was associated with leaving one's home, braving the dangers of the road, and becoming a man after completing multiple stints at the far-away coast.[41] These multi-faceted interpretations of migrant labour formed part of complex moral economies that structured how men and women engaged in migration.

Meanwhile, the African authors of the colonial press drew on the cultural vocabulary of the Swahili Coast in gauging the effects of labour migration on growing cities such as Dar es Salaam and Tanga.[42] Since the nineteenth century, Waswahili had distinguished their own, civilized habitus as *waungwana*, which was rooted in Islam, with what they saw as the barbarity of the *washenzi*, the savages, from inland societies.[43] German colonizers and their African allies adopted this terminology to single out unwanted labour migrants. Thus, Martin Ganisya of the Lutheran mission in Dar es Salaam explained that many recent arrivals to the city were not used to the coast's climate, shunned hard work, became sick and were therefore labelled as '*mshenzi*'. To avoid this, he provided readers with a seven-point list to be consulted 'if we want to come to the coast to work.' It included being in good health, obtaining work fit for one's abilities, acquiring savings and returning home immediately if one could no longer work.[44] As a former slave, Ganisya was one of the most Westernized interlocutors of the Germans and became convinced that European rule had inducted Africans to civilization.[45] He did not explain how sick or incapacitated migrants were to leave towns on their own. Other authors also had little patience for the *washenzi*. Ali Muhamadi complained that 'a man works for a European for one month only' and 'when he has received his wage of 20 Rupees he no longer goes to work; he says: Bwana, I can't work. He goes home. When the Rupees are spent, he goes back to work. But the Europeans, the Banians, and the Indians they receive wealth by using their intelligence only.'[46] In Muhamadi's opinion, migrant workers lacked commitment to wage labour. Similarly, government teacher Mtawa complained about workers' mobility and demanded that they should fulfil their contract with one employer rather than work for multiple ones.[47] Muhamadi's and Mtawa's critiques illustrate the degree to which African workers were able to shape working conditions amid the colony's permanent labour shortage.[48] In German East Africa, pervasive corporal punishment and forced labour co-existed with considerable worker autonomy.[49] Workers' ability to quit jobs also frustrated senior government teacher Alfred Juma from Tanga, who complained that workers did not promptly return after being granted leave:

> When he is permitted a few days to see his elders, he first visits his father and mother for a few days. He is always delayed on the way, because he intends to brag that he has money and he wants to be known as a rich man. In this way he spends the money for a lot of ostentation and games that do not fit him, such as *ngoma* ...[50]

The *ngoma* dance societies criticized by Juma had already provided town dwellers with communal recreation and relief under Zanzibari rule. In lavish rituals, two societies of neighbouring quarters or towns would compete with each other. Competitions provided opportunities to invert the existing social hierarchy, taunt superiors and blow off steam.[51] Under German rule, *ngoma* spread inland as labour migration and the reliance of the colonial state on Swahili-speaking intermediaries carried the culture of the coast inland. *Ngoma* societies now brandished brass instruments and addressed their officers by German military titles.[52] What Juma and other authors singled out as 'ostentation' and the need to 'brag', workers likely considered important parts of their recreation outside the workplace. In this sense, abandoning an employer was not a symptom of lacking appreciation for the sacredness of contracts but rooted in workers' desire to avoid abusive employers and to ensure the reproduction of their labour power.

While German East Africa's Swahili newspapers abided by dominant colonial discourses of alleged African laziness, some African authors drew a more complex picture. In *Pwani na Bara*, the former slave turned mission teacher Daniel Kasuku described colonial workplaces such as the head of the central railway as areas where people from different parts of the territory interacted with each other and exchanged skills.[53]

Others objected to the widespread vilification of inland migrants. For instance, M. Ruben Nyangye argued that whether or not one was a *mshenzi* depended solely on the quality of one's work and not on the superficial adoption of coastal culture: 'Every person of any tribe (*kabila*) who cannot fulfill his or her work with beauty and devotion, who does not protect his or her home, who does not have intelligence, except for anger and evil, is a *mshenzi*.'[54] Some migrants were hailed as trailblazers of the colonial culture of diligence. Among these were the Wanyamwezi, who had been pioneers of the nineteenth-century caravan trade.[55] Mwabondo Mwinyi Matano lauded them for their industriousness while he chided his fellow Waswahili for allegedly seeking free gifts.[56] He also demanded that those who shunned physical labour had to embrace working in 'loincloths and sacks' and give up their pretence of 'neatness' – a veiled critique of the idea that physical labour was beneath the *waungwana*.[57]

Whether the Wanyamwezi were industrious workers or cultureless vagrants led to a debate in *Rafiki yangu*. In August 1912, Melkior from Nachingwea contended that 'the Wanyamwezi lack culture [*desturi*]' because they worked as 'boys' for Europeans and followed them around wherever they went. Invoking the Nyamwezi evangelist Bonifasi Mnyofu, he decried that migrants left their wives, children and elders behind to work on farms.[58] In a searing reply, Paulo Kondemzigo rejected Melkior's critique. Although he conceded that porterage caused problems for women and children, he roundly defended labour migration:

> In the inland country of the Germans [*Katika bara ya nchi ya Wadachi*] there are no men as strong as us. We know every trade, [and] since old times we have carried the loads of the Europeans everywhere. While the people of the coast are prevented by their laziness from building railways and laying tracks, we take up hoes and pickaxes, and we smash rocks and hills ... Now the railway has reached Tabora; soon we will send it to Ujiji! You see? And the plantations of the coast you

pride yourselves of, whose work are they? Who planted rubber trees and sisal? It is not you Melkior, but our tribe, us Wanyanwezi![59]

Kondemzigo's pride reflected that by the end of German rule, Wanyamwezi had indeed become one of the backbones of the colonial economy.[60] At the same time, his polemic against the 'laziness' of the Muslim population of the coast corresponded with similar verbal attacks by Christian missionaries.[61] Kondemzigo's account thus highlights how narratives of the migrant worker in German East Africa became interlaced with local traditions of porterage and European colonial policy. Labour migration not only created a specific culture of work, but also produced distinct narratives of being a worker.

Struggles over narratives of work also loomed large in Cameroon. Under German rule, colonial newspapers frequently covered labour issues in the colony.[62] The translation and proliferation of the Christian work ethic into vernacular languages had started around the mid-nineteenth century.[63] Since 1903 and 1906, respectively, the German Protestant and Baptist missions published the Duala monthlys *Mulee-Ngea* (The Guide) and *Muendi Ma Musango* (Messenger of Peace).[64] Cameroon also boasted the first, albeit short-lived, newspaper published by an African in the German colonies. In 1908, Mpundu Akwa, the son of Chief Dika Akwa, inaugurated the bilingual *Elolombe ya Kamerun* (The Sun of Kamerun) in Duala and German.[65] Funded by collection drives among the Akwa, the paper was published by the Hamburg businessman Hans Mahner-Mons. Its more than fifty pages aimed to foster understanding between the Duala and the colonial power. However, *Elolombe* also included excerpts from the letters of a Duala mission teacher 'M.', who reported on the prevalence of chain gangs and forced labour in the colony. In M.'s view, forced labourers had caused the Duala 'dishonour'. They were petty criminals who had committed crimes out of hunger or the abundant opportunities in local trading stores. Trade had allegedly spoiled the Duala 'and estranged them entirely from manual labor'.[66] Yet M. opined that "this trickery, which is, after all, irreconcilable with the proud nature of the Duala, is merely a temporary phenomenon. As soon as the people [*das Volk*] has learned to lift its hands and accepted the blessing of honest manual labour, there will be no more talk of that 'larcenous character'".[67] Despite this seeming embrace of the colonial ideal of the submissive African worker, the District Office Duala outlawed further collection drives, which led to the paper's demise after its second issue that year.[68]

Under the French mandate, a growing number of vernacular journals appeared on a regular basis.[69] One of these was *Jumwele la Bana ba Kamerun*, the multi-language 'indigenous' supplement of the French colonial newspaper *L'Eveil des Camerounais*. In 1935, a certain Abogo Soupa warned prospective migrants in *Jumwele*'s pages of moving to Cameroon's economic capital: The town of Douala was 'wonderful' indeed, but not for those who had no work or did not work. The administration would disregard non-workers who would be prompted to 'return to their own land' to grow crops. Compatriots who had not yet arrived had to stay away, as should, in the words of Soupa, 'our' women, who were supposed to 'marry and become useful wives' instead of moving to Douala and 'lead the evil life'.[70] According to Thierry Amougou, *L'Eveil* was not only edited by settlers, but also became the mouthpiece of Douala's popular rotating saving associations (*miemba*, also known as *tontines*), which acted as mutual aid societies.[71] The founding of *L'Eveil des Camerounais* probably formed part of French efforts to confront certain Duala demands and exploit inter-African rivalries. Between 1935 and 1936, French administrators sought to reorganize Douala's local leadership structure. Two new important *chefferies* with a Beti and a *Dahoméen* at their heads were installed and formally accorded the same status as the superior Duala chiefs. They would, respectively, direct 'foreigners' from within or from outside the administered territory upon their arrival in Douala. In contrast, those Duala suspected of 'subversive' activities were resettled and their *miemba* newly formed or re-founded.[72]

A closer look at Eugène Schneider, the journal editor, supports the interpretation of *L'Eveil* as an instrument of divide-and-rule politics.[73] As late as 1937, Schneider was celebrated as a 'colonial *par excellence*' and man of the first hour by fellow colonial veterans when he was decorated with the *légion d'honneur* order.[74] According to Hunter, *L'Eveil* 'presented itself not only as a space in which Africans could air their ideas, but also as a channel of communication between Europeans and Africans that would help prevent misunderstandings on both sides'.[75] The paper thus not only created 'political subjects, but also imperial ones' by providing a platform for the exchange of ideas.[76] However, the opportunity of some to express themselves usually meant the silencing of others. While the paper accommodated subjects that dovetailed with the narrative of colonial progress, it never questioned the underlying distribution of power, particularly the land question – which would re-emerge during Cameroon's war for independence. Regarding labour questions, Abogo Soupa's article could be read in the context of Duala clans' involvement in disputes over urban real estate.[77] After the Second World War, labour administrators noticed that some of the Duala feared for the loss of privileges acquired in working closely with the administration.[78] Thus, attempting to slow down the influx of ever more new arrivals and defending one's own professional privileges might have been one motivation why some town dwellers adopted the administration's view on labour migration during the interwar years.

Migrant workers became symbols of colonial economies geared towards commodity exports. Colonial governments and their African and European agents propagated the idea that these essential workers were still anomalies in growing cities. The colonial narrative of the migrant worker espoused diligence and fulfilment of contract, but the motives of African workers, the nature of labour markets and of work itself often made this unfeasible. In fact, the ideal of the permanent, 'stabilized' male wage worker would never be matched by an equivalent number of Africans who were able or willing to profit from the supposed promises of permanent employment. By the mid-1950s, there were about 4–5 million wage labourers in all of Africa, less than 5 per cent of the total African population.[79]

Demanding publics

That many Cameroonians did not share the colonial view of labour migration becomes clear when looking beyond the confines of colonial newspapers. Mandate and trusteeship introduced a degree of expert and moral oversight to colonial rule.[80]

One facet of this oversight was the right of the inhabitants of mandated territories to petition the Permanent Mandates Commission. However, petitions could only be received by the PMC if they had been submitted through the mandatory.[81] Mandatory powers were thus able to hold back potentially irksome submissions. Consequently, the total number of petitions from the French and British B mandates Cameroon, Togo and Tanganyika remained limited.[82] Despite these limitations, inhabitants of Cameroon still managed to submit a few dozen petitions to the Allied powers and, subsequently, to the PMC.[83] In 1930, a Duala petition, which was drafted in German, listed a 'growing urban proletariat' amongst other social and political ills, including the lack of medical care and education, legal inequality, as well as the 'barbaric behavior towards the *indigène*' in general.[84] Similarly, a June 1931 petition by Vincent Ganty, the 'European delegate of the Cameroonian Negro Citizens' (*Délégué en Europe des citoyens nègres camerounais*), criticized 'inhuman behaviour' at construction sites and plantations as well as widespread forced labour. Regarding towns, Ganty observed: 'Men are harassed daily by incessant recruitment for different works and often at important distances from their villages, six days and more; the administration neither gives pay nor food. But they do receive terrific beatings. Women suffer an otherwise identical but in general degrading fate for twentieth century civilization.'[85] Beti and other newspaper authors thus only referred to one dimension of colonial labour mobility. In contrast, petitioners like Ganty anticipated the economic and social emphasis of later petitioners, who articulated their criticism by mirroring the colonial rhetoric of the civilizing mission.

No petitions by Black Tanganyikans reached the League of Nations during the interwar years. Those received by the PMC were drafted by Indian merchants who spoke out against British racial discrimination and European settlers who advocated for the 'Closer Union' of Tanganyika with Kenya and Uganda.[86] But the absence of African petitions was not tantamount to a lack of debate about the nature of work. The discussions about labour led under German rule continued during the mandate in the government newspaper *Mambo Leo* (Current Affairs) and in the independent *Kwetu* (Our Home).[87] Both addressed a still small educated elite, but with a circulation of 15,000 in 1938, *Mambo Leo* reached a wider audience than the papers of the German period.[88] *Kwetu* was a much smaller operation that was founded by the Uganda-born and self-educated Erica Fiah. The paper's independence was based on its editor's prior success as a government clerk and the subsequent founding of his own store in Dar es Salaam.[89] In the pages of *Kwetu* and *Mambo Leo*, readers continued to frame their narratives of work in the coastal language of status, but also began to touch on larger social developments, including rising unemployment, inequality and the expansion of wage labour. Concern with these issues reflected the crisis of Tanganyika's economy between the wars. The years from 1932 to 1947 have been called 'the worst that Tanganyikan workers have experienced'.[90] The Great Depression slashed the government's budget and prices for raw materials, undermining the two pillars of wage employment.[91] The resulting over-supply of cheap, unskilled labour depressed wages, while costs of living in cities rose. As a result, the interwar period saw the first appearance of widespread urban unemployment – or underemployment, as one observer phrased it.[92] While this development was most pronounced in Dar es Salaam, it also affected inland towns. In

February 1939, for instance, one commentator observed that 'we see many people in big towns that do not have work, except by getting the necessities of life by robbing people that are molested and concern themselves with work'.[93] Young men, so-called hooligans (*wahuni*), were singled out as potentially dangerous urban vagrants.[94] One reader of *Mambo Leo* distinguished a whole range of the urban precariat, explaining that '[*w*]*ahuni* are the children who sleep like trash in barrels, and they are the ones that are called the catnapping company, their occupation being to satisfy themselves through theft etc'.[95] For others, a *mhuni* simply meant anyone who 'has no work'.[96]

Concerns regarding the *wahuni* mostly related to crime and town-dwellers' sense of decorum, but sometimes intersected with organized worker action. In September 1939, for instance, *Mambo Leo* blamed the strike of Tanga dockworkers on '*wahuni* who do not work'.[97] While the government newspaper echoed the official view of labour activism as 'disturbances', *Kwetu* sometimes took the side of disaffected workers. Fiah highlighted the plight of the washerwomen and -men (*madobi*) who suffered from abuse by European employers and low wages.[98] Thomas L. M. Marealle, the future Paramount Chief of the Chagga, wrote in his capacity as labour officer in Mbeya that 'individual representation is hopeless' and that African government employees had to defend their collective interests in a Civil Servants Association like European and Indian employees.[99] He also demanded that unskilled workers should receive a living wage of at least 30 shillings that would allow them to support themselves and their families.[100] The paper also re-published a piece by the *Tanganyika Standard* on dismal working conditions in the Public Works Department and decried the generally low wages for unskilled labor.[101] Rather than localized struggles, Fiah understood these issues as part of a larger crisis of colonialism brought about by the Depression. Paraphrasing a speech by the West Indian economist W. Arthur Lewis made during the Conference on Civil Liberty in the Colonial Empire held in London in February 1941, he explained that 'labour problems' arose because 'prices and imports had fallen, exports had diminished, unemployment had increased, social services had been cut and development which had been proposed had to be postponed'.[102] Commenting on Jomo Kenyatta's condemnation of forced labour in Kenya, the editor asked poignantly: 'Who will deny that labour conditions in Kenya are virtually of serfdom? What is the meaning of the "squatter" system anyway? Can you force a free people to sell the greater number of their cattle under a "destocking" law ... What is the real difference between Tanganyika as a Mandate and Kenya as a Colony? If gold is found on tribal land for example, will the Crown not evict the native inhabitants at short notice?'[103] Despite these misgivings, Fiah was not a radical and could also dismiss calls for higher wages as misguided because for 'all ... rightly trained men ... work is first, their pay second'.[104] Moreover, he supported the government's policy of removing alleged *wahuni* from cities, arguing 'that [in] matters of work in cities etc. it is up to the government to see that people do not uselessly crowd cities'.[105]

Anxieties about unemployment were connected to a general critique of wage labour as detrimental to society. Poets such as Seif Hasil from Kilwa lamented that '[t]he money from wages is not a blessing' because it encouraged workers' profligacy on payday and thereby caused widespread indebtedness. While '[t]he day laborers are struggling,' he considered 'those who cultivate cotton' blessed because 'they paid their taxes'.[106] Gereon Mbawila complained that young people streamed to the coast and received high wages despite lacking any skills. This was particularly frustrating since he had been learning a trade for three years but was far from finished.[107] Similarly, H. Alie and others criticized young men's obsession with becoming a clerk, arguing that teaching, farming, blacksmithing or *kupima dhahabu* (weighing gold) would also lead to advancement: 'All occupations are like the limbs of man, one limb has benefits for its side'.[108] Others lamented that arrogant clerks considered all other workers *washenzi* that they could order around.[109] The relationship between wage earners and farmers received particular scrutiny. Edi Hamisi argued that the latter assisted wage earners by getting up at three in the morning and bringing their cassava to market so that servants and clerks could buy them on their way to work.[110] In contrast, Alli Athmani rejected the view that 'the farmer is an assistant to the clerk'. Instead, he considered the farmer a 'caretaker' (*mlezi*) of urban wage earners because 'the work of agriculture is celebrated across the world'.[111] K. Abner Nyanda Kilala from Shinyanga agreed, reminding Hamisi that 'before clerking was available, agriculture existed in our Africa since ancient times'.[112] Meanwhile, Frank Scheza from Tanga, the centre of the territory's extensive sisal plantations, saw the relationship between town and country in a more symbiotic light, noting that urban food markets transformed the clerk's salary into the farmer's income: 'the farmer and the clerk cooperate in their work ... since a quarter of the clerk's salary becomes the benefit of the farmer; and the harvest of the farmer is his own repletion (*shibe*) and that of the clerk and others'.[113]

As a solution to the ills of unemployment and low wages, both *Mambo Leo* and *Kwetu* called for government intervention while advocating self-help based on the ideas of Booker T. Washington and James Emman Kwegyir Aggrey. In 1941, Fiah demanded the realization of the recent finding by Lord Moyne, the Secretary of State for the Colonies, that Africans' standard of living had to be raised. This could not be achieved

> by word but by action. It will not be possible to improve social conditions until and unless the Territory's native population is freed from the bondage of poverty brought about by low pays for Africans. No sane mind can hope for social improvement when the average wage paid to labourers remains at 9/ – and that of educated Africans at Shs. 40/ – or 60/-. War conditions have had their effects upon the African as prices for every imported article have gone high.[114]

At the same time, Fiah informed his readers that they should read *Kwetu* '[i]f you do not want to be a loafer in your life'.[115] Mission-educated teachers such as Simeon Mbaruku Muya of the Christian Missionary Society (CMS) reminded allegedly idle readers 'that without work there is no life', and that agriculture offered the best possibility to realize one's potential.[116] In 1926, the Reverend Samwel Chiponde of the Universities Mission to Central Africa (UMCA) lauded the virtues of hard work in a seven-part excerpt from Booker T. Washington's first autobiography *Up From Slavery* in *Mambo Leo*. Chiponde, who had been the editor of the territory's first Christian newspaper, the UMCA's *Msimulizi* (The Narrator), introduced the series by explaining that it would help readers 'in matters of civilization'.[117] In his view, Washington represented a role model because

270 *Narratives, Nations, and Other World Products*

he had worked hard to support his family and still managed to obtain an education.[118] For British officials, Washington's ideology of gradualism and meritocracy proved convenient in dismissing complaints by disaffected candidates for coveted white-collar positions: some men were born to be clerks, while most were born to be farmers.[119] That these ideas resonated with *Mambo Leo*'s predominantly urban, educated audience can be gleaned from the fact that readers inquired about an outstanding part of the *Up From Slavery* series.[120] The discussion of Washington reflected the global spread of his ideas. Two decades earlier, African-American reformers and German colonizers had brought his ideal of racial uplift through industrial education to German-ruled Togo and – albeit to a lesser degree – to German East Africa.[121] After the First World War, Washington's successors at Tuskegee continued to promote his ideals globally through institutions such as the Phelps-Stokes Fund and the League of Nations.[122] In this context, Washington's ideology intersected with the work of Pan-Africanist J. E. K. Aggrey. In 1924, Aggrey had visited Tanganyika for two weeks as a member of the Phelps-Stokes Commission on education.[123] The presence of an American-educated, African-born polymath inspired members of the local elite. In *Mambo Leo*, readers invoked Aggrey's Pan-African teachings to call on fellow Africans to follow the example of Europeans, but without giving up their own traditions.[124] Similarly, Fiah seized on Aggrey's notion of racial pride in asserting the rights of Africans against the colonial power.[125] These local appropriations of global ideas formed part of a larger discourse over the meaning of civilization (*ustaarabu*) and development (*maendeleo*) in the interwar period.[126] What it meant to be a worker was one facet of this debate.

While narratives about wage labour could thus bring readers together, such narratives also excluded others from colonial society. Established town-dwellers accused the unemployed of causing crime and the depression of wages. In both *Kwetu* and *Mambo Leo*, readers also criticized Indian civil servants for receiving higher wages and blamed them for the unfair treatment of their Black colleagues.[127] Some authors were more circumspect, warning their audience of scapegoating Indian clerks.[128] James Brennan has highlighted how the identification of purported enemies became central to a local language of race, nation and identity in Tanganyika.[129] Although the vilification of Indians and *wahuni* reflected changing boundaries of colonial society, it followed the same trend as debates about *washenzi* under German rule. Indeed, the newspapers of the German and British colonial period shared the same discourse of authoritarian development based on government intervention, civilizational uplift and racial self-help.

Compared to these debates about work in Tanganyika, interwar petitions from Cameroon only dealt occasionally with social and economic issues. In contrast, the tens of thousands of individual letters that left Cameroon after the Second World War covered a broad range of political, social and economic grievances.[130] In both Cameroon and Tanganyika, the right of the administered populations to voice concerns on a global stage shaped the path towards independence. In Article 87, the UN Charta specified that the Trusteeship Council 'may [...] accept petitions and examine them in consultation with the administering authority', as well as 'provide for periodic visits to the respective trust territories at times agreed upon with the administering authority'. This correspondence – sometimes accompanied by photographs, press cuttings, ballot papers, lists of signatures or other addenda – was classified as petitions and communications by the UN Fourth Committee, the Trusteeship Council. Despite French efforts to silence African demands, individuals and groups from the French administered Cameroon made by far the most use of this instrument among all trusteeship territories. In contrast to the *c.* 324 communications sent from Tanganyika – where the British were also intent on limiting the number of submissions – petitioners from French-Cameroon dispatched tens of thousands of petitions to the Trusteeship Council.[131]

To stem this tide, the council devised the category of petitions concerned with 'general problems' – as opposed to those dealing with 'specific' ones which would necessitate it to take action.[132] This bureaucratic form allowed the committee to process petitions in a summary manner rather than reviewing them individually. Meanwhile, the administering authorities tried to obstruct petitioning by alleging that complaints were either unfounded or made up by 'communists'. At first glance, the nature of submissions made such claims not entirely unreasonable. Petitions from a certain village or on a certain issue sometimes arrived in a row and contained parts which seemed to have been based on prepared standard texts, especially when it came to quoting laws or voicing protest against political repression. Many of the petitioners were also backed by an existing association or local party committee of the UPC and TANU. While petitions thus shared common features, the grievances expressed in most remained specific and genuine. But standardized wordings and sentences were also an outcome of largely illiterate societies, where letter-writers often assisted in formulating a client's concerns. The documents thus should be seen as negotiated outcomes shaped by multiple intermediaries, including union activists. Before the controversy over a Cameroonian independence referendum in 1959, the handing over of bundles of petitions that opposed claims for 'Unification and Independence' against 'We want the French to remain' thus came to shape the trajectory of trusteeship.[133] The sheer number of Cameroonian petitions compelled the UN Fourth Committee to change its rules of procedure to process these submissions. Yet the administrative authorities and their UN representatives often refused to acknowledge individual petitions by pointing to authors' alleged or actual affiliation with a banned political party or group. Instead of answering controversial claims, French authorities compiled registers of petitioners' names.[134] Trustees' aim to preserve colonialism thus overshadowed the social and economic concerns of petitioners.

Many petitions offer glimpses into how African workers saw themselves and the world they were living in. In their claims for political rights, these petitions echo the development of Cameroonian and Tanganyikan nationalism. Petitioners frequently called for independence, the re-unification of French and British Cameroon, and rejected plans for a settler-led union of East African territories.[135] At the same time, petitions illustrate that anti-colonialism drew on economic and social grievances, particularly about labour relations. In both territories, claims revolved around the persistence of forced labour. In 1959, for instance, the African workers of *Société R.W. King* in Cameroon accused their European employer of having joined forces with the administration to 'harm and sabotage the Cameroonian worker'. The petitioners insisted that the forced labour regime, a 'diabolic and inhuman system', persisted as a 'way to extinguish the Cameroonians like a [lamp] light'.[136] In 1953, unemployed associations also denounced that the 'two curses' of forced labour and the *indigénat* were still in existence.[137] In Tanganyika, such allegations sometimes harked back to the memory of slavery. In 1948, the head of the Tanganyika African Association in Arusha decried that the present system of labour recruitment was 'a complete Slavery and very oppressive to the Africans [sic]'. Defying the model of the stabilized wage earner, he insisted that it was 'the desire of Africans ... to work and not to enter into a contract', the stipulations of which he was deliberately held in the dark about.[138] Similarly, A. M. Mlay, the vice chairman of the Chagga Cultural Association, demanded from the 1951 UN Visiting Mission that the Northern Province Labor Utilization Board should be abolished since it 'is more of a slave market than a centralization of manpower ... Dr. Livingstone would turn in his grave were he to know how the inhabitants of the country he opened up in the 80's "for commerce and prosperity" are treated in the name of production'.[139] On the one hand, this conflation of colonial labour recruitment with slavery reflects the gradual embrace of a social-democratic rhetoric employed by the ILO and the Fabian Bureau since the interwar period.[140] On the other hand, these 'late' invocations of slavery point to an awareness across Tanganyika that slavery only ended upon national independence in 1961, rather than with its formal abolition in 1922.[141]

Other complaints addressed the slighting of labour regulations, denial of benefits and dismissals without notice.[142] In criticizing the precarity of their employment, West and East African workers exposed the contradictions between official rhetoric and the reality of exploitation in what they considered peripheral extractive economies. After the Second World War, both Cameroon and Tanganyika became the subject of colonial development initiatives in the guise of the *Fonds d'Investissements pour le Développement Economique et Social* (FIDES) and initiatives such as the groundnut scheme.[143] The social and economic progress of trusteeship populations thus became a central trope in legitimizing European investment. In Cameroon, these efforts focused on infrastructure and less on agricultural, social or educational programmes. The fallout of this enforced colonial development could be seen especially in cities, which experienced rapid inflation and burgeoning urbanization.[144] Leading members of the Tanganyika African Government's Servants Association (TAGSA) also understood these contradictions. M. J. H. Lugazia, A. K. Sykes and F. Bumbura Jumbe lamented that despite the creation of an East African Salaries Commission in 1953, salaries were still not in line with the rising cost of living. Criticizing the 1954 UN Visiting Mission for failing to act on the data they had supplied in two previous petitions, they explained that 'in a society like ours, where the strings tightening the price controlling mechanism are so lose [sic], nearly every commodity easily slips out of the price controlling machine, [and] such continual spiral of prices of articles of both internal and external origin has tremendous [power] nullifying the salaries of the Junior officers to a state of subsistence level, and even below this in urban areas'.[145] For the TAGSA members, it was Tanganyika's peripheral position in a global extractive economy that lay at the heart of their local grievances.

In Cameroon, the social outcomes of short-term colonial development policies similarly sharpened the gap between the few who had secured more stable employment and the many who were subject to labour recruitment but left without tangible benefits. A petition dated 12 November 1954, authored by the Edéa branch of an association called the 'Regional Committee for the Defense of African Unemployed in Cameroon', offers insights into some of the intentions behind petitioning.[146] Before describing their actual grievances, the unemployed informed the UN that they had authorized 'our Comrade Um Nyobe, Secretary-General of the UPC [Union of the Peoples of Cameroon]' to speak as 'popular delegate of all progressive and assertive [*revendicatives*] levels of society [*couches sociales*]'. They lamented that the unemployed enjoyed none of the social benefits guaranteed to other workers, '[e]xcept for repression and arrest' to obtain taxes from them. According to the committee, its growing membership was caused by the dismissal of all union and UPC members from their services. The unemployed then listed nine specific measures of redress, which included the opening of construction works 'of interest to the unemployed', stringent adherence to the Labor Code, Union liberties and free speech, social security measures (75 per cent of the territory's current *minimum vital*), the creation of a regional labour office, an end to arbitrary repression against the unemployed and an end to their obligation to pay taxes and to European workers' presence in the region.[147] Attaching four photographs of their group, the petitioners explained to the Fourth Committee that 'we send you some pictures to contradict the government's statement that there are no unemployed in Edéa'.[148]

The photographs reveal the proximity of the Committee to the Cameroonian independence movement. In one of them, Committee members perform a gesture of acclamation utilized during nationalist assemblies and speeches. This gesture can be found on several other photographs that were transmitted by different groups from French-administered Cameroon to the UN, including from UPC committees in hiding (the so-called *maquis*). While the photograph therefore represents a remarkable testimony of self-assertion, it had little effect on the course of the committee's petition. Just as African nationalism developed from everyday life contexts, petitions often developed against the backdrop of local social inequalities – and that usually meant, in territories administered as extractive economies, inequalities of labour.

Negotiating narratives of labour in global arenas

Although many of the UN petitions from Tanganyika and Cameroon criticized social inequalities caused by colonialism, some also reflected diverging opinions. These differences came out clearest in disputes over the consequences of urbanizing African cities. One particularly contested topic was the effects of urbanization on women and family life. In 1948, for instance, the leadership of the TAA complained to the UN Visiting Mission that worker housing isolated men and thereby 'leads to a breaking down of family life and encourages immorality which leads eventually to all types of diseases resulting from loose morals'.[149] The civil servants of the TAA championed the idea of the male breadwinner to achieve better working conditions and to advance their vision of appropriate gender relations. Safer workers' compounds would not only ensure the safety of male labour, but also the moral integrity of stay-at-home mothers.

274 *Narratives, Nations, and Other World Products*

Others saw things differently. In 1952, J. A. Zimba, a member of the *King's African Rifles*, tackled the question 'Is a Woman's Place in the Home?' in the pages of *Mambo Leo*. The winner of the paper's monthly English essay competition argued that UN oversight of Tanganyika had bolstered his conviction that women could do any job a man could do. Invoking an unnamed female Indian UN delegate – Hansa Jivraj Mehta, the vice chairman of the UN Human Rights Commission – and 'school mistresses, women doctors, women administrative assistants and women social welfare workers' in Tanganyika, Zimba proclaimed that women had 'the same mental abilities available in a man and can therefore tackle many kinds of work'.[150] Although he praised women's natural aptitude for work, the Tabora resident qualified his call for equal opportunities by recommending specific careers to them: 'Telephone Operating, telegraph working, wireless operating, typing, general clerical duties, welfare work, microscope work, and also as nurses and doctors and teachers'. After all, '[w]omen are physically more delicate than men, therefore we should not expect too much from them as regards heavy manual labor'.[151] Women's fragile bodies, as it were, still required male tutelage. The paper's editor accordingly noted the 'pity' that among the essay submissions 'no woman was among those who put their views on paper'.[152]

Zimba's article echoed both British and French educational policies that encouraged girls to take up work related to sewing, childcare and nutrition. Although such initiatives furthered female education, they obscured much of the lived reality of women's work. Few were trained in professions or married to someone who was able to afford life in a city. The majority performed hard labour on farms and plantations and marketed produce on markets, which often required carrying goods for long distances. They also toiled as construction workers who collected, washed or transported material for colonial infrastructure projects, taking their children with them who in turn had to contribute to the family's income.[153]

Through petitions, Cameroonian women protested against violations of their political, economic and social rights. The *Union démocratique des femmes camerounaises* organized or assisted in writing an estimated 7,000 petitions.[154] In one dating from 1949, women from Douala deplored a 'policy of disregard' which kept them in a state of 'inferiority'. They pointed to the persistence of forced labour and the discriminatory *indigénat* regime, identifying both as the 'cause of the disorganization of the Cameroonian family'. In addition to their demand to end the repression and racial discrimination under trusteeship, they requested that women and their children be given access to healthcare, schooling and vocational training, that they should be free as European women to sell alcohol, that they receive the same liberties to sell food at public and private construction sites, and that the use of agricultural machinery became compulsory 'in order to libertate women of working with the hoe' on plantations or in palm oil extraction.[155] Such petitions fit in with the broader politics of the Cameroonian independence movement, in which women's committees and local organizations mobilized members and collected signatures.[156] Working women also relied on recourse to the UN to demand better detention conditions when their husbands were imprisoned.[157]

Although East African women also stood at the forefront of nationalist politics, they did not participate equally in petitioning. In Tanganyika, the Women's Section of

TANU and its leader-cum-singer Bibi Titi Mohamed led the organization's membership drive in Dar es Salaam.[158] Lucy Lameck, a trained nurse who studied at Ruskin College, Oxford and Western Michigan University, fought for women's rights in the Kilimanjaro Native Cooperative Union and as one of the first female parliamentarians.[159] Yet none of the 355 Tanganyikan submissions to the UN that were accepted as petitions were authored by women.[160] One possible reason for this difference in female petitioning, which also affected the diverging total numbers of petitions, lay in the prominence of reformist ideas of British socialism in Tanganyika. Nationalist leaders maintained close ties to organizations such as the TUC and the Fabian Bureau, which rejected communist methods of agitation.[161] Lameck's scholarship to Oxford, for example, was funded by the TUC.[162] Of course, such ideological ties did not preclude women's participation, but they contrasted markedly with the more radical rhetoric by the UPC and its allies in the French Communist Party.[163]

Apart from women's role in the workplace, petitioners disagreed over whether to denounce or support colonialism. Not every petition was drafted in opposition to colonial rule. In Cameroon, former associates of the Germans such as Duala notables had called for a return of the former colonial power during the Paris Peace Conference. When demands for independence increased after the Second World War, loyalists again rallied around the current administering power. Two such petitions from Cameroon stem from employees of two important French public construction works companies, *Société de Construction de Batignolles (SCB)* and its partner company *Hersent*. The *Hersent* employees sought to 'voice a lively protest against the anti-Cameroonian intrigues by UPC's General Secretary Um Nyobe Ruben who not in the least represents the working masses in the territory, especially not in Sanaga Maritime' region. '[T]his person without mandate, representing a party of agitation and hatred should be put in his place, that is, oblivion.'[164] Similarly, the *SCB* petition stated that African *personnel* did not agree with Um Nyobe's political movement, which 'not in the least would represent their interests' and consisted of a 'bunch of vagabonds full of hatred, in no way representing the mass of the Cameroonian workers'.[165] This appropriation of the communist notion of the working masses suggests that these petitions might have been prefabricated by company or government representatives.[166] At the same time, African workers who enjoyed professional privileges risked losing them if they showed themselves disloyal. In any case, loyalist petitions reflect a broader French strategy towards the UN: balancing the critical petitions of the administered population with other, more favourable ones. The 'mass of the Cameroonian workers' label became crucial in French justifications of trusteeship. Just as anti-government parties and unions were sidelined by pro-French organizations, French authorities sought to undermine criticism through submissions by loyal French Cameroonians. During the wave of protests after 1955 alone, about 25,000 petitions that supported the independence movement were paralleled by around 5,000 counter-petitions in favour of close future relationships with the French.[167]

In Tanganyika, there were far fewer actual or fabricated petitions of loyalty. When petitioners expressed support for the British they did so because of the disappointment over what they saw as the UN's unkept promises.[168] Members of a later Visiting Missions were shocked when the employees of the Uzaramo Native Treasury demanded to know:

276 *Narratives, Nations, and Other World Products*

> What is U.N.O. and why do the delegates come to Tanganyika? U.N. Missions have come here several times in the past but concrete benefits resulting from their visits are not evident ... The Government of Tanganyika does its best but in a young country like this there is insufficient money to pay for the development required. It is requested therefore that the United Nations Organisation assists with financial aid in this development.[169]

The absence of loyalist submissions and the smaller number of petitions does not necessarily mean that Tanganyika's inhabitants were more content with late colonial rule.

As already suggested above, British rule in Tanganyika differed in key respects from French rule in Cameroon. As we have seen, one reason for the larger number of petitions from Cameroon was that the French employed them to defend colonial rule. While both administrations relied on forced labour until after 1945, the French *indigénat* bred additional grievances through arbitrary taxes, punishments and forced conscription. The British granted limited political rights to Tanganyika's African population in the 1950s with the ultimate, if somewhat disingenuous, goal of independence. Meanwhile, the French refused to countenance a future of Cameroon outside the French Empire amid colonial wars in Indochina and Algeria.[170] Although the British were similarly embattled from Kenya to Malaya, they faced a different kind of nationalist movement in Tanganyika. In contrast to the UPC, TANU did not enjoy a close relationship with labour unions. Personal ties to the Tanganyika Federation of Labor through its president, the later Minister of Labor Rashidi Kawawa, did not prevent the rapid dismantling of union autonomy after independence.[171] Moreover, both TANU and the TFL embraced ideas of the British Labour Party that emphasized keeping unions out of politics. Kawawa and other leaders received training from Labour-affiliated organizations such as the TUC, the Fabian Bureau and the non-communist trade unions organized in the International Confederation of Free Trade Unions (ICFTU).[172] In contrast, the UPC emerged in conjunction with the *L'Union des Syndicats Confédérés du Cameroun* (USCC) and was considered by officials to be the local arm of the French Communist Party.[173]

Conclusion

> The worker gets poorer the more wealth he produces, the more his production increases in power and scope. The worker himself becomes a cheap product with every product he creates ... Work not only produces goods, it produces itself and the worker as its product.[174]

When Karl Marx described the effects of alienation on workers, he was thinking about the repercussions of industrial capitalism in nineteenth-century Europe. Marx famously considered the non-Western world the harbour of a static 'Oriental despotism' that would be swept away by the at once destructive and creative forces of capitalism and colonial rule.[175] Consequently, postcolonial scholars have widely rejected the

Work Narratives
277

universality of Marx's narrative.[176] But his insight that the nature of work *produces* a certain kind of worker is still useful in thinking about how global economic and political integration since the fifteenth century has engendered narratives of labour.

In colonial Cameroon and Tanzania, such narratives stood at the centre of emerging, globally inflected perceptions of politics and society. Despite the limitations imposed by censorship, colonial newspapers such as *Kiongozi*, *L'Eveil*, *Mambo Leo* and *Kwetu* provided a forum in which African authors could probe the impact of colonial labour policies and situate migrant labour in local traditions dating back to the long-distance trade of the nineteenth century. African petitioners to the League and UN not only denounced colonial forced labour, but also formulated ideas about work and its impact on society. The ideas spelled out in newspapers and petitions became 'world products' to the extent that they represented Africans' past and present interactions with the outside world. At the same time, they illustrate how workers, nationalists and intellectuals adopted globally circulating discourses of development, racial uplift and nationalism. In light of imperial attempts to contain the emancipatory potential of trusteeship, colonial newspapers and African petitions thus bear witness to the efforts of the continent's inhabitants to stake claims in the development of their societies and their place in the wider world.

Notes

1   See, for example, Walter Rodney, *A History of the Upper Guinea Coast, 1545–1800* (Oxford: Clarendon Press, 1970); Abdul Sheriff, *Slaves, Spices, & Ivory in Zanzibar: Integration of an East African Commercial Empire into the World Economy, 1770–1873* (Athens, OH: Ohio University Press, 1987).

2   Frederick Cooper, 'What Is the Concept of Globalization Good for? An African Historian's Perspective', *African Affairs* 100, no. 399 (2001): 189–213.

3   Karin Hofmeester, Jan Lucassen, and Filipa Ribeiro da Silva, 'No Global Labor History without Africa: Reciprocal Comparison and beyond', *History in Africa* 41, no. 1 (2014): 261.

4   Gareth Austin, 'Reciprocal Comparison and African History: Tackling Conceptual Eurocentrism in the Study of Africa's Economic Past', *African Studies Review* 50, no. 3 (2007): 1–28.

5   Frederick Cooper, 'Urban Space, Industrial Time, and Wage Labor in Africa', in *Struggle for the City: Migrant Labor, Capital, and the State in Urban Africa*, ed. Frederick Cooper (Beverly Hills: Sage Publications, 1983), 7–50; Keletso E. Atkins, *The Moon Is Dead! Give Us Our Money!: The Cultural Origins of an African Work Ethic, Natal, South Africa, 1843–1900* (London: Currey, 1993); Patrick Harries, *Work, Culture, and Identity: Migrant Laborers in Mozambique and South Africa, c.1860–1910* (Portsmouth, NH: Heinemann, 1994).

6   In this respect, we draw on Emma Hunter, *Political Thought and the Public Sphere in Tanzania: Freedom, Democracy and Citizenship in the Era of Decolonization* (New York: Cambridge University Press, 2015).

7   Jan Lucassen (ed.), *Global Labour History: A State of the Art* (New York: P. Lang, 2006); Marcel van der Linden, *Workers of the World: Essays toward a Global Labor History* (Boston: Brill, 2008); Andreas Eckert (ed.), *Global Histories of*

278   *Narratives, Nations, and Other World Products*

Work (Berlin: De Gruyter Oldenbourg, 2016); Karin Hofmeester and Marcel van der Linden, (eds.), *Handbook the Global History of Work* (Berlin: De Gruyter Oldenbourg, 2018); Stefano Bellucci and Andreas Eckert (eds.), *General Labour History of Africa: Workers, Employers and Governments, 20th–21st Centuries* (Woodbridge, Suffolk: James Currey, 2019).

8   Zachary Kagan Guthrie, 'Introduction: Histories of Mobility, Histories of Labor, Histories of Africa', *African Economic History* 44, no. 1 (2016): 1–17.

9   Axel Fleisch and Rhiannon Stephens (eds.), *Doing Conceptual History in Africa* (New York: Berghahn Books, 2016); Jörn Leonhard and Willibald Steinmetz (eds.), *Semantiken von Arbeit: Diachrone und vergleichende Perspektiven* (Köln: Böhlau Verlag, 2016).

10   Ralph A. Austen and Jonathan Derrick, *Middlemen of the Cameroons Rivers: The Duala and Their Hinterland, c. 1600–c. 1960* (New York: Cambridge University Press, 1999); Andreas Eckert, *Grundbesitz, Landkonflikte und kolonialer Wandel: Douala 1880 bis 1960* (Stuttgart: Steiner, 1999); Thaddeus R. Sunseri, *Vilimani: Labor Migration and Rural Change in Early Colonial Tanzania* (Portsmouth, NH: Heinemann, 2002); Stephen J. Rockel, *Carriers of Culture: Labor on the Road in Nineteenth-Century East Africa* (Portsmouth, NH: Heinemann, 2006).

11   See Robert Brain and Tambi E. Mbuagbaw, *A History of the Cameroon* (London: Longman, 1974); Ghislaine Lydon, *On Trans-Saharan Trails: Islamic Law, Trade Networks, and Cross-Cultural Exchange in Nineteenth-Century Western Africa* (New York: Cambridge University Press, 2009); Randall Lee Pouwels, *Horn and Crescent: Cultural Change and Traditional Islam on the East African Coast, 800–1900* (New York: Cambridge University Press, 1987).

12   Susan Pedersen, 'The Meaning of the Mandates System: An Argument', *Geschichte und Gesellschaft* 32 (2006): 560–82; Michael D. Callahan, *A Sacred Trust: The League of Nations and Africa, 1929–1946* (Brighton: Sussex Academic Press, 2004); R. M. Douglas, Michael D. Callahan, and Elizabeth Bishop, *Imperialism on Trial: International Oversight of Colonial Rule in Historical Perspective* (Lanham, MD: Lexington Books, 2006); Michael D. Callahan, *Mandates and Empire: The League of Nations and Africa, 1914–1931* (Brighton: Sussex Academic Press, 2008); Alex Lichtenstein and Michelle Moyd, 'Introduction: The League of Nations Mandates and the Temporality of Deferral', *The American Historical Review* 124, no. 5 (2019): 1673–5.

13   Adalbert Owona, 'A l'aube du nationalisme camerounais: La curieuse figure de Vincent Ganty', *Revue française d'histoire d'outre-mer* 56, no. 204 (1969): 199–235; Ullrich Lohrmann, *Voices from Tanganyika: Great Britain, the United Nations and the Decolonization of a Trust Territory, 1946–1961* (Münster: LIT Verlag, 2007); Tilman Dedering, 'Petitioning Geneva: Transnational Aspects of Protest and Resistance in South West Africa/Namibia after the First World War', *Journal of Southern African Studies* 35, no. 4 (2009): 785–801; Paul Stacey, '"The Chiefs, Elders, and People Have for Many Years Suffered Untold Hardships": Protests by Coalitions of the Excluded in British Northern Togoland, UN Trusteeship Territory, 1950–7', *The Journal of African History* 55, no. 3 (2014): 423–44.

14   Natasha Wheatley, 'Mandatory Interpretation: Legal Hermeneutics and the New International Order in Arab and Jewish Petitions to the League of Nations', *Past & Present* 227, no. 1 (2015): 205–48.

15   Meredith Terretta, '"We Had Been Fooled into Thinking That the UN Watches over the Entire World": Human Rights, UN Trust Territories, and Africa's Decolonization',

Human Rights Quarterly 34, no. 2 (2012): 358; on women, see Meredith Terretta, *Petitioning for Our Rights, Fighting for Our Nation. The History of the Democratic Union of Cameroonian Women, 1949–1960* (Mankon: African Books Collective, 2013); Kerstin Stubenvoll, 'Arbeit, Treuhand und Dekolonisation. Ungleiche Teilhabe und Selbstbehauptung im Kameruner Arbeits – und Gewerkschaftswesen, 1944 bis 1959/60' (PhD diss., Humboldt University, Berlin, 2019).

16 On these modes see J.-A. Mbembe and Steven Rendall, 'African Modes of Self-Writing', *Public Culture* 14, no. 1 (2002): 239–73; on newspapers, see Derek R. Peterson, Emma Hunter, and Stephanie Newell (eds.), *African Print Cultures: Newspapers and Their Publics in the Twentieth Century* (Ann Arbor: University of Michigan Press, 2016).

17 Sheriff, *Slaves, Spices, & Ivory.*

18 Jeremy Prestholdt, *Domesticating the World: African Consumerism and the Genealogies of Globalization* (Berkeley: University of California Press, 2008).

19 Rockel, *Carriers of Culture*, 97–130.

20 Sonja Malzner and Anne D. Peiter, *Der Träger, Zu einer »tragenden« Figur der Kolonialgeschichte* (Bielefeld: transcript Verlag, 2018).

21 Patrice Mandeng, *Auswirkungen der deutschen Kolonialherrschaft in Kamerun: Die Arbeitskräftebeschaffung in den Südbezirken Kameruns während der deutschen Kolonialherrschaft 1884–1914* (Hamburg: Buske, 1973), 36–8.

22 Michelle Liebst, 'African Workers and the Universities' Mission to Central Africa in Zanzibar, 1864–1900', *Journal of Eastern African Studies* 8, no. 3 (2014): 366–81.

23 Tristan Oestermann, *Kautschuk und Arbeit in Kamerun unter deutscher Kolonialherrschaft 1880–1913* (Köln: Böhlau, 2022).

24 Sunseri, *Vilimani*, 57. On porterage see Andreas Greiner, *Human Porterage and Colonial State Formation in German East Africa, 1880s–1914: Tensions of Transport* (Cham: Palgrave Macmillan, 2022); on female migrants, see Husseina Dinani, 'Gendered Migrant Labour and the Political Economy of Wage Labour and Cash Crops in Late Colonial and Independence Southern Tanzania', *Gender & History* 31, no. 3 (2019): 565–83.

25 Mandeng, *Auswirkungen*, 99–134; on the central railway in Tanzania, see Michael Rösser, *Prisms of Work. Labour, Recruitment and Command in German East Africa* (Berlin, Boston: de Gruyter, 2023).

26 Sunseri, *Vilimani*, 54.

27 Mandeng, *Auswirkungen*, 79, 81.

28 James F. Scotton, 'Growth of the Vernacular Press in Colonial East Africa: Patterns of Government Control' (PhD diss., The University of Wisconsin, Madison, 1971), 32.

29 Fabian Krautwald, 'The Bearers of News: Print and Power in German East Africa', *The Journal of African History* 62, no. 1 (2021): 5–28.

30 Hilde Lemke, 'Die Suaheli-Zeitungen und Zeitschriften in Deutsch-Ostafrika' (PhD diss., University of Leipzig, Leipzig, 1929), 31–40; Martin Sturmer, *The Media History of Tanzania* (Mtwara: Ndanda Mission Press, 1998), 38–42; Jörg Haustein, 'Provincializing Representation. East African Islam in the German Colonial Press', in *Religion, Media, and Marginality in Modern Africa*, ed. Felicitas Becker, Joel Cabrita and Marie Rodet (Athens, OH: Ohio University Press, 2018), 70–92.

31 Sebastian Conrad, *Globalisation and the Nation in Imperial Germany* (New York: Cambridge University Press, 2010), 82.

32 Harald Sippel, '"Wie erzieht man am besten den Neger zur Plantagen-Arbeit?" Die Ideologie der Arbeitserziehung und ihre rechtliche Umsetzung in der Kolonie

Deutsch-Ostafrika', in *Arbeit in Afrika*, ed. Kurt Beck and Gerd Spittler (Münster: LIT Verlag, 1996), 311–33.

33 Conrad, *Globalisation and the Nation*, 85–91.

34 Kiongozi, 'Maisha mema', *Kiongozi*, April 1910.

35 Kiongozi, 'Faida ya kuangalia nyakati za mwaka', *Kiongozi*, December 1910.

36 Akida Raphael Mpelembe, 'Faida ya kazi', *Kiongozi*, December 1911.

37 Mshirazi, 'Hasara ya ukaidi', *Kiongozi*, May 1911.

38 Mb. M[winyi].-M.[atano], 'Bora ni kazi, si kutapia mshahara', *Kiongozi*, March 1907.

39 M.[shirazi] Ch.[ui], 'Kuepukana na faida ya kazi', *Kiongozi*, May 1912.

40 dt., 'Mwendeleo wa watu', *Kiongozi*, October 1911.

41 For the case of Njombe, which became one of the major colonial labor reserves, see Blandina K. Giblin and James L. Giblin, *A History of the Excluded: Making Family a Refuge from State in Twentieth-Century Tanzania* (Athens, OH: Ohio University Press, 2005), 114.

42 On urban development see Jürgen Becher, *Dar es Salaam, Tanga und Tabora: Stadtenwicklung in Tansania unter deutscher Kolonialherrschaft (1885–1914)* (Stuttgart: Steiner, 1997); Franck Raimbault, 'Dar-es-Salaam: histoire d'une société urbaine coloniale en Afrique Orientale allemande (1891–1914)' (PhD diss., Université Paris 1 Panthéon-Sorbonne, Paris, 2007); Patrick Hege, 'Sights and Sites of Colonial Construction: Race, Space, and Urban Design in German Occupied Daressalam, 1850–1917' (PhD diss., Humboldt University, Berlin, 2018).

43 Jonathon Glassman, *Feasts and Riot: Revelry, Rebellion, and Popular Consciousness on the Swahili Coast, 1856–1888* (Dar es Salaam: Mkuki Na Nyota, 1995), 61–3; on the equal importance of place as source of identity see Steven Fabian, *Making Identity on the Swahili Coast: Urban Life, Community, and Belonging in Bagamoyo* (Cambridge: Cambridge University Press, 2019).

44 Martini Ganisya, 'Pwani ndiko kwenyi mali?', *Pwani na Bara*, May 1912.

45 John Iliffe, *A Modern History of Tanganyika* (Cambridge: Cambridge University Press, 1979), 256–7, 334; see also Jürgen Becher, 'Martin Ganyisha. Eine afrikanische Missionskarriere', in *Alles unter Kontrolle: Disziplinierungsprozesse im kolonialen Tansania (1850–1960)*, ed. Albert Wirz, Andreas Eckert and Katrin Bromber (Köln: Köppe, 2003), 170–80.

46 Ali Muhamadi, 'Imara kazini', *Kiongozi*, March 1911.

47 [Mwalimu] Mtawa, 'Tulizeni roho zenu katika kazi zenu!', *Kiongozi*, June 1907.

48 Sunseri, *Vilimani*, 138–48.

49 At any time, an estimated ten to twenty per cent of all workers were penal labor. See Sunseri, 55–6; on corporal punishment, see Martin Schröder, *Prügelstrafe und Züchtigungsrecht in den deutschen Schutzgebieten Schwarzafrikas* (Münster: LIT Verlag, 1997).

50 A.[lfred] J.[uma], 'Asili ya kuvunja dasturi njema', *Kiongozi*, December 1907.

51 Glassman, *Feasts and Riot*, 155–72.

52 T. O. Ranger, *Dance and Society in Eastern Africa, 1890–1970: The Beni Ngoma* (Berkeley: University of California Press, 1975), 33–44.

53 Daniel Kasuku, 'Heri wenyi huruma', *Pwani na Bara*, March 1910. On Kasuku see Paul Döring, *Morgendämmerung in Deutsch-Ostafrika: Ein Rundgang durch die ostafrikanische Mission* (Berlin: Warneck, 1900), 53.

54 M. Ruben Nyangye, 'Maana yake "Mshenzi"', *Pwani na Bara*, August 1914.

55 On Nyamwezi labor migration see Rachel J. Taylor, 'Crafting Cosmopolitanism. Nyamwezi Male Labor, Acquisition and Honor, 1750–1914' (PhD diss., Northwestern University, Evanston, 2018).

Work Narratives   281

56 Mb. M.[wabondo]-M.[atano], 'Asili njema', *Kiongozi,* July 1908.
57 Mwabondo Mwinyimatano, 'Situmie umardadi juu ya kazi', *Kiongozi,* May 1906.
58 Melkior wa Chingwea, 'Sifa ya Wanyamwezi', *Rafiki yangu,* August 1912.
59 Paulo Kondemzigo, 'Sifa ya Wanyamwezi. Majibu kwa Melkior Chingwea', *Rafiki yangu,* October 1912. For a slightly different translation see John Iliffe, *A Modern History of Tanganyika* (Cambridge: Cambridge University Press, 1979), 162–3.
60 Ibid., 162; Sunseri, *Vilimani,* 168.
61 Haustein, 'Provincializing Representation'.
62 Albert Gouaffo, *Wissens – und Kulturtransfer im kolonialen Kontext: Das Beispiel Kamerun-Deutschland (1884–1919)* (Würzburg: Königshausen & Neumann, 2007), 22.
63 Manassé Mintsa-Ze, 'La situation de l'édition au Cameroun des origines à 1970', Mémoire, École Nationale Supérieure de Bibliothécaires, Montpellier 1979.
64 Henry Muluh and Bertha Ndoh, 'Evolution of the Media in Cameroon', in *Journalism and Mass Communication in Africa: Cameroon,* ed. Festus Eribo and Enoh Tanjong (Oxford: Lexington Books, 2002), 3–16.
65 A. Rüger, 'Die Duala und die Kolonialmacht 1884–1914. Eine Studie über die historischen Ursprünge des afrikanischen Antikolonialismus', in *Kamerun unter deutscher Kolonialherrschaft,* ed. Helmuth Stoecker (Berlin: Rütten & Loening, 1960), 214–18.
66 'Aus den Briefen eines "Wilden"', *Elolombe ya Kamerun,* January 1908, vii–viii, viii.
67 Ibid., vii.
68 Rüger, 'Die Duala', 217.
69 These included *Kalat'a Mwendi: onola baboledi o mumbwa, Jumwele la Bana Ba Kamerun / L'eveil des Camerounais, Ngengeti: l'étoile, Ngengeti ni Sadi, Dikalo* and its supplement *Pare.* Some issues of these journals can be consulted in the archives of the *Société des missions évangéliques de Paris.*
70 Abogo Soupa, 'La Vie à Douala', *L'Eveil des Cameorunais / Jumwele la Bana ba Kamerun,* 5 May 1935, 1.
71 Thierry Amougou, *Dualisme Financier et Développement au Cameroun: Une Approche Néo-Braudelienne et Systémique* (Louvain: Université Catholique de Louvain, 2010), 259.
72 Among them Musango ma Bonadoo. See Philippe Nken Ndjeng, *L'idée nationale dans le Cameroun francophone: 1920–1960* (Paris: L'Harmattan, 2012), 86–7; for the reorganization of Douala's leadership see Eckert, *Grundbesitz.*
73 See Emma Hunter, '"Our Common Humanity": Print, Power, and the Colonial Press in Interwar Tanganyika and French Cameroun', *Journal of Global History* 7, no. 2 (2012): 298.
74 Before moving to Cameroon, Schneider had worked for a mining company in Ivory Coast and was part of a group of hardliners; see 'Schneider', *Les Annales Coloniales,* 19 March 1937, 1. He was also a staunch Gaullist who supported the Allies until the journal ceased publication in July 1940. See Jonathan Derrick, 'Free French and Africans in Douala, 1940–41', *Journal of the Historical Society of Nigeria* 10, no. 2 (1980): 53–70.
75 Hunter, '"Our Common Humanity"', 296.
76 Ibid.
77 *Bonado* territories were among the first to be expropriated by the Germans in 1914. Demands for their return increased during the 1930s. See Jonathan Derrick, 'Elitisme colonial au Cameroun. Le cas des Douala dans les années trente', in *Histoire du Cameroun (XIXe siècle–début XXe siècle),* ed. M. Z. Njeuma (Paris: L'Harmattan,

1989), 163–202; allegations that these groups were estate speculators go back to German times. See Eckert, *Grundbesitz*, 95.

78 The second group with such privileges were so-called Dahoméens, African employees trained in other colonial administrations, Dahomé (or Dahomey, today's Benin) among them. See J. Guilbot, *Petite étude sur la main-d'œuvre à Douala* (Yaoundé: Impr. du gouvernement, 1947).

79 Thomas Hodgkin, *Nationalism in Colonial Africa* (London: Muller, 1956), 117–18; Andreas Eckert, 'Wage Labour', in *General Labour History of Africa: Workers, Employers and Governments, 20th–21st Centuries*, ed. Stefano Bellucci and Andreas Eckert (Woodbridge: James Currey, 2019), 38–9.

80 Pedersen, 'The meaning'; Dedering, 'Petitioning Geneva'.

81 Quincy Wright, *Mandates under the League of Nations* (Chicago: University of Chicago Press, 1930), 169.

82 Paul Joseph Hibbeln, '"A Sacred Trust of Civilization": The B Mandates under Britain, France, and the League of Nations Permanent Mandates Commission, 1919–1939' (PhD diss., The Ohio State University, Columbus, 2002), 90–2.

83 Michael Goebel, *Anti-Imperial Metropolis: Interwar Paris and the Seeds of Third World Nationalism* (New York: Cambridge University Press, 2015), 276.

84 See the French Overseas ministry's *Direction des Affaires politiques* letter to the *Commissaire* in French-mandated Cameroon, urging the latter to draft a point-by-point reaction to the petition with a view to the Mandates Commission's reaction, Paris, 17 April 1930, Archives Nationales du Cameroun, Yaoundé, APA 10890 Pétitions Douala, 61.

85 See Annexe III, Arch. Féd. Ydé, APA 10.187. Petition du Délégué en Europe des citoyens nègres camerounais à la S.D.N, cit. in Owona, 'A l'aube du nationalisme', 217; On Ganty and political claims, see Goebel, *Anti-Imperial Metropolis*, 276.

86 Callahan, *Mandates and Empire*, 100–2; Callahan, *A Sacred Trust*, 229.

87 On both papers see, among others, Hunter, *Political Thought*; James R. Brennan, *Taifa: Making Nation and Race in Urban Tanzania* (Athens, OH: Ohio University Press, 2012); Sturmer, *Media History*.

88 Hunter, '"Our Common Humanity"', 285.

89 N. J. Westcott, 'An East African Radical: The Life of Erica Fiah', *The Journal of African History* 22, no. 1 (1981): 85–101.

90 John Iliffe, 'Wage Labor and Urbanization', in *Tanzania under Colonial Rule*, ed. Martin H. Y. Kaniki (London: Longman, 1980), 287.

91 Iliffe, *Modern History*, 342–6.

92 E. C. Baker, 'Memorandum on the Social Conditions of Dar es Salaam', 4 June 1931, SOAS Library Special Collections, 76.

93 S. K. Elinisamehe Manasse, 'Kazi ya wavivu', *Mambo Leo*, February 1939, 23.

94 On the *wahuni* see Andrew Burton, *African Underclass: Urbanisation, Crime & Colonial Order in Dar Es Salaam* (Athens, OH: Ohio University Press, 2005), 5–6, 74–5.

95 Malim Mikidadi Hadji Mwinyibonde, 'Ustaarabu Unafukuzwa na Wahuni', *Mambo Leo*, April 1939, 54; see also M. F. Kassam, 'Wahuni wa Dar es Salaam', *Kwetu*, 13 January 1942, 5.

96 A. S. M. Peter Kisumo, T. R. B. Mchewe, 'Lofa ni mtu gani?', *Mambo Leo*, March 1940, 57.

97 Anon., 'Machafuko mjini Tanga', *Mambo Leo*, September 1939, 143; on the history of the strike, see John Iliffe, 'A History of the Dockworkers of Dar Es Salaam', *Tanzania Notes and Records* 71 (1970): 119–48.

98 'Ukatili juu ya bin adamu', *Kwetu,* 2 August 1938, 22.

99 Thomas L. M. Marealle, 'African Civil Servants Association', *Kwetu,* 5 November 1940, 1–2. On Marealle, see Andreas Eckert, '"I Do Not Wish to Be a Tale Teller." Afrikanische Eliten in British-Tanganyika. Das Beispiel Thomas Marealle', in *Lesarten Eines Globalen Prozesses: Quellen Und Interpretationen Zur Geschichte Der Europäischen Expansion,* ed. Andreas Eckert and Gesine Krüger (Hamburg: LIT Verlag, 1998), 172–86.

100 T. L. M. Marealle, 'African Progress Is Retarded because of the Lack of Money (Translation from Swahili)', *Kwetu,* Special Number, November-December 1941, 11–14, 12.

101 A. R. El-Amawi, 'Working for P.W.D.', *Kwetu,* 3 August 1939, 13; 'Labour', *Kwetu,* 18 December 1940, 1.

102 'A State of Slavery and Fascist Regimentation', *Kwetu,* 6 May 1941, 6.

103 Ibid., 2.

104 'Work', *Kwetu,* 12 March 1940, 4.

105 'Kazi na Waafrika', *Kwetu,* 6 May 1941, 2. On forced removals see Burton, *African Underclass,* 76–81, 101–11.

106 Seif Hashil, 'Mshahara fedha isiyo baraka', *Mambo Leo,* April 1938, 71. On the cycle of indebtedness of many town-dwellers see Baker, 'Memorandum', 46.

107 Gereon Mbawila, 'Ustaarabu ati Uliko ni Pwani', *Mambo Leo,* October 1930, 181.

108 H. Alie, 'Tusikimbilie kazi moja tu', *Mambo Leo,* February 1939, 32.

109 Juma S. Mkanyila, 'Kazi ni kazi vibaya kwiba', *Mambo Leo,* March 1939, 46.

110 Edi Hamisi, 'Mtu wa mshahara ni kama ng'ombe tasa ulimwenguni', *Mambo Leo,* February 1939, 15.

111 Alli Athmani Kirimia, 'Mtu wa Mshahara', *Mambo Leo,* June 1939, 98.

112 K. Abner Nyanda Kilala, 'Mtu wa Mshahara', *Mambo Leo,* September 1939, 158.

113 Frank Scheza, Zigi Segoma, 'Mkulima na mtu wa mshahara', *Mambo Leo,* March 1939, 47.

114 'A Word on the Labour Department's Annual Report 1940', *Kwetu,* 8 December 1941, 2.

115 'Ndugu zetu someni haya', *Kwetu,* 18 November 1937, 2.

116 Mwalimu Simeon Mbaruku Muya, 'Maendeleo ya Wenyeji wa Afrika', *Mambo Leo,* August, 1936, 132.

117 Samwel Chiponde, 'Booker T. Washington. Sehemu ya kwanza', *Mambo Leo,* May 1926, 377. On Chiponde see Morgan Robinson, *A Language for the World. The Standardization of Swahili* (Athens, OH: Ohio University Press, 2022).

118 Chiponde, 'Booker T. Washington. Sehemu ya kwanza', 377. See also M. O. Abbasi, 'Msingi wa ustaarabu. Mbiu ya Kwetu,' *Kwetu,* 29 February 1944, 3.

119 Mtengenezaji, 'Tusidharau kazi iliyo Nyonge', *Mambo Leo,* September 1930, 146.

120 'Majibu kwa Waandikaji', *Mambo Leo,* August 1930, 141.

121 Angela Zimmerman, *Alabama in Africa: Booker T. Washington, the German Empire, and the Globalization of the New South* (Princeton, NJ: Princeton University Press, 2010), 112–73.

122 Zimmerman, *Alabama in Africa,* 198–202.

123 Brennan, *Taifa,* 123–4; on Aggrey, see, among others, Sylvia M. Jacobs, 'James Emman Kwegyir Aggrey: An African Intellectual in the United States', *The Journal of Negro History* 81, no. 1/4 (1996): 47–61.

124 E. Bilindaya, 'Usijilaumu Ngoja Ulaumiwe', *Mambo Leo,* January 1938, 18.

125 'Editorial note', *Kwetu,* 9 December 1939, 1. On the importance of Aggrey for Fiah see Westcott, 'An East African Radical', 95.

284   *Narratives, Nations, and Other World Products*

126 Emma Hunter, 'A History of Maendeleo: The Concept of "Development" in Tanganyika's Late Colonial Public Sphere', in *Developing Africa: Concepts and Practices in Twentieth-Century Colonialism*, ed. Joseph Morgan Hodge, Gerald Hödl, and Martina Kopf (Manchester: Manchester University Press, 2014), 87–107.

127 See, for instance, K. Elias Amos, 'Waafrika Hawaendelei kwa kukosa Mali', *Kwetu*, 16 July 1941, 4; African of Africa, 'African Lead a Hard Life [sic]', *Kwetu*, 1 August 1941, 1–2; 'Waafrika hawaendelei kwa kukosa mali', *Kwetu*, 7 September 1941, 4; 'A Word on the Labour Department's Annual Report 1940', *Kwetu*, 8 December 1941, 2.

128 Ernest Nyibenda, 'Tunataka Mishahara kama ya Wahindi?', *Kwetu*, Special Number, February 1945, 5.

129 Brennan, *Taifa*, 118–58.

130 On the interwar LoN-petitions, see Eckert, *Grundbesitz*, 55–7; in 1931, Ganty deposited three Doula petitions with the SDN that, among other topics, spoke of 'le traitement inhumain des chantiers d'Ottele, les conditions de travail dans les plantations, […] le travail forcé.' See Philippe Dewitte, *Les mouvements nègres en France, 1919–1939* (Paris: L'Harmattan, 1985), 324; for the long history of Duala petitions see Andreas Eckert, 'Petitions, Politics, and Urban Transformations: Duala Petitions, 1860s to 1930s', in *Sources and Methods for African History and Culture: Essays in Honour of Adam Jones*, ed. Geert Castryck, Silke Strickrodt and Katja Werthmann (Leipzig: Leipziger Universitätsverlag, 2016), 377–92; on claim-making of plantation workers in British-administered Cameroon cf. Caroline Authaler, *Deutsche Plantagen in Britisch-Kamerun. Internationale Normen und lokale Realitäten, 1925–1940* (Köln: Böhlau Verlag, 2018).

131 On the numbers see Jean Beauté and Charles Rousseau, *Le droit de pétition dans les territoires sous tutelle* (Paris: Librairie générale de droit et de jurisprudence, 1962), 212; Lohrmann, *Voices from Tanganyika*, 580; Terretta, 'We Had Been Fooled,' 331, who estimates that 45,000 petitions were sent in 1956 alone.

132 Jean Beauté, 'Fonctions et pouvoirs. Article 87', in *La Charte des Nations Unies. Commentaire article par article*, ed. Jean-Pierre Cot and Alain Pellet (Paris/Bruxelles: Association française pour les Nations Unies, 1985), 1211–12.

133 United Nations Archives (UNA), S-0504-0049, United Nations Visiting Mission to the Trust Territories of the Cameroons under British Administration and the Cameroons under French Administration, 1955. Report on the Cameroons, under French Administration, 1956, 49–50.

134 Vgl. Archives Nationales d'Outre-Mer, Aix-en-Provence (ANOM), DPCT 10.

135 Terretta, 'We Had Been Fooled'; Terretta, *Petitioning for Our Rights*, 138; Lohrmann, *Voices from Tanganyika*, 497, 519–25; Kerstin Stubenvoll, 'Arbeit, Treuhand und Dekolonisation'.

136 Terretta, *Petitioning for Our Rights*, 138.

137 Bibliothèque Cujas, Paris (CUJAS), ONU 2885, T/PET.5/229, Pétition de l'Association des chômeurs de la Région Sanaga Maritime, 23 décembre 1953.

138 UNA, S-0441-630, 130/5/06 T/PET. 2/61, President Msambo [?], Memorandum of the Tanganyika African Association, Northern Province Branch, Arusha, To the United Nations' Missions When Visited Arusha, 9 September 1948 [sic].

139 UNA, S-0441-0563, 130/5/02 T/PET. 2/134, A. M. Mlay, Vice Chairman, Memorandum by the Chagga Cultural Association to the Visiting Mission of the United Nations, 11 September 1951.

140 Frederick Cooper, 'Conditions Analogous to Slavery. Imperialism and Free Labor Ideology in Africa', in *Beyond Slavery: Explorations of Race, Labor, and Citizenship*

in Postemancipation Societies, ed. Thomas C. Holt, Rebecca J. Scott, and Frederick Cooper (Chapel Hill: University of North Carolina Press, 2000), 107–50; Daniel R. Smith, *The Influence of the Fabian Colonial Bureau on the Independence Movement in Tanganyika* (Athens, OH: Ohio University, 1985).

141 Felicitas Becker, 'Common Themes, Individual Voices', in *African Voices on Slavery and the Slave Trade*, ed. Sandra E. Greene, Martin A. Klein and Alice Bellagamba (New York: Cambridge University Press, 2013), 71–87.

142 CUJAS, ONU 2855, T/PET.5/225, Pétition de l'Assemblée Centrale des Chômeurs du Cameroun concernant le Cameroun sous Administration français, Douala, 2 décembre 1953, 2.

143 On Cameroon, cf. Martin-René Atangana, *French Investment in Colonial Cameroon: The FIDES Era (1946–1957)* (New York: Peter Lang, 2009); on Tanganyika, see Matteo Rizzo, 'What Was Left of the Groundnut Scheme? Development Disaster and Labour Market in Southern Tanganyika 1946–1952', *Journal of Agrarian Change* 6, no. 2 (2006): 205–38.

144 On Douala, see Austen and Derrick, *Middlemen*, 178; on Dar es Salaam, see Burton, *African Underclass*; James R. Brennan, Andrew Burton, and Yusufu Q. Lawi (eds.), *Dar Es Salaam: Histories from an Emerging African Metropolis* (East Lansing, MI: Michigan State University Press, 2007).

145 UNA, S-0441-565, 130/5/02 T/PET. 2/188, J. H. Lugazia, General President, A. K. Sykes, General Secretary, F. Bumbura Jumbe, General Treasurer, Tanganyika African Government Servants Association, Dar es Salaam Headquarters, to the Secretary, United Nations Visiting Mission, Dar es Salaam, 30 August 1954, 1–16.

146 UNA, S-0441-5710, TR 130/05/02, T/PET.5/550, Comité de Défense des Chômeurs Africains du Cameroun. Comité Régional de la Sanaga-Maritime. Petitions [sic], 12 November 1954.

147 UNA, S-0441-5710, TR 130/05/02, T/PET.5/550, Comité de Défense des Chômeurs Africains du Cameroun. Comité Régional de la Sanaga-Maritime. Petitions [sic], 12 November 1954, 2.

148 Ibid.

149 UNA, S-0441-630, 130/5/06 T/PET. 2/61, Memorandum of the Tanganyika African Association Headquarters to the United Nations' Mission Whilst in Tanganyika at Dar es Salaam, 20 September 1948, 3–6, 3.

150 J. A. Zimba, 'Is a Woman's Place in the Home?', *Mambo Leo*, Julai 1952, 74.

151 Zimba, 'Woman's Place'.

152 PRO, 'Monthly English Essay Competition', *Mambo Leo*, Julai 1952, 74.

153 On female and child labor in colonial Tanzania see Issa G. Shivji, *Law, State, and the Working Class in Tanzania, c. 1920–1964* (Portsmouth, NH: Heinemann, 1986), 64–72; Karin Pallaver, 'From Subsistence Farmers to Guardians of Food Security and Well-Being. Shifts and Continuities in Female Labour Relations in Tanzania (1800-2000)', *African Economic History* 50, no. 1 (2022): 67–92.

154 Terretta, *Petitioning for Our Rights*, 23.

155 UNA, S-0441-628, 130/05/03, Petition des femmes camerounaises, UPC, Comité feminin, Douala, 20 November 1949.

156 See the UN count of 142 petitions and attached lists with 6,201 signatures in UNA, S-0443-0017, TR 132 (1), T.PET.5/L.172, 29 November 1956, 2.

157 See, for example, the tailor Christine Essoumba, who complained about her husband Nicolas' situation in Mokolo prison, Northern Cameroon, UNA, S-0441-569, 130/05/02, T.PET/5.119, 26 January 1953.

158 Chambi Chachage and Jacqueline Mgumia. 'Bibi Titi Mohamed', in *Oxford Research Encyclopedia of African History*, 31 March 2020, https://oxfordre.com/africanhistory/view/10.1093/acrefore/9780190277734.001.0001/acrefore-9780190277734-e-473 (accessed 13 July 2023).

159 Susan Geiger, *TANU Women: Gender and Culture in the Making of Tanganyikan Nationalism, 1955-1965* (Dar es Salaam: Mkuki Na Nyota, 1997), 129-34.

160 Lohrmann, *Voices from Tanganyika*, 151, 154.

161 Shivji, *Law, State, and the Working Class*, 189-92.

162 Geiger, *TANU Women*, 131.

163 On the UPC's radicalism see, among others, Achille Mbembe, *La naissance du maquis dans le Sud-Cameroun, 1920-1960: histoire des usages de la raison en colonie* (Paris: Karthala, 1996); Simon Nken, *L'U.P.C.: de la solidarité idéologique à la division stratégique, 1948-1962* (Paris: Anibwé, 2010).

164 ANY 1 AC 75 Pétitions, n° 281, Le personnel Africain du Barrage d'Edéa to Monsieur le Président de la Mission de visite de l'O.N.U., Edéa, le 31 octobre 1952.

165 ANY 1 AC 75 Pétitions, n° 333 'Personnel Africain de la Société de Construction des Batignolles. Carrière des Travaux d'extension du Port de Douala et le Pont sur le Wouri, à Edéa' (22 signatures Pour les ouvrieurs [sic] illetrés ne sachant écrire illisible). [not dated, probably 1952 or less likely 1955].

166 In contrast to petitions sponsored by liberation movements, the two in question stood out for their brevity, low degree of personal involvement, and thorough command of French syntax. Their authors therefore likely hailed from the circles of literate government or commercial employees.

167 ILO TC 11, T./L.647, Examination of Petitions. Interim report of the Committee on Communications from the Cameroons under French administration, 15 March 1956.

168 Lohrmann, *Voices from Tanganyika*, 531-9.

169 UNA, S-0441-0565, 130/5/02 T/PET. 2/189, Memorandum Presented to the U.N.O. Delegates by Employees of the Uzaramo Native Treasury, Dar es Salaam, 20 December 1954.

170 Marc Michel, *La France au Cameroun, 1919-1960: 'partir pour mieux rester'?* (Paris: Les Indes savantes, 2018).

171 William H. Friedland, *Vuta Kamba. The Development of Trade Unions in Tanganyika* (Stanford: Stanford University Press, 1969).

172 Shivji, *Law, State, and the Working Class*, 190.

173 Léon Kaptue, *Travail et main-d'œuvre au Cameroun sous régime français, 1916-1952* (Paris: L'Harmattan, 1986), 196-7; Yves Mintoogue, '"L'indigène" comme acteur politique. Militantisme et formes de participation politique dans l'Union des Populations du Cameroun (UPC), 1948-1955' (Mémoire du Master de Recherche, Université Paris 1, 2010), 62-4.

174 Karl Marx, *Ökonomisch-philosophische Manuskripte*, ed. Barbara Zehnpfennig (Hamburg: Meiner, 2005), 56. Authors' translation.

175 Edward W. Said, *Orientalism* (New York: Vintage Books, 1994), 153-6.

176 For an overview of the resulting debates see Kolja Lindner, 'Eurocentrisme, postcolonialisme et marxisme: nouveaux regards?', *Raisons politiques* 63, no. 3 (2016): 161-77.

15

Russia in global economic history: On modernization and its discontents

Alessandro Stanziani

Since the eighteenth century, Russia had the unique privilege of being constantly associated to a double dilemma in terms of modernity (temporalities) and its spatial limits: Is Russia like Europe or Asia? Is it modern or backward?

In every instance, answers to these questions reflected a response to structural transformations in states, societies and economies: The global transformations of the world gave birth to attempts of a narrative which led in turn to a quest for universalism, or, at the opposite, to the identification of 'national' culture and 'specificities' to explain peculiarities or deviances from the universal plot – the last being eventually accommodated into a universal path, based upon 'Russian', not Western, 'values' and 'categories'.

This paper will not seek to study all the multiple relevant fields in which these tensions between the Russian specificity versus commonality with Europe were expressed; I will mostly focus on the notion of backwardness in history writing, in general history and economic history in particular. In fact, since the eighteenth century onwards, the notion of backwardness stood at the very core of debates concerning Russian 'modernization' and, therefore, its confrontation with global trends. The identification of what 'Russia' and 'Russian' means took place in connection with multiple processes: empire and state building in Russia itself since the fifteenth century onwards, which took a new dimension in the eighteenth century when the idea of modernization, progress and civilization become widespread with the cultural and economic expansion of Western Europe. In this case, Russia and Europe more or less idealized and mirrored each other in the definition of progress and backwardness, not only in 'cultural' development but also in economic dynamics. Scales of narratives became central: Russian as well as European authors were obliged to fix both time and space scales – on the one hand, they had to decide whether Russia included Asiatic areas or also new southern regions seized from the Ottomans. They also had to decide whether 'Europe' meant England, France or something larger. On the other hand, discussions focused on the question of knowing whether one had to start from 'the origins'; for example, a more or less mythical foundation of Rus', of the 'Kingdom of England', or rather from the advent of the 'modern', in turn starting with the 'great discoveries', Peter the Great, the Glorious Revolution, the French Revolution, capitalism (after feudalism), and so on and so forth.

I will start with the eighteenth century, when the universal ambition of the Enlightenment confronted Russian 'specificities' in economic life and politics, then move to the nineteenth century and Marxism, before moving to the Bolshevik revolution and its aftermath, as each stage revisited the backwardness problem in the narrative of Russia and the world. The last part of this chapter will discuss the Russian 'national' economy and history during the Cold War and its aftermath. Over the longue durée, Russia served as a necessary counterpoint to Enlightenment, Marxist and liberal narratives about global economic history and the conditions of modernization; Russia served as a fictional constant, an idealized mirror, on a feudal or traditional past for the modernizers to elegize. At the same time, Russian intellectuals flipped the mirror back on Russian readers themselves to offer a script of Russian exceptionalism to justify models of what would later become called 'development' or the necessary – though peculiar – road for catching up and industrializing.

Russia's backwardness in the Enlightenment

'Enlightenment' thinking developed in response to global dynamics: encounters with other worlds no longer fuelled the exoticism and wonderment of previous centuries, but instead raised questions about which values, economic systems and types of warfare could dominate and whether or not this new order of priorities was acceptable. Could European values be exported or did local realities have to be taken into account? Was it appropriate for trade and economics to be based on profit rather than on ethical values (and if so, which values could they supplant?) Was it legitimate to use slavery and finance as instruments for imperial expansion?

The Enlightenment brought about changes in human knowledge as a result of global and interconnected structural transformations. The point here is not to determine which region exported 'modernity' or was 'the most modern', based on a scale of values defined once and for all, but to understand the origins and impact of these reciprocal evolutions and influences. Thus, the invention of backwardness in Western economic and philosophical thought owes a great deal to the attention given to Russia and Poland after the start of the eighteenth century.[1] The definition of backwardness and of its main element – labour – lied at the nexus of three interrelated debates: over serfdom in Eastern European, slavery in the colonies and guild reform in France. It is the connection between these three debates that makes the definition of labour, and the distinction between free and forced labour, take on certain characteristics and not others. In the course of the eighteenth century, the work of slaves, serfs and apprentices was judged not just by ethical standards but increasingly by its economic efficiency. On that basis, hierarchies were justified, such as the 'backwardness' of the colonies relative to the West, of Eastern relative to Western Europe and of France relative to England. Turgot, one of the leading economists of the time and future comptroller-general (i.e. finance minister), who had read closely the accounts of travellers to Russia, likened the 'serf to the land' (*serf de la glèbe*, the famous expression popularized by Montesquieu twenty years earlier) to the Russian serf and to the slave; he even spoke of slavery to the land. In France, serfdom to the land belonged to the past. Likewise, the slave in the colonies and the Russian serf would soon become vestiges of the past, though for now they remained justified by the backwardness of the colonies and Russia.[2]

The normative ambitions of political economy seemed to be borne out by the interest with which enlightened monarchs in France as well as Russia read these works. In 1763, Voltaire completed his history of Peter the Great and sent a copy to Catherine II.[3] In this work, as in his letters to Catherine, Voltaire adopted a cautious attitude towards Russian serfdom, indicating that it would be premature to emancipate the people without first enlightening them.[4] For his part, Diderot, who was flattered by Catherine's attention, wondered: 'Does the servitude of the peasants not influence [their] culture? Doesn't the lack of peasant property have a negative effect?' His response was laconic: 'I don't know whether there is any country where the peasant loves the soil and his home more than in Russia. Our free provinces do not have much more grain than those that are not free.'[5] Diderot believed at the time in the reforming potential of Catherine and the French monarchy; based on this belief, he distinguished between nations that had already achieved their highest level of civilization and were starting to degenerate and those that remained closer to nature and could strive for a higher level of order and morals while avoiding the evils of civilization. He placed America and Russia among the latter.[6]

The Pugachev uprising in Russia, and the protests by masters and apprentices against the abolition of the guilds in France, rapidly led to a revision of the enlightened monarchs' projects, both in France and in Russia. The guilds were restored in 1776, the same year that the United States declared its independence and Adam Smith published *The Wealth of Nations*. With the end of Catherine's reforms, a new alignment of forces seemed to be taking shape. Voltaire, hitherto close to the thinking of the physiocrats, began to attack Necker and Quesnay and questioned the idea that economic liberty equalled justice.[7]

The 1780s therefore brought a radicalization of the *philosophes'* positions on the French monarchy, Russia and, ultimately, slavery. Rather than reforms implemented by monarchs, who were henceforth regarded as despots, it was considered better to trust in popular movements. From the 1780s on, Diderot and Condillac associated their scepticism about enlightened despotism with a more general criticism of European civilization. As Condillac suggested, 'Too much communication with Europe was less likely to civilize (*policer*) the Russians than to make them adopt the vices of civilized nations.'[8] From this point of view, the Russian reforms called for similar reforms in France and its colonies. The majority of the *philosophes* held this attitude.[9]

These approaches of the Enlightenment to progress and backwardness had an important impact in Russia itself. The conditions for this influence rooted in the strong cultural, political and commercial exchanges between Europe and Russia, but also in the fact that the Russian Empire as well had to face challenges partially similar and partially different from those of other areas. In particular, the consolidation of the Russian Empire passed through not only the usual diplomatic activity and networking but also through a modernization of the army and, as a consequence, of the Russian fiscal state and economy. These needs and the reforms Peter, then Catherine, enhanced sought precisely to respond to this stake. In the intellectual and political debate, these questions transmuted into that of knowing whether the Enlightenment (and which version of it) was suitable to Russia. No doubt we can see the influence of more radical, even revolutionary thinkers on that careful reader of Raynal, Aleksandr Radishchev.[10] However, in part because Catherine and hence the censors were reticent, even hostile, and in part because of the leanings of the Russian reformers and the Enlightenment philosophers who inspired them, this kind of radical outlook remained in the minority in Russia. Instead, Catherine encouraged her collaborators and young economists to familiarize themselves with and disseminate the ideas of the physiocrats. Mikhail Shcherbatov was not entirely wrong in claiming to be inspired by the French *philosophes* when he suggested keeping Peter the Great's Table of Ranks.[11] Like Voltaire and Diderot in the same era, he emphasized that the peasants were not yet ready for freedom and that, under certain circumstances, serf labour was not necessarily less productive than free labour, because it protected the serf from economic and climatic hazards. Even Vasilii Tatishchev, though distant in many ways from Shcherbatov, took up the argument (dear to Enlightenment philosophy) about the education of the peasant, which, he concluded, would eliminate the threat of revolts even while ensuring a more rational organization of labour.[12]

In 1739, Vasily Tatishchev, a proponent like Peter of the Russian 'Westernisation', published a history of Russia dating back to ancient times (*Istoriia Rossiiskaia s samykh drevneishikh vremen*). His five-volume opus, the fruit of twenty years of research, was based on Russian chronicles, his own travels, observations and extensive reading of Western literature.[13] Along with other European and Asian authors during this period, Tatishchev criticized conventional histories – the *Letopises* (chronicles)[14] and synopses – which he called mythologies. He took on the task of separating historical truth from falsehood. He conceived of Russian history as imperial and universal, and therefore devoted special attention to the empire's non-Russian populations and the specific origin of its slaves.[15] Tatishchev's universal history had to contend with the interpretation of Mikhail Lomonosov, who aimed to show that Russians and the populations of the North (Germanic and northern European) were not merely interconnected but in fact one and the same people. At the Academy of Sciences, Lomonosov set out to identify the purely Slavic origins of Russia, which, in view of its age and civilization, he considered comparable to Rome and Byzantium. Based on these principles, Lomonosov produced a four-volume history of ancient Russia (*Drevniaia rossiskaia istoriia*).[16] His critique of the sources resulted in a Russocentric history. In 1783–4, Catherine II published her own *Remarques concernant l'histoire de la Russie* in an attempt to demonstrate the ancient origin of the Slavs and their language. This rewriting of the country's history, begun in the mid-eighteenth century, was used to justify Russian imperial expansion into Ukraine, Poland and Lithuania based on the specificity of Slavs and their presence outside Russia *strictu sensu* since antiquity. In Russia, as in Western Europe when confronted to 'backward' peasants in the mainland and indigenous people in the colonies, the new historiography made a clear-cut distinction between oral tradition (peasants and nomads) and written documents as well as between myth and genuine history.

Among the economists, it was without a doubt Storch who most violently criticized the slave system, and this despite his role at the University of St. Petersburg and the Academy of Sciences. A disciple of both Smith and political arithmetic, he attacked the cumbersome guild system in Europe as well as forced labour in the colonies, Russia and the United States. At the same time, he drew an important distinction: 'only in Eastern Europe has the improvement of their (slaves, serfs) lot been delayed by the slowness with which progress has occurred in the growth of wealth and civilization; but as these are everywhere advancing at a rapid pace, it is probable that here too, little by little, slavery and serfdom will disappear.' However, he opposed the immediate abolition of serfdom, which would provoke riots as well as the collapse of Russia's economy and society. He instead envisioned gradual reforms, beginning with giving the serfs more responsibility by assigning them a share of the revenues, expanding the use of *obrok* (quitrent) at the expense of *barshchina* (corvee) and, most of all, educating the landowners more fully about new management techniques.[17]

Like the other German cameralists, Storch was not only well-versed in Smith's work and an advocate of his ideas; he also drew inspiration from the reforms being undertaken in the German lands where, as recent research shows, the evolution of serfdom had begun before the arrival of Napoleon's armies and the civil code.[18] Translated into various European languages, Storch's work was widely used by Jean-Baptiste Say, generations of the 'German historical school' and lastly the principal Russian thinkers of the turn of the nineteenth century.[19] The sources and wide distribution of Storch's writings confirm the breadth of the debate about labour, freedom and progress underway across Europe at the turn of the eighteenth and nineteenth centuries.

At some point, the idea that wage labour was the worst form of slavery was accepted by much of the Russian elite. That is why in the twenty years preceding emancipation, the debate on serfdom intersected with that about the commune and then about Russia's 'uniqueness' vis-à-vis the West.[20] It was not so much the abolition of serfdom that was discussed, but the when and how, and consequently the status of the commune and of property. The emphasis on the commune and private property made it possible to relegate to the background the details of what emancipation was supposed to mean and just what kind of labour contract and labour relations would be put in place after the emancipation.[21]

Confirmation of this argument can be found in the way that Russian liberal thinkers envisioned labour in these years. Consider the case of Ivan Vernadskii, professor of Political Economy and Statistics at the University of Kiev and then at the University of Moscow, and his wife Mariia.[22] Their starting point was Adam Smith exalted by nineteenth-century liberal thinkers, namely, the theorist of the division of labour. Mariia Vernadskaia echoed Say's interpretation of Smith that since the division of labour is the core principle of the economy, it is the basis on which all forms of organization, including slavery and serfdom, should be judged. Say concluded that serfdom should be condemned solely for moral reasons, despite sometimes being advantageous by strictly economic calculations. Vernadskaia arrived at the same conclusion and argued that East Indian plantations were an example of efficient division of labour.[23]

In sum, the Enlightenment had difficulties in reconciling Russia and progress, insofar, on the Western side, Russia was identified as a laboratory to enhance the philosopher's role and his idea of progress, mostly teleological. On the Russian side, this gave rise to a kind of forced or anyhow modernization from above. However, during the nineteenth century, in Russia, the tension between modernization and

292   *Narratives, Nations, and Other World Products*

backwardness, the national case and the global dynamics, transmuted into two major connected stakes: the debates on capitalism, its laws and the peasant commune; the approach to history, whether a 'sciences' with its laws or something different. This was the peculiar context in which Marx's thought penetrated Russia.

Russia and Marx

During much of the nineteenth century, and particularly after the 1850s, the question arose in the main countries of Europe as to whether or not the 'historical laws of development' were the same everywhere. Like Russia's political and intellectual elites, its nobility was ultimately less afraid of the peasants' emancipation than of their proletarianization; and as the latter became the focus of the discussion, the nobles gradually came to accept the abolition of serfdom.

In the first volume of *Das Kapital*, and in the *Critique of Political Economy* and *The Communist Manifesto*, Marx accused classical political economy of putting forward abstract theories and laws that failed to take into account the historically situated nature of capitalism. He opposed the abstraction of economics to concrete, empirical analysis of societies and their history. In reality, he was less critical of models in general than of those, like the authors in the classical school, who de-historicized capitalism. Indeed, his approach led him to identify simultaneously the historical singularity of capitalism and its 'general laws'. According to this schema, the passage from feudalism to capitalism is valid everywhere, along with the main characteristics of capitalist dynamics: the alienation and commoditization of labour, the monetization of trade and commodity fetishism that inevitably accompany the trend towards a lower profit rate, alternating periods of crisis and expansion and the existence of the famous 'reserve army' of proletarians. In fact, this schema, which he claimed to be universal, corresponded to Britain, or more accurately, to a stylized description of its history sketched out by Marx. Here historical determinism and the philosophy of history come together in a positivist approach in which history serves less to question than to validate a general schema.

This approach was at odds, however, with the views of Russian intellectuals and revolutionaries. The opposition between Slavophiles and Westernizers in nineteenth-century Russia stemmed precisely from the issue that concerns us here: Eurocentrism in the studies on Russia, in its epistemological and historical dimensions. In fact, the debate over the commune was inseparable from the comparison between Russia and the West. This comparison became the keystone in the tensions between Slavophiles and Westernizers and later between populists and Marxists. The issue was precisely whether there was a global tendency at work in economies and societies or whether historical singularities could shape its direction. In Europe, Chernyshevsky asserted, land was privatized for the benefit of a minority and against the interests of the majority of peasants, who were forced to become proletarized. Drawing on the work of Sismondi, he noted that, compared with individual ownership, community ownership indeed produces less value but it also ensures greater well-being to families. 'The commune is automatically assumed to prevent innovation' because the commune crisis in Russia is not linked, as it is in Europe, to economic development but to tax pressure brought to bear by the state.[24] The debate over the commune was therefore inseparable from the comparison between Russia and the West; this comparison became the keystone in the tensions between Slavophiles and Westernizers and later between populists and Marxists.[25] The issue was precisely whether there was a global tendency at work in economies and societies or whether historical singularities could shape its direction. This debate was at once ideological (the role of the peasantry in the revolution), empirical (how to prove the arguments used) and methodological (how to make comparisons).[26] That is why this debate inevitably ended up being combined with the debate over method in the science of society: unlike the more or less idealized Indians, the Russian case immediately appeared more problematic to Marx, for two main reasons. First, Russia was not properly 'Europe' but it was not 'Asiatic despotism' neither. Where did it have to be put? Second, Russian intelligentsia directly interacted with Marx and contributed to shape his thought; this was not the case in India. Thus, in 1867, a Russian intelligent, Chernyshevsky, close to socialist ideals wrote that 'Those who invoke private property, think that progress in sociology and economics, as in natural science, consists in moving from simple to more complex forms. This process may well be true in biology, but in society we observe the opposite phenomenon. Progress consists in gradual simplification. From this point of view, by limiting specialization, the commune does not contribute to backwardness but rather anticipates the future evolution of the developed countries.'[27]

This passage testifies to the connection between an epistemological question – the analogies and differences between human and natural sciences – and the idea of progress. Capitalism, the peasant commune, Russia and Europe could be compared, but according to a well-defined methodology. In 1869, Mikhailovsky took charge of giving this approach a precise epistemological framework. He claimed that the evolution of humankind was not the result of necessity but of individual will. That is why the methods of the natural sciences cannot be applied to the science of society and, in general, progress is not expressed in the division of labour and specialization but on the contrary in undifferentiation and cooperation. Like Chernyshevsky, Mikhailovsky criticized the division of labour and the market in order to attack the specialization of knowledge. 'Specialization prevents us from grasping the connections between the various aspects of a phenomenon.' In the case of Mikhailovsky, however, this demand was supplemented by a relatively new element. In mentioning the 'Historical School' and chair socialism he was proposing a philosophy of history in which the individual was the linchpin ('the word "progress" has meaning only in relation to the individual'), even though individual demands were supposed to be subordinated to those of society. Among the forms of social and economic organization, the peasant commune was most apt to comply with this principle.[28] But how were these conclusions to be reconciled with the Marxist thought with which these authors associated themselves?

In 1872, members of these same populist circles, above all Daniel's on, translated the first volume of *Das Kapital* into Russian. In the translation itself, however, Marx's categories were displaced. In particular, very often – though not systematically – *Werth* was translated as *stoimost'* (production costs) instead of *tsennost'* (value). Hence the confusion between the notion of value (*tsennost'*) and that of price (*tsen'*) in Russian

294   *Narratives, Nations, and Other World Products*

Marxist thought not only during the Tsarist but also during the soviet period.[29] The translation of *Das Kapital* into Russian exacerbated these conflicts from several standpoints: first ideological and political, then intellectual (Russia and its historical itinerary) and finally methodological – could Marxist categories properly account for the reality in Russia?

In fact, from the early 1870s, Tkachev, Mikhailovsky and Vera Zasulich questioned Marx and Engels regarding the commune and the 'laws of development': was it possible to follow a different development path from the one in the West and thus achieve socialism without going through a capitalist stage?

In a letter addressed to Mikhailovsky in 1877, Marx said he thought Russia could take a different route from the one in the West. Four years later, in a letter to Vera Zasulich, he wrote that the peasant commune was the basis for the social regeneration of Russia.[30] In the same letter, Marx changed his mind about the impact of British colonialism on India; in the 1850s (*Grundrisse, Critique of Political Economy*), he had maintained that the introduction of private land ownership was a considerable improvement. Now he concluded, on the contrary, that this measure had helped to impoverish India.

By turning his focus towards Russia and Asia and empirically casting doubt on his theory, Marx ended up unlocking it. Of course this change has to be understood within the political and intellectual dynamic in Russia at the time. The evolution of the country and the debate taking place there prompted Marx to introduce some leeway into his approach and theory. Conversely, the difficulties in finding translations and equivalent terms for Marx's text in Russian indicated the more fundamental problem of exporting Marx's categories into other contexts. It marks the limit of a particular form of Eurocentrism that sought to model economics on the natural sciences. This type of Eurocentrism has never disappeared from Marxist thought in all its variants.

It is not by chance that Engels always refused to take into consideration the French and the Russian editions of *Das Kapital* and referred to the German one in order to encourage further translations and 'preserve' Marx's thought. In Russia itself these questions were vigorously debated; in the 1880s and early 1890s, populist authors like Danielson (Russian translator of Marx) supported the theory of multiple paths to modernity and therefore the possibility of reaching socialism through the modernization of the peasant commune without passing through capitalism. On the other hand, 'orthodox' Marxists like Plekhanov and then Lenin defended Engels' interpretation of Marx, stressing a single path of development. The publication of the third volume of *Das Kapital* in 1895 immediately provoked a sharp debate among all European socialists. Some Russian intellectuals, like Struve and Bulgakov,[31] considered that the third volume offered a different theory than the first whereby value was not only produced through labour, but also with capital and land. This opened the way to a non-revolutionary approach to socialism that stressed re-distribution within capitalism. These Russian interpretations influenced the well-known emergence of 'revisionism' in Germany (Bernstein) and provoked the sharp reactions of 'orthodox Marxists' in Russia (Plekhanov, Lenin), in Germany (Kautsky) and the rest of Europe. In his well-known 'The Development of Capitalism in Russia', published in 1899, Lenin sought to show that in Russia capitalism was quickly developing and therefore, according to 'orthodox' Marxism, the revolution will follow, under the leadership of the social-democratic party.

This debate continued until the Russian revolution of 1905 and the role the peasantry played in it encouraged Lenin to imagine a new political orientation in which the revolutionary proletariat and the peasants could join forces against capitalism. This was not revisionism, but a way of appropriating populist ideas and seeking to win more support in the countryside. However, this was not to happen until 1917 and beyond.

Meanwhile, a new liberal historiography emerged in Russia, seeking to show at once the country's 'backwardness', the progress under way and hence the measures that still needed to be taken. This historiography was often oriented towards Great Britain, the idealized model of liberalism. Authors such as Maksim Kovalevskii strove to demonstrate first the necessity of historical laws (drawing especially on Henri Maine and his theory of the transition from customary worlds to modern worlds); second, how Russia deviated from those laws; and third, how those gaps could be closed if new measures were adopted, for example, by establishing a parliament and privatizing peasant communities.[32] Other historians, such as Boris Chicherin (1828–1904) and Aleksandr' Kornilov (1862–1925),[33] complained, like Dostoievskii before them, about revolutionary extremists that were impeding the modernization process in Russia.[34] These authors, together with Pavel Miliukov (1859–1943),[35] a historian and politician who belonged to the constitutional democratic party, highlighted the importance of institutional reforms and used the example of the British and in part Russian history to prove their argument.[36] These historians were opposed by theorists described (partly by their adversaries, and partly by themselves) as 'orthodox' Marxists, who criticized not only the liberals but also the Marxist 'revisionists'.

In short, during the last quarter of the nineteenth century and up through the First World War, Russian discussions raised the question of knowing if in history and in political economy one single or multiple paths to modernity were available. The fact that these discussions circulated all around Europe at that time reflected the undergoing convulsion of aristocratic capitalism, of societies where peasants, peasant workers, landowners and rentiers still played a role. We know now, that, unlike conventional interpretations, aristocratic capitalism was important not only in Central and Eastern Europe, but also in Western Europe, for sure until the 1870s and possibly as long as the First World War.[37] In this context, Russia was not exceptional, nor was it particularly stagnant. During the second half of the nineteenth century and up through 1914, the rate of growth and commercialization of Russian agriculture was accelerated.[38] Russia experienced rates of growth similar to those of Germany, France, America, Japan, Norway, Canada and the UK.[39] This growth was based upon the quickly transforming peasant commune, labour intensification and pluri-activity.

The problem was not growth by itself but this kind of growth in the global context: it took place at the very moment when most Western countries expressed the so-called second industrial revolution, a capital intensive process where huge plants and machines replaced small units and labour. Pluri-activity disappeared and urbanization increased.

The First World War brought this global process to Russia and the revolution mostly was a reaction to the second industrial revolution and the great transformation

296 *Narratives, Nations, and Other World Products*

of capitalism. Peasants' unrest were above all directed against the interdiction of seasonal migrations, against requisition of wheat and fixed prices, but also against speculators, and against the increasing use of war prisoners and refugees on noble estates to replace local peasants at war.[40] In short, unrests were not against markets in general, but against war capitalism, standardization and capital intensive production in the industry; they were also supportive of short-term and short-range migration and against definitive proletarization, on the one hand, trans-imperial and global migration, on the other hand. The new regime had the difficult task to reconcile these reactions with Marx's theory.

Soviet Russia and the world history

The Bolshevik revolution fundamentally altered the way we conceive of history, even beyond political judgements. The construction of temporalities hinges in large part on this revolution, the images it evokes and its political role. Among the issues surrounding the October revolution and its history, we find future-oriented history; Russia as a model or an exception, and thus the nature of 'historical laws'; the possibilities of seeing the revolution reproduced elsewhere, above all outside Europe; and the absolutely central role of history in justifying or criticizing the revolution, and conversely its role in political debate. Even today, this influence is obvious in the shift in focus from a forward-looking history, capable of predicting the future, to a history of its failure and the attempt to explain it without falling into the trap of historical necessity yet again. In the end, the Bolshevik revolution reopened the debate concerning 'truth' in history, along at least three main quarrels: whether these theses can be proven without access to archives; the role of propaganda in historiographical construction, only to end, after 1989, with almost blind faith in the archive documents finally available. For the past century, all these problems arising from within the notion of history and of its methods have been heavily conditioned by the Russian revolution. In every case, the connections to the globality of history are clear: revolution, by its very nature, raises the question of whether it is exceptional or supposedly universal, local or worldwide. The globality of historiographical constructions is expressed in historiographical methods and reciprocal influences as well as in the disparities between the ways history is conceived and practised in the USSR and in the West, and how these debates were passed on to the 'Third World' after the Second World War.

The revolution of 1917 had a radical effect, in Russia first of all, where the use of history was crucial to legitimize the seizure of power by the Bolsheviks. Trotsky and Menshevik authors saw the revolution as a deviation from the 'normal' path of historical development. Liberal and socialist authors held the same view.[41] Lenin, on the other hand, altered his earlier position and henceforth justified Russia as an exceptional case, demonstrating the possibility of carrying out a revolution and arriving at a socialist society without going through capitalism. This was the context in which Soviet historiography was introduced. Mikhail Pokrovskii, an official historian of the revolution and of the regime in its early years, tried to reconcile 'the universal laws of history' with the revolution of 1917.[42]

'Before 1917', declared Pokrovskii, 'I maintained that the same regularity (*zakonomernost'*) existed in the field of social phenomena as in the field of chemical and biological phenomena, and that there was no difference between these disciplines. Today my position has changed. There is an essential difference between the natural sciences and the science of society. While in fact all science expresses the development of the forces of production, the social system and class struggle, it is also true that these phenomena are expressed differently by the different disciplines. Unlike the natural sciences, the science of society directly expresses class struggle.'[43]

During the 1920s, the desire to 'accelerate' the pace of history gradually came to dominate other concerns. The end of the New Economic Policy (NEP), forced collectivization and the purges of the 1930s altered the Soviet conception of history. Although most of the existing historians disappeared during the purges, by 1934 history had nevertheless become a required subject in primary and secondary schools, and the number of history chairs grew in the universities.[44] That same year, and again two years later, Stalin, Zhdanov and Kirov wrote a history textbook in which they rejected Pokrovskii's approach, concluding that henceforth the history of the USSR should be the history of its peoples and nationalities, and should also include European and world history.[45] Soviet-style global history was therefore part of a discipline that wanted to take all aspects of human beings into consideration, while subordinating 'culture' and the superstructure of economic dynamics. It was also a history that strove to reconcile socialism in a single country with the aim to 'show the way' to the rest of humanity. In spite of the contradictions, this conception of history had considerable influence all over the world, not only among the multiple, often conflictual Marxist approaches, but also oriented non-Marxist interpretation of history and in particular the tensions between the nation and the global in so many areas as Europe, China, India, Africa and the Americas. During the first half of the twentieth century, history had a political impact that was not only critical, but different from the influence it had had in other periods. The fall of the Central and Eastern European empires and the often-extreme nationalism of the states that succeeded them, the birth of the USSR and the new global role of the United States and Japan fundamentally changed the maps and even the very idea of 'development' as well as the role of the West in this context. Nationalist tensions rose in Europe, Asia and Latin America, and relationships between independence movements and colonial powers grew increasingly strained in Africa during the interwar period. Against this backdrop, history became an indispensable political instrument in several respects: its arguments were supposed to confirm (or deny) the dynamics under way. The historic role of the nation was crucial, first of all in the way it was presented empirically, when it became important to demonstrate, for example, the presence of a longstanding 'national spirit'. This attitude was expressed in discussions about the tools of historiography; in India, Germany, the USSR, Mexico, Brazil, China and Argentina, the tensions between 'genuine history' and fiction, erudition, languages and social models, and 'primary' and 'secondary' sources surfaced in political discussions, influencing historians' attitudes and the role they assigned to their discipline in relation to political debate. This was the context in

298 *Narratives, Nations, and Other World Products*

which the 'real' history of revolutionary Russia, India, Aryan Germany and fascist Italy came into being.

In political economy, these tensions were expressed in those between the so-called 'genetic' and the 'teleological' approach to the plan. The first orientation (Bukharin, Chayanov and Groman) considered that history was important as well as a dose of markets within a socialist economy. Therefore, growth and plan's target must conform to the structure of the economy and to Russian 'specificities'. At the opposite, Strumilin and several Bolshevik leaders argued that the plan had to set first its goals and then means will be uncovered, if necessary by strength. The underlying idea was to 'accelerate' the soviet path of growth in order to compete with the West and erase backwardness. Stalinism and planning as a bureaucratic tool will rely upon the latter approach. Neo nationalism and 'socialism in one country', as it was defined in the 1930s, converged.

Russia and backwardness during Cold War

Alexander Gershenkron is justly famous for *Economic Backwardness in Historical Perspective*. Indeed, like Max Weber and many others before him, Gershenkron began by drawing up the list of Western characteristics on which his comparison would be based; he too emphasized cities, the bourgeoisie, markets and private property. Yet unlike Marx and to some extent Weber, he thought it was possible to arrive at industrialization (but not capitalism) without a bourgeoisie. In place of this component, 'backward' countries (to use the jargon of the 1960s and 1970s) such as Prussia and Russia had 'substituting factors', notably the state. This is a very clever solution to the problem raised by the need to reconcile particular features, historical specificities and general dynamics. If backwardness and diversity go together, then it is possible to conceive of alternative paths.[46] His model postulates that the more backward an economy is at the outset of economic development, the more likely a bourgeois, middle entrepreneurial class will lack and the more institutional substitutes will be required. In particular, taking the example of Germany and Russia, Gershenkron argued that the lack of bourgeoisie was compensated by the major role of the State. In late-comer countries, capital-intensive industries and large-size units, instead of agriculture and consumption units, take the lead. However, contrary to appearances, like Weber, Gershenkron does not compare Russia to England in specific historical contexts. Instead he opposes an ideal image of the West (and of England in particular) to an equally ideal image of nineteenth-century Russia. English economic development is associated with the early introduction of a parliament, privatization of the commons and hence the formation of a proletariat available for agriculture and industry. In contrast, Russia is associated with market towns – and therefore with a bourgeoisie – as well as the presence of an absentee landed gentry living off serfdom.

This work was part of a broad debate in the 1950s and 1960s: with decolonization, economists raised the problem of (under)development and what should be done to remedy it. In the context of the Cold War, this issue was inseparable from the question regarding which economic and political form the new states would take: capitalism or socialism. The components of this debate were globalized; they not only compared the economic achievements of the USSR to those of the West, but also the trajectories of China, India and the countries in the Americas, Africa and Asia that acquired their independence at the time (see also Chapter 16). Not only Gershenkron, but many other economists as well emphasized the need to put these debates in 'historical perspective.' This position warrants reflection on at least three levels: why backwardness, why Russia and why the historical perspective. Backwardness supposes a notion of progress and a comparative scale to measure it; in turn, progress/backwardness involves a teleological notion of time and henceforth an equally peculiar approach to 'history', conceived as a background to confirm or invalidate pre-existing theories. This circularity around the notion of backwardness is quite widespread in economic history for the past three centuries. In this attitude, the 'Russian case' certainly played a central role because of its analytical and political relevance. All the authors who made use of this approach were eager to distinguish themselves from the Stalinist-Soviet variant and from planners oriented towards a *tabula rasa* approach and a radical rethinking of society and the economy. Forced collectivization in the USSR and the Great Leap Forward in China took this direction. They relied on the work of 1920s Soviet economists who had challenged 'historical' approaches, accusing them of trying to perpetuate elements of the old system in the new one.

Nevertheless, in the 1950s and 1960s, few economists adopted this position, especially after the publication of the Khrushchev's report denouncing Stalinist abuses and the rediscovery of the New Economic Policy (NEP) in the USSR. It was in this context that history resumed a central role in economic debate. Walt Rostow put forward his theory of stages of growth in open opposition to socialism; he showed that the stages of growth were universal and that it was impossible to follow elsewhere the soviet path. Rostow delivered a more radical critique of state planning. History served to validate the Western-style itinerary and the arrow of time moved in only one direction. Paradoxically, Rostow reproduced Marx's argument according to which the most advanced countries showed the way and the future to backward countries. This universalist approach did not win unanimous support within development economics in the 1950s and 1960s. The responses put forward reveal a distinct evolution; during the 1950s, the various authors – both Marxist and non-Marxist – tended to give priority to industrialization as the key to escaping from underdevelopment and poverty. In this context, the rural peasant economy was seen as conducive to backwardness insofar as it had a limited ability to commercialize its production or supply workers for industry.[47]

Nevertheless, this approach came under sharper attack beginning in the early 1960s. Several elements were involved, which includes the Khrushchev report; the denunciation of collectivization and Stalin's crimes; the rediscovery of the NEP; Bukharin and Chayanov; and the peasant agriculture as a factor in economic development. Numerous authors used these elements to propose a solution midway between capitalism and socialism (the famous Third Way), consisting essentially of integrating the peasant world into an increasingly market based economy. These authors criticized industrialization and proletarization as one and the same form of 'modernization'.

These criticisms of the industrial model seemed to be borne out in the course of the 1960s and 1970s when the debt and backwardness of the former colonies became more pronounced. As critics noted at the time, the policies that were adopted generated crises in peasant economies, but they did not ensure the rise of industry.[48] The neo-populists then used the NEP in Russia and the works of Chayanov to highlight the possibility of growth founded on the peasant commune. This explains how Russian development and the debate between 'populists' and 'Marxists' from the 1870s to 1914 could be used in discussions regarding the most suitable development policies for Asia, Africa and Latin America in the 1960s.[49] Numerous Marxist economists and anthropologists denied any possible long-term existence of a 'peasant mode of production,' as this system would not offer support for the industrialization process, which is necessary to emerge from backwardness. These authors repeat the criticisms of Chayanov expressed by Russian Marxists – his theory was deemed ahistorical and unable to account for the real dynamism of the agrarian economy, which was by definition subordinated to the choice of industrial capital.[50] Some of these authors spoke Russian and were interested in the original debate that took place in the USSR; Mark Harrison, in particular, translated and continued the work of 'agrarian Marxists.'

At the opposite extreme, the authors who believed that the process of development should take into consideration local specificities – and that the peasant economy makes it possible to reconcile growth, commercialization and job protection – found in Chayanov one of the precursors of these arguments.[51] The flag-bearer of this trend was the Romanian N. Georgescu-Roegen, who had partly been educated in the United States during the 1930s, and who emigrated there permanently in 1948. He was strongly linked both professionally and personally to other famous émigré economist from Austria (J. Schumpeter) and the Soviet Union (Wassily Leontief).

In the USSR, beginning in 1954, and increasingly after the 20th Congress of the Communist Party in 1956, there was a huge increase in studies on Russian economists and statisticians from the turn of the century and first planners.[52] Among the stated goals, two directly take their place within the economic thought of the 1920s: the attention given to more effective planning, as had been proposed by the specialists of the Gosplan and the Zemplan; and the requirement to improve agricultural yields, especially the provisioning of cities, following the suggestions of Chayanov and social agronomists. Now Russian 'specificity' was associated to that of many developing countries, in a scale which was not national, nor global in the Marxist term, but which sought to identify a 'third way' more or less anchored to pre-soviet socialism. Destalinization in the USSR and decolonization in the world went together (on the reorientation of the Soviet Empire, see Chapter 7).

Epilogue

The debate on under-development underwent a reorientation with the decline of Keynesian and Marxist arguments and the success of the monetarist positions of the IMF. This outcome would be confirmed by the fall of the Berlin Wall and the collapse of the USSR. The end of the Cold War thus greatly reduced interest in the debate on development that took place in the USSR during the 1920s. Using the theory of transaction costs and the information economy, Joseph Stiglitz, a Nobel Prize winner in economics, revealed the limits of free market equilibrium along with the distortions

Russia in Global Economic History 301

produced by the Soviet bureaucracy and by managed economies in general.[53] Stiglitz acknowledges the imperfections of free markets, in particular, information and prices are incomplete and do not lead, by themselves, to an efficient equilibrium as postulated by the standard neoclassical theory. At the same time, Stiglitz considers that the solution cannot be found in the plan for, as the Soviet experience shows, planners have less information (and more corruption) than market and the outcome will be even worse than in market economies. He thus suggests that appropriate institutions can correct and help the market without suffocating it.

We may observe that, in these approaches, the same model is employed to talk about the market in nineteenth-century Africa, serfdom in Russia or fairs in Europe in the modern period: it is no accident that neo-institutional economics speaks less about capitalism than about the market economy. This approach calls into question the classifications of economic systems proposed by traditional neo-classical and Marxist literatures (capitalism, peasant economy, feudalism, etc.). Instead we find a typology of organizations that evolve strictly in relation to the institutional context. In the case of the USSR, did economic weakness cause political decline or, on the contrary, did Soviet institutions close the market and thereby bring about its inevitable collapse?

This question, which may seem innocuous to historians, was important for development policy insofar as the debate, especially in the 1990s, was focussed on knowing whether, in post-socialist countries in particular, it was first necessary to set up market institutions and a democratic political system in order to have a market, or conversely whether the market would give rise through its very development to adequate institutions.[54] The issue appears to have been resolved since then because, contrary to the politically correct arguments that always sought to link capitalism to democracy, the experiences in China and Russia in recent years confirm that this equation is by no means obvious. Nationalism, global capitalism and the lack of democracy are increasingly bound one each other.

Notes

1 Albert Lortholary, *Le mirage russe en France au XVIIIe siècle* (Paris: Éditions contemporaines, 1948); Jan Struys, *Les voyages en Moscovie, en Tatarie, Perse, aux Indes et en plusieurs pays étrangers* (Amsterdam: Van Meers, 1681); Pierre de la Martinière, *Voyages des païs septentrionaux* (Paris: L. Vendame, 1671); John Perry, *État présent de la grande Russie* (The Hague: H. Dusanzet, 1717); John Cook, *Voyages and Travels through the Russian Empire, Tartary, and Part of the Kingdom of Persia* (Edinburgh: no publ., 1770).

2 Anne Robert Jacques Turgot, *Oeuvres et documents le concernant*, 5 vols., ed. Gustave Schelle (Paris: Félix Alcan, 1913–23), 2, 375. See also Turgot, 'Plan de deux discours sur l'histoire universelle', in Ibid., 1, 275–324.

3 Voltaire, *Histoire de l'Empire de Russie sous Pierre le Grand* (Paris: Geneva, Cramer, 1763), reissued in Voltaire, *Oeuvres historiques*, ed. René Pomeau (Paris: Pléiade, 1957).

4 Voltaire, 'Letters to Catherine II of 1762, 1765, and 1766', in Voltaire, *Correspondance*, 107 vols., ed. Théodore Bersterman (Geneva: Institut et Musée Voltaire, 1953–65).

5   Denis Diderot, 'Propriété des terres et agriculture: 4 questions', and 'Questions à Catherine II sur la situation économique de l'Empire de Russie', in *Diderot et Catherine II,* ed. Maurice Tourneux (Paris: Calmann Lévy, 1899), reproduced in Denis Diderot, *Mémoires pour Catherine II* (Paris: Garnier, 1966). The quotation is from the edition of 1899, 813–17.

6   Diderot, 'Observations sur le Nakaz de Catherine II', in *Oeuvres politiques* (Paris: Garnier, 1963), 365.

7   See Gilbert Faccarello, 'Galiani, Necker and Turgot: A Debate on Economic Reform and Policy in Eighteenth-Century France', in *Studies in the History of French Political Economy from Bodin to Walras,* ed. G. Faccarello (New York and London: Routledge, 1998), 120–95, particularly 179 fn. 23.

8   Bennot-Etienne abbé de Condillac, *Oeuvres de Condillac,* 23 vols. (Paris: C. Houel an VI, 1798), vol. 20, 63–4.

9   On Condorcet, see Yves Benot, 'Condorcet journaliste et le combat anti-esclavagiste', in *Condorcet mathématicien, économiste, philosophe et homme politique,* ed. Pierre Crépel and Christian Gilain (Paris: Minerve, 1989), 376–84.

10   On the influence of Raynal on Radishchev, see Vladimir I. Moriakov, *Iz istorii evoliutsii obshchestvenno-politicheskikh vzgliadov prosvetitelei kontsa XVIII veka: Reinal' i Radishchev* (on the history of the evolution of the socio-political orientations of institutors during the eighteenth century: Raynal and Radishchev) (Moscow: Izdatel'stvo Moskovskogo Universiteta, 1981); Allison Blakely, 'American Influences on Russian Reformists in the Era of the French Revolution', *Russian Review* 52, no. 4 (1993): 451–71. On Nikolai Novikov, see Editor's Note of 1784, reproduced in Nikolai I. Novikov, *Izbrannye sochineniia* (Selected Works) (Moscow: Gosudarstvennoe izdatel'stvo khudozhestvennoi literatury, 1951), 562.

11   See 'Razmotrenie o voprose – mogut li dvoriane zapisyvat'sia v kuptsy' (Notes on the question: can nobles register as merchants?), in Mikhail M. Shcherbatov, *Neizdannye sochineniia* (Unpublished works) (Moscow: Sotsekgiz, 1935), 139–58; Marc Raeff, 'State and Nobility in the Ideology of M.M. Shcherbatov', *American Slavic and East European Review* 19, no. 3 (1960): 363–79; and Elise K. Wirtschafter, *Structures of Society: Imperial Russia's People of Various Ranks* (DeKalb: Northern Illinois University Press, 1994); idem, *Social Identity in Imperial Russia* (DeKalb: Northern Illinois University Press, 1997).

12   Vassilii N. Tatishchev, *Istoriia Rossiiskaia v samykh drevneishikh vremen* (History of Russia since the most ancient times) (Moscow: Imperatorskii Moskovskii Universitet, 1768, re-edition, Moscow: Nauka, 1962) and *Izbrannye trudy po geografii Rossii* (Moscow, 1779; reissued Moscow: Gosudarstvennoe izdatel'stvo geograficheskoi literatury, 1950).

13   Tatishchev *Istoriia Rossiiskaia.*

14   *Polnoe sobranoe russkikh letopisei* (full collection of the Russian chronicles), 43 volumes (Saint-Petersburg, 2002).

15   Anatole Mazour, *Modern Russian Historiography* (Westport, CT: Westview, 1975).

16   Mikhail Lomonosov, *Drevnaia Rossiskaia istoriia ot nachala rossiskogo naroda do konchiny velikogo kniazia Iaroslava Pervogo ili do 1054 goda* (Saint-Petersburg, 1766).

17   Heinrich Storch, *Cours d'économie politique ou exposition des principes qui déterminent la prospérité des nations,* 5 vols. (Saint Petersburg: A. Pliushar, 1815), booklet 5, 255, 258, 261, 279, 291–2. On Storch, see Paul Romeo, 'Heinrich Storch, Adam Smith and the Question of Russian Economic Development', M.A.

Thesis, University of North Carolina, 1996; Roderick E. McGrew, 'Dilemmas of Development: Baron Heinrich Storch, 1766–1835, on the Growth of Imperial Russia', *Jahrbücher für Geschichte Osteuropas* 24, no. 1 (1976): 31–71; and Iuri Iu. Bliumin, *Ocherki ekonomicheskoi mysli* pervoi poloviny XIX veka (Studies of economic thought during the first half of the nineteenth century) (Moscow, Leningrad: Izdatelstvo Akademii nauk, 1940), 173–95.

18   William Hagen, 'Village Life in East-Elbian Germany and Poland, 1400–1800', in *The Peasantries of Europe, from the Fourteenth to the Eighteenth Centuries*, ed. Tom Scott (London: Routledge, 1998), 145–90.

19   Esther Kingston-Mann, *In Search of the True West* (Princeton: Princeton University Press, 1999).

20   Andrzej Walicki is one of countless authors who have analysed the debate between the Slavophiles and Westernizers during this era. See A. Walicki, *The Slavophile Controversy: History of a Conservative Utopia in Nineteenth-Century Russia* (New York: Oxford University Press, 1975).

21   Vissarion G. Belinskii, *Polnoe sobranie sochinenii* [Complete works], 13 vols. (Moscow: AN SSSR, 1953–59), in particular, vol. 12, 444–68; Ivan A. Aksakov, *Sochinenii (Works)*, 7 vols. (Moscow: Tip. M. G. Volchaninova, 1886–87); Terence Emmons, *The Russian Landed Gentry and the Peasant Emancipation of 1861* (Berkeley: University of California Press, 1968); Lidia G. Zakharova and John Bushnell (eds.), *The Great Reforms in Russia* (Bloomington: Indiana University Press, 1994).

22   Vladimir Vernadskii, *Politicheskoe ravnovesie i Angliia* (Moscow: Univer. tipografiia, 1854); *Ocherk istorii politicheskoi ekonomii* (Saint Petersburg: Red. Ekon. Uzak., 1858); and *Prospekt politicheskoi ekonomii* (Saint Petersburg: Red. Ekon. Uzaz., 1858). On Vernadskii, see V. N. Rozental', 'Obshchestvenno-politicheskaia programma russkogo liberalizma v seredine 50-kh godov XIXe veka', *Istoricheskie zapiski* 70 (1961): 197–222.

23   Mariia Vernadskaia, *Sobranie sochinenii* [Selected works] (Saint Petersburg: Red. Ekon. Uzak., 1862), 76.

24   Nikolai G. Chernyshevskii, 'Ob Obshchinnom vladenii', [On community ownership], 1858, reproduced in *Sochineniia*, Works, vol. 2 (Geneva: Elpidine, 1879).

25   V. G. Belinskii, *Polnoe sobranie sochinenii*, (Complete works), 13 vols. (Moscow: AN SSSR, 1953–59), 12, 444–68; I. A. Aksakov, *Sochinenii (Works)*, 7 vols. (Moscow: Tip. M.G. Volchaninova, 1886–7), v. 2; A. S. Khomiakov, *Polnoe sobranie sochinenii*, 8 vols. (Moscow: Universitetskaia tipografiia, 1900), v. 3; P. A. Zaionchkovskii, *The Abolition of Serfdom in Rusisa* (Gulf Breeze: Academic International Press, 1978); Terence Emmons, *The Russian Landed Gentry and the Peasant Emancipation of 1861* (Berkeley: University of California Press, 1968); L. G. Zakharova and J. Bushnell (eds.), *The Great Reforms in Russia* (Bloomington: Indiana University Press, 1994); N. A. Tsagalov, *Ocherki russkoi ekonomicheskoi mysli perioda padeniia krepostnogoprava* (Studies on Russian economic thought during the fall of serfdom) (Moscow: Gosudarstvennoe izdatel'stvo politicheskoi literatury, 1956); and V. N. Chicherin, *Sobstvennost' i gosudarstvo* (property and the state) 2 vols. (Moscow, 1882–83; new edition, St. Petersburg: Izdatel'stvo Russkoi Khristianskoi gumanitarnoi akademii, 2005).

26   Alessandro Stanziani, *L'économie en révolution, le cas russe. 1870–1930* (Paris: Albin Michel, 1998).

27   Chernyshevskii, 'Ob Obshchinnom vladenii'.

28 Mikhail Mikhailovskii, 'Chto takoe progress', (What is progress), 1869, 'Analogicheskii metod v obshchestvennoi nauke', (The analogical method in social science) 1869; "'Bor'ba za individual'nost'', (The struggle for individuality), in *Sochineniia* (Saint-Petersburg: Izdanie Russkoe Bogatstvo, vol. 1, 1909).

29 Petr Struve, 'Vvedenie' ([preface]) to Karl Marx, *Kapital* (Popova: Saint Petersburg, 1899), XXVIII–XXIX; Mikhail Tugan-Baranovskii, *Osnovy politicheskoi ekonomii* (Slovo: Saint Petersburg, 1905–11), 57–8.

30 Alessandro Stanziani, *L'économie en révolution*. For the letters between Marx and the Russians: Teodor Shanin (ed.), *Late Marx and the Russian Road, Marx and the 'peripheries of capitalism'* (New York: Monthly Review Press, 1983).

31 Serguei Bulgakov, 'Tretij tom "Kapitala" K. Marksa', *Russkaja mysl'* 3 (1895): 1–20; Struve, 'Vvedenie' ([preface]).

32 Maksim Kovalevskii, *Modern Customs and Ancient Laws of Russia* (Union, NJ: Lawbook Exchange, 2000).

33 Boris Nikolaevich Chicherin, *Oblastnye uchrezhdeniia Rosii v XVII veke* (Regional administrations of seventeenth century Russia) (Moscow, 1856).

34 Vera Kaplan, *Historians and Historical Societies in the Public Life of Imperial Russia* (Bloomington: Indiana University Press, 2017).

35 Pavel Nikolaevich Miliukov, *Ocherki po istorii russkoi kul'tury* (Studies on the history of Russian culture) 3 vols. (Saint-Petersburg, 1896–1903).

36 R. A. Kireeva, *Gosudarstvennaia Shkola: istoricheskaia kontseptiia K.D. Kavelina i B.N. Chicherina* (Moscow: Natsia I kultura, 2004); Gary Hambourg, 'Inventing the State School of Historians, 1840–1995', in *Historiography of Imperial Russia: the Profession and Writing of History in a Multinational State*, ed. Terry Sanders (Armonk: Sharpe, 1999), 98–117.

37 Arno Mayer, *The Persistence of the Old Regime. Europe to War* (London: Verso, 1982); Patrick O'Brien, *Economic Growth in Britain and France, 1780–1914. Two Paths to the Twentieth Century* (London: Unwin, 1987). Charles Feinstein and Sidney Pollard (eds.), *Studies in Capital Formation in the United Kingdom, 1750–1920* (Oxford: Clarendon Press, 1988).

38 Paul Gregory, *Russian National Income 1885–1913* (Cambridge: Cambridge University Press, 1982; paperback 2004); Alessandro Stanziani, *L'économie en revolution. Le cas russe, 1870–1930* (Paris: Albin Michel, 1998); Peter Gatrell, *The Tsarist Economy, 1850–1917* (London: Batsford, 1986).

39 Gregory, *Russian*, 126–30; 168–94.

40 Aaron B. Retish, *Russia's Peasants in Revolution and Civil War: Citizenship, Identity, and the Creation of the Soviet State, 1914–1922* (Cambridge: Cambridge University Press, 2008). Ol'ga S. Porshneva, Krest'iane, rabochie i soldaty Rossii nakanune i v gody pervoi mirovoi voiny (Peasants, workers and soldiers in Russia at the eve and during WWI) (Moscow, 2004). Joshua A. Sanborn, *Drafting the Russian Nation: Military Conscription, Total War, and Mass Politics, 1905–1925* (DeKalb, IL, 2003); Lars Lih, *Bread and Authority in Russia, 1914–1921* (Berkeley, CA, 1990).

41 Samuel H. Baron and Nancy W. Heer (eds.), *Windows on the Russian Past: Essays on Soviet Historiography since Stalin* (Columbus, OH: Anchor Press, 1977); John Barber, *Soviet Historians in Crisis, 1928–1932* (New York: Holmes and Meier, 1981).

42 Mikhail Pokrovskii, 'Obshchestvennye nauki v SSSR za 10 let' (Social sciences in the USSR in the past ten years), *Vestnik kommunisticheskoi akademii* no. 26 (1928): 3–30.

43 Pokrovskii, 'Obshchstvennye nauki', 23.

44 John Barber, *Soviet Historians in Crisis, 1928-1932* (London: MacMillan, 1981).

45 Harun Yilmaz, *National Identities in Soviet Historiography* (London: Routledge, 2015).

46 Alexander Gershenkron, *Economic Backwardness in Historical Perspective* (Cambridge, MA: Harvard University Press, 1962).

47 Among the proponents of this approach, see: Paul Rosenstein-Rodan, 'Problems of Industrialization of Eastern and Souteastern Europe', *Economic Journal* 53 (June–September 1943): 202–11; Ragnar Nurske, *Problems of Capital Formation in Underdeveloped Countries* (Oxford: Basil Blackwell, 1953); W. A. Lewis, *The Theory of Economic Growth* (London: Allen and Unwin, 1955).

48 Gunnar Myrdal, *Economic Theory and Underdevelopped Regions* (London: Duckworth, 1956); Paul Baran, *The Political Economy of Growth* (John Calder: New York, 1957).

49 Alexander Mendel, *Dilemmas of Progress in Tsarist Russia. Legal Marxism and Legal Populism* (Cambridge, MA: Harvard University Press, 1961); Paul Rosenstein-Rodan, 'Problems of Industrialization of Eastern and South-eastern Europe', *Economic Journal* 53 (June–September 1943): 202–11; Gunner Myrdal, *Economic Theory and Underdeveloped Regions* (London: Duckworth, 1956).

50 K. Vergopoulos Samir Amin, *La question paysanne et le capitalisme* (Anthropos: Paris, 1974); J. Ennew, P. Hirst, and K. Tribe, 'Peasantry as an Economic Category', *The Journal of Peasant Studies* 4, no. 4 (1977); U. Patnaik, 'Neo-Populism and Marxism: The Chayanovian Veiw of the Agrarian Question and Its Fundamental Fallacy', *The Journal of Peasant Studies*, no. 6 (1979): 375–420; U. Patnaik, 'Reply to Nicholas Georgescu-Roegen', *The Journal of Peasant Studies* 8, no. 2 (1981).

51 Nikolai Georgescu-Roegen, 'Economic Theory on Agrarian Development', *Oxford Economic Papers* XII (1960): 1–40.

52 E. V. Bazhanova, *Istoriia ekonomicheskoi mysli narodov SSSR s drevneishikh vremen do 1917 g* (History of economic thought in the USSR since the ancient times) (Moscow: Nauka, 1959); N. K. Figurovskaja, *Agrarnye problemy v sovetskoi ekonomicheskoi literature 20kh godov* (The agrarian problems in the soviet economic literature of the 1920s) (Moscow: Ekonomika, 1978).

53 Joseph Stiglitz, *Whither Socialism?* (Harvard: MIT Press, 1994).

54 Gregory Yavlinsky, *Laissez Faire versus Policy-Led Transformation, Lessons of the Economic Reforms in Russia* (Moscow: Center for Economic and Political Research, 1996); Shafiqul Islam and Michael Mandelbaum (eds.), *Making Markets Economic Transformations in Eastern Europe and the Post-Soviet States* (New York: Council of Foreign Relations, 1993).

16

Mapping economic interdependence: Creating the periphery in the interwar period

Jeremy Adelman, Laetitia Lenel and Pablo Pryluka

Introduction

In late 2018, protestors from around France donned their yellow vests – known as *gilets jaunes* – to denounce the government's tax hike on diesel fuel, a tax meant to curb carbon emissions and raise revenues. French manifestations of a worldwide phenomenon, a backlash against cosmopolitan elites and their urbane ways, the *gilets jaunes* were irate. The prominent right-wing journalist, Éric Zemmour, rushed to their defence. Zemmour erupted on the news channel BFMTV: 'You have the real French, real Italians, real English, real Americans, who live in this periphery, farther and farther away from the centers where wealth is created.' He denounced 'metropolitan France', and by implication the tuned-out metropolitans elsewhere. 'Here', he claimed, 'the periphery is making itself heard!'[1]

Nowadays, being marginalized, pushed to the periphery, estranged in one's own country and feeling pushed around by world forces, is the dominant rhetoric of outrage against globalization and economic integration. It comes as a shock: the recent strain of patriotic chest-thumping revived a strain of nationalism which many had believed passé because globalization had seemed to have buried small-world imaginaries under the triumphs of one-world supply chains, financialization and the rise of the cosmopolitan city. Instead, an increasing number of people see globalization as a threat to the survival of, if not their kin, their nation.

The backlash against domestic inequalities and spreading precarity has its echo in a long-standing dispute over the meaning of global interdependence.[2] If there was once a conviction that global convergence was destiny, the *gilets jaunes* and their angry cousins around the world have countered with stories of divergence, fracture and even of collapse. The war over the narrative of global togetherness is one chapter in a larger saga concerning, as Quinn Slobodian has argued, 'how we see the world economy'.[3] Indeed, the promise to reverse the deleterious effects of economic globalization has emerged as a central strategy of the current breed of ethno-nativist politicians and a core explanation of their success. This strategy rests on a narrative about what it means to be made marginal or peripheral in a world controlled by distant concentrations of power from commanding heights beyond the clouds.

Where did this idea of the periphery of something wider come from? Our chapter aims to understand how efforts to describe the world economy gave birth to the notion of periphery after 1914. We look in particular at the interwar years as a moment in which observers, critics and a new breed of actors, notably economists, began to imagine a world order that had moved from one of empires to one of trading states. Up to 1914, there was no shortage of thinking about, as well as celebrating and lambasting, imperial integration – with much of the controversy being about the cores of empires. After the First World War, with empires in trouble and references to self-determination on the march, advocates of global integration appealed to an idyll of sovereign nation-states laced together by trade. As Charles Kindleberger and others have pointed out, this transition did not come without turbulences. With Great Britain having lost its hegemonic status and the United States not yet willing to assume the role of hegemonic leader, the interwar period was marked by instability and uncertainty.[4]

This was the context in which a search for a new, postimperial narrative of global integration took hold. This groping spurred hopes for an alternative, better future, one that would overcome the frictions and asymmetries that had caused the imperial wars of 1914. Doing so required creating a rhetoric of postimperial equality. There was a view, announced in both Lenin's and Wilson's promise of a postimperial age of self-determination,[5] that what would emerge from the ashes of the First World War was an arrangement of mutually economically dependent but politically sovereign nation-states. Economic interdependence would replace the incentive to fight; sovereignty would eclipse the incentive to be predatory. A new 'world economy' and a world of nation-states would replace the snarling and eventually ruinous competition between empires.

But the narrative of postimperial interdependence carried an additional burden: how to explain postimperial inequalities and asymmetries that were legacies of empire? Where did the story of new world fusion leave former colonial societies or latecomers to a game dominated by industrial empires? In this emergent arrangement, the keywords of the plotline shifted from colonies of empires to peripheries or margins of a world economy – societies nominally released from the formalities of political subjugation but economically laced to rules and institutions made by others. With the imagining of a world economy to replace the imperial one came a critique and anxiety about the ways in which integration created a new hierarchy, not so much of empires and colonies, but of core nations and peripheral zones. What defined one's place in the order was not formal control but informal mechanisms of power and the structural conditions of subordination. To speak, therefore, of a world economy meant confronting its geographical unevenness, unfairness and the vulnerability of some societies to the predatory temptations of others.

The result: after 1918, two ideas came to the fore at once; the first was the idea and pursuit of rebuilding a world economy premised on open markets and a new interdependent order to eclipse the imperial model of 1914. The second was the necessary, if hidden, idea and recognition of the inequality and asymmetry built within such an order. To borrow a metaphor from music, in the new peace there was a point and a counterpoint, each cueing the other to make a harmony, one sounding notes of integration while another resonated inequality. The building of the world economy has been the dominant point. It has dominated our view of the interwar era. While the peacemakers gathered in Paris to plan the new arrangement, there was also much repairing to be done to the international payments system. Brussels hosted the first 'International Financial Conference' – one of many gatherings that would grapple with the problem of a world and especially Europe awash in debt, as well as the issue of currency stabilization. Moreover, such gatherings sought to replace the disequilibrium brought by war with a new financial and trading order capable of governing a world economy. Within a decade, economic worldmakers had to confront the drive to raise tariff barriers, competitive devaluations and the rash of sauve-qui-peut policies that prioritized national survival over world integration as well as the protection of national producers from international competitors. These menaces, and a commitment to rebuild economic interdependence, spawned a movement to envision a discipline able to reveal and manage the codes of material interdependence. In so doing, this movement mapped out models of interdependence that had to grapple with the unfairness of the world economy and the uneven distribution of power between cores and peripheries – inequalities and differences that did not merely precede, but were in fact the effects of integration itself.

This chapter is about the overlooked counterpoint. It argues that the birth of modern thinking about the world economy and interdependence also sired the notion of periphery, of a new kind of asymmetry structured into the rebooted internationalism. The idea that integration produces economic margins lays the groundwork for what would become by the 1960s, in the full-flush of Thirdworldist narratives, dependency theory. Ours is a story about the origins of the concept that preceded and informed struggles for decolonization: the recognition of an economic periphery attached a narrative about economic injustice to a material and moral critique of the world system in the latter half of the twentieth century.

One might say that that critique has now been globalized: the backlash against economic unfairness nowadays is no longer a rhetoric only of the so-called 'developing' countries, or maybe not anymore at all. In recent years, it has predominantly become a Western narrative that is picked up by Brexiteers, French protesters at the Champs-Élysées and America's 'left-behinds' alike.

To explore the genesis of this narrative, our chapter looks at three different lines of argument about interdependence, which illustrate its intricate origins. First, it describes how, coming from places as different as Argentina and China, Alejandro Bunge and Sun Yat-sen imagined the peripheral status of their countries in the dying days of the First World War, and set the stage for what would later become the grammar of 'dependency' theory. The heirs to this style of thinking ranged from Jawaharlal Nehru to Canadian economists like Harold Innis. Second, it investigates how the ways in which American and European economic geographers – who counted their regions among what they called the 'core' – evaluated and depicted economic interdependence to restore a balance between cores and peripheries within a liberal, free-trade, regime. While by no means exhaustive, the descriptions and visualizations of both these strands of thinking allow us to trace the expectations and fears that accompanied the development of commerce in a moment of crisis and breakdown. This gave rise to a third type of argument about interdependence: the resurgence of

310 *Narratives, Nations, and Other World Products*

neo-mercantilist regimes aiming to replace a broken liberal-multilateral system with coercive, bilateral, regional arrangements that consolidated the hierarchy of cores and peripheries exemplified by thinking about German and Japanese trading regimes. Peripheries, in the weaponized economic statecraft of the 1930s, became the sites for predation and resistance. Few bothered to hide the view that the world economy was a deeply stratified one.

Finding the periphery on the periphery

The 1890s had sparked some reflection in India and elsewhere about unfair trade. One can think of Thorstein Veblen worrying from the American Midwest about wheat prices and the plight of farmers or complaints by statisticians like Dadabhai Naoroji about how British taxes 'drained' Indian wealth. But it was only after the First World War that peripheral consciousness took shape. Consternation over the social question and the irruption of mass political participation after 1918 had created the conditions for more inclusive democratic regimes and the institutionalization of new ways to channel the anxieties of popular sectors. Such a new scenario complicated the future of the globalization process started around the 1870s. How to balance the old rigidity of the gold standard system, deepen suffrage and spread the idea of nation-building? Then, as now, worldmakers faced a trilemma. They could, with difficulty, manage a combination of any two objectives, but never three at once. The trilemma therefore alluded, to basic new questions about the international global order.[6]

If European authorities and commentators struggled to restore financial stability while creating a new balance of forces, voices from the fringes argued against the possibility of such a harmonious portrait of the world economy. The First World War had highlighted the ways in which export economies fell prey to shocks and policies beyond their control. Latin America was no exception. Facing the economic instability created by the War and later the Great Depression, the export boom that had prevailed since the 1870s sputtered, stalled and finally imploded in ways that seemed to render implausible the idea of restoring an old world.[7] The disenchantment was most acute in precisely those places where the economy had benefited most from the old imperial order, only to now be confronted with the fog and uncertainty of the new one. This was notably apparent as it concerned Argentina. For the South American country, these waning days of globalization marked the end of an export model based on raw materials and foodstuff. The years of the *granero del mundo* were coming to a close, and with it, the 'conservative order' that ruled it – in 1916, Argentina had its first presidential election with secret suffrage. The local economy underwent structural changes, but so did the way in which Argentina traded with other nations.[8]

In this context, the Argentine economist Alejandro Bunge gained notoriety as one of the most active intellectuals and policymakers in the country, one who actively sought to write a new script for the country's economic destiny.[9] Trained in Argentina and Germany, he took an active role in the creation of the *Departamento Nacional del Trabajo*, from where he produced some of the first statistics on the standard of living of the working class in Argentina. While doing so, he saw the gradual collapse of

Argentina's export economy and the social and economic consequences of this trade stalemate – the Great War had reshuffled the rules of the world economy.[10] Bunge read into these changes: In a world with greater room for economic isolation, governments in Latin American countries had the prerogative (and the duty) to protect their national economies from external shocks through tariffs and the regulation of capital flows.[11]

For Bunge, protectionism became a tool to forge the integration of Argentina's national economy and to promote a new kind of integration into the global economy. On a local level, Argentina needed to protect national industries to leave behind its previous economic model, based on export-led growth. This would have two consequences. On the one hand, it would encourage the development of industrial cities, exposing internal migrants to a modern urban way of life. On the other, trade tariffs were intended to protect regional industries in Argentina and thereby help integrate the country. Bunge thought this was an urgent task. Argentina showed sharp differences between economic regions, divided by circumferences that had their centre in Buenos Aires, the capital city.[12]

The result was a new way of thinking about economic geography across and within countries. Bunge called this a *país abanico* (a fan-like country), by which he meant relations that radiated according to levels of population density, economic activity, cultural development as well as the standard of living, as one receded from Buenos Aires. In his view, the same applied at an international level, radiating out of economic cores like London. To him, protectionism was also a way to ensure that the edges of the fan were not deprived of the fruits of flow from trade, for trade tariffs could stimulate regional production and thus help improve local conditions through economic

Figure 16.1 Alejandro Bunge ARGENTINA, *país abanico*.[13]

growth.[14] State interventionism, by aiming to industrialize the country and reframing its role in the global economy, could help develop 'forgotten' regions of Argentina.

Making the fringes more visible also underscored the risks and perils of being on the fringes. A modern, industrial and cohesive country would be more insulated from external shocks, for instance. Bunge was among the first who pointed out the country's vulnerability to the fluctuations of a global economy in which 'economic interdependence' forged by the 'civilized' parts of the planet affected 'the rest'. His observation was grounded on a comparison between the value of the local goods exported and the value of the ones imported in Europe and the United States – what, later on, economic literature would define as 'terms of trade'. With this world of relative values in mind, Bunge described how the value of local exports plummeted while foreign credit almost disappeared during the mid-1930s. These were the unintended and structural consequences of international trade. Neither Argentina nor the core economies had intentionally attempted to foster these inequalities – they were the expectable output of the global economy.[15] Bunge identified the existence of an international regime that did not affect all nations and regions in the same way. To smooth the impact of external shocks, states should have at hand economic tools to navigate through a more complex and unstable ocean of trade and exchange. Policymakers should create a new institutional order able to provide effective answers when facing these previously unknown challenges.[16]

One solution was regional integration, to help exporters contend with the market power of importers. Bunge followed closely the first attempts to create a European economic unity. After the publication of what he referred to as the *Manifiesto de los banqueros e industriales internacionales* in October 1926, he provided a thorough reflection on the consequences of Versailles and how bankers and merchants of Europe saw the establishment of a better understanding among their nations as pivotal. Although the establishment of the European Union was still a long way off, the first steps towards regional cooperation provided Bunge with the opportunity to call for an analogous project in South America. From his perspective, the strength of both Europe and the United States relied partially on their economic power as integrated markets. Measured with an array of different economic indicators, it seemed clear to Bunge that South America should be able to compete with them as an economic unit, mainly because each country isolated had no option but to succumb under the expansion of the other two giants. He therefore advocated the creation of a Custom Union of the South (*Unión Aduanera del Sud*), capable of intruding, as he laid out in graphic form, on the alliance of the North Atlantic powers.[17]

This vision of integration as unfair and unequal, as creating a stratified world of industrializers and the rest, and a grasping for dreamy projects took hold elsewhere as well. If Argentina had been a great beneficiary of Victorian convergence, China decidedly had not. By the end of the Boxer Rebellion, there was a veritable scramble for control of – if not partition of – the Middle Kingdom. Several allies had drafted plans to partition China in the wake of the Eight-Nation intervention to subdue the rebels. For Chinese reforming intellectuals, this threat of being further marginalized emboldened them to double down on catching up. If China could not catch up, they felt, it would be dissected. This drove many reformers to follow Western ways with

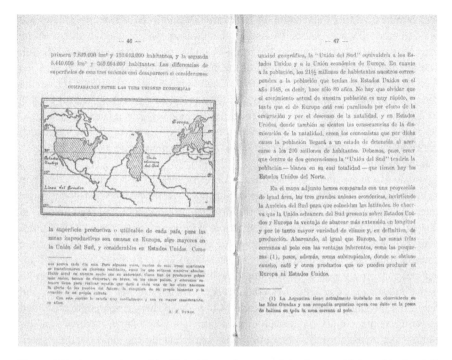

Figure 16.2 A comparison of the United States, Europe and the Customs Union of the South.[18]

ever more zeal. But that strategy lost its charm when the news leaked out in the spring of 1919 that the Paris peacemakers had flipped the German concession in Shandong province to Japan. The result was a wave of violent indignation known as the May Fourth movement.

Chinese reformers were therefore caught between a desire to catch up using Western methods and a growing suspicion that the 'West' and the great powers (including Japan) would wield their might to keep China down. One who took this all in and began to chart China's place in the new world order was the father of Chinese republicanism, Sun Yat-sen. He's receiving something of a renewed interest in the current thinking in Beijing. One can see why. Angry at the West for its hypocrisy, yet nostalgic for Chinese peace and prosperity, he dreamed big about an alternative order. But in the meantime, he fretted about the one he confronted in 1919, which led him to reckon with a world order in which China had slid from being once the hub to becoming a marginal player in the global game.

Still, he warned, even peripheral parts can present weak links in the chain of interdependence. Sun sat down in Canton in 1921 to map out what we would now call a 'strategy' for Chinese development. His manifesto, *The International Development of China*, argued that his country 'is now prey of militaristic and capitalistic powers – a greater bone of contention than the Balkan Peninsula'.[19] In a sense, he turned J. A. Hobson on his head.[20] In his famous 1902 study of imperialism, Hobson had argued that the problems of capitalism in the *metropole* drove magnates in London, Berlin and Washington to subject 'inferior races' to their will and create empires that careened to war. Sun insisted that the creation of backwardness and inferiority in *peripheries* was what threatened world peace. By creating the have-nots in an interdependent world, empires produced weak links in the chain of integration. As far as we can tell, Sun was the first to connect development of the peripheries to global peace and security; without a solution to 'the China Question' another war was inevitable; the key to the problem was economic prosperity; the key to China's prosperity meant solving its backwardness. While advanced countries were deep into a 'second industrial revolution', China could not enter the first, he argued. Because of the ways in which outsiders imposed treaties on a feeble state, China, like many other parts of the world, was out of sync with modernization.

What was to be done? An optimist, and disinclined to apocalyptic visions, Sun saw China's needs as the world's opportunity. Development could deepen global interdependence while giving it more internal stability; but this required, Sun insisted, that great powers reverse transfers of resources back to peripheries. China's backwardness could be seen as a market for others' machinery and technology; the country could also 'absorb all the surplus capital as quickly as the Industrial Nations can possibly produce'. By redistributing capital and capital goods to help China build native industries, other countries could bulk up their producer goods sectors and help close the gap in historical trajectories. China could then be spared its continued targeting by mercantilists, especially from a more predatory Japan – which Sun saw as the chief menace – and instead more fully participate in the global trading order. In this fashion, an 'International Development Scheme' might provide a model of cooperation for what Sun envisioned as a post-Darwinian world.[21]

The key to his scheme was a vast network of railways, canals, roads and dams – in short, infrastructure – built with foreign capital. The plan would have two effects. First, it would integrate a fractured national market within China and help restore some domestic stability. Second, it would draw hinterlands into trading networks with the wider world and in so doing make apparent to China's neighbours and Westerners the greater advantages resulting from commerce rather than plunder and extraction.

The scheme foreshadowed scrambles in India and Latin America to industrialize by protecting domestic markets and nurturing native manufacturing – what is called import substitution industrialization – at the expense of trade with the metropolitan economies. It echoed Bunge's ruminations. But there are two differences between their narratives that are worth noting. First, for Bunge, Argentina's peripherality was the result of being locked into the status of primary goods exporter to industrial powers. China, on the other hand, had been a manufacturer that fell behind with the First Industrial Revolution. There was an emerging recognition that not all peripheries were the same. Second, Sun's grand scheme for investment and infrastructure – unlike Bunge's – made an ethical appeal to a different kind of self-interest. If Bunge was concerned with the national question at home, Sun had bigger quarry in mind. He placed China's health as a cause for the rest. So interdependent had become the global order that redressing injustices was key to world peace.

The War and its aftermath set off the drive to re-envision the world economy in a way that would overcome injustices of the past. The search for new economic narratives and new geographies echoed the anti-colonial upsurge of 1919 in parts of

Figure 16.3 Sun Yat-sen, *The International Development of China*.*

Latin America, through Africa and Asia. In a sense, the recognition of the periphery's place in the new world order was first given attention by the periphery itself.

Landscapes of integration

While Bunge and Sun fretted about life and livelihoods on the edges of the international system after the War, a new generation of actors and institutional settings, many associated with the League of Nations and its affiliates, sought to rebuild free-trade multilateralism out of the imperial ashes in Europe. Their joint goal was to stabilize and integrate the trading and payments system thrown into disequilibrium by the conflict – and to rebuild a 'world economy' after empire.

When 2000 delegates met in London in summer 1924 to hold the first World Power Conference (power as in energy – already signalling the importance of resources to 'power' the world economy), one of their main goals was to survey 'what steps, if any, could be taken to provide adequate opportunities for the co-operation of all nations

---

* Sun Yat-sen, The International Development of China, Appendix.

in the development of power resources'.[22] Cooperation was the new catchphrase. Engineers, scientists and politicians alike argued that cooperation could benefit all, as it allowed the nations of the world to 'all advance together'.[23] Commentators rejoiced and praised the meeting as the dawn of a new era, with political boundaries fading. The delegates of the conference 'saw only the peoples of the world as brothers', heralded a report in the newly founded British journal *Economic Geography*.[24]

What a new tone this was. For a long time, European and American economic geographers had dismissed huge parts of the world as irrelevant to human development or at the receiving end of civilizing missions. In fact, economic geography had been defined by its focus on regions that geographers deemed viable for economic development.[25] Take, for example, the research of Ellsworth Huntington, professor of geography at Yale University. Nine years before engineers, scientists and politicians met in London, Huntington had compared how the output of piece-rate workers in selected factories in Pennsylvania and Connecticut and the daily and weekly marks of students at two academies varied throughout the year and correlated them with the change in temperature over the year. From these measurements, Huntington had deduced what he called the 'ideal climate' for physical and mental work.[26] On this basis, he had constructed a map of the world in which he showed the degree of energy 'which we should expect among normal Europeans in various regions on the basis of climate' (Figure 16.4).[27] Finding a 'striking resemblance between the distribution of climatic energy and of civilization',[28] Huntington had concluded that 'civilization' was directly linked to work output, which he thought to be conditioned by climate.

Huntington had not been alone with his deterministic – and racist – ideas. On the contrary, they seem characteristic of Euro-American approaches in economic

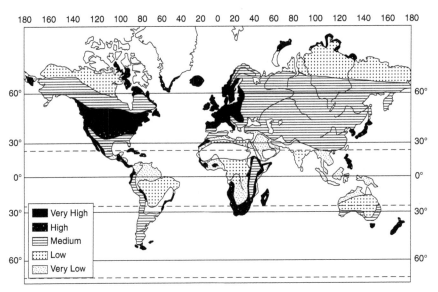

Figure 16.4 Ellsworth Huntington, *The Distribution of Human Energy on the Basis of Climate*.[29]

geography before the First World War. As in Huntington's work, large parts of the world were excluded from the 'world economy' because of their physical conditions.[30] The First World War and its aftermath, however, challenged the notion of an almost static economic order, according to which strong regions could become better but weak regions were doomed to remain weak forever. Faced with domestic economic instability and stagnation, European observers became increasingly aware of European dependence on overseas markets in the course of the 1920s.[31]

'The progress of even the most advanced nations is clearly seen to be limited by the conditions of the whole', explained Daniel Nicol Dunlop, director of the British Electrical and Allied Manufacturer's Association, in his foreword to the transactions of the London conference.[32] It does, argued Dunlop, therefore 'not pay in the long run to deal unfairly with any nation'.[33] What a new tone indeed. Or was it? In fact, the conference quickly proved to be foremost a means for the Great Powers to maintain and enlarge their power. Reports on the British Empire, Canada and the United States were compiled to convince readers and investors of their 'magnificent power resources [...] and the efficient and economic manner in which they have so far been utilized'.[34] Readers were alluded to the '[a]mple natural resources' and 'abundant supplies' of natural sources of power of the respective countries,[35] with photographs of their technological achievements accompanying the enthusiastic descriptions. Held in London during the British Empire Exhibition, the conference was yet another means to demonstrate Western vigour. While the reports also included some of the first geological and hydraulic surveys of regions that had previously been uncharted, most of the surveys covered colonies. So-called skeleton maps, still incomplete in many regards, were envisioned to show how certain sites 'could be converted into sources of power'.[36] Prepared by American or British engineers, the reports were intended to demonstrate the economic value of the colonies so as to attract investors.[37] Tellingly, no South American and only one Japanese participated in a discussion on *Resources of European, Asiatic and South American Countries*.[38]

Unlike Ellsworth Huntington and his colleagues, most economic geographers writing in the interwar period did not exclude any regions from the picture. Instead, they postulated a law-like evolution of economic development open to all or most regions. Different regions were classified according to their 'degree of civilization' or their 'stage of development'.[39] As the geographers and engineers meeting in London in 1924 saw it, 'undeveloped corner[s]' of the world could develop by improving their knowledge and usage of natural resources.[40] Here, underdevelopment was understood not as a syndrome, but as the starting point from which backward regions or 'outlying parts of the world'[41] would follow the trajectory traced out by developed regions.[42] From that perspective, the assumed distance between core and periphery could be measured in time.[43]

The new 'master' narrative of economic development was a reaction to an increasing awareness of the dynamic nature of economic interdependence. 'Up until the last third of the nineteenth century, the United States was predominantly a colonial country: it belonged to the peripheral-capitalist countries such as Russia, South America and the East Indies. It provided the necessary physical capital in the form of food and raw materials to Western European capitalism', explained the German economist Werner

Sombart in 1927. 'Now, capitalism has raised its head in the United States, demanding what only Western Europe used to demand: the necessary physical capital from those areas that are now peripheral to American capitalism.'[44] The quick industrialization of the United States and its rise as a world power convinced contemporaries of the temporary character of the global order. Countries that had formerly belonged to what Sombart called the 'passive and serving', so-called 'peripheral countries' could suddenly, so it seemed, turn 'active and directing', moving up to 'the capitalist Center'.[45] Outlining a linear, law-like development process valid for all countries, then, was an attempt to overcome the uncertainty of the future by narrating and visualizing the world order of interlocked spaces that were divided by resources and power, thereby maintaining Western economic power and predominance. The attendees of the first World Power Conference did not intend to overcome the distinction between Westerners and Resterners – which Bunge and Sun yearned for. Instead, their vision of a world economic geography preserved and naturalized the distinction. While they repeatedly stressed that knowledge should be 'pooled for the common good',[46] attendees seemed mainly concerned with the further development and expansion of what they called the 'developed' corners of the world. Certainly, other countries could and should extend their utilization of natural resources as well. However, this was important only insofar as their resources should 'be transmitted into Europe to keep the wheels and furnaces and spindles going'.[47] Industrialization was still the privilege of a few. It was precisely this strain of hierarchical thinking that fuelled Bunge's and Sun Yat-sen's critical counterpoints.

Spatial thinking and raw power

Both post-1919 peripheral and new core thinkers plotted an integrating world trading order from the nineteenth century as the framing through which a new geography could be envisioned – and reimaged – to suit a global regime after 1919. This kind of spatial thinking enacted a specific 'Politics of Time'.[48] Western economic geographers characterized the Resterners as 'not yet developed'. Likewise, peripheral penseurs drafted plans for how their countries could catch up. The definition of being peripheral, then, was not just locational, but being, as it were, 'behind the times' – what would soon be called 'backward'. Despite all differences, there was a surprising agreement among peripheral and new core thinkers that all nations would eventually follow the same path. From this perspective, the relationship between core and periphery seemed unquestioned; the one set the example for the other to follow.

The Great Depression shattered the story-telling habits about the relations between cores and peripheries. It triggered a new register, one that grew darker and more ominous as the 1930s unfolded, and sired narratives that would justify a more coercive view of core-periphery relations. Writing in the early 1930s, Erich W. Zimmermann, a German economist who had immigrated to the United States in 1911, deplored the 'fateful inequality of long-run potentialities (...) which today divides the world into strong and weak, active and passive, lenders and borrowers, riders and ridden'.[49] Coming of age at the height of Germany's colonial expansion, Zimmermann described the modern world economy as a 'resource hierarchy', which had brought about 'an ominous geographical and racial division of the earth'.[50] While the power and metal industries had become 'the basis of modern machine civilization', thus determining the location of interdependent industries like transportation and communication, industries like agriculture, which did not form a part of 'the industrial organism', had gravitated towards the periphery.[51] This was a direct result of the industrial revolution, which had endowed certain branches of production, using certain resources and selling certain commodities, with extraordinary economic power while leaving out others. By elevating certain nations above others, the industrial revolution had proven 'a great divider of economic powers'.[52] Zimmermann visualized this divide in a diagram, with an inner nucleus of concentric circles (A-E) representing the power-metal system. Around this nucleus was a so-called 'twilight zone' (F-F1) entailing manufacturing industries not organically tied up with the 'centre of power' and a 'periphery' or 'peripheral corona' (G), which Zimmermann described as 'the habitat of the ruled, of the passive elements of the world's economic system' (see Figure 16.5).[53]

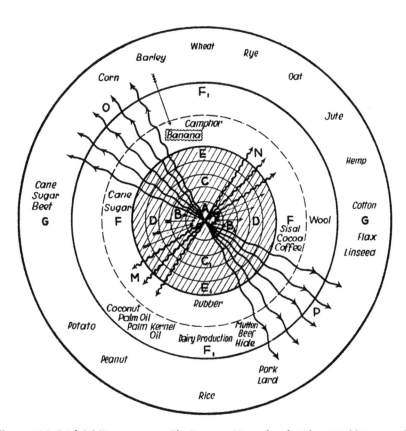

Figure 16.5 Erich W. Zimmermann, *The Resource Hierarchy of Modern World Economy*.[54]

Zimmermann's diagram lays bare the geometrical patterns of the periphery. Here, the world was visualized as a circular shape with industrialized nations at the centre and agricultural countries situated along the circumference of the circle. As in combinatorial topology, each connection between two points along what geometricians called the 'periphery' had to pass the centre of the circle.[55]

In contrast to the postwar voices like Sun and Bunge, and the hopeful economic statecrafters planning the postimperial world in the 1920s, Zimmermann did not believe that the marginalized regions would catch up. Instead, Zimmermann argued that the inequality between different regions would further increase, as regions applying the capitalistic mode of production would possess intrinsic advantages over those not equally able to apply it.[56] Once locked into an international division of labour, the periphery's destiny was set, the story foretold. For Zimmermann, this was a dangerous process. As he explained, '[H]oggish abuse of a superiority not of their making is the surest way of preparing for the downfall' of industrial powers and of the present resource hierarchy.[57] '[T]he "outs" will not stand by idle, and hungrily watch the "ins" feast', predicted Zimmermann. 'Counter-colonization will be the answer to colonization.'[58]

While Zimmermann was expressing a hope that the powers of the core might take a more benign outlook, and curb their 'hoggish' urges, others were less sanguine. The Canadian economic historian, Harold A. Innis, for example, was laying the tracks for what would later be coined as the 'staple theory' of growth – of how peripheral societies were constructed in a way that meant that they could not replicate industrial core models and conceded that a global division of labour created hierarchies. His 1930 *The Fur Trade in Canada* explored the contours of a distinctly peripheral – he used the terms 'center' and 'margin' – location in a world order, a location from which it was all but impossible to escape. Bunge's and Sun Yat-sen's hopes that peripheries might become new cores struck him as implausible. At best, what peripheries could do was encourage sectors around the export base, to diversify within their dependency on core economies. So, as Canada moved through a series of export cycles, from fur to lumber, to mining and agriculture, it could diversify – but it could never cast off realities that it was vulnerable to the decisions and shocks made elsewhere. Akin to Bunge's *país abánico*, with lines of dependence radiating from metropoles, it was Canada's predicament to be caught in the shift between two 'metropole' economic orders, from being a periphery in the British imperial system to being a margin to the American informal empire. Indeed, Innis went so far as to say that margins could have margins, peripheries peripheries – so that the Maritime provinces of Canada were to the power in Ontario what Canada was to the United States, and anticipated frictions between regions of raw material producers within national spaces as between national spaces.[59]

It is true that some economic geographers still envisioned an order in which certain parts of the world would dominate others. What the Great Depression did was lay bare the coercive features of this domination – and eventually the heightened, and eventually more violent, forms of resistance in the peripheries. From the openness of the 1920s, a new mood of closure and potential destruction set in. In the scramble for control and domination of the weak, even the great powers felt threatened. Suddenly, from all sides, a panic spread that any part of the world order could become peripheral. Or, in the case of the former 'core countries', lose their hegemonic status. 'Today more or less everywhere – in the Far East, India, South America, South Africa – industrial regions are in being, or coming into being, which, owing to their low scales of wages, will face us with a deadly competition. The unassailable privileges of the white races have been thrown away, squandered, betrayed', explained the German philosopher Oswald Spengler in 1932. 'The exploited world is beginning to take its revenge on the lords.'[60]

Fear and competition rekindled arguments and anxieties in public discourse about resources, distribution of power, competition and the need to claim and grab what one could as long as one could. The spectre of Malthusian scarcity grew, along with the generalized panic about decaying bodies, dwindling resources and diminishing returns. The frontier became less the zone of Zimmermann's hope for a new consciousness of interdependence and more a material and metaphoric obsession of Malthusians who sought land, oil, coal and control over the seas to brace peripheries to homelands of struggling, hungry and underemployed citizens. Core thinkers increasingly imagined peripheries as new sites for imposing a favourable trade balance – to ensure that wealth in the cores could accumulate, thanks to systematic drainage from peripheries. It was not just that the old liberal order was in peril, and that peripheries were more vulnerable to shocks and instabilities, it was that their very dependence presented opportunities for cores to shed lingering commitments to open trade and to take advantage of peripheries.

The result was a recognition that the power imbalance in the geography of integration created incentives for predatory and aggressive modes of integration. Later, this would become more recognizable in the vocabulary of what would be called 'dependency theory'. But one of the first to alight upon the ways in which co-dependency between cores and peripheries affected outlooks and policies was Albert O. Hirschman. For Hirschman, co-dependency constructed perceptions of interests, not the other way around. This insight cast the spotlight on power asymmetries in the making of the world order, and not as by-products of integration. Hirschman took note of this asymmetry as early as the mid-1930s in his studies of Mussolini's expansionist adventures in Italy when he was a doctoral student in Trieste. But it was not until he relocated to Paris and began to work at the Rockefeller Foundation-funded *Institut de Recherches Economiques et Sociales* at the Sorbonne that he began to catalogue a more systematic drive on the part of powerful trade partners to bully weaker ones into unfair but systematically structured trade deals. The danger was not that autarky was creeping back. It was the reconstruction of world trade 'on strictly separate national lines' because it could exploit what Zimmermann was pointing out: structural differences in global trade between fringes and centres.[61]

In what would become his first book *National Power and the Structure of Foreign Trade* (1945), Hirschman argued that there was a turn away from a 'greater geographic dispersion of commercial relations' of open trade towards a narrowed vision of interdependence with commercial policy as a 'weapon' to 'influence the geographical distribution of foreign trade' in favour of those with power at the expense of those without. The 1930s revived not autarky but mercantilist statecraft. Though he had witnessed Mussolini's economic pressures and efforts to blackmail Balkan neighbours and African trade partners, and he could have fastened on Japanese economic policies around the Pacific Rim and British Imperial Preferences, his case study was Germany and the Nazi policies towards Central and Southeastern Europe, in which unfair deals, exclusive contracts, most-favoured nation clauses and currency clearing restrictions strapped food and staple-producing Balkan and Central Europe near peripheries to the raw power of the industrial Nazi economy. The liberal idyll that free trade could transform unequal space into a single system for 'mutual benefit from commercial intercourse to the various countries trading together' had lost its persuasiveness. Now, the goal was not to reduce dependency, but to deepen it and stratify it around the interests of strong nations, to recompose the map into a world of powerful cores partitioning peripheries into ancillary or marginal zones.[62]

Hirschman's alternative was to rebuild open trade and interdependence by internationalizing the power to control it – in effect, to denationalize commercial policy for the benefit of the whole by ensuring that dominant cores could not subdue dependent peripheries. It was not enough to rely on the myth of enlightened self-interest separate from realities of raw power. It was too easy to moralize and to decry aggressors, to ignore the fact that they were simply exploiting a reality of the world economy: that it was composed of uneven parts, peripheries and cores, margins and metropoles, in an interdependent order that was incapable of safeguarding itself without thinking about what mercantilists had seen all along – that wealth and power were indissolubly connected. Instead, he envisioned active restraining mechanisms and real authority to curb national economic aggressors who sought to bend interdependence to their will – to create rules that placed peripheries at the centre of the concern about global interdependence in order to remove the temptations to dominate them.

If Zimmermann, Hirschman, Innis and others dreamed of an economic order that took consideration of the periphery as a vital, if exploited, component of an interdependent regime, others from the periphery argued for a more radical alternative: to dismantle the political empires that made the core-periphery relations possible. These early components of dependency theory, from the margins, got attached to anti-colonial struggles to level the global field. In so doing, ideas of world economic reform and integration acquired an altogether more adversarial turn. The crisis of the 1930s sharpened the edge of economic anti-colonialism.

Consider the example of Jawaharlal Nehru. Nehru layered on to Indian nationalism and yearnings for self-determination a critique of the wider global-imperial order, one that tied India's backwardness to its colonial status, and its colonial status to British predatory policy, which trapped India in a backward condition. His was an economic narrative that dreamed of a world free of domination as a condition of political sovereignty. In this narrative, becoming peripheral had produced underdevelopment. Being underdeveloped was not what made societies peripheral. This was a powerful shift in the vision of global economic order, one which would fuel arguments for a more radical change in the rules of interdependence after 1945.

Nehru railed against British exploitation – and his vision represented an important step in how narratives of global economic interdependence forked in the 1920s and 1930s, as one vision saw membership in global empire as a key to modernization, while others argued that only a break with empire would put colonies on the path to development. 'The only way to right [injustice and exploitation] is to do away with the domination of any one class over another', he told an audience in Lahore in 1920. 'The exploitation of India and other countries', he exclaimed in *Whither India?*, 'brought so much wealth to England that some of it trickled down to the working class and their standard of living rose'.[63] Since colonies actually lost by staying within the prevailing system, the solution was to drive the British out of India, to break with the old imperial uplift story of progress. The wave of colonial resistance from the 1930s and decolonization in the two ensuing decades ensured that this contesting narrative tradition grew and spread – to become a global rival to the one that old imperialists trumpeted. What fuelled it was the sense that the wider system was in disarray and crisis, that old empires were doomed to crack up.

In this redistributive narrative, not only did development require reversing the geographical flow of resources from the peripheries to cores, it also required an internal shakeup organized by the postcolonial state. Anti-colonialism and domestic economic planning therefore came as a package. Nehru established the National Planning Committee in 1938 as the cornerstone for the new vision of an internal and external transformation. It borrowed from the Soviet model and added elements from American mega-projects, like the Tennessee Valley Authority. When the colonial state imprisoned much of the anti-British activists, the formal planning drive got suspended. But this only cleared the way for Indian capitalists to develop their own planning fever – albeit shorn of more radical, redistributionist urges. The 1944 *Plan of Economic Development for India* was more pro-capitalist, more open to trade; but it insisted on domestic industrialization and state support to reduce dependence on the old metropole – in terms that Bunge and Sun would have easily recognized, but clad in an anti-colonial discourse they would not have. Known as the Bombay Plan it offered a competing, more moderate, contesting narrative.[64]

From the margins, therefore, came a clamour for a redistributive model of integration. This was a geographical imaginary with policy implications devoted to one part of the world – the have-nots – at the expense of another part – the haves. Justice for the margins took on an explicitly redistributionist mien, and its claims acquired more antagonistic features. To challenge deep-seated norms, rules and institutions, it fell to national planners, the new heroes of the story, to punch through the entrenched hindrances. Neo-classical economics rested on notions of flexibility, substitutability and curves upon which to plot the workings of some interchangeable, free-flowing system, tweakable and adjustable to keep the equilibrium. When it came to what would soon become called the 'Third World', the assumptions had to be flipped. There could be no fair and equitable flow of world income without a radical redistribution and redesign of the institutional structures that laced the world economy together.

Conclusion

This chapter has taken the twenty years from 1919 and 1939 as an arc that brought the idea of a periphery in a world economy into view. What started as an effort on the part of peripheral thinkers from China, Argentina, Eastern Europe and India, to think about the specifics of place and location in a global economic geography, turned into a general effort to map the world economy as comprised of differentiated spaces and units that did not share the same resources, fortunes – and fates. By the eve of the Depression there was a growing recognition that, from the periphery's perspective, integration and interdependence did not necessarily yield to convergence, understood as the uplift and equalizing of histories of the future. But once it was conceded that interdependence could produce more differentiation, it was possible to recognize the power asymmetries in the very makeup of the world economy. One further step enabled a new brand of realists to see how global economic integration could be put to the service of an altogether darker view of dependency, one which justified the brazen use of economic inequality to pursue politically aggrandizing ends. One more step in this formulation turned a concern about the fate of the peripheries into a critique of the institutions, notably empires, that strapped cores and peripheries together into regimes of asymmetrical interdependence.

It is worth noting that the view that peripheries were at the mercy of cores could cut both ways. It could justify predatory policies, condoning the strong coercing the weak. It also helped justify peripheral thinkers who challenged the benign, traditional, liberal discourse about interdependence as necessarily good for all sides. This set the stage for more radical anti-colonial thinking by the 1940s and 1950s, a strain of thinking associated with the Bandung moment and calls for the redistribution of global wealth. The result was a fundamental contest between two disparate, rivalrous and eventually warring conceptions of the world economy – and of the place of peripheries in it.

The dualist view of the world economy consisting of cores and peripheries endures. The fall of the Berlin Wall and narratives of globalization claimed to replace the old standoffs of Cold War and Third World revolutionaries with flat-world imagery of free markets and open borders. This was a view that was always more popular in financial hubs like New York, London and Hong Kong than in the *barrios* of Buenos Aires or Mumbai. But the voices of discontent were muted by the chest-thumping celebration about the end of history and the marvels of the market. The financial debacle of 2008 brought the myth to its knees and gave new life to the dualist view of the world economy. In our times, irate protesters, from the Occupy movement to the *gilets jaunes*, may sit at very different ends of the political spectrum. But they are the heirs of interwar debates and thinking about unjust integration. Those who claim to be peripheral promise to lend a voice to those left behind, to make their country great again in the global struggle for power by reversing their marginality. Economic integration and globalization, in this view, produce cores and peripheries, permitting some to rise while others fall. Not surprisingly, Western anxieties about becoming peripheral coincided with the industrialization of the former peripheries, especially China.

Narratives of economic integration and justice are not only surprisingly persistent, but also extremely powerful. As Rogers Smith has argued, 'stories of peoplehood do not merely serve interests, they also help to constitute them'.[65] Indeed, what started as an attempt to describe the economic interdependence of nations has become a powerful narrative that helps to form common identities and common interests – and to win elections. The notions of core and periphery, originally invented to visualize trade relationships between nations and regions in the quest for alternatives, have

Mapping Economic Interdependence 325

recently become dominant means of self-description and ascription, often employed to achieve and maintain power.

Notes

1 Elizabeth Zerovsky, 'The Rights of Man Are the Death of France', *New York Times Magazine*, 10 February 2019.

2 Branko Milanović, *Global Inequality: A New Approach for the Age of Globalization* (Cambridge: Harvard University Press, 2016).

3 Quinn Slobodian, 'How to See the World Economy: Statistics, Maps, and Schumpeter's Camera in the First Age of Globalization', *Journal of Global History* 10, no. 2 (2015): 307–32.

4 Charles Poor Kindleberger, *The World in Depression 1929–1939* (Berkeley: University of California Press, 1973); see also Robert Gilpin, *U.S. Power and the Multinational Corporation: The Political Economy of Foreign Direct Investment*, The Political Economy of International Relations Series (New York: Basic Books, 1975); Stephen D. Krasner, 'State Power and the Structure of International Trade', *World Politics* 28, no. 3 (April 1976): 317–47.

5 Erez Manela, *The Wilsonian Moment: Self-Determination and the International Origins of Anticolonial Nationalism* (New York: Oxford University Press, 2007).

6 Barry J. Eichengreen, *Globalizing Capital: A History of the International Monetary System* (Princeton: Princeton University Press, 1998); Dani Rodrik, *The Globalization Paradox: Why Global Markets, States, and Democracy Can't Coexist* (Oxford: Oxford University Press, 2011).

7 Luis Bértola and José Antonio Ocampo, *The Economic Development of Latin America since Independence* (Oxford: Oxford University Press, 2012).

8 Fernando Rocchi, *Chimneys in the Desert: Industrialization in Argentina during the Export Boom Years, 1870–1930* (Stanford: Stanford University Press, 2006).

9 Coming from this background, Bunge not only gathered data on the economic reality of the country, but also established fruitful ties with different institutions and experts in Europe and the United States in the 1920s and 1930s. He became a pioneer in Latin America not only because of the amount of economic information collected, but also for his role as translator of many of the most updated economic theories into the local and regional context. See Hernán González Bollo, *La teodicea estadística de Alejandro E. Bunge, 1880–1943* (Buenos Aires: Imago Mundi, 2012).

10 Argentina Dirección General de Estadística, *Intercambio Económico de La República. 1910–1917*, ed. Alejandro E. Bunge (Buenos Aires: Talleres gráficos argentinos de L. J. Rosso y cía, 1918), 8–9.

11 Alejandro E. Bunge, *Los Problemas Económicos Del Presente* (Buenos Aires: A.E. Bunge, 1920), 15.

12 While in a first work he divided the country into two regions, in the second one he mentioned three of them. See Alejandro Bunge, *La Economía Argentina*, vol. 1 (Buenos Aires: Agencia General de Librerías y Publicaciones, 1928), 89–91; Alejandro Bunge, *Una Nueva Argentina* (Buenos Aires: G. Kraft ltda, 1940), 225.

13 Bunge, *Una Nueva Argentina*, vol. 1, 225.

14 Bunge, *La Economía Argentina*, vol. 1, 117–18.

15 Bunge, *Una Nueva Argentina*, 207.

16 Despite his analysis, Bunge never used the terms 'core' and 'periphery', which would become popular after the work of one of his disciples, Raúl Prebisch, founder of the Economic Commission for Latin America and father of Latin American economic structuralism. See Joseph LeRoy Love, 'Economic Ideas and Ideologies in Latin America since the 1930s', in *The Cambridge History of Latin America*, ed. Leslie Bethell, vol. VI (New York: Cambridge University Press, 1994), 393–460.

17 Bunge dealt with this topic in two different moments. See Alejandro Bunge, *La Economía Argentina*, vol. 4 (Buenos Aires: Agencia General de Librerías y Publicaciones, 1928), 43; Bunge, *Una Nueva Argentina*, 283.

18 Bunge, *La Economía Argentina*, vol. 4, 46.

19 Sun Yat-sen, *The International Development of China* (New York: Putnam & Sons, 1922), 45.

20 John Hobson, *Imperialism: A Study* (New York: James Pott & Co., 1922).

21 Sun Yat-sen, *The International Development of China*.

22 Daniel Nicol Dunlop, 'Foreword', in *The Transactions of the First World Power Conference*, vol. 1 (London: Percy Lund Humphries & Co Ltd, 1925), ix.

23 Dunlop, 'Foreword', vii.

24 Cf., for example, the report in the newly founded British journal *Economic Geography*. 'Like seers of a single state they [the delegates] surveyed the whole field of potential power; and whether they viewed the waterfalls from the equatorial plateau of Africa and the cascades from the jagged crests of the Alps, the oil fields of America and Persia, or the coal mines of Canada and China, their broad and clear vision recognized no political boundaries, no separate sovereignties. They saw only the peoples of the world as brothers', see 'Power', *Economic Geography* 1, no. 2 (1925): 132.

25 Cf., for example, the definition by Wellington and Whittlesey, '[E]conomic geography is concerned with man quite as much as with the natural environment, and that man may make and does make a choice as to how his economic life is ordered. It should not be forgotten, however, that nature sets broad limits within which men can live and work successfully', Jones D. Wellington and D. S. Whittlesey, *An Introduction to Economic Geography* (Chicago: The University of Chicago Press, 1925).

26 Ellsworth Huntington, *Civilization and Climate* (New Haven: Yale University Press, 1915), 129–37.

27 Huntington, *Civilization and Climate*, 137.

28 Ibid., 148.

29 Ibid., 142.

30 Cf, for example, J. G. Bartholomew, *An Atlas of Economic Geography* (London: Oxford University Press, 1914), 10–11. The British geographer John Bartholomew organized different regions according to their ascribed stage of commercial development. Bartholomew described some regions as 'capable of Commercial Development but at present underdeveloped', and labelled other regions – among them large parts of North Africa, Australia, Canada, Iceland and Russia, and small parts of Latin America – as 'incapable of Commercial Development' because of their physical conditions.

31 'Wovon hat Europa in dem letzten Jahrhundert vor dem Kriege gelebt? Jedenfalls nicht aus sich selbst', noted A. Fraenkel in a 1926 article. A. Fraenkel, 'Die Bedeutung der überseeischen Märkte für Europa', *Weltwirtschaftliches Archiv* 23 (1926): 211.

32 Dunlop, 'Foreword', vii.

33 Ibid., viii.

34 Charles Camsell, 'Power Resources: Their Development and Utilization in Canada. Foreword', in *Transactions of the First World Power Conference*, vol. 1 (London: Percy Lund Humphries & Co Ltd, 1925), 157.

35 Cf., for example, 'The Power Resources of the Commonwealth of Australia and the Mandated Territory of New Guinea', in *Transactions of the First World Power Conference*, vol. 1 (London: Percy Lund Humphries & Co Ltd, 1925), 6.

36 H. N. G. Cobbe, 'Notes on the Recent Preliminary Examinations of Water Power Sites in British Guiana, South America', in *Transactions of the First World Power Conference*, vol. 1 (London: Percy Lund Humphries & Co Ltd, 1925), 148.

37 'En attendant, on espère que les pionniers industriels, les financiers, et les ingénieurs hydro-électriens ne perdent point de vue les opportunités que présente une colonie britannique, qui, située dans la région tropicale, est néanmoins salubre', wrote, for example, an engineer in his report on British Guiana, Cobbe, 'Notes on the Recent Preliminary Examinations of Water Power Sites in British Guiana, South America', 155.

38 Cf. 'Resources of European, Asiatic and South American Countries. Discussion', in *Transactions of the First World Power Conference* (London: Percy Lund Humphries & Co Ltd, 1925), 1417–23.

39 Cf., for example, Eduard Kürschner, 'General Review of the Power Resources of Yugo-Slavia, Their Present Exploitation and the Possibilities of Their Development in the Future', in *Transactions of the First World Power Conference*, vol. 1 (London: Percy Lund Humphries & Co Ltd, 1925), 1411/1412.

40 Cf. Cobbe, 'Notes on the Recent Preliminary Examinations of Water Power Sites in British Guiana, South America', 147; Dunlop, 'Foreword', vii.

41 John Donaldson, *International Economic Relations. A Treatise on World Economy and World Politics* (New York: Longmans, Green & Co., 1928), 607.

42 Cf. Joseph LeRoy Love, *Crafting the Third World. Theorizing Underdevelopment in Rumania and Brazil* (Stanford: Stanford University Press, 1996), 41.

43 Dipesh Chakrabarty, *Provincializing Europe. Postcolonial Thought and Historical Difference* (Princeton: Princeton University Press, 2000), 8.

44 Werner Sombart, *Das Wirtschaftsleben im Zeitalter des Hochkapitalismus* (Munich; Leipzig: Duncker & Humblot, 1927), 302–3.

45 Sombart, *Das Wirtschaftsleben im Zeitalter des Hochkapitalismus*, XIV; on Sombart as the first to distinguish between centre and periphery in the world economic system, see Joseph LeRoy Love, 'The Latin American Contribution to Center-Periphery Perspectives: History and Prospect', in *Cores, Peripheries, and Globalization: Essays in Honor of Ivan T. Berend*, ed. Peter Hanns Reill and Balázs A. Szelényi (Budapest; New York: Central European University Press, 2011), 26.

46 'Resources of European, Asiatic and South American Countries. Discussion', 1417.

47 George Otis Smith, 'A World of Power', *Economic Geography* 1, no. 2 (1925): 137.

48 Johannes Fabian, *Time and the Other: How Anthropology Makes Its Object* (New York: Columbia University Press, 1983).

49 Erich W. Zimmermann, *World Resources and Industries. A Functional Appraisal of the Availability of Agricultural and Industrial Resources* (New York; London: Harper & Brothers Publishers, 1933), 806.

50 Zimmermann, *World Resources and Industries*, 806.

51 Erich W. Zimmermann, 'The Resource Hierarchy of Modern World Economy', *Weltwirtschaftliches Archiv* 33 (1931): 454.

52 Zimmermann, 'The Resource Hierarchy of Modern World Economy', 435.

53 Zimmermann, *World Resources and Industries*, 807.

54 Zimmermann, 'The Resource Hierarchy of Modern World Economy', 457.

55 Otto Hölder, *Die Mathematische Methode. Logisch-Erkenntnistheoretische Untersuchungen im Gebiete der Mathematik, Mechanik und Physik* (Berlin: Julius Springer, 1924), 317.

56 Cf. Zimmermann, 'The Resource Hierarchy of Modern World Economy', 453–4.

57 Zimmermann, 'The Resource Hierarchy of Modern World Economy', 463.

58 Zimmermann, *World Resources and Industries*, 807.

59 The result, Harold A. Innis argued, was the need for a social science adapted to world geographies. See for instance 'The Teaching of Economic History in Canada', (originally published in 1929) in his *Essays in Canadian Economic History* (Toronto: University of Toronto Press, 1956), p. 3: 'A new country presents certain definite problems which appear insoluble from the standpoint of the application of economic theory as worked out in the older highly industrialized countries'.

60 Oswald Spengler, *Man and Technics. A Contribution to a Philosophy of Life* (1932; repr., New York: Alfred A. Knopf, 1963), 101–2.

61 Albert O. Hirschman, *National Power and the Structure of Foreign Trade* (Berkeley; Los Angeles: University of California Press, 1945), 79.

62 Hirschman, *National Power and the Structure of Foreign Trade*, 8.

63 Jawaharlal Nehru, 'Whither India?' (1933), in *India's Freedom* (London: Unwin Books, 1962), 21.

64 David C. Engerman, *The Price of Aid: The Economic Cold War in India* (Cambridge: Harvard University Press, 2018), 27–8.

65 Rogers M. Smith, *Stories of Peoplehood: The Politics and Morals of Political Membership*, Contemporary Political Theory (Cambridge; New York: Cambridge University Press, 2003), 45.

Coda: Narratives in an embattled world

Dominic Sachsenmaier

Pressures on globalization narratives

There are times when dominant narratives seem to have lost touch with the world they claim to describe. The people who once had propounded them fall silent or lose interest and switch to other paradigms, and in a parallel move, their opponents no longer treat them as powerful threats. Within a rather short period of time, narratives that had been widely recognized as powerful visions for the future can seem to belong to the past. They are ready to be moved from political battlefields, debating halls and sites of social resistance to the historian's work desk.

Probably, we are currently living through transformations of this scale. As Jeremy Adelman and Andreas Eckert discuss in their introduction to this volume, many narratives related to globalization have lost much of their earlier standing – and their shaping powers. The authors identify a variety of factors for the decline of the globalization narrative and argue that its demise stems from a combination of long-term developments and short-term events. They stress that earlier assumptions of the weakening roles of national politics and states have proven to be wrong and that national narratives have returned powerfully to the global stage. They outline how nationalism has emerged as an important reservoir for currents flowing from diverse political springs such as identity politics and social protest movements. As a result, they say, of a complex network of multiple developments occurring in many parts of the world, 'the language of the nation became the rhetoric of resistance' to globalization.[1] At the same time, Adelman and Eckert emphasize that concrete regional or global crises further eroded the fundaments of the earlier globalization narrative. In this context, they emphasize the impact of the global financial crisis of 2008, which they argue visibly weakened the idea that the world's future would be characterized by global integration. In other words, global moments, that is, events that are relevant to many parts of the world, have led to an erosion of assumptions related to the idea of globalization.

While the globalization narrative was not completely dead in the late 2010s, new political, social and economic realities have further marginalized its presence. The corona pandemic and the Ukraine War have particularly eroded the expectation that worldwide integration processes would eventually render the nation-state obsolete.

During the two main crises of the early 2020s, notions of the globally most influential social milieus changed. We can assume that after the re-empowerment of states and military forces, multinational corporations and other globalization drivers are no longer the main objects of global concern. Instead, the possibility of major inter-state conflicts or even new world wars evokes much greater fear. As part of the same shift in expectations, narratives about the world's most powerful groups are no longer the same as before. Whereas in the early 2010s it was still possible to imagine social groups like investment bankers, business consultants and world travellers as the globally most powerful groups of our time, now their place has been taken by state ministers, generals and other decision-makers intrinsically connected to state power. In the past few years, many national governments have shown that they can put great limits on the global agency of major corporations. The latter no longer appear as unrelenting forces that drive the world further towards neoliberal integration; rather, public debates have shifted to concepts like global polarization and 'de-globalization'. Moreover, the imagined temporalities of the present have changed: while the era of globalization was widely defined as post-Cold War, the Cold War is now increasingly mentioned as a comparison that can help us conceptualize our global future. Terms like 'New Cold War' have become buzzwords in the discussions about the future patterns of world order, and they quite frequently appear in publication titles.[2]

When people discuss the 'end of globalization', they usually mean that a short period of three to four decades is coming to an end. While it is possible to think of 'globalization' in much longer historical terms,[3] that concept often connotes more specifically an age of neoliberal dominance in the world economy and global politics. Quite in line with this, the concept of 'globalization' has its own global history, and it isn't very long. The origins of the expression are unclear, and scholars still disagree on where – and in what language – it was coined. But the search for the early history of the term is just a hunt for a historical detail: what really matters is its border-crossing, ever-growing presence in the first decades after the end of the Cold War. If hardly anyone had heard of 'globalization' during the early 1980s, by the start of the millennium the term had become a global phenomenon.[4] It got translated into an exceptionally wide range of languages and was highly important in very varied professional and social contexts. Japanese businessmen referred to 'globalization' just as Canadian academics did, so did Turkish journalists, Indian activists and Brazilian politicians. The term seemed to be as young as it was ubiquitous; it smacked of connectivity and neoliberalism, and the speed of its worldwide spread seemed to symbolize global futures that were already in the offing.

Competing visions of globalization

Obviously, widely spread narratives are not monolithic and aren't disseminated across the world with identical contents and storylines. Just as there are no uniform articulations of nationhood, there has never been a singular globalization narrative. What there is exists as a wealth of assumptions, tropes and concepts. It is impossible to compress the 'globalization narrative' into a clear-cut definition, but we can still dissect some key assumptions that have been linked to globalization.[5] Among them was the idea that global capitalism, especially through the activities of multinational corporations, was becoming more powerful than political players in general and nation-states in particular. There was also the expectation that, for better or for worse, global connections constituted the most important transformative forces, that they had the potential to profoundly alter the nature of political, social and cultural belonging, and that this process would lead to social and political formations that would – while hard to predict in their exact forms – be definitely post-national in character.[6]

Widely circulated narratives typically get disseminated by a multitude of players (social groups, political camps, professional milieus, etc.) that have few elements in common and which may not even agree on basic values.[7] The globalization narrative is no exception: Its main elements were shared by a broad range of groups with distinctly different views of globalization. There were many voices that warned of its negative potential and concluded that the forces of global integration (at least in the forms visible in the 1990s and early 2000s) needed to be reversed. One very influential critique was that a massive spread of global corporate structures would disempower the political sector and work against the interests of the vast majority of people around the world. In many countries, significant movements on the left expressed great concerns that in an age of neoliberalism, corporate giants would have the potential to bypass state policies and that they, by implication, could afford to ignore social responsibilities. The widespread critique that globalization would inevitably deepen the gaps between the world's haves and have-nots was typically tied to a host of related concerns. Among those were, for example, the idea that corporate globalization would enhance the hegemonic powers of the West, most notably the United States, an idea that was often linked to the assumption that globalization would not erode political power everywhere, but would help Washington amass even more of it. Other groups highlighted globalization's negative impact on the environment, pointing to factors ranging from pressures on biodiversity to the threat of global warming.

On the other side of the globalization narrative were groups that, even as they acknowledged the problems emanating from global corporate structures, saw some positive potential in the supposedly declining role of nation-states and the prospect of an increasingly boundaryless world. Some academic circles pointed to the new possibilities that came with global public spheres and believed that a global *demos* could potentially be formed that would eventually place planetary concerns like environmental protectionism onto national policymaking.[8] For those who believed the power of the nation-state was waning anyhow, it seemed reasonable to imagine that new social movements would have a realistic chance to create a better world order, one no longer based primarily on inter-state relations and hegemonies.

From a different background and heading in a different direction, some in business circles also threw their weight behind globalization. Some not only developed economic visions, but saw – or claimed to see – the prospect of global integration as a way to overcome many sociopolitical challenges. For example, a document entitled 'Globalization: Threat or Opportunity' published by the International Monetary Fund in 2000 came to the following conclusion:

As globalization has progressed, living conditions (particularly when measured by broader indicators of wellbeing) have improved significantly in virtually all countries. However, the strongest gains have been made by the advanced countries and only some of the developing countries. ... But it is wrong to jump to the conclusion that globalization has caused the divergence, or that nothing can be done to improve the situation. ... The international community should endeavor – by strengthening the international financial system, through trade, and through aid – to help the poorest countries integrate into the world economy, grow more rapidly, and reduce poverty. That is the way to ensure all people in all countries have access to the benefits of globalization.[9]

It would be possible to map out in more detail the patterns and rhythms in the range of globalization narratives during the long turn of the millennium, that is, the last decades of the twentieth and the first decades of the twenty-first century. As all decent global historical scholarship does, we could look more closely at both local specificities and border-crossing entanglements, focusing within this framework on different social carrier groups, professional contexts and public spheres within which key assumptions about globalization were being disseminated. Case studies could investigate business circles, academic networks, political parties, religious groups, nongovernmental organizations and other agents that defined themselves at least partly by their position on neoliberalism and, more specifically, the idea of globalization. The results would deepen our insights into a wealth of transfers and exchanges that characterized the era in which globalization was accompanied by the transformation of communication (public and private), first through the internet and then by social media channels.

The reterritorialization of political consciousness

Additional research on the dissemination of globalization narratives would also bring to light more details, locally and globally, about the great struggles between deterritorialization and reterritorialization of power that have come to characterize our still young twenty-first century.[10] We still do not fully understand the processes that led to a significant change of direction: that the nation-state's significance first seemed to be diminished by the forces of deterritorialization and globalization, but that now, instead of the end of the nation-state, people are debating the end of globalization. As I argue later in this article, this curve towards post-national and then re-national narratives didn't take place all over the world, but was still one of the most powerful political transformations of our time. The crises of 2008 and the early 2020s accelerated this transformation, but the demise of the globalization narrative has been complex and protracted, a process without a clear beginning or end. As early as the late 1990s and early 2000s, scholars debated aspects of de-globalization, even using this term in publication titles.[11] True, the majority of people referring to deglobalization in these years pointed to some local exceptions to a general trend, while others only brought up 'deglobalization' as a counter-vision to the ongoing forces of globalization.[12] But the expectation that global integration had its limits and that it would be a reversible process, is arguably as old as the globalization narrative itself. What has changed is the relative strength of each narrative.

Similar things can be said about another big trend that has been entangled with the declining weight of the globalization narrative and the stratification of political consciousness, namely the growing importance of national imaginaries and the re-empowerment of state agencies. Particularly in its global-local, or glocal, dimensions, this major transformation is still not sufficiently understood. As Adelman and Eckert mention, forces on both the left and the right pushed the nation-state back into the centre of political power. What is more, the growing emphasis on national political agendas has been accompanied on both sides by critiques of globalization. To be sure, there are great differences between the left- and right-wing critiques: Narratives on the left are typically not opposed to any kind of internationalism but to the neoliberal forces of globalization. Right-wing critiques of globalization, on the other hand, are often accompanied by ethno-centrism and cultural essentialism – and usually reject more broadly visions of alternative globalization.

While the basic differences between the two camps are well known, a detailed exploration of some key narratives would help us better understand the complex reconfigurations on the political left and the political right that many states and societies have witnessed in the past two or three decades. To a high degree, these developments were locally specific and conditioned by conditions in single national arenas. In countries like France, established parties on the political left and right disintegrated, giving rise to new parties that are hard to define as either left or right. In other countries, left- and right-wing parties united to defend the nation against international oppression. A prominent example occurred during the Greek financial crisis when Alexis Tsipras led a coalition government from 2015 to 2019 based on alliances that had been long been unthinkable in Athens. Tsipras was a member of Syriza, a party formed in the early 2000s as a coalition of radical and more moderate left-wing forces that was dominated by pro-EU forces. In 2015, Syriza entered a coalition government with a decidedly patriotic and Eurosceptic party called the Independent Greeks – National Patriotic Alliance (ANEL).[13] Throughout their joint governance, the relationship between the parties was tense, but in addition to political pragmatism, their coalition was held together by the idea that Athens needed to fight for the rights of the common Greek people against international exploitative systems, notably the European Union, but also institutions like the International Monetary Fund.[14] While ideological differences remained (for instance, in attitudes towards immigrants), the Greek case shows how left-wing internationalist visions and right-wing ethno-culturalist identities could find common ground in defining the nation as a territory of resistance against larger forces of international capital.

Greece has been an outlier in a rather powerful global trend because its leading party, while emphasizing the nation-state, retained an allegiance to some kind of socialist internationalist vision. In most other countries that experienced a neo-national turn, the reconfiguration of politics has brought decidedly right-wing, neo-authoritarian movements to power. In some cases, new interactions between the political left and right strengthened the latter: In Turkey, some former leftist parties ended up as staunch supporters of Erdogan's authoritarian AKP, which enforced many

Islamist policies and had a strong and religiously grounded nationalist rhetoric. At the same time, Erdogan's party presented itself as the true advocate of the poor, and indeed for a while it strengthened the Turkish welfare sector. Similar things could be said about Modi's Bharatiya Janata Party in India or Bolsonaro's Partido Liberal in Brazil. This alleged socialist vein of right-wing movements is nothing new: in many cases during the twentieth century, right-wing movements incorporated left-wing political language and positioned themselves as the true advocates of the masses. The new emphasis on national interests is usually connected with a narrative that suggests that it is necessary to take a particular country back from global interest groups.[15] Compared to the new creed that sees the nation-state as an endangered space that needs to be protected through self-empowerment, the early 2000s visions of a global civil society look rather pale. They linger on in currents such as the Fridays-For-Future Movement, but in many parts of the world, the momentum is clearly on the side of nationalists.

It is very hard to come up with a clear typology of neo-nationalist movements, and it might even be harder to think globally about the root causes of their rather synchronous rise. Politicians who rallied against international treaties like Donald Trump (against the Transatlantic Trade and Investment Partnership) and Boris Johnson (pro Brexit) came to power in large economies like the United States and Great Britain that in the earlier globalization narrative had been seen as strongholds of neoliberalism. But shifts towards neo-national politics also occurred in wealthy welfare states like Sweden or France and in places with rather poor economies and a highly unequal income distribution like Brazil and the Philippines. They grew fast in secularized societies like the Netherlands, but also experienced a triumphant rise in countries like India, Israel and Turkey, where religious forces actively supported right-wing leaders.

The few elements that all these arenas of neo-nationalism have in common all relate to political communication.[16] The advent of social media had a huge impact on political cultures around the world, and as a new form of mass-communication they opened the way for additional forms of demagogy, the fostering of stereotypes and the manipulation of mass identities.[17] In the early days of the internet, many scholars believed that the new online communication would accelerate the demise of nation-states, and similar points were made about the advent of the social media a few years later. In reality, however, the new communication technologies may have been a major force underlying the reterritorialization of politics – even though they originally figured as powerful symbols of a borderless world. It will probably take historical scholarship time to explore in detail (globally and locally) the connections between new communication media and the waning presence of globalization narratives.[18]

Neo-nationalism and power politics

While the nation-state has been often invoked as a stronghold of resistance to the forces of globalization, its potential for self-empowerment varies widely in different parts of the world. Much depended on circumstances, and these, of course, can differ dramatically, not only in terms of local factors like political cultures and systems of governance but also in terms of the potential for state agency. On the extreme end, there are countries – particularly in parts of Sub-Saharan Africa or Central Asia – where the state has failed to serve as a stabilizing institution and nationhood is not widely recognized as a promising form of peoplehood.[19] In cases like Afghanistan or Somalia, national narratives are hardly mobilized in defence of local interests, and forms of religious, ethnic or clan-type belonging are much stronger than national affiliations.

Then there are a large number of countries where the state is institutionally functional but internationally feeble, which is highly significant in an era of mounting global conflicts. In these states, influential political narratives portray the nation-state as the only realistic form of shelter in stormy times, but they cannot possibly suggest that the state can act as an independent player on the international stage. A wide array of countries, ranging from Canada to Hungary to South Korea, fall into this category: Some are economically or even fiscally reliant on transnational bodies like the European Union or ASEAN; some depend on military protection through alliances like NATO. For neo-nationalist groups in such countries, there is a tension between two main narratives: On one hand, the new commitment to the nation-state is partly based on the idea that globalization undermined the political sector's authority and worked against the interest of the common people. On the other hand, it is increasingly clear that even the scenario of a completely post-global world (however that may look like) would not mean radical national independence, and that the threats seemingly presented by global capitalism could also be found in more regional economic blocks or security systems. Such structural contradictions will likely shape much of the domestic situation in states around the world and will probably have a large impact on important political narratives. In most states, articulations of national pride cannot possibly come with radical national sovereignty, which means that many newly elected right-wing governments will fall short of their election promises.

The third category of countries are nation-states in which, after the collapse of globalization narratives, political groups can at least claim that a renewed emphasis on national agency can give them the ability to unilaterally shape the world around them. Very few countries fall into this category. Certainly the United States and China, the two rival powers of our current age, do, and also in states like in India and Russia, the idea of the nation as a completely sovereign entity doesn't sound entirely absurd and hence is an essential ingredient in political debates. Social and political groups in such powers can present radically nationalist visions without having to consider the logics and necessities of international co-dependencies. What they come up with won't necessarily correspond to political and economic realities, but they have the necessary narrative space to articulate these positions.

Discrepancies between claims and reality or expectations and possibilities can lead to grave miscalculations, however. The war in Ukraine is arguably the most significant example of our current age: The Kremlin decision to launch a full-scale attack on its southwestern neighbour in February 2022 was based on a complex amalgam of assumptions, but Russia's widely narrated belief that it is a great power with the ability and right to shape its surrounding macro-region played a crucial role. Russian militarism and authoritarianism have a strong domestic history, with Putin's policies having long been backed by significant parts of society and powerful institutions that include large parts of the Orthodox Church.[20] Many narratives that provide the discursive support structure for the Kremlin's policies have grown from these internal seedbeds, some of which seek to connect the Russian future with Soviet or even imperial Tsarist traditions.

At the same time, the origins of the current Russian political climate also relate to international entanglements that date from when the globalization narrative dominated. The effort to introduce a neoliberal order at a staggering pace during the early 1990s had a lasting impact on many former Soviet societies, most notably Russia.[21] There the so-called 'shock therapy' led to an economic crisis of historic proportions, with the poverty rate climbing by a staggering 2,500 per cent between 1988 and 1994, so that eventually about half the population fell into that category.[22] This fostered an opinion climate in which globalization and all the transformations commonly associated with that term, including Westernization, were broadly seen as inimical to national interests. This development also affected institutions commonly associated with the term 'globalization', including Western influence, a market economy and the rule of law. What this meant is that already in the early 1990s, some of the most important political narratives in Russia turned explicitly against the idea of global integration and towards the idea of nationhood, glorifying the latter as the only historically legitimate, politically honest and ultimately reliable vision for the future.

Not from global to national: Narrative trajectories in China

China's experiences in the age of globalization differ profoundly from Russia's. Since the Reform and Opening Period during the 1980s, the graphs of the Chinese economy have pointed a very different direction. Until a few years ago, the nominal GDP of the People's Republic was growing by an average of about 10 per cent a year, and in a mere four decades, the country's total economic output has grown about forty to fifty times. Just when Russia dove into the economic abyss, around 1993 to 1994, the Chinese economy experienced record growth rates of 13 or even 14 per cent per annum.[23] This development not only turned the Chinese economy into the world's second largest, it profoundly altered the relationship between Russia and China. While in 1995, the Russian economy was – despite the sharp economic downturn in the preceding years – still more than 40 per cent of the Chinese economy, the latter is now ten times larger than the Russian Federation's. And while in the 1990s, the Russian GDP per capita was still substantially larger than China's, the difference is now merely 20 per cent.

The massive disproportion between the Chinese and Russian economies has had great implications for the relationship between the two countries, which is now dominated by Beijing and is often discussed as an example of shifting global powers.[24] But I want to take the interpretation of this data in a different direction and focus on the relationship between notions of globalization and nationhood on both sides of the Amur River. Whereas in Russia, the integration into the world market was managed as an instant shift towards neoliberal policies, the Chinese economy was opened much more slowly, and similar things could be said about its integration into the global economy. During the early 1990s, the central government in Beijing watched the situation in Russia very carefully, drawing the lesson that economic reforms needed to remain under political tutelage and that the Chinese Communist Party (CCP) should not loosen the political and fiscal reins too fast. For a while, the party released its control over the economy only gradually, and only within a controlled space, it gave the private sector some leeway to work out its own version of internationalization. The latter hasn't been an irreversible process: recently, the CCP has become far more restrictive vis-à-vis private companies, as part of its broader turn towards authoritarian policies.

For several decades after the end of the Cold War, the main Chinese narratives pertaining to globalization and the nation differed dramatically not only from Russia, but from broader global trends. In Chinese narratives, globalization was not typically understood as a force that would deepen the gaps between the world's haves and have-nots or a process that served Western hegemony. Generally speaking, globalization and nation-building were not treated as rival forces but as parts of the same process. The historian Wang Jiafeng phrased this mindset as 'the more national, the more global',[25] and many Chinese scholars and public figures came to a similar conclusion during the late 1990s and at least the first decade of the 2000s. They treated globalization not as a process that would ultimately undermine the capabilities of the nation-state, but as a force that could potentially empower it. More specifically, globalization was frequently interpreted as the latest form of modernization processes that, the assumption went, would ultimately render states more competitive and hence give them more agency in a world that otherwise would be dominated by the old club of the advanced economies.[26] Quite a few voices expressed the hope that through globalization, China would finally gain much-desired international agency, while at the same time its society and economy would change as the result of international influences.[27]

There are several relevant historical backgrounds for the combination of nationalism and globalism that characterized many important narratives in China around the long turn of the millennium. First, there is the general historical background of Chinese nationalism: Starting from the late 1800s or early 1900s, when Chinese modernizers argued that the ailing Qing Empire had to be transformed into a modern state, they presented the nationhood as something China needed to emulate and learn from the great powers of the world. A growing number of intellectuals understood nation-building, ranging from infrastructure projects to the cultivation of a new historiography, as an endeavour that should be inspired by allegedly successful modernizers like Great Britain, France, the United States and Japan.[28] Many key concepts for the new national era – including the term for 'nation' itself (*guojia*) – demonstrated these close international connections, since they were either newly created, mimicked globally circulating terms or were taken from Japanese reinterpretations of older Chinese terms.[29] To be sure, none of the main protagonists on China's political and intellectual stage seriously believed in the idea of modernization as profound Westernization: Most maintained that China had to find its own path into modernity, and that foreign models should be adapted to the specific cultural, social and political conditions of the former Qing empire. Moreover, the visionaries of the early twentieth century were far from operating with concepts like globalization, but they started a

338 *Narratives, Nations, and Other World Products*

tradition of conceptualizing nation-building, international connectedness and global transformation as closely related processes.

During the early or mid-1900s, this close affiliation between nationalism and the belief in deeper international connections was not unusual, and similar currents can be observed in many countries in Africa, Asia and elsewhere. But in the Chinese case, the idea of an intrinsic link between nationalist and internationalist visions has been very resilient, so that even during the heyday of the globalization narrative, the concept of the nation remained widely unchallenged. One reason for the resilience of the synthesis between nationhood and globalism was China's paths and patterns during the second half of the twentieth century. Under Mao, the Chinese Communist Party positioned itself as a highly experimental force that would embark on both radical domestic transformations and a profound reshaping of the global order. The Cultural Revolution can be read as one such episode, with the radical attacks on most symbols of Chinese tradition and the crackdown on artists and intellectuals accompanied by attempts to posit Maoism as a global ideology.[30] A few years after Mao's death, under Deng Xiaoping, the Chinese Communist Party broke with many principles of Maoism, as Bao Maohong discusses in more detail in his contribution to this volume,[31] but the narrative that it took particularly daring steps within the encounter zone of China and the world remained. The market reforms and the shift to developmentalism of the 1980s walked many untried paths, and they were presented as such, perhaps most famously expressed in Deng's famous dictum that China needed to 'grope for stones while crossing the river'.

A major component of Deng's experiment was that it was a controlled experiment, and on that basis, his government tried to connect the future of the nation with some form of globalization. Even as the Chinese Communist Party opened ever-wider sectors of society and the economy, it remained in charge. Deng and the other leaders agreed that they needed to leave much of the political sector, especially party rule, untouched as they embarked on changes that they often defined as the outcome of globalization. While the Chinese Communist Party did experience some change (for instance, it began admitting private entrepreneurs as members in the early 2000s), it was determined to keep massive societal and economic transformations from compromising Chinese sovereignty. The upper echelons looked not only to Russia, but to the Chinese past, particularly the century between the Opium Wars and the Civil War, seeing both as outcomes that had to be avoided. As Xavier Paulès explores in his multifaceted study in this volume, that century is often narrated as a time of humiliation, fragmentation and a loss of China's agency to international players.[32] The CCP positions itself as a historical force that can successfully place China into a globalizing world while simultaneously strengthening the People's Republic's agency. For several decades, it looked as if this would indeed be possible: in contrast to small or mid-sized countries, China's massive demographic and geographical weight (and the PRC's substantial market size) made it possible for Beijing to maintain an unusually high level of unilateral power under the conditions of globalization. For many Chinese viewers, national power seemed to grow because of globalization.

Within that general framework, the term 'globalization' or *quanqiuhua* in Chinese, could mean many different things and sustain many different narratives. The Chinese government liked to depict globalization as a wave that the PRC could ride more successfully than other countries, and use, so the narrative went, to create a new degree of self-empowerment. Corporate players liked to describe globalization as new market opportunities, both abroad (for Chinese firms) and at home, where foreign investors would help create new opportunities for the Chinese labour market. For that reason, Chinese labour was typically not opposed to globalization, seeing it as offering new job opportunities and rising living standards, greater mobility and the prospect of joining the global middle classes. Even intellectuals and civil society groups who were more or less openly opposed to one-party rule usually saw globalization favourably. They hoped that growing global connections would bring greater degrees of diversity in Chinese society and that more international travellers flowing in and out of China would make it harder for Beijing to isolate the country and resort to authoritarian rule.

Well into the 2010s, few significant political, social or economic groups in China regarded globalization as a threat to nationhood. To the contrary, a broad range of groups supported globalization in the name of nation-building, even as they fundamentally disagreed over basic political values and their historicity. For instance, some circles inside and outside the government still define present-day China as largely shaped by twentieth-century revolutions[33] while others prefer to think in terms of longer civilizational continuities.[34] Yet both camps – and other groups on opposite sides such as party loyalists and democratic reformists, neoliberal entrepreneurs and steadfast communists – see promise in the concept of globalization, often including it in their narratives about the future of the Chinese state and society. A pro-globalization outlook could mean hope for a more pluralistic, less authoritarian China, but it could also imply a triumphalist version of nationalism closely tied to visions of the PRC as the new global superpower.

Starting in the early 2020s, this basic situation changed, as China began experiencing a wide range of crises. The economy is no longer as dynamic as during the golden decades of the Chinese economic miracle, and this slowdown quickly translates into social pressure: Youth unemployment has risen to a staggering 20 per cent, and migrant workers can no longer be sure to find jobs in cities. For a variety of reasons (the pandemic, mounting tensions with the United States, etc.), foreign investors have moved out of China, and the number of international residents has dwindled. At the same time, the Chinese government has stepped up its authoritarian policies and developed new forms of control over the education system, the internet and social media, and cultural life. In addition, the Chinese media are increasingly debating a major military conflict with the United States and other powers as a realistic scenario.

In these multiple crises and the macro-narratives that come with them, the concept of globalization is not central. As the key domestic struggles have moved on to other themes, few agents express a strong opposition to globalization (however it might be defined); they don't bother, because the concept is no longer important for their political agendas. This might suggest that now, in China as elsewhere, narratives of nationhood have grown at the expense of narratives of globalization and that the two are no longer seen as connected. In the future, some of the main political visionaries in China might increasingly come to define the prospects of global connection and nation-building as a zero-sum game.

340 *Narratives, Nations, and Other World Products*

Going further than that, it might even be the case that Chinese nationalistic narratives increasingly turn against narratives of the global. We can see hints of that in the political landscapes of Hong Kong after the crackdown on the protests in 2019 and 2020.[35] Anti-China protesters frequently narrate Hong Kong as a global city that has long served as a bridge between China and the world at large and thus did not fully belong to either side, which – one influential narrative goes – was one of the main reasons for its economic successes in the age of globalization. But the PRC government and many chauvinistic voices in China often portray Hong Kong as one of the most significant sites of China's century of humiliation. This allows for narratives that depict Hong Kong's globality as a source of chaos and support the idea that the Chinese state needs to restore order. In other words, the nation is presented as a great antithesis to globalism, and in the Chinese case, this comes along with an increasingly muscular rhetoric about the PRC's economic and military power.

Uncertain futures

In their introduction, Jeremy Adelman and Andreas Eckert point out that 'in a competitive, overheating and now plague-filled world, citizens have been left to find shelter in the bosom of the nation – and summoned to its defense'. Indeed, militarization, self-strengthening and even authoritarian rule are some of the most powerful trends of our time, and narratives play a major part in this newest version of the great game. Global futures remain highly uncertain; virtually anything seems possible. We could enter another era of great power rivalries or even global war, but it is also possible that the forces behind the current resurgence of the nation-state will run out of steam. Perhaps the current impulse to hold tightly to nations and states as visionary concepts will grow weaker, because like globalization before, the forces of statehood will prove unable to solve the real problems of our time. A radically Westphalian state system will almost certainly have a harder time solving shared planetary problems like global warming or refugee crises than a transnationally entangled one, and the weaknesses of the national principle may become more apparent than they are now.

One can at least hope that the dominance of neo-national paradigms might prove weaker than it currently appears. Just as the era dominated by globalization saw multiple narratives, the current crescendo of nation-centred outlooks is not monolithic. As discussed, the trajectories of national narratives and even articulations of authoritarianism differ significantly around the world, so that what currently looks like a powerful global transformation might break apart into different trajectories, some of which could again be postnational in character. There are already many cracks apparent in our neo-national world: Many kinds of agents – intellectuals, activists and businesspeople, just to name a few – are opposed to the current renationalization project, and at least for the time being, powerful transnational political institutions remain in place. In addition, far more than during the 1930s, today's world is characterized by strong border-crossing social communities like migrant networks and diasporic communities. Like global intellectual networks, social movements and even multinational economic players, they may turn out to be significant counterforces to the reterritorialization of politics. Only time will tell how far the current forces of fragmentation and polarization will take this world.

Notes

1 Jeremy Adelman and Andreas Eckert, 'A World of Narratives', 1–16.
2 For example, Ho-fung Hung, *Clash of Empires: From 'Chimerica 'to the 'New Cold War'* (Cambridge: Cambridge University Press, 2022); and Seth Schindler, Jessica DiCarlo, and Dinesh Paudel, 'The New Cold War and the Rise of the 21st-century Infrastructure State', *Transactions of the Institute of British Geographers* 47, no. 2 (June 2022): 331–46.
3 For overviews of this topic, see for example Sebastian Conrad, *What Is Global History?* (Princeton: Princeton University Press, 2016), 141–62; and Pamela Kyle Crossley, *What Is Global History?* (Cambridge: Polity Press, 2007).
4 For a brief account, see Dominic Sachsenmaier, *Global Perspectives on Global History: Theories and Approaches in a Connected World* (Cambridge: Cambridge University Press, 2011), 66–7.
5 Quite a number of overviews and collections of relevant debates have been published, for example Frank J. Lechner and John Boli, eds., *The Globalization Reader* (Hoboken, NJ: John Wiley & Sons, 2020); and John Benyon and David Dunkerley, *Globalization: The Reader* (London: Routledge, 2014).
6 Some prominent theorists (many of whom remained highly critical of the prospect of globalization) opined that new forces of connectivity like cheaper international travel and novel communication technologies would bring about a new information age and a global network society. See for example, Manuel Castells, *The Rise of the Network Society, the Information Age: Economy, Society, and Culture*, vol. I (Cambridge, MA; Oxford, UK: Blackwell, 1996); and Bruce Mazlish, *The Idea of Humanity in a Global Era* (New York: Palgrave Macmillan, 2009).
7 For overviews of theories and methods for the study of narratives, see for example David Herman, et al., *Narrative Theory: Core Concepts and Critical Debates* (Columbus: Ohio State University Press, 2012).
8 For example, Richard Falk and Andrew Strauss, 'Toward Global Parliament', *Foreign Affairs* 80, no. 1 (2001): 212–20; Mary Kaldor, 'The Idea of Global Civil Society', *International Affairs* 79, no. 3 (2003): 583–93; and Jan Aart Scholte, 'Global Civil Society', *Globalization: Critical Concepts in Sociology* 3 (2003): 279–302.
9 IMF Staff, 'Globalization: Threat or Opportunity?', *IMF Issues Briefs*, published 12 April 2000, https://www.imf.org/external/np/exr/ib/2000/041200to.htm (accessed 20 September 2023).
10 On this topic, see for example Charles Maier, *Once Within Borders: Territories of Power, Wealth, and Belonging since 1500* (Cambridge, MA: The Belknap Press of Harvard University Press, 2016).
11 For instance, Michel S. Laguerre, 'Japantown: The Deglobalization of an Ethnopole', in *The Global Ethnopolis: Chinatown, Japantown and Manilatown in American Society*, ed. Michel S. Laguerre (London: Palgrave Macmillan, 2000), 53–75; or Karen Fog Olwig, 'Narrating Deglobalization: Danish Perceptions of a Lost Empire', *Global Networks: A Journal of Transnational Affairs* 3, no. 3 (June 2003): 207–22.

12 Others referred to 'deglobalization' primarily as an important alternative vision for the future – for example: Lord Meghnad Desai, 'The Possibility of Deglobalization', in *Globalization, Social Capital and Inequality: Contested Concepts, Contested Experiences*, ed. Wilfred Dolfsma and Charlie Dannreuther (Northampton, MA: Edward Elgar, 2003), 1–14; and Walden Bello, *Deglobalization: Ideas for a New World* (London: Zed Books, 2002).

13 See for example Paris Aslanidis and Cristóbal Rovira Kaltwasser, 'Dealing with Populists in Government: The SYRIZA-ANEL Coalition in Greece', *Democratization* 23, no. 6 (March 2016): 1077–91; and Yannis Stavrakakis and Giorgos Katsambekis, 'Left-wing Populism in the European Periphery: The Case of SYRIZA', *Journal of Political Ideologies* 19, no. 2 (June 2014): 119–42.

14 For some reflections on the political rhetoric of the early Tsipras government, see Dimitrios Kotroyannos, 'Alexis Tsipras und der rhetorische Diskurs als Politik (Alexis Tsipras and the Rhetorical Discourse as Politics)', 16 April 2016, available at SSRN: https://ssrn.com/abstract=2768793.

15 While anti-refugee politics can be interpreted as a form as anti-globalism, many right-wing governments also position themselves against historically rooted local minorities. An example are the anti-Muslim policies of the BJP in India. See for instance Milan Vaishnav, *The BJP in Power: Indian Democracy and Religious Nationalism* (Washington, DC: Carnegie Endowment for International Peace, 2019). Retrieved from https://carnegieendowment. org/files/BJP_In_Power_final.pdf, accessed June 18 (2023).

16 See for example, Ekaterina Zhuravskaya, Maria Petrova, and Ruben Enikolopov, 'Political Effects of the Internet and Social Media', *Annual Review of Economics* 12, no. 1 (August 2020): 415–38; and Shelley Boulianne, 'Revolution in the Making? Social Media Effects across the Globe', *Information, Communication & Society* 22, no. 1 (2019): 39–54.

17 Needless to say, also the traditional print media, television and the radio made forms of mass-demagogy possible, but the social media add another layer (and audiovisual form) of political manipulation.

18 Significant research energy, particularly in the social sciences, has been spent on exploring the globality of recent right-wing movements, but much of this work is based on classic comparative perspectives that tend to treat single cases as isolated units of analysis.

19 Generally, on a typology of states: Francis Fukuyama, *State-Building, Governance and World Order in the 21st Century* (Ithaca: Cornell University Press, 2014). On Afghanistan, see for example Thomas J. Barfield, *Afghanistan: A Cultural and Political History*, 2nd edition (Princeton: Princeton University Press, 2023).

20 See for example Marlene Laruelle, *Russian Nationalism: Imaginaries, Doctrines, and Political Battlefields* (London: Taylor & Francis, 2019). While the political right is strong in Russia, it would be erroneous to downplay the divisions between different political camps there. On this topic see, for example, Samuel A. Greene and Graeme B. Robertson, *Putin v. the People: The Perilous Politics of a Divided Russia* (New Haven, CT: Yale University Press, 2019).

21 For more details, see for example Philipp Ther, *How the West Lost the Peace: The Great Transformation since the Cold War*, trans. Jessica Spengler (London: Polity, 2023), particularly 139–57.

22 See Clara E. Mattei, *The Capital Order: How Economists Invented Austerity and Paved the Way to Fascism* (Chicago: University of Chicago Press, 2022); and Naomi Klein,

The Shock Doctrine: The Rise of Disaster Capitalism (New York: Henry Holt and Company, 2007).

23   The data of the World Bank, the International Monetary Fund and the United Nations slightly differ from one another, but the main picture is the same.

24   Artyom Lukin, 'The Russia-China Entente and its Future', *International Politics* 58, no. 3 (June 2021): 363–80.

25   Wang Jiafeng, 'Some Reflection on Modernization Theory and Globalization Theory', *Chinese Studies in History* 43, no. 1 (2009): 92.

26   For example, Pu Changgen, 'Quanqiuhua yu zhongguo yingdui' [Globalization and Chinese Responses], *Yazhou yanjiu* [Asian Studies] 44 (2002): 7–23; and Cao, Tianyu, *Xiandaihua, quanqiuhua yu zhongguo daolu* [Modernization, Globalization and China's Path] (Beijing: Shehui kexue wenxian chubanshe, 2003). See also Yan Yunxiang, 'Managed Globalization: State Power and Cultural Transition in China', in *Many Globalizations: Cultural Diversity in the Contemporary World*, ed. Peter Berger and Samuel Huntington (New York; Oxford: Oxford University Press, 2002), 19–47.

27   See for example Liu Kang, *Globalization and Cultural Trends in China* (Honolulu: University of Hawai'i Press, 2004); see also Sachsenmaier, *Global Perspectives on Global History*, 206–11.

28   See for example Klaus Mühlhahn, *Making China Modern: From the Great Qing to Xi Jinping* (Cambridge, MA: Harvard University Press, 2019); and Tang Xiaobing, *Global Space and the Nationalist Discourse of Modernity: The Historical Thinking of Liang Qichao* (Stanford: Stanford University Press, 1996).

29   A broader account of conceptual transformations in Chinese is Lydia H. Liu, *Translingual Practice: Literature, National Culture, and Translated Modernity – China, 1900–1937* (Stanford: Stanford University Press, 1996).

30   For more details, see Julia Lovell, *Maoism: A Global History* (London: Bodley Head, 2019).

31   Bao Maohong, 'Narratives of Power: Political Thoughts and World History Construction in Modern China', 35–50.

32   Xavier Paulès, 'Going Beyond the "Western Impact" Narrative: China as a World Power, 1839–1949', 51–66.

33   For example, Wang Hui, 'Twentieth-Century China as an Object of Thought: An Introduction, Part 1 the Birth of the Century: The Chinese Revolution and the Logic of Politics', *Modern China* 46, no. 1 (2020): 3–48; and Dominic Sachsenmaier, 'Twentieth-Century China as an Object of Thought: Global and Local Historical Reflections', *Modern China* 46, no. 3 (2020): 227–49.

34   Reflections on this topic: Ge Zhaoguang, *What Is China?: Territory, Ethnicity, Culture, and History* (Cambridge, MA: Harvard University Press, 2018).

35   For a longer perspective, see Francis Lap Fung Lee and Chi Kit Chan, 'Political Events and Cultural Othering: Impact of Protests and Elections on Identities in Post-Handover Hong Kong, 1997–2021', *Journal of Contemporary China* (December 2022): 1–15.

Bibliography

Adelman, Jeremy, and Andreas Eckert. 2024. 'A World of Narratives'. In *A World of Narratives: Nations, Empires, and Other World Products: An Anthology of the Global*

History Collaborative, edited by Jeremy Adelman and Andreas Eckert, 1–16. London: Bloomsbury.

Aslanidis, Paris, and Cristóbal Rovira Kaltwasser. 2016. 'Dealing with Populists in Government: The SYRIZA-ANEL Coalition in Greece'. *Democratization* 23, no. 6: 1077–91.

Bao, Maohong. 2024. 'Narratives of Power: Political Thoughts and World History Construction in Modern China'. In *A World of Narratives: Nations, Empires, and Other World Products: An Anthology of the Global History Collaborative*, edited by Jeremy Adelman and Andreas Eckert, 35–50. London: Bloomsbury.

Barfield, Thomas J. 2023. *Afghanistan: A Cultural and Political History*, 2nd Edition. Princeton: Princeton University Press.

Bello, Walden. 2002. *Deglobalization: Ideas for a New World*. London: Zed Books.

Benyon, John, and David Dunkerley. 2014. *Globalization: The Reader*. London: Routledge.

Boulianne, Shelley. 2019. 'Revolution in the Making? Social Media Effects across the Globe'. *Information, Communication & Society* 22, no. 1: 39–54.

Cao, Tianyu. 2003. *Xiandaihua, quanqiuhua yu zhongguo daolu* [Modernization, Globalization and China's Path]. Beijing: Shehui kexue wenxian chubanshe.

Castells, Manuel. 1996. *The Rise of the Network Society, The Information Age: Economy, Society and Culture*. Vol. I. Cambridge, MA and Oxford: Blackwell.

Conrad, Sebastian. 2016. *What Is Global History?* Princeton: Princeton University Press.

Crossley, Pamela Kyle. 2007. *What Is Global History?* Cambridge: Polity Press.

Desai, Lord Meghnad. 2003. 'The Possibility of Deglobalization'. In *Globalization, Social Capital and Inequality: Contested Concepts, Contested Experiences*, edited by Wilfred Dolfsma and Charlie Dannreuther, 1–14. Northampton: Edward Elgar.

Falk, Richard, and Andrew Strauss. 2001. 'Toward Global Parliament'. *Foreign Affairs* 80, no. 1: 212–20.

Fukuyama, Francis. 2014. *State-Building, Governance and World Order in the 21st Century*. Ithaca: Cornell University Press.

Ge, Zhaoguang. 2018. *What Is China?: Territory, Ethnicity, Culture, and History*. Cambridge, MA: Harvard University Press.

Greene, Samuel A., and Graeme B. Robertson. 2019. *Putin v. the People: The Perilous Politics of a Divided Russia*. New Haven: Yale University Press.

Herman, David, James Phelan, Peter J. Rabinowitz, Brian Richardson, and Robyn Warhol. 2012. *Narrative Theory: Core Concepts and Critical Debates*. Columbus: Ohio State University Press.

Hung, Ho-fung. 2022. *Clash of Empires: From 'Chimerica' to the 'New Cold War'*. Cambridge: Cambridge University Press.

IMF Staff. 2000. 'Globalization: Threat or Opportunity?' *IMF Issues Briefs*. Published 12 April 2000. https://www.imf.org/external/np/exr/ib/2000/041200to.htm

Kaldor, Mary. 2003. 'The Idea of Global Civil Society'. *International Affairs* 79, no. 3: 583–93.

Klein, Naomi. 2007. *The Shock Doctrine: The Rise of Disaster Capitalism*. New York: Henry Holt and Company.

Kotroyannos, Dimitrios. 2016. 'Alexis Tsipras und der rhetorische Diskurs als Politik [Alexis Tsipras and the Rhetorical Discourse as Politics]'. 16 April 2016. Available at SSRN: https://ssrn.com/abstract=2768793.

Laguerre, Michel S. 2000. 'Japantown: The Deglobalization of an Ethnopole'. In *The Global Ethnopolis: Chinatown, Japantown and Manilatown in American Society*, edited by Michel S. Laguerre, 53–75. London: Palgrave Macmillan.

Laruelle, Marlene. 2019. *Russian Nationalism: Imaginaries, Doctrines, and Political Battlefields*. London: Taylor & Francis.

Lechner, Frank J., and John Boli, eds. 2020. *The Globalization Reader*. Hoboken: John Wiley & Sons.

Lee, Francis Lap Fung, and Chi Kit Chan. 2022. 'Political Events and Cultural Othering: Impact of Protests and Elections on Identities in Post-Handover Hong Kong, 1997–2021'. *Journal of Contemporary China* 33 (December): 1–15.

Liu, Kang. 2004. *Globalization and Cultural Trends in China*. Honolulu: University of Hawai'i Press.

Liu, Lydia H. 1996. *Translingual Practice: Literature, National Culture, and Translated Modernity – China, 1900–1937*. Stanford: Stanford University Press.

Lovell, Julia. 2019. *Maoism: A Global History*. London: Bodley Head.

Lukin, Artyom. 2021. 'The Russia-China Entente and Its Future'. *International Politics* 58, no. 3: 363–80.

Maier, Charles. 2016. *Once within Borders, Territories of Power, Wealth, and Belonging since 1500*. Cambridge, MA: The Belknap Press of Harvard University Press.

Mattei, Clara E. 2022. *The Capital Order: How Economists Invented Austerity and Paved the Way to Fascism*. Chicago: University of Chicago Press.

Mazlish, Bruce. 2009. *The Idea of Humanity in a Global Era*. New York: Palgrave Macmillan.

Mühlhahn, Klaus. 2019. *Making China Modern: From the Great Qing to Xi Jinping*. Cambridge, MA: Harvard University Press.

Olwig, Karen Fog. 2003. 'Narrating Deglobalization: Danish Perceptions of a Lost Empire'. *Global Networks: A Journal of Transnational Affairs* 3, no. 3: 207–22.

Paulès, Xavier. 2024. 'Going beyond the "Western Impact" Narrative: China as a World Power, 1839–1949'. In *A World of Narratives: Nations, Empires, and Other World Products: An Anthology of the Global History Collaborative*, edited by Jeremy Adelman and Andreas Eckert, 51–66. London: Bloomsbury.

Pu, Changgen. 2002. 'Quanqiuhua yu zhongguo yingdui' [Globalization and Chinese Responses]. *Yazhou yanjiu* [*Asian Studies*] 44: 7–23.

Sachsenmaier, Dominic. 2011. *Global Perspectives on Global History: Theories and Approaches in a Connected World*. Cambridge: Cambridge University Press.

Sachsenmaier, Dominic. 2020. 'Twentieth-Century China as an Object of Thought: Global and Local Historical Reflections'. *Modern China* 46, no. 3: 227–49.

Schindler, Seth, Jessica DiCarlo, and Dinesh Paudel. 2022. 'The New Cold War and the Rise of the 21st-century Infrastructure State'. *Transactions of the Institute of British Geographers* 47, no. 2: 331–46.

Scholte, Jan Aart. 2003. 'Global Civil Society'. *Globalization: Critical Concepts in Sociology* 3: 279–302.

Stavrakakis, Yannis, and Giorgos Katsambekis. 2014. 'Left-wing Populism in the European Periphery: The Case of SYRIZA'. *Journal of Political Ideologies* 19, no. 2: 119–42.

Tang, Xiaobing. 1996. *Global Space and the Nationalist Discourse of Modernity: The Historical Thinking of Liang Qichao*. Stanford: Stanford University Press.

Ther, Philipp. 2023. *How the West Lost the Peace: The Great Transformation since the Cold War*. Translated by Jessica Spengler. London: Polity.

Vaishnav, Milan. 2019. *The BJP in Power: Indian Democracy and Religious Nationalism*. Washington, DC: Carnegie Endowment for International Peace. Retrieved from https://carnegieendowment.org/files/BJP_In_Power_final.pdf.

Wang, Hui. 2020. 'Twentieth-Century China as an Object of Thought: An Introduction, Part 1 The Birth of the Century: The Chinese Revolution and the Logic of Politics'. *Modern China* 46, no. 1: 3–48.

Wang, Jiafeng. 2009. 'Some Reflection on Modernization Theory and Globalization Theory'. *Chinese Studies in History* 43, no. 1: 72–98.

Yan, Yunxiang. 2002. 'Managed Globalization: State Power and Cultural Transition in China'. In *Many Globalizations: Cultural Diversity in the Contemporary World*, edited by Peter Berger and Samuel Huntington, 19–47. New York and Oxford: Oxford University Press.

Zhuravskaya, Ekaterina, Maria Petrova, and Ruben Enikolopov. 2020. 'Political Effects of the Internet and Social Media'. *Annual Review of Economics* 12, no. 1: 415–38.

Index

aerial bombardment 103–18
  active defence 109–10
  air-defence programmes 109–11, 116
  air raids 103–4, 106–13, 115–17
  atomic bombs 104, 117, 139
  civil-defence 104–6, 109–13, 115–18
  firebombing raids 104, 107, 115
  passive air defence 109
  poison-gas attack from air 106–7,
    110
  resilience 109–17
  transnational narrative of resilience
    117–18
  war and global history 104–9
Afghanistan 131, 133–4, 138–40, 335
Africa/Africans 6, 10, 23–4, 26, 40, 43, 58,
  89–90, 93, 129, 131–2, 136, 139,
  149, 175, 185, 204, 224, 226,
  239–41, 248–50, 252, 259–62,
  266, 297, 299, 315, 322, 338.
  See also specific countries
Afro-Asian 133, 136, 192
Aggrey, James Emman Kwegyir 269–70
Ajiashi 97
Akwa, Mpundu 265
Alberdi, Juan Batista, *Bases y puntos de
  partida para la organización
  política de la República
  Argentina* 226
Aliev, Heydar 136
alternative globalization 128, 333. *See also*
  globalization
alternative modernization 128. *See also*
  modernization
Álvarez, Luis Echeverría 177
Americanism 173–4. *See also* The United
  States
American Revolution 21, 225
Amin, Samir 177, 217 n.35
Anglo-Japanese Alliance (1902) 95
anthropology 185, 252–3

anti-colonial/anti-colonialism 8, 36–7, 40,
  43, 131–2, 186, 193–4, 323–4.
  See also colonialism
anti-globalism 342 n.15
anti-globalization 5, 15 n.10
anti-hegemonic 39–40, 203. *See also*
  hegemony/hegemonic
anti-imperialism/anti-imperialist 36–7,
  40, 48, 133, 175, 184. *See also*
  imperialism
anti-refugee politics 342 n.15. *See also*
  refugees
anti-Semitism 10
anti-slavery 24–9, 246. *See also* slave/slavery
Arai Hakuseki, *Seiyō Kibun* (*Accounts on
  Seiyō*) 98 n.9
Aravamudan, Srinivas 247–8
  Tropicopolitains 256 n.45
Archipelago 88–9, 192, 194
Argentina 7–8, 167, 225–8, 297, 309–12,
  314, 323
  Law Number 346 (1869) 228
  Law of Immigration and Colonization
    (1876) 226–7
  país abanico, Bunge's 311
Armitage, David, 'The Declaration of
  Independence' 19, 28
Asia/Asian 4, 13, 23–4, 36–8, 40, 42–3,
  55, 60–2, 79, 87–8, 92–3, 95–6,
  98 n.5, 104, 109, 136, 139, 175,
  185, 192, 224, 297, 299, 315,
  338. *See also specific countries*
Asia-Pacific 106, 112
Asia Pacific War (1941–5) 105
Asiatic Society of Japan 92
assimilation 26, 220, 229
Athens, Greece 3, 333
Atlantic Charter/Charterists 171–2
Auezov, Mukhtar 136
Australia 39, 52, 55, 58–9, 105, 153, 227
Austria/Cisleithania 155

348 *Index*

Austria-Hungary (Austro-Hungarian
Empire) 129, 148–51, 158, 185
Ausgleich of 1867 155
Austrian constitutional law 151
constitutional relationship to Bosnia
Herzegovina 151–2
occupation of Bosnia Herzegovina
148–9, 151, 153
split sovereignty 154–6
Austrian Habsburg monarchy 223
authentic/authenticity 75–6, 79–80
authoritarian/authoritarianism 105, 169–70,
195, 270, 333, 335, 337, 339–40
autochthony 6–7
autonomous republics 129–30. *See also*
Soviet republics
Azerbaijan 131, 136–7

Ba'ath Party 137
Baernreither, Joseph Maria 160 n.16
Baldwin, Stanley 108
Balkans 8, 148–51, 313, 321–2
Ballard, Mary 242, 254 n.10
Bandung Conference (1955) 40, 42, 133,
136, 175, 324
Bankokushi (*History of Ten Thousand
Countries of the World*) 100
n.27, 100 n.30
Banks, Joseph 252
baquan (*bacouen/bacouan*) 59
barbarians 36–7, 67, 89, 221
barbarism 23–4, 107, 229, 248
Barka, Mehdi Ben 175
Bartholomew, John 326 n.30
Battle for Seattle 180
Beiou Kairan Jikki 68
Belgium 22, 67
Brussels 8, 309
Benjamin, Walter 173
Bentham, Jeremy 7, 185
Berlin Conference of 1884–5 149
BIE (Bureau International des
Expositions) 83 n.10
biological racism 27
biombo 89
Bismarck, Otto von 148–9
Black, C.E. 46
Blumenbach, Johannn Frederich 252–3,
258 n.85

Bohls, Elizabeth 241, 244
Bolivia/Bolivian forest 139, 205, 209–11,
214–15
Bolivian diplomacy 211
counter-hegemonic sovereignty
213–14
forest as empowerment narrative 212
global and political counter-narrative
213
national counter-narrative 209–11
proceso de cambio (process of change)
in 211
sovereign defence of forest 211
Tipnis 212
Bolshevik revolution 288, 296
Bolsheviks/ Bolshevism 129–32, 166, 169,
288, 296, 298
borderlands 9, 147, 150
Bosnia Herzegovina 147–9, 154–7
Austria-Hungary's occupation of
148–9, 151, 153–4
constitutional relationship to Austria-
Hungary 151–2
internationalized sovereignty 152
jurisdictional scaling 150–2
legal typologies 152–4
peasants revolt against Muslim
landlords 147
sovereignty 148–50
bourgeoisie 41–3, 132–3, 298
Bove, Jose, *Confederation Paysanne* 180
Brandt, Willy 178
Brandt Report 178, 204
Brazil 10, 22–4, 297, 334
Amazon forest 24, 211–13, 217 n.20
Bolsonaro's Partido Liberal 334
Bretton Woods System 171–3, 176–7
Brezhnev, Leonid 129, 134, 137–8, 141
BRIC (Brazil, Russia, India, China) forum
204
Britain/Britons 4, 22–3, 26–7, 51, 67,
103–8, 110–16, 118, 132, 184,
206–7, 223, 228, 243, 248, 260,
317, 323, 334. *See also* Great
Britain
British Air Raids Precautions
Department 112
the British Museum 4, 7, 72
Corn Laws, abolition of 22

Imperial Preferences 323
Myth of Blitz 117
traditional British phlegm 118
British India 23, 131
Brown, Ernest 114
Buddhism/Buddhist 54, 70, 73, 76, 187–9, 191, 195
Thai Buddhism 188–9
Bukharin, Nikolai Ivanovich 298–9
Bunge, Alejandro 309–12, 314–15, 320, 323, 325 n.9, 325 n.12
Custom Union of the South (*Unión Aduanera del Sud*) 312
Manifiesto de los banqueros e industriales internacionales 312
país abanico (Argentina) 311

Calavita, Kitty 232
Calder, Angus, 'Myth of the Blitz' 113
Cambodia 58, 61
Cameroon 259–61, 265–7, 270–7
Canada 39, 58–9, 105, 153, 227, 295, 317, 320
capitalism 4, 25, 43, 47, 133, 167–8, 170, 172–3, 233, 287, 292, 294–6, 298, 301, 313, 317–18
global capitalism 20, 167, 301, 331, 335
industrial capitalism 20, 276
capital mobility 9, 180
caravan culture 261, 264
Caribbean islands 4, 22, 27, 242–3
Carlos, Juan 5
Catherine II 289–90
Remarques concernant l'histoire de la Russie 290
Caucasus/Caucasian 104, 131, 137, 142, 252
censorship 260, 262, 277, 290
Central Asia/Asians 12, 38, 94, 127–32, 134–6, 139–41
Central Asian elites 12, 127–30, 133–4, 138–9
cotton 132
Russian-dominated 130
Soviet Central Asia 12, 127, 130, 133–4, 142
Central Bureau of Communist Organizations of the Peoples of the East 131

Chambers, Ephraim, *Cyclopaedia: Or an Universal Dictionary of Arts and Sciences* 247
Charter of Economic Rights and Duties of States 177
Charter of the United Nations 203, 214, 270
Chayanov, Alexander 298–300
Che Guevara 175–6
Chen Jiageng 陳嘉庚 (Tan Kah Kee) 56
Chen Jingxi 陳景熙, *Overseas Chinese Organizations and the Dissemination of Chinese Culture* (*Huaren shetuan yu Zhongguo wenhua chuanbo* 華人社團與中華文化傳播) 57
Chernyshevsky, Nikolay 292–3
Chiang Kai-shek 112
Chicherin, Boris 295
Chile 139, 177
China/Chinese 10, 12, 23, 36–7, 39, 41–2, 44, 48, 91–2, 95, 97, 98 n.5, 106, 109, 111, 117, 131–2, 134, 138, 140, 152, 169, 192, 227, 231, 232, 297, 299, 301, 308, 312–14, 323–4, 335
during 1839–1949 51
anti-Hu-Feng Counter Revolutionary Clique incident 41
Beijing 95, 142, 313, 336, 338–9
Belt and Road Initiative 142
Boxer Rebellion (1900) 95, 312
the century of humiliation (*bainian guochi* 百年國恥) 51, 62
Chinese Communist Party (CCP) 51, 337–8
Chinese influence 52, 56, 60, 62
Chinese languages 53–4, 57, 59–62, 105
Cantonese 57–9, 61–2
Hainan 57, 62
Hakka 57, 62
Hokkien 57, 59, 61–2
Teochow 57, 61–2
Chinese Nationalists 112–13, 118, 337, 340
Chinese Restriction 227, 235 n.17
Chinese Revolution of 1911–12 57
Chongqing 103, 112, 117

cookbooks of Chinese recipes 61
cultural exchanges 52–4
cultural influence 54, 60, 62
Cultural Revolution 64 n.33, 338
diaspora 12, 52, 55, 57, 60–2, 64 n.34
dissemination of popular cultures
    (between 1839 and 1949) 60–2
economic growth of 35
gambling games 57–60
Great Leap Forward in 299
Hong Kong 5, 10, 37, 180, 324, 340
library in 56, 64 n.33
Manchus/Manchuria 37, 55, 95, 169,
    207
migrants 52, 54–5, 57–61, 227, 231–2
museums 103
narrative trajectories in 336–40
Northern Barbarian 37
Opium War (1840) 35–6, 38
Overseas Chinese studies (*see* Overseas
    Chinese studies (*huaqiao huaren
    yanjiu* 華僑華人研究))
Peking University 38–9, 46
in pre-modern Japan, elements of 88–9
Reform and Opening Period 336
Shanghai 99 n.14
smokers in 1900s 61
special economic zones (*jingji tequ*
    經濟特區) 55
Sun Yat-sen University 35, 45
Taiwan 94–5
vaccine for Covid 9
Warring States 39
Western impact narrative/nationalist
    narratives 51–4, 58, 62
world history in 36–48
Xinjiang 5, 138–9
youth unemployment in 339
Zhonghua 37
Chiponde, Samwel 269
Chitrabongs, M. L. Chittawadi 190
Christianism/Christianity 93, 147–8, 170,
    188, 192, 211, 251–2, 265
Chulalongkorn (Rama V), King 189–91
Churchill, Winston 20, 113–14, 171
citizenship 4, 6, 13, 153, 220, 226, 232
global citizen/citizenship 6, 10, 19
national citizenship 6, 195, 228
civilian morale 104, 108, 117–18

civilian resilience 12, 103, 116
civilization 3, 5, 23–4, 43, 79, 90–2, 112,
    148, 156, 170, 173–4, 188–9,
    192, 225, 229–30, 233, 240,
    263, 267, 269–70, 287, 289–91,
    316–17, 319
Civil Servants Association 268
climate change 211–13
Cohen, Paul, *Discovering History in China:
    American Historical Writing on
    the Recent Chinese Past* 53
Cold War 36, 39–41, 127–8, 137, 179,
    184, 186, 204, 206, 288, 324,
    330, 337
Russia and backwardness during
    298–300
Colijn, Hendrik 193
colonial governmentality 184–5, 191,
    195–6
colonialism 23, 35, 42–3, 47, 129, 131,
    149, 165, 174–5, 184, 186–7,
    189, 259–60, 268, 271, 273, 275,
    294. *See also* anti-colonial/anti-
    colonialism
colonial oppression 127, 167
colonization 24, 130, 183–4, 187, 190, 195,
    197, 229–30, 241, 252, 320
commodity 4, 8, 10, 105, 115, 171, 176,
    178, 184, 245, 259, 261, 266,
    272, 292, 319
Communist International (Comintern)
    41, 131
Communist University of the Toilers of
    the East 131
Condillac, Bennot-Etienne abbé de 289
Conference of Peace Partisans in Baghdad
    (1959) 136
Conference on Civil Liberty in the
    Colonial Empire, London 268
Congo 149, 153
Congo Free State 158
Congress of Berlin 148, 158, 161 n.26
Conrad, Sebastian, *What Is Global
    History?* 2
Constitution of Paraguay (1870) 228
Convention Relating to International
    Exhibitions (1928) 83 n.10
convergence 1, 26–7, 33 n.36, 166–8, 174,
    176, 178, 180, 227, 307, 312, 324

Index

351

cooperation, international 37, 45–6, 105, 110, 157, 173, 176, 204, 207–9, 293, 312, 314, 316
'Corporate America Flag,' *Adbusters*' 180
cosmopolitans/cosmopolitanism 1, 8, 19–20, 29, 36–8, 105, 112, 307
cotton/cotton textiles 22–3, 25, 98 n.5, 127, 132, 140–1, 268
Covid-19 pandemic 5, 9, 215, 253 n.1, 329, 339
Creoles 219, 240, 251
cricket (*adu jangkrik*) 58
cross-border interactions 9, 165, 176, 181, 205
Cuba 23–4, 57–8, 138, 153, 175, 227, 235 n.17
Cyprus 149, 153–4
Czechoslovakia 110, 142

Dahoméen 266, 282 n.78
Dai Nihonshi (*The Great History of Japan*) 99–100 n.24
Dai-nippon Kaikyō kyōkai (Islamic Society of the Great Japan) 101 n.37
Dai-tōa Kyōeiken (The Greater East Asia Co-prosperity Sphere) 96
Dai-tōashi (History of Greater East Asia) 96
Dasgupta, Swapan 11
Datsu-a Nyū-ō (Leave Asia, Enter Europe) 101 n.33
Davis, Jefferson 21–3, 29
decentralization 6
decolonization 8, 13, 127–32, 135, 138, 142, 148, 186, 195, 203–4, 214, 298, 300, 309, 323
 destalinization as 132–4
 Indonesian-Dutch war of 195
de Gaulle, Charles 203
de-globalization 5, 330, 332
Dekker, Eduard Douwes 193
democratization 6, 84 n.32
Deng Xiaoping 鄧小平 36, 39, 44–8, 55, 131, 338
 reform and open door policy 44–6, 48
Dening, Esler 207–9
Denmark 67, 110
dependency theory 30, 213, 217 n.35, 321–2

deregulation 179
destalinization 127–9, 135, 140, 300
 as second decolonization 132–4
deterritorialization 332
dialects (*fangyan* 方言) 57, 167, 187, 262
diaspora 63 n.3
 Chinese 12, 52, 55, 57, 60–2, 64 n.34
Diderot, Denis 289–90
diversity 58, 129–30, 205, 298, 339
dongyang 90–1
Douglass, Frederick 28, 33 n.27
Douhet, Guilio 107
Duala 261, 265–7, 274–5
Duara, Prasenjit, redemptive societies 66 n.55
Du Bois, W. E. B. 29
Dunlop, Daniel Nicol 317
Dutch East India Company 223
Dutch East Indies 183, 191–5, 223
 Ethical policy 193–4

'East' (*vostok*) 131, 134, 136–7
economic crisis 6, 8, 10, 336
economic geography 174, 309, 311, 316–18, 324
economic integration 128, 165–7, 169, 171, 174, 177–9, 307, 324
economic interdependence 13, 170–1, 174, 308–9, 312, 317, 322, 324
economic miracle 118, 339
economic power 134, 166, 177, 312, 318–19
Eden, Anthony 206
egalitarian 20, 26, 29
Egypt 3, 92, 136, 149, 154
Elolombe ya Kamerun (The Sun of Kamerun) 265
emancipation 22, 24–6, 127, 129, 131, 141, 193, 291–2
Emirate of Bukhara 130
Engels, Friedrich 294
England 22–3, 153, 174, 228, 244, 246–7, 287–8, 298, 323
 Hull 108, 114, 117
 Portsmouth 114
 Southampton 114
 Victoria & Albert Museum 72
Enlightenment 14, 130, 148, 240, 242–3, 249, 252, 257 n.56, 288–92

Index

Eurasia/Eurasian 38, 88–9, 91, 112
Euro-American 21, 23, 29, 47, 316
Eurocentric/Eurocentrism 21, 38, 42–3, 62, 184, 212, 259, 292, 294
European Union 2, 4, 142, 312, 333, 335
Europe/European 2–5, 7–9, 21–3, 26, 28, 36–41, 47, 52, 71, 74–5, 80, 87, 89–93, 95, 98 n.8, 99 n.19, 104–6, 109, 111, 116, 128–31, 134, 141, 149–52, 168–9, 174–6, 178, 185, 193, 223, 226–8, 252, 259, 262, 268, 287–8, 291–3, 295, 297, 301, 312–13, 315, 317, 323. *See also specific countries*
    Central Europe 97 n.2, 131, 169, 223, 322
    competition policy 176–7
    Eastern Europe 107, 169, 223, 288, 291, 295, 297, 323
    European colonialism 128, 131, 174, 184
    European Economic Commission 177
    European governmentality 184, 189
    European integration 175–7
    Western Europe 2, 24, 36–7, 41, 47, 88, 175, 287–8, 290, 295, 317–18
exceptionalism 11, 19–20, 27, 29, 288
exotic/exoticism 73–5, 80, 92, 288
Expo Vienna 1873 67–9, 80, 82 n.5
    invitation to Japan 72–5
    Japanese Garden at 74

Fairbank, John 52
Fairchild, Henry Pratt 229–30
fantan 番攤, gambling game 58–60
Farage, Nigel 8–9
fascist 104, 169, 297
Fenian uprising in Ireland 185
Fenwick, Charles 153
Ferdinand, Franz 147
feudal/feudalism 35, 37, 40, 42–3, 47, 67, 71, 77, 93, 287–8, 292–3, 301
'Finest Hour' 103, 113, 115
Finland 110, 113, 153
First Industrial Revolution 314
First World War 95, 103–8, 115, 129, 147, 149, 166, 178, 229, 260, 262, 295, 308–10, 317. *See also* Second World War
Five-Year Plan 46–7, 132
flat-earth proponents 5, 8–9

Fonds d'Investissements pour le Développement Economique et Social (FIDES) 272
forced labour 116, 118, 260–1, 263, 265, 267–8, 271–2, 274, 276–7, 288, 291
Ford, Henry 173
Fordism/Fordist 168, 172–6
foreign trade 171, 321
Foucault, Michel 184, 196 n.5
France/French 22–3, 27, 45–6, 51, 61, 67, 83 n.10, 92, 106, 111, 132, 168, 175, 180, 184, 191, 228, 260, 271, 275–6, 287–9, 295, 333–4, 337
    French Communist Party 275–6
    French Indochina 61, 132
    French Institute for Advanced Study Fellowship Programme 103
    French Revolution 43, 228, 287
    gilets jaunes 307, 324
    Trente Glorieuses 172–6, 178
Franco-Prussian War 106
Frank, Andre Gunder 177
free agents 220, 230
free labour 21, 25, 290
free market 1, 47, 166–7, 170, 300–1, 324
free trade 8–9, 22–3, 27, 166, 276, 309, 315, 322
Fridays-For-Future Movement 334
Friedman, Thomas 1, 179–80
Friendship Societies 139
Fukuzawa Yukichi 77
    Seiyō Jijō ('Information of the West') 90

Gafurov, Bobozhan 137, 139
Gandhi, Mahatma 194
Ganisya, Martin 263
Ganty, Vincent 267, 284 n.130
Ge Chunyuan 戈春源 58
gender 6, 220, 229, 250, 260, 273
geo-political regionalizations 184, 196 n.2
Georgescu-Roegen, N. 300
German/Germany 10–11, 51, 53, 67, 103–4, 106, 108–9, 111, 113–15, 117–18, 148, 168, 184–5, 213, 232, 295, 297–8, 310, 318, 323
    Augsburg 115–16
    Berlin 107, 111, 116, 148, 158, 313
    Die Sirene (The Siren) magazine 111

fall of the Berlin wall 5, 204, 300, 324
German Zeppelins 106–7
  Hamburg 115–17
  killing of Londoners 115
  Luftschutzgemeinschaft (air-defence
    community) 110
  Luftwaffe 115–16
  migrants 223
  Operation Gomorrah against
    Hamburg 115, 117
  Reich Air Defence League
    (Reichsluftschutzbund/RLB)
    105, 110–11
  self-protection (*Selbstschutz*) 110, 115
  Turkish migrants in 231–2
  Weimar 109–11
Gershenkron, Alexander 298–9
Ghioldi, Rodolfo 139
global capitalism 20, 167, 301, 331, 335
global citizen/citizenship 6, 10, 19. *See also*
    national citizenship
global economy. *See* world economy
global history. *See* world history
global integration 2, 6, 9–10, 14, 20–4,
    26–9, 166, 175, 177, 179, 204,
    219, 240, 243, 308–9, 315–18,
    329, 331–2, 336
global interactions 2–3, 203, 239, 260
global interconnectedness 105, 128, 203
global interdependence 165–6, 170–1,
    175, 181, 307, 314, 322, 324
globalism 8, 337–8, 340
globalization 2, 5–6, 8–10, 35, 47, 54, 105,
    128, 172, 178–80, 240, 249, 252,
    259, 307, 310, 324, 336–40
  alternative globalization 128, 333
  competing visions of 330–2
  decline of globalization narrative 329–30
  political consciousness,
    reterritorialization of 332–4
  socialist globalizations 128
global market. *See* world market
Global North 178
global order 8, 23, 29, 153, 165–6, 186,
    310, 314, 318, 338
Global South 5, 8, 178
Gluck, Carol, 'Modernity in Common:
    Japan and World History' 80
Gobsch, Hanns 106

Goebbels, Joseph 114–15
Goldberg, Jonah 11
Goodrich, Samuel G., *Peter Parley's
    Common School History* 100 n.26
governmentality 184, 195
  colonial governmentality 184–5, 191,
    195–6
  European governmentality 184, 189
  modern governmentality 190
  semi-colonial 189–90
Graham, William 24
Gramsci, Antonio 173
  Prison Notebooks 173
Great Britain 22–3, 25, 27, 51, 67–8,
    92, 105, 206–9, 228, 241, 295,
    308, 334, 337. *See also* Britain/
    Britons
Great Depression 114, 169, 267–8, 310,
    318, 320, 324
Great Exhibition (1851) 68, 83 n.10
Great Patriotic War 103
Great Powers 12–13, 147–8, 151–2, 158,
    167–8, 203, 313–14, 317, 320,
    335, 337, 340
The Great Terror of 1937–8 131
Grotius, Hugo 221–2
Group of 77 (G77) 177
guerrilla 147, 176

Habsburg Monarchy 147–8, 151, 155, 158,
    223
Hall, Catherine 241, 253 n.1
Hall, Hessel Duncan 147, 158 n.1
Hammarskjöld, Dag 203, 205, 215
Hannah-Jones, Nikole, 'A New Origin
    Story' 3
Harrison, Mark 300
Harry Frank Guggenheim Foundation 103
Hasil, Seif 268
Hatta, Mohammad 194
Hayato Ikeda 118
He Fangchuan 何芳川, *History of China's
    cultural exchanges* (*Zhongwai
    wenhua jiaoliu shi* 中外文化交
    流史) 53–4
hegemony/hegemonic 12, 36, 39–40, 139,
    147, 159 n.8, 173, 177, 180, 191,
    193, 308, 321, 331, 337. *See also*
    anti-hegemonic

Henry, E. R. 107
Higginson, Thomas Wentworth 27–8
Hindutva-nationalism 3, 9
Hiroshima and Nagasaki 104, 117–18
Hirschman, Albert O. 170–2, 321–2
 *National Power and the Structure of
 Foreign Trade* 171, 321
historical narratives 48, 51, 62, 79, 131,
 170, 239–40
Hitler, Adolf 8, 113, 115–16
Hobsbawm, Eric 20, 23
Hobson, J. A. 313
Ho Chi Minh 131–2, 138
Holocaust 7, 10–11
home front 103–6, 108–9, 113
honchō. See Japan/Japanese
hooligans (*wahuni*) 268, 270
household air defence (*katei bōkū*) 110
huaqiao studies 52, 56–9, 62
 in China since 1980s 55–6
Huguenots, French 223
human history 38, 43, 93, 234 n.3, 240
humanity 26, 168, 246–7, 257 n.56,
 297
human mobility 13, 219–22, 225, 227,
 232–3
Humboldt Foundation 103
humiliation 51, 62, 338, 340
Hunter, Robert M. T. 22–3, 25–6, 266
Huntington, Elsworth 316–17
 'The Distribution of Human Energy on
 the Basis of Climate' 316

Ibrahim, Abdül Reşit 101 n.34
identity politics 1, 191, 329
immigration/immigrant(s) 107, 219–20
 modern immigration 220, 224
 nation-states and modern theories of
 224–30
 normative immigrant 220, 226–7
Imperial Diet 93
imperialism 27, 35, 43, 47, 51, 53, 62, 104,
 149, 151–2, 167, 184, 207–8,
 227, 241, 243, 313. *See also* anti-
 imperialism/anti-imperialist
Imperial Japan 105–6
inclusion 2, 6, 19, 52, 106
Independent Greeks – National Patriotic
 Alliance (ANEL) 333

India/Indian 1, 9–10, 23–4, 38, 54, 89, 92,
 98 n.5, 133–4, 169, 174, 194,
 268, 293, 297, 299, 310, 314,
 321–3
 Bharatiya Janata Party 334
 Bombay Plan (*Plan of Economic
 Development for India* (1944))
 323
 Rebellion in India (1857) 185
indigenization (*korenizatsiia*) 131, 134–5,
 141
Indonesia 12, 175, 183–4, 186, 196
 Aceh (Nord-Sumatra) 192
 Cultivation System (1830 and 1870) 192
 Dutch territorial expansion 192
 genealogies of development in colonial
 191–5
 Java 58, 60, 192
 nationalism 193–4
 Outer Islands (Borneo, Celebes,
 Papua) 192
 Pembangunan 195
 Perhimpunan Indonesia student
 association 194
Indonesian-Dutch war of decolonization
 195
Indonesia Merdeka (Indonesia Free)
 magazine 194
industrial capitalism 20, 276
industrialization 46–7, 129, 131–2, 135,
 140, 142, 228, 233, 299, 314,
 318, 323–4
industrial production 37, 173
inflation 166, 177, 272
Innis, Harold 309, 320, 322
internal colonialism 186, 189
internal colonization 183–4
 of Siam 187–91
International Bank for Reconstruction
 and Development (World Bank)
 172
International Confederation of Free Trade
 Unions (ICFTU) 276
International Development Scheme 314
International Financial Conference,
 Brussels 309
international frontier 147, 158 n.2
internationalism 8, 40, 170, 186, 309
 liberal internationalism 8, 175

Index

internationalization 178, 337
international laws 7–8, 13, 149, 151–4, 157–8, 220–2, 224–5
International Monetary Fund (IMF) 5, 172, 333
'Globalization: Threat or Opportunity' 331
international political economy 165
Iran 134, 137–8, 140, 178
Iraq 136–7
Islam/Islamic 95, 101 n.34, 101 n.37, 136–7, 140, 260, 262–3. *See also* Muslims
Israel 10, 231, 334
Italy 53, 67, 110–11, 118, 148, 297
Itō Hirobumi 101 n.34
Iwakura Embassy group 67–9, 72–3, 80, 85 n.36, 87
Iwakura Mission 87, 92–3, 95, 98 n.6
Iwakura Tomomi 67, 89

Jackson, Peter A. 189–90
Jani, Disha 183
Japanese Co-Prosperity in the Pacific 169
Japan/Japanese 24, 32 n.25, 35, 37–9, 46, 48, 51–3, 67–8, 89, 91, 106, 109, 111, 116–18, 152, 169, 176, 184, 194, 205–8, 214, 216 n.8, 295, 297, 313–14, 322, 337
  Air Defence Law (1937) 110
  air-defence policies 116
  Ancient Temples and Shrines Preservation Law 81
  archipelago 88–9
  art objects/artworks 77
  Asiatic Society of Japan 92
  authentic/authenticity 75–6, 79
  bombing Chinese urban areas 104
  Boshin War 70
  China/Chinese elements in premodern Japan 88–9
  culture/cultural diplomacy 79–81, 96, 97 n.2
  Daigaku-kengen of 1871 69–72
  Edict for the Preservation of Antiquities and Old Items (*Koki kyubutsu hozon-kata*) 71, 77, 81
  educational/school system 92

enkyu shoshin (detesting the old and respecting the new) 70
and European modernity 89–91
Expo 1867 Paris 83 n.15
Expo 1876 Philadelphia 77, 79
Expo 1878 Paris 77, 79
Expo 1889 Paris 75
Expo 1893 Chicago 77, 79, 84 n.25
  Japanese Pavilion at 75–6
Expo 1900 Paris 79
Expo 1904 St. Louis 81
Expo 1915 San Francisco 76, 77
Expo 1862 London 68
Expo 1873 Vienna (*see* Expo Vienna 1873)
fukoku kyohei slogan 68–9, 74
Great Kantō Earthquake of 1923 108–9
historical writings 92–3
'History of the Empire' 92–3
Hokkaido island 93
Houou-do in *Byodo-in*, Kyoto 76
Imperial Museum/Imperial Household Museum 78
  administrative mandates of 78
  characteristic ideas 78–9
  invitation to Expo 1873 Vienna 72–5
Japanese Bushido 118
Kokumin bōkū (Civil defence) magazine 111–12
language of general revolution processes 82 n.3
Law for the Protection of Cultural Properties (1950) 81
national museum 71–2, 77–8, 80
National Treasures Preservation Law (1929) 81
Ogasawara island 93
policymakers 68–9, 76, 79–82
Ryukyu island 90, 93
self-consciousness of 87–9, 97
Status-of-Forces Agreement (SOFA) 206, 208–9
Tokugawa era (1603–1867) 87, 89–90
Tokugawa shogunate 67–8, 70–1, 82 n.2
Tokyo 108–9, 117
  bombing of 116
  Tokyo National Museum 84 n.32
  Tokyo-Yokohama earthquake of 1923 109

two-faced strategy 69–75, 81
US firebombing of Japanese cities
(1945) 104
warfare of peacetime 68, 74, 79–81
water paintings 76
Jefferson, Thomas 20
Notes on the State of Virginia 235 n.15
Jellinek, Georg 152–3
Johnson, Boris 334
Johnson, Samuel, *Dictionary of the English
Language* 245
*The Journal of Overseas Chinese History
Studies* (*Huaqiao huaren lishi
yanjiu* 华侨华人历史研究) 55
Juma, Alfred 263–4

Kaikyōken Kenkyūsho (the Research
Institute on Kaikyōken)
101 n.37
kaikyōken (Muslim world) 95–6, 101 n.38
Kaikyō sekai (The Islamic World) 101 n.37
kara. See China/Chinese
Kassem, Abd al-Karim 137
Kazakhs/Kazakhstan 127, 130–2, 134–6,
138–41
Alma-Ata 127, 135, 142 n.1
Almaty 127, 136, 141
Baikonur cosmodrome 127
Kazakh steppes 127, 130
Medeu (Russian *Medeo*) Gorge 135–6
Semipalatinsk nuclear test site 127, 139
Shimbulak 136
Turkestan 127, 130, 132, 142
Winter Olympics 141–2
kazi ulaya (European work) 263
Kazushige Ugaki 108
Kendall, Edward Augustus, *Travels
Through the Northern Parts of
the United States in 1807 and
1808* 219
Kenya 267–8, 276
Keynesian/Keynesianism 174, 176–8, 300
Keynes, John Maynard 167–70, 173,
176–8, 180
'Carthaginian Peace' 168
*The Economic Consequences of the
Peace* 168
General Theory 173
Khanate of Khiva 130

Khmer 61
Khoikhoi 223
Khrushchev, Nikita 129, 132–4, 136–41,
299
Kim Il-sung 132
Kindleberger, Charles 308
Kingdom of Hungary 155
Kiongozi (The Guide or Leader)
newspaper 262, 277
Klein, Felix 10
Klein, Naomi, *No Logo* 180
Kobe incident (1952) 205–9, 214, 216 n.8
Kokusai Bunka Shinko Kai (KBS) 81
Kollesberg, Theodor Dantscher von 154,
156, 158
Kolonialpolitik 148
Kondemzigo, Paulo 264–5
Konoe Ayamaro 101 n.37
Korea 38, 58, 88, 91–2, 94–5, 116, 205–9,
216 n.5, 219
Korean War 132, 205–9
Kornilov, Aleksandr' 295
Koskenniemi, Martti 151
koumoujin (red-haired people) 89
Kovalevskii, Maksim 295
Kuki Ryūichi 77–9, 81, 84 n.33
Kume Kunitake 68, 87, 89–91, 93, 97, 99
nn.14–15
Kunaev, Dinmukhamed 134–6
Kunyu Wanguo Quantu map 89–90
kurofune (black ships) 89
Kuwabara Jitsuzo, *Tōyōshi for High School
Students* 94–5, 97
Kwetu (Our Home) newspaper 267–70,
277
Kyrgyz/Kyrgyzstan 127, 130, 132, 134, 139

labour migration/migrants 259–66
accusation against employer 271
caravan culture 261, 264
demand for labourers/workers 261–6
European work (*kazi ulaya*) 263
forced labour 116, 118, 260–1, 263,
265, 267–8, 271–2, 274, 276–7,
288, 291
and plantation 240–1, 247, 261
wage labour 173, 259–60, 262–3,
266–8, 270, 291
laissez-faire economics 176, 179

Lam, Carrie 10
Lamp, Karl 157
landscape aesthetics 244
Laporte, Dominique 196 n.5
Latin America 24–5, 39–40, 43, 131, 139, 204, 210, 213, 228, 297, 300, 310–11, 314–15
League of Nations 152, 184–5, 204, 259–60, 267, 270, 315
Leclerc, Georges-Louis, compte de Buffon 244, 249
legitimacy 13, 148–9, 152, 158, 165, 172, 190, 210–11
Le Japon à l'exposition Universelle de 1878 79
Leninism 42–3, 45
Lenin, Vladimir 129, 131, 167–8, 170–1, 294–6, 308
  Imperialism, the Highest Stage of Capitalism 167
L'Eveil des Camerounais newspaper 265–6, 277
Lewis, W. Arthur 268
L'Histoire du l'art du Japon (Commission impériale du Japon à l'Exposition universelle de Paris, Paris: Maurice de Brunoff, 1900) 84 n.34
liberal internationalism 8, 175
liberalism 170, 295
liberalization 175, 179
Liberation (*jiefang* 解放) 51
Lincoln, Abraham 21, 25, 28–9
Linera, Álvaro García 212
Lingg, Emil 154
Lithuania 141, 290
l'Occident group 99 n.10
Lomonosov, Mikhail 290
Long, Edward
  Black and White (separation) 249–51
  Candid Reflections 248, 250
  on chastity 250
  on complexion of skin 242, 248–50
  family 241–2
  History of Jamaica 239–46, 248, 251–3
    review by *The Monthly Review* 242–4
  on 'Negroes' 239–40, 244, 247–50

orang-utan 239, 249, 256 n.55, 258 n.85
  on species 249
  The Trial of Farmer Carter's Dog Porter, for Murder 246–7, 255 n.35
Long, Samuel 241
Looney Tunes, 'Tokio Jokio' film 112
Lord Mansfield 246–8
  'Delphic *ambiguity*' 247
lottery *zihua* 字花 (*huahui* 花會) 58
L'Union des Syndicats Confédérés du Cameroun (USCC) 276
Luo Rongqu 43, 46
  modernization theory 46–7
  'On Historical Development View of One Axis and Multiple Lines' 47

Machida Hisanari 71–2
Mahalanobis, Prasanta 174
Mahanikai Order 188
Maine, Henri 295
Malay Peninsula 189, 191
Malaysia/Malayan 57, 61, 180, 252, 256 n.55
Mambo Leo (Current Affairs) newspaper 267–70, 274, 277
Mangoenkoesoemo, Tjipto 193
Mantena, Karuna 185
Maoist era (1949–78) 53, 55, 338
Māori Wars in New Zealand 185
Mao Zedong 36, 39–44, 48, 132, 139–40, 338
  'The Great Proletariat Cultural Revolution' 41–3, 45–6
  Party Rectification Campaign (1941) 41
  Three Worlds Theory (Third World) 39–41, 44, 48
Marhaenism 195
Marie-Sklodowska-Curie Actions – COFUND Programme 103
Martin, Terry 130
Marxism/Marxist 40–3, 45, 47–8, 130, 167, 171, 173, 218 n.39, 259, 289, 292–4, 299–301
  orthodox Marxists 294–5
Marx, Karl 40, 43, 276–7, 292, 298–9
  The Communist Manifesto 292
  Critique of Political Economy 292

Das Kapital 292–3
    translation of 293–4
    and Russia 292–6
mass consumption 173–4
mass production 173
mass unemployment 166, 170
Maury, Matthew 24
May Fourth Movement 60, 313
Mbawila, Gereon 269
Mbembe, Achille 10–11, 13
McDonald's 180
Mediterranean Sea 3, 92, 129
Mehta, Hansa Jivraj 274
Meiji Restoration 38, 67, 69, 71, 77, 82 n.3,
    87, 89–90, 100 n.28, 100 n.31
    fukoku kyohei slogan 68–9, 74
    policymakers 81
Memoria 4
mercantile/mercantilists 23, 192, 228, 314,
    321–2
merchants 55, 59, 67, 88, 98 n.5, 105, 196,
    222, 226, 232, 267, 312
Mesopotamia 3, 92
Mestmäcker, Hans-Joachim 176–7, 182 n.24
metropolitan 108, 147, 244, 252, 307, 314
Mexico 23, 27, 221–2, 227, 297
Microsoft 180
The Middle East 2, 97 n.2, 99 n.22, 131–2,
    136, 138, 175, 185
miemba (tontines) 266
migration/migrants 2, 4–5, 8–9, 13, 169,
    220, 296
    Cantonese migrants 58–9
    Chinese 52, 54–5, 57–62, 227, 231–2
    early modern 222–4
    early modern theories of 221–2
    European migrants 226–7, 233
    German migrants 223
    Israeli migrants 231
    labour migration/migrant workers (*see*
        labour migration/migrants)
    lived experience of 220
    mass migration 219, 229
    modern migrants 230–3
    Salvadoran migrants 232
    seasonal 296
    Turkish immigrants 231–2
Mikhailovsky, Nikolay 293–4
Mikoyan, Anastas 137

militarization 176, 340
Miliukov, Pavel 295
Ming dynasty 41
minorities 3, 6, 8–9, 11, 61, 129–30, 139,
    147, 189, 290, 292, 342 n.15
Mitani Hiroshi, *Aikoku, Kakumei, Minshu*
    97 n.1
Miyazaki Ichisada 96
    *Miyazaki Ichisada Zenshū (Complete
        Works of Miyazaki Ichisada),
        Vol. 18: Asian History* 102 n.41
mobilization 5, 105, 134
modernity 6, 20, 47, 80, 89, 142, 184,
    187–9, 191, 193, 220, 287–8,
    294–5, 337
modernization 29, 45–8, 53, 67, 80, 117,
    139, 174–5, 188, 196, 287, 291,
    294–5, 299, 322, 337
Modi, Narendra 3, 5, 9–10
    Bharatiya Janata Party 334
Mohamad, Mahathir 180
Mongkut (Rama IV), King 188
Monnet, Jean 175–6
Montenegro 148
Moore, Henry 242, 254 n.11
moral economy 5, 170–2, 263
Morales, Evo 205, 209, 212–14
Morant Bay Rebellion in Jamaica 185
Morel, Efrain 139
mshenzi 263–4
Mshirazi Chui 262
Muhamadi, Ali 263
Mukhitdinov, Nuritdin 133–4, 136, 138
Mulattos 240, 249, 251–2, 257 n.61
Murphy, Craig 214
Murrow, Edward R. 113
Musil, Robert, *The Man without Qualities*
    149
Muslims 2, 9, 88, 95–7, 101 n.34, 127, 134,
    136–8, 140, 147, 262, 265
    Tatar Muslim 95, 101 n.34, 131
    umma 260
Mussolini, Benito 169, 321
Mutual Assured Destruction (MAD) 204
mythologies 21, 103, 106, 290

nanbanjin (southern barbarians) 89
Nanyō (the Southern Ocean) 91
Naoroji, Dadabhai 310

Index

Napoleon 8, 193, 291
Narzikullov, Ibadullo 140
national citizenship 6, 195, 228. *See also*
  global citizen/citizenship
national emancipation 127, 131
nationalism 2, 4, 8–9, 28, 37, 131, 133,
  167, 169, 175, 183, 193–4, 208,
  219, 271, 273, 301, 307, 322,
  329, 337–8
nationality 128–30, 134, 138, 142, 227–9
nationalization 134, 136, 142, 229
national liberation movements 37, 40,
  43–4, 128, 130
national markets 172, 174, 314
national narratives 1–3, 10, 13, 20, 36,
  69, 79–82, 88, 118, 205, 207,
  209–10, 241, 243, 329, 335, 340
The National Showa Memorial Museum
  (Shōwakan) 103
National Social Science Foundation 46–7
national sovereignty 166, 170–2, 175, 335
  Kobe incident (1952) 207–9
  in Korean War-Era East Asia 205–7
  as narrative of common good 205–9
  and Pachamama as narrative
    partners 211–12
nation-building 6, 68, 80–1, 185, 195,
  337–9
nationhood 3, 6, 19, 26, 227, 330, 335–9
nation-states 1, 7–8, 10, 19–20, 29, 36,
  38, 104, 129, 170, 172, 174–6,
  184–6, 189, 219–20, 227–8, 230,
  233, 308, 329, 331–2, 334, 337
  and modern theories of immigrant
    224–30
NATO 40, 142, 209, 335
natural history 240–1, 244
naturalization 220, 223–5, 227–9, 233, 248
Naturalization Law of 1889, Costa Rica's
  228
natural sciences 293–4, 297
Navarro, Samuel 227
Nazi Germany 105–6, 109–11, 113–16,
  118, 169, 322
'Negroes' 239–40, 244, 246–50, 262
Nehru, Jawaharlal 132, 138, 174, 177, 309,
  322–3
  National Planning Committee (1938)
    323

neo-classical economics 301, 323
neocolonialism 175, 178
neoliberals/neoliberalism 166, 172, 176,
  179, 330–4, 336, 339
neo-nationalism 298, 334, 340
  and power politics 334–6
The Netherlands 67, 132, 184, 194, 228,
  334
New Economic Policy (NEP) 45, 297,
  299–300
New International Economic Order
  (NIEO) 177–8
New Order Suharto regime (1966–98)
  195
The New World 37, 39, 168, 177, 180,
  221–2, 224, 251, 308, 313, 315,
  330
New Zealand 59, 105, 185, 227
ngoma dance societies 264
Nicholas, Tsar 25
Nihonshoki 99 n.24
Nike 180
Nixon, Richard 176
normative immigrant 220, 226–7
North America 47, 57–8, 61, 222–5
Northern Province Labor Utilization
  Board 272
North Korea 132, 138, 205–6
Nyangye, M. Ruben 264
Nye, Joseph 51

Occident/Occidental 38, 87, 90–2, 97,
  99 n.20
Oceania 58, 89, 93
Ogborn, Miles, *The Freedom of Speech.*
  Talk and Slavery in the Anglo-
  Caribbean World 256 n.49
Okakura Kakuzo 84 n.33
Okakura Tenshin 84 n.33
Okuma Shigenobu 72, 101 n.34
The Old World 168, 173, 310
Opium Wars (1839–42 and 1856–60)
  35–6, 38, 51, 53, 61–2, 66 n.62,
  338
Organization of Solidarity with the
  People of Asia, Africa and Latin
  America 175
Orientalist Institutes 137, 139
Oriental Studies 92, 99 n.22, 137

Orient/Oriental/Orientalism 38, 48, 76, 78, 87–8, 91–3, 95, 97, 99 n.17, 138
Origins of the Cataclysm. See Anatomy of the 19th Century
orthodox Marxists/Marxism 294–5
Orwell, George, atrocity campaigns 4
Ottawa Agreements 169
Ottoman Empire 129, 131, 147–8, 151–2, 184–5, 287
Overseas Chinese studies (*huaqiao huaren yanjiu* 華僑華人研究) 52, 57–8, 61–2, 63 n.17
  Chinese emigration during 1839–1949 54–5
  global history 54
  Huaqiao studies in China since 1980s 55–6
  loophole and its causes 56–7
Overy, Richard 105
Ovezov, Balysh 134

Pachamama (Andean Goddess) 210, 213
  and common good as narrative partners 211–12
Pacific Rim 323
Pakistan 138, 140
pan-Africanism 139, 270
Paris Commune Revolution (1871) 43
Paris Peace Conference 275
Parks, Robert Ezra, 'Marginal Man' 230
Parley's Universal History on the Basis of Geography 93, 100 n.27
Party Rectification Campaign (1941) 41
Passenger Cases 225–6
paternalism 134, 193
patriotic narrative 10, 12
Pearl River delta region 57–8, 60
peasants/peasantry 25, 42, 147, 192, 212, 289–90, 292–6, 299–301
Peng Dehuai 41
People's Republic of China (PRC) 39, 41, 44–5, 51, 338–40. *See also* China/Chinese
Perhimpunan Indonesia student association 194
periphery/peripheral countries 8, 14, 20, 127–9, 132, 142, 147, 150, 156, 166, 174–5, 177, 184, 189, 211, 213, 223, 272, 307–8, 310–15, 318–21, 324

Permanent Mandates Commission (PMC) 260, 267
Perry, Matthew 24, 89, 91–2
Peru 52, 222
Peter the Great 287, 289–90
Phelps-Stokes Fund 270
the Philippines 61, 90, 192–4, 227, 334
Pokrovskii, Mikhail 296–7
Poland 24, 105, 110–11, 117, 132, 288, 290
Polanyi, Karl 170–2, 178
  Anatomy of the 19th Century 170
  The Great Transformation 170
Politburo (Presidium) 136
political economy 23, 25, 165, 168, 171, 186, 240–2, 246, 252, 289, 292, 295, 298
polygenesis/polygenism 240, 248, 252–3
populists 195, 292–5, 300
Portugal 22, 132, 167
postcolonial/postcolonialism 6, 128, 130, 141, 148–9, 159 n.7, 173–7, 183–4, 186, 191, 196, 323
postimperial 308, 320
poverty 45, 178, 223, 269, 299, 332, 336
Pragmatic Sanction 157
Prebisch, Raúl 326 n.16
Princip, Gravilo 147
privatization 179, 298
proletarian 12, 40–3, 45, 48, 262, 267, 292
proletarianization 259, 292, 296, 299
pro-slavery 22–9
pro-slavery Southerners 23, 32 n.25
protectionism 170, 311, 331
protectorates 130, 132, 147, 149, 153, 155–6
Provisional Military Investigative Commission 108
Prussia 298
Pufendorf, Samuel van 221–2
Putin, Vladimir 3, 335

Qing dynasty 35–7, 55, 95, 337
Queen Wilhelmina 192

race/racism 7, 10, 23, 26, 29, 37, 104, 220, 239–40, 243, 249–52, 260, 270, 321
RAF 104, 108, 115
Rafiki yangu 262, 264
Rashidov, Sharof 134, 136
Rasulov, Dzhabar 134

Index

rationalization 173, 188
Reagan, Ronald 20
reconstruction 117, 172–3, 226, 321
Redlich, Josef, *Das österreichiche Staats-
und Reichsproblem* (*The
Austrian State- and Imperial
Problem*) 157–8
Redslob, Robert 153, 155
refugees 5, 95, 101 n.34, 148, 181, 221–2,
225, 232, 296, 340
'Regional Committee for the Defense
of African Unemployed in
Cameroon' 273
regional integration 48, 312
Reichsmark bloc 169
Renan, Ernest 4
republicanism 26, 313
republicanization 134
Republican Party (Republicans) 24–9
The Republic of Iraq 137
resilience 12, 103–4, 106, 108–18, 172
resistance 2, 5, 8, 56, 165–6, 225, 232, 310,
320, 323, 329, 333–4
resource hierarchy of modern world
economy 319–20
Resources of European, Asiatic and South
American Countries 317
'Responsibility to Protect' doctrine 148
Resterners 318
Reynolds, Quentin 113–14, 187
rhetoric 1, 8, 20, 29, 56, 90, 148, 167,
188, 229–30, 248, 259, 267,
307, 334
Ricci, Matteo 89
Rifa Chiffà (*Chiffa* lottery) 58
rival narratives 24, 166, 169
Robertson, William, *History of America*
240
Rome 3–4, 290
Roosevelt, Franklin D. 171, 175
Rostow, Walt 299
Rothschild, Emma 241
The Royal Asiatic Society of Great Britain
92
Roy, Manabrenda Nath 131
Rubin, Robert 180
Russian Empire 127, 129, 141, 224, 289
Russia/Russian 14, 24–5, 27, 40, 44, 46, 53,
67, 129, 131–2, 142, 167, 287,
301, 317

and backwardness
during Cold War 298–300
in the Enlightenment 288–92
and China 335–7
Civil War (1918–21) 129
invasion of Ukraine 3–5, 9
Kremlin 335–6
Leningrad 103, 135
and Marx 292–6
modernization 287, 291, 295
Moscow 4, 45, 127–32, 134–7, 140–2
Moscow Youth Festival 128
October revolution 44, 296
peace treaty of San Stefano 148
Russian Revolution 185, 295–6
Russian tsarism 131
second industrial revolution 295
serfs/serfdom 24, 288–9, 291–2, 301
Slavic origins of 290
Slavophiles *vs.* Westernizers 292–3
Soviet Russia and world history 296–8
vaccine for Covid 9
Russo-Japanese war (1904–5) 81, 95

San Francisco Peace Treaty (1952) 206–7
Sanguo yanyi (三國演義) Chinese
literature 60
Sano Tsunetami 72, 83 n.15
Satsuma 71
Saudi Arabia 137, 140
savage/savagery 24, 26, 38, 104, 106, 208,
248, 263
Say, Jean-Baptiste 291
Schayegh, Cyrus 150
Schmidt, Helmut 177
Schneider, Eugène 266, 281 n.74
Schneller, Hans 154
Schurz, Carl 25–6
Sebastiani, Silvia, *The Scottish
Enlightenment. Race, Gender
and the Limits of Progress* 239
second industrial revolution 167, 295,
314
Second World 39–40, 128, 172. *See also*
Third World
Second World War 4, 8, 12, 52, 87–8,
96–7, 103–6, 109, 111–13, 118,
203, 208, 260, 296. *See also*
First World War
Seiyōshi (the 'History of *Seiyō*') 94, 96

362 Index

Seiyō (the Western Ocean) 87, 89–95, 97, 98 n.7, 100 n.30. *See also Tōyō*
self-determination 170, 186, 229, 308, 322
self-empowerment 334, 339
self-regulating market 170
semi-colonial 37, 40, 129, 132, 183, 189–91, 195
semi-feudal 37, 40
Serbia 148, 158, 219, 223
Seth, Suman 252
settler colonialism 165, 222–5
Seward, William Henry 25–7
Sharp, Granville 248
Shcherbatov, Mikhail M. 290
Shiller, Robert J., *Narrative Economics: How Stories Go Viral and Drive Major Economic Events* 11
Shintoism 70
Shiryaku ('Abstract of History') 100 n.27
Siam/Siamese monarchy 183–4, 191–2, 196, 196 n.4. *See also* Thailand/ Thai
    development and progress 188, 191, 194
    internal colonization 187–91
    semi-colonial governmentality 189, 195
Simmel, Georg
    Soziologie 230
    'The Stranger' 230
Singapore 46, 61, 191
Singapore Hokkien-Teochew riots of May 1854 57
Sino-Japanese War (1894–5) 38, 94–5
Sino-Japanese War (1937–45) 56, 111–12
Sino-Soviet split 139
Sino-Soviet Treaty of Friendship, Alliance and Mutual Assistance (1950) 40, 43
slave/slavery 7, 20–3, 26, 51, 224, 239, 243, 245–51, 259–61, 288–9, 291
    and plantation 240–1, 247, 261
    slaveholders 22–5, 27–8
    slave-owners 243–4, 246
    Slave Power 24–5
    slave revolts 245, 252
    slave trade 224–5, 235 n.17, 239, 245–6, 259

Sloane, Hans 4, 7, 240–1
Smith, Able Seamen Derek 206, 208
Smith, Adam 290–1
    The Wealth of Nations 289
smokers in French Indochina 61
Smoot-Hawley tariffs 169
social class 11, 250–1, 297
socialism 37, 40, 43–5, 47, 127, 132–3, 137, 194, 260, 293, 298
    Soviet socialism 129, 142
socialist development 127, 134, 137–9, 175
socialist globalizations 128
socialist revolution 36, 42, 44, 132
Société Asiatique (first academic society on Asia) 92, 99 n.22
Société de Construction de Batignolles (SCB) 275
Société R. W. King 271
soldiers on the home front 109, 113
Solidarity Conference in Cairo (1957–8), Afro-Asian Peoples' 136
Somalia 335
Sombart, Werner 317–18
Somerset case (1772) 246
Somerset, James 248
Song dynasty 55
Soupa, Abogo 265–6
South Africa 8, 153, 223, 227, 321
South America 61, 221, 224, 310, 312, 317, 321
Southeast Asia 13, 55, 59–62, 90–1, 95, 183–4, 187, 189, 191, 194–5, 223
South Kensington Museum. *See* England, Victoria & Albert Museum
sovereign states 19, 93–4, 149, 155, 186, 203–4
sovereignty 7, 26, 28, 40, 48, 93, 128, 148–52, 154, 158, 166, 170, 176, 184–5, 210, 219, 221, 223, 308, 338
    counter-hegemonic sovereignty 213–14
    imperial sovereignty 150
    internationalized sovereignty 152
    national sovereignty (*see* national sovereignty)

quasi-sovereignty 147, 149–50, 153
sovereign defence of Bolivian forest
    211
split sovereignty (Austria-Hungary)
    154–6
Turkish sovereignty 151
Soviet Central Asia 12, 127, 130, 133–5,
    139, 142
Soviet East 131, 136
Soviet federalism 128–9, 139
Soviet Kazakhstan 127, 139
Soviet nationality policy 138, 142
Soviet republics 129–30, 133–4, 137–9,
    142. *See also* autonomous
    republics
Soviet Union 12, 39–42, 45, 48, 105–6,
    109–11, 115, 127–30, 132–3,
    135–7, 140, 142, 169, 300
Spain/Spanish 54, 112–13, 223–4, 226,
    243, 251
    Barcelona 4, 112
    Spaniards 221, 250–1
    Spanish America 22, 250
    Spanish Civil War 4, 104, 112
    Spanish Cuba 22–3
    Spanish Republicans 113, 118
Spengler, Oswald 321
Stalinism 42, 129, 298
Stalin, Joseph 127–9, 131–5, 142, 299
Status-of-Forces Agreement (SOFA) 206,
    208–9
Stephens, Alexander 23, 27
Stiglitz, Joseph 300–1
Stinner, Peter 206, 208
Storch, Heinrich 290–1
Suez crisis in 1956 136
Sukarno 195
Sumatra Treaty of 1824 191–2
Sumner, Charles 24–5, 27, 33 n.29
Sun Yat-sen 36–9, 44, 48, 309, 313–15,
    320, 323
    *The International Development of
    China* manifesto 313, 315
    Pan-Asianism 36–8, 48
Suryaningrat, Suwardi, 'If I were a
    Dutchman' 193
Suslov, Mikhail 138
Süss, Dietmar 113, 117

Sweden 23, 67, 110, 334
Switzerland 67
Syria 136, 138

tabula rasa approach 299
Tacky's war 245–6
Taiping rebellion (1850–64) 54–5
Tajik/Tajikistan 127, 130, 132, 134, 136,
    140–1
Takehiko Kariya 85 n.37
Tanganyika 267–8, 270, 272–6
    Tanganyika African Association 272
    Tanganyika African Government's
        Servants Association (TAGSA)
        272
Tanzania 259–61, 277
    Dar es Salaam 263, 267, 275
Tatishchev, Vassilii N. 290
tax(es) 179, 192, 226–7, 235 n.17, 262,
    269, 273, 276, 293, 307
Tejima Seiich 77
teleology 53, 191
tenjiku. See India/Indian
Tennessee Valley Authority 174, 323
Tezner, Friedrich 154–5
Thailand/Thai 60–1, 183–4, 187–9. *See
    also* Siam/Siamese monarchy
    Bangkok 187, 190–1
    Cultural Mandates (1940s) 188
    elites' project modernity 188–9
    mueang 187–8, 195, 196 n.4
    non-modern social ontology 196 n.4
    Sangha reforms 188
    semi-colonial governmentality
        188–90
    siwilai 187–92, 195
    Tai/ethnic Tai 187
    Tai-Kadai language family 196 n.3
    Thai Buddhism 188–9
    Thai language 60–1
    Thammayut Order of monks 188
    Western/modern toilets 190
Third World 127–8, 136, 140, 142, 175–80,
    296, 323–4. *See also* Second
    World
titular nationalities 130, 134
Tkachev, Pyotr 294
Togo 267, 270

Index

Tongling, Wang, *New History of the Oriental* 38
total war 104, 109
Tōyōshi (the history of *Tōyō*) 87–8, 93–7
  Kuwabara on 94
Tōyō (the Eastern Ocean) 87–97, 98 n.7, 100 n.30. *See also Seiyō*
trade/traders 1, 3, 8–9, 13, 23–4, 29, 169, 172, 181, 265, 288, 310–12, 323
  caravan trade 261, 264
  foreign trade 171, 321
  free trade 8–9, 22–3, 27, 166
  slave (*see* slave/slavery)
  trade agreements 8, 89, 175
transatlantic 26, 28
transnational 1, 5, 12–13, 19, 25, 103–5, 108, 111–12, 116–18, 204, 215, 227, 335, 340
transpatialization 150
Treaty of Berlin 148, 150–1, 154–8, 161 n.27
Treaty of San Stefano 148
Treaty of Versailles 110, 172
Trenchard, Hugh 108
Tricontinental Conference, Havana 175
Trump, Donald 3, 10, 30 n.5, 334
Trusteeship Council 270–1
Tsarist Empire 129–32, 134, 184, 294, 336
Tsipras, Alexis 333
TUC 276
Tunis 24, 154
Turkey/Turkish 148, 153–4, 231–2, 333–4
  Turkish sovereignty 151
Turkmens/Turkmenistan 127, 130, 132, 134, 136, 140–1
Turner, Victor 231–2

Uganda 267
Uighurs 138–9
Ukraine, Russian invasion of 3–5, 9, 140, 142, 290, 329, 335
Ulbrich, Joseph, Austrian constitutional law 151–2
Uldzhabaev, Tursunbai 134
Union démocratique des femmes camerounaises 274
Union of the Peoples of Cameroon (UPC) 273, 275–6

the United Nations 177, 186, 204–6, 209, 212, 214, 216 n.5, 259, 289
  Bolivian forest 210–11
  Charter of the United Nations 203, 214, 270
  Fourth Committee 271, 273
  General Assembly (resolution 63/278) 211
  global narrative of environmental justice 209–10
  Kobe incident (1952) 205–9
  narratives of common good 204–9, 214
    and Pachamama as narrative partners 211–12
  national sovereignty in Korean War-Era East Asia 205–9
  Security Council Resolution 82 205–7, 209
  UN Visiting Mission (1954) 272, 275
the United States 5, 9, 19–23, 38–40, 46–8, 51–3, 55, 58–9, 67, 74, 77, 80, 83 n.10, 87, 89–93, 95, 99 n.19, 100 n.26, 104–6, 113, 133, 137, 140, 153, 158 n.1, 169, 175–6, 184, 206, 216 n.5, 219, 225–7, 229, 231–2, 259, 291, 295, 297, 300, 308, 312–13, 317–18, 320, 331, 334–5, 337, 339
  Act to Encourage Immigration (1864) 235 n.17
  American exceptionalism 19–20, 27, 29, 33 n.36
  anti-slavery 24–9
  Bay of Pigs invasion of Cuba 137–8
  boycotts of brand 180
  Civil Rights Act (1866) 226
  Confederate States of America 28
  The Declaration of Independence 19, 28, 225
  Doolittle Raid in April 1942 116
  emancipation 24–6
  firebombing of Japanese cities (1945) 104
  Fourteenth Amendment 226
  Laws for Naturalization of Foreigners, obstruction of 225

pro-slavery 22–9
San Francisco Earthquake of 1906
  109
slavery 22–4
Status-of-Forces Agreement (SOFA)
  with Japan 206, 208–9
  US Army Air Force 115
  US Civil War 20–1, 28–9
universalism 20, 287
University of Jinan 暨南, Guangzhou 56
Unno, Jūza 107
US-Mexico War (1846–8) 23, 27
USSR 103, 128, 130, 133, 137–41,
  296–301
Usubaliev, Turdakun 134
Uzaramo Native Treasury 275–6
Uzbeks/Uzbekistan 127, 130, 132, 134,
  136–8, 140–1

Valcarcel, Gustavo 139
Vattel, Emer de 221–2
Veblen, Thorstein 173, 310
Vernadskaia, Maria 291
Vernadskii, Ivan 291
Vienna 67–8, 72–3, 150, 155
Vietnam 59–61, 132, 138, 175, 222
  Cao Dai sect (religious movement) 61
Vitoria, Francisco de 221
Volksgemeinschaft (national community)
  113
Voltaire 7, 289–90
von der Groeben, Hans 176
von Liszt, Franz 153

wage labour 173, 259–60, 262–3, 266–8,
  270, 291
Wagener, Gottfried 72–3
Wanyamwezi 264–5
The War of Resistance against Japan
  (1937–45) 103
Warsaw Pact 138
washenzi 263, 269–70
Washington, Booker T., *Up From Slavery*
  in *Mambo Leo* 269–70
Washington Consensus 179
Waswahili 263–4
waungwana 263–4
Weber, Max 298

Webster, Noah
  *An American Dictionary of the English
    Language* 219
  *A Compendious Dictionary of the
    English Language* 219
Wells, H. G. 107
  The War in the Air 106
Western civilization 68, 71, 90
Western games 58
Western impact narrative 51–4, 58,
  61–2
Westernization 71, 336–7
Westphalian state system 340
white race 26, 240, 246, 321
Wilson, Woodrow 7, 20, 186, 308
Wolff, Christian von 221–2
World Bank 5, 172, 343 n.23
World Economic Forum 8
world economy 24–5, 29, 35, 165–71,
  175, 178–9, 181, 184, 186, 228,
  307–12, 314–15, 317–19, 322–4,
  330
world history 1–3, 5, 11–14, 20–1, 35–6,
  54, 113, 118, 149
  in China 36–48, 54, 56
  and Soviet Russia 296–8
  war and 104–9
world integration. *See* global integration
world market 13, 22–3, 28, 45, 138, 166–7,
  169, 170–2, 175, 180, 244, 247,
  336
world power 51, 97, 128, 318
World Power Conference 315, 318
World Trade Organization (WTO) 2, 5, 8,
  35, 180
Wright brothers 106
Wright, Quincy 161 n.27
Wu Han
  General History of the World 42–3, 48
  Hai Rui's Dismissal of Office 41
Wuxia (武俠 knights errant) novels 60

xenophobia 7, 208
xīyang 90–1

Yanagiya Kentaro 75, 78
Yang Renbian 43
Young Turk regime of 1908 151

Yuanmao, Wang 222
yushutsu-kogei (crafts prepared for export) 75

Zade, Mirzo Tursun 136
Zasulich, Vera 294
Zemmour, Éric 2, 11, 307
Zhang Yudong 張禹東, *Overseas Chinese Organizations and the Dissemination of Chinese Culture* (*Huaren shetuan yu Zhongguo wenhua chuanbo* 華人社團與中華文化傳播) 57
Zhongguo tushuguan fenleifa 中國圖書館分類法 (*zhongtufa* 中圖法) system 64 n.33
Zhou Yiliang 41–3, 47
Zhu Xizu 38
Zimba, J. A. 274
Zimmermann, Erich W. 318–21

Printed in the USA
CPSIA information can be obtained
at www.ICGtesting.com
LVHW020805171024
794058LV00003B/87

9 781350 440982